THIRD EDITION

ETHICS AND TECHNOLOGY

Controversies, Questions, and Strategies for Ethical Computing

HERMAN T. TAVANI

Rivier College

WILEY

JOHN WILEY & SONS, INC.

Vice President & Executive Publisher	*Donald Fowley*
Executive Editor	*Beth Lang Golub*
Editorial Assistant	*Mike Berlin*
Marketing Manager	*Christopher Ruel*
Marketing Assistant	*Diana Smith*
Senior Media Editor	*Lauren Sapira*
Production Manager	*Janis Soo*
Assistant Production Editor	*Yee Lyn Song*
Designer	*RDC Publishing Group Sdn Bhd*
Cover Credit	© *Emrah Türüdü/iStockphoto*

This book was set in 10/12 Times Ten Roman by Thomson Digital, and printed and bound by Malloy Lithographers. The cover was printed by Malloy Lithographers.

This book is printed on acid free paper. ∞

Library of Congress Cataloging-in-Publication Data

Tavani, Herman T.
  Ethics and technology : controversies, questions, and strategies for ethical computing / Herman T. Tavani.—3rd ed.
      p. cm.
  Includes bibliographical references and index.
  ISBN 978-0-470-50950-0 (pbk.)
  1. Computer networks—Moral and ethical aspects. I. Title.
  TK5105.5.T385 2011
  175—dc22

                                                                        2009042657

Printed in the United States of America

10 9 8 7 6 5 4 3 2 1

CONTENTS AT A GLANCE

TABLE OF CONTENTS

▶ **CHAPTER 5**

PRIVACY AND CYBERSPACE   132

▶ **CHAPTER 6**

SECURITY IN CYBERSPACE   173

▶ **CHAPTER 7**

CYBERCRIME AND CYBER-RELATED CRIMES   201

▶ **CHAPTER 8**

INTELLECTUAL PROPERTY DISPUTES IN CYBERSPACE   229

▶ **CHAPTER 9**

REGULATING COMMERCE AND SPEECH IN CYBERSPACE   265

▶ **CHAPTER 10**

THE DIGITAL DIVIDE AND THE TRANSFORMATION OF WORK   300

PREFACE

The cyber landscape has evolved significantly since the publication of the first edition of *Ethics and Technology* in June 2003. For example, we have witnessed a proliferation of social networking services (SNSs), such as MySpace, Facebook, and Twitter; blogs now permeate the Internet, comprising what many refer to as the "blogosphere"; YouTube is viewed daily by millions of people around the world, many of whom are also eager to upload onto it their personal videos for everyone to see; and *Wikipedia* has become the default encyclopedia for a generation of students. We have also seen tremendous growth in the number of people who interact in virtual worlds, such as *Second Life*, and who participate in "massively multiplayer online role-playing games," or MMORPGs, such as *World of Warcraft*.

With these new and evolving technologies and online forums, a cluster of social and ethical concerns inevitably arise; some are now intensely debated. For example, is cyberbullying something that should be tolerated in SNSs? Are people who participate in SNSs unwittingly giving up more and more of their personal privacy via Web-mining practices carried out on these forums? Should political blogs be regulated for journalistic standards of accuracy, especially since they can influence the outcomes of political elections? Should behavior that is not tolerated in physical space because it is deemed to be hostile or offensive, or at least inappropriate, be allowed in virtual environments and MMORPGs? Should teenagers who send (or "sext") nude or semi-nude pictures of themselves via their cell phones, or through video-phone technologies such as Skype, be prosecuted for child pornography crimes? These questions are among some of the more recent social and ethical concerns examined in the third edition of *Ethics and Technology*.

Although new technologies emerge, and existing technologies continue to mature and evolve, many of the ethical issues associated with them are basically variations of existing ethical problems. At bottom, these issues reduce to traditional ethical concerns having to do with dignity, respect, fairness, obligations to assist others in need, and so forth. So, we should not infer that the moral landscape itself has been altered because of behaviors made possible by these technologies. We will see that, for the most part, the new issues examined in this edition of *Ethics and Technology* are similar in relevant respects to the kinds of ethical issues we examined in the book's previous editions. However, many emerging technologies present us with challenges that, initially at least, do not seem to fit easily into our conventional ethical categories. So, a major objective of this textbook is to show how those controversies can be analyzed from the perspective of standard ethical concepts and theories.

The purpose of *Ethics and Technology*, as stated in the prefaces to the previous editions of this book, is to introduce students to issues and controversies that comprise the relatively new field of *cyberethics*. The term "cyberethics" is used in this textbook to refer to the field of study that examines moral, legal, and social issues involving cybertechnology. *Cybertechnology*, in turn, refers to a broad spectrum of computing and information technologies that range from stand-alone computers to the cluster of networked computing, information, and communications technologies. Many of these technologies include devices that are connected to privately owned computer networks as well as to the Internet itself.

This textbook examines a wide range of cyberethics issues—from specific issues of moral responsibility that directly affect computer and information-technology (IT) professionals to broader social and ethical concerns that affect each of us in our day-to-day lives. Questions about the roles and responsibilities of computer/IT professionals in developing safe and reliable computer systems are examined under the category of professional ethics. Broader social and ethical concerns associated with cybertechnology are examined under topics such as privacy, security, crime, intellectual property, Internet regulation, and so forth.

▶ NEW IN THE *THIRD EDITION*

New pedagogical material includes

- new and/or updated *scenarios* in each chapter, illustrating both (actual) cases and hypothetical situations, which enable students to apply methodological concepts/frameworks and ethical theories covered in Chapters 1 and 2;
- new *sample arguments* in most chapters, which enable students to apply the tools for argument analysis covered in Chapter 3;
- a newly designed set of study/exercise questions called "Essay/Presentation Questions" in each chapter, which include *unanalyzed scenarios* that can be used for either in-class group projects or outside class assignments;
- additional "review questions" and "discussion questions" at the end of many chapters;
- an updated and revised glossary of key terms used in the book;
- an updated *Ethics and Technology* Web site with new resources and materials for students and instructors.

New issues examined and analyzed include

- ethical and social aspects of blogging, including controversies involving personal blogs (or online diaries) and political blogs;
- privacy concerns generated by Web mining, including the Facebook Beacon controversy;
- controversies surrounding cyberbullying, including the Megan Meier incident on MySpace;
- sexting incidents involving young teenagers vis-à-vis existing child pornography laws;
- violence and pornography in MMORPGs;
- controversies affecting virtual economies and "gold farming" in virtual worlds;

- cyberespionage activities carried out by governments and state-sponsored organizations, and the implications these activities have for the security of our national infrastructure;
- controversies involving "certified ethical hackers" (CEH) who carry out preemptive counter hacking activities on the part of the organizations that hire them.

New models/conceptual frameworks examined include

- the Value Sensitive Design (VSD) model for computer/IT professionals to consider in developing computer/information systems;
- the "contextual-integrity" model of privacy for evaluating privacy-related controversies;

Also included in the new edition are **expanded discussions** of

- ethical relativism, in which the views of ethical absolutism and ethical objectivism are now also critically examined;
- ongoing disputes involving illicit file-sharing of copyrighted material through P2P networks, including controversies surrounding the Pirate Bay site;
- digital rights management (DRM) technology in the context of "interoperability" devices for playing digital music on multiple platforms;
- e-mail spam and "phishing" controversies;
- global dimensions of the digital divide, including an analysis of the question whether affluent nations have a moral obligation to bridge the divide;
- ethical aspects of workplace surveillance and employee-monitoring practices;
- cybersecurity-related controversies affecting hacktivism, cyberterrorism, and information warfare.

In revising the book, I have also eliminated some older, now out-of-date, material. Additionally, I have streamlined some of the material that originally appeared in previous editions of the book but still needs to be carried over into the present edition.

► AUDIENCE AND SCOPE

Because cyberethics is an interdisciplinary field, this textbook aims at reaching several audiences and thus easily runs the risk of failing to meet the needs of any one audience. I have nonetheless attempted to compose a textbook that addresses the needs of computer science, philosophy, social/behavioral science, and library/information science students. Computer science students need a clear understanding of the ethical challenges they will face as computer professionals when they enter the workforce. Philosophy students, on the contrary, should understand how moral issues affecting cybertechnology can be situated in the field of applied ethics in general and then analyzed from the perspective of ethical theory. Social science and behavioral science students will likely want to assess the sociological impact of cybertechnology on our social and political institutions (government, commerce, and education) and sociodemographic groups (affecting gender, race, ethnicity, and social class). And library science and information science students should be aware of the complexities and nuances of current intellectual property laws that threaten unfettered access to electronic information, and should be informed about recent regulatory schemes that threaten to censor certain forms of electronic speech.

Students from other academic disciplines should also find many issues covered in this textbook pertinent to their personal and professional lives; some undergraduates may elect to take a course in social and ethical aspects of technology to satisfy one of their general education requirements. Although *Ethics and Technology* is intended mainly for undergraduate students, it could be used, in conjunction with other texts, in graduate courses as well.

We examine ethical controversies using *scenarios* that include both actual cases and hypothetical examples, wherever appropriate. In some instances I have deliberately constructed provocative scenarios and selected controversial cases to convey the severity of the ethical issues we consider. Some readers may be uncomfortable with, and possibly even offended by, these scenarios and cases—for example, those illustrating unethical practices that negatively affect children and minorities. Although it might have been politically expedient to skip over issues and scenarios that could unintentionally offend certain individuals, I believe that no textbook in applied ethics would do justice to its topic if it failed to expose and examine issues that adversely affect vulnerable groups in society.

Also included in most chapters are s*ample arguments* that are intended to illustrate some of the rationales that have been put forth by various interest groups to defend policies and laws affecting privacy, security, property, and so forth, in cyberspace. Instructors and students can evaluate these arguments via the rules and criteria established in Chapter 3 to see how well, or how poorly, the premises in these arguments succeed in establishing their conclusions.

Exercise questions are included at the end of each chapter. First, basic "review questions" quiz the reader's comprehension of key concepts, themes, issues, and scenarios covered in that chapter. These are followed by higher-level "discussion questions" designed to encourage students to reflect more deeply on some of the controversial issues examined in the chapter. Additionally, a new set of questions, called "essay/presentation questions," is now included in each chapter; these have been added in response to instructors who requested *unanalyzed scenarios* for classroom use. Building on the higher-level nature of the discussion questions, the essay/presentation questions are intended to provide students and instructors with additional resources for analyzing important controversies introduced in the various chapters. As such, these questions can function as in-class resources for group projects or they can serve as outside-class assignments.

Some discussion and essay/presentation questions ask students to compare and contrast arguments and topics that span multiple chapters; for example, students are asked to relate arguments used to defend intellectual property rights, considered in Chapter 8, to arguments for protecting privacy rights, examined in Chapter 5. Other discussion and essay/presentation questions ask students to apply foundational concepts and frameworks, such as ethical theory and critical thinking techniques introduced in Chapters 2 and 3, to the analysis of specific cyberethics issues examined in subsequent chapters. In some cases, these discussion and essay/presentation questions may generate lively debate in the classroom; in other cases, they can serve as a point of departure for various class assignments and group projects. Although no final "solutions" to the issues and dilemmas raised in the discussion and essay/presentation questions are provided in the text, some "strategies" for analyzing them are included in the section of the book's Web site (www.wiley.com/college/tavani) entitled "Strategies for Discussion Questions."

▶ ORGANIZATION AND STRUCTURE OF THE BOOK

Ethics and Technology is organized into twelve chapters. Chapter 1, "Introduction to Cyberethics: Concepts, Perspectives, and Methodological Frameworks," defines key concepts and terms that will appear throughout the book. For example, definitions of terms such as *cyberethics* and *cybertechnology* are introduced in this chapter. We then examine whether any ethical issues involving cybertechnology are unique ethical issues. We also consider how we can approach cyberethics issues from three different perspectives: professional ethics, philosophical ethics, and sociological/descriptive ethics, each of which represents the approach generally taken by a computer scientist, a philosopher, and a social/behavioral scientist. Chapter 1 concludes with a proposal for a comprehensive and interdisciplinary methodological scheme for analyzing cyberethics issues from these perspectives.

In Chapter 2, "Ethical Concepts and Ethical Theories: Establishing and Justifying a Moral System," we examine some of the basic concepts that make up a moral system. We draw a distinction between "ethics" and "morality" by defining ethics as "the study of morality." "Morality," or a moral system, is defined as an informal, public system comprising rules of conduct and principles for evaluating those rules. We then examine consequence-based, duty-based, character-based, and contract-based ethical theories. Chapter 2 concludes with a model that integrates elements of competing ethical theories into one comprehensive and unified theory.

Chapter 3, "Critical Thinking Skills and Logical Arguments: Tools for Evaluating Cyberethics Issues," includes a brief overview of basic concepts and strategies that are essential for debating moral issues in a structured and rational manner. We begin by describing the structure of a logical argument and show how arguments can be constructed and analyzed. Next, we examine a technique for distinguishing between arguments that are valid and invalid, sound and unsound, and inductive and fallacious. We illustrate examples of each type with topics and issues involving cybertechnology and cyberethics. Chapter 3 concludes with some strategies for spotting and labeling "informal" logical fallacies that frequently occur in everyday discourse.

Chapter 4, "Professional Ethics, Codes of Conduct, and Moral Responsibility," examines issues related to professional responsibility for computer/IT professionals. We consider whether there are any special moral responsibilities that computer/IT professionals have *as* professionals. We then examine some professional codes of conducted that have been adopted by computer organizations. We also ask: To what extent are software engineers responsible for the reliability of the computer systems they design and develop, especially applications that include "life-critical" and "safety-critical" software? Are computer/IT professionals ever permitted, or perhaps even required, to "blow the whistle" when they have reasonable evidence to suggest that a computer system is unreliable? Finally, we examine some schemes for analyzing risks associated with the development of safety-critical software.

We discuss privacy issues involving cybertechnology in Chapter 5. First, we examine the concept of privacy as well as some arguments for why privacy is considered an important human value. We then look at how personal privacy is threatened by the kinds of surveillance techniques and data-collection schemes made possible by cybertechnology. Specific data-gathering and data-exchanging techniques are examined in detail. We next consider some challenges that data mining and Web mining pose for protecting personal privacy in public space. In Chapter 5 we also consider whether technology itself, in the form of privacy-enhancing technologies (or PETs), can provide an adequate solution to some privacy issues generated by cybertechnology.

Chapter 6, "Security in Cyberspace," examines security threats in the context of computers and cybertechnology. Initially, we differentiate three distinct senses of "security": data security, system security, and network security. We then examine the concepts of "hacker" and "hacker ethic," and we ask whether computer break-ins can ever be morally justified. Next, we differentiate acts of "hacktivism," cyberterrorism, and information warfare. We then ask whether total security is cyberspace is achievable, and if so whether it would be desirable. Chapter 6 concludes with a brief examination of risk analysis in the context of cybersecurity.

We begin our analysis of cybercrime, in Chapter 7, by considering whether we can construct a profile of a "typical" cybercriminal. We then propose a definition of cybercrime that enables us to distinguish between "cyberspecific" and "cyber-related" crimes to see whether such a distinction would aid in the formulation of more coherent cybercrime laws. We also consider the notion of legal jurisdiction in cyberspace, especially with respect to the prosecution of cybercrimes that involve interstate and international venues. In addition, we examine technological efforts to combat cybercrime, such as controversial uses of encryption and biometric technologies.

Chapters 8 and 9 examine legal issues involving intellectual property and free speech, respectively, as they relate to cyberspace. One objective of Chapter 8, "Intellectual Property Disputes in Cyberspace," is to show why an understanding of the concept of intellectual property is important in an era of digital information. We consider three theories of property rights and make important distinctions among legal concepts such as copyright law, patent protection, and trademarks. Additionally, we consider specific scenarios involving intellectual property disputes, including the original Napster controversy as well as some recent peer-to-peer (P2P) networks that have been used for file sharing. We also examine the Free Software and the Open Source Software initiatives. Finally, we consider a compromise solution that supports and encourages the sharing of digital information in an era when strong copyright legislation seems to discourage that practice.

Chapter 9, "Regulating Commerce and Speech in Cyberspace," looks at additional legal issues, especially as they involve regulatory concerns in cyberspace. We draw distinctions between two different senses of "regulation" as it applies to cyberspace, and we also consider whether the Internet should be understood as a medium or as a "place." We also examine controversies surrounding e-mail spam, which some believe can be viewed as a form of "speech" in cyberspace. We then ask whether all forms of online speech should be granted legal protection; for example, should child pornography, hate speech, and speech that can cause physical harm to others be tolerated in online forums? Finally, we examine the issue of online defamation, and we consider whether Internet service providers (ISPs) should be held liable for the content of information conveyed in their online forums.

Chapter 10 examines a wide range of social equity issues from the perspective of cybertechnology's impact for sociodemographic groups (affecting class, race, and gender) as well for employment and work. The chapter begins with an analysis of global aspects of the "digital divide." We then examine specific issues affecting racial minorities, women, and disabled persons. We also examine social and ethical issues affecting employment in the contemporary workplace, and we ask whether the use of cybertechnology has transformed employment and work. Chapter 10 closes with an analysis of employee privacy and autonomy issues that arise because of surveillance and monitoring techniques used in the contemporary workplace.

In Chapter 11, we examine issues pertaining to two broad themes: *community* and *personal identity* in cyberspace. We begin by analyzing the impact that cybertechnology has for our traditional understanding of the concept of community. In particular, we ask whether online communities, such as Facebook and MySpace, raise any special ethical or social issues. Next, we explore the relationship between online communities and democracy, and we consider whether cybertechnology facilitates democracy or threatens it. We then examine some implications that behaviors made possible by virtual environments and virtual-reality (VR) applications have for our conventional understanding of personal identity. The final section of Chapter 11 examines the impact that developments in artificial intelligence (AI) have for our sense of self and for what it means to be human.

Chapter 12, the final chapter of *Ethics and Technology*, examines some ethical, social, and professional challenges that arise in connection with emerging and converging technologies. We note that cybertechnology is *converging* with non-cybertechnologies, including biotechnology and nanotechnology, generating new fields such as bioinformatics and nanocomputing. We ask whether ethical issues that arise in these new fields warrant special consideration. We also examine some specific challenges for computer professionals engaged in nanocomputing research and development.

A Glossary that defines terms commonly used in the context of computer ethics and cyberethics is also included. However, the glossary is by no means intended as an exhaustive list of such terms. Additional material for this text is available on the book's Web site: www.wiley.com/college/tavani.

▶ THE WEB SITE FOR *ETHICS AND TECHNOLOGY*

Seven appendices for *Ethics and Technology* are available only in online format. Appendices A through E include the full text of five professional codes of ethics: the ACM Code of Ethics and Professional Conduct, the Australian Computer Society Code of Ethics, the British Computer Society Code of Conduct, the IEEE Code of Ethics, and the IEEE-CS/ACM Software Engineering Code of Ethics and Professional Practice, respectively. Specific sections of these codes are included in hardcopy format as well, in relevant sections of Chapter 4. Two appendices, F and G, are also available online. Appendix F contains the section of the *IEEE-CS/ACM Computing Curricula 2001 Final Report* that describes the social, professional, and ethical units of instruction mandated in their computer science curriculum. Appendix G provides some additional critical thinking techniques that expand on the strategies introduced in Chapter 3.

The Web site for *Ethics and Technology* also contains additional resources for instructors and students. Presentation slides in PowerPoint format for Chapters 1–12, as well as graphics (for tables and figures in each chapter), are available in the "Instructor" and "Student" sections of the site. As noted earlier, a section on "Strategies," which includes some techniques for answering the discussion questions included at the end of each of the book's 12 chapters, is also included on this site.

The book's Web site is intended as an additional resource for both instructors and students. It also enables me to "update the book," in between editions, with new issues and scenarios in cyberethics, as they arise. For example, a section entitled "Recent Controversies" is included on the book's Web site. I invite your feedback as to how this site can be continually improved.

▶ A NOTE TO STUDENTS

If you are taking an ethics course for the first time, you might feel uncomfortable with the prospect of embarking on a study of moral issues and controversial topics that might initially cause you discomfort because ethics is sometimes perceived to be preachy, and its subject matter is sometimes viewed as essentially personal and private in nature. Because these are common concerns, I address them early in the textbook. I draw a distinction between an ethicist, who studies morality or a "moral system," and a moralist who may assume to have the correct answers to all of the questions; note that a primary objective of this book is to examine and analyze ethical issues, not to presume that any of us already has *the* correct answer to any of the questions I consider.

To accomplish this objective, I introduce three types of conceptual frameworks early in the textbook. In Chapter 1, I provide a methodological scheme that enables you to identify controversial problems and issues involving cybertechnology *as* ethical issues. The conceptual scheme included in Chapter 2, based on ethical theory, provides some general principles that guide your analysis of specific cases as well as your deliberations about which kinds of solutions to problems should be proposed. A third, and final, conceptual framework is introduced in Chapter 3 in the form of critical thinking techniques, which provides rules and standards that you can use for evaluating the strengths of competing arguments and for defending a particular position that you reach on a certain issue.

This textbook was designed and written for you, the student! Whether or not it succeeds in helping you to meet the objectives of a course in cyberethics is very important to me, so I welcome your feedback on this textbook; and I would sincerely appreciate hearing your ideas on how this textbook could be improved. Please feel free to write to me with your suggestions, comments, and so forth. My email address is htavani@rivier .edu. I look forward to hearing from you!

▶ NOTE TO INSTRUCTORS: A ROADMAP FOR USING THIS BOOK

The chapters that make up *Ethics and Technology* are sequenced so that readers are exposed to foundational issues and conceptual frameworks before they examine specific problems in cyberethics. In some cases, it may not be possible for instructors to cover all of the material in Chapters 1–3. It is strongly recommended, however, that before students are assigned material in Chapter 4, they at least read Sections 1.1, 1.4–1.5, 2.4–2.8, and 3.1. Instructors using this textbook can determine which chapters best accommodate their specific course objectives. Computer science instructors, for example, will likely want to assign Chapter 4, on professional ethics and responsibility, early in the term. Social science instructors, on the other hand, will likely examine issues discussed in Chapters 10 and 11 early in their course. Philosophy instructors may wish to structure their courses beginning with a thorough examination of the material on ethical concepts and ethical theory in Chapter 2 and techniques for evaluating logical arguments in Chapter 3. Issues discussed in Chapter 12 may be of particular interest to CS instructors teaching advanced undergraduate students.

Many textbooks in applied ethics include a requisite chapter on ethical concepts/ theory at the beginning of the book. Unfortunately, they often treat them in a cursory manner; furthermore, these ethical concepts and theories are seldom developed and reinforced in the remaining chapters. Thus, readers often experience a "disconnect" between the material included in the book's opening chapter and the content of the specific cases and issues discussed in subsequent chapters. By incorporating elements of ethical theory into my discussion and analysis of the specific cyberethics issues I examine, I have tried to avoid the "disconnect" between theory and practice that is commonplace in many applied ethics textbooks.

▶ A NOTE TO COMPUTER SCIENCE INSTRUCTORS

Ethics and Technology can be used as the main text in a course dedicated to ethical and social issues in computing, or it can be used as a supplementary textbook for computer science courses in which one or more ethics modules are included. As I suggested in the preceding section, instructors may find it difficult to cover all of the material included in this book in the course of a single semester. And as I also previously suggested, computer science instructors will likely want to ensure that they allocate sufficient course time to the professional ethical issues discussed in Chapter 4. Also of special interest to computer science instructors and their students will be the sections on computer security and risk analysis in Chapter 6; open source code and intellectual property issues in Chapter 8; and regulatory issues affecting software code in Chapter 9. Because computer science instructors may need to limit the amount of class time they devote to covering foundational concepts included in the earlier chapters, I recommend covering at least the critical sections of Chapters 1–3 described previously. This should provide computer science students with some of the tools they will need as professionals to deliberate on ethical issues and to justify the positions they reach.

In designing this textbook, I took into account the guidelines on ethical instruction included in the *Computing Curricula 2001 Final Report*, issued in December 2001 by the IEEE-CS/ACM Joint Task Force on Computing Curricula, which recommends the inclusion of sixteen core hours of instruction on social, ethical, and professional topics in the curriculum for undergraduate computer science students. [See the online Appendix F at www.wiley.com/college/tavani for detailed information about the social/ professional (SP) units in the Computing Curricula 2001.] Each topic prefaced with an SP designation defines one "knowledge area" or a CS "body of knowledge." They are distributed among the following ten units:

SP1: History of computing (e.g., history of computer hardware, software, and networking)

SP2: Social context of computing (e.g., social implications of networked computing, gender-related issues, and international issues)

SP3: Methods and tools of analysis (e.g., identifying assumptions and values, making and evaluating ethical arguments)

SP4: Professional and ethical responsibilities (e.g., the nature of professionalism, codes of ethics, ethical dissent, and whistle-blowing

SP5: Risks and liabilities of computer-based systems (e.g., historical examples of software risks)

SP6: Intellectual property (e.g., foundations of intellectual property, copyrights, patents, and software piracy)

SP7: Privacy and civil liberties (e.g., ethical and legal basis for privacy protection, technological strategies for privacy protection)

SP8: Computer crime (e.g., history and examples of computer crime, hacking, viruses, and crime prevention strategies)

SP9: Economic issues in computing (e.g., monopolies and their economic implications; effect of skilled labor supply)

SP10: Philosophical frameworks (e.g., ethical theory, utilitarianism, relativism)

All ten SP units are covered in this textbook. Material described in SP1 is included in Chapters 1 and 10, and topics included in SP2 are discussed in Chapters 1 and 11. The methods and analytical tools mentioned in SP3 are described at length in Chapters 2 and 3, whereas professional issues involving codes of conduct and professional responsibility described in SP4 are included in Chapters 4 and 12. Also discussed in Chapter 4, as well as in Chapter 6, are issues involving risks and liabilities (SP5). Intellectual property issues (SP6) are discussed in detail in Chapter 8 and in certain sections of Chapter 9, whereas privacy and civil liberty concerns (SP7) are discussed mainly in Chapters 5 and 12. Chapter 7, on computer crime, is devoted to material described in SP8. Economic issues (SP9) are considered in Chapters 9 and 10. And philosophical frameworks of ethics, including ethical theory (SP10), are discussed in Chapter 2.

Table 1 illustrates the corresponding connection between SP units and the chapters of this book.

TABLE 1 SP ("Knowledge") Units and Corresponding Book Chapters

SP (Social/ Professional) Unit	1	2	3	4	5	6	7	8	9	10
Chapter(s)	1, 10	1, 11	2, 3	4, 12	4, 6	8, 9	5, 12	7	9, 10	2

ACKNOWLEDGMENTS

In revising *Ethics and Technology* for a third edition, I have once again drawn from several of my previously published works. Chapters 1–4, on foundational and professional issues in cyberethics, incorporate material from three articles: "The State of Computer Ethics as a Philosophical Field of Inquiry," *Ethics and Information Technology* 3, no. 2 (2001); "Applying an Interdisciplinary Approach to Teaching Computer Ethics," *IEEE Technology and Society Magazine* 21, no. 3 (2002); and "The Uniqueness Debate in Computer Ethics," *Ethics and Information Technology* 4, no. 1 (2002). In Chapter 5, on privacy in cyberspace, I have drawn from material in four works: "Computer Matching and Personal Privacy," *Proceedings of the Symposium on Computers and the Quality of Life* (ACM Press, 1996); "Informational Privacy, Data Mining, and the Internet," *Ethics and Information Technology* 1, no. 2 (1999); "Privacy Enhancing Technologies as a Panacea for Online Privacy Concerns: Some Ethical Considerations," *Journal of Information Ethics* 9, no. 2 (2000); and "Can the 'Contextual Integrity' Model of Privacy Be Applied to Personal Blogs in the Blogosphere?" (co-authored with Frances Grodzinsky), *Proceedings of the Eighth International Conference on Computer Ethics — Philosophical Enquiry* (Nomiki Bibliothiki, 2009).

Chapters 6 and 7, on security and crime in cyberspace, draw from material in three sources: "Social and Ethical Aspects of Information Technology," *Wiley Encyclopedia of Electrical and Electronics Engineering* (1999); "Privacy and Security" in Duncan Langford's book, *Internet Ethics* (Macmillan, 2000); and "Defining Computer Crime: Piracy, Trespass, and Vandalism in Cyberspace" in *Readings in CyberEthics* 2nd ed. (Jones and Bartlett, 2004), co-edited with Richard Spinello. In Chapters 8 and 9, on intellectual property and Internet regulation, I drew from material in "Information Wants to be Shared: An Alternative Approach for Analyzing Intellectual Property Disputes in the Information Age," *Catholic Library World* 73, no. 2 (2002); and "Online File Sharing: Resolving the Tensions between Privacy and Property" (co-authored with Frances Grodzinsky), *Computers and Society* 38, no. 4 (2008).

Chapters 10 and 11, on the digital divide and online communities, incorporate material from "Ethical Reflections on the Digital Divide," *Journal of Information, Communication and Ethics in Society* 1, no. 2 (2003); and "Online Communities, Democratic Ideals, and the Digital Divide" (co-authored with Frances Grodzinsky) in Soraj Hongladarom and Charles Ess's book *Information Technology Ethics: Cultural Perspectives* (Idea Group, 2007). In Chapter 12, on emerging and converging technologies, I incorporated material from my article "Genomic Research and Data-Mining Technology," *Ethics and Information Technology* 6, no. 1 (2004); and from my book, *Ethics Computing, and Genomics* (Jones and Bartlett, 2006).

The third edition of *Ethics and Technology* has benefited from suggestions and comments I received from many anonymous reviewers, as well as from the following colleagues: Philip Brey, Richard Epstein, Don Gotterbarn, Frances Grodzinsky, James Moor, Mark Rosenbaum, and John Weckert. I am especially grateful to Fran Grodzinsky (Sacred Heart University), with whom I have co-authored several papers, for permitting me to incorporate elements of our joint research into relevant sections of this book. I am also grateful to the numerous reviewers and colleagues who commented on the previous editions of this book; many of their helpful suggestions have been carried over to the present edition.

The new edition of the book has also benefited from some helpful comments that I received from students who have used earlier editions of the text. In particular, I would like to thank Karen Johnson and Chuck Heinztelman, former students in the computer ethics course I teach at Rivier College, for pointing me to some sources that I have since incorporated into the current edition of the book.

I am grateful to Rivier College for a Faculty Development Grant during the summer of 2008 that supported my work on this edition of *Ethics and Technology*. I am also grateful to my colleagues in the philosophy department at Rivier, Lloyd Carr and Jerry Dolan, for providing me with a supportive environment in which to teach and write, and for helping me to refine some of the positions I defend in this book.

I also wish to thank the editorial staff at John Wiley & Sons, especially Beth Golub and Mike Berlin, for their support throughout the various stages of the revision process for the book's third edition. And I am grateful to Yee Lyn Song, in Wiley's production group, for her attention to important details in the process of converting my manuscript for the new edition into final book format.

Finally, I must once again thank the two most important people in my life: my wife Joanne, and our daughter Regina. Without their continued support and extraordinary patience, the third edition of this book could not have been completed.

This edition of *Ethics and Technology* is dedicated to the memory of my parents, Flora (Hutton) Tavani and Herman Tavani Sr.

Herman T. Tavani

Nashua, NH

FOREWORD

The computer/information revolution is shaping our world in ways it has been difficult to predict and to appreciate. When mainframe computers were developed in the 1940s and 1950s, some thought only a few computers would ever be needed in society. When personal computers were introduced in the 1980s, they were considered fascinating toys for hobbyists but not something serious businesses would ever use. When Web tools were initially created in the 1990s to enhance the Internet, they were a curiosity. Using the Web to observe the level of a coffee pot across an ocean was intriguing, at least for a few moments, but not of much practical use. Today, armed with the wisdom of hindsight, the impact of such computing advancements seems obvious, if not inevitable, to all of us. What government claims that it does not need computers? What major business does not have a Web address? How many people, even in the poorest of countries, are not aware of the use of cellular phones?

The computer/information revolution has changed our lives and has brought with it significant ethical, social, and professional issues; consider the area of privacy as but one example. Today, surveillance cameras are abundant, and facial recognition systems are effective even under less than ideal observing conditions. Information about buying habits, medical conditions, and human movements can be mined and correlated relentlessly using powerful computers. Individuals' DNA information can easily be collected, stored, and transmitted throughout the world in seconds. This computer/information revolution has brought about unexpected capabilities and possibilities. The revolution is not only technological but also ethical, social, and professional. Our computerized world is perhaps not the world we expected, and, even to the extent that we expected it, it is not a world for which we have well-analyzed policies about how to behave. Now more than ever we need to take cyberethics seriously.

Herman Tavani has written an excellent introduction to the field of cyberethics. His text differs from others in at least three important respects: First, the book is extraordinarily comprehensive and up to date in its subject matter. The text covers all of the standard topics such as codes of conduct, privacy, security, crime, intellectual property, and free speech, and also discusses sometimes overlooked subjects such as democracy, employment, access, and the digital divide. Tavani more than anyone else has tracked and published the bibliographical development of cyberethics over many years, and his expertise with this vast literature shines through in this volume. Second, the book approaches the subject matter of cyberethics from diverse points of view. Tavani examines issues from a social science perspective, from a philosophical perspective, and from a computing professional perspective, and then he suggests ways to integrate these diverse approaches. If the task of cyberethics is multidisciplinary, as many of us believe, then such a diverse but integrated methodology is crucial to accomplishing the task. His book is one of the few that constructs such a methodology. Third, the book is unusually helpful to students and teachers because it contains an entire chapter discussing critical thinking skills and is filled with review and discussion questions.

The cyberage is going to evolve. The future details and applications are, as always, difficult to predict. But it is likely that computing power and bandwidth will continue to grow while computing devices themselves will shrink in size to the nanometer scale. More and more information devices will be inserted into our environment, our cars, our houses, our clothing, and us. Computers will become smarter. They will be made out of new materials, possibly biological. They will operate in new ways, possibly using quantum properties. The distinction between the virtual world and the real world will blur more and more. We need a good book in cyberethics to deal with the present and prepare us for this uncertain future. Tavani's *Ethics and Technology* is such a book.

James H. Moor

Dartmouth College

1

Introduction to Cyberethics: Concepts, Perspectives, and Methodological Frameworks

Our primary objective in Chapter 1 is to introduce some foundational concepts and methodological frameworks that will be used in our analysis of specific cyberethics issues in subsequent chapters of this textbook. To accomplish this objective, we

- define key terms such as *cyberethics* and *cybertechnology*;
- describe key developmental phases in cybertechnology that influenced the evolution of cyberethics as a distinct field of applied ethics;
- consider whether there is anything unique or special about cyberethics issues;
- examine three distinct perspectives for identifying and approaching cyberethics issues;
- propose a comprehensive methodological scheme for analyzing cyberethics issues.

We begin by reflecting briefly on three scenarios, each illustrating a cluster of ethical issues that will be examined in detail in later chapters of this book.

▶ **SCENARIO 1–1:** "The Washingtonienne" Blogger

Jessica Cutler, a former staff assistant to U.S. Senator Michael DeWine (R-Ohio), authored an online diary (on blogger.com) under the pseudonym "The Washingtonienne." In May 2004 she was fired when the contents of her diary appeared in *Wonkette: The DC Gossip*, a popular blog in the Washington D.C. area. Until her diary was discovered and published in *Wonkette*, Cutler assumed that it had been viewed by only a few of her fellow "staffers" (Washington D.C. staff assistants) who were interested in reading about the details of her romantic relationships and sexual encounters. In her diary, Cutler disclosed that she earned an annual salary of only $25,000 as a staffer and that most of her living expenses were "thankfully subsidized by a few generous older gentlemen." She also described some details of her sexual relationships with these men, one of whom was married and an official in the Bush administration. (Cutler did not use the real names of these men but instead referred to them via initials that could easily be linked to their actual identities.) Following her termination as a staffer, in response to the political fallout and the media attention resulting from the publication of her diary, Cutler was offered a book contract with a major publisher. She was also subsequently sued by one of the men implicated in her blog.[1] ■

▶ **SCENARIO 1–2:** Verizon and the Recording Industry

In January 2003, a United States district court in the District of Columbia ruled that Verizon (an Internet service provider or ISP) must comply with a subpoena by the Recording Industry Association of America (RIAA)—an organization that represents the interests of the recording industry. The RIAA, in an effort to stop the unauthorized sharing of music online, requested from Verizon the names of two of its subscribers who allegedly made available more than 600 copyrighted music files on the Internet. Although many ISPs, such as Comcast, and many universities complied with similar subpoenas issued on behalf of the RIAA, Verizon refused to release the names of any of its subscribers. Verizon argued that doing so would violate the privacy rights of its subscribers and would violate specific articles of the U.S. Constitution. So, Verizon appealed the district court's decision. On December 19, 2003, the United States Court of Appeals for the District of Columbia overturned the lower court's decision, ruling in favor of Verizon.[2] ■

▶ **SCENARIO 1–3:** A Cyberstalking Incident

In October 1999, twenty-year-old Amy Boyer was murdered by a young man who had stalked her via the Internet. The stalker, Liam Youens, was able to carry out most of the stalking activities that eventually led to Boyer's death by using a variety of tools and resources generally available to any Internet user. Via standard online search facilities, for example, Youens was able to gather personal information about Boyer. And after paying a small fee to Docusearch.com, an online information company, Youens was able to find out where Boyer lived, where she worked, and so forth. Youens was also able to use another kind of online tool, available to Internet users, to construct two Web sites, both dedicated to his intended victim. On one site, he posted personal information about Boyer as well as a photograph of her; on the other Web site, Youens described, in explicit detail, his plans to murder Boyer.[3] ■

First, consider "The Washingtonienne" scenario, where a wide range of ethical and legal issues arise. These include concerns affecting privacy, confidentiality, anonymity, free speech, defamation, and so forth. For example, did Cutler violate the privacy and confidentiality of her romantic partners through the remarks she made about them in her online diary? Should she be held liable for defamation of character because of the nature of her remarks about these individuals, or was she merely exercising her right to free speech? Was Cutler's expectation of anonymity violated when she was eventually "outed" by *Wonkette*, or was her scenario no different from that of any author or journalist who writes under a pseudonym but whose real identity is eventually discovered and made public? Should Cutler's online diary be considered a "public document" merely because it was on the Web, or did her diary also deserve some privacy protection because of the limited scope of its intended audience? The answers to these questions would seem to depend on specific laws and policies governing blogs and the "blogosphere," which we examine in detail in Chapter 11.

Next, consider the Verizon scenario. Here, several important ethical issues also arise—e.g., concerns involving privacy and surveillance, anonymity and civil liberties, access and equity, property and ownership, and so forth. For example, consider the impact that the RIAA's actions have for a user's expectation of privacy and anonymity while navigating the Internet. Do ISPs such as Comcast and Verizon have an obligation to protect the identity of users who subscribe to their services? Should an Internet user's activities be allowed to be monitored by organizations in the private sector, such as the RIAA? Should users be able to freely exchange MP3 files that contain copyrighted music? Will allowing this practice deprive recording artists, as well as the corporations that represent them, of substantial earnings and possibly even their livelihoods? Does the unauthorized exchange of copyrighted music files over the Internet violate the rights of recording artists? Or is the recording industry attempting to unfairly restrict the opportunity for users to exchange and share information over the Internet? These and similar questions are examined in detail in Chapters 8 and 9.

Third, consider some ethical concerns that arise in the Boyer cyberstalking scenario. These include worries affecting privacy and security, free speech and censorship, and moral responsibility and legal liability. For example, was Boyer's privacy violated because of the way in which personal information about her could be so easily gathered by Liam Youens? Was Youens' "right" to set up a Web site about Amy Boyer without Boyer's knowledge, and without first getting her explicit consent, also a violation of Boyer's rights? And was Youens' alleged right to place on that Web site any kind of information about Boyer he wished to include, regardless of whether that information might be false or defamatory, a right that is protected by free speech? Should the two ISPs that allowed Youens to post such information to Web sites that resided in their domains be held legally liable? And should one of those ISPs be held liable, at least in some contributory sense, for the murder of Amy Boyer, because of the death threat posted on an electronic forum in its domain? Also, do ordinary users who happen to come across a Web site that contains a posting of a death threat directed toward one or more individuals have a moral responsibility to inform those individuals whose lives are threatened? These and similar questions are examined in detail in Chapters 5–7 and 9.

The Washingtonienne, Verizon, and Boyer scenarios provide us with particular contexts in which we can begin to think about a cluster of ethical issues affecting the use of computers and cybertechnology. A number of alternative examples could also have been used to illustrate many of the moral and legal concerns that arise in connection with this technology. In fact, examples abound. One has only to read a daily newspaper or view regular television news programs to be informed about controversial issues involving computers and the Internet, including questions that pertain to property, privacy, security, anonymity, crime, and jurisdiction. Ethical aspects of these issues are examined in the chapters comprising this textbook. In the remainder of Chapter 1, we identify and examine some key foundational concepts and frameworks in cyberethics.

▶ 1.1 DEFINING KEY TERMS: CYBERETHICS AND CYBERTECHNOLOGY

For our purposes, *cyberethics* can be defined as the study of moral, legal, and social issues involving cybertechnology. Cyberethics examines the impact of cybertechnology on our social, legal, and moral systems, and it evaluates the social policies and laws that have been framed in response to issues generated by its development and use. To grasp the significance of these reciprocal relationships, it is important to understand what is meant by the term *cybertechnology*.

1.1.1 What Is Cybertechnology?

Cybertechnology, as used throughout this textbook, refers to a wide range of computing and communications devices, from stand-alone computers to connected, or networked, computing and communications technologies. These technologies include, but need not be limited to, hand-held devices such as PDAs (or personal digital assistants), cell phones, personal computers (desktops and laptops), and mainframe computers. Networked devices can be connected directly to the Internet, or they can be connected to other devices through one or more privately owned computer networks. Privately owned networks, in turn, include local area networks (LANs) and wide area networks (WANs). A LAN is a privately owned network of computers that span a limited geographical area, such as an office building or a small college campus. WANs, on the other hand, are privately owned networks of computers that are interconnected throughout a much broader geographic region.

How exactly are LANs and WANs different from the Internet? In one sense, the Internet can be understood as *the network of interconnected computer networks*. A synthesis of contemporary information and communications technologies, the Internet evolved from an earlier United States Defense Department initiative (in the 1960s) known as the ARPANET. Unlike WANs and LANs, which are privately owned computer networks, the Internet is generally considered to be a public network, in the sense that much of the information available on the Internet resides in "public space" and is thus available to anyone. The Internet, which should be differentiated from the World Wide Web, includes several applications. The Web, based on hypertext transfer protocol (HTTP), is one application; other applications include file transfer protocol (FTP), Telnet, and e-mail. Because many users navigate the Internet by way of the Web, and because the majority of users conduct their online activities almost exclusively on the Web portion of the Internet, it has become very easy to confuse the Web with the Internet.

The Internet and privately owned computer networks, such as WANs and LANs, are perhaps the most common and well-known examples of cybertechnology. However, "cybertechnology" is used in this book to represent the entire range of computing systems, from stand-alone computers to privately owned networks to the Internet itself. "Cyberethics" refers to the study of moral, legal, and social issues involving those technologies.

1.1.2 Why the Term *Cyberethics?*

Many authors have used the term "computer ethics" to describe the field that examines moral issues pertaining to computing and information technology (see, for example, Barger 2008; Johnson 2009). Others use the expression "information ethics" (Capurro 2006) to refer to a cluster of ethical concerns regarding the flow of information that is either enhanced or restricted by computer technology.[4] Because of concerns about ethical issues involving the Internet in particular, some have also used the term "Internet ethics" (Langford 2000). Ethical issues examined in this textbook, however, are not limited to the Internet; they also include privately owned computer networks and interconnected communications technologies—i.e., technologies that we refer to collectively as cybertechnology. Hence, we use "cyberethics" to capture the wide range of moral issues involving cybertechnology.

For our purposes, "cyberethics" is more accurate than "computer ethics" for two reasons. First, the term "computer ethics" can connote ethical issues associated with computing *machines*, and thus could be construed as pertaining to stand-alone or "unconnected computers." Because computing technologies and communications technologies have converged in recent years, resulting in networked systems, a computer system may now be thought of more accurately as a new kind of *medium* than as a machine. Second, the term "computer ethics" might also suggest a field of study that is concerned exclusively with ethical issues affecting computer professionals. Although these issues are very important, and are examined in detail in Chapter 4 as well as in relevant sections of Chapters 6 and 12, we should note that the field of cyberethics is not limited to an analysis of moral issues that affect only professionals.

"Cyberethics" is also more accurate, for our purposes, than "information ethics." For one thing, "information ethics" is ambiguous because it can mean a specific methodological framework—i.e., *Information Ethics* (or *IE*)—for analyzing issues in cyberethics (Floridi 2007).[5] Or it can connote a cluster of ethical issues of particular interest to professionals in the fields of library science and information science (Buchanan and Henderson 2009). In the latter sense, "information ethics" refers to ethical concerns affecting the free flow of, and unfettered access to, information, which include issues such as library censorship and intellectual freedom. (These issues are examined in Chapter 9.) Our analysis of cyberethics issues in this text, however, is not limited to controversies often considered under the heading "information ethics."

Given the wide range of moral issues examined in this book, the term "cyberethics" is also more comprehensive, and more appropriate, than "Internet ethics." Although many of the issues considered under the heading cyberethics often pertain to the Internet, some issues examined in this textbook do not involve the Internet per se—for example, issues associated with computerized monitoring in the workplace, with professional responsibility for designing reliable computer hardware and software systems, and with the implications of cybertechnology for gender and race. We examine ethical issues that cut across the spectrum of devices and networked communication systems comprising cybertechnology, from stand-alone computers to networked systems.

▶ 1.2 THE CYBERETHICS EVOLUTION: FOUR DEVELOPMENTAL PHASES IN CYBERTECHNOLOGY

In describing the key evolutionary phases of cybertechnology and cyberethics, we begin by noting that the meaning of "computer" has evolved significantly since the 1940s. If you were to look up the meaning of that word in a dictionary written before World War II, you would most likely discover that a computer was defined as a person who calculated numbers. In the time period immediately following World War II, the term "computer" came to be identified with a (calculating) machine as opposed to a person (who calculated).[6] By the 1980s, however, computers had shrunk in size considerably and they were beginning to be understood more in terms of desktop machines (that manipulated symbols as well as numbers), or as a new kind of medium for communication, rather than simply as machines that crunch numbers. As computers became increasingly connected to one another, they came to be associated with metaphors such as the "information superhighway" and cyberspace; today, many ordinary users tend to think about computers in terms of various Internet- and Web-based applications made possible by cybertechnology.

In response to some social and ethical issues that were anticipated in connection with the use of electronic computers, the field that we now call cyberethics had its informal and humble beginnings in the late 1940s. It is interesting to note that during this period, when ENIAC (Electronic Numerical Integrator and Calculator)—the first electronic computer, developed at the University of Pennsylvania, became operational in 1946—some analysts confidently predicted that no more than five or six computers would ever need to be built. It is also interesting to point out that during this same period, a few insightful thinkers had already begun to describe some social and ethical concerns that would likely arise in connection with computing and cybertechnology.[7] Although still a relatively young academic field, cyberethics has now matured to a point where several articles about its historical development have appeared in books and scholarly journals. For our purposes, the evolution of cyberethics can be summarized in four distinct *technological phases.*[8]

Phase 1 (1950s and 1960s)

In *Phase 1*, computing technology consisted mainly of huge mainframe computers, such as ENIAC, that were "unconnected" and thus existed as stand-alone machines. One set of ethical and social questions raised during this phase had to do with the impact of computing machines as "giant brains." Today, we might associate these kinds of questions with the field of artificial intelligence (or AI). The following kinds of questions were introduced in Phase 1: Can machines think? If so, should we invent thinking machines? If machines can be intelligent entities, what does this mean for our sense of self? What does it mean to be human?

Another set of ethical and social concerns that arose during Phase 1 could be catalogued under the heading of privacy threats and the fear of Big Brother. For example, some people in the United States feared that the federal government would set up a national database in which extensive amounts of personal information about its citizens would be stored as electronic records. A strong centralized government could then use that information to monitor and control the actions of ordinary citizens. Although networked computers had not yet come on to the scene, work on the ARPANET—the Internet's predecessor, which was funded by an agency in the United States Defense Department—began during this phase, in the 1960s.

Phase 2 (1970s and 1980s)

In *Phase 2*, computing machines and communications devices in the commercial sector began to converge. This convergence, in turn, introduced an era of computer/communications networks. Mainframe computers, minicomputers, microcomputers, and personal computers could now be linked together by way of one or more privately owned computer networks such as LANs and WANs (see Section 1.1.1), and information could readily be exchanged between and among databases accessible to networked computers.

Ethical issues associated with this phase of computing included concerns about personal privacy, intellectual property, and computer crime. Privacy concerns, which had emerged during Phase 1 because of worries about the amount of personal information that could be collected by government agencies and stored in a centralized government-owned database, were exacerbated because electronic records containing personal and confidential information could now also easily be exchanged between two or more commercial databases in the private sector. Concerns affecting intellectual property and proprietary information also emerged during this phase because personal (desktop) computers could be used to duplicate proprietary software programs. And concerns associated with computer crime appeared during this phase because individuals could now use computing devices, including remote computer terminals, to break into and disrupt the computer systems of large organizations.

Phase 3 (1990–Present)

During *Phase 3*, the Internet era, availability of Internet access to the general public has increased significantly. This was facilitated, in no small part, by the development and phenomenal growth of the World Wide Web in the 1990s. The proliferation of Internet- and Web-based technologies has contributed to some additional ethical concerns involving computing technology; for example, issues of free speech, anonymity, jurisdiction, and trust have been hotly disputed during this phase. Should Internet users be free to post any messages they wish on publicly accessible Web sites or even on their own personal Web pages—i.e., is this a user's "right" that is protected by free speech or freedom of expression? Should users be permitted to post anonymous messages on Web pages, or even be allowed to navigate the Web anonymously or under the cover of a pseudonym?

Issues of jurisdiction also arose because there are no clear national or geographical boundaries in cyberspace; if a crime occurs on the Internet, it is not always clear where—i.e., in which legal jurisdiction—it took place and thus it is unclear where it should be prosecuted. And as e-commerce emerged during this phase, potential consumers initially had concerns about trusting online businesses with their financial and personal information. Other ethical and social concerns that arose during Phase 3 include disputes about the public vs. private aspects of personal information that has become increasingly available on the Internet. Concerns of this type have been exacerbated by the amount of personal information included on social networking sites, such as Facebook and MySpace, and on other kinds of interactive Web-based forums (made possible by Web 2.0 technology).

We should note that during Phase 3, both the interface used to interact with computer technology and the devices used to "house" that technology were still much the same as in Phases 1 and 2. A computer was still essentially a box, a CPU, with one or more peripheral devices, such as a video screen, keyboard, or mouse, serving as interfaces to that box. And computers were still viewed as devices essentially external to humans, as things or objects "out there." As cybertechnology continues to evolve, however, it may no longer make sense to try to understand computers simply in terms of objects or devices that are necessarily external to us. Instead, computers will likely become more and more a part of who or what we are as human beings. For example, James Moor (2005) notes that computing devices will soon be a part of our clothing and even our bodies. This brings us to Phase 4.

Phase 4 (Present–Near Future)

Presently we are on the threshold of *Phase 4*, a point at which we have begun to experience an unprecedented level of convergence of technologies. We have already witnessed aspects of technological convergence beginning in Phase 2, where the integration of computing and communications devices resulted in privately owned networked systems, as we noted above. And in Phase 3, the Internet era, we briefly described the convergence of text, video, and sound technologies on the Web, and we noted how the computer began to be viewed much more as a new kind of medium than as a conventional type of machine. The convergence of information technology and biotechnology in recent years has resulted in the emerging fields of bioinformatics and computational genomics; this has also caused some analysts to question whether computers of the future will still be silicon-based or whether some may also possibly be made of biological materials. Additionally, biochip implant technology, which has been enhanced by developments in AI research (described in Chapter 12), has led some to predict that in the not-too-distant future it may become difficult for us to separate certain aspects of our biology from our technology.

Today, computers are also becoming ubiquitous or pervasive; i.e., they are "everywhere" and they permeate both our workplace and our recreational environments. Many of the objects that we encounter in these environments are also beginning to exhibit what Philip Brey (2005) and others call "ambient intelligence," which enables "smart objects" to be connected to one another via wireless technology. Some consider radio frequency identification (RFID) technology (described in detail in Chapter 5) to be the first step in what is now referred to as *pervasive* or *ubiquitous computing* (described in detail in Chapter 12).

What other kinds of technological changes should we anticipate as research and development continues in Phase 4? For one thing, computing devices will likely continue to become more and more indistinguishable from many kinds of noncomputing devices. For another thing, a computer may no longer typically be conceived of as a distinct device or object with which users interact via an explicit interface such as a keyboard, mouse, and video display. We are now beginning to conceive of computers and cybertechnology in drastically different ways. Consider also that computers are becoming less visible—as computers and electronic devices continue to be miniaturized and

TABLE 1.1   Summary of Four Phases of Cyberethics

Phase	Time Period	Technological Features	Associated Issues
1	1950s–1960s	Stand-alone machines (large mainframe computers)	Artificial intelligence (AI), database privacy ("Big Brother").
2	1970s–1980s	Minicomputers and PCs interconnected via privately owned networks	Issues from Phase 1 plus concerns involving intellectual property and software piracy, computer crime, and communications privacy.
3	1990s–present	Internet and World Wide Web	Issues from Phases 1 and 2 plus concerns about free speech, anonymity, legal jurisdiction, virtual communities, etc.
4	Present to near future	convergence of information and communication technologies with nanotechnology and biotechnology	Issues from Phases 1–3 plus concerns about artificial electronic agents ("bots") with decision-making capabilities, and development in nanocomputing, bioinformatics, and pervasive computing.

integrated/embedded in objects, they are also beginning to "disappear" or to become "invisible" as distinct entities.

Many analysts predict that computers will become increasingly smaller in size, ultimately achieving the nano scale. (We examine some ethical implications of nano-technology and nanocomputing in Chapter 12). Many also predict that aspects of nanotechnology, biotechnology, and information technology will continue to converge. However, we will not speculate any further in this chapter about either the future of cybertechnology or the future of cyberethics. The purpose of our brief description of the four phases of cybertechnology mentioned here is to provide a historical context for understanding the origin and evolution of at least some of the ethical concerns affecting cybertechnology that we will examine in this book.

Table 1.1 summarizes key aspects of each phase in the development of cyberethics as a field of applied ethics.

▶ 1.3 ARE CYBERETHICS ISSUES UNIQUE ETHICAL ISSUES?

Few would dispute the claim that the use of cybertechnology has had a significant impact on our moral, legal, and social systems. Some also believe, however, that cybertechnology has introduced new and unique moral problems. Are any of these problems genuinely unique moral issues? There are two schools of thought regarding this question.

Consider once again the three scenarios included in the chapter's opening section. Have any new ethical issues been introduced in these scenarios, or are the issues that arise in each merely examples of existing ethical issues that have been exacerbated in some sense by new technologies used to communicate and disseminate personal information (such as in blogs in the Washingtonienne scenario), distribute and share proprietary information (such as P2P networks and the Verizon scenario), or search for and locate personal information (as in the Boyer scenario)? To see whether any new ethical issues arise because of cybertechnology in general, consider once again the cyberstalking scenario involving Amy Boyer. Here, one could argue that there is nothing really new or unique in the stalking incident that led to Boyer's death, because in the final analysis "crime is crime" and "murder is murder." According to this line of reasoning, whether a murderer happens to use cybertechnology to assist in carrying out a particular homicide is irrelevant. One might further argue that there is nothing special about cyberstalking incidents in general, regardless of whether or not they result in a victim's death. Proponents of this position could point to the fact that stalking activities are hardly new, since these kinds of activities have been carried out in the off-line world for quite some time. So, cybertechnology might be seen simply as the latest in a series of tools or techniques that are now available to aid stalkers in carrying out criminal activities.

Alternatively, some argue that forms of behavior made possible by cybertechnology have indeed raised either new or special ethical problems. Using the example of cyber-stalking to support this view, one might point out the relative ease with which stalking activities can now be carried out. Simply by using a computing device with Internet access, one can stalk persons without having to leave the comfort of his or her home. A stalker can, as Liam Youens did, easily acquire personal information about his or her victim because such information is readily accessible to online search requests. Further-more, a stalker can roam the Internet either anonymously or under the cloak of an alias, or pseudoname. The fact that a user can navigate the Web with relative anonymity makes it much more difficult for law enforcement agents to track down a stalker, either before or after that stalker has caused physical harm to the victim(s).

Also consider issues having to do with *scope* and *scale*: an Internet user can stalk multiple victims simultaneously via the use of multiple "windows" on his or her computer screen. The stalker can also stalk victims who happen to live in states and nations that are geographically distant from the stalker. Stalking activities can now occur on a scale or order of magnitude that could not have been realized in the pre-Internet era. More individuals can now engage in stalking behavior because cybertechnology has made it easy, and, as a result, significantly more people can now become the victims of stalkers.

But do these factors support the claim that cybertechnology has introduced any new and unique ethical issues? Walter Maner (2004) argues that computer use has generated a series of ethical issues that (a) did not exist before the advent of computing, and (b) could not have existed if computer technology had not been invented.[9] Is there any evidence to support Maner's claim? Next we consider two scenarios that, initially at least, might suggest that some new ethical issues have been generated by the use of cybertechnology.

▶ **SCENARIO 1–4:** Developing the Code for a Computerized Weapon System

Sally Bright, a recent graduate from Technical University, has accepted a position as a software engineer for a company called CyberDefense, Inc. This company has a contract with the U.S. Defense Department to develop and deliver applications for the U.S. military. When Sally reports to work on her first day, she is assigned to a controversial project that is developing the software for a computer system designed to deliver chemical weapons to and from remote locations. Sally is conflicted about whether she can, given her personal values, agree to work on this kind of weapon-delivery system, which would not have been possible without computer technology. ■

Is the conflict that Sally faces in this particular scenario one that is new or unique because of computers and cybertechnology? One might argue that the ethical concerns surrounding Sally's choices are unique because they never would have arisen had it not been for the invention of computer technology. In one sense, it is true that ethical concerns having to do with whether or not one should participate in developing a certain kind of computer system did not exist before the advent of computing technology. However, it is true only in a trivial sense. Consider that long before computing technologies were available, engineers were confronted with ethical choices involving whether or not to participate in the design and development of certain kinds of controversial technological systems. Prior to the computer era, for example, they had to make decisions involving the design of aircraft intended to deliver conventional as well as nuclear bombs. So, is the fact that certain technological systems happen to include the use of computer software or computer hardware components morally relevant in this scenario? Have any new or unique ethical issues, in a nontrivial sense of "unique," been generated here? Based on our brief analysis of this scenario, there does not seem to be sufficient evidence to substantiate the claim that one or more new ethical issues have been introduced.

▶ **SCENARIO 1–5:** Digital Piracy

Harry Flick is an undergraduate student at Pleasantville State College. In many ways, Harry's interests are similar to those of typical students who attend his college. But Harry is also very fond of classic movies, especially films that were made before 1950. DVD and videocassette copies of these movies are difficult to find; those that are available tend to be expensive to purchase, and very few are available for loan at libraries. One day, Harry discovers a Web site that has several classic films (in digital form) freely available for downloading. Since the movies are still protected by copyright, however, Harry has some concerns about whether it would be permissible for him to download any of these films (even if only for private use). ■

Is Harry's ethical conflict one that is unique to computers and cybertechnology? Are the ethical issues surrounding Harry's situation new and thus unique to cyber-technology, because the practice of downloading digital media from the Internet—a practice that many in the movie and recording industries call "digital piracy"—would not have been possible if computer technology had not been invented in the first place? If so, this claim would, once again, seem to be true only in a trivial sense. The issue of piracy itself as a moral concern existed before the widespread use of computer technology. For example, people were able to "pirate" audio cassette tapes simply by using two or more analog tape recorders to make unauthorized copies of proprietary material. The important point to note here is that moral issues surrounding the pirating of audio cassette tapes are, at bottom, the same issues underlying the pirating of digital media. They arise in each case because, fundamentally, the behavior associated with unauthorized copying raises moral concerns about property, fairness, rights, and so forth. So, as in Scenario 1–4, there seems to be insufficient evidence to suggest that the ethical issues associated with digital piracy are either new or unique in some nontrivial sense.

1.3.1 Distinguishing between Unique Technological Features and Unique Ethical Issues

Based on our analysis of the two scenarios in the preceding section, we might conclude that there is nothing new or special about the kinds of moral issues associated with cybertechnology. In fact, some philosophers have argued that we have the same old ethical issues reappearing in a new guise. But is such a view accurate?

If we focus primarily on the moral issues themselves *as moral issues*, it would seem that perhaps there is nothing new. Cyber-related concerns involving privacy, property, free speech, etc., can be understood as specific expressions of core (traditional) moral notions, such as autonomy, fairness, justice, responsibility, and respect for persons. However, if instead we focus more closely on cybertechnology itself, we see that there are some interesting and possibly unique features that distinguish this technology from earlier technologies. Maner has argued that computing technology is "uniquely fast," "uniquely complex," and "uniquely coded." But even if cybertechnology has these unique features, does it necessarily follow that any of the moral questions associated with that technology must also be unique? One would commit a logical fallacy if he or she concluded that cyberethics issues must be unique simply because certain features or aspects of cybertechnology are unique. The fallacy can be expressed in the following way:

PREMISE 1. Cybertechnology has some unique technological features.

PREMISE 2. Cybertechnology has generated some ethical concerns.

CONCLUSION. Some ethical concerns generated by cybertechnology must be unique ethical concerns.

As we will see in Chapter 3, this reasoning is fallacious because it assumes that characteristics that apply to a certain technology must also apply to ethical issues generated by that technology.[10]

1.3.2 An Alternative Strategy for Analyzing Claims about the Uniqueness of Cybertechnology

Although it may be difficult to prove conclusively whether or not cybertechnology has generated any new or unique ethical issues, we must not rule out the possibility that many of the controversies associated with this technology warrant special consideration from an ethical perspective. But what, exactly, is so different about issues involving computers and cybertechnology that makes them deserving of special moral consideration? James Moor (2007) points out that computer technology, unlike most previous technologies, is "logically malleable"; it can be shaped and molded to perform a variety of functions. Because noncomputer technologies are typically designed to perform some particular function or task, they lack the universal or general-purpose characteristics that computing technologies possess. For example, microwave ovens and DVD players are technological devices that have been designed to perform specific tasks. Microwave ovens cannot be used to view DVDs, and DVD players cannot be used to defrost, cook, or reheat food. However, a computer, depending on the software used, can perform a range of diverse tasks: it can be instructed to behave as a video game, a word processor, a spreadsheet, a medium to send and receive email messages, or an interface to Web sites. Hence, cybertechnology is extremely malleable.

Moor points out that because of its logical malleability, cybertechnology can generate "new possibilities for human action" that appear to be limitless. Some of these possibilities for action generate what Moor calls "policy vacuums," because we have no explicit policies or laws to guide new choices made possible by computer technology. These vacuums, in turn, need to be filled with either new or revised policies. But what, exactly, does Moor mean by "policy"? Moor (2004) defines policies as "rules of conduct, ranging from formal laws to informal, implicit guidelines for actions."[11] Viewing computer ethics issues in terms of policies is useful, Moor believes, because policies have the right level of generality to consider when we evaluate the morality of conduct. As noted, policies can range from formal laws to informal guidelines. Moor also notes that policies can have "justified exemptions" because they are not absolute; yet policies usually imply a certain "level of obligation" within their contexts.

What action is required when one or more policy vacuums are discovered? A solution to this problem might seem quite simple and straightforward. We might assume that all we need to do is identify the vacuums that have been generated and then fill them with policies and laws. However, this will not always work, because sometimes the new possibilities for human action generated by cybertechnology also introduce "conceptual vacuums," or what Moor calls "conceptual muddles." In these cases, we must first eliminate the muddles by clearing up certain conceptual confusions before we can frame coherent policies and laws.

1.3.3   A Policy Vacuum in Duplicating Computer Software

A critical policy vacuum, which also involved a conceptual muddle, emerged with the advent of personal desktop computers (henceforth referred to generically as PCs). The particular vacuum arose because of the controversy surrounding the copying of software. When PCs became commercially available, many users discovered that they could easily duplicate software programs. They found that they could use their PCs to make copies of proprietary computer programs such as word processing programs, spreadsheets, and video games. Some users assumed that in making copies of these programs they were doing nothing wrong. At that time there were no explicit laws to regulate the subsequent use and distribution of software programs once they had been legally purchased by an individual or by an institution. Although it might be difficult to imagine today, at one time software was not clearly protected by either copyright law or the patent process.

Of course, there were clear laws and policies regarding the theft of physical property. Such laws and policies protected against the theft of personal computers as well as against the theft of a physical disk drive residing in a PC on which the proprietary software programs could easily be duplicated. However, this was not the case with laws and policies regarding the "theft," or unauthorized copying, of software programs that run on computers. Although there were intellectual property laws in place, it had not been determined that software was or should be protected by intellectual property (IP) law: It was unclear whether software should be understood as an idea (which is not protected by IP law), as a form of writing protected by copyright law, or as a set of machine instructions protected by patents. Consequently, many entrepreneurs who designed and manufactured software programs argued for explicit legal protection for their products. A policy vacuum arose with respect to duplicating software: Could a user make a backup copy of a program for herself? Could she share it with a friend? Could she give the original program to a friend? A clear policy was needed to fill this vacuum.

Before we can fill the vacuum regarding software duplication with a coherent policy or law, we first have to resolve a certain conceptual muddle by answering the question: what, exactly, is computer software? Until we can clarify the concept of software itself, we cannot frame a coherent policy as to whether or not we should allow the free duplication of software. Currently there is still much confusion, as well as considerable controversy, as to how laws concerning the exchange (and, in effect, duplication) of proprietary software over the Internet should be framed.

In Moor's scheme, how one resolves the conceptual muddle (or decides the conceptual issue) can have a significant effect on which kinds of policies are acceptable. Getting clear about the conceptual issues is an important first step, but it is not a sufficient condition for being able to formulate a policy. Finally, the justification of a policy requires much factual knowledge, as well as an understanding of normative and ethical principles.

Consider the controversies surrounding the original Napster Web site and the RIAA regarding the free exchange of music over the Internet. Proponents on both sides of this dispute experienced difficulties in making convincing arguments for their respective positions due, in no small part, to confusion regarding the nature and the status of information (digitized music in the form of MP3 files) being exchanged between Internet users and the technology (P2P systems) that facilitated this exchange. Although cyber-technology has made it possible to exchange MP3 files, there is still debate, and arguably a great deal of confusion as well, about whether doing so should necessarily be illegal. Until the conceptual confusions or muddles underlying arguments used in the Napster vs. RIAA case in particular, and about the nature of P2P file-sharing systems in general, are resolved, it is difficult to frame an adequate policy regarding the exchange of MP3 files in P2P transactions.

How does Moor's insight that cyberethics issues need to be analyzed in terms of potential policy vacuums and conceptual muddles contribute to our earlier question as to whether there is anything unique or special about cyberethics? First, we should note that Moor takes no explicit stance on the question as to whether any cyberethics issues are unique. However, he does argue that cyberethics issues deserve special consideration because of the nature of cybertechnology itself, which is significantly different from alternative technologies in terms of the vast number of policy vacuums it generates (Moor 2001). So, even though the ethical issues associated with cybertechnology—that is, issues involving privacy, intellectual property, and so forth—might not be new or unique, they nonetheless can put significant pressure on our conceptual frameworks and nor-mative reasoning to a degree not found in other areas of applied ethics. Thus it would seem to follow, on Moor's line of reasoning, that an independent field of applied ethics that focuses on ethical aspects of cybertechnology is indeed justified.

▶ 1.4 CYBERETHICS AS A BRANCH OF APPLIED ETHICS: THREE DISTINCT PERSPECTIVES

Cyberethics, as a field of study, can be understood as a branch of *applied ethics*. Applied ethics, as opposed to theoretical ethics, examines practical ethical issues. It does so by analyzing those issues from the vantage point of one or more ethical theories. Whereas ethical theory is concerned with establishing logically coherent and consistent criteria in the form of standards and rules for evaluating moral problems, the principal aim of applied ethics is to analyze specific moral problems themselves through the application of ethical theory. As such, those working in fields of applied ethics, or practical ethics, are not inclined to debate some of the finer points of individual ethical theories. Instead, their interest in ethical theory is primarily with how one or more theories can be successfully applied to the analysis of specific moral problems that they happen to be investigating.

For an example of a practical ethics issue involving cybertechnology, consider again the original Napster controversy. Recall that at the heart of this dispute is the question: should proprietary information, in a digital format known as MP3 files, be allowed to be exchanged freely over the Internet? Those advocating the free exchange of MP3 files could appeal to one or more ethical theories to support their position. For example, they might appeal to utilitarianism, an ethical theory that is based on the principle that our policies and laws should be such that they produce the greatest good (happiness) for the greatest number of people. A utilitarian might argue that MP3 files should be distributed freely over the Internet because the consequences of allowing such a practice would make the majority of users happy and would thus contribute to the greatest good for the greatest number of persons affected.

Others might argue that allowing proprietary material to be exchanged freely over the Internet would violate the rights of those who created, and who legally own, the material. Proponents of this view could appeal to a nonutilitarian principle or theory that is grounded in the notion of respecting the rights of individuals. According to this view, an important consideration for an ethical policy is that it protects the rights of individuals—in this case, the rights of those who legally own the proprietary material in question—irrespective of the happiness that might or might not result for the majority of Internet users.

Notice that in our analysis of the dispute over the exchange of MP3 files on the Internet (in the Napster case), the application of two different ethical theories yielded two very different answers to the question of which policy or course of action ought to be adopted. Sometimes, however, the application of different ethical theories to a particular problem will yield similar solutions. We will examine in detail some standard ethical theories, including utilitarianism, in Chapter 2. Our main concern in this textbook is with applied, or practical, ethics issues, and not with ethical theory per se. Wherever appropriate, however, ethical theory will be used to inform our analysis of moral issues involving cybertechnology.

Understanding cyberethics as a field of applied ethics that examines moral issues pertaining to cybertechnology is an important first step. But much more needs to be said about the perspectives that interdisciplinary researchers bring to their analysis of the issues that make up this relatively new field. Most scholars and professionals conducting research in this field of applied ethics have proceeded from one of three different perspectives—professional ethics, philosophical ethics, or sociological/descriptive ethics.[12] Gaining a clearer understanding of what is meant by each of these perspectives is useful at this point.

1.4.1 Perspective #1: Cyberethics as a Field of Professional Ethics

According to those who view cyberethics primarily as a branch of *professional ethics*, the field can best be understood as identifying and analyzing issues of ethical responsibility for computer and information-technology (IT) professionals. Among the cyberethics issues considered from this perspective are those having to do with the computer/IT professional's role in designing, developing, and maintaining computer hardware and software systems. For example, suppose a programmer discovers that a software product she has been working on is about to be released for sale to the public even though that product is unreliable because it contains "buggy" software. Should she blow the whistle?

Those who see cyberethics essentially as a branch of professional ethics would likely draw on analogies from other professional fields, such as medicine and law. They would point out that in medical ethics and legal ethics, the principle focus of analysis is on issues of moral responsibility that affect individuals as members of these *professions*. By analogy, they would go on to argue that the same rationale should apply to the field of cyberethics – i.e., the primary, and possibly even exclusive, focus of cyberethics should be on issues of moral responsibility that affect computer/IT professionals. Don Gotterbarn (1995) can be interpreted as defending a version of this position when he asserts

The only way to make sense of 'Computer Ethics' is to narrow its focus to those actions that are within the control of the individual *moral* computer professional.[13] [Italics Gotterbarn]

So, in this passage, Gotterbarn suggests that the principal focus of computer ethics should be on issues of professional responsibility and not on the broader moral and social implications of that technology.

The analogies Gotterbarn uses to defend his argument are instructive. He notes, for example, that in the past, certain technologies have profoundly altered our lives, especially in the ways that many of us conduct our day-to-day affairs. Consider three such technologies: the printing press, the automobile, and the airplane. Despite the significant and perhaps revolutionary effects of each of these technologies, we do not have "printing press ethics," "automobile ethics," or "airplane ethics." So why, Gotterbarn asks, should we have a field of computer ethics apart from the study of those ethical issues that affect the professionals responsible for the design, development, and delivery of computer systems? In other words, Gotterbarn suggests that it is not the business of computer ethics to examine ethical issues other than those that affect computer professionals.

Professional Ethics and the Computer Science Practitioner

Gotterbarn's view about what the proper focus of computer ethics research and inquiry should be is shared by other practitioners in the discipline of computer science. However, some of those practitioners, as well as many philosophers and social scientists, believe that Gotterbarn's conception of computer ethics as simply a field of professional ethics is too narrow. In fact, some who identify themselves as computer professionals or as "information professionals," and who are otherwise sympathetic to Gotterbarn's overall attention to professional ethics issues, believe that a broader model is needed. For example, Elizabeth Buchanan (2004), in describing the importance of analyzing ethical issues in the "information professions," suggests that some nonprofessional ethics issues must also be examined because of the significant impact they have on noninformation professionals, including ordinary computer users. Consider that these issues can also affect people who have never used a computer.

Of course, Buchanan's category of "informational professional" is considerably broader in scope than Gotterbarn's notion of computer professional. But the central point of her argument still holds, especially in the era of the Internet and the World Wide Web. In the computing era preceding the Web, Gotterbarn's conception of the field as one limited to ethical issues concerning computer professionals might have seemed more plausible than it does today. Now, computers are virtually everywhere, and the ethical issues generated by certain uses of computers and cybertechnology affect virtually everyone, professional and nonprofessional alike.

Despite the critiques leveled against Gotterbarn's conception of the field, his position may turn out to be the most plausible of the three models we consider. Because of the social impact that computer and Internet technologies have had during the past three decades, we have tended to identify many of the ethical issues associated with these technologies, especially concerns affecting privacy and intellectual property, as computer ethics issues. But Deborah Johnson (2000) believes that in the future, computer-related ethical issues, such as privacy and property (that are currently associated with the field of computer ethics), may become part of what she calls "ordinary ethics." In fact, Johnson has suggested that computer ethics, as a separate field of applied ethics, may eventually "go away." However, even if Johnson's prediction turns out to be correct, computer ethics as a field that examines ethical issues affecting responsibility for computer professionals will, in all likelihood, still be needed. In this sense, then, Gotterbarn's original model of computer ethics might turn out to be the correct one in the long term.

Applying the Professional Ethics Model to Specific Scenarios

It is fairly easy to see how the professional ethics model can be used to analyze issues involving professional responsibility that directly impact computer professionals. For example, issues concerned with the development and implementation of critical software would fit closely with the professional model. But can that model be extended to include cases that may only affect computer professionals indirectly?

We can ask how some of the issues in the "Washingtonienne," Verizon, and Boyer scenarios, each described earlier in this chapter, might be analyzed from the perspective of professional ethics. First, consider the Washingtonienne scenario, which initially might seem to be outside the purview of computer ethics vis-à-vis professional ethics. However, some interesting and controversial questions arise that can have implications for computer professionals as well as for professional bloggers. For example, should online service providers hire programmers to design features that would support anonymity for individuals who post certain kinds of personal information (e.g., personal diaries such as Cutler's) to blogs aimed at sharing that information with a limited audience, as opposed to blogs whose content is intended to be available to the entire "online world"? Also, should online service providers be encouraged to include applications that enable bloggers to delete, permanently, some embarrassing information they had entered in a blog in the past—e.g., information that could threaten their current employment (as in the case of Jessica Cutler) or harm their chances or future employment (e.g., if information they had previously posted to a blog were discovered by a prospective employer)?

Consider the example of information about oneself that a person might have carelessly posted on Facebook when he or she was a first-year college student; the question of whether an individual's remarks entered in an online forum should remain there indefinitely (or should be stored in that forum's database in perpetuity) is one that is now hotly debated. Another aspect of the professional ethics model as applied to blogs is whether bloggers themselves should be expected to comply with a professional "blogger code of ethics," as some have proposed. For example, there are ethical codes of conduct that professional journalists are expected to observe. (We examine professional codes of ethics in detail in Chapter 4.)

Next, consider the Verizon scenario, which also might initially appear to be outside the purview of professional ethics. Like the Washingtonienne scenario, however, the Verizon controversy also has professional ethics implications. For example, should computer programmers and computer professionals design systems that allow commercial organizations such as the RIAA to engage in the surveillance of online activities of ordinary users? Should programmers be prohibited from developing P2P applications because they can be abused by some individuals in illicit file-sharing activities? Questions such as these clearly have an impact for computer professionals.

Finally, consider the Boyer scenario. From the vantage point of professional ethics, one might argue that cyberstalking in general and the murder of Amy Boyer in particular are not the kinds of concerns that are the proper business of computer ethics. We saw that someone such as Gotterbarn might ask why a crime that happened to involve the use of a computer should necessarily be construed as an issue for computer ethics. For example, he notes that a murder that happened to be committed with a surgeon's scalpel would not be considered an issue for medical ethics. While murders involving the use of a computer, like all murders, are serious moral and legal problems, Gotterbarn seems to imply that they are not examples of genuine computer ethics issues.

However, Gotterbarn and the advocates for his position are acutely aware that software developed by engineers can have implications that extend far beyond the computing profession itself. So, for example, engineers who develop code that can be used in applications that violate individual privacy may bear some of the responsibility for harms caused by that code. And ISPs who use those software applications could also share some responsibility for privacy violations. Thus, someone approaching the Boyer case from the perspective of professional ethics might ask the following kinds of questions: Was Boyer's right to privacy violated? If so, should the ISPs involved be held morally responsible or legally liable? And should the computer professionals who are employed by those ISPs, or who developed the software code that enabled Boyer's privacy to be violated, also be held responsible?

Many of the ethical issues discussed in this book have implications for computer professionals, either directly or indirectly. Issues that have a direct impact on computer professionals in general, and software engineers in particular, are examined in Chapter 4, which is dedicated to professional ethics. Computer science students and computer professionals will likely also want to assess some of the indirect implications that issues examined in Chapters 5 through 12 also have for the computing profession.

1.4.2 Perspective #2: Cyberethics as a Field of Philosophical Ethics

What, exactly, is *philosophical ethics* and how is it different from professional ethics? Since philosophical methods and tools are also used to analyze issues involving professional ethics, any attempt to distinguish between the two might seem arbitrary, perhaps even odd. For our purposes, however, a useful distinction can be drawn between the two fields because of the approach each takes in addressing ethical issues. Whereas professional ethics issues typically involve concerns of responsibility and obligation affecting individuals as members of a certain profession, philosophical ethics issues include broader concerns—social policies as well as individual behavior—that affect virtually everyone in society. Cybertechnology-related moral issues involving privacy, security, property, and free speech can affect everyone, including individuals who have never even used a computer.

To appreciate the perspective of cyberethics as a branch of philosophical ethics, consider James Moor's classic definition of the field. According to Moor (2007), cyberethics, or what he calls "computer ethics," is

> the analysis of the nature and social impact of computer technology and the corresponding formulation and justification of policies for the ethical use of such technology.[14]

Two points in Moor's definition are worth examining more closely. First, computer ethics (i.e., what we call "cyberethics") is concerned with the social impact of computers and cybertechnology in a broad sense, and not merely the impact of that technology for computer professionals. Secondly, this definition challenges us to reflect on the social impact of cybertechnology in a way that requires a justification for our social policies.

Why is cyberethics, as a field of philosophical ethics dedicated to the study of ethical issues involving cybertechnology, warranted when there aren't similar fields of applied ethics for other technologies? Recall our earlier discussion of Gotterbarn's observation that we do not have fields of applied ethics called "automobile ethics" or "airplane ethics," even though automobile and airplane technologies have significantly affected our day-to-day lives. Moor could respond to Gotterbarn's point by noting that the introduction of automobile and airplane technologies did not affect our social policies and norms in the same kinds of fundamental ways that computer technology has. Of course, we have had to modify and significantly revise certain laws and policies to accommodate the implementation of new kinds of transportation technologies. In the case of automobile technology, we had to extend, and in some cases modify, certain policies and laws previously used to regulate the flow of horse-drawn modes of transportation. And clearly, automobile and airplane technologies have revolutionized transportation, resulting in our ability to travel faster and farther than was possible in previous eras.

What has made the impact of computer technology significantly different from that of other modern technologies? We have already seen that for Moor, three factors contribute to this impact: logical malleability, policy vacuums, and conceptual muddles. Because cybertechnology is logically malleable, its uses often generate policy vacuums and conceptual muddles. In Section 1.3.2 we saw how certain kinds of conceptual muddles contributed to some of the confusion surrounding software piracy issues in general, and the Napster controversy in particular. What implications do these factors have for the standard methodology used by philosophers in the analysis of applied ethics issues?

Methodology and Philosophical Ethics
Philip Brey (2004) notes that the standard methodology used by philosophers to conduct research in applied ethics has three distinct stages in that an ethicist must

1. identify a particular controversial practice as a moral problem,

2. describe and analyze the problem by clarifying concepts and examining the factual data associated with that problem,

3. apply moral theories and principles in the deliberative process in order to reach a position about the particular moral issue.[15]

We have already noted (in Section 1.3) how the first two stages in this methodology can be applied to an analysis of ethical issues associated with digital piracy. We saw that, first, a practice involving the use of cybertechnology to "pirate" or make unauthorized copies of proprietary information was *identified* as morally controversial. At the second stage, the problem was *analyzed* in descriptive and contextual terms to clarify the practice and to situate it in a particular context. In the case of digital piracy, we saw that the concept of piracy could be analyzed in terms of moral issues involving theft and intellectual property theory. When we describe and analyze problems at this stage, we will want to be aware of and address any policy vacuums and conceptual muddles that are relevant.

At the third and final stage, the problem must be *deliberated* over in terms of moral principles (or theories) and logical arguments. Brey describes this stage in the method as the "deliberative process." Here, various arguments are used to justify the application of particular moral principles to the issue under consideration. For example, issues involving digital piracy can be deliberated upon in terms of one or more standard ethical theories, such as utilitarianism (defined in Chapter 2).

Applying the Method of Philosophical Ethics to Specific Scenarios

To see how the philosophical ethics perspective of cyberethics can help us to analyze a cluster of moral issues affecting cybertechnology, we revisit the Washingtonienne, Verizon, and Boyer scenarios introduced in the opening section of this chapter. In applying the philosophical ethics model to these scenarios, our first task is to identify one or more moral issues associated with each. We have already seen that these scenarios illustrate a wide range of ethical issues. For example, we saw that ethical issues associated with the Washingtonienne scenario include free speech, defamation, confidentiality, anonymity, and privacy with respect to blogs and blogging. But what kinds of policy vacuums and conceptual muddles, if any, arise in this case? For one thing, both the nature of a blog and the practices surrounding blogging are relatively new. Thus, not surprisingly, we have very few clear and explicit policies affecting the "blogosphere." To consider why this is so, we begin by asking: what, exactly, is a blog? For example, is it similar to a newspaper or a periodical (such the *New York Times* or *TIME Magazine*), which is held to standards of accuracy and truth? Or is a blog more like a tabloid (such as the *National Inquirer*), in which case there is little expectation of accuracy? Our answers to these questions may determine whether bloggers should be permitted to post anything they wish, without concern of liability for any of their remarks that may be false or defamatory, or both? At present, there are no clear answers to these and related questions surrounding blogs. So, it would seem that explicit policies are needed to regulate blogs and bloggers. But it would also seem that before we can frame explicit policies for blogging, we first need to resolve some important conceptual muddles.

Next, consider the Verizon vs. RIAA scenario. Among the ethical issues identified in that case were concerns affecting privacy, anonymity, surveillance, and intellectual property.[16] We can now ask whether any policy vacuums and conceptual muddles were generated in that case. We noted earlier that the original Napster scenario introduced controversies with respect to sharing proprietary MP3 files online. The Verizon scenario, however, introduces some issues that go beyond that concern. For example, what is an ISP user's expectation of privacy and anonymity while engaged in online activities? Is it permissible for commercial organizations such as the RIAA to monitor an individual's online activities, even when it suspects a user of exchanging proprietary files containing music or movies? Does the RIAA's behavior in this case violate any basic civil liberties guaranteed in the U.S. Constitution or EU Directives? The courts, thus far, have vacillated in their interpretation of these questions. So, arguably, a policy vacuum has emerged with respect to whether commercial organizations such as the RIAA should be allowed to engage in surveillance activities regarding users of P2P systems and whether they should be able to require that ISPs disclose the identities of their subscribers.

Finally, consider the Boyer scenario. Recall that one of the ethical concerns we identified in that scenario of cyberstalking had to do with personal privacy; among the complaints in the wrongful death suit filed by Amy Boyer's stepfather was that his stepdaughter's privacy had been violated. We next ask whether the specific privacy concerns involving the Boyer case have generated any policy vacuums or conceptual muddles. Note that the kind of personal information about Boyer that her stalker was able to retrieve from the Internet would likely be considered "public information," since information of that kind is also generally accessible in public records. Of course, it is now much easier to access public records because of their online availability, in many instances, than it was in the pre-computer era; so we might now ask whether our existing privacy laws and policies regarding the access and flow of personal information are still adequate. In other words, does a policy vacuum exist here? The fact that personal information residing in public databases can now be accessed with relative ease through the use of Internet search facilities would seem to pose a challenge for our existing privacy policies. So it would appear that a policy vacuum has emerged in the Boyer scenario as well.

Next, we ask whether any conceptual vacuums or muddles have also been introduced in the Boyer scenario. Consider criteria that we have traditionally used to distinguish between personal information that is essentially public and personal information that is considered private in nature. Is there also a conceptual muddle here? That is, does the concept of personal information itself need to be reexamined in an age of cybertechnology? (We will address this particular question in Chapter 5, where we examine a set of privacy concerns that some now refer to as the "problem of privacy in public." We will see that our traditional conception of privacy, which has informed our current policies, may indeed need to be rethought in light of vacuums introduced by cybertechnology.) Once the policy vacuums and conceptual muddles have been resolved, we can then move on to the third and final stage, where we deliberate on how best to resolve the privacy issue involving the Boyer scenario. In our discussion of ethical theory in Chapter 2, we will see how this is done.

1.4.3 Perspective #3: Cyberethics as a Field of Sociological/Descriptive Ethics

The two perspectives on cyberethics that we have examined thus far—professional ethics and philosophical ethics—can both be understood as *normative* inquiries into applied ethics issues. Normative inquiries or studies, which focus on evaluating and prescribing moral systems, can be contrasted with *descriptive* inquiries or studies. Descriptive ethics is, or aims to be, nonevaluative in approach; instead, it describes particular moral systems and reports how members of various groups and cultures view particular moral issues. This kind of analysis of ethical and social issues is often used by sociologists and social scientists; hence, our use of the expression "sociological/descriptive perspective" to analyze this methodological framework.

Descriptive vs. Normative Inquiries

Whereas descriptive investigations provide us with information about what *is* the case, normative inquiries evaluate situations from the vantage point of questions having to do with what *ought to be* the case. Those who approach cyberethics from the perspective of descriptive ethics often describe sociological aspects of a particular moral issue, such as the social impact of a specific technology on a particular community or social group. For example, one way of analyzing moral issues surrounding the "digital divide" (examined in Chapter 10) is first to describe the problem in terms of its impact on various sociodemographic groups involving social class, race, and gender. We can investigate whether, in fact, fewer poor people, non-whites, and women have access to cybertechnology than wealthy and middle-class persons, whites, and men. In this case, the investigation is one that is basically descriptive in character. If we were then to inquire whether the lack of access to technology for some groups relative to others was unfair, we would be engaging in a normative inquiry. For example, a normative investigation of this issue would question whether certain groups *should* have more access to cybertechnology than they currently have. The following scenario illustrates an approach to a particular cyberethics issue via the perspective of sociological/descriptive ethics.

► **SCENARIO 1–6:** The Impact of Technology X on Community Y

ABC Corporation, a company that employs 8,000 workers in Community Y, has decided to purchase and implement a new kind of computer/information technology, Technology X. The implementation of Technology X will likely have a significant impact for ABC's employees in particular, as well as for Community Y in general. It is estimated that 3,000 jobs at ABC will be eliminated when the new technology is implemented during the next six months. ■

Does the decision to implement Technology X pose a normative ethical problem for the ABC Corporation, as well as for Community Y? If we analyze the impact that Technology X has with respect to the number of jobs that are gained or lost, our investigation is essentially descriptive in nature. In reporting this phenomenon, we are simply describing or stating what *is/is not* at issue in this case. If, however, we argue that ABC should not implement this new technology (e.g., because it will displace workers in Community Y), then we make a claim that is normative (i.e., a claim about what *ought/ought not* to be the case). For example, one might argue that the workers should not be displaced because of certain contractual obligations that exist between ABC and its employees. Alternatively, one might argue that, if Technology X is implemented, certain factors should be taken into consideration in determining which workers would lose their jobs. Suppose that in the process of eliminating jobs, older workers and minority employees would be disproportionately affected. Would that have affected the way we view the situation?

Our initial account of the impact of Technology X's implementation for Community Y simply reported some descriptive information about the number of jobs that would likely be lost by employees at ABC Corporation, which has sociological implications. As our analysis of this scenario continued, however, we did much more than merely describe what the impact was; we also evaluated the impact for ABC's employees in terms of what we believed *ought* to have been done. In doing so, we shifted from an analysis based on some claims that were merely descriptive to an analysis in which the claims were essentially normative.

Some Benefits of Using the Sociological/Descriptive Approach to Analyze Cyberethics Issues

Why is the examination of cyberethics issues from the sociological/descriptive ethics perspective useful? Huff and Finholt (1994) suggest that focusing on descriptive aspects of social issues can help us to better understand many of the normative features and implications. In other words, when we understand the descriptive features of the social effects of a particular technology, the normative ethical questions become clearer. So, Huff and Finholt believe that analyzing the social impact of cybertechnology from the sociological/descriptive perspective can better prepare us for our subsequent analysis of practical ethical issues affecting our system of policies and laws.

We have already noted that virtually all of our social institutions, from work to education to government to finance, have been affected by cybertechnology. This technology has also had significant impacts on different sociodemographic sectors and segments of our population. The descriptive information that we gather about these groups can provide important information that, in turn, can inform legislators and policy makers who are drafting and revising laws in response to the effects of cybertechnology.

From the perspective of sociological/descriptive ethics, we can also better examine the impact that cybertechnology has for our understanding of concepts such as community and individuality. We can ask, for instance, whether certain developments in social networking technologies used in MySpace and Facebook have affected the way that we conceive traditional notions such as "community" and "neighbor." Is a community essentially a group of individuals with similar interests, or perhaps a similar ideology, irrespective of geographical limitations? Is national identity something that is, or may soon become, anachronistic? While these kinds of questions and issues in and of themselves are more correctly conceived as descriptive rather than normative concerns, they can have significant normative implications for our moral and legal systems as well. Much more will be said about the relationship between descriptive and normative approaches to analyzing ethical issues in Chapters 10 and 11, where we examine the impact of cybertechology on sociodemographic groups and on many of our social and political institutions.

Applying the Sociological/Descriptive Ethics Approach to Specific Scenarios

Consider how someone approaching cyberethics issues from the perspective of sociological/descriptive ethics might analyze the Washingtonienne, Verizon, and Boyer scenarios, described above. In the Washingtonienne case, the focus might be on gathering sociodemographic and socioeconomic data pertaining to the kinds of individuals who are likely to view and interact in blogs. For example, some social scientists might consider the income and educational levels of bloggers, as compared to individuals who engage in alternative kinds of online activities or who do not use the Internet at all. Others might be interested in determining which kinds of users view their blogs and online postings as simply an online outlet for the kind of personal information that traditionally was included only in one's (physical) diary. (Jessica Cutler's behavior seemed to fit this category.) Social and behavioral scientists might further inquire into why some individuals seem to display little-to-no concern about posting intimate details of their romantic and sexual encounters to online forums that could be read, potentially at least, by millions of people. They might also question why some bloggers, as well as many participants in other kinds of online forums such as MySpace and Facebook, are so eager to post personal information, including information about their location (at a given point in time) and about their recreational interests, to online forums, in an era when that kind of information is so easily tracked and recorded by individuals other than those for whom it is intended.

In analyzing the Verizon scenario from the perspective of sociological/descriptive ethics, social scientists might focus their attention on concerns involving "social control" on the part of nongovernmental organizations, such as the RIAA. For example, they might analyze this case from the point of view of user participation in P2P networks to see whether there has been a significant change in the behavior of those who currently use these forums, and whether certain groups are affected more than others, as a result of the RIAA's activities. They might also conduct surveys to see whether, as a result of the RIAA's threats and lawsuits, individuals have a greater fear about file sharing music in P2P systems.

Next consider the Boyer scenario with respect to how it might be analyzed by someone doing research from the point of view of sociological/descriptive ethics. For example, a researcher might inquire into whether there has been an increase in the number of stalking and stalking-related crimes. And if the answer to this question is "yes," the researcher might next question whether such an increase is linked to the widespread availability of cybertechnology. Also, the researcher might consider whether certain groups in the population are now more at risk than others with respect to being stalked in cyberspace. The researcher could inquire whether there are any statistical patterns to suggest that celebrities and certain high-profile individuals, such as politicians and corporate leaders, are more likely to be stalked via cybertechnology than are ordinary individuals. The researcher could ask if women are generally more vulnerable than men to the kinds of threats posed by cyberstalking. And, if they are, are younger, single women more likely to be stalked in cyberspace than women in other subgroups?

Also, a researcher approaching the Boyer scenario from the sociological/descriptive ethics perspective might set out to determine whether a profile for a typical cyberstalker can be established, by pursuing answers to the following kinds of questions: Is a typical cyberstalker someone who is young, white, and male? Is it likely that individuals who never would have thought of physically stalking a victim in geographical space might now be inclined to engage in cyberstalking, perhaps because of the relative ease of doing so with cybertechnology? Or is it the case that some of those same individuals might now be tempted to do so because they believe that they will not likely get caught? Also, has the fact that a potential cyberstalker realizes that he or she can stalk a victim on the Internet under the cloak of relative anonymity contributed to the increase in stalking-related activities? These are a few of the kinds of questions that could be examined from the sociological/descriptive perspective of cyberethics.

Table 1.2 summarizes some key characteristics that differentiate the three main perspectives for approaching cyberethics issues.

TABLE 1.2   Summary of Cyberethics Perspectives

Type of Perspective	Associated Disciplines	Issues Examined
Professional	Computer Science	Professional responsibility
	Engineering	System reliability/safety
	Library/Information Science	Codes of conduct
Philosophical	Philosophy	Privacy and anonymity
	Law	Intellectual property
		Free speech
Sociological/ Descriptive	Sociology Behavioral Sciences	Impact of cybertechnology on governmental/financial/educational institutions and sociodemographic groups

In Chapters 4–12, we examine specific cyberethics questions from the vantage points of three perspectives. Issues considered from the perspective of professional ethics are examined in Chapter 4. Cyberethics issues considered from the perspective of philosophical ethics, such as those involving privacy, security, and intellectual property and free speech, are examined in Chapters 5–9. And several of the issues considered in Chapters 10–12 are examined from the perspective of sociological/descriptive ethics.

▶ 1.5 A COMPREHENSIVE CYBERETHICS METHODOLOGY

The three different perspectives of cyberethics described in the preceding section might suggest that three different kinds of methodologies are needed to analyze the range of issues examined in this textbook. The goal of this section, however, is to show that a single, comprehensive method can be constructed, and that this method will be adequate in guiding us in our analysis of cyberethics issues.

Recall the standard model used in applied ethics, which we briefly examined in Section 1.4.2. There we saw that the standard model includes three stages, i.e., where a researcher must (1) identify an ethical problem, (2) describe and analyze the problem in conceptual and factual terms, and (3) apply ethical theories and principles in the deliberative process. We also saw that Moor argued that the conventional model was not adequate for an analysis of at least some cyberethics issues. Moor believed that additional steps, which address concerns affecting "policy vacuums" and "conceptual muddles," are sometimes needed before we can move from the second to the third stage of the methodological scheme. We must now consider whether the standard model, with Moor's additional steps included, is complete. Brey (2004) suggests that it is not.

Brey believes that while the (revised) standard model might work well in many fields of applied ethics, such as medical ethics, business ethics, and bioethics, it does not always fare well in cyberethics. Brey argues that the standard method, when used to identify ethical aspects of cybertechnology, tends to focus almost exclusively on the *uses* of that technology. As such, the standard method fails to pay sufficient attention to certain features that may be embedded in the technology itself, such as design features that may also have moral implications.

We might be inclined to assume that technology itself is neutral and that only the uses to which a particular technology is put are morally controversial. However, Brey and others believe that it is a mistake to conceive of technology, independent of its uses, as something that is value-free, or unbiased. Instead, they argue, moral values are often embedded or implicit in features built into technologies at the design stage. For example, some feminist critics have pointed out that in the past the ergonomic systems designed for drivers of automobiles were biased toward men and gave virtually no consideration to women. That is, considerations having to do with the average height and typical body dimensions of men were implicitly built into the design specification. These critics also note that decisions about how the ergonomic systems would be designed were all made by men, which likely accounts for the bias embedded in that particular technological system.

1.5.1 Is Cybertechnology Neutral?

As noted in the preceding section, Brey believes that cybertechnology has certain built-in values and biases that are not always obvious or easy to detect. He worries that these biases can easily go unnoticed by computer ethics researchers. An example of how difficult it can be to detect relevant biases and values can be found in a case involving noncybertechnology, such as gun technology. You have probably heard the expression, "Guns don't kill people; people kill people." An assumption underlying this slogan is that guns, independent of their applications or uses, are neutral. That is, guns in and of themselves are neither good nor bad. It would seem that there is an element of truth in this claim—after all, guns in and of themselves do not kill people. And until some person actually handles the gun, no one typically dies as a result of that gun. However, some critics note that the above slogan can be misleading if it is used to convey the claim that guns are neutral in the sense that they are no different from any other technologies or tools when it comes to violence.

Corlann Gee Bush (2006) has argued that gun technology, like all technologies, is biased in certain directions. She argues that certain features inherent in gun technology cause guns to be biased toward violence. To illustrate this bias, Bush appeals to an analogy from physics in which an atom that either loses or gains electrons through ionization becomes charged, or "valenced," in a certain direction. She notes that all technologies, including guns, are similarly valenced in that they tend to favor certain directions rather than others.

Bush concedes that devices other than guns can be used effectively to kill people. For example, a hammer, an ice pick, or even a certain kind of computer hardware device could each be used to kill someone. She argues, however, that guns are "valenced to violence" in a way that other tools and technologies that could also be used to kill people are not. She points out that the mere presence of a gun in a particular situation raises the level of violence. Of course, an assailant could bludgeon someone to death by using a certain kind of computer hardware device. The assailant could also use a hammer to strike several blows to a person's head causing that person's death, or he could even stab someone to death with an ice pick. Although ice picks, hammers, and computer hardware devices *can* each be used to kill people, these objects are less likely to result in the unplanned or accidental death of an individual than would the presence of a gun in a similar situation. They are less likely to result in someone's death because of the respective purposes and functions of ice picks, hammers, and computing devices.

Note that in cases involving the presence of a computer device, an ice pick, or a hammer, an assailant must make physical contact with his victim and must then apply some measure of physical force to carry out the murder. In the case involving a gun, on the other hand, the assailant is not required to make any physical contact at all. But perhaps more importantly, computer hardware devices, hammers, and ice picks are not charged or valenced toward killing someone in the same way guns are. The function of gun technology is such that it lends itself to violence and killing, by virtue of its intended purpose and design, even if a resultant death is not intended. So, if Bush is correct, technology is not neutral.

At this point, you might ask what, exactly, the preceding discussion about technologies being valenced has to do with our concern that computer technology might have embedded biases. Our purpose has been to show that all technologies and, by implication, computer technology, have embedded values and biases. Locating biases in software is important, and in Chapter 10 we examine some specific cases that illustrate gender bias in educational software and video games. Because Brey worries that many computer ethics researchers assume computer technology is inherently neutral, he proposes a method that causes us to question such an assumption. To employ his method, we need to locate what Brey calls "embedded normative values" in computer technology. Exposing such values inherent in various computer technologies is the first step of Brey's "disclosive method of computer ethics."

1.5.2   A "Disclosive" Method for Cyberethics

As noted earlier, Brey believes that the standard, or what he calls "mainstream," applied ethics methodology is not always adequate for identifying moral issues involving cybertechnology. Brey worries that using the standard model we might fail to notice certain features embedded in the design of cybertechnology. He also worries about the standard method of applied ethics because it tends to focus on known moral controversies, and because it fails to identify certain practices involving the use of cybertechnology that have moral import but that are not yet known. Brey refers to such practices as having "morally opaque" (or morally nontransparent) features, which he contrasts with "morally transparent" features.

According to Brey, morally controversial features that are transparent tend to be easily recognized as morally problematic. For example, many people are aware that the practice of placing closed circuit video surveillance cameras in undisclosed locations is controversial from a moral point of view. Brey notes that it is, however, generally much more difficult to discern morally opaque features in technology. These features can be morally opaque for one of two reasons: either they are unknown or they are known but perceived to be morally neutral.[17]

Consider an example of each type of morally opaque (or morally nontransparent) feature. Computerized practices involving data mining (defined in Chapter 5) would be unknown to those who have never heard of the concept of data mining and who are unfamiliar with data mining technology. However, this technology should not be assumed to be morally neutral merely because data mining techniques are unknown to nontechnical people, including many ethicists. Even if such techniques are opaque to many users, data mining practices raise certain moral issues pertaining to personal privacy.

Next consider an example of a morally opaque feature in which a technology is well known. Most Internet users are familiar with search engine technology. What users might fail to recognize, however, is that certain uses of search engines can be morally controversial with respect to personal privacy. Consequently, one of the features of search engine technology can be morally controversial in a sense that it is not obvious or transparent to many people, including those who are very familiar with and who use search engine technology. So, while a well-known technology, such as search engine programs, might appear to be morally neutral, a closer analysis of practices involving this technology will disclose that it has moral implications.

Figure 1.1 illustrates some differences between morally opaque and morally transparent features.

Brey argues that an adequate methodology for computer ethics must first identify, or "disclose," features that, without proper probing and analysis, would go unnoticed as having moral implications. Thus, an extremely important first step in Brey's "disclosive method" is to reveal moral values embedded in the various features and practices associated with cybertechnology itself.

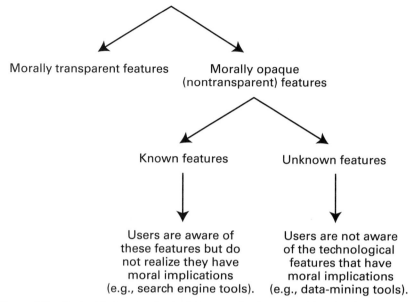

Figure 1.1 Embedded technological features having moral implications.

1.5.3 An Interdisciplinary and Multilevel Method for Analyzing Cyberethics Issues

Brey's disclosive model is *interdisciplinary* because it requires that computer scientists, philosophers, and social scientists collaborate. It is also *multilevel* because conducting computer ethics research requires three levels of analysis:

- disclosure level
- theoretical level
- application level

First of all, the moral values embedded in the design of computer systems must be disclosed. To do this, we need computer scientists because they understand computer technology much better than philosophers and social scientists do. However, social scientists are also needed to evaluate system design and make it more user-friendly. Then philosophers can determine whether existing ethical theories are adequate to test the newly disclosed moral issues or whether more theory is needed. Finally, computer scientists, philosophers, and social scientists must cooperate by applying ethical theory in deliberations about moral issues.[18] In Chapter 2, we examine a range of ethical theories that can be used.

In the deliberations involved in applying ethical theory to a particular moral problem, one remaining methodological step also needs to be resolved. Jeroen van den Hoven (2000) has noted that methodological schemes must also address the "problem of justification of moral judgments." For our purposes, we use the strategies of logical analysis included in Chapter 3 to justify the moral theories we apply to particular issues.

Table 1.3 describes the academic disciplines and the corresponding tasks and functions involved in Brey's disclosive model.

TABLE 1.3 Brey's Disclosive Model

Level	Disciplines Involved	Task/Function
Disclosure	Computer Science Social Science (optional)	Disclose embedded features in computer technology that have moral import
Theoretical	Philosophy	Test newly disclosed features against standard ethical theories
Application	Computer Science Philosophy Social Science	Apply standard or newly revised/formulated ethical theories to the issues

It is in the interdisciplinary spirit of the disclosive methodology proposed by Brey that we will examine the range of cyberethics issues described in Chapters 4–12.

▶ 1.6 A COMPREHENSIVE STRATEGY FOR APPROACHING CYBERETHICS ISSUES

The following methodological scheme, which expands on the original three-step scheme introduced in Section 1.4.2, is intended as a strategy to assist you in identifying and analyzing the specific cyberethics issues examined in this book. Note, however, that this procedure is not intended as a precise algorithm for resolving those issues in some definitive manner. Rather, its purpose is to guide you in the identification, analysis, and deliberation processes by summarizing key points that we have examined in Chapter 1.

Step 1. *Identify* a practice involving cybertechnology, or a feature of that technology, that is controversial from a moral perspective.

    1a. Disclose any hidden or opaque features.

    1b. Assess any descriptive components of the ethical issue via the sociological implications it has for relevant social institutions and sociodemographic groups.

    1c. In analyzing the normative elements of that issue, determine whether there are any specific guidelines, i.e., social policies or ethical codes, that can help resolve the issue (for example, see the relevant professional codes of conduct described in Chapter 4 and Appendixes A–E).

    1d. If the normative ethical issue cannot be resolved through the application of existing policies, codes of conduct, etc., go to Step 2.

Step 2. *Analyze* the ethical issue by clarifying concepts and situating it in a context.

    2a. If a policy vacuums exists, go to Step 2b; otherwise, go to Step 3.

    2b. Clear up any conceptual muddles involving the policy vacuum and go to Step 3.

Step 3. *Deliberate* on the ethical issue. The deliberation process requires two stages.

   3a. Apply one or more ethical theories (see Chapter 2) to the analysis of the moral issue, and then go to Step 3b.

   3b. Justify the position you reached by evaluating it via the standards and criteria for successful logic argumentation (see Chapter 3).

Note that you are now in a position to carry out much of the work required in the first two steps of this methodological scheme. In order to satisfy the requirements in Step 1d, a step that is required in cases involving professional ethics issues, you will need to consult the relevant sections of Chapter 4. Upon completing Chapter 2, you will be able to execute Step 3a; and after completing Chapter 3, you will be able to satisfy the requirements for Step 3b.

▶ 1.7 CHAPTER SUMMARY

In this introductory chapter, we defined several key terms, including *cyberethics* and *cybertechnology*, used throughout this textbook. We also briefly described four evolutionary phases of cyberethics, from its origins as a loosely configured and informal field concerned with ethical and social issues involving stand-alone (mainframe) computers to a more fully developed field that is today concerned with ethical aspects of ubiquitous, networked computers. We then briefly considered whether any cyberethics issues are unique or special in a nontrivial sense. We next examined three different perspectives on cyberethics, showing how computer scientists, philosophers, and social scientists each tend to view the field and approach the issues that comprise it. Within that discussion, we also examined some ways in which embedded values and biases affecting cybertechnology can be disclosed and thus made explicit. Finally, we introduced a comprehensive methodological scheme that incorporates the expertise of computer scientists, philosophers, and social scientists who work in the field of cyberethics.

▶ REVIEW QUESTIONS

1. What, exactly, is *cyberethics*? How is it different from and similar to computer ethics, information ethics, and Internet ethics?
2. What is meant by the term *cybertechnology*? How is it similar to and different from computer technology?
3. Identify and briefly describe some key aspects of each of the "four phases" in the evolution of cyberethics as a field of applied ethics.
4. Why does Walter Maner believe that at least some cyberethics issues are unique? What arguments does he provide to support his view?
5. Why is it important to distinguish between unique technological features and unique ethical issues when evaluating the question, Are cyberethics issues unique?
6. What alternative strategy does James Moor use to analyze the question whether cyberethics issues are unique ethical issues?
7. Why does Moor believe that cybertechnology poses special problems for identifying and analyzing ethical issues?
8. Explain what Moor means by the expressions "logical malleability," "policy vacuum," and "conceptual muddle."
9. What is applied ethics, and how is it different from theoretical ethics?
10. Summarize the principal aspects of the perspective of cyberethics as a field of *professional* ethics.

11. Describe the principal aspects of the perspective of cyberethics as a field of *philosophical* ethics.
12. Summarize the key elements of the perspective of cyberethics as a field of *sociological/descriptive* ethics.
13. Describe the kinds of criteria used to distinguish normative ethical inquiries from those that are essentially descriptive.
14. What are the three elements of the standard, or "mainstream," method for conducting applied ethics research?
15. How is Philip Brey's "disclosive method" of computer ethics different from what Brey calls "mainstream computer ethics"?
16. Describe Corlann Bush's argument for why technology is not neutral.
17. How can Bush's arguments regarding the *nonneutrality* of technology be used to support Brey's point about embedded values in cybertechnology?
18. What does Brey mean by "morally opaque" or "morally nontransparent" features embedded in computer technology?
19. In which ways is Brey's disclosive method "multilevel"? Briefly describe each level in his methodology.
20. In which ways is that method also "multidisciplinary" or interdisciplinary? Which disciplines does it take into consideration?

▶ DISCUSSION QUESTIONS

1. Identify and critically analyze some ethical issues that arise in the "Washingtonienne" scenario. Should Jessica Cutler's anonymity have been protected, and should the contents of her online diary have been protected from their subsequent publication in *Wonkette?* Explain.
2. Describe and critically evaluate some ethical issues that arise in the scenario involving Verizon and the RIAA. Was the RIAA simply protecting its intellectual property interests, or did it go too far in the Verizon case? Explain.
3. List and critically analyze some ethical concerns that arise in the Amy Boyer cyberstalking incident. What actions, if any, can/should ISPs be expected to take to avoid future online stalking incidents that might result in a stalkee's death? Explain.
4. Assess Don Gotterbarn's arguments for the claim that computer ethics is, at bottom, a field of applied ethics whose primary concern should be moral-responsibility issues for computer professionals. Do you agree with his position? Why? How might Gotterbarn's view of the field of computer ethics turn out to be the correct one? Explain.
5. What are some of the benefits of using the sociological/descriptive ethics model for analyzing cyberethics issues? Identify and briefly describe a specific incident where this method can be applied.
6. Recall the key elements of the "comprehensive strategy" for approaching cyberethics that we examined in Section 1.6. Identify a contemporary controversial issue or practice involving cybertechnology and then apply the first two steps of the comprehensive model to it.

▶ ESSAY/PRESENTATION QUESTIONS

1. Think of a controversial practice involving cybertechnology that has not yet been identified as an ethical issue, but which might eventually be recognized as one that has moral implications. Apply Brey's disclosive method to see whether you can isolate any embedded values or biases affecting that practice. Are you also able to identify any morally opaque or morally nontransparent features affecting that practice? Explain.
2. We identified three main perspectives from which cyberethics issues can be examined. Can you think of any additional perspectives from which cyberethics issues might also be analyzed? In addition to the Washingtonienne, Verizon, and Boyer scenarios that we examined, can you think of other cases involving cyberethics issues that would benefit from being analyzed from all three perspectives considered in Chapter 1? Explain.
3. Much has been written about the benefits and risks of participating in social networking services (SNSs) such as Facebook and MySpace, and we briefly described some controversies associated with these forums. To

date, we do not have clear and coherent policies governing one's participation in these forums; nor do we have clear and explicit policies regarding which kinds of personal information from these forums should be accessible to third parties. So, it would seem that these forums can easily generate what James Moor calls "policy vacuums." Moor believes that before we can fill these vacuums with successful policies, we must first identify and resolve any conceptual muddles that arise. How many kinds of conceptual muddles can you identify with respect to the SNSs in which you participate?

4. We briefly considered the question as to whether at least some cyberethics issues are new or unique ethical issues. Can you think of any ethical issues affecting cybertechnology that would not have been possible if computers and cybertechnology had never been developed and implemented? If no cyberethics are unique in a nontrivial sense, how can the field of cyberethics be justified as a distinct field of applied ethics? Explain.

▶ ENDNOTES

1. See Richard Leiby, "The Hill's Sex Diarist Reveals All (Well Some)," *The Washington Post* (May 23, 2004), p. D03. Also available at http://www.washingtonpost.com/wp-dyn/articles/A48909-2004May22.html (accessed July 27, 2008). Also see Grodzinsky and Tavani (2009).
2. See Electronic Privacy Information Center, "Verizon v RIAA." Available at http://epic.org/privacy/copyright/verizon/ (accessed July 30, 2008). Also see Grodzinsky and Tavani (2005).
3. See A. J. Hitchcock, "Cyberstalking and Law Enforcement: Keeping Up With the Web," *Link-UP* (July/August 2000). Available at http://computeme.tripod.com/cyberstalk.html (accessed July 30, 2008). Also see Grodzinsky and Tavani (2004).
4. Some have used a combination of these two expressions. For example, Ess (2009) uses "information and computer ethics" (ICE) to refer to ethical issues affecting "digital media." Also, Capurro (2007) uses the expression "Intercultural Information Ethics" (IIE).
5. Floridi (2007, p. 63) contrasts Information Ethics (IE) with computer ethics (CE), by noting that the former is the "philosophical foundational counterpart of CE."
6. See the interview conducted with Paul Ceruzzi in the BBC/PBS video series, *The Machine That Changed the World* (1990).
7. For example, Bynum (2008) notes that Norbert Weiner, in his writings on cybernetics in the late 1940s, anticipated some of these concerns.
8. My analysis of the four phases in this section is adapted from and expands on Tavani (2001). Note that what I am calling a "technological phase" is not to be confused with something as precise as the expression "computer generation," which is often used to describe specific stages in the evolution of computer hardware systems.
9. Maner (2004, p. 41) argues that computers have generated "entirely new ethical issues, unique to computing, that do not surface in other areas."
10. My analysis of the uniqueness debate here is adapted from Tavani (2002a).
11. Moor (2004), p. 107.
12. My scheme for analyzing computer-ethics issues from these perspectives is adapted from Tavani (2002b).
13. Gotterbarn (1995), p. 21.
14. Moor (2007), p. 31.
15. Brey (2004), pp. 55–56.
16. See, for example, Grodzinsky and Tavani (2005) for an analysis of this case in terms of these issues.
17. For more details on this distinction, see Brey (2004), pp. 56–57.
18. See Brey, pp. 64–65.

▶ REFERENCES

Barger, Robert N. 2008. *Computer Ethics: A Case-Based Approach*. New York: Cambridge University Press.

Brey, Philip. 2004. "Disclosive Computer Ethics." In R. A. Spinello and H. T. Tavani, eds. *Readings in CyberEthics*. 2nd ed. Sudbury MA: Jones and Bartlett Publishers, pp. 55–66. Reprinted from *Computers and Society* 30, no. 4 (2000): 10–16.

Brey, Philip. 2005. "Freedom and Privacy in Ambient Intelligence," *Ethics and Information Technology* 7, no. 4: 157–66.

Buchanan, Elizabeth A. 2004. "Ethical Considerations for the Information Professions." In R. A. Spinello and H. T. Tavani, eds. In *Readings in CyberEthics*. 2nd ed. Sudbury, MA: Jones and Bartlett Publishers, pp. 613–24.

Buchanan, Elizabeth A., and Kathrine A. Henderson. 2009. *Case Studies in Library and Information Science Ethics*. Jefferson NC: McFarland.

Bush, Corlann Gee. 2006. "Women and the Assessment of Technology." In M. Winston and R. Edelbach, eds. *Society, Ethics, and Technology*. 3rd ed. Belmont, CA: Wadsworth, pp. 69–83. Reprinted from J. Rothschild, ed. *Machina Ex Dea*. New York: Teacher's College Press, 1983, pp. 151–70.

Bynum, Terrell Ward. 2008. "Milestones in the History of Information and Computer Ethics." In K. E. Himma and H. T. Tavani, eds. *The Handbook of Information and Computer Ethics*. Hoboken NJ: John Wiley and Sons, pp. 25–48.

Capurro, Rafael. 2007. "Intercultural Information Ethics." In R. Capurro, J. Freübrauer, and T. Hausmanninger, eds. *Localizing the Internet*. Munich: Fink Verlag, pp. 21–38.

Ess, Charles. 2009. *Digital Media Ethics*. London U.K.: Polity Press.

Floridi, Luciano. 2007. "Information Ethics: On the Philosophical Foundations of Computer Ethics." In J. Weckert, ed. *Computer Ethics*. Aldershot U.K.: Ashgate, pp. 63–82. Reprinted from Ethics and Information Technology 1, no. 1 (1999): pp. 37–56.

Gotterbarn, Don. 1995. "Computer Ethics: Responsibility Regained." In D. G. Johnson and H. Nissenbaum, eds. *Computing, Ethics, and Social Values*. Upper Saddle River, NJ: Prentice Hall.

Grodzinsky, Francis S., and Herman T. Tavani. 2004. "Ethical Reflections on Cyberstalking." In R. A. Spinello and H. T. Tavani, eds. *Readings in CyberEthics*. 2nd ed. Sudbury MA: Jones and Bartlett Publishers, pp. 561–70.

Grodzinsky, Frances S., and Herman T. Tavani. 2005. "P2P Networks and the *Verizon v. RIAA* Case." *Ethics and Information Technology* 7, no. 4: 243–50.

Grodzinsky, Frances S., and Herman T. Tavani. 2009. "Can the 'Contextual Integrity' Model of Privacy Be Applied to Personal Blogs in the Blogosphere?" In M. Bottis, ed. *Proceedings of the Eighth International Conference on Computer Ethics—Philosophical Inquiry*. Athens, Greece: Nomiki Bibliothiki, pp. 303–11.

Huff, Chuck, and Thomas Finholt, eds. 1994. *Social Issues in Computing: Putting Computing in its Place*. New York: McGraw Hill.

Johnson, Deborah G. 2000. "The Future of Computer Ethics." In G. Collste, ed. *Ethics in the Age of Information Technology*. Linköping, Sweden: Centre for Applied Ethics, pp. 17–31.

Johnson, Deborah G. 2009. *Computer Ethics*. 4th ed. Upper Saddle River, NJ: Prentice Hall.

Langford, Duncan, ed. 2000. *Internet Ethics*. New York: St. Martin's Press.

Maner, Walter. 2004. "Unique Ethical Problems in Information Technology." In T. W. Bynum and S. Rogerson, eds. *Computer Ethics and Professional Responsibility*. Malden, MA: Blackwell, pp. 39–59. Reprinted from *Science and Engineering Ethics* 2, no. 2 (1996): 137–54.

Moor, James H. 2001. "The Future of Computer Ethics: You Ain't Seen Nothing Yet." *Ethics and Information Technology* 3, no. 2: 89–91.

Moor, James H. 2004. "Just Consequentialism and Computing." In R. A. Spinello and H. T. Tavani, eds. *Readings in CyberEthics*. 2nd ed. Sudbury, MA: Jones and Bartlett Publishers, pp. 407–17. Reprinted from *Ethics and Information Technology* 1, no. 1 (1999): 65–69.

Moor, James H. 2005. "Should We Let Computers Get Under Our Skin?" In R. Cavalier ed. *The Impact of the Internet on Our Moral Lives*. Albany, NY: State University of New York Press, pp. 121–38.

Moor, James H. 2007. "What Is Computer Ethics?" In J. Weckert, ed. *Computer Ethics*. Aldershot, UK: Ashgate, pp. 31–40. Reprinted from *Metaphilosophy* 16, no. 4 (1985): 266–75.

Tavani, Herman T. 2001. "The State of Computer Ethics as a Philosophical Field of Inquiry." *Ethics and Information Technology* 3, no. 2: 97–108.

Tavani, Herman T. 2002a "The Uniqueness Debate in Computer Ethics: What Exactly Is at Issue, and Why Does it Matter?" *Ethics and Information Technology*, 4, no. 1: 37–54.

Tavani, Herman T. 2002b "Applying an Interdisciplinary Approach to Teaching Computer Ethics" *IEEE Technology and Society Magazine* 21, no. 3: 32–38.

van den Hoven, Jeroen. 2000. "Computer Ethics and Moral Methodology." In R. Baird, R. Ramsower, and S. Rosenbaum, eds. *Cyberethics: Social and Moral Issues in the Computer Age*. Amherst, NY: Prometheus Books, pp. 80–94. Reprinted from *Metaphilosophy*, 28, no. 3 (1997): 234–48.

▶ FURTHER READINGS

Abelson, Hal, Ken Ledeen, and Harry Lewis. *Blown to Bits: Your Life, Liberty and Happiness after the Digital Explosion*. Upper Saddle River, NJ: Addison-Wesley, 2008.

Carbo, Toni, and Martha M. Smith. "Global Information Ethics: Intercultural Perspectives on Past and Future Research," *Journal for the American Society for Information Science and Technology* 59, no. 7 (2008): 1111–23.

De Palma, Paul, ed. *Computers in Society 08/09*. 14th ed. New York: McGraw Hill, 2008.

Friedman, Batya, Peter Kahn, and Alan Borning. "Value Sensitive Design and Information Systems." In K. E. Himma and H. T. Tavani, eds. *The Handbook of Information and Computer Ethics*. Hoboken, NJ: John Wiley and Sons, 2008, pp. 69–101.

Maner, Walter. "Heuristic Methods for Computer Ethics." In J. H. Moor and T. W. Bynum, eds. *Cyberphilosophy: The Intersection of Computing and Philosophy*. Malden, MA: Blackwell, 2002, pp. 243–69.

Mitcham, Carl, ed. *Encyclopedia of Science, Technology, and Ethics*. 4 Vols. New York: Macmillan, 2005.

Moor, James H. "Why We Need Better Ethics for Emerging Technologies." In J. van den Hoven and J. Weckert, eds. *Information Technology and Moral Philosophy*. New York: Cambridge University Press, 2008, pp. 26–39.

van den Hoven, Jeroen. "Moral Methodology and Information Technology." In K. E. Himma and H. T. Tavani, eds. *The Handbook of Information and Computer Ethics*. Hoboken, NJ: John Wiley and Sons, 2008, pp. 49–67.

▶ ONLINE RESOURCES

Association for Computing—Special Interest Group on Computers and Society. http://www.sigcas.org/.

Bibliography on Computing, Ethics, and Social Responsibility. http://cyberethics.cbi.msstate.edu/biblio/.

Computer Professionals for Social Responsibility (CPSR). http://cpsr.org/.

Developing on/off-line Computer Ethics (Dolce). http://csethics.uis.edu/dolce/.

Heuristic Methods for Computer Ethics. http://csweb.cs.bgsu.edu/maner/heuristics/maner.pdf.

International Center for Information Ethics (ICIE). http://icie.zkm.de/.

International Society for Ethics and Information Technology. http://www.uwm.edu/Dept/SOIS/cipr/inseit.html.

Research Center for Computing and Society. http://www.southernct.edu/organizations/rccs/.

Ethical Concepts and Ethical Theories: Establishing and Justifying a Moral System

In Chapter 1, we defined cyberethics as the study of moral issues involving cybertechnology. However, we have not yet defined what is meant by *ethics, morality,* and *the study of moral issues.* In Chapter 2 we define these terms as well as other foundational concepts, and we examine a set of ethical theories that will guide us in our deliberation on the specific cyberethics issues we confront in Chapters 4–12. To accomplish the objectives of Chapter 2, we provide answers to the following questions:

- What is ethics, and how is it different from morality or a moral system?
- What are the elements that make up a moral system?
- Where do the rules in a moral system come from, and how are they justified?
- How is a philosophical study of morality different from studying morality from the perspectives of religion and law?
- Is morality essentially a personal, or private, matter, or is it a public phenomenon?
- Is morality simply relative to particular cultures and thus culturally determined?
- How is meaningful dialogue about cyberethics issues that are global in scope possible in a world with diverse cultures and belief systems?
- What roles do classic and contemporary ethical theories play in the analysis of moral issues involving cybertechnology?
- Are traditional ethical theories adequate to handle the wide range of moral controversies affecting cybertechnology?

▶ 2.1 ETHICS AND MORALITY

Ethics is derived from the Greek *ethos*, and the term *morality* has its roots in the Latin *mores*. Both the Greek and the Latin terms refer to notions of custom, habit, behavior, and character. Although "ethics" and "morality" are often used interchangeably in everyday discourse, we draw some important distinctions between the two terms as we will use them in this textbook. First, we define ethics as the study of morality.[1] This definition, of course, raises two further questions:

a. What is *morality*?
b. What is *the study of morality*?

We have begun to answer question (b) in Chapter 1, where we described three approaches to cyberethics issues. You may want to review Section 1.4, which describes how moral issues can be studied from the perspectives of professional ethics, philosophical ethics, and sociological/descriptive ethics. We will say more about the study of morality from a philosophical perspective in Section 2.1.2. Now we begin by answering question (a).

2.1.1 What Is Morality?

There is no universally agreed upon definition of "morality" among ethicists and philosophers. For our purposes, however, *morality* can be defined as a system of rules for guiding human conduct, and principles for evaluating those rules. Note that (i) morality is a *system*, and (ii) it is a system comprised of moral *rules* and *principles*. Moral rules can be understood as rules of conduct, which are very similar to the notion of policies, described in Chapter 1. There, "policies" were defined as rules of conduct that have a wide range of application. According to James Moor (2004), policies range from formal laws to informal, implicit guidelines for actions.

There are two kinds of rules of conduct:

1. *Directives* that guide our conduct as individuals (at the microlevel)
2. *Social policies* framed at the macrolevel

Directives are rules that guide our individual actions and direct us in our moral choices at the "microethical" level (i.e., the level of individual behavior). "Do not steal" and "Do not harm others" are examples of directives. Other kinds of rules guide our conduct at the "macrolevel" (i.e., at the level of social policies and social norms).

Rules of conduct that operate at the macroethical level guide us in both framing and adhering to social policies. For example, rules such as "Proprietary software should not be duplicated without proper authorization," or "Software that can be used to invade the privacy of users should not be developed," are instances of social policies. Notice the correlation between the directive "Do not steal" (a rule of conduct at the microlevel), and the social policy "Unauthorized duplication of software should not be allowed" (a rule of conduct at the macrolevel). In Section 2.1.2 we will see that both types of rules of conduct are derived from a set of "core values" in a moral system.

The rules of conduct in a moral system are evaluated against standards called *principles*. For example, the principle of social utility, which is concerned with

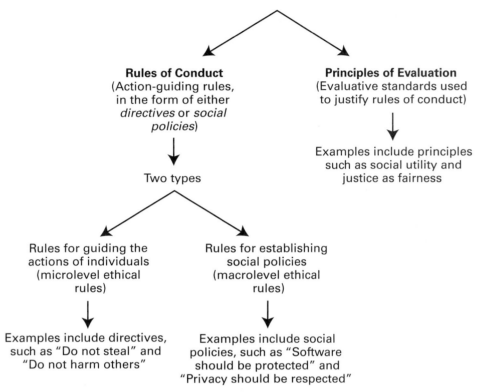

Figure 2.1 Basic components of a moral system.

promoting the greatest good for the greatest number, can be used as a "litmus test" for determining whether the policy "Proprietary software should not be copied without permission" can be justified on moral grounds. In this case, the policy in question could be justified by showing that not allowing the unauthorized copying of software will produce more overall social good than will a policy that permits software to be duplicated freely.

Similarly, the policy "Users should not have their privacy violated" might be justified by appealing to the same principle of social utility. Or a different principle such as "respect for persons," or possibly a principle based on the notion of fairness, might be used to justify the social policy in question. Figure 2.1 illustrates the different kinds of rules and principles that comprise a moral system.

What Kind of a System Is a Moral System?

According to Bernard Gert (2005, 2007), morality is a "system whose purpose is to prevent harm and evils." In addition to preventing harm, a moral system aims at promoting human flourishing. Although there is some disagreement regarding the extent to which the promotion of human flourishing is required of a moral system, virtually all ethicists believe that, at a minimum, the fundamental purpose of a moral system is to prevent or alleviate harm and suffering. We have already seen that at the heart of a moral system are rules of conduct and principles of evaluation. We next consider some other characteristics that define a moral system.

Gert describes a moral system as one that is both public and informal. The system is *public*, he argues, because everyone must know what the rules are that define it. Gert uses the analogy of a game, which has a goal and a corresponding set of rules. The rules are understood by all of the players, and the players use the rules to guide their behavior in legitimately achieving the goal of the game. The players can also use the rules to evaluate or judge the behavior of other players in the game. However, there is one important difference between a moral system and a game: Not everyone is required to participate in a game, but we are all obligated to participate in a moral system.

Morality is also *informal* because, Gert notes, a moral system has no formal authoritative judges presiding over it. Unlike games in professional sports that have rules enforced by referees in a manner that approaches a legal system, morality is less formal. A moral system is more like a game of cards or like a "pickup game" in baseball or basketball. Here the players are aware of the rules, but even in the absence of a formal official or referee to enforce the game's rules, players generally adhere to them.

Gert's model of a moral system includes two additional features: *rationality* and *impartiality*. A moral system is rational in that it is based on principles of logical reason accessible to ordinary persons. Morality cannot involve special knowledge that can be understood only by privileged individuals or groups. The rules in a moral system must be available to all rational persons who, in turn, are *moral agents*, bound by the system of moral rules. We do not hold nonmoral agents (such as pets, young children, and mentally challenged persons) morally responsible for their own actions, but moral agents often have responsibilities to some nonmoral agents.[2]

A moral system is *impartial* in the sense that the moral rules are ideally designed to apply equitably to all participants in the system. In an ideal moral system, all rational persons are willing to accept the rules of the system, even if they do not know in advance what their particular place in that system will be. To ensure that impartiality will be built into a moral system, and that its members will be treated as fairly as possible, Gert invokes the "blindfold of justice" principle. Imagine that you are blindfolded while deciding what the rules of a moral system will be. Since you do not know in advance what position you will occupy in that system, it is in your own best interest to design a system in which everyone will be treated fairly. As an impartial observer who is also rational, you will want to ensure against the prospect of ending up in a group that is treated unfairly.[3]

Table 2.1 summarizes four key features in Gert's model of a moral system.

TABLE 2-1 Four Features of Gert's Moral System

Public	Informal	Rational	Impartial
The rules are known to all of the members.	The rules are informal, not like formal laws in a legal system.	The system is based on principles of logical reason accessible to all its members.	The system is not partial to any one group or individual.

2.1.2 Deriving and Justifying the Rules of a Moral System

Thus far, we have defined morality as a system that is public, informal, rational, and impartial. We have also seen that at the heart of a moral system are rules for guiding the conduct of the members of the system. But where, exactly, do these rules come from? And what criteria can be used to ground or justify these rules? Arguably, the rules of conduct involving individual directives and social policies are justified by the system's evaluative standards, or principles. But how are those principles in turn justified?

On the one hand, rules of conduct for guiding action in the moral system, whether individual directives or social policies, are ultimately derived from certain core *values*. Principles for evaluating rules of conduct, on the other hand, are typically grounded in one of three systems or sources: religion, law, or (philosophical) ethics. Figure 2.2 illustrates how the rules and principles that comprise a moral system are derived and grounded.

We next describe the core values in a society from which the rules of conduct are derived.

Core Values and Their Role in a Moral System

The term *value* comes from the Latin *valere*, which means having worth or being of worth. Values are objects of our desires or interests; examples include happiness, love, and freedom. Some philosophers suggest that that the moral rules and principles comprising a society's moral system are ultimately derived from that society's framework of values.[4]

Philosophers often distinguish between two types of values, *intrinsic* and *instrumental*. Any value that serves some further end or good is called an instrumental value because it is tied to some external standard. Automobiles, computers, and money are examples of goods that have instrumental value. Values such as life and happiness, on the other hand, are *intrinsic* because they are valued for their own sake. Later in this chapter, we will see that utilitarians argue that happiness is an intrinsic value. And in Chapter 5,

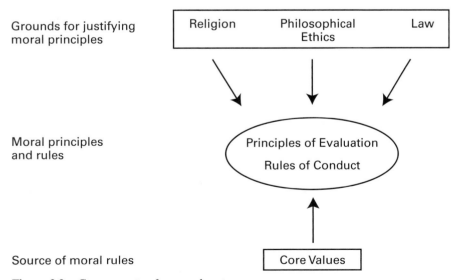

Figure 2.2   Components of a moral system.

we will see that some ethicists believe personal privacy is a value that has both intrinsic and instrumental attributes.

Another approach to cataloguing values is to distinguish *core values*, some of which may or may not also be intrinsic values, from other kinds of values. James Moor (2004), for example, believes that life, happiness, and autonomy are core values because they are basic to a society's thriving and perhaps even to its survival. Autonomy, Moor argues, is essentially a cluster of values that includes ability, security, knowledge, freedom, opportunity, and resources. Although core values might be basic to a society's flourishing, and possibly to that society's survival, it does not follow that each core value is also a moral value.

Sometimes descriptions of morals and values suggest that morals are identical to values. Values, however, can be either moral or nonmoral, and moral values need to be distinguished from the broader set of nonmoral values. Consider again the roles that rationality and impartiality play in a moral system. Rationality informs us that it is in our interest to promote values consistent with our own survival, happiness, and flourishing as individuals. When used to further only our own self-interests, these values are not necessarily moral values. Once we bring in the notion of impartiality, however, we begin to take the moral point of view. When we frame the rules of conduct in a moral system, we articulate one or more core moral values, such as autonomy, fairness, and justice. For example, the rule of conduct "Treat people fairly" is derived from the moral value of impartiality. And our moral values are, in turn, derived from certain core nonmoral values (see Figure 2.3).

Three Approaches for Grounding the Principles in a Moral System

We have seen how the rules of conduct in a moral system can be derived from a society's core values. Now we will consider how the principles that are used to justify the rules of conduct are grounded. As we suggested in Section 2.1.2, the principles are grounded in one of three sources: religion, law, and philosophical ethics. We now consider how a particular moral principle can be justified from the vantage point of each scheme. As an illustration, we can use the rule of conduct "Do not steal," since it underpins many cyberethics controversies involving software piracy and intellectual property. Virtually every moral system includes at least one rule that explicitly condemns stealing. But why, exactly, is stealing morally wrong? This particular rule of conduct is evaluated against one or more principles such as "We should respect persons" or "We should not cause harm to others"; but how are these principles, in turn, justified? The answer depends on whether we take the religious, the legal, or the ethical (philosophical) point of view.

Approach #1: Grounding Moral Principles in a Religious System   Consider the following rationale for why stealing is morally wrong:

Stealing is wrong because it offends God or because it violates one of God's Ten Commandments.

Here the "moral wrongness" in the act of stealing is grounded in religion; stealing, in the Judeo-Christian tradition, is explicitly forbidden by one of the Ten Commandments. From the point of view of these particular institutionalized religions, then, stealing is wrong because it offends God or because it violates the commands of a divine authority.

Grounds for justifying moral principles

Religion
(Obedience to
divine authority)

Philosophical Ethics
(Ethical theory
and logical arguments)

Law
(Obedience to
a legal system)

Moral principles
and rules

Principles of Evaluation
Principles such as social utility, duty, and obligation are
used as standards to evaluate and justify rules of conduct.

Rules of Conduct
Moral rules are derived from basic moral values
(macrolevel rules or social policies, such as "protect privacy";
microlevel rules or directives, such as "do not cheat").

Source of
moral rules

Basic Moral Values
Moral values are derived from core nonmoral values
by using the notion of *impartiality*. (Examples include
autonomy and respect for persons.)

Core Nonmoral Values
Nonmoral values originate from desires and typically
involve *rational* self interests. (Examples include
survival, security, and pleasure.)

Figure 2.3   Components of a moral system: an expanded view.

Furthermore, Christians generally believe that those who steal will be punished in the next life even if they are not caught and punished for their sins in the present life.

One difficulty in applying this rationale in the United States is that American society is pluralistic. While the United States was once a relatively homogeneous culture with roots in the Judeo-Christian tradition, American culture has in recent years become increasingly heterogeneous. People with different religious beliefs or with no religious beliefs at all can disagree with those whose moral beliefs are grounded solely on religious convictions. Because of these differences, many argue that we need to ground the rules and principles of a moral system in criteria other than those provided by organized religions. Some suggest that civil law can provide the foundation needed for a moral system to work.

Approach #2: Grounding Moral Principles in a Legal System   An alternative rationale to the one proposed in the preceding section is as follows:

Stealing is wrong because it violates the law.

One advantage of using law instead of religion as the ground for determining why stealing is wrong is that it eliminates certain kinds of disputes between religious and nonreligious persons and groups. If stealing violates the law of a particular jurisdiction, then the act of stealing can be declared wrong independent of any religious beliefs or disbeliefs—Christian, Muslim, or even agnostic or atheist. And since legal enforcement of rules can be carried out independent of religious beliefs, there is a pragmatic advantage to grounding moral principles (and their corresponding rules) in law rather than in religion: those breaking a civil law can be punished, for example, by either a fine or imprisonment, or both.

But laws are not uniform across political boundaries: Laws vary from nation to nation and state to state within a given nation. In the United States, the unauthorized copying and distribution of proprietary software is explicitly illegal. However, in certain Asian countries, the practice of copying proprietary software is not considered criminal (or even if it is technically viewed as a crime, actual cases of piracy may not be criminally prosecuted). So there can be a diversity of legal systems just as there is a diversity of religious systems.

Perhaps a more serious flaw in using a legal approach is that history has shown that certain laws, although widely accepted, institutionalized, and practiced within a society, have nonetheless been morally wrong. For example, slavery was legally valid in the United States until 1865. And in South Africa, apartheid was legally valid until 1991. So if we attempt to ground moral principles in law, we are still faced with serious challenges. Also, we can ask whether it is possible, or even desirable, to institutionalize morality such that we require specific laws for every possible moral issue?

Approach #3: Grounding Moral Principles in a Philosophical System of Ethics   A third way to approach the problem of how to ground moral systems is to say:

Stealing is wrong because it is wrong.

Notice what this statement implies. The moral rightness or wrongness of stealing is not grounded in any external authority, theological or legal. So regardless of whether God condemns stealing or whether stealing violates existing civil laws, stealing is held to be wrong in itself. On what grounds can such a claim be made? Many philosophers and ethicists argue that reason alone is sufficient to show that stealing is wrong—reason informs us that there is something either in the very act of stealing or in the consequences of the act that makes stealing morally wrong.

In the case of both religion and law, sanctions in the form of punishments can be applied to deter individuals from stealing. In the first case, punishment for immoral behavior is relegated to the afterlife. And in the second case, punishment can be meted out here and now. In the case of philosophical ethics, sanctions take the form of social disapprobation (disapproval) and, possibly, social ostracism, but there is no punishment in a formal sense.

According to the system of philosophical ethics, stealing is morally wrong by criteria that reason alone is sufficient to determine. Of course, we need to specify what these criteria are; we will do this in Sections 2.4–2.7, where we discuss four kinds of ethical theories. Figure 2.3 summarizes the main elements and features of the moral system that we have examined in this section and expands the key features of Figure 2.2.

In Figure 2.3, arrows from both directions ultimately lead to "Rules of Conduct." Using the rules of conduct as our reference point, we see that they are derived from basic moral values, which in turn are derived from a set of core nonmoral values. With the rules of conduct still serving as our point of reference but moving in the opposite direction, we see that these rules are evaluated and justified by a set of moral principles. These moral principles, in turn, are grounded in criteria that are either legal, religious, or philosophical, or some combination of the three.

The Method of Philosophical Ethics: Logical Argumentation and Ethical Theory

In Chapter 1, we briefly described the philosophical method and saw how it could be used to analyze cyberethics issues. We also saw that the method philosophers use to analyze moral issues is normative, in contrast to the descriptive method that is used by many social scientists. We saw that sociological and anthropological studies are descriptive because they describe or report how people in various cultures and groups behave with respect to the rules of a moral system. For example, a sociologist might report that people who live in nations along the Pacific Rim believe that it is morally permissible to make copies of proprietary software for personal use. However, it is one thing simply to report or describe what the members of a particular culture believe about a practice such as duplicating proprietary software, and it is something altogether different to say that people ought to be permitted to make copies of that proprietary material. When we inquire into moral issues from the latter perspective, we engage in a normative investigation.

We have seen that normative analyses of morality can involve religion and law as well as philosophy. We have also seen, however, that what separates philosophy from the other two perspectives of normative analysis is the methodology used to study the moral issues. To approach these issues from the perspective of philosophical ethics is, in effect, to engage in a philosophical study of morality.

If you are taking a course in ethics for the first time, you might wonder what is meant by the phrase "philosophical study." We have already described what is meant by a descriptive study, which is essentially a type of scientific study. Philosophical studies and scientific studies are similar in that they both require that a consistent methodological scheme be used to verify hypotheses and theories; and these verification schemes must satisfy criteria of rationality and impartiality. But philosophical studies differ from scientific studies in one important respect: Whereas scientists typically conduct experiments in a laboratory to confirm or refute one or more hypotheses, philosophers have no physical laboratory to test ethical theories and claims. Instead philosophers confirm or reject the plausibility of the evidence for a certain claim or thesis via the rules of logical argumentation (which we will examine in Chapter 3); these rules are both rational and impartial. Another important feature that distinguishes a philosophical study of morality from other kinds of normative investigation into morality is the use of ethical theory in the analysis and deliberation of the issues.

Ethicists vs. Moralists

We note that ethicists who study morality from the perspective of philosophical methodology, and who thus appeal to logical arguments to justify claims and positions involving morality, are very different from moralists. Moralists often claim to have all of the answers regarding moral questions and issues. Many moralists have been described as "preachy" and "judgmental." And some moralists may have a particular moral agenda to advance. Ethicists, on the other hand, use the philosophical method in analyzing and attempting to resolve moral issues; they must remain open to different sides of a dispute, and their primary focus is on the study of morality and the application of moral theories. As such, they approach moral issues and controversies by way of standards that are both rational (based on logic) and impartial (open to others to verify). We briefly return to some of these important distinctions in our discussion of differences between moral absolutism and moral objectivism, later in this chapter.

▶ 2.2 DISCUSSION STOPPERS AS ROADBLOCKS TO MORAL DISCOURSE

We have suggested that impartial and objective standards, such as those provided by ethical theory and the rules of logical argumentation, can be used in our analysis of moral issues. However, many people might be surprised that tests and standards of any kind can be applied to disputes about morality and moral issues. So before beginning our examination of ethical theory, perhaps we should first acknowledge and try to address some concerns that many people frequently encounter when either they willingly engage in, or find themselves involuntarily drawn into, discussions involving moral issues. We will see why these concerns are often based on some conceptual confusions about the nature of morality itself.

Have you ever been engaged in a serious conversation about a moral issue when, all of a sudden, one party in the discussion interjects with a remark to the effect, "But who's to say what is right or wrong anyway?" Or perhaps someone might interject, "Who are we to impose our values and ideas on others?" Such clichés are just two examples of the kinds of simplistic or nonreflective questions that we are likely to hear in discussions involving moral issues. I call remarks of this type "discussion stoppers" because often they close down prematurely what otherwise might be a useful discussion. These stoppers can take many different forms, and some are more common than others, but we can analyze them in terms of four distinct questions:

1. People disagree about morality, so how can we reach agreement on moral issues?
2. Who am I/who are we to judge others and to impose my/our values on them?
3. Isn't morality simply a private matter?
4. Isn't morality simply a matter that different cultures and groups should determine for themselves?

2.2.1 Discussion Stopper #1: People Disagree on Solutions to Moral Issues

Because different people often have different beliefs as to the correct answer to many moral questions, some infer that there is no hope of reaching any kind of agreement on answers to *any* moral question. And from this inference, some conclude that any meaningful discourse about morality is impossible. Three crucial points that people who draw these and similar inferences about morality fail to recognize, however, are as follows:

   I. Experts in other fields of study, such as science and mathematics, also disagree as to the correct answers to certain questions.

  II. There is common agreement as to answers to some moral questions.

 III. People do not always distinguish between disagreements about general principles and disagreements about factual matters in disputes involving morality.

We briefly examine each of these points.

Experts in Many Fields Disagree on Fundamental Issues

First, we should note that morality is not the only area in which intelligent people have disagreements. Scientists and mathematicians disagree among themselves about core issues in their disciplines, yet we do not dismiss the possibility of meaningful discourse in science and mathematics merely because there is some disagreement among experts in those fields. Consider also that computer scientists disagree among themselves whether open source code is better than proprietary code, whether Linux is a better operating system than Windows XP or Vista, or whether C++ is a better programming language than Java.

One example of how natural scientists can disagree among themselves is apparent in the classic and contemporary debate in physics regarding the nature of light. Some physicists argue that light is ultimately composed of particles, whereas others claim that light is essentially composed of waves. Because physicists can disagree with each other, should we conclude that physics itself must be a totally arbitrary enterprise? Or, alternatively, is it not possible that certain kinds of disagreements among scientists might indeed be healthy for science? The debate about the nature of light has actually contributed to moving the field of physics forward in ways that it otherwise would not progress. In this sense, then, a certain level of disagreement and dispute among scientists is a positive and constructive function in the overall enterprise of scientific discovery. Similarly, why not assume that certain kinds of disagreements in ethics—that is, those that are based on points aimed at achieving constructive resolutions—actually contribute to progress in the field of ethics?

Also note that disagreement exists among contemporary mathematicians as to whether or not numbers are constructed (as opposed to having an independent existence). Because mathematicians disagree about the truth of certain claims pertaining to foundational issues in mathematics, does it follow that the field of mathematics itself is arbitrary? Does it also follow that we should give up any hope of eventually reaching agreement about basic truths in mathematics? And should we dismiss as arbitrary the theories of mathematics as well as the theories of physics, simply because there is some level of disagreement among scholars in both academic fields? Would it be reasonable to do so? If not, then why should ethics be dismissed merely because there is some disagreement among ethicists and among ordinary persons as to the correct answers to some moral issues?

Note that certain conditions (parameters, rules, etc.) must be satisfied in order for a particular claim or a particular theory to qualify as acceptable in debates among scientists and among mathematicians. We will see that certain rules and parameters must also be satisfied in order for a particular claim or theory to qualify as acceptable in debates among ethicists. Just as there are claims and theories in physics and in mathematics that are not considered plausible by the scientific and mathematical communities, similarly, not every claim or theory involving morality is considered reasonable by ethicists. Like mathematicians and scientists, ethicists continue to disagree with one another; for example, they will likely continue to debate about which ethical theories should be applied in the case of cloning and genomic research. But like scientists and mathematicians, ethicists will continue to work within the constraints of certain acceptable rules and parameters in advancing their various theories.

Common Agreement on Some Moral Issues

We can now turn to our second point: People have demonstrated considerable agreement on answers to some moral questions, at least with respect to moral principles. We might be inclined to overlook the significant level of agreement regarding ethical principles, however, because, as Gert (2005, 2007) notes, we tend to associate moral issues with highly controversial concerns such as the death penalty, euthanasia, abortion, and cloning, all involving life and death decisions. We tend to forget that there are also many basic moral principles on which we do agree; for instance, nearly everyone believes that people should tell the truth, keep promises, respect their parents, and refrain from activities involving stealing and cheating. And most people agree that "Murder is wrong." It would be prudent for us to pay closer attention to our beliefs regarding these core moral principles in order to find out why there is such agreement.

So if we agree on many basic moral principles, such as our commonly held beliefs that murder is wrong and stealing is wrong, then why do many people also believe that disputes about moral issues are impossible to resolve? Beliefs and assumptions regarding morality may be based on certain conceptual confusions, and one source of confusion may be our failure to distinguish between the alleged factual matters and the general principles that constitute moral issues. This brings us to our third point.

Disagreements about Principles vs. Disagreements about Facts

Richard De George (1999) has pointed out that in analyzing moral issues we need to be very careful to distinguish our disagreements about moral principles from our disagreements about certain facts, or empirical data, associated with a particular moral issue. For example, in the current debate over intellectual property rights in cyberspace, the dispute is not so much about whether we should accept the moral principle that stealing is wrong, for parties on both sides of the debate would acknowledge that stealing is indeed morally wrong. What they disagree about is whether an activity that involves either the unauthorized copying of proprietary software or the unauthorized exchange of proprietary information over a computer network is itself a form of stealing. In other words, the debate is not about a moral principle, but rather has to do with certain empirical matters, or factual claims.

Recall our discussion of the original Napster controversy in Chapter 1. It might turn out this particular controversy is not a moral dispute but rather a debate over factual claims. And once the factual questions are resolved, the Napster controversy might be understood as one that is, at bottom, nonmoral in nature. Being able to recognize these distinctions will help us to eliminate some of the confusion surrounding issues that initially are perceived to be moral but ultimately may turn out to be nonmoral, or descriptive.

2.2.2 Discussion Stopper #2: Who Am I to Judge Others?

People are often uncomfortable with the prospect of having to evaluate the moral beliefs and practices of others. We generally feel that it is appropriate to *describe* the different moral beliefs that others have but that it is inappropriate to make *judgments* about the moral beliefs held by others. This assumption is problematic on two levels: First, as a matter of descriptive fact, we constantly judge others in the sense that we make certain evaluations about them. And second, from a normative perspective, in certain cases we *should* make judgments (evaluations) about the beliefs and actions of others. We briefly examine both points.

Persons Making Judgments vs. Persons Being Judgmental

First, we need to make an important distinction between "making a judgment" about someone or something and "being a judgmental person." Because someone makes a judgment, or evaluation, about X, it does not follow that he or she is also necessarily being a judgmental person. For example, a person can make the judgment "Linux is a better operating system than Vista" and yet not be a judgmental person. One can also judge that "Mary is a better computer programmer than Harry" without necessarily being judgmental about either Mary or Harry. Being judgmental is a behavioral trait exhibited by those who are strongly opinionated or who tend to speak disparagingly of anyone who holds a position on some topic that is different from their own. "Judging" in the sense of evaluating something, however, does not require that the person making the judgment be a judgmental person.

We routinely judge, or evaluate, others. We judge others whenever we decide whom we will pursue as friends, as lovers, or as colleagues. Judging is an integral part of social interaction. Without judgment at this level, we would not be able to form close friendships, as opposed to mere acquaintances. And we would not be able to choose a spouse or to choose where we wish to live, work, recreate, and so forth.

Judgments Involving Condemnations vs. Judgments Involving Evaluations

Why do we tend to be so uncomfortable with the notion of judging others? Part of our discomfort may have to do with how we currently understand the term "judge." As we saw above, we need to be careful to separate the cognitive act of judging (i.e., making judgments about someone or something) from the behavioral trait of "being judgmental." Consider the biblical injunction that instructs us to refrain from judging others in the sense of condemning them. In that sense of "judge" there would seem to be much wisdom in the biblical injunction.

However, there is also another sense of "judge" that means "evaluate," which is something we are often required to do in our everyday lives. Consider some of the routine judgments, or evaluations, you make when deciding between competing options available to you in your day-to-day life. When you change jobs or purchase a house or an automobile, you make a judgment about which job, house, or automobile you believe is best for your purposes. When you chose the particular college or university that you are attending, you evaluated that particular institution relative to others.

There are also people employed in professions that require them to make judgments. For example, professional sporting associations employ referees and field judges who make decisions or judgments concerning controversial plays. Judges evaluate contest entries to determine which entries are better than others. Think, for example, about the judging that typically occurs in selecting the winning photographs in a camera club contest. Or consider that when a supervisor writes a performance review for an employee, she is making a judgment about the employee's performance.

Are We Ever Required to Make Judgments about Others?

It could be argued that just because we happen to make judgments about others, it doesn't necessarily follow that we ought to judge persons. However, there are certain occasions when we are not only justified in making judgments about others, but we are also morally obligated to do so. Consider, for instance, that in many societies an individual selects the person that he or she will marry, judging (evaluating) whether the person he or she is considering will be a suitable life-long partner in terms of plans, goals, aspirations, etc. In this case, failing to make such judgment would be not only imprudent but also, arguably, immoral. It would be immoral because, in failing to make the appropriate judgments, one would not be granting his or her prospective spouse the kind of consideration that he or she deserves.

Next, consider an example involving child abuse. If you see an adult physically abusing a child in a public place by repeatedly kicking the child, can you not at least judge that the adult's behavior is morally wrong even if you are uncomfortable with making a negative judgment about that particular adult?

Also consider a basic human-rights violation. If you witness members of a community being denied basic human rights, should you not judge that community's practice as morally wrong? For example, if women in Afghanistan are denied education, medical treatment, and jobs solely on the grounds that they are women, is it wrong to make the judgment that such practices, as well as the system that permits those practices, are immoral?

So it would seem that some serious confusions exist with respect to two distinct situations: (1) someone making a judgment about X, and (2) someone being a judgmental person. With that distinction in mind, we can avoid being judgmental and yet still make moral judgments when appropriate, and especially when we are obligated to do so.

2.2.3 Discussion Stopper #3: Morality Is Simply a Private Matter

Many people assume that morality is essentially personal in nature and must, therefore, be simply a private matter. Initially, such a view might seem reasonable, but it is actually both confused and problematic. In fact, "private morality" is essentially an oxymoron, or contradictory notion. For one thing, morality is a *public* phenomenon—recall our discussion of Gert's account of morality as a "public system" in Section 2.1.1, where we saw that a moral system includes a set of public rules that apply to all of the members of that system. Thus morality cannot be reduced to something that is simply private or personal.

We have already seen that morality is a system of normative rules and standards whose content is studied by ethicists in the same way that mathematicians study the content of the field of mathematics. Would it make sense to speak of personal mathematics, personal chemistry, or personal biology? Such notions sound absurd because each discipline has a content area and a set of standards and criteria, all of which are open and available to all to examine. Since public rules make up the content of a moral system, which itself can be studied, we can reasonably ask how it would make sense to speak of private morality.

If morality were simply a private matter, then it would follow that a study of morality could be reduced to a series of descriptive reports about the personal preferences or personal tastes of individuals and groups. But is such an account of morality adequate? Are the moral choices that we make nothing more than mere personal choices? If you happen to prefer chocolate ice cream and I prefer vanilla, or if you prefer to own a laptop computer and I prefer to own a desktop computer, we will probably not choose to debate these preferences. You may have strong personal beliefs as to why chocolate ice cream is better than vanilla and why laptop computers are superior to desktop computers; however, you will most likely respect my preferences for vanilla ice cream and desktop computers, and, in turn, I will respect your preferences.

Do moral choices fit this same kind of model? Suppose you happen to believe that stealing is morally wrong, but I believe that stealing is okay (i.e., morally permissible). One day, I decide to steal your laptop computer. Do you have a right to complain? You would not, if morality is simply a private matter that reflects an individual's personal choices. Your personal preference may be not to steal, whereas my personal preference is for stealing. If morality is grounded simply in terms of the preferences that individuals happen to have, then it would follow that stealing *is* morally permissible for me but *is not* for you. But why stop with stealing? What if I happen to believe that killing human beings is okay?

You can probably see the dangerous implications for a system in which moral rules and standards are reducible to personal preferences and personal beliefs. The view that morality is private and personal can quickly lead to a position that some ethicists describe as *moral subjectivism*. According to this position, what is morally right or wrong can be determined by individuals themselves, so that morality would seem to be in the "eye of the beholder." Moral subjectivism makes pointless any attempt to engage in meaningful ethical dialogue.

2.2.4 Discussion Stopper #4: Morality Is Simply a Matter for Individual Cultures to Decide

Some might assume that morality can best be understood not so much as a private or a personal matter but as something for groups or cultures to determine. According to this view, a moral system is dependent on, or relative to, a particular culture or group. Again, this view might initially seem quite reasonable; it is a position that many social scientists have found attractive. To understand some of the serious problems inherent in this position, it is useful to distinguish between *cultural relativism* and *moral relativism*.

Cultural Relativism
Cultures play a crucial role in the transmission of the values and principles that constitute a moral system. It is through culture that initial beliefs involving morality are transmitted to an individual. In this sense cultures provide their members with what ethicists often refer to as "customary morality," or conventional morality, where one's moral beliefs are typically nonreflective (or perhaps prereflective). For example, if asked whether you believe that acts such as pirating software or invading someone's privacy are wrong, you might simply reply that both kinds of behavior are wrong because your society taught

you that they are wrong. However, is it sufficient for one to believe that these actions are morally wrong merely *because* his or her culture says they are wrong? Imagine, for example, a culture in which the principle "Murder is wrong" is not transmitted to its members. Does it follow that murdering people would be morally permissible for the members of that culture?

The belief that morality is simply a matter for individual cultures to decide is widespread in our contemporary popular culture. This view is often referred to as *cultural relativism*, and at its base is the following assumption:

A. Different cultures have different beliefs about what constitutes morally right and wrong behavior.

Note that this assumption is essentially descriptive in nature, because it makes no normative judgment about either the belief systems of cultures or the behavior of people in those cultures. Although it is generally accepted that different cultures have different conceptions about what is morally right and morally wrong behavior, this position has been challenged by some social scientists who argue that the reported differences between cultures are greatly exaggerated. Other social scientists suggest that all cultures may possess some universal core moral values.[5]

However, let us assume that claim (A) is true and ask whether it logically implies (B).

B. We should not morally evaluate the behavior of people in cultures other than our own (because different cultures have different belief systems about what constitutes morally right and wrong behavior).

Note that (B) is a different kind of claim than (A). Also note that to move from (A) to (B) is to move from cultural relativism to *moral relativism.*

Moral Relativism

What are the differences between the two forms of relativism? We saw that cultural relativism is essentially a descriptive thesis, merely reporting that people's moral beliefs vary from culture to culture. Moral relativism, on the contrary, is a normative thesis because it asserts that one *should not* make moral judgments about the behavior of people who live in cultures other than one's own. However, critics point out that if moral relativists are correct, then any kind of behavior can be morally acceptable—provided that such behavior is approved by the majority of people in a particular culture.

Critics also note that the moral relativist's reasoning is flawed. For example, they point out that sometimes it is appropriate for people to question certain kinds of behavioral practices, regardless of where those practices are carried out. Consider a specific case involving a practice in some cultures and tribes in West Africa, where a ritual of female circumcision is performed. Is it wrong for those living outside these cultures to question this practice from the perspective of morality or human rights? Although this practice has been a tradition for generations, some females living in tribes that still perform it on teenage girls have objected. Let us assume, however, that the majority of members of cultures that practice female circumcision approve it. Would it be inappropriate for those who lived outside of West Africa to question whether it is morally wrong to force some women to experience this ritual against their wishes? And if so, is it inappropriate (perhaps even morally wrong) to question the practice simply because the persons raising such questions are not members of the particular culture?

If we embrace that line of reasoning used by the moral relativist, does it follow that a culture can devise any moral scheme it wishes as long as the majority of its members approve it? If so, is moral relativism a plausible thesis? Perhaps the following scenario can help us to understand further the flawed reasoning in moral relativism.

► **SCENARIO 2–1:** Evaluating Moral Relativism

Two cultures, Culture A and Culture B, adjoin each other geographically. The members of Culture A are fairly peaceful people, tolerant of the diverse beliefs found in all other cultures. And they believe that all cultures should essentially mind their own business when it comes to matters involving morality. Those in Culture B, on the contrary, dislike and are hostile to those outside their culture. Culture B has recently developed a new computer system for delivering chemical weapons that it plans to use in military attacks on other cultures, including Culture A. Since Culture A subscribes to the view of moral relativism, and thus must respect the views of all cultures with regard to their systems of moral beliefs, can it condemn, in a logically consistent manner, Culture B's actions as immoral? ■

Because Culture A embraces moral relativism, it must be tolerant of all of Culture B's practices and actions, as it would in the case of all cultures. Furthermore, Culture A cannot condemn the actions of Culture B, since, in the relativist's view, moral judgments about Culture B can be made only by those who reside in that culture. So, Culture A cannot say that Culture B's actions are morally wrong.

Moral relativists can say only that Cultures A and B are different. They cannot say that one is better than another, or that the behavior in one is morally permissible while the other is morally impermissible. Consider that while the systems for treating Jews used by the Nazis and by the British in the 1940s were clearly different, moral relativists could not say, with any sense of logical consistency, that one system was morally superior to the other. In the same way, Culture B cannot be judged by Culture A to be engaging in morally wrong conduct even though Culture B wishes to destroy A and to kill all of its members. Perhaps you can see that there is a price to pay for being a moral relativist. Is that price worth paying?

Although moral relativism might initially seem attractive as an ethical position, we can now see why it is conceptually flawed. To debate moral issues, we need a conceptual and methodological framework that can provide us with impartial and objective criteria to guide us in our deliberations. Otherwise, ethical debate might quickly reduce to a shouting match in which those with the loudest voices or, perhaps worse yet, those with the "biggest sticks" win the day.

Moral Absolutism and Moral Objectivism

Why is moral relativism so attractive to so many people, despite its logical flaws? Pojman (2006) notes that many people tend to assume that if they reject moral relativism, they must automatically endorse some form of *moral absolutism*. But do they necessarily need to make an either/or choice here? Pojman and others believe that it is possible to hold a view called *ethical objectivism*, which is between the two extremes.[6] Recall our earlier distinction between ethicists and moralists at the end of Section 2.2; the group that we identified there as moralists are similar to moral absolutists in that both believe they have all of the correct answers for every moral question. Whereas absolutists argue that there is only one uniquely correct answer to every moral question, moral relativists assume that there are no universally correct answers to any moral questions. Moral objectivists disagree with both positions; they disagree with absolutists by pointing out that there can be more than one acceptable answer to some moral questions, despite the fact that most cultures agree on the answers to many moral issues. For example, we saw that there is considerable agreement across cultures on principles such as "murder is morally wrong" and that "stealing is morally wrong." However, objectivists also acknowledge that reasonable people can nonetheless disagree on what the correct answers are to some moral questions.

Objectivists also differ from relativists in at least one important respect. Relativists suggest that *any* answer to a moral question can be appropriate, as long the majority in a culture hold that view. Objectivists such as Gert (2005, 2007) counter by arguing that even if there is no uniquely correct answer to every moral question, there are nonetheless many incorrect answers to some of these questions.[7] To illustrate this point, consider an analogy involving a normative dispute that happens to be nonmoral in nature—viz., a debate about who was the greatest baseball player of all time. Reasonable people could disagree on the correct answer to this normative question. For example, some might argue that it was Babe Ruth or Hank Aaron; others could reasonably claim that it was Ty Cobb or Joe DiMaggio. All four answers are objectively plausible. But someone could not reasonably defend the claim that the best baseball player was Danny Ainge or Stan Papi, since those answers are clearly unacceptable (even if we, as individuals, happen to like these former baseball players). So, there are definitely some wrong answers to this normative question, and thus we cannot endorse the "anything goes" view of relativists in defending a rational answer to the question concerning the greatest baseball player of all time. The rationale used in this scenario can be extended to the analysis of normative questions that are moral in nature.

We can now see how moral objectivism offers an alternative to the extreme views of moral relativism and moral absolutism. Unlike moral absolutism, objectivism allows for a plurality of plausible answers to some controversial moral questions, provided that certain rational criteria are satisfied. But unlike relativists, objectivists would not find every answer acceptable, because some answers would fall outside the criteria of (rationally defensible) moral behavior, in the same way that some answers fell outside the criteria for rationally acceptable answers to the normative question about the greatest baseball player. Because moral objectivism allows for the possibility that there may be more than one (rationally) acceptable answer to at least some moral questions, it is compatible with a view that some call "ethical pluralism" (Ess 2006). Although objectivism and pluralism do not entail moral relativism, they allow for multiple ethical theories—provided, of course, that those theories satisfy objective criteria. Because relativism fails to satisfy such criteria, however, it cannot be included in the list of "objective" ethical theories we will examine (such as utilitarianism, deontology, etc.) in the remaining sections of this chapter.

Fortunately, ethical theory can provide us with criteria for objectively analyzing moral issues so that we can avoid the problems of moral relativism without having to endorse moral absolutism. Before proceeding directly to our discussion of ethical theories, however, it would be useful to summarize some of the key points in our analysis of the four discussion stoppers. Table 2.2 summarizes these points.

TABLE 2-2 Summary of Logical Flaws in the Discussion Stoppers

Stopper #1	Stopper #2	Stopper #3	Stopper #4
People disagree on solutions to moral issues.	*Who am I to judge others?*	*Ethics is simply a private matter.*	*Morality is simply a matter for individual cultures to decide.*
1. Fails to recognize that experts in many areas disagree on key issues in their fields.	1. Fails to distinguish between the act of judging and being a judgmental person.	1. Fails to recognize that morality is essentially a public system.	1. Fails to distinguish between descriptive and normative claims about morality.
2. Fails to recognize that there are many moral issues on which people agree.	2. Fails to distinguish between judging as condemning and judging as evaluating.	2. Fails to note that personally-based morality can cause major harm to others.	2. Assumes that people can never reach common agreement on some moral principles.
3. Fails to distinguish between disagreements about principles and disagreements about facts.	3. Fails to recognize that sometimes we are required to make judgments.	3. Confuses moral choices with individual or personal preferences.	3. Assumes that a system is moral because a majority in a culture decides it is moral.

▶ 2.3 WHY DO WE NEED ETHICAL THEORIES?

In our analysis of the four discussion stoppers, we saw some of the obstacles that we encounter when we debate moral issues. Fortunately, there are ethical theories that can guide us in our analysis of moral issues involving cybertechnology. But why do we need something as formal as ethical theory? An essential feature of theory in general is that it guides us in our investigations and analyses. Science uses theory to provide us with general principles and structures with which we can analyze our data. Ethical theory, like scientific theory, provides us with a framework for analyzing moral issues via a scheme that is internally coherent and consistent as well as comprehensive and systematic. To be coherent, a theory's individual elements must fit together to form a unified whole. To be consistent, a theory's component parts cannot contradict each other. To be comprehensive, a theory must be able to be applied broadly to a wide range of actions. And to be systematic, a theory cannot simply address individual symptoms peculiar to specific cases while ignoring general principles that would apply in similar cases.

To see how a theory might either satisfy or fail these criteria, we will look at an analogy involving the way that the U.S. Congress sometimes drafts and enacts a piece of legislation into law. In certain situations, lawmakers respond to a highly publicized and controversial incident by formulating and passing legislation that provides a "Band Aid" fix to a crisis but fails to address the central or core issue of a problem for which it was written. Consider in the following scenario the kind of reasoning that the members of Congress used in passing the Video Privacy Protection Act (also known as the Bork Bill) in 1988.

▶ SCENARIO 2–2: Piecemeal vs. Comprehensive Legislation

Following Judge Robert Bork's nomination to fill a vacancy on the U.S. Supreme Court, the U.S. Congress and the media engaged in an investigative process that preceded the formal confirmation hearings. One news reporter went to the video rental store where Bork rented videos and requested a list of movies that Bork had rented. The reporter allegedly intended to make some observations about the kinds of movies Bork preferred to view, including whether or not Bork had rented any pornographic films. Not surprisingly, many in Congress were appalled when they learned that a reporter could so easily collect this kind of information about Judge Bork. In their hasty response to this incident, Congress passed the Video Privacy Protection Act in order to prevent reporters and other interested parties from finding out which movies individuals rent at video stores.[8]   ■

While some might praise Congress's action as a quick and timely response, others would point out that this particular piece of legislation was piecemeal rather than systematic. For example, was the real issue in this case a matter of keeping others from finding out which videotapes that Bork (or anyone else) happens to rent, or was it a much larger question? Even after the Bork Bill was passed into law, a reporter could still theoretically find out which kinds of books Bork purchased or which kinds of audio-cassette tapes and compact discs he bought. So, rather than being a comprehensive and systematic piece of legislation, the Video Privacy Protection Act was yet one more piece of patchwork legislation that was nonsystematic and noncomprehensive. An ideal law is not merely reactive to a particular incident, nor is it one that is hastily passed because it happens to involve a prominent person rather than ordinary citizens.

How can our brief examination of some flaws in the process used to draft the Bork Bill help us to avoid certain kinds of mistakes in our effort to frame adequate ethical theories? Recall that one of the characteristics of a good theory is that it is general enough to guide us in the examination of more than one case. The Bork Bill is so specific that it fails to serve as a piece of general legislation to protect privacy rights of individuals in analogous situations. Of course, there is a vast difference between laws passed by Congress and the kinds of ethical theories that guide us in moral deliberation. Perhaps we can now see why a good theory will need to be comprehensive, systematic, internally coherent, and logically consistent. We next examine four different kinds of ethical theories: consequence-based, duty-based, contract-based, and character-based. As we examine each theory, see if it meets the criteria that we have determined essential for a successful ethical theory.

▶ 2.4 CONSEQUENCE-BASED ETHICAL THEORIES

Some have argued that the primary goal of a moral system is to produce desirable consequences or outcomes for its members. For these ethicists, the consequences (i.e., the ends achieved) of actions and policies provide the ultimate standard against which moral decisions must be evaluated. So if one must choose between two courses of action—that is, either "Act A" or "Act B"—the morally correct action will be the one that produces the most desirable outcome. Of course, we can further ask the question, "Whose outcome?"—i.e., "the most desirable outcome for whom"? Utilitarians argue that the outcome or consequences for the greatest number of individuals, or the majority, in a given society is paramount in moral deliberation. According to the utilitarian theory,

An individual act (X) or a social policy (Y) is morally permissible if the consequences that result from (X) or (Y) produce the greatest amount of good for the greatest number of persons affected by the act or policy.

Utilitarians stress the "social utility" or social usefulness of particular actions and policies by focusing on the consequences that result from those actions and policies. Jeremy Bentham (1748–1832), who was among the first philosophers to formulate utilitarian ethical theory in a systematic manner, defended this theory via two claims:

I. Social utility is superior to alternative criteria for evaluating moral systems.

II. Social utility can be measured by the amount of happiness produced.

According to (I), the moral value of actions and policies ought to be measured in terms of their social usefulness (rather than via abstract criteria such as individual rights or social justice). The more utility that specific actions and policies have, the more they can be defended as morally permissible actions and policies. In other words, if Policy Y encourages the development of a certain kind of computer software, which in turn would produce more jobs and higher incomes for those living in Community X, then Policy Y would be considered more socially useful and thus the morally correct policy. But how do we measure overall social utility? That is, which criterion can we use to determine the social usefulness of an act or a policy? The answer to this question can be found in (II), which has to do with happiness.

Bentham argued that nature has placed us under two masters, or sovereigns: pleasure and pain. We naturally desire to avoid pain and to seek pleasure or happiness. However, Bentham believed that it is not the maximization of individual pleasure or happiness that is important, but rather generating the greatest amount of happiness for society in general. Since it is assumed that all humans, as individuals, desire happiness, it would follow on utilitarian grounds that those actions and policies that generate the most happiness for the most people are most desirable. Of course, this reasoning assumes:

a. All people desire happiness.

b. Happiness is an intrinsic good that is desired for its own sake.

We can ask utilitarians what proof they have for either (a) or (b). John Stuart Mill (1806–1873) offered the following argument for (a):

> The only possible proof showing that something is audible is that people actually hear it; the only possible proof that something is visible is that people actually see it; and the only possible proof that something is desirable is that people actually desire it.

From the fact that people desire happiness, Mill inferred that promoting happiness ought to be the criterion for justifying a moral system. Unlike other goods that humans desire as means to one or more ends, Mill argued that people desire happiness for its own sake. Thus, he concluded that happiness is an intrinsic good. (Recall our earlier discussion of intrinsic values in Section 2.1.2.)

You might consider applying Mill's line of reasoning to some of your own goals and desires. For example, if someone asked why you are taking a particular college course (such as a course in cyberethics), you might respond that you need to satisfy three credit hours of course work in your major field of study or in your general education requirements. If you were then asked why you need to satisfy those credit hours, you might respond that you would like to earn a college degree. If next someone asks you why you wish to graduate from college, you might reply that you wish to get a good-paying job. If you are then asked why you want a good-paying job, your response might be that you wish to purchase a home and that you would like to be able to save some money. If asked why again, you might reply that saving money would contribute to your financial and emotional security. And if further asked why you want to be financially and emotionally secure, you might respond that ultimately you want to be happy. So, following this line of reasoning, utilitarians conclude that happiness is an intrinsic good—that is, something that is good in and of itself, for its own sake, and not merely a means to some further end or ends.

2.4.1 Act Utilitarianism

We noted above that utilitarians look to the expected outcomes or consequences of an act to determine whether or not that act is morally permissible. However, some critics point out that because utilitarianism tends to focus simply on the roles that individual acts and policies play in producing the overall social good (the greatest good for the greatest number), it is conceptually flawed. Consider a hypothetical scenario in which a new controversial policy is being debated.

▶ **SCENARIO 2–3:** A Critique of Act Utilitarianism

A policy is under consideration in a legislative body in the nation of Newmerica, where 1% of the population would be forced to work as slaves in a manufacturing facility to produce computer chips. Proponents of this policy argue that, if enacted into law, it would result in lower prices for desktop computers for consumers in Newmerica. They argue that it would also likely result in more overall happiness for the nation's citizens because the remaining 99% of the population, who are not enslaved, would be able to purchase personal computers and other computer-based appliances at a much lower price. Hence, 99% of Newmerica's population benefit at the expense of the remaining 1%. This policy clearly seems consistent with the principle of producing the greatest good for the greatest number of Newmerica's population, but should it be enacted into law? ■

The above scenario illustrates a major flaw in at least one version of utilitarianism, viz., *act utilitarianism*. According to act utilitarians,

> An act, X, is morally permissible if the consequences produced by doing X result in the greatest good for the greatest number of persons affected by Act X.

All things being equal, actions that produce the greatest good (happiness) for the greatest number of people seem desirable. However, policies and practices based solely on this principle can also have significant negative implications for those who are not in the majority (i.e., the greatest number). Consider the plight of the unfortunate few who are enslaved in the computer chip processing plant in the above scenario. Because of the possibility that such bizarre cases could occur, some critics who embrace the goals of utilitarianism in general reject act utilitarianism.

Critics who reject the emphasis on the consequences of individual acts point out that in our day-to-day activities we tend not to deliberate on each individual action as if that action were unique. Rather, we are inclined to deliberate on the basis of certain principles or general rules that guide our behavior. For example, consider some principles that may guide your behavior as a consumer. Each time that you enter a computer store, do you ask yourself, "Shall I steal this particular software game in this particular store at this particular time?'' Or have you already formulated certain general principles that guide your individual actions, such as: it is never morally permissible to steal? In the latter case, you are operating at the level of a rule or principle rather than deliberating at the level of individual actions.

2.4.2 Rule Utilitarianism

Some utilitarians argue that the consequences that result from following *rules* or principles, not the consequences of individual acts, ultimately matter in determining whether or not a certain practice is morally permissible. This version of utilitarian theory, called *rule utilitarianism*, can be formulated in the following way:

> An act, X, is morally permissible if the consequences of following the general *rule*, Y, of which act X is an instance, would bring about the greatest good for the greatest number.

Note that here we are looking at the consequences that result from following certain kinds of rules as opposed to consequences resulting from performing individual acts. Rule utilitarianism eliminates as morally permissible those cases in which 1% of the population is enslaved so that that the majority (the remaining 99%) can prosper. Rule utilitarians believe that policies that permit the unjust exploitation of the minority by the majority will have overall negative social consequences and thus will not be consistent with the principle criterion of utilitarian ethical theory.

Rule utilitarianism would seem to be a more plausible ethical theory than act utilitarianism. However, some critics reject all versions of utilitarianism because they believe that no matter how this theory is expressed, utilitarianism is fundamentally flawed. These critics tend to attack one or both of the following aspects of utilitarian theory:

I. Morality is basically tied to the production of happiness or pleasure.

II. Morality can ultimately be decided by consequences (of either acts or policies).

Critics of utilitarianism argue that morality can be grounded neither in consequences nor in happiness. Hence, they argue that some alternative criterion or standard is needed.

▶ 2.5 DUTY-BASED ETHICAL THEORIES

Immanuel Kant (1724–1804) argued that morality must ultimately be grounded in the concept of duty, or obligations that humans have to one another, and never in the consequences of human actions. As such, morality has nothing to do with the promotion of happiness or the achievement of desirable consequences. Thus Kant rejects utilitarianism in particular, and all consequentialist ethical theories in general. He points out that, in some instances, performing our duties may result in our being unhappy and may not necessarily lead to consequences that are considered desirable. Theories in which the notion of duty, or obligation, serves as the foundation for morality are called *deontological* theories because they derive their meaning from the Greek root *deon*, which means duty. How can a deontological theory avoid the problems that plague consequentialist theories such as utilitarianism? Kant provides two answers to this question, one based on our nature as rational creatures, and the other based on the notion that human beings are ends-in-themselves. We briefly consider each of Kant's arguments.

What does Kant mean when he says that humans have a rational nature? Kant argues that what separates us from other kinds of creatures, and what binds us morally, is our rational capacity. Unlike animals who may be motivated only by sensory pleasure, humans have an ability to reason and deliberate. So Kant reasons that if our primary nature were such that we merely seek happiness or pleasure, as utilitarians suggest, then we would not be distinguishable from other creatures in morally relevant ways. But because we have a rational capacity, we are able to reflect upon situations and make moral choices in a way that other kinds of (nonrational) creatures cannot. Kant argues that our rational nature reveals to us that we have certain duties or obligations to each other as "rational beings" in a moral community.

We can next examine Kant's second argument, which concerns the roles of human beings as ends-in-themselves. We have seen that in focusing on criteria involving the happiness of the majority, utilitarians allow, even if unintentionally, that the interests and well-being of some humans can be sacrificed for the ends of the greatest number. Kant argues that a genuinely moral system would never permit some humans to be treated simply as means to the ends of others. He also believes that if we are willing to use a standard based on consequences (such as social utility) to ground our moral system, then that system will ultimately fail to be a moral system. Kant argues that each individual, regardless of his or her wealth, intelligence, privilege, or circumstance, has the same moral worth. From this, Kant infers that each individual, therefore, is an end in him- or herself and thus should never be treated merely as a means to some end. Thus we have a duty to treat fellow humans as ends.

2.5.1 Rule Deontology

Is there a rule or principle that can be used in an objective and impartial way to determine the basis for our moral obligations? For Kant, there is such a standard or objective test, which can be formulated in a principle that he calls the *categorical imperative*. Kant's imperative has a number of variations, and we will briefly examine two of them. One variation of his imperative directs us to

> Act always on that maxim or principle (or rule) that ensures that all individuals will be treated as ends-in-themselves and never merely as a means to an end.

Another variation of the categorical imperative can be paraphrased in the following way:

> Act always on that maxim or principle (or rule) that can be universally binding, without exception, for all human beings.[9]

Kant believed that if everyone followed the categorical imperative, we would have a genuinely moral system. It would be a system based on two essential principles: universality and impartiality. In such as system, every individual would be treated fairly since the same rules would apply universally to all persons. And because Kant's imperative observes the principle of impartiality, it does not allow for one individual or group to be privileged or favored over another. In other words, if it is morally wrong for you to engage in a certain action, then it is also morally wrong for all persons like you—that is, all rational creatures (or moral agents)—to engage in that action. And if you are obligated to perform a certain action, then every moral agent is likewise obligated to perform that action. To illustrate Kant's points about the role that universal principles play in a moral system, consider the following scenario.

▶ **SCENARIO 2–4:** The Principles of Universality and Impartiality

Bill, a student at Technical University, approaches his philosophy instructor, Professor Kanting, after class one day to turn in a paper that is past due. Professor Kanting informs Bill that since the paper is late, he is not sure that he will accept it. But Bill replies to Professor Kanting in a way that suggests that he is actually doing his professor a favor by turning in the paper late. Bill reasons that if he had turned in the paper when it was due, Professor Kanting would have been swamped with papers. Now, however, Kanting will be able to read Bill's paper in a much more leisurely manner, without having the stress of so many papers to grade at once. Professor Kanting then tells Bill that he appreciates his concern about his professor's well being, but he asks Bill to reflect a bit on his rationale in this incident. Specifically, Kanting asks Bill to imagine a case in which all of the students in his class, fearing that their professor would be overwhelmed with papers arriving at the same time, decided to turn their papers in one week late. ∎

On deontological grounds, Bill can only make an exception for himself if everyone else (in this case, every other student in Bill's class) had the right to make exceptions for him- or herself as well. But if everyone did that, then what would happen to the very notion of following rules in a society? It is not that negative consequences would result from this that bothers deontologists such as Kant. Rather, if everyone decided that he or she could make an exception for him- or herself whenever it was convenient to do so, we couldn't even have practices such as promise keeping and truth telling. For those practices to work, they must be universalizable (i.e., apply to all persons equally) and impartial. When we make exceptions for ourselves, we violate the principle of impartiality, and we treat others as means to our ends.

In Kant's deontological scheme, we do not consider the potential consequences of a certain action or of a certain rule to determine whether that act is morally permissible. Rather, the objective rule to be followed—that is, the litmus test for determining when an action will have moral worth—is whether the act complies with the categorical imperative.

For a deontologist such as Kant, enslaving humans would always be immoral, regardless of whether the practice of having slaves might result in greater social utility for the majority (e.g., being able to purchase consumer products at a lower price) than the practice of not allowing slavery. The practice of slavery is immoral, not because it might have negative social consequences in the long term, but because

a. it allows some humans to be used only as a means to an end; and

b. a practice such as slavery could not be consistently applied in an objective, impartial, and universally binding way.

Kant would ask, for example, whether we could consistently impose a universal maxim that would allow slavery. He believed that we could not consistently (in a logically coherent sense) formulate such a principle that would apply to all humans, since we would have to allow that we also be willing to be subject to slavery. If we allow for the practice that some individuals can be enslaved but not others, then we would be allowing for exceptions to the moral rule. We would also be allowing some individuals to be used only as a means to the ends of others rather than as ends-in-themselves.

Although Kant's version of deontological ethics avoids many of the difficulties of utilitarianism, it, too, has been criticized as an inadequate ethical theory. Critics point out, for example, that even if Kant's categorical imperative provides us with as the ultimate test for determining when some particular course of action is our duty, it will not help us in cases where we have two or more conflicting duties. Consider that, in Kant's system, we have duties to both keep promises and tell the truth. Thus, acts such as telling a lie or breaking a promise can never be morally permissible. However, Kant's critics point out that sometimes we encounter situations in which we are required *either* to tell the truth and break a promise *or* to keep a promise and tell a lie. In these cases, we encounter genuine moral dilemmas. Kant's deontological theory does not provide us with a mechanism for resolving such conflicts.

2.5.2 Act Deontology

Although Kant's version of deontology has at least one significant flaw, some philosophers believe that a deontological account of morality is nonetheless the correct kind of ethical theory. They also believe that a deontological ethical theory can be formulated in a way that avoids the charges of Kant's critics. One attempt at reformulating this theory was made by David Ross (1930). Ross rejects utilitarianism for many of the same reasons that Kant does. However, Ross also believes that Kant's version of deontology is not fully adequate.

Ross argues that when two or more moral duties clash, we have to look at individual situations in order to determine which duty will override another. Like act utilitarians, then, Ross stresses the importance of analyzing individual situations to determine the morally appropriate course of action to take. Unlike utilitarians, however, Ross believes that we must not consider the consequences of those actions in deliberating over which course of action morally trumps, or outweighs, another. Like Kant, Ross believes that the notion of duty is the ultimate criterion for determining morality. But unlike Kant, Ross does not believe that blind adherence to certain maxims or rules can work in every case for determining which duties we must ultimately carry out.

Ross believes that we have certain *prima facie* (or self-evident) *duties*, which, all things being equal, we must follow. He provides a list of prima facie duties such as honesty, benevolence, justice, and so forth. For example, each of us has a prima facie duty not to lie and a prima facie duty to keep a promise. And if there are no conflicts in a given situation, then each prima facie duty is also what he calls an *actual duty*. But how are we to determine what our actual duty is in situations where two or more prima facie duties conflict with one another? Ross believes that our ability to determine what our actual duty will be in a particular situation is made possible through a process of "rational intuitionism" (similar to one used in mathematics).[10]

We saw that for Kant, every *prima facie* duty is, in effect, an absolute duty because it applies to every human being without exception. We also saw that Kant's scheme does not provide a procedure for deciding what we should do when two or more duties conflict. However, Ross believes that we can determine what our overriding duty is in such situations by using a deliberative process that requires two steps:

  a. Reflect on the competing *prima facie* duties.

  b. Weigh the evidence at hand to determine which course of action would be required in a particular circumstance.)

The following scenario illustrates how Ross's procedure can be carried out.

▶ **SCENARIO 2–5:** A Dilemma Involving Conflicting Duties

You promise to meet a classmate one evening at 7:00 in the college library to study together for a midterm exam for a computer science course you are taking. While driving in your car to the library, you receive a call on your cell phone informing you that your grandmother has been taken to the hospital and that you should go immediately to the hospital. You consider calling your classmate from your car, but you realize that you don't have his phone number. You also realize that you don't have time to try to reach your classmate by e-mail. What should you do in this case? ◼

All things being equal, you have a moral obligation to keep your promise to your friend. You also have a moral obligation to visit your grandmother in the hospital. On both counts, Kant and Ross are in agreement. But what should we do when the two obligations conflict? For a rule deontologist like Kant, the answer is unclear as to what you should do in this scenario, since you have two absolute duties. For Ross, however, the following procedure for deliberation is used. You would have to weigh between the two prima facie duties in question to determine which will be your actual duty in this particular circumstance. In weighing between the two conflicting duties, your actual duty in this situation would be to visit your grandmother, which means, of course, that you would have to break your promise to your friend. However, in a different kind of situation involving a conflict of the same two duties, your actual duty might be to keep the promise made to your friend and not visit your grandmother in the hospital.

Notice that in cases of weighing between conflicting duties, Ross places the emphasis of deliberation on certain aspects of the particular situation or context, rather than on mere deliberation about the general rules themselves. Unlike utilitarians, however, Ross does not appeal to the consequences of either actions or rules in determining whether a particular course of action is morally acceptable. For one thing, Ross argues that he would have to be omniscient to know what consequences would result from his actions. So, like all deontologists, Ross rejects the criteria of consequences as a viable one for resolving ethical dilemmas.

One difficulty for Ross's position is that, as noted above, it uses a process called "rational intuitionism." Appealing to the intuitive process used in mathematics to justify certain basic mathematical concepts and axioms, Ross believes that the same process can be used in morality. However, his position on moral intuitionism is controversial and has not been widely accepted by contemporary ethicists. And since intuitionism is in an important component in Ross's theory of act deontology, many ethicists who otherwise might be inclined to adopt Ross's theory have been skeptical of it. Nevertheless, variations of that theory have been adopted by contemporary deontologists.

Figure 2.4 summarizes key features that differentiate act and rule utilitarianism and act and rule deontology.

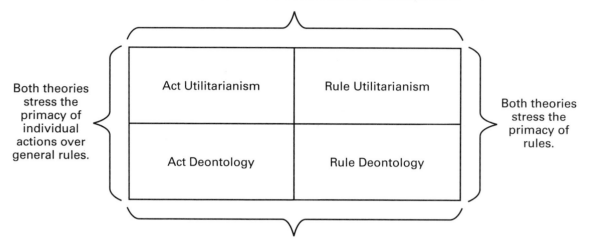

Figure 2.4   Acts vs. rules and consequences vs. duties.

▶ 2.6 CONTRACT-BASED ETHICAL THEORIES

During the past two centuries, consequence-based and duty-based ethical theories have tended to receive the most attention from philosophers and ethicists. However, other kinds of ethical theories, such as those that emphasize criteria involving social contracts and individual rights, have recently begun to receive some serious attention as well. From the perspective of social contract theory, a moral system comes into being by virtue of certain contractual agreements between individuals. One of the earliest formal versions of a contract-based ethical theory can be found in the writings of Thomas Hobbes (1588–1679). In his classic work *Leviathan*, Hobbes describes an original "premoral" state that he calls the "state of nature." It is premoral because there are no moral (or legal) rules yet in existence. In this state, each individual is free to act in ways that satisfy his or her own natural desires. According to Hobbes, our natural (or physical) constitution is such that in the state of nature we act in ways that will enable us to satisfy our desires (or appetites) and to avoid what Hobbes calls our "aversions." While there is a sense of freedom in this natural state, the condition of our day-to-day existence is hardly ideal. In this state, each person must continually fend for herself, and, as a result, each must also avoid the constant threats of others, who are inclined to pursue their own interests and desires.

Hobbes describes this state of nature as one in which life is "solitary, poor, nasty, brutish, and short." Because we are rational creatures, and because we see that it would be in our best interests to band together, Hobbes notes that we eventually establish a formal legal code. In doing this, Hobbes believes that we are willing to surrender some of our "absolute" freedoms to a sovereign. In return, we receive many benefits, including a system of rules and laws that are designed and enforced to protect individuals from being harmed by other members of the system.

One virtue of the social contract model of ethics is that it gives us a motivation for being moral. We see that it is in our individual self-interest to develop a moral system with rules. This type of motivation for establishing a moral system is conspicuously absent in both the utilitarian and deontological theories.[11] So a contract-based ethical theory might seem to have one advantage over them.

2.6.1 Some Criticisms of Contract-Based Theories

Some critics, such as Pojman (2006), point out that contract-based theories provide the foundation for only a minimalist morality. They are minimalist in the sense that we are obligated to behave morally only where an explicit or formal contract exists. So if I have no express contract with you, or if a country such as the United States has no explicit contract with a developing nation, there is no moral obligation for me to help you or for the United States to come to the aid of that developing nation. Of course, we can think of many situations involving morality where there are no express contracts or explicit laws describing our obligations to each other. Yet we also tend to believe that in at least some of these cases we are morally obligated to help others when it is in our power to do so.

Consider the case of Kitty Genovese who was murdered outside her apartment building in New York in 1964, as thirty-eight neighbors in her apartment building watched. During the incident, none of Genovese's neighbors came to her rescue or called the police. When interviewed after the fact, some of her neighbors responded that they did nothing wrong.[12] In one sense, they were correct, since there was no explicit law requiring that they do anything at all. So technically, these neighbors were correct, at least from a legal perspective. But we can certainly ask whether her neighbors had a moral obligation to do something rather than simply be indifferent. It is in this sense, then, that social contract theory can be seen as being minimalist and legalistic, and not a robust theory of morality.

Another way to think about minimalist morality is to think of the difference between two principles: (a) doing no harm, and (b) doing good. A minimalist morality would insist merely that we do not harm others. As such, it does not require that we come to the aid of others. But is that an adequate view of morality? Should we accept such a moral system as complete? If you happen to see a child drowning in water that is four feet deep, and it is in your power to rescue the child, are you not morally obligated to do so? Are you under no moral obligation to assist simply because you may have no explicit legal contract requiring you to rescue that particular child?

According to a minimalist account of morality, you are not *required* to make any effort to save the child. All that is required is that you not actively harm the child (or anyone else). But some argue that a moral system demands much more of us than simply doing no harm. That is, it may also obligate us to do good when it is in our power to do so. According to the latter view of morality, then, if we could rescue the child without any significant inconvenience to ourselves, we would be morally obligated to do so (even if we have no explicit contract).

2.6.2 Rights-Based Contract Theories

Closely associated with social contract ethical theories are rights-based theories of morality. Some philosophers have argued that independent of whether individuals happen to have any legal rights, all humans have certain moral rights or natural rights. Philosophers such as Thomas Aquinas (1225–1274), as well as several of the Founders of the United States, believed that humans possess some natural rights. In the Declaration of Independence, for example, Thomas Jefferson asserted that all humans are entitled to life, liberty, and the pursuit of happiness because these rights are "inalienable" and "self-evident."

Of course, it is one thing for philosophers and legal scholars to assert that humans are endowed with natural or moral rights; and it is something altogether different to ensure that such rights are guaranteed and are protected by the state. Hence, the need for explicit legal rights identified in a governing charter or constitution. Legal rights are grounded in "positive law," or civil law, whereas moral rights or natural rights are not. However, some argue that moral rights are derived from natural law; and because of this, they further argue that these rights exist independently of any legal rights that might happen to be granted to citizens of a certain nation via that nation's system of positive laws.[13]

Philosophers and legal scholars often differentiate between two kinds of legal rights: _positive rights_ and _negative rights_. Having a negative right to something means simply that one has the right not to be interfered with in carrying out the privileges associated with that right. For example, your right to vote and your right to own a computer are both negative rights. They are negative rights in the sense that as a holder of those rights, you have the right (and the expectation) not to be interfered with in exercising your right to go to polls to cast your vote in a particular election or your right to purchase a computer. However, as holder of a negative right, you cannot demand (or even expect) that others must either physically transport you to the voting polls if you are unable to travel there on your own, or provide you with a computer if you cannot afford to purchase one.

Positive rights, it turns out, are very rare. And since those rights tend to be far more controversial than negative rights, philosophers and legal scholars have had a much more difficult time justifying them. In the United States, one's right to receive an education (through the twelfth grade of high school) is a positive right. All American citizens are entitled to such an education; thus they must be provided with a free public education through the twelfth grade. An interesting question, for our purposes, is, what would happen in the event that our formal education process requires that each student own a computer and that he or she has access at home to the Internet? In that case, would students also have to be provided with a home computer and free Internet access? (We take up the question of universal access issues and the "digital divide" in Chapter 10.)

Some would argue that access to adequate health care should also be a positive right as well, because they believe health care is something that citizens have a right to be provided (even if they cannot afford to pay for it). In Canada as well as in many European countries, universal health care is viewed as a positive right. In the United States, however, this is not the case (at least not as of October 2009), and the topic of national health care is presently a hotly disputed political issue.

Discussion about the nature of rights can be both confusing and controversial. In the United States, many conservative political and religious leaders believe that in recent years far too much emphasis has been placed on individual rights. As a result, they believe that we have not paid enough attention to corresponding responsibilities that individuals also have in virtue of possessing those rights. However, we will not pursue that line of controversy here.

▶ 2.7 CHARACTER-BASED ETHICAL THEORIES

A fourth type of ethical theory that must be considered, especially in light of the recent attention it has received, is *virtue ethics* (also sometimes described as "character ethics"). This ethical theory ignores the special roles that consequences, duties, and social contracts play in moral systems, especially with respect to determining the appropriate standard for evaluating moral behavior. Rather, it focuses on criteria having to do with the character development of individuals and their acquisition of good character traits from the kinds of habits they develop. The fundamental principles of virtue ethics were introduced in the writings of Plato and Aristotle nearly 2,500 years ago. In more recent times, virtue ethics has gained respect among ethicists as a viable contemporary ethical theory, in part, through the influential work of Alasdair MacIntyre.[14]

2.7.1 Being a Moral Person vs. Following Moral Rules

Aristotle believed that ethics was something not merely to be studied, but rather to be lived or practiced. In fact, Aristotle thought of ethics as a "practical science," like politics. To become an ethical person, in Aristotle's view, one is required to do more than simply memorize and deliberate on certain kinds of rules. What is also needed, Aristotle argued, is that people develop certain *virtues*. The Greek word for virtue is *arete*, which means excellence. Aristotle believed that to be a moral person, one had to acquire the right virtues (strengths or excellences). Through the proper training and acquisition of good habits and character traits, Aristotle believed that one could achieve moral virtues such as temperance and courage that are needed to "live well."

Because virtue ethics focuses primarily on character development and moral education, it does not need to rely on a system of formal rules. Consider that both utilitarians and deontologists depend on having a system of rules when they ask a question such as, What should we do in such and such a case or situation? For utilitarians, the answer could be found by measuring the anticipated outcomes of following a general rule or principle. And for deontologists the answer can be determined by using a formal rule such as the categorical imperative as a principle for determining which duties you have. For contract theorists, questions involving moral obligation ultimately rest on the principle or rule, What is the nature of my contract, if any, in this particular situation? Virtue ethicists take a very different tack. Instead of asking, "What should I *do* in such and such a situation?" a virtue ethicist asks, *What kind of person should I be*? Hence, the emphasis on *being a moral person*, and not simply on understanding what moral rules are and how they apply in certain situations. Whereas deontological and utilitarian theories are action-oriented and rule-oriented, virtue ethics is "agent-oriented" because it is centered on the moral development and character of the agent herself.

Virtue ethicists believe that a moral person is one who is necessarily disposed to do the right thing. They correctly point out that when we engage in routine acts in our daily lives, including many of our nonnormative actions, we do not deliberate by asking ourselves, What ought I to do in such and such a case? In our earlier criticism of act utilitarianism, we considered a situation in which an individual would be required to deliberate over whether or not to steal an item each time he or she entered a store. A virtue ethicist would point out that if that person had developed the right kind of moral character (through the acquisition of the "correct" moral habits), he or she would not be in a position that required such deliberation. That is, the moral person is already disposed not to steal items from stores (or from fellow human beings) because of the kinds of character traits that he or she has previously developed. And in the example involving the drowning child, considered in our criticism of contract-based ethical theory, a virtue ethicist would also likely point out that a moral person would not have to deliberate. Regardless of whether someone had an explicit legal contract to help rescue the child, the virtue ethicist would point out that a moral person is predisposed to attempt to rescue the child if it were in his or her power to do so.

2.7.2 Acquiring the "Correct" Habits

Consider the following illustration of a disposition to behave in a certain way. When you woke up this morning and began to prepare for your day's events, did you ask yourself the question, Should I brush my teeth today? Most likely, this question never crossed your mind. Why not? The answer, of course, is that you have already developed certain habits such that you are disposed to brush your teeth in the morning without having to question it or even think about it. Of course, the act of brushing one's teeth is not an act that has any moral significance. But it is the process of character formation, especially the development of moral habits, that is crucial to becoming a fully moral person, from the perspective of virtue ethics.

As noted above, Aristotle believed that ethics was something to be lived and practiced, not simply studied. Thus some philosophers and ethicists believe that to teach ethics, one must first be an ethical person. The teacher who instructs students on the virtues but who himself lacks them would be a poor model for aspiring students. James Moor (2002) suggests that virtue ethics instruction is the "first level" in teaching (computer) ethics. He believes that building habits of character such as kindness, truthfulness, honesty, trustworthiness, helpfulness, generosity, and justice are important prerequisites in preparing for the second level of instruction. Once students have mastered the virtues, they can then move to the second level where they learn the established rules of a moral system.

Some instructors have argued that their students are better able to relate to classroom examples that involve virtue ethics than to those illustrating other traditional theories. For this reason, Frances Grodzinsky (2001) has suggested that aspects of virtue ethics should be incorporated into the ethics training for computing professionals. Grodzinsky believes that aspiring computer professionals who wish to develop an appropriate level of sensitivity to ethical aspects of their profession often find the principles of virtue ethics far more useful than the kinds of rigid rules required in ethical theories such as utilitarianism and deontology. She notes that action-guiding rules associated with utilitarian and deontological theories often tend to be perceived by students as too abstract and formal. On the contrary, however, many of those students are able to grasp what it means to develop certain character traits and thus become (or be) a certain kind of person.

It would seem that the re-emergence of virtue ethics, despite the fact that its origins can be traced back to classical Greece, has provided ethicists with some fresh insights. However, we should also note that virtue ethics is not without its critics. One of the chief drawbacks of taking virtue ethics as a complete theory of ethics is that it neither helps

TABLE 2-3   Four Types of Ethical Theory

Type of Theory	Advantages	Disadvantages
Consequence-based (Utilitarian)	Stresses promotion of happiness and utility	Ignores concerns of justice for the minority population
Duty-based (Deontology)	Stresses the role of duty and respect for persons	Underestimates the importance of happiness and social utility
Contract-based (Rights)	Provides a motivation for morality	Offers only a minimal morality
Character-based (Virtue)	Stresses character development and moral education	Depends on homogeneous community standards for morality

resolve conflicts that can arise among the competing virtues nor encourages examination of consequences. Some critics point out that a virtue- or character-based ethics would seem to have a better chance of taking hold in a society that is homogeneous rather than in one that is heterogeneous or pluralistic. The ancient Greek society could be considered fairly homogeneous in the sense that the world that Plato and Aristotle inhabited included a consensus as to what the ideal values, including the moral education of the young, were. In contemporary America, which is much more heterogeneous than classical Greek society, we have a diversity of views about which ideals and values are most important.

It is also worth pointing out that character-based ethical systems would most likely flourish in cultures where the emphasis placed on community life is stronger than that accorded to the role of individuals themselves. Beginning with the Enlightenment period in the West in the seventeenth and eighteenth centuries, considerable emphasis has been placed on the importance of individual autonomy and individual rights. As you might already have suspected, aspects of utilitarianism, deontological ethics, and contractualist ethics are strongly tied to the notions of individual rights and responsibilities. In the ancient Greek world of Aristotle's time, the notion of community was paramount. Thus virtue ethics faces certain challenges in contemporary Western society that it would not have had to endure in the classical Greek *polis*, or city-state.

▶ 2.8 INTEGRATING ASPECTS OF CLASSICAL ETHICAL THEORIES INTO A SINGLE COMPREHENSIVE THEORY

We have completed our examination of the four main types of ethical theories, and we have noted some of the strengths and weaknesses of each theory. Consequentialist theories such as utilitarianism are useful because they aim at promoting happiness and the social good. Yet, we also saw that utilitarians tend to ignore the importance of justice and fairness in their preoccupation with promoting social utility for the majority. Deontologists, on the contrary, stress the importance of obligation and respect for all persons, and thus emphasize the principles of fairness and justice. However, we saw that deontologists fail to pay sufficient attention to the promotion of happiness and the social good.

Contract theory seems useful in that it provides a motivation for being moral and it enables us to articulate which explicit moral obligations we have and do not have, both as individuals and as a society. However, the weakness of the social contract view is that it provides us with only a minimalist theory of morality. Virtue ethics stresses character development and the acquisition of good habits on the part of individuals, but its disadvantage is that it depends on homogeneous community standards for determining the correct virtues. Thus each theory has its weakness, despite its strengths. Table 2–3 summarizes the advantages and disadvantages of the each of the four ethical theories we examined.

Because of problems with the four types of traditional ethical theories that we considered, some have advocated for alternative ethical theories including feminist ethics. Alison Adam (2008) has drawn from some of the insights of Carol Gilligan,[15] as well as from other authors who have contributed to the literature on feminist ethics, in making her case for why at least some computer ethics issues would be better understood if they were analyzed from the perspective of feminist ethical theory. We examine Adam's arguments for a "gender-informed" computer ethics in Chapter 10, where we consider gender issues affecting cybertechnology.

Others have proposed ways in which elements of two or more traditional theories can be integrated into a single, more comprehensive framework. For example, Bernard Gert (2005, 2007) has integrated aspects of two theories by incorporating Kant's insights on the importance of impartiality with the claims of utilitarians about consequences, but he thinks that each theory, in itself, is inadequate. Gert has also shown how his moral system, which he calls "common morality," can be directly applied to issues involving computer ethics such as copying proprietary software.[16] Recall our discussion of Gert's notion of the moral system and its corresponding "moral rules" in Section 2.1.1.

Influenced by the work of Gert and others, Moor (2004) has proposed a scheme that integrates aspects of utilitarian and deontological theories into a framework he calls "just consequentialism." We next examine some key aspects of this theory.

2.8.1 Moor's Just-Consequentialist Theory and Its Application to Cybertechnology

Moor believes that only an ethical approach that combines considerations of consequences of action with more traditional deontological considerations of duties, rights, and justice can provide us with a defensible ethical theory—viz., just consequentialism—that yields a useful framework for applied ethics. Moor begins by considering what kind of conduct we want ethics to regulate. He believes first and foremost everyone wants to be protected against suffering unnecessary harms. We don't want to be killed or suffer great pain or have our freedom taken away. Human nature is such that people value the same kind of basic goods (life, happiness, abilities, security, knowledge, freedom, opportunities, and resources). The specifics of these may be manifest somewhat differently in different cultures (some kinds of freedom may be more important in some cultures than others, for example), but the general set of goods, which Moor calls "core values" (see Section 2.1.2), is shared by all. Losing any of these goods counts as harm, and all of us want ethics to protect us from others causing us harm. This point is captured by the familiar ethical maxim "Do no harm," described earlier. Stealing someone's computer causes a loss of resources to that person, and lying about software bugs undermines the purchaser's knowledge. Thus it is not surprising that we regard stealing and lying as unethical activities in light of their harmful consequences.

Another desirable objective of ethics, according to Moor, is to support justice, rights, and duties. We want others to keep their promises and agreements, to obey the law, and to fulfill their duties in whatever roles they play. These specific obligations are generated within societies, and to the extent that they spring from just agreements, laws, and social situations, we justifiably expect others to fulfill their duties toward us. For example, we want a software engineer to produce reliable software. We believe it is her duty as a professional to develop effective and safe software and that we have a right to expect good quality when we buy it. Another familiar maxim of ethics is "Do your duty," where "duty" here designates specific duties people acquire by their roles in society such as a signer of contract, a citizen, a parent, an employer, or an employee. Violating one's just duty, such as knowingly designing defective software for later production and sales, in the absence of contravening considerations, is clearly unethical.

Moor believes that if all we had to do to be ethical were to do no harm and perform our duties, ethics would be challenging but at least easy to understand. But, as Moor argues, the ethical life is not nearly so simple. Often actions involve a mixture of goods and evils as well as conflicts among duties. Sometimes we need to make exceptions to our general policies for action. How do we decide what to do? His answer involves two steps: the deliberation stage and the selection stage. First, at the *deliberation stage*, we should consider the various possible policies for action from an impartial point of view. Impartial does not mean that everyone is treated the same but that the policy is regarded as a rule governing the situation without consideration to the particular individuals who happen to be involved. This is what Gert has in mind by his "blindfold of justice" (see Section 2.1.1) or what Rawls suggests with his "veil of ignorance." This is a technique to establish the justice of a policy—it will not be just if one will not accept the policy as a general rule of conduct, not knowing who plays which roles in the situation.

For example, consider the cyberstalking scenario discussed in Chapter 1, in which Liam Youens stalked Amy Boyer on the Internet and eventually murdered her. Let us assume that Youens was obsessed with his victim and got significant gratification out of his deeds. If we consider a policy for justifying such an action impartially, we will clearly reject it. We will not endorse a policy of allowing someone to stalk and kill us even if such murderers get significant pleasure from it. It is easy to reject such a policy as unjust and unethical when considered from an impartial point of view.

However, many policies will pass the impartiality test, and we will still need to consider whether we should adopt them. We need to move to the second step in the decision-making process, the *selection stage*, and weigh carefully the good consequences and the bad consequences of the remaining policies. In this second step, it may be less of a choice between ethical vs. unethical policies than between better vs. worse policies. Although we may be able to at least partially rank policies, legitimate disagreements about the rankings often exist.

For instance, consider the controversial issues as to whether we should adjust or even have a policy of intellectual property protection. For many years in many places there were no laws protecting intellectual property. It is far from clear that this situation was unjust or even bad. A culture might maintain that sharing information and invention is more valuable to the society's members' welfare and the society's cohesiveness than trying to protect intellectual property. Witness the rationale given for the "open source movement" in software development. Critics of this movement, however, might maintain that having intellectual-property protection laws is important to protect creators and to produce innovative products for everyone's benefit.

According to Moor, it is important to keep in mind that although we may disagree about the merits of various policies and how to rank them, rational discussion of the relevant policies is very possible and highly desirable. People may overlook values embedded in a situation and may change their rankings once informed. People may not be fully aware of the consequences of various policies. Moor does not believe that complete agreement on controversial policies can or necessarily should be reached, as people may ultimately rank benefits and harms differently. Nevertheless, considerable consensus about some policies being better than others can often be generated. Moor points out that frequently much of the disagreement hinges on differences about the facts of the case than on value differences. (Recall our early analysis of differences involving "disagreements about principles" and "disagreements about facts" in Section 2.2.1, in our discussion of discussion stoppers in ethics.) It would radically change much of the debate about the need for protecting MP3 files, for example, if it could be demonstrated that, *as a matter of fact*, downloading MP3 files to preview them dramatically increases sales or if it could be demonstrated that, *as a matter of fact*, downloading MP3 files to preview them dramatically decreased the quality of music that was produced.

2.8.2 Key Elements in Moor's Just-Consequentialist Framework

Moor's ethical framework of just consequentialism can be summarized in terms of a strategy that includes the following steps:

1. *Deliberate* over various policies from an impartial point of view to determine whether they meet the criteria for being ethical policies. A policy is ethical, if it

   a. does not cause any unnecessary harms to individuals and groups, and

   b. supports individual rights, the fulfilling of duties, etc.

2. *Select* the best policy from the set of just policies arrived at in the deliberation stage by ranking ethical policies in terms of benefits and (justifiable) harms. In doing this, be sure to

   a. weigh carefully between the good consequences and bad consequences in the ethical policies, and

   b. distinguish between disagreements about facts and disagreements about principles and values, when deciding which particular ethical policy should be adopted. (Knowledge about the facts surrounding a particular case should inform the decision-making process.)

As we noted in our discussion of virtue ethics in Section 2.7.2, Moor points out that developing the appropriate habits of character such as kindness, truthfulness, honesty, trustworthiness, helpfulness, generosity, and justice is an important prerequisite in moral behavior. So if one has not already developed the "correct" habits required for moral behavior, it may be difficult for an individual to successfully carry out the steps in Moor's just-consequentialist model. In this sense, elements of virtue ethics or character-based ethics are also presupposed in Moor's framework.

We apply the just-consequentialist framework, wherever appropriate, in suggesting policies in response to moral issues that arise from specific cyberethics issues examined in Chapters 4–12 of this textbook.

▶ 2.9 CHAPTER SUMMARY

In this chapter, we defined ethics as the study of morality. In elaborating on that definition, we drew some useful distinctions between morality (as a system of rules and principles) and ethics (as the study of that system). Acknowledging the distinction between normative and descriptive studies of morality, we saw that normative investigations into morality can be conducted from the perspectives of religion and law as well as from philosophy. We also noted that only philosophical ethics offers a method to analyze moral issues based exclusively on the application of ethical theory and logical argumentation. We briefly identified and analyzed some common "discussion stoppers" that are frequently invoked in ways that prematurely close down, even if unintentionally, the possibility of constructive ethical dialogue.

We also examined the roles that ethical theories ideally play in guiding us in our moral deliberations about cyberethics issues. We saw that consequence-based, duty-based, contract-based, and character-based theories each had certain strengths and weaknesses. Finally, we examined James Moor's proposal for a framework that incorporates aspects of consequence-based and duty-based theories (and to some extent character-based theories) into one unified, comprehensive theory, called "just consequentialism." We summarized Moor's framework into a two-step process that we will use, wherever possible, in our analysis of the cyberethics issues examined in this textbook.

▶ REVIEW QUESTIONS

1. What is *ethics*, and how can it be distinguished from *morality*?
2. What is meant by a *moral system*?
3. What are some of the key differences between the "rules of conduct" and the "principles of evaluation" that comprise a moral system? Give an example of each.
4. Describe the key differences between rules of conduct that are individual "directives" and those that are "social policies." Provide an example of each.
5. What does Bernard Gert mean when he describes morality in terms of a system that is both "public" and "informal"?
6. Describe how the ideals of "rationality" and "impartiality" function in Gert's moral system.
7. What are *values*, and what are some of the key differences between moral values and nonmoral values? Provide some examples of "basic moral values" and "core nonmoral values."
8. How do religion, law, and philosophy each provide different grounds for justifying a moral principle? How can each perspective be applied to the analysis of the moral principle "Stealing is wrong?"
9. What are the basic differences separating ethicists from moralists?
10. Identify and briefly summarize four different kinds of "discussion stoppers" in ethical discourse.
11. Why are these "discussion stoppers" problematic for the advancement of dialogue and debate about ethical issues?
12. What is moral relativism? How is it different from cultural relativism?
13. What is moral objectivism, and how is it different from moral absolutism?
14. What is ethical theory, and what important functions do ethical theories play in the analysis of moral issues?

15. What are the distinguishing features of consequence-based ethical theories?
16. Describe some of the key differences between act utilitarianism and rule utilitarianism.
17. Which features distinguish duty-based ethical theories from alternative types of theories?
18. Describe some of the main differences between act deontology and rule deontology.
19. What is meant by the expression "contract-based" ethical theories?
20. What features distinguish "character-based" (or "virtue-based") ethical theories from alternative schemes of morality?

► DISCUSSION QUESTIONS

1. Why does Gert believe that the notion of "personal morality" is an oxymoron? For Gert, how is a moral system both similar to, and different from, a game? Apply Gert's notion of a moral system to the analysis of a contemporary ethical issue affecting cybertechnology. Analyze that issue in terms of the four features that comprise a moral system for Gert.
2. What is the method of philosophical ethics, and what is a "philosophical study"? How is a philosophical study used in an analysis of moral issues? How does a philosophical study differ from a descriptive study? Why are sociological and anthropological studies of morality usually descriptive rather than normative in nature?
3. Why do we need ethical theories? How are ethical theories similar to, but different from, scientific theories? Why would informal principles such as the "golden rule" and "following one's conscience" be inadequate for analyzing ethical issues? How does the example of the Video Privacy Protection Act (also known as the "Bork Bill") illustrate the inadequacy of approaching a problem with a "band-aid fix"—i.e., from an approach that is neither comprehensive nor systematic?
4. How does James Moor's "just consequentialist" theory incorporate aspects of utilitarian and deontological theories into one comprehensive ethical framework? Describe the strategies used in the two different stages of Moor's theory: the deliberation and the selection stage. Identify a contemporary moral issue affecting cybertechnology, and apply Moor's just consequentialist theory to it.

► ESSAY/PRESENTATION QUESTIONS

1. Recall the four types of "discussion stoppers" that we examined in this chapter. Is that collection of "stoppers" complete? Can you think of any additional discussion stoppers that might also block or shut down moral discourse? Why is it so easy to fall victim to one or more of those stoppers when discussing moral issues in general, as well as moral issues involving the use of cybertechnology in particular?
2. Consider the following situation. You have just been appointed to the board of directors of XYZ.com. Unfortunately, the dot-com company has been experiencing some difficult financial times, resulting in revenue losses in three of the last four quarters. As you assume your new position, you discover that two proposals are on the table. Each proposal has been put forth as a means for dealing with XYZ's immediate financial problems. Proposal #1 recommends that all employees be retained, but that an immediate freeze on salary increases (raises) for all employees be imposed for the next six months. (Employees may even be asked to take a 5% cut in pay if things do not improve by the end of that period.) Proposal #2 recommends that wages not be frozen, but that 5% of the XYZ's work force be laid off. (One piece of reasoning behind this proposal is that taking more drastic measures will "protect" 95% of XYZ's workers and will send a message to Wall Street and local investors that XYZ is serious about improving its financial position and that it will soon be a stable company once again.) The board is evenly split, seven members favoring proposal# 1 and seven favoring proposal #2. Yours will be the tie-breaking vote. In your deliberation, describe how an *act utilitarian*, a *rule utilitarian*, a *rule deontologist*, and an *act deontologist* would each reach a solution to this dilemma. Which solution seems most plausible?
3. Imagine a scenario in which the United States government, with the approval of the majority of Americans, decides to round up all Arab-Americans and relocate them into internment camps. Also, imagine that you

have a friend who is an American citizen of Arab descent. She asks you to protect her from the authorities. You have known this person all of your life, and you are convinced that she is a loyal American. So you agree to hide her in the third floor of your house. Next, imagine that a United States federal agent knocks on your door and asks if you know the whereabouts of the person you are hiding. How would you respond to that agent? You now face a genuine moral dilemma because you cannot both keep your promise to your friend and tell the truth to the federal agent. Initially, your gut reaction might suggest that the solution to your dilemma is really quite simple. For example, you might believe that a far greater good will be served by lying to the federal agent than by breaking your promise to your friend. However, to embrace the moral principle inherent in that line of reasoning is to fall back into utilitarianism. And we have already seen some of the difficulties that can result from trying to be a consistent and thoroughgoing utilitarian. Furthermore, could you consistently universalize a moral principle that states: Whenever you must choose between telling the truth to authorities and breaking a promise to a friend, always honor your promise? Will that principle work in every case? Will Ross's theory help in this situation? Explain.

4. Are any of the four traditional ethical theories we examined—i.e., consequence-based, duty based, contract-based, and character-based—adequate to handle moral issues that arise as a result of cybertechnology? If not, is an alternative kind of ethical theory needed, as some have argued (e.g., Adam 2008)? Or can a comprehensive, integrated theory, such as the one proposed by James Moor (i.e., his theory of "just consequentialism") be used successfully to resolve moral issues involving cybertechnology? Explain.

▶ ENDNOTES

1. This is a classic definition of ethics that has been articulated and defended by many philosophers. See, for example, Paul W. Taylor's *Principles of Ethics: An Introduction* (Belmont CA: Wadsworth, 1980).
2. "Agency" and "moral agency" are philosophically complex notions that are debated in the philosophical literature; unfortunately, however, an examination of these notions is beyond the scope of this chapter and book.
3. Gert's "blindfold of justice" is similar in some ways to John Rawls' well-known "veil of ignorance," articulated in Rawls' class work *A Theory of Justice* (rev. ed. 1999). However, the two notions also differ in key respects.
4. See, for example, Pojman (2006).
5. For example, some critics point out that while the differences affecting moral beliefs might seem apparent at the surface level, a deeper analysis will suggest universal or core moral beliefs that are merely articulated differently via particular customs and practices at the surface level.
6. Bernard Gert suggests that his ten "moral rules" are objective in nature. However, Gert does not use the label "objectivism" to describe his moral system.
7. Although Gert does not call himself a moral objectivist, I interpret his position to be compatible with the view I describe as moral objectivism.
8. See http://epic.org/privacy/vppa/.
9. The variations expressed here are paraphrases of Kant's categorical imperative.
10. For more detail on this strategy, see Ross (1930).
11. Pojman (2006) explains in more detail how this kind of theory provides a motivation for being moral.
12. For the original account of this incident, see "Queens Woman is Stabbed to Death in Front of Home," *New York Times* (March 14, 1964).
13. This is a basic distinction in Natural Law, a theory of ethics that we are not able to examine in detail in this chapter.
14. See, for example, MacIntyre's *After Virtue* (Notre Dame IN: University of Notre Dame Press, 1981).
15. Gilligan's classic book *In a Different Voice* (Cambridge MA: Harvard University Press, 1982) has influenced feminist ethics.
16. See Gert (2004).

▶ REFERENCES

Adam, Alison. 2008. "The Gender Agenda in Computer Ethics." In K. E. Himma and H. T. Tavani, eds. The Handbook of Information and Computer Ethics. Hoboken, NJ: John Wiley and Sons, pp. 589–619.
Aristotle. *Nicomachean Ethics*. Trans. M. Oswald. New York: Bobbs-Merrill, 1962.

Bentham, Jeremy. 1948. *Introduction to the Principles of Morals and Legislation*. W. Harrison, ed. London: Oxford University Press.

De George, Richard T. 1999. *Business Ethics*. 5th ed. Upper Saddle River NJ: Prentice Hall.

Ess, Charles. 2006. "Ethical Pluralism and Global Information Ethics." *Ethics and Information Technology* 8, no. 4: 215–66. p. 63–82. Reprinted from *Ethics and Information Technology* 1, no. 1 (1999): 37–56.

Gert, Bernard. 2004. "Common Morality and Computing." In R. A. Spinello and H. T. Tavani, eds. *Readings in CyberEthics*. 2nd ed. Sudbury MA: Jones and Bartlett, pp. 96–106.

Gert, Bernard. 2005. *Morality: Its Nature and Justification*. Rev. ed. New York: Oxford University Press.

Gert, Bernard. 2007. *Common Morality: Deciding What to Do*. New York: Oxford University Press.

Grodzinsky, Frances S. 2001. "The Practitioner from Within: Revisiting the Virtues." In R. A. Spinello and H. T. Tavani, eds. *Readings in CyberEthics*. Sudbury MA: Jones and Bartlett, pp. 580–91. Reprinted from *Computers and Society* 29, no. 1 (1999): 9–15.

Hobbes, Thomas. 1962. *Leviathan*. New York: Collier Books.

Kant, Immanuel. 1965. *Fundamental Principles of the Metaphysics of Morals*. Trans. T. K. Abbott. London: Longman's.

Mill, John Stuart. 1965. *Utilitarianism*. New York: Bobbs-Merrill.

Moor, James H. 2002. "The Importance of Virtue in Teaching Computer Ethics." In M. Ochi et al., eds. *Proceedings of the Foundations of Information Ethics*. Hiroshima, Japan: Hiroshima University Press, pp. 29–38.

Moor, James H. 2004. "Just Consequentialism and Computing." In R. A. Spinello and H. T. Tavani, eds. *Readings in CyberEthics*. 2nd ed. Sudbury MA: Jones and Bartlett, pp. 107–13.

Pojman, Louis P. 2006. *Ethics: Discovering Right and Wrong*. 5th ed. Belmont CA: Wadsworth.

Rawls, John. 1999. *A Theory of Justice*. Rev. ed. New York: Oxford University Press.

Ross, W. D. 1930. *The Right and the Good*. London: Oxford University Press.

▶ FURTHER READINGS

Arthur, John, ed. *Morality and Moral Controversies*. 7th ed. Upper Saddle River NJ: Prentice Hall, 2005.

Cahn, Steven, and Peter Markie, eds. *Ethics: History, Theory, and Contemporary Issues*. New York: Oxford University Press, 2006.

Hinman, Lawrence, M. *Ethics—A Pluralistic Approach to Moral Theory*. 4th ed. Belmont CA: Wadsworth Publishing, 2008.

Pojman, Louis P. *How Should We Live?—An Introduction to Ethics*. Belmont CA: Wadsworth Publishing, 2005.

Rachels, James. *The Elements of Moral Philosophy*. 5th ed. New York: McGraw-Hill, 2006.

Sterba, James. *Morality in Practice*. 7th ed. Belmont CA: Wadsworth Publishing, 2004.

Triplett, Timm. "Bernard Gert's *Morality* and Its Application to Computer Ethics," *Ethics and Information Technology* 4, no. 1 (2002): 79–92.

3

Critical Thinking Skills and Logical Arguments: Tools for Evaluating Cyberethics Issues

You may wonder why a chapter dedicated to critical thinking skills is included in a book on cyberethics. To appreciate the important role that these skills play in our examination of cyberethics issues, recall the methodological framework that we developed in Chapter 1. There we saw that the final step of that methodology requires that we defend or justify our position by evaluating it against the rules of logical argumentation.[1] In Chapter 3 we examine some basic critical thinking concepts we need to do this. To accomplish these objectives, we

- examine the structure of a *logical argument* and show how arguments are used in resolving disputes affecting ethical aspects of cybertechnology;
- evaluate the strength of arguments by distinguishing between arguments that are valid and invalid, sound and unsound, inductive and fallacious;
- identify some common logical fallacies that occur in everyday reasoning and show how they apply to arguments affecting cyberethics issues.

Additional material on critical thinking skills is included in Appendix G, available at www.wiley.com/college/tavani.

▶ 3.1 CRITICAL THINKING AND LOGICAL ARGUMENTS

Critical thinking is a branch of informal logic. According to Brooke Moore and Richard Parker (2009), critical thinking includes a "variety of deliberative processes" that assist us in evaluating arguments and analyzing claims. Claims, also called statements or assertions, comprise a form of reasoning called a logical argument or argument.

For our purposes, an *argument* can be defined as a reasoning form or structure that attempts to establish the truth of one claim (called a *conclusion*) based on the assumed truth of the evidence in other claims (called *premises*) provided to support the conclusion. Thus, an argument is a *form of reasoning* that has two important characteristics or features in that it

    i.   includes at least two claims;

    ii. aims at establishing a conclusion (i.e., the truth of one claim) based on evidence provided by one or more other claims, called premises.

We will see that whereas arguments are either valid or invalid, the claims that comprise them are either true or false. First, however, we examine an important role that arguments can play when someone is trying to support or defend a position in a dispute.

3.1.1   The Role of an Argument in a Dispute Involving Cybertechnology

Consider a hypothetical dispute about whether a controversial and powerful new computer chip—code-named Chip X—is being developed in Japan. This new chip is alleged to be so powerful in speed and performance that it will eclipse any computer chips that manufacturers in the United States, such as Intel or AMD, will be capable of producing during the next several years. Chip X will also enable the manufacturer to monitor certain activities of those users whose computers contain the chip in ways that pose serious threats to personal privacy.

Suppose I claim that Chip X is currently under development by Mishito Corporation. Let us further suppose that you are skeptical about my claim. There are a number of ways I could attempt to convince you: I could persuade you to accompany me on a trip to Japan to see first-hand whether or not Chip X is being developed there. In this case, we could obtain direct evidence about my claim. But if you are unable or are unwilling to accompany me to Japan, I will have to use some other, less direct mode of verification to convince you. For example, I could show you a copy of the design specifications for Chip X, extracted from a confidential Mishito Corporation document that I happened to acquire. Or perhaps I could ask a mutual colleague of ours who recently studied as an exchange student at the University of Hiroshima, where the field testing for this new chip is being carried out, to corroborate my claim regarding Chip X. That is, I can put together various pieces of evidence to construct a logical argument that supports my claim.

Now we are in a position to debate the merits of my argument regarding Chip X without having to go to Japan to verify the truth of my claim. Before we debate the strength of my argument, however, we must first understand some essential features of an argument's *structure*.

3.1.2   The Basic Structure of an Argument

We noted in Section 3.1 that an argument consists of two or more claims, one of which is called the conclusion; the others are called the premises. The standard form for representing an argument is to list the premises first and then state the conclusion. The following structure represents an argument's standard form:

PREMISE 1

PREMISE 2 (optional)

PREMISE 3 (optional)

.

.

.

PREMISE *n* (optional)

CONCLUSION

To support my claim that Chip X is currently being developed in Japan, in the conclusion of my argument I would need to list the evidence in the form of one or more premises. For example, I could use the following argument form:

> **PREMISE 1**. When I recently visited the Computer Science Department at the University of Hiroshima in Japan, I noticed that graduate students and professors there were field-testing a new computer chip, whose code name is Chip X.
>
> **PREMISE 2**. I have a copy of the design specifications for Chip X, which shows that it will be several times faster than any chip currently available in the United States.
>
> **PREMISE 3**. Lee Smith, a mutual colleague of ours who was recently an exchange student in the computer science program at the University of Hiroshima and who participated in the field-testing of Chip X, will corroborate my claim.
>
> **CONCLUSION**. Chip X is currently being developed in Japan.

This particular argument includes three premises and a conclusion; additional premises could be added. However, an argument requires at least one premise along with a conclusion. In this section, we are concerned only with argument structure and not with how strong the argument might be. An argument, however weak, still qualifies as an argument if it has one or more premises and a conclusion.

You might have observed that the claim expressed in the conclusion to our argument about Chip X could also be verified (i.e., determined to be either true or false) independent of the evidence provided in the argument's premises. Since the conclusion contains a statement that is descriptive, or empirical (i.e., capable of being observed through sensory experience), the truth or falsity of the conclusion could be resolved in this case simply by going to Japan to see whether such a chip was actually being developed there.

However, not all arguments have empirical or descriptive statements as their conclusions. Suppose that I want to convince you that people should be able to include information on their Web sites about how to build bombs. Further, suppose that my reason for holding this view is based on the principle that people are allowed to write books on how to build bombs, and authors of Web sites should have the same rights and freedoms as authors of books. And suppose I base my reasoning for this claim on the right of authors to express themselves as guaranteed in the First Amendment of the United States Constitution. My argument could be constructed as follows:

PREMISE 1. A person's right to author a book on how to build a bomb is protected by the First Amendment (of the U.S. Constitution).

PREMISE 2. Authoring material in a book is similar to authoring material on the Web.

CONCLUSION. A person's right to author material on the Web about how to build a bomb ought to be protected by the First Amendment.

Notice how this argument differs from the preceding one. For one thing, we can't simply go to Japan to determine whether this conclusion is true or false. For another, the conclusion contains a normative statement (one that includes "ought"). Unlike the previous argument, which contained a descriptive statement in its conclusion that could be verified independently of the argument, we depend on the *form of reasoning* alone to help us determine whether the conclusion is true. In doing this, we will *assume* that the premises in this argument are true and then ask whether the conclusion would logically follow from them.

Initially, the reasoning in this argument might seem plausible: the person constructing the argument cleverly uses an analogy based on a legal right that applies in physical space. So, we might assume that any legal rights that citizens enjoy in physical space should automatically be extended to cyberspace.

In this argument, we are also asked to consider certain features or characteristics that are common to both (printed) books and Web sites. Clearly, we can draw a number of analogies here. For example, both books and Web sites can communicate and disseminate information to readers; each is authored by one or more persons; and so forth. However, there is a danger in pushing some of these analogies too far: Whereas books are tangible items existing in physical space, Web sites are not. And the scope of a Web site allows it to be accessed by members of the international community, some of whom may have no access to books or may lack sufficient funds to purchase books. We begin to see many dissimilarities between books and Web sites, so we must be cautious about drawing conclusions when reasoning by analogy. Later in this chapter, we will see why arguments of this kind are not valid.

Next, consider a case in which someone tries to convince you that Internet users should not expect to retain their privacy when they engage in online activities, because the Internet is essentially a public forum or public space. Notice that, as stated, the conclusion of the argument precedes the premise. However, we can convert the argument into standard form as follows:

> **PREMISE**. The Internet is in public space.
>
> **CONCLUSION**. Those who use the Internet should not expect to retain any personal privacy.

Is the argument convincing? Before we evaluate this argument's reasoning, we should point out that a key term in the premise is unclear or imprecise: we first need to understand what is meant by public space. We also need to consider whether the Internet can indeed be considered a public space or, for that matter, any kind of space at all. (In Chapter 9, we consider arguments as to whether the Internet is best conceived of as a "place," like a bookstore, or as a broadcast medium, like television and radio.)

But let us assume that the premise in this argument is true. Does it follow that Internet users should have no expectations about retaining their personal privacy? Consider, for example, that while public rest rooms and pubic telephone booths both reside in public space, people expect to retain some privacy while using those facilities. (We will consider issues involving personal privacy in public space in our discussion of privacy and cyberspace in Chapter 5.)

So the argument does not appear to be very convincing; the conclusion would not likely follow from the premise, even when the premise is assumed true. In fact, the argument is fallacious, and in Section 3.7, we will see why—that is, we will identify which rules it breaks. First, however, we consider some strategies for constructing arguments.

▶ 3.2 CONSTRUCTING AN ARGUMENT

Think of some situations in which arguments are used by those in powerful positions, as well as by ordinary persons. Lawyers, for example, use arguments to try to persuade juries; and politicians often use arguments to convey their positions to their constituencies. All of us use arguments when we try to convince a friend, a spouse, or a boss about some point or other. If you try to convince your parents that they should buy you a new iPod, for example, you will most likely be making an argument of some sort. Ultimately, arguments will succeed or not succeed depending on how well they are constructed and how strong the reasoning mechanisms they use are. We refer to those features as argument strength, and we examine that concept in Section 3.3 in our discussion of valid vs. invalid arguments. In this section, we focus on how arguments are constructed.

Arguments often appear as editorials in newspapers and periodicals where they are sometimes expressed in prose forms that can obscure the argument, making it difficult to isolate and analyze. When this happens we must locate the arguments concealed in the text before we can analyze them. Consider the political debate over the need for a new national missile defense (NMD) system, which has been controversial from both a domestic and an international perspective. A fairly straightforward argument in favor of NMD in the editorial section of a newspaper might look something like the following:

> We must build a national missile defense system because without such a system we are vulnerable to nuclear attacks from rogue nations that might arise in the future. Engineers and computer scientists have testified that they can design a computer-guided missile defense system that is effective, safe, and reliable. It is our obligation as Americans to take whatever measures we can to protect the safety of our citizens.

Before we analyze this argument, however, it is perhaps worth making a few parenthetical remarks about certain events leading up to NMD. The debate in the U.S. Congress over NMD that occurred during the George W. Bush administration can be viewed as an updated version of the earlier "Star Wars" debate, officially known as the Strategic Defense Initiative (or SDI). That debate, which took place during the Reagan administration in the 1980s, was significant for cyberethics because it was one of the first ethical controversies to catch the attention of a group of computer ethics pioneers.[2] We will examine some specific ethical issues pertaining to Star Wars and NMD of interest to computer professionals in Chapter 4. Our primary purpose in this chapter, however, is to consider the NMD controversy only insofar as it illustrates how logical arguments can be constructed and analyzed.

There has been strong support for NMD among many conservative politicians in the United States. As suggested above, a proponent of the NMD system could construct an argument for his or her case by first asserting that without such a new missile system, the United States is vulnerable to future attacks from potential "rogue" nations that might acquire nuclear weapons. The proponent might next want to assure us that there is sufficient and compelling evidence that such a missile defense system would be safe and reliable. Finally, the NMD supporter might assume the following principle: "We must do whatever is necessary to preserve the safety of America and its people." The structure of the proponent's argument can be represented as follows:

PREMISE 1. Without the new NMD, the United States is vulnerable to nuclear attacks in the future from rogue nations.

PREMISE 2. Computer scientists and engineers have testified before Congress that they can design a computer-guided missile defense system that is both safe and reliable.

PREMISE 3. The United States must do whatever is necessary to preserve the military defense of the nation and the safety of its citizens.

CONCLUSION. The United States should build the new NMD.

Thus far, we have considered only the structure of this argument. That is, we have described its two basic components—its premises and conclusion—and we have represented it in standard logical form. Now we ask: Is the reasoning used in the argument strong? Are there rules that will enable us to determine this? To answer these questions, we first need to understand the difference between valid and invalid arguments.

▶ 3.3 VALID ARGUMENTS

The first question we could ask about the sample argument described in the preceding section is whether its reasoning is strong or weak—that is, is the argument's reasoning *valid* or is it *invalid*? "Valid" and "invalid" are technical terms in logic. Whereas claims (the individual statements that make up an argument) are either true or false, arguments will be either valid or invalid; it is incorrect to refer to an argument as either true or false, and it is incorrect to refer to a claim as either valid or invalid.

How can we determine whether a particular argument is valid or invalid? In formal systems of logic, elaborate schemes that consist of symbols, rules, and tables have been constructed for determining when arguments are valid or invalid. But fortunately we can use an informal system developed by John Nolt (2002). That system does not require that we know anything about the *actual* truth or falsity of the claims in an argument's premise(s) in order to determine whether an argument is valid or invalid. Instead, we need only to determine whether the argument's conclusion would necessarily follow from its premises, when those premises are all *assumed* to be true.[3] In other words, we ask,

> Is the relationship between the premises and the conclusion such that if all of the premises in the argument are assumed true, it would be impossible for the conclusion to be false?

The concern here is with the relationship of truth conditions that obtain *between* the premises and the conclusion. The premises and the conclusion could be true or false independent of each other, but that is not relevant for testing the argument's validity. We ask only whether the assumed truth of the premises is sufficient to guarantee the truth of the conclusion. If the answer is yes, then the argument is valid. If, however, it is logically possible for the argument's conclusion to be false at the same time that its premises are true, then the argument is invalid.

You can apply this test for validity to the argument for the new national missile defense system that we considered above. Imagine that all of the argument's premises are true statements. Is it possible—that is, could you conceive of a possible instance such that—when those premises are true, the conclusion could still be false? Of course, the premises could be imagined to be false, and the conclusion could be imagined to be false as well. But the relevant questions here are: What happens when all of the premises are imagined to be true? Could the claim in the argument's conclusion (i.e., "The United States should build the new NMD.") be false, even when Premises 1–3 are assumed true? The answer is yes. Hence, the argument is invalid.

The Counterexample Strategy

To show that an argument is invalid, all we need to do is to produce one *counterexample* to the argument. A counterexample is

> a logically possible case in which the argument's conclusion could be imagined to be false while (at the same time) the argument's premises are assumed true.[4]

In the NMD argument, we can coherently imagine a logically possible situation (i.e., a situation that does not involve a logical contradiction) where the conclusion "The United States should build the new NMD" is false when the claims stated in Premises 1–3 are assumed true. For example, we can imagine a situation or case in which all three premises are true but some alternative strategy not involving the development of a new missile defense system could provide for the safety of America. So a counterexample is possible; thus the argument is invalid.

Note, however, although this particular argument has been shown to be invalid, it does not follow that the argument's conclusion is, in fact, false. All that has been shown is that the argument is invalid because the form of reasoning it uses does not succeed in guaranteeing that the conclusion must be true. It is still possible, of course, that the conclusion could be true. But a different argument would need to be constructed to show that the inference is valid.

Suppose we added a fourth premise, "The new NMD system is necessary to preserve the defense and safety of the United States and its citizens," to the argument. The amended argument would be as follows:

PREMISE 1. Without the new NMD, the United States is vulnerable to nuclear attacks in the future from rogue nations.

PREMISE 2. Computer scientists and engineers have testified before Congress that they can design a computer-guided missile defense system that is both safe and reliable.

PREMISE 3. The United States must do whatever is necessary to preserve the military defense of the nation and the safety of its citizens.

PREMISE 4. The new NMD system is necessary to preserve the defense and safety of the United States and its citizens.

CONCLUSION. The United States should build the new NMD.

This argument would now be valid. If all of its premises are assumed true, then the conclusion cannot be false. Of course, we could next ask whether all of the premises in this argument are in fact true. Premises 1 and 2 are fairly uncontroversial claims, though Premise 2 might be challenged by programmers who believe that building a completely reliable computer system is not possible. However, both Premises 3 and 4 are controversial: Premise 4 can be shown to be false if it can be demonstrated that the United States could be adequately protected without the newly proposed missile defense system; Premise 3, which is a normative statement, can also be shown to be false if, for instance, we can provide an exception to the principle included in it. For one thing, we

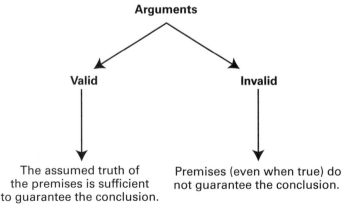

Figure 3-1   Valid and invalid arguments.

could ask both whether indeed the United States *must* do whatever is necessary to make the United States safe and what exactly we mean by the phrase "whatever is necessary"? For example, what if making the United States safe entailed closing down all systems of transportation, all government offices, and all schools for an indefinite period of time that could go on for years? It might protect United States citizens but would it be an acceptable alternative? And United States citizens might be willing to make trade-offs rather than shut down major institutions essential to their day-to-day lives. So Premise 3, as stated, is also false. However, even if all of the premises are eventually shown to be false, the argument itself is still valid because its conclusion follows from the premises if they are assumed true.

Figure 3.1 illustrates the basic distinction between valid and invalid arguments. Next consider the following argument.

PREMISE 1. People who own iMac computers are smarter than those who own PCs.

PREMISE 2. My roommate owns an iMac computer.

PREMISE 3. I own a PC.

CONCLUSION. My roommate is smarter than me.

This argument meets all of the criteria for validity: *if* all three of the premises in this argument are assumed true, then the conclusion ("My roommate is smarter than me.") must be true. In other words, no counterexample to this argument's reasoning form is possible. However, the argument's validity alone is not sufficient to establish that the argument succeeds in the final analysis (as we will see in the following sections). It shows only that when all of the premises are assumed true, the conclusion would also be true.

This argument, like all valid arguments, is valid in virtue of its *logical form*; an argument's logical form, not its content, determines its validity and invalidity. An example of a valid logical form is as follows:

PREMISE 1. Every A is a B.

PREMISE 2. C is an A.

CONCLUSION. C is a B.

Any argument that has this form is valid, regardless of the content represented by A, B, or C. As long as the premises "Every A is a B" and "C is an A" are both assumed true, there is no way that the conclusion "C is a B" could be coherently conceived to be false. Even if the two premises in this particular argument turn out to be false in the actual world, the argument continues to be valid by virtue of its logical form.

We can now see that it is important to separate two distinct questions:

a. What is the *strength of reasoning* of the argument (i.e., is it valid or invalid)?

b. Are the argument's premises true in the actual world?

To say that an argument is valid does not necessarily mean that its premises are true in the actual world. An argument can be valid in terms of its logical form and yet still be unsound. One more step is required for an argument to qualify as a *sound argument*. To be sound, all of the premises (included in the valid argument) must be true in the real world, and not merely assumed true as in the case of the test for validity. For information on how to determine whether a statement is true or false, see Appendix G, available at www.wiley.com/college/tavani.

▶ 3.4 SOUND ARGUMENTS

To assume that the premises of an argument are true is an important first step in the process of evaluating arguments, because doing so enables us to determine the logical relationship between the argument's premise(s) and conclusion and thus determine the argument's strength of reasoning. The reasoning strength will be one of either validity or invalidity. If we can produce one counterexample by showing a possible case where the argument's conclusion can be false even when all of its premises are assumed true, we have shown the argument to be invalid. If the argument is shown to be invalid, we can stop here for the time being. To show that the argument was valid, all that we had to do was to show that no counterexample was possible. And to do that, we considered the hypothetical or assumed truth of the argument's premises vis-à-vis the argument's conclusion. If the argument is valid, then we must determine if it is sound by going on to the next step, where we test the premises to see whether they are true or false in the actual world.

Consider again the two arguments in the preceding section: one involving an NMD system, and the other involving the intelligence of iMac users. Both arguments were shown to be valid. (The argument defending the need for an NMD system had to be modified, but once we modified it, it met the criteria for validity.) We can now further examine each argument to see if it is also sound. An argument will be sound if (a) the argument is valid and (b) all of the premises are actually true (and not merely assumed to be true).

First consider the NMD system. If one or more of Premises 1–4 are false, then the argument will be unsound. Premise 3, "The United States must do whatever is necessary to preserve the military defense of the nation and the safety of its citizens," is clearly questionable. Surely, the goal of national defense is one of the highest priorities of a political administration. But we have already seen that the phrase "whatever is necessary" is problematic. For example, would such a principle give the United States government the right to use *any* means that it happened to deem necessary to bring about some desired end?

Suppose some government officials believed that it was necessary to put all non-United States citizens under house arrest? Or suppose that some of those officials believed that all United States citizens should be subject to constant search and seizure, both within and outside their homes? Would these measures be acceptable? Perhaps under the most severe and dire circumstances some proposals of this type might seem plausible. But it is still not exactly clear that such drastic measures would be necessary. So Premise 3 in the missile defense argument cannot be confirmed to be true, even if Premises 1, 2, and 4 can. Thus this argument is not sound even though it is valid. Because it is unsound, the argument does not succeed. However, once again we should be careful to note that even when an argument is unsound, or even when it is invalid, it does not necessarily follow that the argument's conclusion is false. Rather, we can only infer that the evidence given, that is, the particular premises used to support the argument's conclusion, is not adequate because (when used alone) the premises fail to meet certain logical requirements.

Returning to the argument involving claims about the intelligence of iMac users, we saw that when we assume the truth of all three premises of that argument, the conclusion cannot be imagined to be false; hence the argument is valid. But is it also sound? We need to examine each premise in more detail. Premises 2 and 3—"My roommate owns an iMac computer" and "I own a PC," respectively—are relatively easy to verify because both are descriptive claims. To see if they are true or false, we simply go to the dormitory room or to the apartment where my roommate and I live and observe whether my roommate indeed owns an iMac computer and whether I own a PC.

Premise 1—"People who own iMac computers are smarter than those who own PCs"—however, is more controversial and hence more difficult to verify than the other premises. Clearly, more evidence would be needed to show that Premise 1 is true; in fact, it certainly seems suspect. So despite the fact that the argument is valid in virtue of its logical form, we cannot yet say that it is sound. Thus the argument would appear, at best, to be not sound, but inconclusive.

As you might suspect, sound arguments are not very common, and often they are about matters that are either trivial or uncontroversial. Consider the following argument:

PREMISE 1. CEOs of major computer corporations are high-school graduates.
PREMISE 2. Bill Gates was the CEO of a major computer corporation.

CONCLUSION. Bill Gates is a high-school graduate.

This argument is clearly valid because no counterexample can be constructed; that is, there is no possible case where Premises 1 and 2 could both be (assumed) true and the conclusion could be false at the same time. As it turns out, the premises are also true in the actual world, so this argument is sound; however, it is also not terribly informative. Perhaps you can now see why there are so few sound arguments that are also informative: relatively few valid arguments are sound, and relatively few sound arguments are informative or nontrivial.

Figure 3.2 illustrates the basic differences between valid arguments that are sound and those that are unsound.

At this point, you might ask, what good is a valid argument if it contains false premises? You might also wonder whether certain types of invalid arguments whose premises are true in the actual world are stronger than valid arguments that contain one or more false premises.

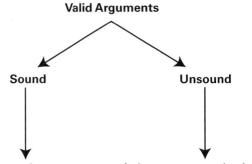

Figure 3-2   Sound and unsound (valid) arguments.

▶ 3.5 INVALID ARGUMENTS

Consider the following argument:

PREMISE 1. All CEOs of major United States computer corporations have been United States citizens.

PREMISE 2. Bill Gates is a United States citizen.

CONCLUSION. Bill Gates has been a CEO of a major computer corporation in the United States.

Even though all three of the claims included in this argument (i.e., the two premises and the conclusion) are true in the actual world, we can show that this argument is invalid by producing at least one counterexample. We can imagine a possible case where the premises in this argument are both true, but the conclusion—that Bill Gates has been CEO of a major computer corporation—is false. For example, we can imagine him as a consultant or a programmer, or he could be employed outside the computer field. However, there is even a more serious flaw in this argument: If we substitute for "Bill Gates" the names Al Gore, Michael Jordan, Julia Roberts, or Rudolph Giuliani, we see that although each of these persons is a United States citizen, none has been a CEO of a major computer corporation. Yet by the logic used in the argument, it would follow that if any of these people is a United States citizen, then he or she must also be or have been a CEO. We have shown that this argument is invalid. If you noticed that the reasoning in this argument was weak, now you know exactly why.

We next determine whether the following argument is valid or invalid:

PREMISE 1. Most CEOs of major computer corporations are college graduates.

PREMISE 2. Steve Ballmer is the CEO of a major computer corporation.

CONCLUSION. Steve Ballmer is a college graduate.

Notice that all of the statements included in this argument happen to be true in the real world. But is the reasoning valid? Clearly not. All we need is one counterexample to show why. If we substitute the name "Bill Gates" for "Steve Ballmer," the present CEO of Microsoft, the premises of the argument remain true but the conclusion is false. The argument is invalid, but because the premises are true, this particular invalid argument is stronger overall than either of the two arguments we considered that were valid but unsound. Overall argument strength, as opposed to an argument's strength of reasoning, takes into account the actual truth condition of the argument's premises. We saw that an argument's strength of reasoning is concerned only with the hypothetical or assumed truth of those premises.

▶ 3.6 INDUCTIVE ARGUMENTS

Not all invalid arguments are necessarily weak arguments; in fact, some are quite strong. Hence, we should not automatically discard every invalid argument simply because it is not valid. Some invalid arguments are *inductive*. Although inductive arguments do not necessarily guarantee the truth of their conclusions in the way that valid arguments do, inductive arguments nonetheless provide a high degree of probability for their conclusions. Those invalid arguments that are not inductive are fallacious arguments; we will discuss them in the next section. In this section, we describe the criteria that must be satisfied for an argument to be inductive.

Let's determine the strength of reasoning of the following argument:

> **PREMISE 1**. Seventy-five percent of people who own iPods also own iMac computers.
> **PREMISE 2**. My roommate currently owns an iPod.
>
> **CONCLUSION**. My roommate also owns an iMac computer.

Based on the technique discussed earlier in this chapter, we can see that this argument is not valid: a counterexample to the argument is possible. For instance, we can assume that both premises are true while the conclusion ("My roommate owns an iMac computer") is false. There is no contradiction in doing this since my roommate could be among the 25% of people who currently own iPods but who never owned iMacs. So clearly the argument is invalid.

This argument and the argument in the preceding section designed to show that Bill Gates is the CEO of a major computer corporation are both invalid, but they are different in their strength of reasoning. The argument that tried to show that Gates must be or have been a CEO because "Gates is a United States citizen" and "all CEOs of major computer corporations have been United States citizens" has weak reasoning. On the other hand, the form of reasoning used in the argument to show that my roommate owns an iMac computer is much stronger. In fact, the conclusion ("My roommate owns an iMac computer") is *very likely* to be true when we assume the truth of both premises. Hence this (invalid) argument is inductive.

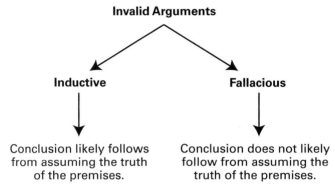

Figure 3-3   Inductive and fallacious (invalid) arguments.

As suggested above, some inductive arguments, although invalid, can be stronger overall than some valid arguments. But how is that possible? We have seen examples of valid arguments that contained premises that were false in the actual world. Inductive arguments consisting of premises that are all true in the actual world are generally stronger than arguments that are valid but unsound. As you consider the various arguments involving privacy, free speech, security, etc., in Chapters 4 through 9, determine which ones meet the criteria of being inductive with all true premises. Such arguments will be much more successful in establishing their positions (i.e., they will be much stronger) than will deductive arguments that contain one or more false premises.

Figure 3.3 illustrates the basic differences between invalid arguments that are inductive and invalid arguments that are fallacious.

▶ 3.7 FALLACIOUS ARGUMENTS

Recall the argument that we considered in Section 3.5 to show that Bill Gates was the CEO of a major computer corporation. All of the statements or claims in that particular argument were true in the actual world, so the argument might have seemed fairly strong. Yet, because we could produce a counterexample (and, in fact, we saw that we could easily produce several counterexamples), clearly the argument was invalid.

We next ask whether the argument is inductive or fallacious. That is, how likely is it that the argument's conclusion, "Gates has been the CEO of a major computer corporation," would be true based simply on the assumed truth of the argument's premises? Even though the conclusion could be true—and even though it is, in fact, true—the truth or falsity would have to be established on grounds other than those given in the premises used to support the conclusion that Gates has been a CEO. Hence this argument is *fallacious*.

Note that an argument's being fallacious has nothing to with the actual truth or falsity of its premises, so you have probably noticed a certain irony with respect to an argument's strength of reasoning. We have seen that an argument can be valid and yet contain one or more false premises and a false conclusion; and, conversely, an argument can be fallacious despite the fact that all of its premises as well as its conclusion could be true.

Recall an argument that we examined in Section 3.1.2:

> **PREMISE**. The Internet is in public space.
>
> **CONCLUSION**. Those who use the Internet should not expect to retain any personal privacy.

We noted earlier that this argument is fallacious, and we can now better understand the reason why. When we evaluate the argument's strength of reasoning, that is, whether it is valid or invalid, we first ask if a counterexample can be produced. Let us assume that the premise — The Internet is in public space — is true. Is it possible for that statement to be true, and for the conclusion (Internet users cannot expect to retain their privacy) to be false, at the same time? The answer would appear to be "yes." So a counterexample can be produced, and the argument is invalid. We can next ask whether the argument is inductive or fallacious. In the argument's current form, the conclusion does not likely follow from the premise, even when that premise is assumed true. So the argument is fallacious.

Also recall an argument that we examined in Chapter 1 for the view that at least some ethical issues involving cybertechnology must be unique. The argument had the following form:

> **PREMISE 1**. Cybertechnology has some unique technological features.
> **PREMISE 2**. Cybertechnology has generated some ethical concerns.
>
> **CONCLUSION**. Ethical concerns generated because of unique technological features in cybertechnology must be unique ethical concerns.

You can no doubt see why this argument is fallacious. First, we construct a counterexample to show the argument is invalid; that is, we can imagine a case where both premises are true, but the conclusion is false. For example, we can imagine some ethical concern that is generated by unique technological feature of cybertechnology is a traditional ethical problem and thus is not new or unique. Furthermore, we can construct a range of possible cases where both premises are assumed true, but the conclusion could be false. (In fact, in the majority of such cases, the conclusion would not likely be true merely because of what is assumed to be true in the premises). As we noted in Chapter 1, this argument wrongly assumes that a characteristic that applies to the technology — viz., uniqueness — must also apply to the ethical issues generated by this technology. Of course, it is possible that some cyberethics issues may turn out to be unique ethical issues. But if that happens, it is not because of the evidence supplied in the premises of the above argument.

Figure 3.4 presents an overview of the different kinds of argument forms that we have examined in this chapter.

In Section 3.9, we will examine some "informal logical fallacies" that tend to recur in everyday reasoning. There, we will also examine techniques for spotting some of the

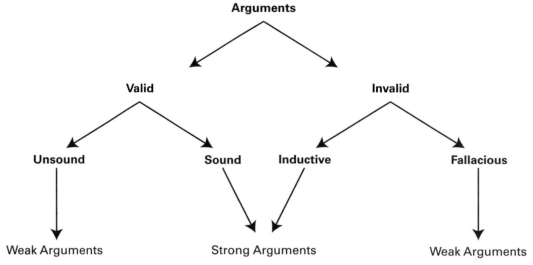

Figure 3-4 Comprehensive view of arguments.

more common fallacies, or "fallacy types," that occur in ordinary discourse. These techniques do not require the counterexample strategy that we used to distinguish invalid from valid arguments. First, however, we include a scheme that summarizes the techniques we have used thus far to differentiate among valid and invalid, sound and unsound, and inductive and fallacious arguments.

► 3.8 A SEVEN-STEP STRATEGY FOR EVALUATING ARGUMENTS

The following strategy, which consists of seven steps, summarizes the techniques we used in Sections 3.3–3.6 to evaluate an argument's overall strength of reasoning:

Step 1. Convert the argument into standard form. (List the premises, followed by the conclusion.)

Step 2. Test the argument for its strength of reasoning to see whether it valid or invalid. Strategy: Assume the premises to be true, and ask yourself whether the conclusion must also be true when those premises are assumed true. Is a counterexample to the argument possible?

Step 3. Is the argument valid?
If yes, go to Step 4.
If no, go to Step 5.

Step 4. Is the (valid) argument also sound? That is, are the premises true in the actual world?
Strategy: To determine whether a claim is true or false in the actual world, see the guidelines in Appendix G (available at www.wiley.com/college/tavani).

   a. If the argument is valid and if all of the premises are true in the actual world, then the argument is also sound.

b. If the argument is valid, but one or more premises can be shown to be false, then the argument is unsound. (Note that if one or more premises are unable to be verified, i.e., determined to be either true or false, then the overall argument is inconclusive.)

Step 5. Is the (invalid) argument inductive or fallacious?
Strategy: To determine this, ask how likely the conclusion would be true when the premises are assumed true.

a. If the conclusion would likely be true because the premises are assumed true (i.e., the evidence for the conclusion is strong), the argument is inductive.

b. If the conclusion would not likely be true even when the premises are assumed true, the argument is fallacious.
Note: Keep in mind that a fallacious argument can be made up of individual claims or statements that are themselves true in the actual world.

Step 6. Determine whether the premises in your argument are either true or false in the actual world.
Strategy: Consult the guidelines for determining the truth or falsity of statements in Appendix G, available at www.wiley.com/college/tavani.

Step 7. Make an overall assessment of the argument by determining both (a) the argument's strength of reasoning (valid, inductive, or fallacious) *and* (b) the truth conditions of each of the argument's premises.
Strategy: Determine, for example, whether the argument's overall strength is

• inductive with all true premises,

• inductive with some false premises,

• fallacious with a mixture of true and false premises,

• some other combination.

Remember that an inductive argument with premises that are all true can be stronger overall than a valid argument with one or more false premises.

We should note that some less formal techniques are also available for spotting fallacious arguments. In the next section we will see that there is an informal, and arguably simpler, way of identifying and cataloging many logical fallacies that frequently appear in everyday discourse.

▶ 3.9 IDENTIFYING SOME COMMON FALLACIES

Contrary to what many people assume, "fallacy" does not mean false statement; rather, it means *faulty reasoning*. As we saw in Section 3.6, it is possible for an argument to contain all true statements and still be fallacious. (We also saw that an argument can contain all false statements and still be valid, solely by virtue of its logical form.)

At this point, you might be unsure about your ability to recognize a fallacious argument without using the counterexample strategy described in this chapter or without applying some of the more sophisticated rules that comprise formal systems of logic. Because so many fallacies appear in everyday reasoning, logicians have categorized them in ways that are convenient for us to recognize. We refer to these kinds of fallacious arguments as *informal logical fallacies*.

The following ten informal fallacies, or "fallacy types," each illustrated with one or more examples involving computers and cybertechnology, are typical of fallacious arguments that surface time and again in ordinary everyday discourse.

3.9.1 *Ad Hominem* Argument

In the *ad hominem* argument, an attack is directed to the person rather than to the substance of the person's argument. For example, imagine that the late Senator Ted Kennedy had opposed a bill before Congress that supported the construction of a controversial national missile defense system (we saw an argument for this view in Section 3.2). Further suppose that Kennedy opposed the bill even though its passage would have meant thousands of new jobs for computer professionals in Massachusetts. Next imagine that a proponent of this legislation, Senator Smith, offered the following objection to Kennedy's position:

> How can we take seriously a position regarding the future of our national defense that has been proposed by a senator who has been arrested for drunken driving and who has been involved in extramarital affairs?

What is wrong with Senator Smith's attack, and why does the reasoning used in it commit a logical fallacy? Note that Senator Smith did not attack the merits or weaknesses of Kennedy's position on the national missile defense system; rather he attacked the personal character of the senator. Even if Kennedy's personal character was questionable, that point was irrelevant to whether the bill he opposed should be passed or defeated, or whether it was a well-conceived piece of legislation or one that was ill-founded. Unfortunately, the debate over the merits or deficiencies of the bill could be cut short, or at least temporarily derailed, because of the *ad hominem* attack.

One might object that if Kennedy's character had been attacked in this scenario because of allegations that were made against him on different grounds—e.g., a charge that he had sold secrets to foreign governments—then the personal attack against Kennedy might have been justified. Although national security-related allegations might have greater relevance in the argument as to why Kennedy's position on the missile defense system debate should not have been taken seriously, the argument would still be fallacious because the attack fails to focus on the merits of the issues being debated; instead it focuses on a person's character.

3.9.2 Slippery Slope Argument

The slippery slope argument has the form, "X could possibly be abused; therefore, we should not allow X." For example, one might argue:

> We should not continue to allow computer manufacturers to build computer systems that include CD burners. If we allow them to do so, young users will burn copies of copyrighted music illegally. If the rate of unauthorized copying of music continues, recording artists will lose more money. If they lose more money, the entire music industry could be in jeopardy. If the music industry in America declines, the entire U.S. economy will suffer. So, we must prohibit computer manufacturers from providing CD burners as part of the computer systems they build.

It should be fairly easy to spot the fallacy here: The author assumes that allowing computer manufacturers to continue to include CD burners as part of their computer systems will inevitable lead to an abusive slippery slope that logically implies a downturn in the overall U.S. economy. It is certainly possible that in the future, the U.S. economy does experience a down-turn while computer manufacturers continue to produce computers with CD burners. And it may well be that some users abuse CD burners to make unauthorized copies of music. However, any claim that the bad economy was an inevitable result of the use of CD burners in computers cannot be substantiated merely in terms of the evidence provided in the above argument.

3.9.3 Fallacy of Appeal to Authority

Arguments that conform to the fallacy of authority (*argumentum ad vericundiam*) have the following form:

> **PREMISE 1**. X is an authority in field Y.
> **PREMISE 2**. X said Z.
>
> **CONCLUSION**. Z.

As an example, imagine that Tim Berners-Lee, who designed the HTTP protocol that became the standard for the World Wide Web, has agreed to do an advertisement for Twitter, a social networking service (SNS). Further imagine that someone draws the following inference from the ad:

> Tim Berners-Lee believes that Twitter is superior to SNSs such as Facebook and MySpace. And Berners-Lee is clearly an expert on matters involving the Web and the Internet. So, Twitter must be superior to alternative SNSs such as Facebook and MySpace.

Can you spot the fallacy here? It is true that Berners-Lee is an expert on Web design; it may also be true that Twitter is superior to alternative SNSs (e.g., in certain respects). However, is the argument's conclusion that Twitter is superior to Facebook and Myspace, even if true, warranted by the premises? Simply because Berners-Lee wrote the code that became the standard protocol for the World Wide Web, and thus is an expert on some matters involving the Web, does that make him an authority on SNSs?

3.9.4 False Cause Fallacy

The false cause argument (*post hoc ergo propter hoc*—after this, therefore because of this) reasons from the fact that event X preceded event Y to the conclusion that event X is necessarily the cause of event Y. Consider the following argument about the Micro-soft's Vista operating system:

> Shortly after the release of the Microsoft Vista operating system in early 2007, Microsoft's stock plummeted severely. Hence, there is no doubt that the release of Vista is responsible for the decline in Microsoft's loss in the stock market.

Can you identify the fallacy in the above argument? Even though it might be tempting to attribute Microsoft's decline in the price of its stock to the release of the Vista operating system, the person making this argument has overlooked the possibility of other factors that might have caused this decline. For example, maybe there were factors in the economy in early 2007 that affected all high-tech stock prices at that time, or maybe there were overall declines in the stock market during that period.

3.9.5 Begging the Question

An argument commits the fallacy of begging the question when its premise(s) presuppose the truth of the conclusion it is trying to establish. In such a case, the reasoning is circular. Consider the following argument:

> Object-oriented programming (OOP) languages are superior to nonstructured programming languages because OOP languages are structured.

Why is this reasoning fallacious? Here the author of the argument has reasoned in a circle—instead of establishing that OOP languages are superior, the author assumes that to be the case; that is, the truth of the premise presupposes the truth of the conclusion, rather than supplying evidence for the conclusion.

3.9.6 Fallacy of Composition/Fallacy of Division

The fallacy of composition confuses the characteristics that apply to the parts of a whole, or to the individual members of a group, with the characteristics of the whole itself. For example, consider the following form of reasoning:

> The new XYZ desktop computer is the best system on the market. XYZ has the fastest processor currently available on any PC, it comes with twice the amount of RAM than any of its competitors, and it comes equipped with a suite of office applications that are superior to those on any currently available system. Also, its monitor has the best resolution and graphic display currently available on any commercial desktop computer.

Here the fallacy should be obvious. Each of the component parts of this desktop computer is the best that is currently available. However, it clearly does not follow that the system will necessarily be the best one available. The connections between the various parts of this system might not be well designed; we are not told how reliable the computer system is vis-à-vis its competitors. These kinds of flaws are apparent in all argument forms that commit the fallacy of composition. A film that has the best cast (Tom Hanks, Julia Roberts), one of the best directors (Steven Spielberg), and one of the best soundtrack composers (John Williams) might still be a flop. The quality of the individual parts does not necessarily guarantee the same quality in the overall product.

Next consider the flip side of this fallacy: the fallacy of division. The fallacy of division mistakenly infers that the same attributes or characteristics that apply to the whole or to the group must also apply to every part of the whole or to every member of the group. See if you can spot the fallacy in the following argument:

Harvard University is the highest-ranked university in the U.S. Thus, Harvard must have the nation's best computer science department.

Does the conclusion to the above argument follow from its premise? Clearly not! Harvard might be ranked first overall among universities in the United States, but the possibility remains that MIT, Stanford University, or some other institution has the nation's highest-ranked computer science department.

3.9.7 Fallacy of Ambiguity

Fallacious reasoning can occur whenever one or more terms are used ambiguously; ambiguous terms have more than one interpretation, and it is not always clear which interpretation the author intends. Consider the following argument:

Humans can think, and highly sophisticated artificial intelligence (AI) computer systems can think; therefore, highly sophisticated AI computer systems are human.

In this case, it is possible that both premises are true in the actual world. However, the sense in which AI computer systems are said to think is not necessarily the same sense in which humans, in fact, think. Here, the term "think" is used ambiguously. So even if it is true that computers can think in one sense of that term, it doesn't necessarily follow that computers can think in the same sense that humans do. Even if computers and humans could both think in the same sense, it doesn't follow that computers must be human. Consider that animals do many things in ways that are similar to humans, yet we do not infer that animals are humans. (One might object to the above argument being called a fallacy by noting that if thinking is defined as something that only humans could do, then, by definition, computers would have to be human. While this kind of move might avoid the fallacy of ambiguity, it introduces other problems since the premise "computers can think" would now be questionable.)

Another variation of the fallacy of ambiguity can be found in the following argument:

Computers have memory. Humans have memory. Having a memory enables humans to recall some of their childhood experiences. Therefore, computers can recall experiences from their childhood.

Notice that memory is used in two different senses in the above argument.

Although both examples of the fallacy of ambiguity illustrate exaggerated cases, many arguments used in everyday language commit variations of this fallacy.

3.9.8 Appeal to the People (*Argumentum ad Populum*)

Sometimes people appeal to the notion that there is strength in numbers. I remember once seeing a jacket to a record album that contained the following expression: "Fifty million Elvis fans can't be wrong." Is that true? Does it follow that because Elvis Presley had fifty million fans, that those numbers alone were sufficient to prove that Elvis was a great recording artist. Do sheer numbers count? Suppose that 150 million Americans believed that slavery was okay. Would that mean that slavery must be okay? The fallacy of the appeal to the people assumes that because X is popular, or because the majority of people agree with X, then X must be an acceptable standard. The following argument commits the fallacy of popular appeal.

The majority of Americans believe that it is perfectly acceptable to share copyrighted music over the Internet. So, despite the objections of greedy entrepreneurs in the recording industry, peer-to-peer (P2P) networks such as LimeWire and Pirate Bay should be allowed to serve the wishes of the American people.

You should be able to spot the fallacy in this argument quite easily. Perhaps there are good reasons for why LimeWire should be allowed to operate as a site for downloading music. However, those reasons have not been well articulated in this argument. What if the majority of Americans believed that all software should be distributed free of charge, does it follow that it should? The appeal to popular opinion has been an effective strategy, and in a democracy there are cases where such an appeal is clearly warranted and appropriate. The fallacy, of course, is to assume that every kind of issue—especially those concerning moral questions—can be decided in terms of a popular referendum.

3.9.9 The Many/Any Fallacy

This fallacy assumes that because many things of a certain kind have a feature, anything of that kind has that feature. It has the following form:

> **PREMISE**. Many items of a certain kind, A, have property B.
>
> **CONCLUSION**. Any item of the kind A has B.

Clearly, many items of a certain kind can have a property B without all of them having B. Note that many intellectual-property-protection policies could be justifiable, but does it follow that any intellectual-property-protection policy is justifiable? Similarly, we can ask whether it follows from the fact that many sorting algorithms are efficient that *any* sorting algorithm is efficient. In his description of this fallacy, James Moor (2004) made the point that there are many acceptable ways to travel from Boston to Madrid. For example, one could travel to Madrid from Boston via flights connecting in London, Paris, Zurich, and so forth. However, it doesn't follow that any way of traveling between the two cities is acceptable. Consider that traveling from Boston to Madrid via the South Pole or even by way of Bangkok, Thailand would not be acceptable, at least not for most travelers.

Consider how a variation on this fallacy could arise in a discussion involving the use of programming languages to write a particular kind of software application. Theoretically, there are many programming languages—Basic, Fortran, Ada, Cobol, Java, C++, and so forth—that *could* be used to write the code for a particular kind of software application, but it doesn't follow that any programming language can be used to write the code *efficiently*. While there might be legitimate disputes as to whether C++ or Java is better for writing a particular Internet application, most programmers would agree that for Internet applications either of these two languages is superior to Fortran or Cobol.

3.9.10 The Virtuality Fallacy

Recently coined by James Moor, the *virtuality fallacy* has the following form:

PREMISE 1. X exists in cyberspace

PREMISE 2. Cyberspace is virtual.

CONCLUSION. X (or the effect of X) is not real.[5]

Those who defend questionable forms of online behavior, such as launching viruses and engaging in unauthorized entries into computer systems, sometimes suggest that these activities cause no real harm to people. Some reason that because these activities are virtual activities carried out in the virtual world, their effects are only virtual and thus not real. You should be able to spot the fallacy in this line of reasoning. Imagine that someone has posted an insulting remark about you on Facebook or some other online forum. Arguably, the locus of offense is in cyberspace or virtual space as opposed to real (physical) space. Does it follow that the harm is not real, or that the particular harm caused to you is any less real than it would have been had it occurred in a physical setting? In Chapter 11, we examine some arguments used by members of virtual communities who reason that no real harm to real people can result in electronic forums in virtual space. There, we will see how the virtuality fallacy applies.

We have considered some techniques for identifying fallacy types in ordinary language. The common fallacy types identified in this section represent only a small sample of those identified and labeled by logicians and philosophers. Yet all have one feature in common: their reasoning is so weak that even when the premises are assumed true, the conclusion would not likely be true because of weak or insufficient evidence. You can make up labels of your own for some of the fallacious arguments we have encountered, which have not yet been given labels. For example, consider the fallacious argument we examined in Section 3.7 that tried to show that computer ethics issues must be unique because computers have some unique technical features and because computers raise ethical issues. We can call this the "Computer Ethics is Unique Fallacy." Also consider the fallacy we considered in this chapter, which reasoned that Internet users should have no expectation of personal privacy while they are online because the Internet is in public space. We could label this the "Privacy in Public Fallacy." You can no doubt come up with additional labels for fallacious arguments that you encounter in your analysis of cyberethics issues.

These techniques for spotting logical fallacies in ordinary, everyday discourse are useful in helping us to evaluate some of the arguments we will examine in the remaining chapters in this textbook. We should also note that some authors, including John Artz (2000), have suggested that "narrative reasoning" in the form of stories, as opposed to strict logical reasoning (even in the informal sense used in this chapter), can be more useful in helping us to understand and evaluate some cyberethics issues. However, we will not pursue this debate here, because the aim of Chapter 3 has been to show how conventional critical thinking skills and the tools associated with logical argumentation can be applied to cyberethics issues.

▶ 3.10 CHAPTER SUMMARY

In this chapter, we considered some basic critical thinking skills and we examined both the structure and the strength of logical arguments. We considered key criteria for differentiating among arguments that were valid and invalid, sound and unsound, and inductive and fallacious. We then considered a seven-step strategy for determining an argument's overall strength of reasoning. We also identified ten common fallacies, or "fallacy types," that illustrated flaws in reasoning that pertain to cybertechnology and cyberethics issues; and we considered some techniques that will help us to spot additional informal logical fallacies that occur in everyday reasoning. In the remaining chapters of this textbook, we will see how the critical thinking skills introduced in Chapter 3 can be used to evaluate arguments affecting many cyberethics disputes.

▶ REVIEW QUESTIONS

1. What is critical thinking, and how can it be applied to ethical issues involving cybertechnology?
2. What is a logical argument, and how is it different from a claim or a statement?
3. Identify and briefly describe the two important characteristics or features of an argument?
4. What role or purpose do arguments play in helping us to resolve issues in cyberethics?
5. Describe the basic structure of an argument.
6. What is meant by "argument strength" (as opposed to argument structure)?
7. What is the essential difference between an argument that is valid and one that is invalid? Construct an example of each.
8. What is a counterexample, and how can it be used to show that an argument is invalid?
9. How is it possible for an argument to be valid but not successful?
10. What is required for an argument to be sound? Construct an example of a sound argument.
11. What is the main difference between invalid arguments that are inductive and invalid arguments that are fallacious? Construct an example of each.
12. What is an "informal logical fallacy"? Why do logicians and philosophers give specific labels to some common fallacies that occur in everyday reasoning?
13. What is the *Ad Hominem Fallacy*? Provide an example of this fallacy involving either an issue in cyberethics or an aspect of cybertechnology.
14. What is the *Slippery Slope Fallacy*? Provide an example of this fallacy involving either an issue in cyberethics or an aspect of cybertechnology.
15. What is the *Fallacy of Appeal to Authority (Ad Vericundiam)*? Provide an example of this fallacy involving either an issue in cyberethics or an aspect of cybertechnology.
16. What is the *False Cause Fallacy*? Provide an example of this fallacy involving either an issue in cyberethics or an aspect of cybertechnology.
17. What is the difference between the *Fallacy of Composition* and the *Fallacy of Division*? Provide an example of each fallacy involving either an issue in cyberethics or an aspect of cybertechnology.
18. What is the *Fallacy of Ambiguity*? Provide an example of this fallacy involving either an issue in cyberethics or an aspect of cybertechnology.
19. What is the *Fallacy of Appeal to the People (Ad Populum)*? Provide an example of this fallacy involving either an issue in cyberethics or an aspect of cybertechnology.
20. What is the *Virtuality Fallacy*? Provide an example of this fallacy involving either an issue in cyberethics or an aspect of cybertechnology.

▶ DISCUSSION QUESTIONS

1. Construct your own argument for the view that your university should/should not have the right to monitor student e-mail. Next, analyze your argument to see if it is either valid or invalid.

If it is valid, determine whether it is also sound. If it is invalid, determine whether it is inductive or fallacious.

2. Construct an argument for or against the development of a new national missile defense (NMD) system, which we discussed in the text. Modify the argument in ways that make it inductive, and then valid. Can you construct the argument in a way that it is also sound? Next, construct an argument for the opposite point of view re NMD and assess it in the same way as before.

3. Identify some of the arguments that have been made on both sides in the debate about sharing proprietary MP3 files on the Internet. Evaluate the arguments in terms of their strength of reasoning. Can you find any valid arguments? Can you find any inductive arguments?

4. Construct an argument for or against the view that privacy protection should be improved for ordinary users who conduct searches on Google. Next evaluate your arguments against the rules for valid, inductive, and fallacious arguments. Does your argument contain any of the informal fallacies we examined in Section 3.9?

▶ ESSAY/PRESENTATION QUESTIONS

1. Based on what you have learned in this chapter, construct an argument to support or refute the view that all undergraduate students should be required to take a course in cyberethics. Apply the seven-step strategy (for distinguishing between arguments that are valid, inductive, and fallacious) to your argument.

2. Locate a recent article that describes some moral, legal, or social issue involving cybertechnology. How many invalid arguments can you find in that article? How many of these invalid arguments are also fallacious? Can you identify in that article any of the common fallacy types that we described in this chapter?

▶ ENDNOTES

1. Many ethics instructors now recognize the importance of rigorous critical thinking skills for analyzing issues examined in ethics courses, and an increasing number of introductory ethics and applied ethics textbooks include a separate chapter on logical arguments and critical thinking. See, for example, Bowyer (2001), Vaughn (2008), and Waller (2008).

2. An analysis of issues and arguments surrounding the classic SDI controversy and NMD are included in Bowyer (2001, 2002) and in Yurcik and Doss (2002).

3. Both the methodology and the terminology that I use in this chapter for argument evaluation closely follow a model of informal logic used by Nolt (2002).

4. This definition of counterexample closely follows Nolt's.

5. Moor described this fallacy type in a talk entitled "Just Consequentialism and Computing," presented at the *2000–2001 Humanities Lecture Series*, Rivier College, Nashua NH, February 2001.

▶ REFERENCES

Artz, John M. 2000. "Narrative vs. Logical Reasoning in Computer Ethics." In R. Baird, R. Ramsower, and S. Rosenbaum, eds. *Cyberethics: Social and Moral Issues in the Computer Age.* Amherst NY: Prometheus, pp. 73–79.

Bowyer, Kevin W. 2001. "Critical Thinking Skills." Chap. 2 in *Ethics and Computing: Living in a Computerized World.* 2nd ed. New York: IEEE Press.

Bowyer, Kevin W. 2002. "Star Wars Revisited: Ethics and Safety Critical Software." *IEEE Technology and Society* 21, no. 1: 13–26.

Moor, James H. 2004. "Reason, Relativity, and Responsibility in Computer Ethics." In R. A. Spinello and H. T. Tavani, eds. *Readings in CyberEthics.* 2nd ed. Sudbury MA: Jones and Bartlett, pp. 40–54.

Moore, Brooke Noel, and Richard Parker. 2009. *Critical Thinking.* 9th ed. New York: McGraw-Hill.

Nolt, John E. 2002. *Informal Logic: Possible Worlds and Imagination.* New York: McGraw Hill.

Vaughn, Lewis. 2008. *Doing Ethics: Moral Reasoning and Contemporary Issues.* New York: W. W. Norton.

Waller, Bruce N. 2008. *Consider Ethics.* 2nd ed. New York: Pearson.

Yurcik, William, and David Doss. 2002. "Software Technology Issues for a U.S. National Missile Defense System." *IEEE Technology and Society Magazine* 21, no. 2: 36–46.

▶ FURTHER READINGS

Artz, John M. "The Role of Emotion in Reason," *Computers and Society* 30, no. 1 (2000) 14–16.

Barker, Steven. *The Elements of Logic*. 6th ed. New York: McGraw Hill, 2003.

Bergmann, Marie, James H. Moor, and Jack Nelson. *The Logic Book*. 5th ed. New York: McGraw Hill, 2009.

Copi, Irving M., and Carl Cohen. *Introduction to Logic*. 13th ed. Upper Saddle River NJ: Prentice Hall, 2009.

Hurley, Patrick. *A Concise Introduction to Logic*. 10th ed. Belmont CA: Wadsworth Publishing, 2009.

Kahane, Howard, and Nancy Cavender. *Logic and Contemporary Rhetoric: The Use of Reason in Everyday Life*. 11th ed. Belmont CA: Wadsworth Publishing, 2010.

Rudinow, Joel, and Vincent Barry. *Invitation to Critical Thinking*. 6th ed. Belmont CA: Wadsworth Publishing, 2008.

Ruggeiro, Vincent R. *Thinking Critically About Ethical Issues*. 7th ed. New York: McGraw-Hill, 2008.

4

Professional Ethics, Codes of Conduct, and Moral Responsibility

In this chapter, we examine a range of issues often categorized under the general heading "professional ethics." More specifically, we analyze the following questions:

- What do we mean by "professional ethics" in a computing or information-technology (IT) context?

- Do professionals working in the computing/IT field have any special moral responsibilities?

- What are professional codes of ethics, and what important functions do they serve in the computing/IT profession?

- What is "whistle-blowing," and when is it permissible or perhaps even required for computer/IT professionals?

- Which standards of moral responsibility, legal liability, and accountability should apply in cases of computer malfunctions, especially in safety-critical computer systems?

- Which conditions must be satisfied in order to have an adequate model of risk analysis for the development of software, especially for safety-critical and life-critical systems?

- What kinds of criteria are required for a comprehensive software design methodology?

Issues involving software reliability and risk are also examined from the perspective of cybersecurity, in Chapter 6, where concerns about the vulnerability and reliability of computer systems are considered from the vantage point of attacks on computer systems from external sources, such as malicious hackers. In this chapter, our concern with unreliable computer systems centers primarily on issues that arise as a result of malfunctions and errors generated from "internal" sources; that is, we are concerned with reliability and safety issues that can be traced to the coding and testing of software and to the manufacturing of hardware components used in computer systems.

A principal objective of this chapter is to determine the extent to which computer/IT professionals should be held accountable for malfunctions involving computer systems. Consider two incidents, now viewed as classic cases, which occurred in the 1980s. In July 1988, the USS *Vincennes*, a United States Navy ship equipped with the Aegis Radar System, accidentally shot down an Iranian passenger airliner, killing 290 people. A poorly designed user interface to the computerized radar system contributed significantly to this accident.[1] Between June 1985 and January 1987, a series of malfunctions involving the Therac-25, a computerized radiation therapy machine, resulted in six serious accidents and three deaths. The problem was eventually traced to a bug in a software program that, in certain instances, caused massive overdoses of radiation to be administered to patients.[2]

Both the Therac-25 and the Aegis incidents are examined in detail in this chapter, in Sections 4.5.2 and 4.6, respectively. Accidents of this type are sometimes categorized as "computer error" or "computer malfunction." But who, exactly, is responsible for these computer errors and malfunctions? It would seem reasonable to hold the manufacturers of unreliable computer systems legally liable for harms caused by faulty design interfaces or by "buggy" software. But we must also ask to what extent the computer/IT professionals, especially the software engineers who design and develop "safety-critical" and "life-critical" applications, bear responsibility for the harmful consequences that result from unreliable computer systems.

While the Aegis and Therac incidents each raise concerns about professional responsibility for safety-critical and life-critical systems, our analysis of responsibility and reliability issues in Chapter 4 is also concerned with failures and malfunctions of computer systems, which might not be "safety-critical," but which can cause businesses and ordinary users to lose work, time, and money. For example, problems in the computerized baggage system at the new Denver International Airport caused both damage to luggage and routing problems, which cost the airport millions of dollars and significantly delayed its opening. Before examining specific cases involving unreliable computer systems, however, we first briefly consider some foundational issues in professional ethics.

▶ 4.1 PROFESSIONAL ETHICS

Recall that in Chapter 1 we described professional ethics as one of the three main perspectives through which cyberethics issues can be identified and analyzed. We saw that, when applied to computing, professional ethics is a field of applied ethics concerned with moral issues that affect computer professionals. You may also recall from our discussion of professional ethics in Chapter 1 that Don Gotterbarn suggested that professional ethics is the principal, perhaps even exclusive, perspective through which ethical issues involving the computing field should be examined.[3] Although this claim is controversial and will not be further considered here, we have devoted this chapter to an analysis of computer ethics issues from the vantage point of professional ethics.

Why have a category called "professional ethics"? After all, one could reasonably argue that independent of whether a particular moral issue happens to arise in either a professional or a nonprofessional context, ethics is ethics; the same basic ethical rules apply to professionals as to ordinary individuals. In response, many ethicists argue that some moral issues affecting professionals are sufficiently distinct and specialized to warrant a separate field of study. Some ethicists also argue that, at least in certain cases, professionals have special moral obligations, which exceed those of ordinary individuals. To grasp the essential points in the arguments advanced by these ethicists, it is useful first to understand what is meant by "profession" and "professional."

4.1.1 What Is a Profession?

The meaning of "profession" has evolved significantly over time. Harris, Pritchard, and Rabins (2004) note that the term was once associated with people "professing a religious or monastic life," before taking on a more secular meaning in the late seventeenth century, when it was first used to refer to one who "professed to be duly qualified."[4] In more recent times, a profession has come to be associated with a certain kind of vocation or an occupation in which a person has a specific set of skills or a mastery of knowledge in a particular field.

A profession can be distinguished from many ordinary occupations in terms of certain kinds of characteristics, such as having a code of ethics. Consider that the field of computing/IT has a number of professional societies with ethical codes (see Section 4.3), as do professions such as medicine and law. However, the computing/IT profession also differs from traditional professions such as medicine and law in at least one key respect. While many doctors and lawyers work in private practice, most computer/ IT professionals are not self-employed; even though some work as independent consultants, most are employed by corporations. So, some may question whether the computer/IT field is a "true profession." But Robert Barger (2008) argues that it qualifies as a genuine profession because the field satisfies two criteria that have traditionally characterized a profession: (1) expert knowledge, which he describes as a "special technical knowledge that is certified by some authority and is not possessed by the layperson"; and (2) autonomy with respect to "independence in conducting one's professional practice."[5]

4.1.2 Who Is a Professional?

As in the case of "profession," the term "professional" has also evolved over time. Traditional professionals included lawyers, medical doctors, and professors. In our current and expanded use of that term, we refer to a broader range of professional categories, such as real-estate professionals, marketing professionals, and so forth. A defining attribute of traditional professions, such as medicine and law, is that members often find themselves in situations in which their decisions and actions can have significant social effects; for example, medical doctors can prescribe the use of certain drugs for their patients, who otherwise would have no legal access to them, and lawyers are bound by special obligations such as client confidentiality that would not apply if they were acting as ordinary citizens. In these cases, a professional's roles and responsibilities can exceed those of ordinary individuals. Sometimes these roles and responsibilities are said to *differentiate* professionals from nonprofessional persons.

Elizabeth Buchanan (2004) believes that the roles and responsibilities of professionals are differentiated from ordinary individuals because:

. . . professionals are experts in a field, which provides them an advantage over the lay person and that professional's work has the potential to impact—either positively or negatively—the general public at large.[6]

Buchanan goes on to note that "information professionals" have the potential to adversely affect an "increasingly large and diverse clientele by failing to act responsibly, fairly, timely, and appropriately." So it would seem that these roles and responsibilities differentiate professionals working in the fields of computing and information technology from ordinary individuals. The extent to which a computer/IT professional's roles and responsibilities are "highly differentiated," however, is a matter of some dispute. To understand why this is so, it would first help to understand what, exactly, is meant by the expression "computer/IT professional."

4.1.3 Who Is a Computer/IT Professional?

Broadly speaking, a *computer/IT professional* is anyone employed in the computing and IT fields—from software and hardware engineers, to specialists such as support personnel, network administrators, and computer repair technicians. Computer professionals can also include faculty and instructors who teach in computer science and information management departments at universities, as well as in industry settings. We could possibly even extend "computer/IT professional" to include professionals who are responsible for providing unfettered access to electronic information in libraries, although they may prefer to describe themselves as "information professionals" or "information science professionals."[7]

A computer/IT professional might also be thought of in more narrow terms, in which case only software engineers would be included. Of course, there are various gradients in between the two ends of this spectrum. A computer/IT professional could be defined in a way that would exclude professionals in the fields of communications and library science, yet still include professionals whose computer-specific job descriptions extend beyond software engineering per se, such as software technical writers, software quality analysts, and managers and supervisors who play key roles in the software development process and make up a *software engineering team*.[8]

For purposes of this chapter, we will consider "computer/IT professionals" to include software/hardware engineers and software/hardware engineering teams, as well as computer science instructors in colleges, universities, and industry settings who are responsible for educating and training the members of software engineering teams. We will also include IT professionals in end-user support roles (e.g., network administrators and computer support personnel) in our definition of computer professionals. However, we will not include lawyers, accountants, nurses, or other professionals who are employed by computer companies or who work closely with computers as part of their regular employment.

▶ 4.2 DO COMPUTER/IT PROFESSIONALS HAVE ANY SPECIAL MORAL RESPONSIBILITIES?

Some ethicists believe that all professionals, regardless of their practice, have special moral obligations *as professionals*. But are there also specific moral obligations that apply to computer/IT professionals in the more narrow sense in which we have defined the term? As noted above, many computer/IT professionals are software engineers or members of software engineering teams. An important question for us to ask is: Does this group of professionals have any special moral obligations that differentiate them from other professionals who work in the computing/IT field? Gotterbarn (2001) believes that because software engineers and their teams are responsible for developing safety-critical systems, they have significant opportunities to

    i. do good or cause harm,

    ii. enable others to do good or cause harm,

   iii. influence others to do good or cause harm.

Thus Gotterbarn suggests that the roles and responsibilities involved in the development of safety-critical systems is a differentiating factor.

4.2.1 Safety-Critical Software

What, exactly, is safety-critical software? Kevin Bowyer (2001) points out that the phrase "safety-critical system" is often used to refer to computer systems that can have a "direct life-threatening impact." He notes that, under this definition, examples of safety-critical software applications typically include

- aircraft and air traffic control systems,
- mass transportation systems,
- nuclear reactors,
- missile systems,
- medical treatment systems.

However, Bowyer believes that an understanding of safety-critical systems that includes only these examples is too narrow. He suggests that a broader definition be adopted in which safety-critical systems are also understood as software applications used in the design of physical systems and structures whose failures can also have an impact that is life threatening. Here, the range of safety-critical applications can be expanded to include software used in the

- design of bridges and buildings,
- selection of water disposal sites,
- development of analytical models for medical treatment.[9]

We use the expanded sense of "safety-critical software" in this chapter. And we examine two important cases of computer malfunctions involving safety-critical software in our discussions of moral-accountability and risk-assessment issues in Sections 4.5 and 4.6, respectively.

▶ 4.3 PROFESSIONAL CODES OF ETHICS AND CODES OF CONDUCT

We have already seen that many professions have established professional societies, which in turn have adopted codes of conduct. For example, the medical profession established the American Medical Association (AMA), and the legal profession established the American Bar Association (ABA). Both associations have formal codes of ethics/conduct for their members. The computing profession has also established a number of professional societies, the largest of which are the Association for Computing Machinery (ACM) and the Institute for Electrical and Electronics Engineers-Computer Society (IEEE-CS). Both organizations have adopted professional codes of ethics, and the full texts of these two codes are included in Appendixes A and E (www.wiley.com/college/tavani), as well as at the ACM and IEEE sites.

Both the ACM and the IEEE codes contain general statements about what is expected, and in some cases what is required, to be a member in good standing. The IEEE Code of Ethics contains ten general directives; the first four instruct members to

1. accept responsibility in making engineering decisions consistent with the safety, health, and welfare of the public . . . ;
2. avoid real or perceived conflicts of interest wherever possible . . . ;
3. be honest . . . ;
4. reject bribery in all its forms; . . . [10]

The ACM Code of Ethics and Professional Conduct, on the other hand, is more complex. It contains twenty-four imperatives, formulated as statements of personal responsibility. Like the IEEE Code, the ACM Code also lists general moral imperatives:

1.1 contribute to society and human well being,

1.2 avoid harm to others,

1.3 be honest and trustworthy,

1.4 be fair and take action not to discriminate,

1.5 honor property copyrights and patents,

1.6 give proper credit for intellectual property,

1.7 respect the privacy of others,

1.8 honor confidentiality.

From these general imperatives, a list of more specific professional responsibilities follows. These include the directives:

2.1 Strive to achieve the highest quality . . . in . . . work.

2.2 Acquire and maintain professional competence.

These directives are then followed by six "organizational leadership imperatives," which include:

3.1 Articulate social responsibilities of members . . .

3.2 Manage personnel and resources to design and build information that enhance the quality of working life.

The fourth component of the ACM Code stresses "compliance with the code," and consists of two imperatives:

4.1 Uphold and promote the principles of this code.

4.2 Treat violations of this code as inconsistent with membership of the ACM. [11]

4.3.1 The Purpose of Professional Codes

Professional codes of ethics serve a variety of functions. For example, Gotterbarn and Miller (2009) note that these codes are often perceived as a way to "regulate members of a profession." Bynum and Rogerson (2004) believe that for computer/IT professionals, codes of ethics have five important functions: inspiration, education, guidance, account-ability, and enforcement. For example, they point out that codes *inspire* members of the profession by "identifying values and ideals" to which members can aspire. Bynum and Rogerson believe that codes *educate* by informing members about the profession's values and standards, and that they *guide* members by specifying "standards of good practice." Additionally, codes describe the level of *accountability* and responsibility that is expected and demanded by a professional society. Finally, codes have an *enforcement* function with regard to behavior deemed to be "ethically unacceptable" in a society.[12] Martin and Schinzinger (2004) describe this feature as a "disciplinary or penal function" that codes can serve when members violate one or more policies stipulated by the professional code.

To be effective, a professional code must be broad, yet specific. Perlman and Varma (2002) point out that a code must be broad enough to cover the ethical conflicts and concerns likely to arise in its professional field (such as computing), but, at the same time, a code cannot be so broad that it reaches to extraneous incidents. It must also be sufficiently specific to serve as a guide to making sound decisions for practical action in actual circumstances that are likely to arise in the computing field. To accomplish the first objective, Perlman and Varma believe that a code needs to encompass the principles that guide professions in general, and ethics in particular. And to satisfy the second objective, a code is measured by the degree to which its rules serve as "effective guides" for computer/IT professionals and practitioners. Perlman and Varma also note that in engineering contexts, professional codes face a special challenge because the practice of engineering often dictates secrecy, whereas the ethics of engineering requires transparency, or openness.

4.3.2 Some Criticisms of Professional Codes

Initially, it might seem surprising that anyone would be critical of professional codes in general or of specific codes developed for computer professionals. However, critics of professional codes of ethics have pointed out that the ethical codes adopted by professional computer societies have no "teeth." For example, violations of the ACM or the IEEE codes, unlike violations of professional codes in the fields of medicine and law, do not necessarily threaten the employment of those who violate them. Also, computer professionals are not usually required to be members of either the ACM or the IEEE to be employed in the computing field or to practice as computer professionals.

Michael Davis (1995) has pointed out some ways in which professional codes are often dismissed. For example, he notes that they are often perceived as "self-serving, unrealistic, inconsistent, mere guides for novices, too vague, or unnecessary."[13] To Davis's list, we could add one more characteristic—professional codes also tend to be incomplete. Ben Fairweather (2004) believes that codes of conduct for computing professionals have been influenced by a conception of computer and information ethics that is limited to four traditional areas of concern: privacy, accuracy, property, and accessibility. He argues that a professional code built on a foundation that includes such a narrow range of ethical concerns can provide certain loopholes for unethical behavior in an organization.

John Ladd (1995) has criticized ethical codes on slightly different grounds, arguing that these codes rest on a series of confusions that are both "intellectual and moral." His complex arguments can, for our purposes, be summarized in three main points. First, Ladd notes that ethics is basically an "open ended, reflective, and critical intellectual activity." Because ethics is a field of study that consists of issues to be examined, explored, discussed, deliberated, and argued, it requires a process of deliberation and argumentation. (Recall our definition of ethics in Chapter 2.) Directives listed in a professional code may give an employee the mistaken notion that all he or she needs to do is to locate a directive and then blindly follow it. More importantly, however, Ladd notes that individuals are not told what to do in a situation where two or more of a code's principles or directives conflict with one another. Here the individual needs to deliberate; yet professional codes do not typically provide any hierarchy of principles or any mechanism for choosing one directive over another.

Second, Ladd is critical of codes because of the confusions they introduce with respect to responsibilities involving microethics vs. macroethics issues (i.e., confusions about which responsibilities apply to individual professionals and which responsibilities apply to the profession itself). Recall that we briefly discussed the microethical/macroethical distinction in Chapter 2. In the context of professional ethics, microethical issues apply to personal relationships between individual professionals and other individuals, such as clients. Macroethical issues, on the contrary, apply to social problems that confront members of a profession collectively, or as a group. As such, most microethical issues involve the application of ordinary moral notions (such as honesty and civility) that would also hold when dealing with other individuals in nonprofessional contexts. Macroethical issues, however, are more complex, since they involve the formulation of policies at the level of social organizations. Ladd believes that we need to distinguish between questions such as "Which responsibilities do I, as a computer professional, have in such and such a situation?" and "Which responsibilities does the computing profession, as a profession, have in such and such a situation?" He concludes that professional codes of ethics cannot help us to make this important distinction.

Third, Ladd believes that attaching disciplinary procedures and sanctions to codes effectively turns them into legal rules or "authoritative rules of conduct" rather than ethical rules. The role of ethics in general, he argues, is to appraise, criticize, and even defend the principles, rules, and regulations, but it is not to dictate or to punish. Also, when individuals are compelled to obey directives, they are deprived of their autonomy, that is, their ability to choose, which is crucial in moral deliberation. So Ladd argues that professional codes rest on some mistaken notions about both the nature and the purpose of morality, which ultimately result in a series of intellectual and moral confusions.

4.3.3 Defending Professional Codes

It is very important to point out at this stage of our discussion of professional codes that not everyone has been critical of them. In fact, even some critics who have identified specific limitations or weaknesses in professional codes have also defended and praised them. For example, Robert Barger (2003), who concedes that the hope of finding a single professional code that everyone would accept might seem "dim," also notes that we should not infer that an effort to do so is futile. And Davis, whose criticisms of professional codes were described in the previous section, has argued that codes are extremely important for engineering professionals because they are central to guiding individual engineers in how to behave morally as professionals. Since an engineer cannot always rely on his or her own private conscience when making moral decisions, Davis believes that codes play an essential role in "advising individual engineers in how to conduct themselves."[14] He also believes that codes of conduct can help individual engineers to better understand "engineering as a profession." Bynum and Rogerson (2004), who also describe some positive functions that codes serve, point out that we should acknowledge the "limitations of codes." For example, they note that professional codes should not be viewed simply as laws or algorithms, or as "exhaustive checklists."

Gotterbarn (2000) has suggested that some of the criticism leveled against professional codes might be eliminated if we think of them as serving three important, but distinct, functions; that is,

- Codes of ethics
- Codes of conduct
- Codes of practice

Gotterbarn describes *codes of ethics* as "aspirational," because they often serve as mission statements for the profession and can thus provide vision and objectives. *Codes of conduct*, on the other hand, address the professional and the professional's attitude and behavior. Finally, *codes of practice* relate to operational activities within a profession. Gotterbarn points out that the degree of enforcement possible with respect to specific violations of a professional code is dependent on the type of code violated. For example, he notes that violations involving codes of ethics, which are primarily aspirational, are often considered no more than "light concerns." Consequently, violations of these codes may not have any serious consequences for individuals. Violations involving codes of conduct, on the other hand, can range from warnings given to an individual to the possibility of exclusion from practicing in a profession. Violations of codes of practice go one step further, however, in that they may also lead to legal action.

Gotterbarn notes that the hierarchy in the three types of codes parallels the three levels of obligation owed by professionals. The first level includes a set of ethical values, such as integrity and justice, which professionals share with other humans by virtue of a shared humanity. The second level of responsibility is shared by all professionals, regardless of their fields of specialization. The third (and deeper) level comprises several obligations that derive directly from elements unique to a particular professional practice, such as software engineering. This threefold distinction is incorporated in a professional code developed by a joint task force of the IEEE-CS/ACM, which we examine in the next section.

Table 4.1 lists some of the strengths and weaknesses of professional codes.

4.3.4 The IEEE-CS/ACM Software Engineering Code of Ethics and Professional Practice

In the 1990s, the ACM and IEEE approved a joint code of ethics for software engineers: the IEEE-CS/ACM Software Engineering Code of Ethics and Professional Practice

TABLE 4.1 Some Strengths and Weaknesses of Professional Codes

Strengths	Weaknesses
Codes inspire the members of a profession to behave ethically.	Directives included in many codes tend to be too general and too vague.
Codes guide the members of a profession in ethical choices.	Codes are not always helpful when two or more directives conflict.
Codes educate the members of a profession about their professional obligations.	A professional code's directives are never complete or exhaustive.
Codes discipline members when they violate one or more of the code's directives.	Codes are ineffective (have no"teeth") in disciplinary matters.
Codes "sensitize" members of a profession to ethical issues and alert them to ethical aspects they otherwise might overlook.	Directives in codes are sometimes inconsistent with one another.
Codes inform the public about the nature and roles of the profession.	Codes do not always distinguish between microethics issues and macroethics issues.
Codes enhance the profession in the eyes of the public.	Codes can be self-serving for the profession.

(SECEPP). Gotterbarn (2001) believes that as a code for computer professionals, SECEPP is unique for two reasons: First, it is intended as *the* code for the software engineering profession, unlike the individual codes (such as those of the ACM and IEEE) designed for particular professional societies within the computing profession. Second, Gotterbarn believes that SECEPP is distinctive in that it has been adopted by two international computing societies: ACM and IEEE-CS.

SECEPP is organized into two main parts: a short version and a longer, or full, version. Each version has its own preamble, and the full text for each version is included in Appendix E (www.wiley.com/college/tavani). SECEPP comprises eight core principles:

1. PUBLIC—Software engineers shall act consistently with the public interest.

2. CLIENT AND EMPLOYER—Software engineers shall act in a manner that is in the best interests of their client and employer, consistent with the public interest.

3. PRODUCT—Software engineers shall ensure that their products and related modifications meet the highest professional standards possible.

4. JUDGMENT—Software engineers shall maintain integrity and independence in their professional judgment.

5. MANAGEMENT—Software engineering managers and leaders shall subscribe to and promote an ethical approach to the management of software development and maintenance.

6. PROFESSION—Software engineers shall advance the integrity and reputation of the profession consistent with the public interest.

7. COLLEAGUES—Software engineers shall be fair to and supportive of their colleagues.

8. SELF—Software engineers shall participate in lifelong learning regarding the practice of their profession and shall promote an ethical approach to the practice of the profession.[15]

Does SECEPP Provide an Appropriate Balance between Generality and Specificity?

We noted above that professional codes are often criticized for being too vague and too general to be useful, yet there is also the danger of being too specific. If a professional code is too specific, it might fail to instruct members about general principles regarding ethical behavior and ethical decision making. SECEPP does include some very specific language, but it also has general prescriptions found in most professional codes. And, at the general level, SECEPP emphasizes the profession's obligation to the public at large, including concern for the public's health, safety, and welfare. For example, in the preamble to the full version of the code, software engineers are encouraged to

- consider broadly who is affected by their work;
- examine if they and their colleagues are treating other human beings with due respect;
- consider how the public, if reasonably well informed, would view their decisions;
- analyze how the least empowered will be affected by their decisions.

The preamble to the short version of SECEPP summarizes aspirations at a high level of abstraction. The specific clauses included in the full version, on the other hand, give examples of how these aspirations change the way software engineering professionals act *as* professionals. The code's principal authors note that "without the aspirations, the details can become legalistic and tedious; without the details, the aspirations can become high sounding but empty; together, the aspirations and the details form a cohesive code."[16] SECEPP's supporters believe that this code achieves an ideal balance between the general and the specific.

Does SECEPP Avoid Criticisms of Earlier Professional Codes?

One criticism often directed at professional codes is that they are incomplete; recall Ben Fairweather's argument in Section 4.3.2. Another criticism notes that most codes provide no mechanism for choosing between principles when two or more of them conflict; recall John Ladd's critique, also included in Section 4.3.2. Gotterbarn (2000) believes that SECEPP has overcome both difficulties.

Regarding the charge of incompleteness, Gotterbarn is willing to concede that the principles included in SECEPP are not intended to be exhaustive. He also acknowledges that no code could reasonably anticipate every possible moral controversy that can arise. However, he believes that SECEPP addresses the problem of completeness by providing "general guidance for ethical decision making." Gotterbarn argues that ethical tensions that arise can best be addressed by "thoughtful consideration of fundamental principles, rather than blind reliance on detailed regulations." He also points out that SECEPP should not be viewed as a simple algorithm that generates ethical decisions. And Gotterbarn notes that the individual principles that comprise SECEPP are not intended to be used in isolation from one another.

With respect to the second major criticism of professional codes, Gotterbarn points out that SECEPP has a "hierarchy of principles." This hierarchy enables engineers to prioritize their roles and responsibilities and to determine which ones are overriding when two or more conflict. Recall the list of eight principles that make up SECEPP: the ordering of these principles is intended to offer some guidance in cases where two or more rules conflict. SECEPP's hierarchy of principles states that concern for the health, safety, and welfare of the public is primary in all ethical judgments.

4.3.5 Educating Computer Professionals about the Existence of Codes of Ethics

How are future computer professionals supposed to discover that codes of ethics are available for them? Of course, the same question applies to professionals already working in the field who are not members of the ACM or the IEEE and who do not hold undergraduate degrees in computer science. We consider each question separately.

With respect to future computer professionals, a formal process is already in place to instruct undergraduate students about professional computing codes. A joint IEEE-CS/ ACM task force on curriculum issued a report titled *IEEE-CS/ACM Computing Curricula 2001*, recommending that sixteen core hours of instruction on social, ethical, and professional topics be included in the curriculum for undergraduate computer science students. Ethics instruction is organized into ten units (see Appendix F at www. wiley.com/college/tavani for detailed information about the content for each unit). One unit (SP5) specifically addresses the question of professional codes, stating that explicit instruction be given on "professional and ethical responsibilities (the nature of professionalism, codes of ethics, ethical dissent and whistleblowing)."

We next consider the second question regarding education about codes of conduct: How should those already employed in the computer field learn about the professional codes that apply to them? Perlman and Varma (2002) suggest that instruction about ethical codes could be integrated into training programs in the workplace. They note, for example, that newly hired engineers could be assigned mentors, who themselves have been trained in ethical awareness in the engineering profession. Consider that some companies, such as Lockheed Martin, have had official *ethics officers* who can assist in implementing such training programs.

4.3.6 Some Concluding Thoughts on Professional Codes

You can examine the full texts of the ACM, Australian Computer Society (ACS), British Computer Society (BCS), IEEE, and SECEPP Codes of Ethics in Appendixes A through E, respectively, which are available at www.wiley.com/college/tavani. (The full text for each code is also available at the respective Web site for each professional society.) You can then decide for yourself whether these codes are too general and too vague, as some critics suggest, or whether they are too narrow in scope, as other critics have argued. You can also determine whether SECEPP is sufficiently robust in terms of its breadth and depth to withstand the criticisms of earlier professional codes.

In defense of professional codes, it would be unfair to ask too much of them; for example, there are certain kinds of professional decisions that codes of ethics cannot help us make. If you are entering the computing profession, you might ask yourself a number of questions along the following lines. Should I work for a software company that has contracts with the United States Department of Defense? Should I accept a position with a software company that designs computer systems that could be used in warfare? Should

I work for a large corporation such as Microsoft, which has been sued by the United States Government for violating antitrust laws? Should I work on software projects that will advance computing and global communication in developing countries? Professional codes were never designed or intended to answer these kinds of questions.

Computer/IT professionals will continue to face new challenges that cannot possibly be anticipated in an organization's code of conduct. These challenges affect not only individuals, as computing professionals, but also can sometimes affect the computing profession itself. For example, Ben Schneiderman (2002) has questioned whether the ACM should take a leadership role in response to challenges involving terrorism in the aftermath of September 11, 2001. Should the ACM, through the technical expertise of its members, attempt to educate and inform policy makers with regard to laws involving the use of cybertechnology in combating terrorism? This question is controversial, and the ACM has taken no official stance on it. There does not appear to be any explicit language in the ACM Code of Ethics to guide the organization and its members with regard to questions like this one.

So professional codes clearly have some limitations, especially if one looks to them for advice in how to make professional career choices or for trying to determine the extent to which a computer/IT professional should be involved in policy issues that affect society at large. However, we should be careful not to underestimate the important contributions that well-developed professional codes, such as SECEPP, have made to the computing profession thus far. Critics may be correct in pointing out that following the directives of a professional code can never be a substitute for the kind of careful moral deliberation that is needed in certain controversial cases. Nevertheless, well-developed codes of conduct provide professionals with an important first step in the overall ethical deliberation process.

▶ 4.4 CONFLICTS OF PROFESSIONAL RESPONSIBILITY: EMPLOYEE LOYALTY AND WHISTLE-BLOWING

What exactly is employee loyalty? Do employees and employers have a special obligation of loyalty to each other? Should loyalty to one's employer ever preclude an employee's "blowing the whistle" in critical situations? In which cases can whistle-blowing be justified? Each of these questions is examined in this section.

4.4.1 Do Employees Have an Obligation of Loyalty to Employers?

Many ethicists believe that while loyalty may not be an obligation that is absolute, we nonetheless have a *prima facie* obligation of loyalty in employment contexts. In other words, all things being equal, an employee should be loyal to his or her employer and vice versa. What is the origin of the concept of employee loyalty in an engineering context? Carl Mitcham (1997) points out that, historically, engineers believed that they had a basic obligation to be loyal to institutional authority. Originally, an engineer was a "soldier who designed military fortifications or operated engines of war, such as catapults."[17] Mitcham notes that early civil engineering could be viewed as peacetime military engineering in which engineers were "duty bound to obey their employer," which was often some branch of the government. So it may well be the case that this historical precedent has contributed to the sense of loyalty many engineers currently have for their institutions and employers.

Does employee loyalty still make sense in the context of a large computer corporation in the twenty-first century? Skeptics might argue that loyalty makes sense only in employment contexts where there is mutual commitment on the part of both parties involved—employer and employee. In good economic times, employees may have the sense that their employers are very loyal to them. And in the past, it was not uncommon for employees in many professional fields to expect to be able to spend their entire career working for one employer, provided he or she was a loyal employee. But downturns in the U.S. economy, especially during the past three decades, have caused many employers to reassess their obligations to employees. As a result of significant downsizing in many corporations in the 1980s and 1990s, and continuing into this century, employees can reasonably question the degree of loyalty that their employers offer them. In fairness to corporations, however, CEOs also have an obligation of loyalty to stockholders to ensure that the company remains viable and profitable. This obligation can sometimes conflict with a corporation's obligations to its employees.

In one sense, the skeptic's arguments seem plausible. Consider, for instance, how many corporations have gone through downsizing and restructuring phases in which loyal employees who have served a company faithfully for several years have been laid off or dismissed as part of restructuring plans. Also consider that many computer programming jobs in the United States are now being "outsourced" by major corporations, such as IBM, to countries where programmers are willing to write the software code for much lower wages. (We examine the trend of outsourcing computer programming jobs in our discussion of globalization and cybertechnology in Chapter 10.) Not only does this practice raise questions for employee loyalty, but it could also affect the future of the computer profession in the United States if young people are discouraged from entering the programming field because of having their high-skilled jobs eliminated via outsourcing (Baker and Kripalani 2005).

On the contrary, however, some employers have shown what would certainly appear to be a strong sense of loyalty to employees. For example, there have been instances where an employer will keep an employee on the payroll even though that employee has a chronic illness that causes her to miss several months of work. There have also been cases in which several employees have been kept on by a company despite the fact that their medical conditions have caused the corporation's health insurance costs to increase significantly, thereby reducing the company's overall earnings. You may also have heard of a case involving the owner of Malden Mills, whose physical plant in Massachusetts was destroyed by fire. The mill's proprietor, Aaron Feuerstein, could have been excused from any future obligations to his employees, and he could have chosen to rebuild his facility in a different state or country where employees would work for lower wages. Instead, Feuerstein continued to pay and provide benefits for his employees while a new facility was being built in Massachusetts. So there have been instances in which employers have been very loyal to their employees.

How should the notion of employee loyalty apply in computing/IT contexts? Do computer/IT professionals necessarily have an obligation to be loyal to their employers? A thorough examination of the arguments on both sides of this issue, unfortunately, would take us beyond the scope of this chapter, so we will assume that, all things being equal, computer/IT professionals should be loyal to their employers.

However, sometimes an employee's obligation of loyalty can come into conflict with other obligations, such as those to society in general, especially where health and safety considerations are at stake. How are computer/IT professionals supposed to balance their obligation of loyalty to an employer against their obligations of loyalty that lie elsewhere? Even if a computer/IT professional has a *prima facie* obligation of loyalty to his or her employer (i.e., all things being equal), does it follow that he or she has an absolute obligation of loyalty? Consider that computer/IT professionals, because of the nature of the critical-safety projects they work on, can also have an obligation to society as a whole, especially since safety and health issues can arise. Divided loyalties of this type, of course, can result in serious conflicts for employees, and in certain cases the moral dilemmas they generate are so profound that an employee must determine whether to blow the whistle.

4.4.2 Whistle-Blowing

What, exactly, is whistle-blowing? Sisela Bok (2003) defines a whistle-blower as an individual who makes "revelations meant to call attention to negligence, abuses, or dangers that threaten the public interest." She goes on to note that whistle-blowers often "sound an alarm" from within the organizations in which they work. Bok also notes that whistle-blowing can be viewed as a form of *dissent*, because those who blow the whistle make public their disagreement with their employers or with some authority. Although Bok defends whistle-blowing in certain cases, where other alternatives have been "considered and rejected," she also believes that it should remain as a "last alternative" due to its "destructive side effects."[18]

Determining When to Blow the Whistle

When should an employee blow the whistle? Consider a whistle-blowing incident in which Colleen Rowley, an FBI employee, came forth to describe how critical messages had failed to be sent up the Federal Bureau's chain of command in the days immediately preceding the tragic events of September 11, 2001. Was it appropriate for her to blow the whistle on her supervisor? Was she disloyal to her supervisor and her fellow employees in doing so?

Should individuals in positions of authority in corporations such as Enron and WorldCom have blown the corporate whistle about their illegal accounting practices, which were discovered in early 2002? One could argue that failing to blow the whistle in the Enron case resulted in thousands of people losing their retirement savings and, in some cases, their entire life savings.

There are, no doubt, cases where a decision to blow the whistle might have saved human lives. Consider, for example, the Space Shuttle *Challenger* disaster in January 1986, which resulted in the deaths of the seven crew members. Engineers who designed the space shuttle were aware of the safety risks in launching the shuttle in cooler temperatures. In fact, some engineers, when learning the *Challenger* was scheduled for launch on a cool January morning, went to their supervisors to express their concerns. However, a decision was made to stick with the original launch date. Having received no support from their supervisors, should those engineers have gone directly to the press? Would whistle-blowing at that level have saved the lives of the *Challenger*'s crew?

You may have heard of a now classic case involving the Ford Pinto (automobile), which had a gas tank that was unsafe. (The trial concluded in 1980.) The faulty design of the Pinto's gas tank caused the car to catch on fire when involved in certain collisions, even at lower speeds. In some cases these fires caused the deaths of Pinto drivers and passengers. Many of the engineers who worked on the Pinto's design were aware that its gas tank was unsafe, and they strongly recommended that the design be changed. However, a management decision was made at Ford to go ahead and produce Pintos with unsafe gas tanks. Should the engineers involved have gone public? This particular incident has since sparked considerable debate about when it is appropriate for an employee to blow the whistle.

In cases such as the Challenger and the Pinto, many believe that the engineers involved had a responsibility to blow the whistle on management. We next briefly examine two classic cases of whistle-blowing in a computing/engineering context: one that that occurred in the late 1960s/early 1970s, and another in the early 1980s.

▶ **SCENARIO 4–1:** Whistle-Blowing and BART

An incident at BART (Bay Area Rapid Transit) in California became highly publicized in the 1970s. It involved a computerized mass transit system, which was then under development. The system had some difficulties in the development phase—e.g., it was both behind schedule and over budget. Additionally, some employees working on the project believed that the system was not safe. In particular, three engineers working on the project were concerned about the safety of the transit system's ATC (automatic train control) system. They decided to take their concerns to their immediate managers but were not satisfied with the answers they received. So, the three engineers next took their concerns to the organization's board of directors. Once again, however, they were dissatisfied with the lack of support from the board. At that point, the engineers decided to blow the whistle. Shortly afterwards, they were fired.[19]   ▪

Since the BART incident, whistle-blowing laws at both the federal and state levels have been passed. In addition to the federal Whistle-blower Protection Act of 1989, many states, such as Florida, have passed their own laws to protect whistle-blowers. However, not all states have done this, and the level of protection granted to whistle-blowers in states where legislation has been enacted varies considerably; many individuals feel that it is still too risky to go public with their concerns.

▶ **SCENARIO 4–2:** Whistle-Blowing and SDI

In the early 1980s, a U.S. military proposal called the Strategic Defense Initiative (SDI) was introduced and debated. SDI, also referred to as "Star Wars" in the media, was a national missile defense (NMD) system that would provide a "defense shield" against incoming ballistic missiles. The SDI proposal, which was vigorously supported by the Reagan administration, soon became very controversial. While SDI's supporters argued that the missile system was essential for America's national defense, critics argued that the system was unreliable. One critic, David Parnas, decided to go public with his concerns about SDI.[20]   ▪

David Parnas, a consultant on the Star Wars project, was paid $1,000 per day for his expertise. However, shortly after he joined the SDI project team, Parnas became convinced that it was not possible to construct SDI software that could confidently be expected to work when needed. His conclusion that SDI was inadequate was based on concerns he had about the design specifications and the testing of the software involved. Parnas (1990) argued that the specifications were not known with sufficient confidence and that the SDI software would not be able to undergo adequate testing. Additionally, Parnas determined that there would not be sufficient time during an attack to repair and reinstall software that failed.

When Parnas went public with his position, some of SDI's supporters accused him of disloyalty and of acting out of his own self-interest. Many of Parnas's defenders, however, pointed out that Parnas walked away from a lucrative consulting contract. Did Parnas do the right thing? It is interesting to note that William Yurcik and David Doss (2002) believe that the arguments used by Parnas in the case of SDI also apply in the controversy involving the most recent national missile defense (NMD) proposal put forth by the Bush administration in early 2001. In Chapter 3, we briefly examined some arguments advanced for and against the NMD proposal.

Can Professional Codes Guide Engineers in Whistle-blowing Decisions?

As noted above, legislation has been enacted at both the federal and the state levels in the U.S. to protect employees who go public with certain kinds of information. We also noted that individual state laws vary considerably with the amount and kind of protection offered to whistle-blowers. It would seem appropriate to ask what measures the engineering and computing professions themselves have taken to protect whistle-blowers. Perhaps a more fundamental question is, What kind of guidance do the ethical codes adopted by engineering and computing professions provide members when they are confronted with specific dilemmas that could lead to a whistle-blowing decision? Sections 6.12 and 6.13 of SECEPP state that an engineer is obligated to

- express concerns to the people involved when significant violations of this Code are detected unless this is impossible, counterproductive, or dangerous;
- report significant violations of this Code to appropriate authorities when it is clear that consultation with people involved in these significant violations is impossible, counterproductive, or dangerous.

Although guidelines such as these are useful, many believe that they are still too vague. It would be helpful if engineers had more straightforward criteria for determining when they are permitted, or perhaps even required, to blow the whistle.

Being Morally Permitted vs. Being Morally Required to Blow the Whistle

Richard De George (1999) has offered some specific conditions for when an engineer is (a) *morally permitted* to blow the whistle, and (b) *morally obligated* to do so. De George believes that engineers and other workers are morally permitted to go public with information about the safety of a product if three conditions are satisfied. For our purposes, we can summarize De George's three conditions as follows:[21]

1. The product will do "serious and considerable harm" to the public.
2. The engineers have reported the "serious threat" to their immediate supervisor.
3. The engineers have "exhausted the internal procedures and possibilities" within the company, including going to the board of directors, having received no support from their immediate supervisor.

Although De George argues that one is morally permitted to blow the whistle when conditions 1 through 3 are satisfied, he does not believe that a person is yet morally required to do so. To have a strict moral obligation to blow the whistle, De George believes that two additional conditions must be satisfied:

4. The engineers have "accessible, documented evidence that would convince a reasonable, impartial, observer that one's view of the situation is correct."

5. The engineers have "good reasons to believe that by going public the necessary changes will be brought about."[22]

Applying De George's Criteria

De George provides us with a carefully developed and articulate model in which to assess whistle-blowing in an engineering context. Next, we apply De George's model to the BART and the SDI cases, described above. In the BART case, the engineers involved would seem to have satisfied De George's first three conditions; thus whistle-blowing in their case was morally permissible. But were they also morally obligated to blow the whistle? The engineer's actions would also seem to have satisfied condition 4, but the requirements for condition 5 may be less clear. It is not yet obvious from the account that we considered thus far that the engineers had "good reasons" for believing that going public would necessarily bring about the intended changes. Additionally, we should note that De George also includes a caveat with condition 5, pointing out that the engineer's chance of "being successful must be worth the risk one takes and the danger to which one is exposed."[23]

Next, consider the SDI case. One difference is that this case, unlike BART, involves one person as opposed to a group of engineers. Another difference is that Parnas's position was challenged by an expert who offered a different analysis of the risks involved. While it is not clear that Parnas was morally obligated to blow the whistle on SDI, it would seem that he satisfied De George's first three criteria for being morally permitted to do so.

Of course, we can question whether De George's criteria are too stringent, as some have suggested, or whether they are too lenient as others have argued.[24] However, we will not pursue that debate here. Nor will we question the merits of De George's whistle-blowing model outside the context of an engineering environment. We conclude our discussion by noting that one virtue of De George's model is that it provides clear and straightforward guidelines for engineers to consider in a morally complex case without also requiring them to be what De George calls "moral heroes" or "moral saints."

4.4.3 An Alternative Strategy for Understanding Professional Responsibility

Michael McFarland offers an alternative model with regard to whistle-blowing, arguing that engineers must see themselves in a "wider social context." He claims that unless individual engineers

a. see their work in relation to society, an adequate account of their ethical responsibilities cannot be given.

b. learn to act in collaboration with others, both inside and outside their profession, they will not be able to meet their responsibilities.[25]

McFarland suggests that, collectively, engineers might be held to a higher standard of social responsibility than ordinary individuals, but that the onus of responsibility should not fall directly on engineers as individual engineers. Rather, it should be shouldered by engineers as members of the engineering profession.

McFarland's model is based on the assumption that, as moral agents, we have a *prima facie* obligation to come to the aid of others. In describing the nature of this obligation, he uses a nonengineering analogy involving the Kitty Genovese case. (We briefly examined this incident in Chapter 2.) Recall that Genovese was murdered in New York City in 1964 as 38 people in and around her apartment building watched or listened. It has since been argued that if some of Genovese's neighbors had banded together to come to her aid, she would have survived. The analogy for engineers that McFarland wishes to draw is that when no other sources of help are available, engineers should take responsibility by banding together.

McFarland recognizes that if engineers act as individuals, they might not always have the ability to help. If they act collectively, however, they might be able to accomplish goals that would otherwise not be possible. Consider that if Genovese's neighbors had acted individually to intervene in her behalf, they might have put themselves at great risk. However, if they had acted collectively as a group, the neighbors could have overcome Genovese's assailant. Thus McFarland's model encourages engineers to shift their thinking about responsibility issues from the level of individual responsibility (the microethical level) to responsibility at the broader level of the profession itself (the macroethical level).

► 4.5 MORAL RESPONSIBILITY, LEGAL LIABILITY, AND ACCOUNTABILITY

Thus far, our examination of issues involving the moral responsibility of computing/IT professionals has focused mainly on questions concerning employee loyalty and whistle-blowing. We have seen that some of these questions have centered on the responsibilities of computing/IT professionals as individuals, whereas others have dealt with responsibilities facing the computing/IT profession itself. We have also noted that these questions illustrate essential differences between issues of responsibility involving microethics and macroethics. However, we have not yet fully considered the concept of moral responsibility itself.

Philosophers often describe the concept of responsibility in terms of certain conditions that must be satisfied. Two such conditions are *causality* and *intent*. In other words, some agent, X, is held morally responsible for an act, Y, if X caused Y. Here, a person could be held responsible even if he or she did not intend the outcome. Consider that Robert Morris, the Cornell graduate student who launched the "Internet worm" in 1988, claimed that he did not intend that the Internet be brought to a standstill. Nonetheless, Morris was held responsible for the outcome *caused* by his unleashing the computer worm. Agents can also be held responsible when they *intend* for something to happen, even if they ultimately fail to cause (or to bring about) the intended outcome. For example, consider a scenario in which a disgruntled student intends to blow up a college's computer lab, but at the last minute is discovered and prevented from doing so. Even though the student failed to carry out his objective—cause the bomb to detonate in the computer lab—we hold the student morally culpable because of his intentions.

The term "responsibility" is often used in nonmoral contexts; for example, we speak of a power surge being responsible for the crash of a computer system. But we do not attribute blame to the utilities company that generated the electricity that ultimately caused the computer to crash. The utilities company and the power surge are responsible only in the nonmoral sense. By considering whether we can blame an agent for an action, we can determine if we can hold the agent morally responsible—the sense of "responsible" that concerns us in this chapter.

4.5.1 Distinguishing Responsibility from Liability and Accountability

It would be helpful at this point to distinguish responsibility from the related notions of liability and accountability. Responsibility differs from liability in that *liability* is a legal concept, sometimes used in the narrow sense of "strict liability." To be strictly liable for harm is to be liable to compensate for it even though one did not necessarily bring it about through faulty action. Here, the moral notion of blame may be left out. A property owner may be legally liable for an injury to a guest who falls in the property owner's house, but it does not necessarily follow that the property owner was also morally responsible for any resulting injury. (We elaborate on the notion of liability in Section 4.5.4, where we examine the legal liability of producers of defective computer software.)

Helen Nissenbaum (2007) distinguishes between responsibility and accountability by suggesting that responsibility is only part of what is covered by the "robust and intuitive notion of accountability." In Nissenbaum's scheme, *accountability* is a broader concept than responsibility, and means that someone, or some group of individuals, or perhaps even an entire organization, is *answerable*. In a computing context, she notes that accountability means

> there will be someone, or several people to *answer* not only for malfunctions in life-critical systems that cause or risk grave injuries and cause infrastructure and large monetary losses, but even for the malfunctions that cause individual losses of time, convenience, and contentment.[26]

Table 4.2 summarizes the elements we have used to differentiate moral responsibility, legal liability, and accountability.

Nissenbaum believes that the notion of accountability has been "systematically undermined" in the computer era, despite the fact that we are increasingly dependent on safety-critical and life-critical systems controlled by computers. In Section 4.2, we saw that safety-critical applications included software used in aircraft and air traffic control

TABLE 4.2 Responsibility, Legal Liability, and Accountability

Moral Responsibility	Legal Liability	Accountability
Attributes blame (or praise) to individuals.	Does not attribute blame or fault to those held liable.	Does not necessarily attribute blame (in a moral sense).
Usually attributed to individuals rather than collectivities or groups.	Typically applies to corporations and property owners.	Can apply to individuals, groups of individuals, and corporations.
Notions of guilt and shame apply, but no legal punishment or compensation need result.	Compensation can be required even when responsibility in a formal sense is not admitted.	Someone or some group is answerable (i.e., it goes beyond mere liability).

systems, in nuclear reactors, in missile systems, and in medical treatment systems, as well as in the selection of water disposal sites and in the design of bridges and buildings. Nissenbaum argues that a major barrier to attributing accountability to the developers of safety-critical software is the problem of "many hands."

4.5.2 Accountability and the Problem of "Many Hands"

Computer systems are typically developed in large organizational settings. Because these systems are the products of engineering teams or of corporations, as opposed to the products of a single programmer working in isolation, many individuals (or many "hands") are involved in their development. Thus it is very likely that no single individual grasps all of the code used in developing a particular safety-critical system.[27] As a result, it is difficult to determine who exactly is accountable whenever one of these safety-critical systems results in personal injury or harm to individuals; it is not always clear whether the manufacturer of the system hardware (the machine) or the engineering teams that developed the system's software, or both, should be held accountable.

When thinking about the problem of many hands from the perspective of strict moral responsibility, as opposed to accountability, two difficulties arise: first, we tend to attribute moral responsibility for an accident to an individual, but not to groups or "collectivities." Thus we sometimes encounter difficulties when we try to attribute blame to an organization. Nissenbaum suggests that by using "accountability" we can avoid the tendency to think only at the level of individuals in matters typically associated with assigning moral responsibility.

The second difficulty arises because the concept of moral responsibility is often thought of as exclusionary, as Ladd (1995) points out. In other words, if we can show that *A* is responsible for *C*, then we might infer that *B* cannot be held responsible for *C*. Ladd believes that moral responsibility should be viewed as nonexclusionary because both *A* and *B* (and possibly others) can be responsible for *C*. Nissenbaum suggests that we can avoid this confusion if we use "accountability" instead of "responsibility": holding Sally accountable for making unauthorized copies of proprietary software does not necessarily preclude holding Harry accountable as well, as when Harry pays Sally for making copies of the pirated software.

So Nissenbaum believes that holding one individual accountable for some harm need not necessarily let others off the hook, because several individuals may be accountable. Nor does it mean letting organizations off the hook, because they too may be accountable. As Nissenbaum puts the matter, "We should hold each fully accountable because many hands ought not necessarily lighten the burden of accountability." The following scenario (involving the Therac-25 machine, which we described briefly in the opening section of this chapter) illustrates how the involvement of "many hands" can obscure the process in determining accountability for accidents affecting some safety-critical systems.

▶ **SCENARIO 4–3:** The Therac-25 Machine

The Therac-25 was a computer-controlled radiation treatment machine built by Atomic Energy of Canada Limited (AECL). Between 1985–1987, there were six reported incidents in which patients were severely overdosed by the Therac-25. As a result of the severe radiation burn caused by the excessive radiation dosages, three individuals died and two others had irreversible injuries.[28] ■

Eventually the Therac-25 malfunction was traced not to a single source but to numerous faults, including two significant software coding errors ("bugs") and a faulty microswitch. One bug involved radiation dosage errors: if a subsequent request to change a previously entered radiation dosage was entered in a certain sequence through the user interface, a software bug caused the new entry to be ignored, and the entry instructing the original dosage was used. Instead of receiving 200 RADs, one radiation patient received 20,000 RADs; this patient died shortly afterwards from excessive radiation (Leveson and Turner 2001).

Several interesting questions regarding the locus of responsibility were raised in the wake of the Therac-25 accidents. Who, exactly, should be held accountable for the deaths and injuries that resulted from the computer malfunction? Is the hospital, which may be found legally liable, also accountable in a larger sense? Should the company that manufactured and sold the Therac system to the hospital be held accountable? Were the engineers and programmers who worked on the design and development of this system ultimately responsible for the injuries and deaths caused to the radiation patients? Should they be held liable?

When engineers design physical structures such as bridges and airplanes, certain levels of redundancy and tolerance are built into those systems. For example, one missed detail in the construction of a bridge will not cause it to collapse, nor will one missed detail in the assembly of one of the physical components of an airplane's subsystems necessarily cause the plane to crash. However, one errant line of software code can cause a program to crash, and in a safety-critical software application, one errant line of code can result in deaths, as well as in serious injuries. (Of course, this problem is compounded when computers are networked together because software bugs in one computer system can be propagated across a network.)

4.5.3 Could an Industry-wide Standard Help Resolve the "Many Hands" Problem?

Because of the severity of the malfunctions that can arise in life-critical and safety-critical systems, some have proposed that an industry-wide standard be adopted to help ensure the development of more reliable computer systems. Robert Steele (2000), who has called for a "standard of due diligence" for the computing profession, points out that consumers would not purchase automobiles if they believed that the tires would fall off while they are driving. Yet, he notes, consumers are expected to purchase computer systems that are often unreliable.

Nissenbaum argues that a "substantive standard" for the computing/IT profession is not only needed, it should be "clarified and vigorously promoted." According to Nissenbaum, guidelines for producing safer and more reliable computers should include a standard that incorporates

- a formal analysis of system modules as well as of the entire system,
- meaningful quality assurance and independent auditing, and
- built-in redundancy.[29]

Nissenbaum believes that a standard of care comprising these criteria would provide a nonarbitrary means for determining accountability; it would offer a tool for distinguishing between malfunctions due to inadequate practices and those that occur in spite of a programmer or designer's best efforts. Nissenbaum also suggests that if such standard of care had existed at the time Therac-25 was produced, the software developers of the system could have been held accountable for the deaths and injuries that resulted.

4.5.4 Legal Liability and Moral Accountability

In Section 4.5.1, we saw that legal liability can be distinguished from both moral responsibility and accountability. Nissenbaum believes that in computer/IT contexts, it is important to keep "accountability" distinct from "liability to compensate." She concedes that liability offers a partial solution to problems resulting from computer malfunctions, because at least it addresses the needs of the victims; however, she also notes that accepting liability as a substitute for accountability can further obscure the process of determining who is accountable for computer malfunctions.

Is it reasonable to hold computer corporations legally liable for products they sell that are either unreliable or defective? Supporters of liability law believe that holding owners legally liable makes sense because owners are typically in the best position to directly control their property. Nissenbaum believes that because ownership implies a "bundle of rights," it should also imply responsibilities such as being liable. Software owners (who are also usually the software's producers) are in the best position to directly affect the quality of the software they release to the public. Yet, ironically, the trend in the software industry, Nissenbaum points out, is to "demand maximal property protection while denying, to the extent possible, accountability." Software manufacturers frequently include disclaimers of liability on their products such as "This software is sold as is."

Nissenbaum also suggests that strict liability would shift the accountability to the producers of defective software, thereby addressing an anomaly (perhaps even a paradox) with respect to our current understanding of overall accountability: While liability laws protect the public against potential harm, most producers of software deny accountability for software errors. Producers sometimes base their argument on the notion that software is prone to error in ways that surpass other technologies. Nissenbaum concludes that strict liability laws can send a message cautioning software producers to take extraordinary care to produce safe and reliable systems. Strict liability laws may also cause manufacturers to reassess the level of risk tolerated in the process of developing software.

▶ 4.6 RISK ASSESSMENT IN THE SOFTWARE DEVELOPMENT PROCESS

Some analysts have suggested that in order to reduce software failures, we must first address issues involving the level of risk currently associated with the development of computer systems. Gotterbarn (2004) argues that ethical risks associated with the entire "software development life cycle" must also be taken into consideration. For Gotterbarn, the life cycle of software includes the maintenance phase as well as the design and development stages.

Bruce Schneir (2004) notes that in the context of computer/IT security, risk assessment models can be used to make informed decisions about the most cost-effective controls in order to limit risks to one's assets. Gotterbarn worries that while much attention has been paid to cost-effectiveness, very little thought has been given to ethical considerations in the models of risk used in the software development process. In these models, risk has typically been understood in terms of scheduling, budgeting, or specification requirements. Gotterbarn argues that software can satisfy all three conditions and still fail to meet an acceptable standard of risk assessment. To see how this is possible, we examine a case involving the Aegis Radar System, which was briefly described in the opening section of this chapter.

▶ **SCENARIO 4–4:** The Aegis Radar System

The Aegis Radar System was developed by the United States Navy. Its purpose was to enable U.S. ships to monitor space around them. A serious incident involving the Aegis system occurred in July 1988 on board the USS *Vincennes*. The ship accidentally shot down an Iranian passenger aircraft, killing 230 people. Many believe that a contributing element to—and arguably the key reason for—the accident was the poor design of the Aegis system's user interface.[30]   ∎

In response to the *Vincennes* incident, some critics have argued that system designers need to realize the importance of building features that affect human abilities and limitations into the interfaces of safety-critical systems. Some analysts believe that accidents such as the one involving the Aegis system on the *Vincennes* are inevitable because they result from the mathematical errors in calculation. Critics of this interpretation, however, believe that the Aegis accident was an error of engineering judgment, that is, an error not reducible to engineering science or to mathematics. They also believe that similar errors could be better understood if an adequate model of risk assessment were used.

The Aegis Radar System met all of the requirements that the developer and customer had set for it; in fact, it satisfied the three conditions specified above: it was on schedule, it was within budget, and it satisfied design specification requirements. Yet the use of the Aegis system resulted in the deaths of 230 airline passengers. Are risks involving accidents of this magnitude acceptable in schemes for the development of software?

Gotterbarn suggests that software failures like the one involving the Aegis system are the result of two defects in current models of risk assessment for software development:

1. an overly narrow conception of risk, and
2. a limited notion of system stakeholders.

With respect to (1), Gotterbarn argues that a model of risk assessment based solely on cost effectiveness and using only criteria such as budget and schedule is overly narrow. He suggests that the assessment model be enlarged to include social, political, and ethical issues. Regarding (2), Gotterbarn notes that the only stakeholders typically given consideration in risk assessment models for software development are the software developers and the customers, and he argues that this limited notion of "system stakeholders" leads to the development of systems that have unanticipated negative effects. Gotterbarn concludes that unless an adequate risk model for software development is framed, we may be doomed to experiencing future computer malfunctions similar to that of the Aegis system on the USS *Vincennes*.[31]

We will discuss software risk, reliability, and vulnerability in detail in Chapter 6, which examines computer security issues. In Chapter 6, we focus on risks affecting intrusions into computer systems from external sources such as malicious hackers. A model for analyzing risk, especially as it applies to securing our computer network-dependent infrastructure, is also included in that chapter.

▶ 4.7 VALUE SENSITIVE DESIGN: A COMPREHENSIVE DEVELOPMENT METHODOLOGY

We have seen that there are good reasons for expanding the notion of "stakeholder" and for ensuring that considerations affecting stakeholders are built into the process of designing software systems. Some analysts argue that we also need to build into the design process a strategy that more broadly examines the potential impact that software development has for "human values." In Chapter 1, we saw that Philip Brey (2004) argued that computer technology is not value-free or neutral, as some software engineers and computer practitioners might assume, but instead contains features that impact our system of moral and nonmoral values. These values are often embedded in the technology's features, even if no one consciously intended to build them into it. The first step in Brey's "disclosive method" requires that we identify and disclose these values, which often times can be "opaque" or nontransparent, at an early stage in the design process. You may want to review Brey's model (in Section 1.5.2) at this point to identify the various stages included in his disclosive method.

Brey's model has been influenced in part by a movement called *Value Sensitive Design* or *VSD*. Friedman, Kahn and Borning (2008) define VSD as

> a theoretically grounded approach to the design of technology that accounts for human values in a principled and comprehensive manner throughout the design process.[32]

The VSD model is very complex, and a complete analysis of this carefully articulated framework is not possible here. But it is useful to look at some crucial elements of this model, because it can provide us with the outlines for a design strategy that is comprehensive and robust. According to Friedman, Kahn, and Borning, VSD has eight key components, in that it

1. seeks to be proactive: to influence the design of technology early in and throughout the design process.
2. enlarges the arena in which values arise to include not only the work place . . . but also education, the home, commerce, online communities, and public life.
3. contributes a unique methodology that employs conceptual, empirical, and technical investigations.
4. enlarges the scope of human values beyond those of cooperation . . . and participation . . . to include all values, especially those with moral import.
5. distinguishes between usability and human values with ethical import.
6. identifies and takes seriously two classes of stakeholders: direct and indirect.
7. is an interactional theory.
8. builds from the psychological proposition that certain values are universally held.[33]

Although each component is important to the success of the overall design process for VSD, we limit our examination to the third component, which distinguishes among three kinds of investigations—conceptual, empirical, and technical—that differentiate VSD from alternative models. To illustrate how this component is implemented, the authors analyze a series of design cases, one of which involves the design of cookies technology (described in detail in Chapter 5) in connection with the informed consent process affecting Web browsers.

In applying their three-part investigation model to the design of cookies technology, Friedman et al. note that the value of informed consent is involved and that this value is important because it protects other human values such as privacy, autonomy, and trust. So, at the level of *conceptual investigations*, the first level in the process, they consider the following questions:

a. What values are implicated?

b. How should we engage in trade-offs among competing values in the design, implementation, and use of information systems (e.g., autonomy vs. security, or anonymity vs. trust)?

c. Should moral values (e.g., a right to privacy) have greater weight than, or even trump, nonmoral values (e.g., aesthetic preferences)?[34]

The authors note that the conceptual investigation reveals that a "philosophically informed" analysis of the value of informed consent is needed, which in turn shows that the idea of *consent* encompasses a range of conditions that include "voluntariness, comprehension, and agreement." The kinds of questions asked at the level of conceptual investigations might easily be overlooked in a standard design specification for cookies technology. Yet they are the kinds of questions that Friedman et al. believe ought to be asked before designing that technology, rather than being addressed after the technology has been developed.

Next, *empirical investigations* are needed to evaluate the "success of a particular design" within the "human context" in which the "technical artifact"—in this case, cookies for Web browsers—is situated. Empirical investigations can be applied in situations where the activity affecting the technology can be "observed, measured, or documented." Investigations at this level are followed by *technical investigations*, which

i. involve the proactive design of systems to support values identified in the conceptual investigation, and

ii. focus on how existing technological properties and underlying mechanisms support or hinder human values.[35]

In a retrospective analysis of their technical investigation of the cookies technology embedded in the Netscape Navigator and the Internet Explorer browsers, Friedman et al. describe their evaluations over a five-year period. Their analysis includes the users' perceptions regarding the use of cookies and how the implementation of that technology evolved in light of VSD.

Our analysis of VSD in this section has been limited primarily to an examination of one critical element or component of the overall design strategy—viz., the three-part investigations scheme. It has also been limited to a consideration of human values inherent in the design of only one technology (cookies). We should also note that designing cookies technology would not typically fall into the category of designing safety-critical or life-critical software, which can have a more significant impact for human values. Nonetheless, our brief examination of VSD shows how this model can inform the design process used in all software development.

We have also seen how this model can help to ensure that human values are taken into consideration at the outset rather than in later stages of the software design process. We conclude this section and chapter by noting that VSD provides software developers and software engineering teams with explicit criteria for a design strategy that is considerably more comprehensive in scope than alternative strategies.

▶ 4.8 CHAPTER SUMMARY

In this chapter, we examined some ethical problems that confront computer/IT professionals, and we focused on the kinds of issues and challenges that software engineers and their team members sometimes face in the development of safety-critical software. We saw that professional codes of ethics/conduct are useful insofar as they inspire and educate professionals entering and working in the field of computing and information technology. We also saw, however, that many professional codes have serious limitations. We noted that the IEEE-CS/ACM Software Engineering Code of Ethics and Professional Practice (SECEPP) was designed to avoid many of the shortcomings of earlier professional codes of ethics.

We also considered questions having to do with employee loyalty, especially in cases where computer/IT professionals have conflicting obligations to society and the public good. We examined circumstances where engineers are permitted to blow the whistle vs. being required to blow the whistle. We also saw how the role of accountability has been undermined in the computer era, for both individual computer/IT professionals and the computer profession as a whole. We saw that because accountability is diffused by the problem of "many hands," it is not always easy to determine where accountability and responsibility for computer malfunctions and errors in safety-critical software systems ultimately lie. Next, we considered a proposal for revising the conventional models of risk assessment used in developing software for safety-critical systems. Finally, we briefly examined the VSD model and its implications for the software design process.

Among the professional ethics concerns affecting computers and cybertechnology that were not considered in this chapter are issues surrounding "open" vs. "closed" software development methodologies. Some ethical aspects of methodologies used in software development are examined in Chapter 8 in our discussion of open source software (OSS) and free software foundation (FSF) development. An ethical issue that also has implications for computer professionals but not examined in this chapter involves the global outsourcing of programming jobs. This controversy is examined in Chapter 10 in connection with our discussion of globalization and the transformation of work. Another professional ethics question not considered in Chapter 4 is whether computer professionals should participate in nanocomputing research and development, given certain kinds of controversies surrounding nanotechnology. This question is examined in Chapter 12.

▶ REVIEW QUESTIONS

1. What is professional ethics?
2. What is a profession, and who is a professional?
3. Who is a computer/IT professional?
4. Do computer/IT professionals have special moral responsibilities that ordinary computer users do not have?
5. How do Don Gotterbarn, Keith Miller, and Simon Rogerson propose that we define the profession of software engineering?
6. According to Gotterbarn, what responsibilities do software engineers and their teams have that differentiate them from other professionals working in the computer field?
7. How is "safety-critical software" defined by Kevin Bowyer?
8. What are professional codes of ethics, and what functions do they serve?
9. Briefly describe John Ladd's criticisms of professional codes.
10. Explain Gotterbarn's threefold distinction: codes of ethics, codes of conduct, and codes of practice.
11. Do Gotterbarn's distinctions help to eliminate any of the criticisms that have been raised against professional codes?
12. How does the IEEE-CS/ACM Software Engineering Code of Ethics and Professional Practice (SECEPP) improve on earlier professional codes affecting software engineers?
13. What, exactly, is whistle-blowing?
14. Can professional codes guide engineers in determining when it would be appropriate to blow the whistle?
15. What does Helen Nissenbaum mean by *accountability*?
16. How is Nissenbaum's notion of accountability different from both liability and responsibility?
17. What does Nissenbaum mean by "the problem of many hands" in a computing/IT context?
18. Describe the conventional criteria used in assessing risk in the software-development process.
19. According to Gotterbarn, what is required for an adequate model of risk analysis for the development of safety-critical systems?
20. What is the Value Sensitive Design (VSD) method?

▶ DISCUSSION QUESTIONS

1. Describe some virtues of the ethical codes of conduct adopted by professional societies such as the ACM and IEEE-CS, and list some shortcomings of these professional codes as well. In the final analysis, do the advantages of having a code outweigh the prospects of not having one? Use either an actual or a hypothetical case to establish the main points in your answer.
2. Evaluate Richard DeGeorge's criteria for when it is morally permissible, as opposed to when it is morally required for an engineer to blow the whistle. Apply these criteria to a recent controversy where you believe that blowing the whistle would have been either morally permissible or morally required.
3. Revisit Michael McFarlands's argument for the position we described as an "alternative strategy" (in Section 4.4.3) for understanding the concept of professional responsibility for engineers. Is it a practical alternative? How could this model help individual engineers who, as members of the broader engineering profession, find themselves in a situation where they believe it would be appropriate to blow the whistle?
4. Review the Value Sensitive Design (VSD) method. How might VSD have been applied in the Aegis case? Do you believe it would have made a difference in the design of the final software? Can you think of other cases where VSD might have made a difference? Should VSD, or something similar to it, be required for the design of all safety-critical and life-critical software?

▶ ESSAY/PRESENTATION QUESTIONS

1. Do you believe that a coherent and comprehensive code of conduct for computing and IT professionals is possible? If so, which of the codes mentioned in this chapter best approximates such a code? In framing your

response to this question, consult the full descriptions of the five professional codes included in Appendixes A through E on the book's Web site (www.wiley.com/college/tavani).

2. You have been working for the XYZ Computer Corporation as an entry-level software engineer since you graduated from college last May. You have done very well so far; you are respected by management, are well liked by your fellow employees, and have been assigned to a team of engineers that has consistently worked on the most critical and valued projects and contracts that XYZ Corp. has secured. Their most recent contract is for a United States defense project involving the missile defense system, and again you have been assigned to the team that will develop software for this project. However, you are staunchly opposed to the project's objectives, so you ask to be reassigned. Your supervisor and coworkers, as well as upper management, are disappointed to learn of your strong feelings about this project. You are asked to reconsider your views, and you are promised a bonus and a substantial pay increase if you agree to work on this project during the next year. You also discover from a colleague that refusing to work on this project would greatly diminish your career advancement at XYZ and may even make you vulnerable to future layoffs. To compound matters, you and your spouse are expecting your first child in about three months and you recently purchased a home. What would you do? Describe the process of ethical deliberation that you would undertake in trying to resolve this dilemma.

3. For the past six months you have worked on a project to develop a transportation-related software program for the city of Agropolis, a project designed to make some much needed improvements to Agropolis's system of public transportation. You and your team of programmers have worked very hard on this project, but you have encountered difficulties that could not possibly have been anticipated in the original design plan; these difficulties have put your project significantly behind schedule. The city transportation planners are nervous, because they depend on the software from your company to get the new transportation system up and running. And the management at your company is very uncomfortable because it signed a contract to deliver the required software on time. Although the software is not yet foolproof, testing thus far reveals that it works about 99% of the time. The few glitches that remain apply only to the transportation system's backup code, which arguably would be needed in only the most severe emergencies. Residents of the city are also eager to have the new transportation system in place.

   A decision is made by the management of your company and by the managers of the city transportation system to go ahead and implement the software as it is. They base their decision on the probability that a backup system would not be needed for several months (at which time the remaining bugs should be fixed). A decision was also made by management on both sides not to announce publicly that the software still has a few bugs. You and a few of your coworkers believe that the bugs are more dangerous than management is willing to admit. What would you do in this case? Would you be willing to blow the whistle? Defend your position.

4. Recall the various arguments that we examined as to when it is appropriate, and sometimes mandatory, for software engineers and IT professionals to blow the whistle. The criteria for when whistle-blowing is permissible, at least for those working in some federal government agencies, may have changed recently. In November 2002, the Homeland Security Act passed in both houses of Congress and was signed into law by President Bush. On one interpretation of the new law, whistle-blowing acts similar to that of Colleen Rowley—who blew the whistle on her FBI superiors who failed to act on information in the days preceding September 11—would be illegal and thus a punishable offense. What implications could this have for software engineers and other computer professionals whose employment comes under the auspices of the Homeland Security Department? In this case, what set of rules should computer professionals follow?

▶ ENDNOTES

1. See George C. Wilson. "Navy Missile Downs Iranian Jetliner on 4th of July," *Washington Post* (July 4, 1998), p. A01.
2. Leveson and Turner (2001).
3. See, for example, Gotterbarn (1995).
4. Harris, Pritchard, and Rabins (2004), p. 9.
5. Barger (2008), p. 85.

6. Buchanan (204), p. 620.
7. Buchanan suggests that an "information professional" can be conceived of along these lines.
8. Gotterbarn, Miller, and Rogerson (1999) suggest that a software engineering team can be thought of as those who contribute by direct participation to "the analysis, specification, design, development, certification, maintenance and testing of software systems."
9. See Bowyer (2001), p. 165.
10. The full text of IEEE Code of Ethics is available at http://www.ieee.org/web/membership/ethics/code_ethics.html.
11. The full text of the ACM Code of ethics is available at http://web.mit.edu/afs/athena.mit.edu/course/2/2.95j/Codes-of-Ethics/ACM-Code-of-Ethics.html.
12. For a full description of these five features, see Bynum and Rogerson (2004), pp. 135–36.
13. Davis (1995), p. 586.
14. Ibid., p. 586.
15. The text of both versions of this code (short and full) is available at http://seeri.etsu.edu/Codes/TheSECode.htm.
16. Gotterbarn, Miller, and Rogerson (1999).
17. Mitcham (1997), p. 262.
18. Bok (2003), p. 53.
19. For more details on this case, see Bok, pp. 51–52.
20. For more information on this case, see Bowyer (2002).
21. The full text for these three conditions is included in De George (1999), pp. 251–53.
22. See De George, pp. 250–56, for the full text of his five conditions for whistle-blowing.
23. De George, pp. 255–56. De George's fourth and fifth conditions are also presented in summarized form here.
24. See Johnson (1991) for some classic articles that critique De George's model for whistle-blowing.
25. McFarland (1991), pp. 159–60.
26. Nissenabum (2007), p. 274. [Italics Added]
27. See Nissenbaum, p. 275. There she also includes additional guidelines such as "independent auditing" and "excellent documentation."
28. For more detail, see Leveson and Turner (2001).
29. See Nissenbaum, p. 279. There she also includes some additional guidelines.
30. For more information on this case, see Gotterbarn (2004).
31. See Gotterbarn (2004), p. 675. An expanded version of his model is included in Gotterbarn, Clear, and Kwan (2008).
32. Friedman, Kahn, and Borning (2008), p. 70.
33. Ibid., pp. 85–86.
34. Ibid., p. 72.
35. Ibid., p. 73.

▶ REFERENCES

Baker, Stephen and Manjeet Kripalani. 2005. "Software: Programming Jobs Are Heading Overseas by the Thousands: Is There a Way for the U.S. to Stay on Top? In P. De Palma, ed. *Annual Editions: Computers in Society 05/06*. Dubuque IA: McGraw-Hill/Dushkin, pp. 47–51.

Barger, Robert N. 2003. "Can We Find a Single Ethical Code?" In M. David Ermann and Michele S. Shauf, eds. *Computers, Ethics, and Society*. New York: Oxford University Pres, pp. 42–47.

Barger, Robert N. 2008. *Computer Ethics: A Case-Based Approach*. New York: Cambridge University Press.

Bok, Sisela. 2003. "The Morality of Whistle Blowing." In M. David Ermann and Michele S. Shauf,eds. *Computers, Ethics, and Society*. New York: Oxford University Pres, pp. 47–54.

Bowyer, Kevin, ed. 2001. *Ethics and Computing: Living Responsibly in a Computerized World*. 2nd ed. New York: IEEE Press.

Buchanan, Elizabeth A. 2004. "Ethical Considerations for the Information Professions." In R. A. Spinello and H. T. Tavani, eds. *Readings in CyberEthics*. 2nd ed. Sudbury MA: Jones and Bartlett Publishers, pp. 613–24.

Davis, Michael. 1995. "Thinking Like an Engineer." In D. G. Johnson and H. Nissenbaum, eds. *Computing Ethics and Social Values*. Englewood Cliffs NJ: Prentice Hall, pp. 586–97.

De George, Richard T. 1999. *Business Ethics*. 3rd ed. Upper Saddle River NJ: Prentice Hall.

Fairweather, N. Ben. 2004. "No PAPA: Why Incomplete Codes of Ethics are Worse Than None at All." In T. W. Bynum and S. Rogerson, eds. *Computer Ethics and Professional Responsibility*. Malden MA: Blackwell, pp. 142–56.

Friedman, Batya, Peter H. Kahn, Jr., and Alan Borning. 2008. "Value Sensitive Design and Information Systems." In K. E. Himma and H. T. Tavani, eds. *The Handbook of Information and Computer Ethics*. Hoboken NJ: John Wiley and Sons, pp. 69–101.

Gotterbarn, Don. 1995. "Computer Ethics: Responsibility Regained." In D. G. Johnson and H. Nissenbaum, eds. *Computers, Ethics and Social Values*. Englewood Cliffs NJ: Prentice Hall, pp. 18–24.

Gotterbarn, Don. 2000. "Computer Professionals and YOUR Responsibilities." In D. Langford, ed. *Internet Ethics*. New York: St. Martin's Press, pp. 200–19.

Gotterbarn, Don. 2001. "The Ethical Software Engineer." In K. W. Bowyer, ed. *Ethics and Computing: Living Responsibly in a Computerized World*. 2nd ed. New York: IEEE Press, p. 67.

Gotterbarn, Don. 2004. "Reducing Software Failures: Address Ethical Risks With Software Development Impact Statements." In R. A. Spinello and H. T. Tavani, eds. *Readings in CyberEthics*. 2nd ed. Sudbury MA: Jones and Bartlett Publishers, pp. 674–89.

Gotterbarn, Don, Tony Clear, and Choon-Tuck Kwan. 2008. "A Practical Mechanism for Ethical Risk Assessment—A SoDIS Inspection." In K. E. Himma and H. T. Tavani, eds. *The Handbook of Information and Computer Ethics*. Hoboken NJ: John Wiley and Sons, pp. 429–71.

Gotterbarn, Don, and Keith Miller. 2009. "The Public is Priority: Making Decisions Using the Software Code of Ethics," *IEEE Computer*, Vol. 42 No. 6, pp. 66–73.

Gotterbarn, Don Keith Miller, and Simon Rogerson. 1999. "Software Engineering Code of Ethics Approved." *Communications of the ACM* 42, no. 10: 102–07.

Harris, Charles E., Michael S. Pritchard, and Michael J. Rabins. 2004. *Engineering Ethics: Concepts and Cases*. 3rd ed. Belmont CA: Wadsworth.

Johnson, Deborah G., ed. 1991. *Ethical Issues in Engineering*. Englewood Cliffs NJ: Prentice Hall.

Ladd, John. 1995. "The Quest for a Code of Professional Ethics: An Intellectual and Moral Confusion." In D. G. Johnson and H. Nissenbaum, eds. *Computers, Ethics and Social Values*. Englewood Cliffs NJ: Prentice Hall, pp. 580–85.

Leveson, Nancy G., and Clark S. Turner. 2001. "An Investigation of the Therac-25 Accidents." In K. W. Bowyer, ed. *Ethics and Computing: Living Responsibly in a Computerized World*. 2nd ed. New York: IEEE Press, pp. 200–24. Reprinted from *IEEE Computer* 26, no. 7 (1993): 18–41.

Martin, Michael W., and Roland Schinzinger. 2004. *Ethics in Engineering*. 4th ed. New York: McGraw-Hill.

McFarland, Michael C. 1991. "The Public Health, Safety, and Welfare: An Analysis of the Social Responsibility of Engineers." In D. G. Johnson, ed. *Ethical Issues in Engineering*. Englewood Cliffs NJ: Prentice Hall, pp. 159–74.

Mitcham, Carl. 1997. "Engineering Design Research and Social Responsibility." In K. Schrader Frechette and L. Westra, eds. *Technology and Values*. Lanham MD: Rowman and Littlefield, pp. 261–78.

Nissenbaum, Helen. 2007. "Computing and Accountability." In J. Weckert, ed. *Computer Ethics*. Aldershot UK: Ashgate, pp. 273–80. Reprinted from *Communications of the ACM* 37 (1994): 37–40.

Parnas, David Lorge. 1990. "Professional Responsibility to Blow the Whistle on SDI." In M. D. Ermann, M. B. Williams, and C. Guiterrez, eds. *Computers, Ethics, and Society*. New York: Oxford University Press, 359–72.

Perlman, Bruce, and Roli Varma. 2002. "Improving Engineering Practice," *IEEE Technology and Society* 21, no. 1: 40–47.

Schneiderman, Ben. 2002. "ACM's Computing Professionals Face New Challenges." *Communications of the ACM* 45, no. 2: 31–34.

Schneir, Bruce. 2004. *Secrets and Lies: Digital Security in a Networked World*. Rev. ed. New York: John Wiley & Sons.

Yurcik, William, and David Doss. 2002. "Software Technology Issues for a U.S. National Missile Defense System." *IEEE Technology and Society* 21, no. 2: 36–46.

▶ FURTHER READINGS

Birsch, Douglas. "Moral Responsibility for Harm Caused by Computer System Failures." *Ethics and Information Technology* 6, no. 4 (2004): 233–45.

Buchanan, Elizabeth A., and Kathrine A. Henderson. *Case Studies in Library and Information Science Ethics*. Jefferson NC: McFarland, 2009.

Fleddermann, Charles. *Engineering Ethics*. 3rd ed. Upper Saddle River NJ: Prentice Hall, 2008.

Huff, Chuck. "Unintentional Power in the Design of Computer Systems." In R. A. Spinello and H. T. Tavani, eds. *Readings in CyberEthics*. Sudbury MA: Jones and Bartlett Publishers, 2004, pp. 651–58.

Miller, Keith W., and David K. Larson. "Agile Software Development: Human Values and Culture." *IEEE Technology and Society Magazine* 24, no. 4 (2005): 36–42.

Moor, James H. "If Aristotle Were a Computing Professional." In R. Baird, R. Ramsower, and Rosenbaum, eds. *Cyberethics: Social and Moral Issues in the Computer Age*. Amherst NY: Prometheus, 2000, pp. 34–40.

Rashid, Awais, John Weckert, and Richard Lucas. "Software Engineering Ethics in a Digital World." *IEEE Computer* 42, no. 6 (2009): 34–41.

Rowan, John, and Samuel Zinaich, eds. 2003. *Ethics for the Professions*. Belmont CA: Wadsworth.

Unger, Stephen H. "Making Computer Professionals and Other Engineers Low-Priced Commodities." *IEEE Technology and Society Magazine* 23, no. 2 (2004): 36–40.

CHAPTER

5

Privacy and Cyberspace

Of all the ethical issues associated with the use of cybertechnology, perhaps none has received more media attention than concern about the loss of personal privacy. In this chapter, we examine issues involving privacy and cybertechnology by asking the following questions:

- How are privacy concerns generated by the use of cybertechnology different from privacy issues raised by earlier technologies?
- What, exactly, is personal privacy, and why is it valued?
- How do computerized techniques used to gather and collect information, such as Internet "cookies" and RFID technology, raise concerns for personal privacy?
- How do the transfer and exchange of personal information across and between databases, carried out in computerized merging and matching operations, threaten personal privacy?
- How do tools used to "mine" personal data exacerbate existing privacy concerns involving cybertechnology?
- Can personal information we disclose to friends in social networking services, such as Facebook and MySpace, be used in ways that threaten our privacy?
- How do the use of Internet search engines and the availability of online public records contribute to the problem of protecting "privacy in public"?
- Do the kinds of privacy-enhancing tools currently available to Internet users provide them with adequate protection for their online personal information?
- Are current privacy laws and data protection schemes adequate?

Concerns about privacy can affect many aspects of an individual's life—from commerce to healthcare to work to recreation. For example, we speak of consumer privacy, medical and healthcare privacy, employee and workplace privacy, and so forth. Unfortunately, we cannot examine all of these categories of privacy in a single chapter. So we will have to postpone our analysis of certain kinds of privacy issues until later chapters in the book. For example, we will examine some ways that medical/genetic privacy issues are aggravated by cybertechnology in our discussion of bioinformatics in Chapter 12, and we will examine some particular employee/workplace privacy issues affected by the use of cybertechnology in our discussion of workplace surveillance and employee monitoring in Chapter 10. Some cyber-related privacy concerns that conflict with cyber security issues and national security interests will be examined in Chapter 6. In our discussion of emerging and converging technologies in Chapter 12, we examine some issues that affect a relatively new category of privacy concern called "location privacy," which arise because of the use of embedded chips, RFID technology, and global positioning systems.

Although some cyber-related privacy concerns are specific to one or more spheres or sectors—i.e., employment, healthcare, and so forth—others cut across multiple dimensions of our lives, affecting virtually all persons regardless of their employment or health status. The privacy issues involving cybertechnology examined in this chapter affect each of us, whether or not we have ever owned or even used a networked computer. Consider that in carrying out many of our day-to-day activities, we supply information to organizations that use computers to record, store, and exchange those data. These activities can include information we provide in filling out various forms, or they can include information acquired from our commercial transactions in a bank or a store. Also consider that many people now engage in online commerce activities, and this raises some additional consumer-related privacy worries. But users who navigate the Web solely for recreational purposes are also at risk with respect to their privacy. For example, personal data about one's interests and preferences can be acquired by organizations and by individuals whose need for this information is not always obvious. Furthermore, personal data about us collected via our online activities and transactions can then be sold to third parties.

Also consider that applications such as Google Street View (a feature of Google Earth and Google Maps) make use of satellite cameras and global positioning system (GPS) software that enable Internet users to zoom in on your house or place of employment and potentially record information about you. Additionally, closed circuit television cameras (CCTVs) located in public places and in shopping malls record many of your daily movements as you casually stroll through those environments. So even if you have never used a computer, cell phone, or any form of cybertechnology, your privacy is threatened in ways that were not possible in the past.

In this chapter, we examine a wide range of privacy concerns affecting the day-to-day activities of ordinary individuals carried out in both online and offline contexts. We also note, however, that cybertechnology is not the first technology to threaten personal privacy. We begin by looking at some ways to distinguish current issues associated with cybertechnology from privacy concerns involving earlier technologies.

▶ 5.1 ARE PRIVACY CONCERNS ASSOCIATED WITH CYBERTECHNOLOGY UNIQUE OR SPECIAL?

Concerns about personal privacy existed long before the advent of computers and cybertechnology. Prior to the information era, for example, the camera and the telephone presented challenges for privacy, so we can ask: what, if anything, is special about the privacy concerns that are associated with cybertechnology? Consider the impact that changes in technology have had on privacy with respect to the

- *amount* of personal information that can be gathered,
- *speed* at which personal information can be transmitted,

- *duration* of time that the information can be retained,
- *kind* of information that can be acquired and exchanged.

Cybertechnology makes it possible to collect and store much more information about individuals than was possible in the pre-computer era. The *amount* of personal information that could be collected in the pre-computer era was determined by practical considerations, such as the physical space required to store the data and the time and difficulty involved in collecting the data. Today, of course, digitized information that can be stored electronically in computer databases takes up very little storage space and can be collected with relative ease.

Consider the speed at which information is exchanged and transferred between databases. At one time, records had to be physically transported between filing destinations; the time it took to move them depended upon the transportation systems—e.g., motor vehicles, trains, airplanes, and so forth—that carried the records. Now, of course, records can be transferred between electronic databases in milliseconds through wireless technologies, high-speed cable lines, or even ordinary telephone lines.

With so much information being collected and transferred so rapidly, many have expressed concerns about its accuracy as well as the difficulties in tracking down and correcting any inaccuracies that might have been transferred. In an interview conducted for the BBC TV series *The Machine that Changed the World*, Harvard law professor Arthur Miller points out that trying to correct such information is like "chasing a greased pig"—you may get your hands on the pig, but it is very difficult to keep the pig firmly in your grip.[1] Although issues concerning the accuracy of personal information are clearly distinguishable from those concerning privacy per se, accuracy issues are frequently associated with privacy issues, and both are impacted by cybertechnology.

Also consider the *duration* of information—that is, how long information can be kept. Before the information era, information was manually recorded and stored in file cabinets and then in large physical repositories; it is unlikely that report cards my parents received as high school students still exist somewhere as physical records in file cabinets, for at that time, report cards were not computerized but instead existed, literally, as ink marks on paper. But the report cards my daughter received when she was a high school student were both generated and stored using computer technology. As an electronic record, her report card can be kept indefinitely, and the grades she receives as a high school student (as well as the grades she received in elementary school and in college) can follow her throughout her life.

In the past, practices involving the retention of personal data were perhaps more "forgiving." Because of practical limitations, such as physical storage space, that affected how long personal data could be kept on file, much of the personal information collected and stored had to be destroyed after a certain number of years. Since information could not be archived indefinitely, people with blemished records sometimes had the opportunity to start over again—deleting records from the past provided a kind of frontier from which one could "go West" and begin again. Today, of course, one's electronic dossier would follow on the trip west, precluding the possibility of starting over with a clean slate. We can argue whether the current means of data retention is a good thing, but it is difficult to dispute the claim that now, because of cybertechnology, each of us has what Arthur Miller describes as a "womb-to-tomb dossier."

Cybertechnology has also generated privacy concerns because of the *kind* of personal information that can now be collected. For example, every time you engage in an electronic transaction, such as making a purchase with a credit card or withdrawing money from an ATM, transactional information is collected and stored in several computer databases; this information can then be transferred electronically across commercial networks to agencies that request it. Personal information, retrieved from transactional information that is stored in computer databases, has been used to construct electronic dossiers containing detailed information about an individual's commercial transactions, including purchases made and places traveled—information that can reveal patterns in a person's preferences and habits.

Although the privacy concerns that we now associate with cybertechnology may not be totally new, or even different in kind, from those we associate with earlier technologies, few would dispute the claim that cybertechnology has exacerbated them. In Sections 5.4–5.7, we examine specific uses of cybertechnology that raise concerns for personal privacy. First, however, we examine the concept of personal privacy to better understand what privacy is and why we value it.

▶ 5.2 WHAT IS PERSONAL PRIVACY?

Although many definitions of privacy have been put forth, there is no universally agreed upon definition of this concept. To illustrate this point, consider some of the metaphors that are typically associated with privacy. Sometimes we speak of privacy as something that can be *lost* or *diminished*, suggesting that privacy can be understood in terms of a repository of personal information that can be either diminished altogether or gradually eroded. Contrast this view with descriptions of privacy as something that can be *intruded upon* or *invaded*, where privacy can be understood in terms of a spatial metaphor, such as a zone, that deserves protection. Alternatively, privacy is sometimes described as something that can be violated or breached, when we think of it in terms of either a right or an interest that deserves legal protection. Because of these different conceptions of privacy, we will see that it is useful to distinguish between the notions of one's having privacy (in a descriptive sense) and one's having a (normative) right to privacy. We will say more about this distinction in Section 5.2.4.

Privacy analysts have pointed out that in the United States, the meaning of privacy has evolved since the eighteenth century. Initially, privacy was understood in terms of freedom from (physical) intrusion. Later it became associated with freedom from interference into one's personal affairs, including one's ability to make decisions freely. Most recently, privacy has come to be closely identified with concerns affecting access to and control of personal information—a view that is also referred to as "informational privacy." Although the main emphasis in this chapter is on informational privacy, we also briefly examine the other two views.

5.2.1 Accessibility Privacy: Freedom from Unwarranted Intrusion

In a seminal paper on privacy, Samuel Warren and Louis Brandeis suggested that privacy could be understood as "being let alone" or "being free from intrusion." Appearing in the *Harvard Law Review* in 1890, the Warren and Brandeis article made the first explicit reference to privacy as a legal right in the United States. Many Americans are astonished to find out that there is no explicit mention of privacy in either the Constitution or its first ten amendments, the Bill of Rights. However, some legal scholars believe that a right to privacy can be inferred from the Fourth Amendment, which protects citizens against unreasonable searches and seizures of personal affects (i.e., papers, artifacts, etc.) by the government. Many legal scholars believe that the Fourth Amendment also provides legal grounds for a right to privacy protection from nongovernmental intrusion as well.

Warren and Brandeis also suggested that our legal right to privacy is grounded in our "right to inviolate personality." In part, they were responding to a certain use of a new technology—not the computer, of course, but rather the camera—which had begun to threaten individual privacy in new ways.[2] Photographs of people began to appear in newspapers, for example, in gossip columns, along with stories that were defamatory and sometimes even false. Warren and Brandeis believed that individuals have a (legal) right not be intruded upon in this manner. Because this definition of privacy as freedom from unwarranted intrusion focuses on the harm that can be caused through physical access to a person or to a person's possessions, Judith DeCew and others have described this view as *accessibility privacy*.[3]

5.2.2 Decisional Privacy: Freedom from Interference in One's Personal Affairs

Privacy is also sometimes conceived of as freedom from interference in one's personal choices, plans, and decisions; some refer to this view as *decisional privacy*. This kind of privacy has also been associated with reproductive technologies having to do with contraception. In *Griswold v. Connecticut* (1965), the court ruled that a person's right to get counseling about contraceptive techniques could not be denied by state laws. The view of privacy as freedom from external interference into one's personal affairs has since been appealed to in legal arguments in a series of controversial court cases, such as those involving abortion and euthanasia. For example, this view of privacy was appealed to in the landmark Supreme Court decision on abortion (*Roe v. Wade* 1973), as well as in a state court's decision involving Karen Ann Quinlan's right to be removed from life-support systems and thus her "right to die."[4] Because it focuses on one's right not to be interfered with, decisional privacy can be distinguished from both accessibility privacy and informational privacy.

5.2.3 Informational Privacy: Control over the Flow of Personal Information

Because of the increasing use of technology to gather and store personal information, many contemporary analysts view privacy as one's ability to restrict access to and control the flow of one's personal information. Privacy concerns are now often framed in terms of questions such as: Who should have access to one's personal information? To what extent can individuals control the ways in which information about them can be gathered, stored, mined, combined, recombined, exchanged, and sold? These are our concerns in this chapter, where we focus on *informational privacy*.

Table 5.1 summarizes the three views of privacy.

5.2.4 A Comprehensive Account of Privacy

James Moor (2000) has introduced an account of privacy that incorporates important elements of the nonintrusion, noninterference, and informational views of privacy. According to Moor,

TABLE 5.1 Three Views of Privacy

Accessibility Privacy	Privacy is defined as one's physically being let alone, or being free from intrusion into one's physical space.
Decisional Privacy	Privacy is defined as freedom from interference in one's choices and decisions.
Informational Privacy	Privacy is defined as control over the flow of one's personal information, including the transfer and exchange of that information.

> An individual [has] privacy *in a situation* with regard to others if and only if in that situation the individual [is] *protected from intrusion, interference,* and *information access* by others:[5] [Italics added]

An important element in this definition is Moor's notion of "situation," which he deliberately leaves broad so that it can apply to a range of contexts, or zones, that can be "declared private." For example, a situation can be an "activity" or a "relationship," or it can be the "storage and access of information" in a computer.

Central to Moor's theory is a distinction between *naturally private* and *normatively private* situations, enabling us to differentiate between the conditions required for (a) having privacy, and (b) having a right to privacy. This distinction, in turn, enables us to differentiate between a loss of privacy and a violation of privacy. In a naturally private situation, individuals are protected from access and interference from others by natural means, for example, physical boundaries such as those one enjoys while hiking alone in the woods. In this case, privacy can be *lost* but not *violated,* because there are no norms—conventional, legal, or ethical—according to which one has a *right*, or even an expectation, to be protected. In a normatively private situation, on the other hand, individuals are protected by conventional norms (e.g., formal laws and informal policies) because they involve certain kinds of zones or contexts that we have determined to need normative protection. The following two scenarios will help us to differentiate between normative and natural (or descriptive) privacy.

▶ **SCENARIO 5–1:** Descriptive Privacy

Mary arrives in the computer lab at her university at 11:00 PM to work on a paper that is due the next day. No one else is in lab at the time that Mary arrives there, and no one enters the lab until 11:45 PM, when Tom—the computer lab coordinator—returns to close the lab for the evening. As Tom enters, he sees Mary typing on one of the PCs in the lab. Mary seems startled as she looks up from her computer and discovers that Tom is gazing at her. ∎

Did Mary lose her privacy when Tom entered the lab and saw her? Was her privacy violated? Before Tom noticed her in the lab, we could say that Mary had privacy in the descriptive, or natural, sense of the term because no one was physically observing her while she was in the lab. When Tom entered and noticed that Mary was typing on a computer, Mary lost her natural (or descriptive) privacy in that situation. However, we should not infer that her privacy was violated in this incident, because a university's computer lab is not the kind of situation or zone that is declared normatively private and thus protected.

▶ **SCENARIO 5–2:** Normative Privacy

Tom decides to follow Mary, from a distance, as she leaves the computer lab to return to her (off-campus) apartment. He carefully follows her to the apartment building, and then stealthily follows

Mary up the stairway to the corridor leading to her apartment. Once Mary is safely inside her apartment, Tom peeps through a keyhole in the door. He observes Mary as she interacts with her computer in her apartment. ■

Has Mary's privacy been violated in this scenario? In both scenarios, Tom observes Mary interacting with a computer. In the first scenario, the observation occurred in a public place. There, Mary may have lost some privacy in a descriptive or natural sense, but she had no expectation of preserving her privacy in that particular situation. In the second scenario, Mary not only lost her privacy, but her privacy was violated as well, because apartments are examples of zones or "situations" that we, as a society, have declared normatively private.

We have explicit rules governing these situations with respect to privacy protection. Note that it was not merely the fact that Tom had observed Mary's interactions with a computer that resulted in her privacy being violated in the second scenario. Rather, it was because Tom had observed her doing this in a normatively protected situation. So, there was nothing in the information per se that Tom acquired about Mary that threatened her privacy; it was the situation or context in which information about Mary was acquired that caused her privacy to be violated in the second scenario.

5.2.5 Privacy as "Contextual Integrity"

We have seen the important role that a situation, or context, plays in Moor's privacy theory. But some critics argue that the meaning of a situation or context is either too broad or too vague. Helen Nissenbaum (2004a) elaborates on the notion of a context in her model of privacy as "contextual integrity," where she links adequate privacy protection to "norms of specific contexts." She notes that the things we do, including the transactions and events that occur in our daily lives, all take place in some context or other. In her scheme, contexts include "spheres of life" such as education, politics, the marketplace, and so forth.

Nissenbaum's privacy framework requires that the processes used in gathering and disseminating information (a) are "appropriate to a particular context," and (b) comply with norms that govern the flow of personal information in a given context.[6] She refers to these two types of informational norms as

1. norms of appropriateness,
2. norms of distribution.

Whereas norms of appropriateness determine whether a given type of personal information is either appropriate or inappropriate to divulge within a particular context, norms of distribution restrict or limit the flow of information within and across contexts. When either norm has been "breached," a violation of privacy occurs; conversely, the contextual integrity of the flow of personal information is maintained when both kinds of norms are "respected."[7]

As in the case of Moor's privacy model, Nissenbaum's theory demonstrates why we must always attend to the context in which information flows, and not to the nature of the information itself, in determining whether normative protection is needed. To illustrate some of the nuances in her framework of privacy as contextual integrity, consider the following scenario in which a professor collects information about students in his seminar.

▶ **SCENARIO 5–3:** Preserving Contextual Integrity in a University Seminar

Professor Roberts teaches a seminar on social issues in computing to upper-division undergraduate students at his university. Approximately half of the students who enroll in his seminar each semester are computer science students, whereas the other half are students majoring in humanities, business, etc. At the first meeting of each seminar, Professor Robert asks students to fill out an index card on which they include information about their major, their year of study (junior, senior, etc.), the names of any previous computer science courses they may have taken (if they are non-CS majors), their preferred e-mail address, and what they hope to acquire from this course. Professor Roberts then records this information in his electronic grade book. ■

Has Professor Roberts done anything wrong in requesting and collecting this information? For the most part, it is information that he could have gathered from the registrar's office at his university—e.g., information about which CS courses the students took, and so forth. But Roberts finds it much more convenient to collect information in the classroom, and he informs the students that he uses that information in determining which kinds of assignments he will decide to give to the class in general, and which kinds of criteria he will use to assign students to various group projects.

Because Professor Roberts has informed the students about how the information they provided to him will be used in the context of the classroom, and because the students have consented to give him the information, no privacy violation seems to have occurred. In fact, the process used by Professor Roberts satisfies the conditions for Nissenbaum's norm of appropriateness with respect to contextual integrity.

Next, suppose that Professor Roberts has lunch a few weeks later with a former student of his, Phil, who recently graduated and now has a job as a software engineer for a publishing company. Phil's company plans to release its first issue of a new magazine aimed at recent CS graduates, and it has launched an advertising campaign designed to attract undergraduate CS majors who will soon graduate. Phil asks Professor Roberts for the names of the CS majors in the seminar he is teaching. Professor Roberts is initially inclined to identify some students that Phil would likely know from classes that he had taken the previous year at the university. But should Professor Roberts reveal those names to Phil?

If he did, Professor Roberts would violate the privacy norm of distribution within the context of the seminar he is teaching. Consider that the students gave information about themselves to Professor Roberts for use in the context of that seminar. While his use of that information for purposes of the seminar is context-appropriate, passing on (i.e., distributing) any of that information to Phil is not, because it would violate the integrity of that context. Even though the information about the students that Professor Roberts has collected is not highly sensitive or confidential information, it was given to him for use only in the context of the seminar he is teaching. Insofar as Professor Roberts uses the information in that context, he preserves its integrity. But if he elects to distribute the information outside that context, he violates its integrity and breaches the privacy of his students.

▶ 5.3 WHY IS PRIVACY IMPORTANT?

Of what value is privacy? Why does privacy matter, and why should we care about it? In 1999, Scott McNealy, then CEO of Sun Microsystems, uttered his now famous remark to a group of reporters: "You have zero privacy anyway. Get over it." Is the idea of personal privacy merely a relic of the past? Michael Froomkin (2000) and Simson Garfinkel (2000) both speak of the "death of privacy." But not everyone has conceded defeat in the battle over privacy. Some privacy advocates staunchly believe that we should be vigilant about retaining what little privacy we may still have. Others note that we do not appreciate the value of privacy until we lose it, and by then it is usually too late. They point out that once privacy has been lost, it is difficult, if not impossible, to get back. So perhaps we should heed their warnings and try to protect privacy to the degree that we can.

We might also question whether the current privacy debate needs to be better understood in terms of differences that reflect generational attitudes. For many so-called Millennials, who are now college-aged, privacy does not always seem to be of paramount importance. Most Millennials, as well as many members of Generations X and Y, seem all too eager to share their personal information widely on social networking services such as Facebook, and many also seem willing to post "away messages" on AIM or Skype that disclose their whereabouts at a given moment to a wide range of people. But for many older Americans, including Baby Boomers, privacy is something that is generally still valued. So the relative importance of privacy may vary considerably among the generations; however, we will proceed on the assumption that privacy has value and thus is important.

Is privacy universally valued? Or is it valued mainly in Western, industrialized societies where greater importance is placed on the individual? It has been argued that some non-Western nations and cultures do not value individual privacy as much as we do in the West. Alan Westin (1967) believes that countries with strong democratic political institutions consider privacy more important than do less democratic ones. Nations such as Singapore and the People's Republic of China seem to place less importance on individual privacy and greater significance on broader social values, which are perceived to benefit the state's community objectives. Even in countries such as Israel, with strong democratic systems but an even stronger priority for national security, individual privacy may not be as important a value as it is in most democratic nations. So, even though privacy has at least some universal appeal, it is not valued to the same degree in all nations and cultures. As a result, it may be difficult to get universal agreement on privacy laws and policies in cyberspace.

5.3.1 Is Privacy an Intrinsic Value?

Is privacy something that is valued for its own sake—that is, does it have intrinsic value? Or is it valued as a means to an end, in which case it has only instrumental worth? Recall our discussion of intrinsic and instrumental values in Chapter 2. There we saw that happiness has intrinsic value because it is desired for its own sake. Money, on the other hand, has instrumental value since it is desired as a means to some further end or ends.

While few would argue that privacy is an intrinsic value, desired for its own sake, others, including Charles Fried (1990), argue that while privacy is instrumental, it is not merely instrumental. Fried suggests that unlike most instrumental values that are simply one means among others for achieving a desired end, privacy is also essential, that is, necessary to achieve important human ends, such as trust and friendship. We tend to associate intrinsic values with necessary conditions and instrumental values with contingent, or nonnecessary conditions; so while privacy is instrumental in that it is a means to certain human ends, Fried argues that it is also a necessary condition for achieving those ends.

Although agreeing with Fried's claim that privacy is more than merely an instrumental value, James Moor (2004) takes a different approach to illustrate this point. Like Fried, Moor argues that privacy itself is not an intrinsic value. Moor believes that privacy is the articulation, or "expression," of the "core value" *security*, which in turn is essential across cultures, for human flourishing. (We examine the concept of security as it relates to privacy in Chapter 6). And like Fried, Moor shows why privacy is necessary to achieve certain ends. Moor further suggests that as information technology insinuates itself more and more into our everyday lives, privacy becomes increasingly important for articulating, or expressing, the core value security.

Judith DeCew (2006) argues that because privacy acts as a "shield" to protect us in various ways, its value lies in the "freedom and independence" it provides for us. She notes that privacy shields us from interference as well as from "pressures that preclude self-expression and the development of relationships."[8] Privacy also serves as a shield, in DeCew's view, in that it protects us from coercion and the "pressure to conform." She also believes that the loss of privacy leaves us vulnerable and threatened because we are likely to become more conformist and less individualistic.

5.3.2 Privacy as a Social Value

Based on the insights of DeCew and others, one might infer that privacy is a value that simply benefits individuals. However, some authors have pointed out the social value that privacy also provides, noting that privacy is essential for democracy. Priscilla Regan (1995) points out that we often frame debates over privacy simply in terms of how to balance privacy interests as individual goods against interests involving the larger social good; in such debates, Regan believes, interests benefiting the social good will generally override concerns regarding individual privacy. If, however, privacy is understood as not solely concerned with individual good but as contributing to the broader social good, then in debates involving the balancing of competing values, individual privacy might have a greater chance of receiving equal consideration.

Since privacy can be of value for greater social goods, such as democracy, as well as for individual autonomy and choice, it would seem that it is important and worth protecting. But privacy is increasingly threatened by new cyber and cyber-related technologies. In Sections 5.4–5.6, we examine how privacy is threatened by three different kinds of practices that use cybertechnology:

a. *data gathering* techniques used to collect and record personal information, often without the knowledge and consent of users;

b. *data exchange* techniques used to transfer and exchange personal data across and between computer databases, typically without the knowledge and consent of users;

c. *data mining* techniques used to search large databases in order to generate consumer profiles based on the behavioral patterns of certain groups.

▶ 5.4 GATHERING PERSONAL DATA: MONITORING, RECORDING, AND TRACKING TECHNIQUES

Collecting and recording data about people is hardly new. Since the Roman era, and possibly before then, governments have collected and recorded census information. Not all data gathering and data recording practices have caused controversy about privacy. However, cybertechnology makes it possible to collect data about individuals without their knowledge and consent. In this section, we examine some controversial ways in which cybertechnology is used to gather and record personal data, as well as to monitor and track the activities and locations of individuals.

5.4.1 "Dataveillance" Techniques

Some believe that the greatest threat posed to personal privacy by cybertechnology lies in its capacity for surveillance and monitoring. Others worry less about the monitoring per se and more about the vast amounts of transactional data recorded using cybertechnology. Roger Clarke uses the term *dataveillance* to capture both the surveillance (data monitoring) and data recording techniques made possible by computer technology.[9] There are, then, two distinct controversies about dataveillance: one having to do with surveillance as a form of data monitoring, and one having to do with the recording and processing of data once the data are collected. We examine both controversies, beginning with a look at data monitoring aspects of surveillance.

First, we should note the obvious, but relevant, point that privacy threats associated with surveillance are by no means peculiar to cybertechnology. Long before the advent of cybertechnology, individuals (e.g., private investigators and stalkers) as well as organizations, including governmental agencies all over the world, have used both electronic and nonelectronic devices to monitor individuals and groups.

Telephone conversations have been subject to government surveillance by wiretapping, but phone conversations have also been monitored in the private sector as well; for example, telephone conversations between consumers and businesses are frequently monitored, sometimes without the knowledge and consent of the consumers who are party to them. So surveillance is by no means a recent concern, or, for that matter, is it associated solely or even mainly with the use of cybertechnology to monitor and record an individual's online activities. However, now video cameras can monitor consumers' movements while they shop at certain stores, and scanning devices such as those used by "intelligent highway vehicle systems," such as E-ZPass, subject motorists to a type of surveillance while they drive through tollbooths.

In the past, it was not uncommon for companies to hire individuals to monitor the performance of employees in the workplace. Now, however, there are "invisible supervisors," that is, computers, that can continuously monitor the activities of employees around the clock without failing to record a single activity of the employee. We will discuss workplace monitoring in greater detail, including recent arguments that have been used both to defend and to denounce computerized monitoring, in Chapter 10, where we consider workplace issues involving cybertechnology. In the remainder of this section, we consider surveillance techniques that involve monitoring and recording personal data in both off- and online activities.

Although users may not always realize that they are under surveillance, their online activities are tracked by Web site owners and operators to determine how frequently users visit their sites and to draw conclusions about the preferences users show while accessing their sites. We next consider some controversies associated with a type of online surveillance technology known as *cookies*.

5.4.2 Internet Cookies

Cookies are files that Web sites send to and retrieve from the computer systems of Web users, enabling Web site owners to collect information about an individual's online browsing preferences whenever a person visits a Web site. The use of cookies by Web site owners and operators has generated considerable controversy, in large part because of the novel way that information about Web users is collected and stored. Data recorded about the user are stored on a file placed on the hard drive of the user's computer system; this information can then be retrieved from the user's system and resubmitted to a Web site the next time the user accesses that site. No other data gathering mechanism actually stores the data it collects about a particular user on that user's computer system. It is also important to note that the exchange of data between the user and Web site typically occurs without the user's knowledge and consent.

Those who defend the use of cookies tend to be owners and operators of Web sites. Proprietors of these sites maintain that they are performing a service for repeat users of a Web site by customizing the user's means of information retrieval. They also point out that, because of cookies, they are able to provide a user with a list of preferences for future visits to that Web site. Privacy advocates, on the other hand, see the matter quite differently. They argue that activities involving the monitoring and recording of an individual's activities while visiting a Web site and the subsequent downloading of that information onto a user's computer (without informing the user) clearly cross the privacy line. Some privacy advocates also point out that information gathered about a user via cookies can eventually be acquired by online advertising agencies, who can then target that user for online ads.

Initially, you might feel a sense of relief in discovering that, generally, owners and operators of one Web site cannot access cookies-related information pertaining to a user's activities on another Web site. However, information about a user's activities on different Web sites can, under certain circumstances, be compiled and aggregated by online advertising agencies such as DoubleClick that pay to place advertisements in the form of banners on Web sites. The ad banners include a link from a host's Web page to the advertising agency's URL (uniform resource locator), so when a user accesses a Web page that contains an advertisement from DoubleClick, cookies can be sent to the user's system not only from the Web site requested by the user but also from the online advertising agency operating on that site. The advertising agency can then retrieve the cookie from the user's system and use the information it acquires about that user in its marketing advertisements. DoubleClick can also acquire information about that user from data in cookies that it retrieves from other Web sites the user has visited and where DoubleClick also advertises. The information can then be combined and cross-referenced in ways that enable a marketing profile of that user's online activities to be constructed and used in more direct advertisements.

Some see DoubleClick's practices as especially worrisome because DoubleClick attempted to purchase a database company called Abacus; had the acquisition gone through, Doubleclick could have compiled personal information from the two unrelated databases. We will discuss some of the implications of such a practice for privacy in a later section of this chapter that examines some techniques and practices involved in merging computerized records.

Several privacy advocates have argued that because cookies technology involves monitoring and recording a user's activities while visiting Web sites (without the user's knowledge and consent) as well as the subsequent downloading of that information onto a user's computer system, it violates the user's privacy. To assist Internet users in their concerns about cookies, a number of privacy-enhancing tools, which are discussed in detail in Section 5.8, have been made available. In the newer versions of most Web browsers, users have an option to disable cookies, so that they can either opt-in or opt-out of cookies, assuming that they (i) are aware of cookies technology, and (ii) know how to enable/disable that technology on their Web browsers.

Many privacy advocates object to the fact that the default status for most Web browsers is such that cookies will automatically be accepted unless explicitly overridden by the user. As we noted above, cookies technology involves downloading the information it gathers about users onto the user's computer system. So, cookies technology also raises concerns involving encroachment or intrusion into a user's physical space as well as privacy concerns regarding the clandestine method used to gather data about users who visit Web sites.

5.4.3 RFID Technology

Another mode of surveillance made possible by cybertechnology involves the use of RFID (radio frequency identification) technology. In its simplest form, RFID technology consists of a tag (microchip) and a reader. The tag has an electronic circuit, which stores data, and an antenna that broadcasts data by radio waves in response to a signal from a reader. The reader also contains an antenna that receives the radio signal, and it has a demodulator that transforms the analog radio information into suitable data for any computer processing that will be done (Lockton and Rosenberg 2005).

Although the commercial use of RFIDs was intended mainly for the unique identification of real-world objects (e.g., items sold in supermarkets), the tags can also be used to monitor those objects after they are sold. For example, Helen Nissenbaum (2004a) notes that prior to the use of RFID tags

> . . . customers could assume that sales assistants, store managers, or company leaders recorded point-of-sale information. RFID tags extend the duration of the relationships, making available to . . . others a range of information about customers that was not previously available.[10]

In one sense, the use of these tags in inventory control would seem uncontroversial. For example, Simson Garfinkel (2002) notes that a company such as Playtex could place an RFID tag in each bra to make sure that shipments of bras headed for Asia are not diverted to New York. He also points out, however, that a man with a handheld (RFID) reader in his pocket who is standing next to a woman wearing such a bra can learn the make and size of her bra. Additionally, and perhaps more controversially, RFID technology can be used for tracking the owners of the items that have these tags. So, on the one hand, RFID transponders in the form of ''smart labels'' make it much easier to track inventory and protect goods from theft or imitation. On the other hand, these tags pose a significant threat to individual privacy. Critics of this technology, which include organizations such as the Electronic Privacy Information Center (EPIC) and the American Civil Liberties Union (ACLU), worry about the accumulation of RFID transaction data by RFID owners and how those data will be used in the future.

RFID technology is already widely used in America—as Garfinkel notes, it has been incorporated into everything from automobile keys to inventory control systems to passports. If you have an E-ZPass (or some other intelligent highway system) transponder in your car, for example, you are already carrying a wireless tag; E-ZPass uses the serial number to debit your account when your car passes through a tollbooth. Garfinkel also notes that these tags have started to appear in clothing. For example, Texas Instruments and the Gap conducted a three-month test in which every piece of denim in a store in Atlanta received a wireless ID tag.

Ranchers in the United States track cattle by implanting RFID tags in the animals' ears. In the future, major cities and municipalities might require RFID tags for pets; in Taiwan, owners of domesticated dogs are now required to have a microchip containing an RFID tag, which identifies the animal's owner and residence, inserted in their pet dog's ear. Policies requiring RFID tags for humans, especially for children and the elderly, may also be established in the future. In the United States, some nursing homes already provide their patients with RFID bracelets. Alison Adam (2005) notes that chips (containing RFID technology) can be implanted in children so that they can be tracked if abducted; however, she worries that we may come to rely too heavily on these technologies to care for children.

According to Garfinkel (2004), roughly 40 million Americans carry some form of RFID device in their pocket every day. This might suggest that people are comfortable with RFID technology. However, the fact that this technology is now included in chips embedded in humans, which enables them to be tracked, has raised concerns for many privacy advocates.

In light of these concerns, Garfinkel (2002) has proposed an "RFID Bill of Rights" to protect individuals and guide businesses that use RFID tags. In this scheme, individuals would have the right to (a) know whether products contain RFID tags, (b) have RFID tags removed or deactivated when they purchase products, and (c) know when, where, and why the tags are being read.

Like Internet cookies and other online data gathering and surveillance techniques, RFID clearly threatens individual privacy. But unlike surveillance concerns associated with cookies, which track a user's habits while visiting Web sites, RFID technology can be used to track an individual's location in the offline world. We examine some specific privacy and surveillance concerns affecting RFID in connection with "location privacy" and "pervasive surveillance" issues in Chapter 12 in our discussion of ubiquitous communication and ambient intelligence.

5.4.4 Cybertechnology and Government Surveillance

Thus far, we have examined some surveillance techniques involving cybertechnology that are used mainly in the business and commercial sectors to monitor the activities of consumers and to record data about them. Another mode of surveillance that is also associated with cybertechnology involves governments and government agencies that monitor the activities of citizens, a practice that is sometimes referred to as "domestic spying." As already noted, this practice is not exactly new, but as the technologies used by governments to monitor their citizens' activities become more sophisticated, intrusive, and pervasive, the threats posed to privacy and civil liberties become exacerbated.

Some cybertechnologies, despite their initial objectives and intent, can facilitate government surveillance. Consider, for example, that the cell phone companies in the United States are required by the Federal Communications Commission (FCC) to install a Global Positioning System (GPS) locator chip, in compliance with an "enhanced 911 mandate," in all of the cell phones manufactured after December 2005. This technology, which assists 911 operators in emergencies, also enables any cell phone user to be tracked within 100 meters of his or her location. However, privacy advocates worry that this information can also be used by the government to spy on individuals.

Government agencies currently use a variety of technologies that enable them to intercept and read private e-mail messages. In Chapter 6, we will see that this practice, initiated by the George W. Bush administration to monitor e-mail between U.S. residents and people living outside the United States, has been controversial. And in Section 5.7.1 we will see why the U.S. Government's decision to subpoena the records of online search requests made by users of search engines such as Google, which are recorded and archived in computer databases, has also been controversial. In Chapter 7, we describe in detail some of the specific technologies (such as Internet pen registers, keystroke monitoring, encryption, and biometric technologies) and some of the programs (such as the Carnivore and the Total Information Awareness project) that have been used by government agencies in the United States to conduct surveillance on individuals. There, we will also see why these technologies and programs, which have been used to combat terrorism and crime in cyberspace, have been controversial from the point of view of privacy and civil liberties.

While few would object to the desirable ends that increased security provides, we will see that many oppose the means—i.e., the specific technologies and programs supporting surveillance operations, as well as legislation such as the USA Patriot Act— that the U.S. Government has used to achieve its objectives. In Chapter 7, we will see why the Patriot Act, enacted into law in October 2001 and renewed in March 2006, has been controversial from the point of view of civil liberties. Our purpose in this section has been to briefly describe how government surveillance of citizens illustrates one more way that cybertechnology both contributes to and enhances the ability of organizations to gather and record data about individuals.

▶ 5.5 EXCHANGING PERSONAL DATA: MERGING AND MATCHING ELECTRONIC RECORDS

In the previous section we examined ways in which personal data could be gathered using surveillance techniques and then recorded electronically in computer databases. Other tools have been devised to transfer and exchange those records across and between computer databases. Simply collecting and recording personal data, per se, might not seem terribly controversial if, for example, the data were never used, transferred, exchanged, combined, or recombined. Some would argue, however, that the mere collection of personal data is problematic from a privacy perspective, assuming that if data are being collected, there must be some motive or purpose for their collection. Of course, the reason, as many now realize, is that transactions involving the sale and exchange of personal data are a growing business.

Much of the personal data gathered electronically by one organization is later exchanged with other organizations; indeed, the very existence of certain institutions depends on the exchange and sale of personal information. Many now believe that professional information gathering organizations, such as Equifax, Experion (formerly TRW), and Trans Union (credit reporting bureaus), as well as the Medical Information Bureau (MIB), violate the privacy of individuals because of the techniques they use to facilitate the exchange of personal information across and between databases. These techniques are known as computer merging and computer matching.

5.5.1 Merging Computerized Records

Few would dispute the claim that organizations, in both the public and the private sectors, have a legitimate need for information about individuals in order to make intelligent decisions concerning those individuals. For example, if you are applying for a credit card, it would be reasonable for the credit company to request information about you. However, few would also disagree with the claim that individuals should have a right to keep some personal information private. A crucial question, then, is: What kind of control can an individual expect to retain over the personal information that he or she has given to an organization? Can, for example, an individual expect that personal information provided to an organization for legitimate use in a specific context will remain within that organization? Or will it instead by exchanged with other organizations who can then combine or merge it with existing information?

Computer merging is the technique of extracting information from two or more unrelated databases that contain information about some individual or group of individuals, and then integrating that information into a composite file. It occurs whenever two or more disparate pieces of information contained in separate databases are combined. Consider the following sequence of events in which you voluntarily give information about yourself to three different organizations. First, you give information about your income and credit history to a lending institution in order to secure a loan. You next give information about your age and medical history to an insurance company to purchase life insurance. You then give information about your views on certain social issues to a political organization you wish to join. Each of these organizations can be said to have a legitimate need for information to make certain decisions about you—insurance companies have a legitimate need to know about your age and medical history before agreeing to sell you life insurance, and lending institutions have a legitimate need to know about your income and credit history before agreeing to lend you money to purchase a house or a car. And insofar as you voluntarily give these organizations the information requested, no breach of your privacy has occurred.

Now suppose that without your knowledge and consent, information about you that resides in the insurance company's database is transferred and merged with information about you that resides in the lending institution's database or in the political organization's database. Even though you voluntarily gave certain information about yourself to three different organizations, and even though you voluntarily authorized each organization to have the information, it does not follow that you authorized any one organization to have some combination of that information.[11] When organizations merge information about you in a way that you did not specifically authorize, the "contextual integrity" of your information has been violated. (Recall Nissenbaum's criteria for preserving the contextual integrity of personal information described in Section 5.2.5.)

Next, consider a case of computer merging involving DoubleClick, an online advertising company. In our discussion of cookies technology in the previous section, we described how DoubleClick used cookies to compile data from multiple Web sites on which it placed DoubleClick ad banners. DoubleClick can compile the cookies-related information it received from its advertisement banners that are clicked on by users at multiple Web sites. If, for example, DoubleClick advertised on 1,000 Web sites, it could retrieve cookie files from any user who visited any of those sites. Thus DoubleClick can compile and cross-reference cookies-related information in ways that individual Web site proprietors cannot. This, in turn, has caused concern among DoubleClick's critics, including privacy advocates.

► **SCENARIO 5–4:** Merging Personal Information in Unrelated Computer Databases

DoubleClick planned to purchase Abacus Direct Corporation, a database company, in late 1999. Abacus's databases contained not only records of consumer's catalogue purchases but also actual names and telephone numbers that had been collected by Abacus primarily from offline transactions. With this acquisition, DoubleClick could merge records in the Abacus database with its own database, which consisted of information gained primarily from Internet cookies files. And with its newly merged data, DoubleClick would have an information mosaic about individuals that included not merely anonymous and indirect information (such as IP addresses and ISP-related information) but also direct personal information. The Web profiles in DoubleClick's original database, gathered via cookies, included data about which Web sites that users (who are identified and tracked via an IP address) visit, how long they visit a particular site, and so on. That information could now be compared to and combined with explicit personal information (gathered offline and stored in Abacus's databases), including names, addresses, and phone numbers.[12] ■

The planned merger involving the two companies, which generated considerable controversy at the time, was cancelled in January 2000, when Double Click was sued by a woman who complained that her right to privacy had been violated. The woman claimed that DoubleClick's business practices were deceptive, because the company had quietly reversed an earlier policy by which it provided businesses with only anonymous data about Internet users (acquired from cookies files). Because of public pressure, Double-Click backed off from its proposal to purchase Abacus, but many users were able to see for the first time the privacy threats that can result from merging electronic data. However, DoubleClick continued to function as an online advertising company, and in March 2008, it was acquired by Google.

5.5.2 Matching Computerized Records

Computer matching is a variation of the technology used to merge computerized records. It involves cross-checking information in two or more unrelated databases to produce matching records, or "hits." In federal and state government applications, this technique has been used by various agencies and departments for the express purpose of creating a new file containing a list of potential law violators, as well as individuals who have actually broken the law or who are suspected of having broken the law.[13]

Consider a scenario in which you complete a series of forms for various federal and state government agencies, such as the Internal Revenue Service (IRS), your state government's motor vehicle registration department, or your local government's property tax assessment department. You supply the specific information requested and, in addition, you include general information requested on each form, such as your social security number and driver's license number, which can be used as identifiers in matching records about you that reside in multiple databases. The information is then electronically stored in the agencies' respective databases, and routine checks (matches) can be made against information (records) contained in those databases. For example, your property tax records can be matched against your federal tax records to see whether you own an expensive house but declared only a small income. Records in an IRS database of divorced or single fathers can be matched against a database containing records of mothers receiving welfare payments to generate a list of potential deadbeat parents.

In filling out the various governmental forms, you agreed to give some information to each government agency. It is by no means clear, however, that you authorized information given to any one agency to be exchanged with other agencies. You had no say in the way information that you authorized for use in one context was subsequently used in another. Because of this contextual violation of personal information, some have argued that practices involving computerized matching of records containing personal data raise serious threats for personal privacy. The debate over computerized record matching has been hotly contested, and it has been denounced because of its implications for stereotyping and profiling certain classes or groups of individuals. Computerized record matching has also been criticized by civil liberties groups who fear that such a practice might lead to a new form of social control.

Defenders of this practice justify the matching of computer records because it enables us to track down deadbeat parents, welfare cheats, and the like. Although few would object to the ends that could be achieved, we can question whether the practice of computerized matching is compatible with individual privacy. Even if computerized record matching does help to root out governmental waste and fraud, as Kusserow (1995) argues, would that fact alone justify such a practice? Consider this counterexample: Suppose that 24-hour video surveillance and daily drug testing of all government employees also help to root out government waste and fraud—would such means also be justifiable in order to reach the desired end?

Proponents of computer matching might argue that 24-hour video surveillance and daily drug testing of government workers would violate the privacy of workers in ways that matching computerized records does not. However, critics such as Shattuck (1995) have pointed out that computer matches have been made even when there was no suspicion that a particular individual or group of individuals had violated the law. For example, computer records of entire categories of individuals, such as government employees, have been matched against databases containing records of welfare recipients on the chance that a "hit" will identify one or more welfare cheats. One line of argumentation sometimes used to defend a practice such as computer matching against the charge of violating privacy rights is as follows:

PREMISE 1. Privacy is a legal right.

PREMISE 2. Legal rights are not absolute.

PREMISE 3. When one violates the law (i.e., commits a crime), one forfeits one's legal rights.

CONCLUSION. Criminals have forfeited their legal right to privacy.

Initially, this line of reasoning seems quite plausible, but does it apply in the case of computerized record matching? First of all, this argument assumes that we have an explicit legal right to privacy. Let us assume, for the sake of argument, that we have such a right and that all legal rights are (or ought to be) conditional only. Even with the addition of these two assumptions, problems remain: for example, those who maintain that a deadbeat parent has, in violating the law, given up his right to privacy seem to either disregard or ignore any right to privacy accorded to individuals who have not broken the law. For it was only by matching the records of mostly innocent individuals whose names were included in multiple government databases that a "hit," identifying one or more alleged criminals, was generated. So even if criminals do forfeit their right to privacy, the process of identifying these criminals via computerized record matching entails that several noncriminals will be required to forfeit that right as well.

Next, consider a computerized matching technique involving biometric identifiers that also has been used by some government agencies.

▶ **SCENARIO 5–5:** Using Biometric Technology at Super Bowl XXXV

At Super Bowl XXXV in January 2001, a facial recognition technology scanned the faces of individuals entering the stadium. The digitized facial images were then instantly matched against images in a centralized database of suspected criminals and terrorists. The fans who attended the sporting advent were not told that their faces were being scanned. The day after the super bowl, many learned what had happened via a newspaper story, which caused considerable controversy at the time. Many privacy advocates and civil liberties proponents criticized the tactics used by the government.[14]   ■

Although this incident generated some controversy in early 2001, the attitudes of many Americans who were initially critical of the government's use of biometrics at Super Bowl XXXV changed later that year, following the tragic events of September 11. We will examine this biometric technique in greater detail in Chapter 7, where we discuss cybercrime. However, it is useful at this point to show how this biometric-based matching technique differs from the computerized record-matching practice involving government workers, which we considered earlier in this section.

Initially, one might argue that the biometric-based matching technique used to scan and match faces of individuals at stadiums and airports, as well as other public places, is essentially no different from the computerized record-matching operations previously used to catch welfare cheats and deadbeat parents. But in traditional computerized record matching, all of the databases involved contain records of individuals who were (or should have been) assumed to be innocent. As we saw, records of government workers (presumed to be innocent) were matched against records of welfare recipients (also presumed to be innocent) to ferret out any persons who just happen to be in both groups. In the case of the face recognition program used at Super Bowl XXXV, however, images of persons entering the football stadium were matched against a database of persons already known (or at least suspected) to be criminals and terrorists. So the objectives of the targeted matches at Super Bowl XXXV were much more specific than were those of the "fishing expeditions" used in traditional computerized record-matching practices. Perhaps this is one reason why the biometric-based matching operations aimed at catching terrorists and dangerous criminals have been less controversial than traditional record-matching practices used by federal and state governments.

▶ 5.6 MINING PERSONAL DATA

A form of data analysis that uses techniques gained from research and development in artificial intelligence (AI), described in Chapter 11, has been used to "mine" personal data. Formally referred to as Knowledge Discovery in Databases, or KDD, the process is now more commonly known as *data mining*. Essentially, data mining involves the indirect gathering of personal information through an analysis of implicit patterns discoverable in data. Data mining activities can generate new and sometimes nonobvious classifications or categories; as a result, individuals whose data are mined can become identified with or linked to certain newly created groups that they might never have imagined to exist. This is further complicated by the fact that current privacy laws offer individuals no protection with respect to how information about them acquired through data mining activities is subsequently used, even though important decisions can be made about those individuals based on the patterns found in the mined personal data. So, data mining technology can be used in ways that raise special concerns for personal privacy.

5.6.1 How Does Data Mining Threaten Personal Privacy?

What is so special about the privacy concerns raised by data mining? For example, how do they differ from privacy issues introduced by more traditional data retrieval techniques, such as computerized merging and matching operations that we examined in Section 5.5? For one thing, privacy laws as well as informal data protection guidelines have been established for protecting personal data that are

- *explicit* in databases (in the form of specific electronic records),
- *confidential* in nature (e.g., data involving medical, financial, or academic records),
- exchanged between or across databases.

However, virtually no legal or normative protections apply to personal data manipulated in the data mining process, where personal information is typically

- *implicit* in the data,
- *nonconfidential* in nature,
- *not exchanged* between databases.

Unlike personal data that reside in explicit records in databases, information acquired about persons via data mining is often derived from implicit patterns in the data. The patterns can suggest "new" facts, relationships, or associations about a person, placing that person in a "newly discovered" category or group. Also, because most personal data collected and used in data mining applications is considered neither confidential nor intimate in nature, there is a tendency to presume that such data must by default be *public* data. And unlike the personal data that are often exchanged between or across two or more databases in traditional database retrieval processes, in the data mining process personal data are often manipulated within a single database, and typically within a large *data warehouse*.

Next consider a scenario involving data mining practices at a bank in determining whether or not to grant loans. As you consider the privacy issues raised in the following scenario, keep in mind Nissenbaum's distinction between "norms of appropriateness" and "norms of distribution" for determining contextual integrity (described in Section 5.2.5).

▶ **SCENARIO 5–6:** Data Mining at the XYZ Bank

Lee, a junior executive at ABC Marketing Inc., has recently applied for an automobile loan at the XYZ Bank. To secure the loan, Lee agrees to complete the usual forms required by the bank for loan transactions. He indicates that he has been employed at the ABC Marketing Company for more than three years and that his current annual salary is $210,000. He also indicates that he has $30,000 in a separate savings account, a portion of which he intends to use as a down payment for a new BMW. On the loan form, Lee also indicates that he is currently repaying a $15,000 personal loan used to finance a family vacation to Europe the previous year.

Next, the bank's computing center runs a data mining program on information in its customer databases and discovers a number of patterns. One reveals that executives earning more than $200,000 but less than $300,000 annually, who purchase luxury cars (such as BMWs), and who take their families on international vacations, are also likely start their own businesses within their first five years of employment. A second data mining algorithm reveals that the majority of marketing entrepreneurs declare bankruptcy within one year of starting their own businesses. The data mining algorithms can be interpreted to suggest that Lee is a member of a group that neither he nor possibly even the loan officers at the bank had ever known to exist—viz., the group of marketing executives likely to start a business and then declare bankruptcy within a year. With this new category and new information about Lee, the bank determines that Lee, and people that fit into Lee's group, are long-term credit risks.[15]   ■

Does the mining of data about Lee by the XYZ Bank raise concerns for privacy? At one level, the transaction between Lee and the bank seems appropriate. To borrow money from XYZ Bank, Lee has authorized the bank to have the information about him, that is, his current employment, salary, savings, outstanding loans, and so forth, that it needs to make an informed decision as to whether or not to grant him the loan. So, if we appeal to Nissenbaum's framework of privacy as contextual integrity, it would seem that there is no breach of privacy in terms of norms of appropriateness. However, Lee gave the bank information about him for use in one context, viz., to make a decision about whether or not he should be granted a loan to purchase a new automobile. He was assured that the information given to the bank would not be exchanged with a third party without first getting Lee's explicit consent. So, unlike cases involving the computerized merging and matching of records that we considered in Section 5.5, no information about Lee was either exchanged or cross-referenced between databases—i.e., there is no breach of the norms of distribution (in Nissenbaum's model). However, it is unclear whether the bank has agreed not to use the information it now has in its databases about Lee for certain in-house analyses.

Although Lee voluntarily gave the bank information about his annual salary, about previous vacation loans, and about the type of automobile he intended to purchase, he gave each piece of information for a specific purpose and use, in order that the bank could make a meaningful determination about Lee's request for an automobile loan. It is, however, by no means clear that Lee authorized the bank to use disparate pieces of that information for more general data mining analyses that would reveal patterns involving Lee that neither he nor the bank could have anticipated at the outset. Using Lee's information for this purpose would now raise questions about "appropriateness" in the context involving Lee and Bank XYZ.

The mining of data in Lee's case is controversial from a privacy perspective for several reasons. For one thing, the information that Lee is someone likely to start his own business, which would probably lead to his declaring personal bankruptcy, was not explicit in any of the data (records) about Lee; rather it was implicit in patterns of data about people similar to Lee in certain respects but vastly different from him in other respects. For another thing, Lee's case illustrates how data mining can generate new categories and groups such that the people whom the data mining analysis identifies with those groups would very likely have no idea that they would be included as members. And we have seen that, in the case of Lee, certain decisions can be made about members of these newly generated groups simply by virtue of those individuals being identified as members. For example, it is doubtful that Lee would have known that he was a member of a group of professional individuals likely to start a business, and that he was a member of a group whose businesses were likely to end in bankruptcy. The "discovery" of such groups is, of course, a result of the use of data mining tools.

Even though no information about Lee was exchanged with databases outside XYZ, the bank did use information about Lee internally in a way that he had not explicitly authorized. And it is in this sense—unauthorized internal use by data users—that data mining raises serious concerns for personal privacy. Note also that even if Lee had been granted the loan for the automobile, the bank's data mining practices would still have raised serious privacy concerns with respect to the contextual integrity of his personal information. Lee was merely one of many bank customers who had voluntarily given certain personal information about themselves to the bank for use in one context—in this example, a loan request—and subsequently had that information used in ways that they did not specifically authorize.

Consumer Profiling

Of course, Lee's case is merely hypothetical. But some recent evidence now suggests that banks and consumer credit organizations are using data mining techniques to determine an individual's "credit worthiness" in ways that are not so different from the example involving Lee. In these cases, a consumer's credit rating could actually be determined via profiling schemes that can suggest "guilt by association." For example, a consumer could have the spending limit on her credit card reduced, or have that card revoked altogether, because of where she shops or where she lives. In the economic turndown in 2008–2009, many homes were lost to foreclosure. So people living in neighborhoods where there was a high rate of foreclosures, or people holding mortgages with certain banks or lending institutions that have experienced high rates of home foreclosures, may be considered credit risks by virtue of their association with either a certain neighborhood or bank-profiling, even though they have been responsible in paying their mortgages and other loans on time. Similarly, if individuals shop at a certain kind of retail store, say Wal-Mart, information about their purchases at such a store can associate them with other individuals who shop there, and who may have a higher-than-average default rate on their credit cards.

Mike Stuckey (2008) describes an incident where a 37-year old computer consultant had two of his American Express cards canceled and the limit on a third card reduced.

The consumer was told that the credit card company's decision was based in part on criteria having to do with *where* he shopped and with *who* held his mortgage. American Express informed this customer that included in the criteria it uses to decide to reduce the spending limit on someone's credit card are the company's

> "credit experience with customers who have made purchases at establishments where you have recently used your card."

> "analysis of the credit risk associated with customers who have residential loans from the creditor(s) indicated in your credit report."

While there has been suspicion for some time that credit card companies engage in the kind of profiling scheme used by American Express, consumer advocates and credit analysts believe that this may be the first time that a major credit company has admitted to using such criteria. In its defense, however, American Express claims that it needs to analyze its exposure to risk as it reviews its cardholder's credit profiles in light of the economic turndown in 2008–2009 (Stuckey 2008).

We have seen how data mining can be used to threaten consumer privacy. But can it also be used to protect consumers against fraudulent activities? Perhaps not surprisingly, data mining, like other technologies, can be viewed as a "double-edged sword" with respect to consumers' interests, as the following story suggests. One day in 2008, I was informed by my credit card company that a purchase, which the company apparently viewed as suspicious or questionable, had been charged earlier that day to my credit card account. When asked about the purchase, I informed the company's representative that it had not been made by me, and I also thanked the person for notifying me so promptly about this transaction. The company representative then immediately cancelled my existing credit card and issued me a new card with a new account number.

Why did the company suspect that the purchase made that day with my credit card was questionable? It would seem that the data mining algorithms used by the credit card company to determine the patterns of my purchases—which kinds of purchases and credit card transactions I typically make, with whom and where I make them, and when—also revealed the anomaly of the questionable purchase made that day with my credit card. So in this instance, data mining appeared to have been used in a way that protected the interests of a consumer.

In Table 5.2, we summarize some of the differences in mining, matching, and merging techniques used to process personal information.

TABLE 5.2 Mining, Matching, and Merging Techniques for Manipulating Personal Data

*Data **Merging***	A data-exchange process in which personal data from two or more sources is combined to create a "mosaic" of individuals that would not be discernable from the individual pieces of data alone.
*Data **Matching***	A technique in which two or more unrelated pieces of personal information are cross-referenced and compared to generate a match, or "hit," that suggests a person's connection with two or more groups.
*Data **Mining***	A technique for "unearthing" implicit patterns in large single databases, or "data warehouses," revealing statistical data that associates individuals with nonobvious groups; user profiles can be constructed from these patterns.

5.6.2 Web Mining

Initially, the mining of personal data depended on large (offline) commercial databases called data warehouses, which stored the data, consisting primarily of transactional information. Data mining techniques are now also used by commercial Web sites to analyze data about Internet users, which can then be sold to third parties. This process is sometimes referred to as "Web mining," which has been defined as the application of data mining techniques to discover patterns from the Web.[16] The kinds of patterns discovered from Web mining can be useful to marketers in promotional campaigns. The following scenario, involving Facebook, illustrates how mining is done on the Web.

▶ **SCENARIO 5–7:** The Facebook Beacon Controversy

Facebook (originally called "The Facebook") is a popular social networking service (SNS) founded by Mark Zuckerberg in 2004, when he was a student at Harvard University. As in the case of other SNSs (examined in detail in Chapter 11), Facebook enables its members to share information about themselves with "friends" and to make additional friends through its range of services. In November 2007, Facebook announced a marketing initiative called Facebook Beacon, which would let Facebook friends share information about what they do online, including the purchases they make, on their Facebook profile. Although this feature, made possible by external Web sites that sent data about individuals to Facebook, enabled users to share their online activities with their friends, it also allowed targeted advertisements by the Web sites sending the data. Essentially, Beacon allowed affiliate Web sites (including Blockbuster, Fandago, and many others) to send stories about a user's online activities to Facebook, which were then displayed to that user's "friends" in the form of news feeds and Social Ads.

However, the Beacon initiative proved to be very controversial; for one reason, it disclosed what purchases users made at certain Web sites. Also, when Facebook introduced Beacon, it stated that it would not share any personally identifiable information in the Social Ads, and it claimed that users would only see those ads to the extent that they were willing to share that information with others. But Facebook was soon criticized for collecting more user information for advertisers than it had originally admitted. In December 2007, Zuckerberg publicly apologized for the way that the Beacon project had been set up, admitting that it was established as an "opt-out" system instead of an "opt-in" system. So, by default, if a Facebook user did not explicitly decline to share something, Beacon would share the advertising information with that person's friends via the user's profile.[17] ∎

Many Facebook users complained when they discovered what was happening with the information about their online purchases and activities. But were the practices used in the Beacon program incompatible with Facebook's privacy policy at that time? Facebook's original privacy agreement stated:

> We may use information about you that we collect from other sources, including but not limited to newspapers and Internet sources such as blogs, instant messaging services, Facebook Platform developers, and other users of Facebook, to supplement your profile.

A controversial clause in its privacy policy was Facebook's right to sell a user's data to private companies, which stated

> We may share your information with third parties, including responsible companies with which we have a relationship.

However, Facebook officials claimed that they had never provided, nor had they intended to provide, users' information to third-party companies. But Facebook nonetheless decided to change its privacy policy in response to the controversy generated by Beacon.[18]

The Beacon controversy also generated other privacy concerns for Facebook users, independent of Web mining. One concern had to do with Facebook's policy for users wishing to delete their accounts. Some users worried about what would happen to the personal information that Facebook had collected about them while their accounts were active. Did Facebook own that information? Could it be used in future Web mining or sold to third parties, or both? Facebook's initial policy stated that users could only "deactivate" their accounts. Once deactivated, the user's profile would no longer be visible on Facebook. However, that information would remain on Facebook's servers. Again, many users were not satisfied, because they wished to delete their accounts permanently. For example, some users wished to permanently remove information that may have been embarrassing or highly sensitive, including photos of them drinking at parties or in their dormitory rooms. In response to pressure from users, Facebook changed its policy for deleting accounts in February 2008. The new policy enables users to contact Facebook to request that their accounts be permanently deleted.

The Facebook Beacon controversy illustrates how easily personal data can be mined on the Web. Because the amount of data on the Internet is so vast, one might assume that it is impossible to mine those data in ways that could be useful. However, current data mining tools employ sophisticated and advanced AI technology that enable the users of those tools to "comb" through massive amounts of data that would not have been possible to analyze with traditional information retrieval techniques. Also, sophisticated search engines, including *metasearch* engines, "crawl" through the Web in order to uncover general patterns in information retrieved from their requests across multiple Web sites. In Section 5.7.1, we examine some specific ways in which the use of Internet search engines raise privacy concerns even though the kind of personal information retrieved from online search facilities might not seem to need explicit privacy protection. To see why such protection might indeed be needed in these cases, however, we first examine some questions underlying a concern that Helen Nissenabum (2004a, b) calls the "problem of privacy in public."

▶ 5.7 PROTECTING PERSONAL PRIVACY IN PUBLIC SPACE

Thus far, we have examined how cybertechnology can be used to gather, exchange, and mine personal information. With the exception of data mining, which manipulates personal, but nonconfidential information, the kind of personal information gathered and exchanged was often confidential and intimate in nature. For example, we saw how financial and medical records could be exchanged between two or more databases using computerized merging and matching. This confidential and very personal information is referred to as nonpublic personal information (NPI). Privacy analysts are now concerned about a different kind of personal information—public personal information (PPI), which is neither confidential nor intimate and which is also being gathered, exchanged, and mined using cybertechnology.

PPI includes information such as where you work or attend school or what kind of car you drive; it is information about you as a particular person. PPI has not enjoyed the privacy protection that has been granted to NPI.

Until recently, most concerns about personal information that was gathered and exchanged electronically were limited to NPI, and because of the attention it has received, privacy laws and policies were established to protect NPI. But now privacy advocates are extending their concern to PPI; they are arguing that PPI deserves greater legal and normative protection than it currently has. As noted above, Nissenbaum refers to this challenge as the problem of protecting privacy in public.

Why should the collection and exchange of PPI raise privacy concerns? Suppose that I discover some information about you: you are a junior at Technical University, you frequently attend your university's football games, and you are actively involved in your university's computer science club. In one sense, the information that I have discovered about you is personal, because it is about *you* (as a person), but it is also public, because it pertains to things that you do in the public sphere. Should you be worried that this information about you is so easily available?

In the past, the public availability of such seemingly harmless and uncontroversial information about you was no cause for concern. Imagine that eighty years ago a citizen petitioned his or her congressperson to draft legislation protecting the privacy of each citizen's movements in public places. It would have been difficult then to make a strong case for such legislation; no one would have seen any need to protect that kind of personal information. But now some are arguing that we need to protect privacy in public, that our earlier assumptions are no longer tenable. Nissenbaum (2004b) believes that many in the commercial sector proceed from an assumption that she believes is "erroneous"—viz., "There is a realm of public information about persons to which no privacy norms apply."[19] Keep this assumption in mind as you consider the following scenario.

▶ **SCENARIO 5–8:** Shopping at SuperMart

One day, you decide to shop for groceries at SuperMart. If I happen to see you enter or leave SuperMart, or if we are both shopping in this store at the same time, I now have information that you shop (or, at least, have once shopped) at SuperMart. (This information could be considered "public" because it was acquired in a public forum and because it is neither intimate nor confidential in nature.) If I also happen to pass by you in one of the aisles at SuperMart, I can observe the contents of your shopping basket; I may notice that you are purchasing several bottles of wine but relatively little food. Again, I have acquired this information about you by observing your activity in a public forum. ▪

Because the information I have acquired about you in the above scenario can be considered public information, it would not warrant any legal privacy protection. And even though this information is about *you as a person*, it is not the kind of personal information to which we, as a society, would typically grant normative privacy protection. What, exactly, is the privacy problem regarding the kind of personal information about your public activities in shopping at SuperMart? Why should you be concerned about information that is gathered about what you do at SuperMart or, for that matter, in any public place? Let us continue the shopping metaphor, but this time we consider shopping that takes place in cyberspace.

▶ **SCENARIO 5–9:** Shopping at Nile.com

Imagine that you visit an online bookstore called *Nile.com* to locate a particular book that you are considering purchasing. Because you are visiting this book store via a computer located in your own home, you cannot be observed by people in physical space nor can you be seen by other customers on the *Nile.com* Web site. However, from the moment you log on to *Nile.com*, information about you is being intentionally gathered and carefully recorded—i.e., information about the exact time that you entered Nile, as well as the exact time that you leave. As you make contact with the Nile Web site, Nile requests a cookie file from your computer to determine whether you have previously visited this site. If you have visited this site before and have clicked on items that interested you, Nile can find a record of these items. The information stored in that cookie file can also be used by Nile to alert you to newly released books that it believes might interest you, based on an analysis of the data Nile collected from your previous visits to its site. ■

The information that Nile now has about you does not seem categorically different from the information that SuperMart might also have about you (assuming that you used that store's "courtesy card" or discount card in making your purchases). However, there are significant differences in the ways that information about you can be gathered, recorded, and then used as a result of your shopping at each store.

When you shopped in physical space at SuperMart, only your actual purchases could be recorded and stored in SuperMart's databases. Items that might have only caught your attention and items that you might also have picked up or even placed in your cart at one point while shopping but did not eventually purchase at the check-out register are not recorded by SuperMart's data collection system. However, as you shop, or even browse, at Nile, there is a record of virtually every move you make—every book that you search, review, etc., as well as the one(s) you purchase. Yet, just like the information gathered about your shopping habits in physical space at SuperMart, this personal information that Nile has gathered about your browsing and shopping habits online is considered and treated as public information.

Now we can see why some people worry about having their movements in cyberspace tracked and recorded. The information Nile gathered about you is, in effect, *Nile's* information, even though it pertains to *you* as a person; Nile now owns that information about you, as well as the information it has about its other customers, and is, in principle at least, free to do with that information whatever it chooses. On the one hand, the information seems fairly innocuous—after all, who really cares which books you happen to browse or purchase? On the other hand, however, this information can be combined with other information about your online transactions at additional Web sites to create a consumer profile of you, which can then be sold to a third party.

One argument that online entrepreneurs might advance to defend these business practices is that if a user puts information about him- or herself into the public domain of the Internet, then that information is no longer private. Of course, one response to this line of reasoning could be to question whether users clearly understand the ways that data they submit might subsequently be used.

In the Nile.com scenario, Nile used information about you in ways that you neither authorized nor intended—an example of the kind of practice that Nissenbaum (2004a) describes as violating "contextual integrity" (see Section 5.2.5). Also, we can question whether businesses, such as Nile, should be able to "own" the information about us that they collect and then do with that information whatever they please for as long as they want? Joseph Fulda (2004) questions whether the old legal rule which states, "Anything put by a person in the public domain can be viewed as public information," should still apply. He admits that such a rule may have served us well, but only before data were "mined" to produce profiles and other kinds of patterns about individuals.[20]

5.7.1 Search Engines and the Disclosure of Personal Information

Internet search engines are valuable for directing us to available online resources for academic research, commerce, recreation, and so forth; so it might be surprising to find that search engine technology, too, can be controversial from the perspective of personal privacy. How can search engine technology conflict with personal privacy? At least two different kinds of concerns affecting privacy arise because of practices involving search engines: (1) search engine companies such as Google record and archive each search request made by users, and (2) search engines enable users to acquire a wealth of personal information about individuals, with relative ease. We begin with a brief examination of (1).

Google and the Controversy Surrounding Records of Users' Searches
Google creates a record of every search made on its site, which it then archives. The topic searched for, as well as the date and time the specific search request is made by a user, are included in the record. These data can be linked to the IP address and the ISP of the user requesting the search. So individual searches made by a particular user could theoretically be analyzed in ways that suggest patterns of that individual's online behavior, and, perhaps more controversially, these records could later be subpoenaed in court cases. Yet many, if not most, Google users were unaware of the company's policy regarding the recording and archiving of users' search requests.

On the one hand, this information might seem relatively innocuous—after all, who would be interested in knowing about the kinds of searches we conduct on the Internet, and who would want to use this information against us? On the other hand, however, consider a student who is writing a research paper on Internet pornography. Records of this user's search requests could reveal several queries that individual made about pornographic Web sites, which in turn might suggest that this student is interested in viewing pornography. In January 2006, Google users discovered that any worries they may have had about the lack of privacy protection concerning their Internet searches were justified.

▶ **SCENARIO 5–10:** Tracking Your Search Requests on Google

In 2005, the Bush administration informed Google that it must turn over a list of all users' queries entered into its search engine during a one-week period (the exact dates were not specified by Google). But Google refused to comply with the subpoena on the grounds that the privacy rights of its users would be violated. Both Yahoo Inc. and Microsoft Corp. MSN, companies that operated the second- and third-most-used search engines, respectively, also had their search records subpoenaed by the Bush administration. Yahoo, unlike Google, complied with the subpoena. It was not clear whether Microsoft also turned over its records to the government, since it declined to say one way or another.[21]   ■

The Bush administration's decision to seek information about the search requests of ordinary users has drawn significant criticism from many privacy advocates. Although the Bush administration claimed that it had the authority to seek electronic information in order to fight the "war on terror" and to prevent another September 11-like attack, the records at issue in this particular case had to do with the number of users requesting information about, or inadvertently being sent to, pornographic Web sites. The Bush administration was interested in gathering data to support its stance on the Child Internet Pornography Act (CIPA), which had been challenged in a U.S. District Court (see Chapter 9). So, many critics were quick to point out that the Bush administration's rationale for obtaining records of search requests made by ordinary citizens seemed politically and ideologically motivated, and had nothing to do with protecting national security.

Using Search Engines to Acquire Information about Persons

It is not only the fact that an individual's search requests are recorded and archived by major companies such as Google that make Internet search engines controversial from the perspective of personal privacy. Search engine-related privacy issues also arise because ordinary individuals can be the subjects of search requests. Consider that search engines can be used to acquire a wealth of personal information about individuals, and with relative ease. In some cases that information resides in public records, many of which are now available to Internet users; in other cases, it resides in commercial databases (such as *docusearch.com*) and is available to Internet users for a small fee. (Recall our discussion in Chapter 1 of how Liam Youens acquired this kind of information in stalking Amy Boyer.)

We have already seen how search engines can be used for malicious purposes such as stalking. In fact, one search facility—Gawker-Stalker (www.gawker.com/stalker)—has been designed specifically for the purpose of stalking famous people, including celebrities. For example, suppose that Matt Damon is spotted ordering a drink at an up-scale café in Boston. The individual who spots Damon can send a "tip" via e-mail to Gawker-Stalker, informing the site's users of Damon's whereabouts. The Gawker site then provides its users, via precise GPS software, with information about exactly where, and at what time, Damon was sighted. Users interested in stalking Damon can then follow his movements electronically, via the Gawker site, or they can locate and follow him in physical space, if they are in the same geographical vicinity as Damon.

But it is not just celebrities who are vulnerable to information about them being acquired by others via search engines. Consider the amount and kind of personal information about ordinary individuals that is now available to search engines. In some cases, that information may have been placed on the Internet inadvertently, without the knowledge and consent of those affected. Yet information about those persons can be located by an Internet user who simply enters their names in a search engine program's entry box. Marie Wright and John Kakalik (2000) note that certain information about individuals that was once difficult to find and even more difficult to cross-reference is now readily accessible and collectible through online automated search facilities.

The fact that one can search the Internet for information about someone does not seem terribly controversial. After all, people regularly place information about themselves on Web sites (or perhaps they authorize someone else to do it for them) and on social networking services such as Facebook and MySpace. Also, one might assume that, by virtue of the fact that this kind of personal information is available to the public, it should be viewed as public information. But should such information about persons be unprotected by privacy norms merely because it is now more easily accessible for viewing by the public?

We have seen how the use of search engines can threaten the privacy of individuals in two distinct ways: (1) by recording and archiving records of a user's search queries that reveal the topic of the search and the time the request was made by the user, and (2) by providing users of search engines with personal information about individuals who may have no idea of the wealth of personal information about them that is available online and have no control over how it is accessed and by whom it is accessed. The latter concern is further complicated by the fact that individuals who are the subject of online searches enjoy no normative protection because of the presumed "public" nature of the personal information about them that is available via online searches. We next consider some controversies that involve access to personal information that resides in public records available online.

5.7.2 Accessing Online Public Records

Another kind of personal information that can also be considered public in nature is information about us stored in records located in municipal buildings, which are accessible to the general public. Public records have generally been available to anyone willing to go to those municipal buildings and request hardcopy versions of them. Some municipalities charge a small fee to retrieve and copy the requested records. Many of these public records can now also be accessed online. Has this changed anything?

Consider that information merchants were always able to physically or manually collect all of the public records they could acquire. But early "information entrepreneurs" without computer technology would have had to hire legions of clerks to collect the (publicly available) data, sort the data according to some scheme, and then compile and print the data for sale. The process would have been physically impractical and hardly profitable, given the labor it involved; it would probably never have occurred to anyone even to attempt it prior to the advent of sophisticated information technology.

We could ask why public records were made public in the first place. Were they made public so that information merchants could profit from them, or were they instituted to serve broader societal and governmental ends? In order for governmental agencies at all levels to operate efficiently, records containing personal information are needed. For example, municipal governments need real estate information for tax assessment purposes, state governments need information about motor vehicle owners and operators, and federal governments need social security and income tax information. Records have to be easily accessible to and transferable and exchangeable between governmental agencies at various levels. Since they contain information that is neither confidential nor intimate, they are, with good reason, public records. It has been assumed that the availability of public records causes no harm to individuals, and that communities are better served because of the access and flow of those records for what seems to be legitimate purposes. But information gathering companies now access those public records, manipulate them to discover patterns useful to businesses, and then sell that information to third parties.

Many information merchants seem to assume that offices responsible for maintaining public records now have a legal obligation to make *all* public records available online. Their presumption is that the government has no right to restrict or limit, in any way, information that has been deemed appropriate for inclusion in public records. Is this a reasonable presumption? Consider two incidents, one involving public records at the city level and the other at the state level, that have caused controversy.

▶ **SCENARIO 5–11:** Accessing Online Public Records in Pleasantville

The city of Pleasantville has recently approved a plan to make all of its public records, including real estate records, available online; with a networked computer, one will be able to enter the address of any house in Pleasantville and retrieve the current tax assessment for the house, the price paid by the most recent owner, and a description of the physical layout of the house, including the location of doors and windows. Many of Pleasantville's citizens soon become outraged when they learn that this information is available over the Internet, even though the same information had previously been available as public records, stored in physical file cabinets at City Hall.[22] ■

Why should the residents of Pleasantville be so concerned? For one thing, some might worry that prospective burglars could plan break-ins by accessing the detailed physical layouts of their homes, which were readily available online. We should note that public records in the form of motor vehicle information have also been made available online, and, as in the Pleasantville scenario involving access to records about one's home, this practice has also outraged many citizens.

▶ **SCENARIO 5–12:** Accessing Online Motor Vehicle Records in the State of Oregon

In the 1990s, Oregon placed the state's motor vehicle records on the Internet. An independent computer consultant used the means available to any private citizen to purchase data from Oregon's Department of Motor Vehicles, which was already available offline to anyone willing to pay a small fee. Once he purchased the information and converted it to electronic format, the consultant set up a Web site where any Internet user could, for a small fee, enter an Oregon license plate number and obtain the name and address of the owner of the registered vehicle. Many of Oregon's residents were outraged when they heard about this practice; eventually, the state's governor intervened and persuaded the consultant to close down the Web site.[23] ■

We ask again, What was the purpose of making such records public in the first place? There is no reason to believe that it was to facilitate commerce in the private sector. Of course, selling information, as the State of Oregon did, is now an important source of revenue for many state governments. But we also need to consider the privacy (and other ethical) implications of states selling information about their residents to online merchants, especially in an era where technology makes it so easy to erode personal privacy. Can technology also provide us with tools to protect our privacy?

▶ 5.8 PRIVACY-ENHANCING TECHNOLOGIES

We have seen how cybertechnology has exacerbated privacy concerns. Ironically, perhaps, cybertechnology also provides tools that can help users to protect their privacy. For example, *privacy-enhancing technologies* or *PETs* have been developed to help users protect (a) their personal identity while navigating the Internet, and (b) the privacy of their online communications (such as e-mail). An example of (b) is encryption tools that encode and decode e-mail messages. We will examine encryption technology in Chapter 6. Here we consider whether PETs actually accomplish (a).

Some PETs enable users to navigate the Internet either anonymously or pseudony-mously; one of the best-known anonymity tools is available from *Anonymizer.com*. It is important to note that although Anonymizer users enjoy anonymity while visiting Web sites, they are not anonymous to *Anonymizer.com* or to their own ISPs. A user's activities on a Web site can be recorded in server log files and can thus be traced back to a specific ISP and IP address. To enjoy complete anonymity on the Internet, online users need tools that do not require them to place their trust in a single "third party" (such as Anonymizer).

Although PETs assist users in navigating the Web with relative anonymity, they are not useful for e-commerce transactions in which users must reveal their actual identities. Many e-commerce sites now provide users with a stated privacy policy that is backed by certified "trustmarks" or trust seals (discussed in more detail in Section 5.9.1). These trust agreements between users and e-commerce sites can also be viewed as PETs in that they are intended to protect a user's privacy during a consumer transaction. But are they adequate to the task? To answer this question, we next analyze PETs in relation to two specific challenges: consumer education and informed consent.[24]

5.8.1 Educating Users about PETs

How are users supposed to find out about PETs? There is currently no requirement for commercial Web sites to inform users about the existence of PETs or to make those tools available to them. Furthermore, online consumers must not only discover that PETs are available, but they must also learn how to use these tools. So at present, responsibility for learning about PETs and how to use them is incumbent upon consumers. Is it reasonable and is it fair to expect users to be responsible for these tasks?

PGP (Pretty Good Privacy), one of the more popular PETs, has been available for some time. The PGP tool PGPcookie.cutter, which is freely available on the Internet, was one of the early tools that enabled users to bypass cookies. Today, most Web browsers allow users to reject cookies, but the default setting on many browsers automatically accepts cookies unless the user explicitly rejects them.

We could reasonably ask why the default setting should not be changed such that Web sites would have to get a user's permission to send a cookie file to that user's computer system. The Web site could inform, and possibly educate, the user about the existence of cookies, and then ask whether he or she is willing to accept them. Why not presume that users do not want cookie information recorded and stored on their computer systems, and then set the default conditions on Web browsers accordingly? And why not further presume that users do not want their personal data used in ways they did not explicitly authorize when they initially disclosed it in a commercial transaction? Following Judith DeCew (1997, 2006), we could "presume in favor of privacy" and then develop ways that would allow individuals to determine for themselves how and when that presumption should be overridden. (This is part of a process that DeCew refers to as "dynamic negotiation.") Independent of questions about where the presumption should reside — that is, in favor of the privacy of individuals or in favor of commercial interests — the widespread application and use of PETs will require a massive educational effort.

5.8.2 PETs and the Principle of Informed Consent

Even if the consumer-education-related issues involving PETs can be resolved, other questions need to be asked. For example, do PETs adequately support users in making *informed* decisions about the disclosure of their personal data in commercial transactions? Traditionally, the principle of informed consent has been the model, or standard, in contexts involving the disclosure of one's personal data. However, users who willingly consent to provide information about themselves for one purpose (e.g., in one transaction) may have no idea how that information can also be used in secondary applications.

Some in the commercial sector argue that because no one is forcing users to reveal personal data, the disclosure of such data is done on a completely voluntary basis. Assume that a user has willingly consented to disclose personal data in an e-commerce transaction. Has the user also consented to having that information used for for additional, "secondary" purposes? Recall our discussion in Section 5.6 about data mining, where we saw that specific information given by a consumer for use in one context could be subsequently "mined."

We can also ask whether businesses that collect personal data could possibly know in advance exactly how those data will be used in secondary and future applications? When data mining technology is involved, for example, it would seem that businesses could *not* adequately inform users about exactly how their personal data might be used in secondary applications. What kind of *informed* choice, then, could users make in these cases? (In Chapter 12, we examine how the principle of informed consent has become nontransparent or "opaque" in cases of genomic research that employ data mining technology.)

Some in the e-commerce sector have responded to critics by pointing out that in most cases users are provided with the means to either "opt-in" or "opt-out" of having their personal data collected, as well as having those data made available for secondary use. But the default is such that if no option is specified by the user when he or she discloses personal data for use in one context, then those disclosed personal data are also available for secondary use. Hence, the policy is "presumed consent," not informed consent. Is that presumption fair to online consumers?

Because PETs provide users with some ways of protecting their identity and also provide them some choice in controlling the flow of their personal information, they would seem to be an empowering rather than a disabling technology. But PETs alone are insufficient for resolving many privacy concerns affecting consumers.

▶ 5.9 PRIVACY LEGISLATION AND INDUSTRY SELF-REGULATION

We saw in the previous section that even though PETs offer users a means to protect their identity in certain kinds of activities, they are not the "magic bullet" many of their staunchest supporters have suggested. Recognizing the limitations of PETs, some privacy advocates believe that stronger privacy laws will protect consumers, whereas others in the commercial sector, for example, believe that additional privacy legislation is neither necessary nor desirable. Instead, they suggest strong industry controls regulated by standards.

Generally, privacy advocates have been either skeptical or suspicious of voluntary controls, including industry standards for "self-regulation initiatives." Instead, they argue for stricter privacy legislation and data protection principles to protect the interests of users. We begin this section with a look at certain self-regulatory schemes for privacy protection that is provided to consumers by industry standards.

5.9.1 Industry Self-regulation Initiatives Regarding Privacy

Many industry advocates for the use of "voluntary controls" to address the privacy concerns of users admit that tools such as PETs might not be adequate to protect the privacy of consumers engaged in e-commerce transactions. However, they also believe that alternatives to privacy legislation are possible. These advocates point to the establishment of industry standards that have already been accepted and implemented. These standards are similar to PETs in the sense that they are intended to protect a user's privacy, but unlike PETs in that they are not themselves tools.

An industry-backed privacy initiative called TRUSTe, which is self-regulatory, ensures that Web sites adhere to the privacy policies they advertise. TRUSTe uses a branded system of "trustmarks" (graphic symbols), which represent a Web site's privacy policy regarding personal information. Trustmarks provide consumers with the assurance that a Web site's privacy practices accurately reflect its stated policies. Through this PET-like feature, users can file a complaint to TRUSTe if the Web site bearing its trust seal does not abide by the stated policies. Any Web site that bears the TRUSTe mark and wishes to retain that seal must satisfy several conditions: The Web site must clearly explain in advance its general information-collecting practices, including which personally identifiable data will be collected, what the information will be used for, and with whom the information will be shared. Also, the Web site must disclose whether the user will be able to correct and update personally identifiable information, and whether the user information will be removed from that Web site's database upon request (Wright and Kakalik 2000). Web sites that bear a trust seal but do not conform to these conditions can have their seal revoked. And Web sites displaying trust seals, such as TRUSTe, are subject to periodic and unannounced audits of their sites.

Critics point out that the practical application of TRUSTe and similar tools may prove difficult. The amount of information users are required to provide may discourage some users from carefully reading and thus adequately understanding what is expected from them. Various warnings these tools display may appear unfriendly and thus work against the ideal of easy Web site access and use; "friendlier" trustmarks or graphic icons might result in users being supplied with less direct information that is important to protecting their privacy. Advocates of tools such as TRUSTe argue that since users will be better able to make informed choices regarding electronic purchasing and other types of online transactions, those users would clearly benefit from programs such as TRUSTe.

Critics worry that such programs do not go far enough. Consider, for example, the case of *Toysmart.com*, an e-commerce site that operated in Massachusetts. Consumers who purchased items from Toysmart were assured, via an online trust seal, that their personal data would be protected. The vendor's policy stated that personal information disclosed to Toysmart would be used internally but would not be sold to or exchanged with external vendors. So, users who dealt with Toysmart expected that their personal data would remain in that company's databases and not be further disclosed or sold to a third party. In the spring of 2000, however, Toysmart was forced to file for bankruptcy.[25]

In the bankruptcy process, Toysmart solicited bids for its assets, which included its databases containing the names of customers. Were the parties interested in purchasing that information under any obligation to adhere to the privacy policy that Toysmart had established with its clients? If not, whoever either took over Toysmart or purchased its databases, would, in principle, be free to do whatever they wished with the personal information in them, despite the fact that such information was given to Toysmart by clients under the belief that information about them would be protected indefinitely.

The Toysmart incident illustrates a situation in which users exercised control over their personal information in one context—that is, in electing whether to disclose information about themselves to Toysmart in online transactions—based on specific conditions stated in Toysmart's privacy policy. However, it also turned out that these individuals were not guaranteed that the personal information they disclosed to Toysmart would be protected in the future. Thus it would seem that controls beyond those provided by trustmarks and e-commerce vendors are needed. Such controls, in the form of policies and laws, would ensure that a zone of privacy is established and enforced to protect individuals against subsequent (unauthorized) uses of the personal information they disclose in online activities.

5.9.2 Privacy Laws and Data Protection Principles

Many nations have passed or are currently in the process of seriously considering strong privacy legislation. The United States, however, has not taken the lead on legislation initiatives; some would argue that the United States is woefully behind the European nations in this regard. In fact, in the United States there is currently very little privacy protection in legal statutes. In 1974, Congress passed the Privacy Act, which has been criticized both for containing far too many loopholes and for lacking adequate provisions for enforcement. It applies only to records in federal agencies and thus is not applicable in the private sector. Subsequent privacy legislation in the United States has resulted mostly in a "patchwork" of individual state and federal laws that are neither systematic nor coherent. (Recall our discussion of the Video Privacy Protection Act, also known as the "Bork Bill," in Chapter 2.) In April 2003, the Health Insurance Portability and Accountability Act (HIPAA), which provides protection for "individually identifiable" medical records from "inappropriate use and disclosure," was enacted into law. (HIPAA is examined in Chapter 12 in connection with our discussion of bioinformatics.) But the kind of privacy protection provided by HIPAA does not apply to an individual's nonmedical/health records such as consumer data.

Another U.S. law that affects individual privacy, and which privacy critics view as a controversial piece of legislation, is the USA Patriot Act. Because this Act has implications for issues that affect computer security and crime, we consider it in more detail in Chapter 7. In this chapter our primary focus on legislation affecting privacy has been concerned with consumer-related privacy issues.

Generally, the United States government has resisted requests from privacy advocates for stronger consumer privacy laws, siding instead with business interests in the private sector who believe that such legislation would undermine economic efficiency and thus adversely impact the overall economy. Critics point out, however, that many of those businesses who have subsidiary companies or separate business operations in countries with strong privacy laws and regulations, such as nations in Western Europe, have found little difficulty in complying with the privacy laws of the host countries; profits for those American-owned companies have not suffered because of their compliance. In any event, there is now increased pressure on the United States government to enact stricter privacy laws and on American businesses to adopt stricter privacy polices and practices because of global e-commerce pressures, especially from Canada and the European Union (EU).

EU nations have, through the implementation of strict data protection principles, been far more aggressive than the United States in addressing privacy concerns of individuals. In 1980, most Western European nations signed on to the Organization for Economic Cooperation and Development (OECD) Principles, and in the early 1990s the European community began to consider synthesizing the data protection laws of the individual European nations.[26] The European Community has since instituted a series of directives, including the EU Directive 95/46/EC of the European Parliament and of the Council of Europe of 24 October 1995, which is referred to as the EU Directive on Data Protection, designed to protect the personal data of its citizens by prohibiting the "transborder flow" of such data to countries that lack adequate protection of personal data.[27]

Dag Elgesem (2004) has pointed out that a central focus of the EU Directive, unlike earlier privacy legislation in Europe that focused simply on the recording and the storage of personal information, is on the *processing* and *flow* of personal data. Several principles make up the European Directive; among them are the principles of Data Quality, Legitimate Purposes, Sensitive Data, and The Right to Be Informed. Whereas the Data Quality Principle is concerned with protecting the data subject's reasonable expectations concerning the processing of data about that subject, the Legitimate Purposes Principle lists the purposes for which the processing of personal data about the data subject are considered legitimate. What helps to ensure that each of these principles is enforced on behalf of data subjects is the presence of privacy protection commissions and boards in the various European nations. As in the case of Canada, which has also set up privacy oversight agencies with a Privacy Commissioner in each of its provinces, many European countries have their own data protection agencies.

Thus far, we have considered various kinds of proposals aimed at addressing privacy concerns. Some have called for stricter privacy laws on the part of governments and for the formation of privacy oversight commissions to enforce those laws. Others call for more serious self-regulatory measures by those in the commercial sector. And some proposals have suggested the need for technological solutions that empower online users by providing them with privacy-enhancing tools. Can these various proposals, or at least relevant aspects of them, be successfully combined or integrated into one comprehensive proposal?

While there has been no uniform consensus on a comprehensive privacy policy, especially one that could be implemented across international borders, there does seem to be considerable agreement on at least one point: any comprehensive privacy policy should be as transparent as possible. In examining James Moor's theory of privacy in Section 5.2.4, we saw that personal privacy could be protected in "situations" or zones that were declared "normatively private." We also saw that Moor requires that the rules for setting up normatively private situations be "public" and open to debate. This point is made explicit in his *Publicity Principle*, which states that the rules and conditions governing private situations should be "clear and known to persons affected by them" (Moor 2000). Thus a critical element in Moor's model for an adequate privacy policy is openness, or transparency, so that all parties in the "situation," or context, are kept abreast of what the rules are at any given point in time. In this sense, Moor's publicity principle would seem to provide a key foundational element in any comprehensive privacy policy that incorporates legislation, self-regulation, and privacy-enhancing tools.

▶ 5.10 CHAPTER SUMMARY

We began by examining some ways that cybertechnology has exacerbated privacy concerns introduced by earlier technologies. We then briefly examined the concept of privacy and some theories that have attempted to explain and justify privacy. We saw that "informational privacy" could be distinguished from "accessibility privacy" and "decisional privacy," and that Moor's privacy theory was able to integrate key components of three traditional theories into one comprehensive theory of privacy. We also saw that privacy is an important value, essential for human ends such as friendship, autonomy, and democracy.

We saw how nonpublic personal information (NPI) is threatened by data gathering and data exchanging techniques, including computerized matching and merging of records. And we also saw how public personal information (PPI) is threatened by data mining technology. We examined some privacy threats posed by the use of RFID technology, Internet cookies, and search engine technology. We also considered whether technology itself, in the form of privacy-enhancing technologies or PETs, could be used to preserve personal privacy or whether stronger privacy legislation and better industry self-regulation are needed.

We also noted at the outset that not all computer-related privacy concerns could be examined in Chapter 5. For example, specific kinds of privacy concerns pertaining to computerized monitoring in the workplace are discussed in Chapter 10, and privacy issues affecting computerized medical and healthcare information are examined in Chapter 12. Also examined in Chapter 12 are surveillance concerns affecting "location privacy" made possible by pervasive computing and global positioning system (GPS) technologies. Although some privacy concerns affecting personal information about individuals collected by governmental organizations were also briefly considered in this chapter, additional privacy issues in this area are examined in Chapter 6 in the context of our discussion of computer security. Our main focus in Chapter 5 has been with privacy and cybertechnology concerns affecting the collection, exchange, and mining of personal data acquired from a typical individual's day-to-day activities, both on- and offline.

▶ REVIEW QUESTIONS

1. Identify and briefly describe four ways in which the privacy threats posed by cybertechnology differ from those posed by earlier technologies.
2. What is personal privacy, and why is privacy difficult to define?
3. Describe some important characteristics that differentiate "accessibility privacy," "decisional privacy," and "informational privacy."
4. How does James Moor's theory of privacy combine key elements of these three views of privacy? What does Moor mean by a "situation," and how does he distinguish between "natural privacy" and "normative privacy"?
5. Why is privacy valued? Is privacy an intrinsic value or is it an instrumental value? Explain.
6. Is privacy a social value, or is it simply an individual good?
7. What does Roger Clarke mean by "dataveillance"? Why do dataveillance techniques threaten personal privacy?
8. What are Internet cookies, and why are they considered controversial from the perspective of personal privacy?
9. What is RFID technology, and why is it a threat to privacy?

10. Explain computerized merging. Why is it controversial from the perspective of personal privacy?

11. Describe the technique known as computerized matching? What problems does it raise for personal privacy?

12. What is data mining, and why is it considered controversial?

13. What is the difference between public personal information (PPI) and nonpublic personal information (NPI)?

14. What is meant by "privacy in public"? Describe the problem of protecting personal privacy in public space.

15. Why are certain aspects and uses of Internet search engines controversial from a privacy perspective?

16. Why does online access to public records pose problems for personal privacy?

17. What are privacy-enhancing technologies (PETs)? How is their effectiveness challenged by concerns related to (user) education and informed consent?

18. Describe some of the voluntary controls and self-regulation initiatives that have been proposed by representatives from industry and e-commerce. Are they adequate solutions?

19. What are some of the criticisms of U.S. privacy laws such as HIPAA and the Privacy Act of 1974?

20. Describe some principles included in the European Union (EU) Directive on Data Protection. What do you believe to be some of the strengths and weaknesses of those principles when compared to privacy laws in America?

► DISCUSSION QUESTIONS

1. Review Helen Nissenbaum's framework of privacy in terms of "contextual integrity." What are the differences between what she calls "norms of appropriateness" and "norms of distribution"? Give an example of how either or both norms can be breached in a specific context.

2. Through the use of currently available online tools and search facilities, ordinary users can easily acquire personal information about others. In fact, anyone who has Internet access can, via a search engine such as Google, find information about us that we ourselves might have had no idea is publicly available there. Does this use of search engines threaten the privacy or ordinary people? Explain.

3. In debates regarding access and control of personal information, it is sometimes argued that an appropriate balance needs to be struck between individuals and organizations: individuals claim that they should be able to control who has access to their information, and organizations, including government and business groups, claim to need that information in order to make appropriate decisions. How can a reasonable resolution be reached that would satisfy both parties?

4. Reexamine the arguments made by the U.S. Government and by Google regarding the government's requests for information about users' search requests made during the summer of 2005. Are the government's reasons for why it should have access to that information reasonable? Does Google have an obligation to protect the personal information of its users, with respect to disclosing information about their searches? Could this obligation be overridden by certain kinds of national defense interests? If, for example, the government claimed to need the information to prevent a potential terrorist attack, would that have changed your analysis of the situation? Or does the government have the right, and possibly an obligation to the majority of its citizens, to monitor the searches if doing so could positively affect the outcome of child pornography legislation?

► ESSAY/PRESENTATION QUESTIONS

1. Initially, privacy concerns involving computer technology arose because citizens feared that a strong centralized government could easily collect and store data about them. In the 1960s, for example, there was talk of constructing a national computerized database in the United States, and many were concerned that George Orwell's prediction of Big Brother in his classic book *1984* had finally arrived. The centralized database, however, never materialized. Prior to September 11, 2001, some privacy advocates suggested that we have fewer reasons to be concerned about the federal government's role in privacy intrusions (Big Brother) than we do about privacy threats from the commercial sector (Big Bucks and Big Browser). Is that assessment still accurate? Defend your answer.

2. Apply Helen Nissenbaum's framework of "privacy as contextual integrity" (examined in Section 5.2.5) to personal blogs that contain online personal diaries, such as the "Washingtonienne" (involving Jessica Cutler) scenario that we briefly described in Chapter 1. (At this point, you may want to revisit Scenario 1–1 in Chapter 1.) An important question that we were unable to analyze in our earlier analysis of that case was whether Cutler's privacy had been violated. Using Nissenbaum's framework, however, we can further refine our initial question by asking whether the incident violated the integrity of the norms of appropriateness or the norms of distribution, or both, in that context. Consider that, when Cutler set up her blog, she did not bother to protect it with a password. Is that point relevant in your assessment? Because the information included in her blog could, in principle, be read by anyone on the Internet, could Cutler plausibly claim that her privacy had been violated when her online diary was discovered and then posted in *Wonkette*, the Washington DC online gossip column? Also consider the six men implicated in her blog? Was it appropriate for her to include that information in her online diary? Did the distribution of information about them via Cutler's diary violate their privacy? Explain.

3. In the days and weeks immediately following the tragic events of September 11, 2001, some political leaders claimed that extraordinary times call for extraordinary measures; in times of war, basic civil liberties and freedoms, such as privacy, need to be severely restricted for the sake of national security and safety. Perhaps, as a nation, the value that we have traditionally attached to privacy has diminished significantly since then. Initially, the majority of American citizens strongly supported the Patriot Act, which passed by an overwhelming margin in both houses of Congress and was enacted into law on October 21, 2001. However, between 2001 and 2005 support for this act diminished considerably. Many privacy advocates believe that it goes too far and thus erodes basic civil liberties. Some critics also fear that certain provisions included in the act could easily be abused. Examine some of the details of the Patriot Act (which can be viewed on the Web), and determine whether its measures are as extreme as its critics suggest. Are those measures consistent with the value of privacy, which Americans claim to embrace? Do privacy interests need to be reassessed, and possibly recalibrated, in light of ongoing threats from terrorists?

4. We suggested at the beginning of this chapter that concerns about the loss of privacy may have a generational dimension or element—i.e., younger people may be less concerned about privacy loss involving cybertechnology than older people. To further explore this possibility, conduct a series of informal interviews with individuals that represent three generations: Millennials, Gen X/Y, and Baby Boomers. Ask members of each group how much they value their privacy and how much of it they are willing to trade off for the convenience of cybertechnology. Compare the results of the answers you get from the three groups. Are their respective views about the importance of privacy as far apart as some might expect? Explain.

► ENDNOTES

1. See the interview with Arthur Miller in the video "The World at Your Fingertips" in the BBC/PBS Series, *The Machine That Changed the World*, 1990.
2. See Warren and Brandeis (1890).
3. See DeCew (1997) for a fuller account of accessibility privacy.
4. For a discussion of the right to privacy in the Quinlan case, see "Court at the End of Life – The Right to Privacy: Karen Ann Quinlan" at http://www.libraryindex.com/pages/582/Court-End-Life-RIGHT-PRIVACY-KAREN-ANN-QUINLAN.html.
5. Moor (2000), p. 207.
6. Nissenbaum (2004a), p. 137.
7. Ibid., p. 135.
8. DeCew (2006), p. 121. Moor (2006, p.114) also describes privacy as a kind of "shield" that protects us.
9. See Clarke's account of dataveillance. Available at http://www.rogerclarke.com/DV/ (accessed April 5, 2009).
10. Nissenbaum (2004a), p. 135.
11. Mason (2007, p. 42) makes a similar point when he notes that "I may authorize one institution to collect 'A' about me, and another institution to collect 'B' about me: but I might not want anyone to possess 'A and B' about me at the same time."
12. See, for example, Scott Chapman and Gurpreet S. Dhillon (2002). "Privacy and the Internet: The Case of DoubleClick, Inc." In G. Dhillon, ed. *Social Information in the Information Age: issues and Controversies*. Hershey PA: Idea Group, pp. 75–88.
13. My discussion of computerized matching here draws from Tavani (1996).

14. For more information about this incident, see Brey (2004).
15. This scenario is adapted from Tavani (1999).
16. See "Web Mining," *Wikipedia.* Available at http://en.wikipedia.org/wiki/Web_mining (accessed May 18, 2009).
17. See http://en.wikipedia.org/wiki/Facebook (accessed May 18, 2009).
18. Ibid.
19. Nissenbaum (2004b), p. 455.
20. Fulda (2004), p. 472.
21. See, for example, Antone Gonsalves (2006). "Yahoo, MSN, AOL Gave Search Data To Bush Administration Lawyers." *Information Week*, January 19. Available at http://www.informationweek.com/news/security/government/showArticle. jhtml?articleID=177102061 (accessed August 10, 2008).
22. This scenario is based in part on a real controversy involving online public records in Merrimack NH.
23. See Scanlan (2001) for a more detailed account of this scenario.
24. My analysis of PETs in this section draws from Tavani (2000).
25. For more information about this scenario, see Nicholas Morehead (2000). "Toysmart: Bankruptcy Litmus Test." *Wired* 7, no. 12. Available at http://www.wired.com/techbiz/media/news/2000/07/37517 (accessed August 11, 2008).
26. See http://www.oecd.org/document/18/0,3343,en_2649_34255_1815186_1_1_1_1,00.html.
27. See http://www.cdt.org/privacy/eudirective/EU_Directive_.html.

▶ REFERENCES

Adam, Alison. 2005. "Chips in Our Children: Can We Inscribe Privacy in a Machine?" *Ethics and Information Technology* 7, no. 4: 233–42.

Brey, Philip. 2004. "Ethical Aspects of Facial Recognition Systems in Public Places." In R. A. Spinello and H. T. Tavani, eds. *Readings in Cyberethics.* 2nd ed. Sudbury MA: Jones and Bartlett, pp. 585–600.

DeCew, Judith W. 1997. *In Pursuit of Privacy: Law, Ethics, and the Rise of Technology.* Ithaca NY: Cornell University Press.

DeCew, Judith W. 2006. "Privacy and Policy for Genetic Research." In H. T. Tavani, ed. *Ethics, Computing, and Genomics.* Sudbury MA: Jones and Bartlett, pp. 121–35.

Elgesem, Dag. 2004. "The Structure of Rights in Directive 95/46/EC on the Protection of Individuals with Regard to the Processing of Personal Data and the Free Movement of Such Data." In R. A. Spinello and H. T. Tavani. eds. *Readings in CyberEthics.* 2nd ed. Sudbury MA: Jones and Bartlett Publishers, pp. 418–35.

Fried, Charles. 1990. "Privacy: A Rational Context." In M. D. Ermann, M. B. Williams, and C. Gutierrez, eds. *Computers, Ethics, and Society.* New York: Oxford University Press, pp. 51–67.

Froomkin, Michael. 2000. "The Death of Privacy?" *Stanford Law Review* 52. Available at www.law.miami.edu/~froomkin/ articles/privacy-deathof.pdf.

Fulda, Joseph S. 2004. "Data Mining and Privacy." In R. A. Spinello and H. Tavani, eds. *Readings in CyberEthics.* 2nd ed. Sudbury MA: Jones and Bartlett Publishers, pp. 471–75.

Garfinkel, Simson. 2000. *Database Nation: The Death of Privacy in the 21st Century.* Cambridge MA: O'Reilly and Associates.

Garfinkel, Simson. 2002. "RFID Bill of Rights." *Technology Review*, October. Available online at www.technologyreview.com/ articles/02/10/garfinkel1002.asp. (accessed August 10, 2008).

Garfinkel, Simson. 2004. "RFID Rights." *Technology Review*, November. Available online at http://www.technologyreview. com/Infotech/13902/?a=f (accessed August 10, 2008).

Grodzinsky, Frances S., and Herman T. Tavani. 2008. "Online File Sharing: Resolving the Tensions between Privacy and Property Interests." *Computers and Society* 38, no. 4: 28–39.

Kusserow, Richard P. 1995. "The Government Needs Computer Matching to Root Out Waste and Fraud." In D. G. Johnson and H. Nissenbaum, eds. *Computers, Ethics, and Social Values.* Englewood Cliffs NJ: Prentice Hall, pp. 299–304.

Lockton Vance, and Richard S. Rosenberg. 2005. "RFID: The Next Serious Threat to Privacy." *Ethics and Information Technology* 7, no. 4: 221–31.

Mason, Richard O. 2007. "Four Ethical Issues of the Information Age." In J. Weckert, ed. *Computer Ethics.* Aldershot UK: Ashgate, pp. 31–40. Reprinted from *MIS Quarterly* 10: 5–12.

Moor, James H. 2000. "Towards a Theory of Privacy for the Information Age." In R. M. Baird, R. Ramsower, and S. E. Rosenbaum, eds. *Cyberethics: Moral, Social, and Legal Issues in the Computer Age.* Amherst NY: Prometheus Books, pp. 200–12.

Moor, James H. 2004. "Reason, Relativity, and Responsibility in Computer Ethics." In R. A. Spinello and H. T. Tavani, eds. *Readings in CyberEthics.* 2nd ed. Sudbury MA: Jones and Bartlett Publishers, pp. 40–54.

Moor, James H. 2006. "Using Genetic Information While Protecting the Privacy of the Soul." In H. T. Tavani, ed. *Ethics, Computing, and Genomics*. Sudbury MA: Jones and Bartlett, pp. 109–19.

Nissenbaum, Helen. 2004a. "Privacy as Contextual Integrity." *Washington Law Review* 79, no. 1: 119–57.

Nissenbaum, Helen. 2004b. "Toward an Approach to Privacy in Public: Challenges of Information Technology." In R. A. Spinello and H. T. Tavani, eds. *Readings in CyberEthics*. 2nd ed. Sudbury MA: Jones and Bartlett, pp. 450–61. Reprinted from *Ethics and Behavior* 7, no. 3 (1997): 207–19.

Regan, Priscilla M. 1995. *Legislating Privacy: Technology, Social Values, and Public Policy*. Chapel Hill NC: The University of North Carolina Press.

Scanlan, Michael. 2001. "Informational Privacy and Moral Values." *Ethics and Information Technology* 3, no. 1: 3–12.

Shattuck, John. 1995. "Computer Matching is a Serious Threat to Individual Rights." In D. G. Johnson and H. Nissenbaum, eds. *Computers, Ethics and Social Values*. Englewood Cliffs NJ: Prentice Hall, pp. 310–14.

Stuckey, Mike. 2008. "Amex Rates Credit Risk by Where You Live, Shop." *MSNBC.Com*. Available at http://www.msnbc.msn.com/id/27055285/ (accessed May 18, 2009).

Tavani, Herman T. 1996. "Computer Matching and Personal Privacy: Can They Be Compatible?" In C. Huff, ed. *Proceedings of the Symposium on Computers and the Quality of Life*. New York: ACM Press, pp. 97–101.

Tavani, Herman T. 1999. "Informational Privacy, Data Mining and the Internet." *Ethics and Information Technology* 1, no. 2: 137–45.

Tavani, Herman T. 2000. "Privacy-Enhancing Technologies as a Panacea for Online Privacy Concerns: Some Ethical Considerations" *Journal of Information Ethics* 9, no. 2: 26–36.

Tavani Herman T., and James H. Moor. 2001. "Privacy Protection, Control Over Information, and Privacy-Enhancing Technologies." *Computers and Society* 31, no. 1: 6–11.

Warren, Samuel, and Louis Brandeis. 1890. "The Right to Privacy." *Harvard Law Review* 4, no. 5: 193–220.

Westin, Alan F. 1967. *Privacy and Freedom*. New York: Atheneum Press.

Wright, Marie, and John Kakalik. 2000. "The Erosion of Privacy." In R. M. Baird, R. Ramsower, and S. E. Rosenbaum, eds. *Cyberethics: Moral, Social, and Legal Issues in the Computer Age*. Amherst NY: Prometheus Books, pp. 162–70.

▶ FURTHER READINGS

Alfino, Mark. "Misplacing Privacy." *Journal of Information Ethics* 10, no. 1 (2001): 5–8.

Cavoukian, Anne. "Tag, You're It: Privacy Implications of Radio Frequency Identification Technology." February 2004. Available at http://www.ipc.on.ca/docs/rfid.pdf.

Dubbeld, Lynsey. "Limits on Surveillance: Frictions, Fragilities and Failures in the Operation of Camera Surveillance." *Journal of Information, Communication and Ethics in Society* 2, no. 1 (2004): 9–19.

Mizutani, Masahiko, James Dorsey, and James H. Moor. "The Internet and Japanese Conception of Privacy." *Ethics and Information Technology* 6, no. 2 (2004): 121–28.

Rosen, Jeffrey. *The Unwanted Gaze: The Destruction of Privacy in America*. New York: Random House, 2000.

Solove, Daniel J. *The Digital Person: Technology and Privacy in the Information Age*. New York: New York University Press, 2004.

Yao-Hua, Lü. "Privacy and Data Privacy Issues in Contemporary China." *Ethics and Information Technology* 7, no. 1 (2005): 7–15.

Zimmer, Michael. "Surveillance, Privacy, and the Ethics of Vehicle Safety Communication Technologies." *Ethics and Information Technology* 7, no. 4 (2005): 201–10.

6

Security in Cyberspace

Can computer break-ins ever be justified on ethical grounds? This is one of many cybersecurity issues that we will examine in Chapter 6. Other questions include

- What is cybersecurity, and how are security issues involving computers and cybertechnology different from privacy issues in cyberspace?

- How are violations involving cybersecurity similar to and different from issues of cybercrime?

- Which key features differentiate data security, system security, and network security?

- What is meant by "hacking" and the "hacker ethic"?

- Can certain kinds of "hacktivism" be viewed as acts of "electronic civil disobedience"?

- What is the difference between cyberterrorism and information warfare?

- Is total security in cyberspace a reasonable expectation and goal?

- How can risk analysis models help us achieve greater security in cyberspace?

You may recall that we briefly discussed the concept of risk analysis in Chapter 4, in connection with issues affecting professional ethics and professional responsibility. In the final section of this chapter, our analysis of risk centers on the evaluation of models that can make cyberspace more secure. We begin our analysis of security issues in cyberspace with a brief discussion of some basic concepts and definitions.

▶ 6.1 SECURITY IN THE CONTEXT OF CYBERTECHNOLOGY

What, exactly, do we mean by "computer security" and "cybersecurity"? Like privacy, *security*—especially, in the context of computing and cybertechnology—has no universally agreed-upon definition. The expressions *computer security* and *cybersecurity* are often associated with issues having to do with "reliability," "availability," "safety," "integrity," "confidentiality," and "privacy" of data and computer databases. Richard Epstein (2007) believes that security concerns affecting computers and cybertechnology can be viewed in terms of three key elements, which he also notes are sometimes referred to as the "big three" issues:

- confidentiality,
- integrity,
- accessibility.

Whereas confidentiality is "about preventing unauthorized persons from gaining access to unauthorized information," integrity, in computer security contexts, is about "preventing an attacker from modifying data." In Epstein's scheme, accessibility has to do with "making sure that resources are available for authorized users."[1]

Are any additional elements or criteria useful for understanding cybersecurity? Peter Neumann (2004) notes that, in addition to providing desired confidentiality, integrity, and accessibility, cybersecurity aims at preventing "misuse, accidents, and malfunctions" with respect to computer systems. Neumann also notes, however, that cybersecurity can be a "double-edged sword"; for example, it can be used to protect privacy, but it can also be used to undermine "freedom of access" to information for users.[2]

In defining cybersecurity, it is important to point out that sometimes issues involving security in cyberspace overlap with concerns pertaining to cybercrime; other times they intersect with issues involving privacy. We briefly examine some ways in which security issues intersect and overlap with both kinds of concerns, also noting how security concerns can be distinguished from those of privacy and crime.

6.1.1 Cybersecurity as Related to Cybercrime

How are cybersecurity violations both similar to and different from cybercrime? Virtually every security violation involving cybertechnology is criminal, but not every crime in cyberspace necessarily involves a breach, or violation, of cybersecurity. Consider three cyber-related crimes that have no direct implications for cybersecurity: a pedophile can use a computer to solicit sex with young children, a drug dealer can use the Internet to traffic in drugs, and a college student can use a computer network to download copyrighted music.

Although each of these activities is clearly illegal, it is not clear that any of them necessarily result from insecure computers. Perhaps greater security mechanisms on computer networks could deter crimes and detect criminals in cyberspace, but cyber-related crimes involving pedophilia, drug trafficking, and downloading music do not typically result from security flaws in computer system design, nor do these crimes occur because of computer systems that are undependable.

There are, then, important distinctions between issues of security and crime involving cybertechnology. We will discuss cybercrime in Chapter 7, and focus our attention in this chapter on actual and potential threats to security in cyberspace.

Just as cybersecurity overlaps with cybercrime, security concerns involving cyber-technology also intersect with worries about personal privacy. We discussed some of these privacy-related concerns in our discussion of confidentiality and data integrity in Chapter 5. Now we ask: How are issues pertaining to security in cyberspace different from those involving privacy?

6.1.2 Security and Privacy: Some Similarities and Some Differences

The concepts of privacy and security are not always easy to separate, especially when civil liberties and basic human rights are discussed. In the United States, arguments for a right to privacy that appeal to the Fourth Amendment have often been made on the basis of *securing* the person (and the person's papers, and so forth) from the physical intrusion of searches and seizures. Paul Thompson (2001) believes that many of our claims involving a right to privacy are grounded in the notion of security and can be better understood as arguments concerning a "right to being secure."

Although cyber-related issues involving privacy and security often overlap, some important distinctions are nonetheless worth drawing. Cyber-related privacy concerns often arise because people fear losing control over personal information that can be accessed by organizations (especially businesses and government agencies), many of whom claim to have some *legitimate* need for that information in order to make important decisions. Security concerns, on the contrary, typically arise because people worry that personal data or proprietary information, or both, could be retrieved and possibly altered, by unauthorized individuals and organizations.

Privacy and security concerns can be thought of as two sides of a single coin: People need personal privacy and they wish to control who has information about them as well as how that information is accessed by others. Making sure that personal information stored in computer databases is secure is important in helping them achieve and maintain their privacy. In this sense, then, the objectives would seem compatible with, and even complementary to, security. In another sense, however, there is a certain tension between privacy and security. From the perspective of security, the protection of system resources and proprietary data is generally considered more critical, whereas from the vantage point of privacy, the protection of personal information and personal autonomy will receive a higher priority.

Privacy concerns tend to focus on protecting personal data from unauthorized access, abuse, and alteration, reflecting values that preserve individual autonomy and individual respect for persons. And while anonymity tools (discussed in Section 6.6.4) help to protect the privacy of individuals navigating in cyberspace, those tools also cause serious concerns for security because anonymous behavior makes it difficult to identify security violators. So, in some cases, there is a natural tension between security and privacy; at other times, however, the objectives and goals of privacy and security—for example, with respect to confidentiality and data integrity—are the same.[3]

▶ 6.2 THREE CATEGORIES OF CYBERSECURITY

Security issues involving cybertechnology span a range of concerns having to do with three distinct kinds of vulnerabilities:

    I. unauthorized access to *data*, which either are resident in or exchanged between computer systems;

    II. attacks on *system resources* (such as computer hardware, operating system software, and application software) by malicious computer programs;

    III. attacks on *computer networks*, including the infrastructure of privately owned networks and the Internet itself.[4]

We refer to the first of these three categories of security concerns as "data security." The second category of concerns can be described under the heading "system security," and the third can be understood as "network security."

We briefly describe some concerns associated with each category of security.

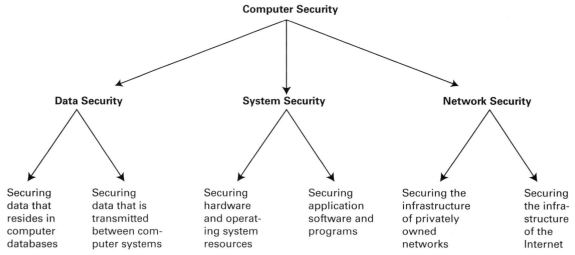

Figure 6-1 Three kinds of computer security.

6.2.1 *Data Security:* **Confidentiality, Integrity, and Availability of Information**

Data security is concerned with vulnerabilities pertaining to unauthorized access to data. Those data can either (a) reside in one or more computer storage devices, or (b) be exchanged between two or more computer systems, or both. In particular, data security issues affect the confidentiality, integrity, and availability of information. Richard Spinello (2000) aptly describes what is required for data security when he points out that

> . . . proprietary or sensitive information under one's custodial care is kept confidential and secure, that information being transmitted is not altered in form or content and cannot be read by unauthorized parties, and that *all* information being disseminated or otherwise made accessible through Web sites and online data repositories is as accurate and reliable as possible.[5] [Italics Spinello]

Three points in this description are worth highlighting. First, the information to be protected can be either *proprietary* or *sensitive*, or both. (Proprietary information, as we will see in Chapter 8, is legally protected by schemes such as copyrights and patents and thus can be "owned" by corporations or by individuals, while sensitive information is generally considered to be intimate or confidential because it includes personal, medical, and financial records.)

Second, the information must be secured not only from tampering and alteration by unauthorized parties, but also from merely being accessed (and read) by those parties. Third, and finally, the stored information must be accurate, readily available, and accessible to authorized parties. So not only must the information residing in a computer database or in a password-protected Web site be available at optimal times, it must be able to be accessed by authorized users at any time—i.e., accessible "on demand."

6.2.2 *System Security:* **Viruses, Worms, and Malware**

System security is concerned with vulnerabilities to system resources such as computer hardware, operating system software, and application software. As such, it is concerned with various kinds of viruses, worms, and related "malicious programs" that can disrupt and sometimes destroy computer systems. What are the differences between computer viruses and worms? According to Ed Skoudis (2004), a virus is a self-replicating piece of software code that "attaches itself to other programs and usually requires human action to propagate." He defines a worm in contrast as a self-replicating piece of code that "spreads via networks and usually doesn't require human interaction to propagate." Michael Simpson (2006) points out that worms replicate and propagate without needing a host or program.

Some security analysts differentiate further between the two types of disruptive programs by pointing out that a worm is less virulent than a virus. However, worms can spread more quickly than viruses, because worms, unlike viruses, do not need any human action to trigger them. We already noted that viruses cannot run on their own and are often activated when an unsuspecting user opens an e-mail attachment. Worms, on the contrary, can move from machine to machine across networks and can have parts of themselves running on different machines. Consider some effects of two notorious worms: *Code Red* and *Conficker*.

▶ **SCENARIO 6-1:** The Code Red Worm

In the summer of 2001, Internet users were warned about an impending attack by a malicious program called the *Code Red Worm*, which took advantage of a flaw in Microsoft's NT operating system. The worm was designed to infect systems during the first eighteen days of a given month and then activate on the nineteenth day, at which time the "infected computers" would target additional computers. The worm would then sit dormant in the newly infected computers until the first day of the next month, when the reactivated worm would spread further by infecting more systems. Code Red infected an estimated 395,000 servers in less than 14 hours.[6] ■

▶ **SCENARIO 6-2:** The Conficker Worm

In early 2009, the Conficker Worm—also referred to as Kido, Downup, and Downadup—gained international attention, as many braced for an attack on April 1 of that year. The worm spread quickly via a "buffer overflow" vulnerability in the Microsoft Windows operating system. Later versions of Conficker also spread through network file systems and USB drives. George Lawton (2009) notes that the worm turned the computers it infected into "a botnet capable of launching mass attacks" and that in a four-day period in early January 2009, the number of "individual infections grew from 2.4 million to 8.9 million." Among the international organizations affected by Conficker were the German armed forces and the U.K. Ministry of Defense.[7] ■

Some worms and viruses have become well known, not only in the computer community but in the popular media as well. For example, you may have heard of the ILOVEYOU virus (also known as the "Love Bug") that wreaked havoc for computer users around the world in 2000. Other "classic" viruses and worms have had names such as "Michaelangelo," "Melissa," "Slammer," and "Blaster." If the distinction between viruses and worms were not confusing enough, some analysts suggest that we further differentiate disruptive programs to include Trojan horses and logic bombs. A *Trojan horse* often appears to be a benign program, but it can do significant system damage behind the scenes. *Logic bombs*, on the contrary, check for certain conditions or states in a computer system and then execute when one of those conditions arises. Some now refer collectively to these various kinds of "malicious programs," including viruses and worms, under the single heading "malware." According to Simpson (2006), malware can take many forms and can also include "spyware."

The effects of malware can range from minor annoyances with individual computer systems, to preventing an entire organization from operating, to shutting down computer networks, to disrupting major segments of the Internet.

6.2.3 *Network Security:* **Protecting our Infrastructure**

A third category of computer security, which we call *network security*, is concerned with securing computer networks—i.e., from large, privately owned computer networks (such as WANs) to the Internet itself—against various kinds of attacks. The Internet's infrastructure, which includes the set of protocols that makes communication across the individual computer networks possible, has been the victim of several attacks. These attacks have ranged from programs launched by individuals with malicious intentions to individuals who claimed their intentions were benign. In many cases, these attacks have severely disrupted activities on segments of the Internet. In a few cases, they have also rendered the Internet virtually inoperable.

In 1988, many ordinary users (and perhaps even some security experts as well) realized for the first time just how vulnerable the Internet was to these kinds of attacks when Robert Morris unleashed a program, later described as the "Internet worm," that disabled much of the Internet.[8] Several Internet disruptions caused by various kinds of malware have since followed. We should note that it is not always easy to determine whether a major computer network disruption is the result of the work of malicious individuals who launch various kinds of malware or is due to the failure of some aspect of the network infrastructure itself. For example, a significant power outage experienced by the AT&T long distance telephone service in 1990 was attributed to a software glitch in the system's programming code that caused the network to crash. However, as we will see in our discussion of cyberterrorism in Section 6.4, some have questioned the official explanation given by AT&T.

Because most nations depend on a secure cyberspace for their national infrastructure, including power grids, there is now increased concern over threats from international hacking groups, including governments and state-sponsored organizations. The following scenario illustrates how vulnerable our national infrastructure may be to attacks by foreign governments.

▶ **SCENARIO 6–3:** The GhostNet Controversy

In March 2009, The Information Warfare Monitor (IWM), a Canadian organization that monitors cyberespionage, discovered a network of at least 1,295 compromised computers in 103 countries. Approximately 30% of these were considered "high-value" targets, which (according to the IWM Report) included ministries of foreign affairs, embassies, international organizations, news media, and nongovernmental organizations (NGOs). The computer systems were compromised in ways that suggested China was responsible, but the IWM report refused to identify any one nation. The circumstantial evidence implicating China was tied to the fact that IWM's investigation was launched in response to a request by the Dali Lama, the exiled leader of Tibet (and long-time enemy of the Chinese government), who reported that his computer network had been hacked. (The IWM report referred to the cyberespionage system as "GhostNet" because it resembled the ghOst RAT trojan horse malware that was traced back to Hainan, China.) The IWM report concluded that regardless of which country or countries were responsible for the cyberespionage, the discovery of these activities should serve as a warning to policy makers that network security requires serious attention.[9] ∎

In one sense, this scenario might initially seem to be more concerned with information warfare, which we discuss in Section 6.5, than with network security. However, the GhostNet controversy has also raised concerns about the vulnerability of a nation's network-based infrastructure, including its power grids. We will return to the GhostNet controversy later in this chapter in our discussion of information warfare.

Thus far, we have differentiated three distinct kinds of security concerns, and we have briefly described various kinds of malicious programs. We have also differentiated security issues from concerns involving crime and privacy in cyberspace. However, we have said very little—at least directly—about ethical aspects of computer security.

▶ 6.3 ETHICAL ASPECTS OF CYBERSECURITY

An important objective of this chapter is to determine what ethically is at stake with respect to computer security. In previous chapters we saw that ethical concerns arise because of issues having to do with autonomy, respect, fairness, and so forth. So, how do ethical concerns arise in the context of cybersecurity? To be autonomous, individuals need to have some control over how information about them is gathered and used. Having secure computers means that users can have greater control over the information about them that is stored electronically; it also helps to ensure that this information is kept confidential.

However, there is also another side to questions surrounding ethics and security. In the preceding section, we saw that in cyberspace, some individuals have not only caused minor nuisances but have also disrupted major networks, resulting in severe financial loss and significant physical damage. These activities are facilitated in part by anonymity tools that enable users to navigate the Web without having to reveal their true identities. While these tools might help to protect an individual's privacy, they also pose a risk for cybersecurity. So, some proponents of stronger security argue that individual freedom and autonomy may have to yield to public safety and security.

6.3.1 Hacking and the "Hacker Ethic"

Individuals who have launched malicious programs of various kinds, which we collectively refer to as malware, have commonly been described in the media as computer *hackers*. Who are hackers, and what is hacking in the context of computers and cybertechnology? According to Simpson (2006), a hacker is anyone who "accesses a computer system or network without authorization from the owner." He defines "crackers," on the contrary, as hackers who break into a computer system with "the intention of doing harm or destroying data." Note that we will further examine the concept of hacking as well as the profile of a "typical" computer criminal in our discussion of cybercrime in Chapter 7, where we discuss hacking as it relates to crime and criminal behavior. In this chapter, we examine hacking and the notion of a "hacker ethic" as it relates to cybersecurity.

Many in the computer science community are unhappy with how the word "hacker," which now has a derogatory connotation, is used in the conventional media. Kaufman, Perlman, and Speciner (2002), for example, describe "true computer hackers" in a very different way—i.e., as individuals who play with computers for the "pure intellectual challenge" and as "master programmers, incorruptibly honest, unmotivated by money, and careful not to harm anyone." They go on to note that people identified in the media as hackers tend to be malicious individuals who are neither brilliant nor accomplished; furthermore, Kaufman, Perlman, and Speciner claim that these individuals who call themselves hackers have stolen a "beautiful word" that had been used to describe "some remarkable and wonderful people." The authors also note that "early hackers" have been described as individuals who aimed at accessing computer systems to see how they worked, not to cause any harm to those systems.

In this chapter, we use "hacker" in the sense of the term often attributed to early computer enthusiasts. In documenting early computer hackers, many of whom were associated with "the MIT culture," some authors have used the expressions "hacker ethic" and "hacker code of ethics." Steven Levy (2001) suggests that a strong and distinctive code of ethics, in which freedom and elegance are primary values, could be found in the hacker community. Levy describes the hacker code as "a philosophy, an ethic, and a dream," based on the following principles:

I. Access to computers should be unlimited and total.

II. All information should be free.

III. Mistrust authority–promote decentralization.

IV. Hackers should be judged by their hacking (not by bogus criteria such as degrees, age, race, or position).

V. You can create art and beauty on a computer.

VI. Computers can change your life for the better.[10]

Perhaps what Levy really describes is not so much a code of ethics but rather a code for the way that hackers approach their craft, that is, in terms of a certain *ethic*, as in "work ethic." Pekka Himanen (2001) has described the hacker ethic as a "new work ethic," which he contrasts with the classic "Protestant work ethic" (coined originally by Max Weber in his classic work *The Protestant Ethic and the Spirit of Capitalism*). In addition to an ethic, hackers also seem to have a distinct "ethos"—that is, they have a distinct way of looking at the world, especially the world of computers.

Many hackers believe that computer systems are inherently flawed and thus need to be improved. As a result, some hackers believe that they need total access to all computer systems in order to take them apart, see how they work, and make the needed improvements. Not surprisingly, then, hackers want to remove any barriers to free access to computers. Many hackers have embraced, either explicitly or implicitly, the following three principles:

1. Information should be free.

2. Hackers provide society with a useful and important service.

3. Activities in cyberspace are virtual in nature and thus do not harm real people in the real (physical) world.

We briefly consider each principle.

Information Should Be Free

Should information be totally free? If so, on what grounds can this claim be justified? The expression "Information wants to be free" has become a mantra for many hackers who see proprietary software and systems as obstacles to realizing the freedom of the Internet, where users would otherwise have total access to information. The debate over whether information should be free, or even to what extent information should be freely accessible to Internet users, is a complicated one. As we shall see in Chapter 8, this debate is rooted in complex property laws and policies that have been disputed in the courts, resulting in Supreme Court decisions. So we will postpone our fuller discussion of this particular point raised by hackers until our analysis of intellectual property in cyberspace. However, a few brief comments need to be made at this point.

Some critics regard the view that information should be free as idealistic or romantic. According to Eugene Spafford (2007), it is also a very naïve view. He points out that if information were free, privacy would not be possible because individuals could not control how information about them was collected and used. Also, it would not be possible to ensure integrity and accuracy of that information, since information that was freely available could always be modified and changed by anyone who happened to access it. So from the points of view of privacy and confidentiality, a world in which all information was literally and completely free would not be desirable. Thus, there would seem to be good reasons for not embracing the principle that information should be free.

Hackers might object, however, by pointing out that they do not claim that all information should be free because they recognize that some information should be kept private. Hence they would argue for a position along the following lines: keep private any information that should be private, and keep free any information that should be free. They recognize that there is much information that should be kept private but is not, and there is much information that should be publicly available but is not.[11]

Hackers Provide Society with an Important Service

Does the second hacker principle fare any better? Many are suspicious of claims that hackers perform a useful service for society by searching for and exposing security holes in cyberspace. According to this rationale, hackers are doing us a favor, because pointing out these security holes will force those responsible for the holes to fix them.

Spafford has produced a series of counterexamples to this version of the hacker argument, and he uses an analogy to counter the hacker's position that exposing security vulnerabilities is doing the computer user community a favor. Spafford asks whether we would permit someone to start a fire in a crowded shopping mall in order to expose the fact that the mall's sprinkler system was not adequate. Similarly, we could also ask whether you would be willing to thank a burglar, who in the process of burglarizing your house, was able to show that your home security system was inadequate. If you would not, then why, Spafford would ask, should we thank hackers for showing us that our computers are insecure? We return to Spafford's argument below in Section 6.3.2.

However, we will see how some nonmalicious hackers have discovered holes in security systems that have also revealed questionable, and possibly illegal, behavior on the part of content providers in cyberspace. For example, a type of hacking activity led to a discovery of a security flaw in a Digital Rights Management (DRM) system (described in Chapter 9) used by Sony BGM. This discovery also revealed that Sony was able to control the computers of customers running its music CDs and to spy on these customers.

So, one might make a utilitarian argument that computer users are better served if such abuses are discovered by nonmalicious hackers.

Hacking Causes Only Virtual Harm, Not Real Harm

According to third principle we identified, unauthorized access in cyberspace causes no real harm because those activities occur only in the *virtual* world. This argument commits a logical fallacy in that it confuses the relationship between the notions of "harm" and "space" by reasoning that

> the virtual world is not the real (physical) world, so any harms that occur in the virtual world are not real harms.

Consider how this reasoning is flawed. If someone sends you an e-mail message in which they unfairly accuse you of being a malicious person, they have communicated with you in cyberspace, which is "virtual," as opposed to physical, space. But does it follow that the content of the e-mail is any less real than if it had been printed in a hardcopy letter that had been sent to you in the physical mail? Would any harm you experience because of the e-mail's content be any less real than the harm you would experience from identical information in a letter written on physical paper? James Moor (2001) has described a variation of this type of reasoning involving incidents in virtual contexts as the "virtuality fallacy," which we briefly examined in Chapter 3. In Chapters 9 and 11, respectively, we will see how harms involving virtual child pornography and a "virtual rape" in cyberspace can arguably cause real harms to real people, even if they involve only virtual (or computer-generated) images or virtual characters.

Of course, nonmalicious hackers could argue that they are not causing any harm, virtual or real. In fact, some might argue that they are helping to reduce the amount of harm that can occur because of abuses of power by content providers on the Internet (as we will see in our analysis of the Sony BMG controversy in Chapter 9).

We have considered some counterexamples for each of the three principles that we identified as key elements in the "hacker code of ethics." And we have considered some ways in which nonmalicious hackers can respond to those counterexamples. In the following section, we consider the question of whether unauthorized access to a computer in the form of an explicit break-in could ever be ethically justified.

6.3.2 Are Computer Break-ins Ever Ethically Justifiable?

Spafford believes that in certain extreme cases, breaking into a computer could be the "right thing to do."[12] He also argues, however, that computer break-ins always cause harm, which suggests that they are not ethically justified. How can Spafford defend what some might interpret as a contradictory claim: sometimes it could be right to do something that is ethically unjustifiable? Spafford asks us to consider a scenario in which vital medical data that resided in a computer are needed in an emergency to save someone's life. Further imagine that the authorized users of the computer system cannot be located. In this case, Spafford believes that breaking into that computer system would be the right thing to do. We might assume that Spafford's rationale in this situation is based on utilitarian grounds because, arguably, a greater good (or at least less harm) would result—and conversely, a greater wrong would be committed if the break-in were not carried out.

However, Spafford does not appeal to utilitarian or consequentialist principles to defend his position. Instead, he bases his argument on deontological grounds (see the discussion of deontological and nonconsequentialist ethical theories in Chapter 2) because he believes that morality is determined by actions, not results. He correctly notes that we cannot evaluate morality based on consequences or results because we would not "know the full scope of those results," which are based on the "sum total of all future effect." Thus, Spafford believes that we must base our moral decisions primarily on the actions themselves and not on possible results. In this sense, his view is compatible with the ethical theory of Act Deontology, which we analyzed in Chapter 2.

Critics might point out that Spafford has not provided us with a general principle for determining which kinds of break-ins are ethically justifiable. But using the act deontologist criteria, Spafford could respond by noting that each extreme situation would have to be analyzed on a case-by-case basis, in order to weigh the seriousness of the particular situation. In deliberating and weighing the specific circumstances involving each of those situations, however, Spafford claims that we cannot simply base our decision on absolute duties (as in Kant's version of rule deontology) or on consequentialist considerations based on the anticipated outcomes of rules and actions. (You may want to review David Ross's account of act deontology in Chapter 2 to see how it applies to Spafford's position on justifying a computer break-in affecting extreme cases.)

Independent of whether some computer break-ins can be justified on moral grounds is the question whether certain forms of hacking, especially for nonmalicious purposes, ought to be legally permissible (a question we examine in detail in Chapter 7). Another interesting question is whether the expression "ethical hacker" is an oxymoron. We should note that at least one organization believes that there can be "ethical hackers," and they offer a program that certifies individuals to engage in authorized hacking activities for companies who employ them. According to the Certified Ethical Hacker (CEH) Web site, an ethical hacker is:

> an individual who is usually employed with the organization and who can be trusted to undertake an attempt to penetrate networks and/or computer systems using the same methods as a Hacker [but] has authorization to probe the target . . . A Certified Ethical Hacker is a skilled professional who understands and knows how to look for the weaknesses and vulnerabilities in target systems and uses the same knowledge and tools as a malicious hacker.[13]

Of course, few would disapprove of training people—whether or not we choose to call them "ethical hackers"—to thwart the malicious actions carried by individuals that, for better or worse, we have traditionally called hackers. And the official process of certifying such individuals would seem to give them a sense of legitimacy. But these are not the kind of hackers—if we still wish to use that term to describe these individuals—whose activities would seem to raise moral concerns. However, insofar as these certified hackers' activities also allow "preemptive" hacking attacks, we can question the moral and legal status of some of their actions. We take up this particular question in Chapter 7.

Additional questions regarding hacking could include whether we should distinguish between "white hat" and "black hat" hackers, and whether we need to distinguish between hacking and "cracking," as some computer security analysts do. We also address these and similar questions in Chapter 7, where we examine legal issues involving hacking in connection with our discussion of cybercrime.

Thus far we have differentiated among three types of cybersecurity concerns—data security, system security, and network security—and we have considered whether, in highly unusual cases, some computer break-ins could be ethically justified. We have not yet considered the various implications that break-ins involving malicious hacker attacks have had for our financial infrastructure, which increasingly depends on available networked computers. Nor have we yet considered some of the threats that certain forms of malicious hacking pose to our national security. In the next two sections we examine both security-related concerns.

▶ 6.4 CYBERTERRORISM

Concerns about the threats posed by cyberterrorism have been on the rise in the United States and around the world. In 2002, the U.S Congress passed legislation that specifically addressed this new kind of terrorism. In May 2009, President Barack Obama responded to pressure to establish a "cybersecurity czar" to address concerns about cyberterrorism. He announced that he would create a top-level post called "Cyber Security Coordinator" to oversee "a new comprehensive approach to securing America's digital infrastructure" and to respond to the threat of cyber attacks from Al Qaeda and other terrorist groups.[14]

What, exactly, is cyberterrorism? Dorothy Denning (2004) defines it as the "convergence of terrorism and cyberspace."[15] As such, cyberterrorism covers politically motivated hacking operations intended to cause grave harm—that is, resulting in either loss of life or severe economic loss, or both. Denning (2007) also notes that acts of cyberterrorism are typically performed by "non-state actors" in their goal of intimidating or coercing governments and societies. In some cases, however, it is difficult to separate acts of malicious hacking (e.g., computer break-ins and cybervandalism) from cyberterrorism. As noted in our discussion of network security in Section 6.2.3, it is sometimes even difficult to determine whether a major computer network disruption is due to a system failure (in either the hardware or software of a networked computer system) or is the result of the work of either malicious hackers or cyberterrorists.

▶ **SCENARIO 6–4:** A Computer Network Failure, or an Instance of Cyberterrorism?

In 1990, the AT&T long distance telephone service experienced a power outage that lasted for several hours and caused its network to crash. As a result, U.S. businesses lost millions of dollars in revenue. Officially, the power outage was attributed to a software bug in the programming code in the AT&T computer system. Some have been suspicious of this explanation, believing instead that the crash was the result of the work of malicious hackers. Others have gone so far as to suggest that this particular incident was the first cyberterrorist attack on the United States infrastructure.[16] ■

The disruption of the AT&T computer system—regardless of how it was caused, or who or what caused it—showed for the first time just how vulnerable certain elements of America's economic infrastructure were to software failures involving networked computers. Immediately following the AT&T incident, the FBI increased surveillance on individuals and organizations it suspected of possessing the combination of skills and motives to damage, disrupt, or possibly bring down altogether elements of the United States infrastructure. Malicious hackers, such as Kevin Mitnick (code named Condor), and individuals in groups, such as Cyberpunks, the Legion of Doom (LOD), and the Masters of Deception (MOD), were closely watched.

To what extent are attacks on our infrastructure and on our military defense systems random attacks perpetrated by mischievous individuals, possibly as pranks, and to what extent are these the attacks of highly coordinated efforts of organized groups? It is not always easy to determine, based simply on the *motives* that separate these individuals and groups.

6.4.1 Cyberterrorism vs. Hacktivism

In 2000, several coordinated cyber attacks perpetrated against major e-commerce Web sites, such a Yahoo and eBay, prevented tens of thousands of people from accessing them. These cyber intrusions, called denial-of-service (DOS) attacks, resulted in severe economic loss for major corporations. Should these DOS attacks be classified as cyberterrorism? Or are they better understood as a form of hacking by individuals with some particular political agenda or ideology—a kind of behavior that Mark Manion and Abby Goodrum (2004) describe as *hacktivism* or "electronic political activism"?

Noting that some hackers and political activists have expressed their outrage over the ways in which the Internet has become increasingly "commodified," Manion and Goodrum question whether the actions taken by these individuals can be viewed as a new form of "civil disobedience" that integrates the talent of traditional computer hackers with the interests and social consciousness of political activists. They also point out that while many hackers continue to be portrayed in the media as vandals, terrorists, and saboteurs, only a few have considered the possibility that at least some of these individuals might be hacktivists. But they also point out that a key factor in making this distinction is to show that political activists are engaging in acts of electronic civil disobedience.

Is the distinction drawn by Manion and Goodrum plausible? Can acts of hacktivism be justified on grounds of civil disobedience? Kenneth Himma (2007) describes the line of reasoning that hacktivists and their supporters use to justify their activities as forms of political activism and civil disobedience via the following argument:

PREMISE 1. Because civil disobedience is justifiable as a protest against injustice, it is permissible to commit digital intrusions as a means of protesting injustice.

PREMISE 2. Insofar as it is permissible to stage a sit-in in a commercial or governmental building to protest, say, laws that violate human rights, it is permissible to intrude on commercial or government networks to protest such laws.

CONCLUSION. Digital intrusions that would otherwise be morally objectionable are morally permissible if they are politically motivated acts of electronic civil disobedience, or hacktivism.[17]

Based on our analysis of arguments in Chapter 3, we see that the form of this argument is valid. But in order to be a sound argument, the premises must also be true;

otherwise the argument will be valid and unsound. Both of the argument's premises are controversial, and they assume that an appropriate analogy can be drawn between civilly disobedient acts in the physical and the electronic realms. But how are we to understand the notion of "electronic civil disobedience"? Manion and Goodrum claim that for an act to qualify as "civilly disobedient," it must satisfy the following conditions:

- No damage done to persons or property
- Nonviolent
- Not for personal profit
- Ethical motivation—the strong conviction that a law is unjust, or unfair, to the extreme detriment of the common good
- Willingness to accept personal responsibility for the outcome of actions.[18]

Based on these criteria, Manion and Goodrum believe that a number of nonviolent, politically motivated "hacks" qualify as electronic civil disobedience (ECD). They cite, as an example, a hack by Eugene Kashpureff in protesting the policy for assigning Internet domain names (described in Chapter 9) as one that meets the condition required for ECD; Kashpureff carried out his act nonanonymously and he was willing to go to jail. Kashpureff's actions also seem to satisfy the other conditions for ECD outlined by Manion and Goodrum.

Denning (2008), however, argues that Manion and Goodrum's analysis of hacktivism suggests that some acts of Web defacement may also be morally justified as ECD insofar as they are "ethically motivated." But she points out that defacing a Web site seems to be incompatible with Manion and Goodrum's first condition for ECD—i.e., "no damage." As Denning notes, defacements can "cause information property damage that is analogous to physical property damage" and both forms of damage can "require resources to repair."[19] So she suggests that at least some of the cases that Manion and Goodman count as hacktivism are questionable, given their own criteria. Such cases might also seem to border on cyberterrorism.

Can a meaningful distinction be drawn between acts of hacktivism and cyberterrorism? Denning (2001) has drawn some helpful distinctions among three related notions: *activism*, *hacktivism*, and *cyberterrorism*. She suggests that activism can be viewed as normal, nondisruptive use of the Internet to support a cause; for example, an activist could use the Internet to discuss issues, form coalitions, and plan and coordinate activities. Activists could engage in browsing the Web, sending e-mail, posting material to a Web site, constructing a Web site dedicated to their political cause or causes, and so forth.

Denning notes that hacktivism, which she describes as the convergence of activism and computer hacking, uses hacking techniques against a target Internet site in a way that (a) intends to disrupt normal operations, but (b) does not intend to cause serious damage. She also notes that these disruptions could be caused by "e-mail bombs" and "low-grade viruses" that cause only minimal disruption but would not result in severe economic damage or loss of life.

Cyberterrorism, as we saw earlier, consists of activities intended to cause great harm, such as loss of life or severe economic damage, or both. For example, a cyberterrorist might attempt to bring down the United States stock market or take control of a transportation unit in order to cause trains to crash. Denning believes that conceptual distinctions can be used to differentiate activism, hacktivism, and cyberterrorism. She also admits, however, that as we progress from activism to cyberterrorism the boundaries become fuzzy. For example, should an e-mail bomb sent by a hacker who is also a political activist be classified as a form of hacktivism or as an act of cyberterrorism? Many in law enforcement would no doubt argue that rather than trying to understand the ideological beliefs, goals, and objectives of those who engage in malicious forms of hacking, much more effort should be devoted to finding ways to deter and catch these individuals. However, the category distinctions that Denning has drawn can help determine the degree of punishment that these individuals should receive.

6.4.2 Cybertechnology and Terrorist Organizations

A major security concern, especially since September 11, 2001, has been how and when terrorist organizations, such as Al Qaeda, might use cybertechnology to carry out their objectives. We now know that the terrorists who carried out the highly coordinated attacks on the Twin Towers of the World Trade Center communicated by e-mail in the days preceding the attack. We also have discovered that many members of Al Qaeda, despite the fact that some operated out of caves in Afghanistan, had fairly sophisticated computer devices. Yet it does not seem that these terrorists have taken full advantage of currently available forms of cybertechnology in executing their campaigns.

Why not? One possible explanation is that they have not yet gained the needed expertise with cybertechnology. This, of course, may change as the next generation of terrorists, who will likely be more skilled in the use of computers and cybertechnology, replace current leadership. Two terrorists gave up their lives in targeting the Navy ship USS *Cole* in 2000. Similar activities might be done remotely in the future via cybertechnology, in which case no terrorists would be required to give up their lives in carrying out their missions. A scenario is also possible in which terrorists gain control of an airplane's onboard computer systems and even block the ability of a pilot to override those controls.

Denning (2007) notes that there is evidence that terrorist groups and "jihadists" are interested in conducting cyberattacks. She also notes that there is evidence to suggest they have at least some capability to carry out such attacks, and that they are undergoing online training on how to develop the necessary skills. She also points out, however, that there is no evidence to suggest either that the threat of cyberattacks from these terrorist groups is imminent or that they have acquired the knowledge or the skills to conduct "highly damaging attacks against critical infrastructure."[20] But Denning also notes that there are "indicators" showing that these terrorist groups have an interest in acquiring the relevant knowledge and skills. As noted earlier, U.S. President Barack Obama created a new post for a Cyber Security Coordinator in 2009 in response to threats of cyber attacks from terrorist groups.

▶ 6.5 INFORMATION WARFARE

In the preceding section, we saw that it is not always easy to differentiate acts of cyberterrorism from those of hacktivism, activism, and cybervandalism. It can also be difficult to distinguish between acts of cyberterrorism and acts of *information warfare* (IW). Denning (1999) defines IW as "operations that target or exploit information media in order to win some objective over an adversary." But certain aspects of cyberterrorism also conform to Denning's definition of IW, so what distinguishes information warfare from cyberterrorism? For one thing, information warfare is a broader concept than cyberterrorism, and for another, it need not involve loss of life or severe economic loss, even though such results can occur.

James Moor (2004) has pointed out that with cybertechnology, the concept of warfare has become "informationally enriched." He notes that while information has always played a vital role in warfare, now its importance is overwhelming, because the battlefield is becoming increasingly computerized. In the past, warfare was conducted by physical means: human beings engaged in combat, using weapons such as guns, tanks, and aircraft. During the first Gulf War, in the early 1990s, we saw for the first time the importance of information technology in contemporary warfare strategies. Arguably, the war was won quickly by the multinational coalition because it had advantages in cybertechnology. Destroying the Iraqi communications technologies at the outset put the Iraqi army at a severe disadvantage. Also, the use of "smart bombs" helped the American military pinpoint targets with accuracy not possible before the advent of computers and computer-related technologies. Moor points out that in the future, warfare may have more to do with information and cybertechnology than with human beings going into combat.

Consider again the GhostNet controversy (described in Scenario 6–3) and its implications for IW. Recall that the Information Warfare Monitor issued a report that included a warning to policy makers to take information security programs seriously. Not only did the report outline the implications that cyberespionage had for a nation's infrastructure, but it also warned of the potential disasters it could have for a nation's military defense. We saw that much of the evidence in that report pointed circumstantially to China, but also suggested that other countries may be involved as well. For example, in 2009, the Associated Press reported that the government of South Korea accused North Korea of running a cyberwarfare unit that attempted to hack into both U.S. and South Korean military networks to gather confidential information and to disrupt service. North Korea was also suspected of launching the cyberattacks (in the form of denial-of-service attacks) in July 2009 that disrupted the Web sites of 27 American and South Korean government agencies as well as commercial Web sites such as the New York Stock Exchange, Nasdaq, and Yahoo's finance section (Shang-Hun and Markoff 2009). In light of these attacks, there were reports that Barack Obama is considering creating a new military command that would gather all Pentagon cyberwar capabilities under one organization.

Some have pointed out that IW, unlike conventional or physical warfare, often tends to be more disruptive than destructive. The "weapons" of IW, consisting of logic bombs, viruses, worms, and DoS attacks deployable from cyberspace, typically strike at a nation's infrastructure. Although these are not the traditional weapons of warfare, the disruption can be more damaging than physical damage from conventional weapons.

An interesting question that has been entertained by some analysts is whether information warfare can meet the conditions required for a "just warfare." For example, one condition that must be satisfied for a war to be carried out "justly" is that a distinction be made between combatants and noncombatants. However, it may not be possible to make this and other kinds of important distinctions affecting just-war requirements in the context of IW. So, some conclude that IW can never be justified solely on moral grounds. Unfortunately, however, an examination of the necessary

TABLE 6.1 Hacktivism, Cyberterrorism, and Information Warfare

Hacktivism	The convergence of political activism and computer hacking techniques to engage in a new form of civil disobedience.
Cyberterrorism	The convergence of cybertechnology and terrorism for carrying out acts of terror in (or via) cyberspace.
Information Warfare	Using information to jam the enemy's communication systems, and using technology to take out an enemy's computer and information systems.

conditions stipulated for just-war theory vis-à-vis IW is beyond the scope of this chapter.[21]

We have discussed various security threats, from malicious hacking to hacktivism, and from cyberterrorism to information warfare, as summarized in Table 6.1. We have also seen that it is not always easy to differentiate clearly among them. What is important, of course, is that we continue to develop measures for deterring, detecting, preventing, and responding to future attacks on computer systems. In the next section, we examine some currently available security countermeasures.

▶ 6.6 SECURITY COUNTERMEASURES

Richard Power defines a *countermeasure* as any "action, device, procedure, technique, or other measure that reduces the vulnerability of a threat to a system."[22] Although we have come to rely increasingly on countermeasures, some security analysts believe that we would not need them as much if better security features were built into computer systems in the first place. For example, Richard Epstein (2007) argues that security considerations need to be factored into the software development process from the outset and that this requires a development team with "knowledgeable personnel." Spafford (2007) argues along similar lines that successful security cannot be thought of as an "add-on" to computer systems; instead, it should be embedded in the systems themselves. We agree with both Epstein and Spafford; however, it would also be prudent to use existing tools and technologies to combat security threats until better security is built into computer systems.

Arguably, the best tactical approach to security threats, at present, is through available security countermeasures. These countermeasures come in a variety of forms. In this section, we briefly examine four common types: firewall technology, antivirus software and antispyware, encryption devices, and anonymity tools.

6.6.1 Firewall Technology

According to Power, a *firewall* is a "system or combination of systems that enforces a boundary between two or more networks."[23] Firewalls not only help to secure systems from unauthorized access to information in databases, but also help prevent unwanted and unauthorized communication into or out of a privately owned network. As Simpson (2006) notes, firewalls serve two purposes in that they control access to (a) all traffic that enters an internal network, and (b) all traffic that leaves an internal network.

Steven Lodin and Christoph Schuba (2001) suggest that a firewall can be compared to a "moat around a castle." Through a system of features consisting of gateways and filters, firewalls are designed to secure the flow of information in and out of a specific network. But firewalls offer very little protection from security threats (such as sabotage) that can occur inside the network. Thus firewalls can be viewed as only one component in a comprehensive scheme for protecting a computer network.

6.6.2   Antivirus Software and Antispyware

Another commonly used security countermeasure is *antivirus software*, which is designed to "inoculate" computer systems against viruses, worms, and other forms of malicious programs. Lee Garber and Richard Raucci (2001) note that work on computer virus theory began more than fifty years ago with computer science pioneer and mathematician John von Neumann, who was among the first to describe the phenomenon "self-replicating systems." (Von Neumann is credited with designing the architecture for the first stored computer program in electronic computers.) Many contemporary antivirus programs are very sophisticated; some are able not only to detect and eliminate viruses but also to delete them as well. Certain antivirus programs can repair "infected files" and can remove "infected sectors" from system memory and disk drives. Because of new and more sophisticated viruses continuously unleashed on the Internet, however, antivirus software can become quickly outdated and obsolete.

A related concern is protecting against *spyware*, which Simpson (2006) defines as something installed on users' computers without their knowledge that records personal information from the source computer and sends it to a destination computer. Many free software programs that can be downloaded from the Internet contain spyware, which can monitor a user's Web surfing activities and send that information back to the host computer. Antispyware programs, such as Spysweeper, have become a standard means of protecting against unwanted spyware. Some ISPs now include spyware-detecting programs as part of their services.

In addition to securing computer systems against attacks by malicious programs, the information transmitted between computer systems needs to be protected. Whereas firewalls and antivirus software protect against incoming malicious programs and hacker break-ins, they do not ensure that information sent beyond the "walls" of the protected system is secure. To ensure the integrity of this information, some users and many organizations have turned to data encryption tools.

6.6.3   Encryption Tools

We already noted that some data security issues arise because of the threat to information that is transmitted over the Internet. In our discussion of privacy in Chapter 5, we saw that certain privacy-enhancing tools (PETs) could be used to protect the content of a user's communications in cyberspace. For example, Pretty Good Privacy (PGP), which was one of the earliest and perhaps best-known PETs, was designed to ensure the confidentiality and integrity of data transmitted via e-mail. PGP employs a technique known as *data encryption*, which can also be viewed as a type of security countermeasure. Another well-known PET used as a security countermeasure is GNU Privacy Guide

(GPG), an open source application. Currently, much information that is transmitted in cyberspace, especially information communicated via e-mail, occurs through messages that are encrypted.

The use of data encryption, or cryptography, techniques in communicating sensitive information is hardly new; in fact, it is believed to date back at least as far as the Roman era, when Julius Caesar encrypted messages he sent to his generals—possibly even as far back as Egyptian hieroglyphics. Essentially, encryption is the act of converting the information in a message, composed in ordinary text (or "plain text"), into "ciphertext." The party receiving the encrypted message then uses a "key" to decrypt the ciphertext back into plain text. So long as both parties have the appropriate key, they can decode a message back into its original form (i.e., plain text). One challenge in ensuring the integrity of encrypted communications has been to make sure that the key, which must remain private, can be successfully communicated. Thus, an encrypted communication will be only as secure and private as its key. In symmetric encryption, the same key is used to code and decode the message.[24]

The cryptographic technique described in the preceding paragraph is generally referred to as private key encryption, a system in which both parties use the same encryption algorithm and the same private key. A more recent technology, called public cryptography, uses two keys: one public and the other private. If *A* wishes to communicate with *B*, *A* uses *B*'s public key to encode the message. That message can then be decoded only with *B*'s private key, which is known only to *B*. Similarly when *B* responds to *A*, *B* uses *A*'s public key to encrypt the message. That message can be decrypted only by using *A*'s private key, known only to *A*. Although information about an individual's public key is accessible to others, that individual's ability to communicate encrypted information is not compromised. Public-key encryption technologies have been used by governmental agencies responsible for protecting national security and military intelligence, preventing terrorism, and enforcing laws.

One group that has been especially interested in the security features made possible by strong forms of encryption is the e-commerce community, which relies on encryption-based technology to authenticate online transactions. *Digital signatures* are a means of ensuring authentication, using public key encryption, between online consumers and merchants. Digital signatures verify that the party alleged to have sent the information in question is, in fact, the party that sent it. VeriSign is one of many companies that use a public-key encryption technology to produce a "digital certificate," which authenticates online transactions between consumers and merchants.[25]

More will be said about encryption in Chapter 7, where we examine certain practices involving the use of cryptography by governmental and law enforcement agencies to combat crime. Our discussion of encryption technology in this section has focused on its role in securing information. We next consider some ways in which anonymity tools can be used as a type of security countermeasure.

6.6.4 Anonymity Tools

Not only do users wish to secure the integrity and confidentiality of their electronic communications, but many also wish to protect their identity while engaging in online activities. The introduction of anonymity tools, such as the Anonymizer (www.anonymizer .com), enable users to navigate the Web either anonymously or pseudonymously.

What is anonymity, and how does it raise ethical concerns involving security in cyberspace? Kathleen Wallace (2008) notes that the term "anonymity" can denote a number of related things, including "namelessness, detachment, unidentifiability, lack of recognition, loss of sense of identity or sense of self, and so on." In one sense, being anonymous means not being recognized or known as an individual with a certain name or identity. However, Wallace (1999) also describes a person as being anonymous when that person has no traits that can be coordinated in way that would make that person "uniquely identifiable."[26] So an individual is anonymous in cyberspace when that person is able to navigate the Internet in a way that his or her personal identity is not revealed. Even though a user's movements in cyberspace can be tracked by data monitoring tools such as cookies (see Chapter 5), an anonymous user cannot be identified beyond certain technical information, such as the user's Internet protocol (IP) address and Internet service provider (ISP).

What kind of value is anonymity? Do we have right (or even an expectation) to anonymity? We noted in Chapter 5 that anonymity is often closely associated with privacy, which is generally believed to be a positive human value. Does a defense of personal privacy necessarily entail that we must embrace anonymity as well? Not all privacy advocates and civil libertarians who currently defend anonymous behavior on the Internet believe that anonymity itself is a core human value or a basic right. For example, some argue that while we have a right to privacy, we have no right to anonymity. Others, however, believe that without some degree of anonymity in cyberspace, users are vulnerable to having all of their movements tracked.

Many users have found the opportunity to interact anonymously or pseudonymously a desirable feature of the Internet, but some security analysts and many law enforcement officials fear that criminals and terrorists will abuse Internet anonymity and thereby exploit that medium for their own sinister ends. So, Internet anonymity has made it possible for individuals to behave in undesirable or even harmful ways and it has also made the process of identifying and catching criminals more difficult. Thus we can reasonably ask whether Internet anonymity should be protected. As Helen Nissenbaum (2004) so aptly puts the matter, "after all is said and done, we would not want to discover that the thing we have fought so hard to protect was not worth protecting after all."[27]

▶ 6.7 IS TOTAL SECURITY IN CYBERSPACE A REASONABLE EXPECTATION?

Richard Epstein (2007) argues that the goal of computer security is to prevent "vulnerabilities that can lead to exploits" from a "malicious intruder" who might want to use that information to achieve malevolent ends. To what extent can that goal be realized? Can total security in cyberspace be achieved? If so, would it be a desirable goal? Different answers to both questions have been given by different computer security experts. Many of us would no doubt prefer a secure cyberspace; however, some security analysts believe that we might not be willing to accept the consequences of such a level of security. More secure systems might require features that would make computer systems less friendly (and thus more difficult to operate). And while businesses might desire more secure systems, they might not want them if they discourage prospective online customers because of stricter security guidelines or requirements. So, stricter security requirements could have a negative financial impact on both computer manufacturers and e-commerce.

6.7.1 Trade-offs in Cybersecurity

In any decisions to produce computer systems with enhanced security features, there are clearly trade-offs that can be measured in cost, convenience, and flexibility. Having more secure computer systems might result in products that are more expensive to purchase, for both individual consumers and businesses. Would consumers be willing to spend more money for more security? And would commercial organizations be willing to incur costs that might be prohibitive because of the sheer numbers of computer systems with enhanced security that they would need to purchase at higher prices? Nonmonetary costs could be measured in terms of restrictions to user autonomy—more secure systems could eliminate anonymity and reduce privacy. And we've discussed how more secure systems might result in computers that are less user-friendly—and thus less convenient and less flexible.

But there are certain levels of insecurity that most of us seem willing to accept. For example, most of us drive automobiles, despite the fact that they are vulnerable to collisions and breakdowns that result in the deaths of thousands of motorists and pedestrians each year. Of course, we could invest billions of dollars in programs designed to make cars safer, but how much are we willing (or able) to spend for safer cars? Would consumers spend $90,000 on average for a car that was slightly, or even significantly, safer than current standard automobiles? Could they afford to do so?

We might, as a society, decide that it would be safer to drive and ride in armored vehicles. We could design automobiles to be more like military-style tanks in order to reduce the number of deaths and injuries that result from the use of automobiles. But even if we could figure out how to produce such vehicles economically, we would still have to be sure they offered convenience and flexibility. As a society, we have decided that we will accept a certain level of risk associated with automobile fatalities and injuries rather than either driving tanks (for automobiles) or not driving motor vehicles altogether. Can we, and should we, accept similar levels of risk associated with computer security? In the final section of this chapter, we examine computer security issues from the vantage point of risk analysis.

6.7.2 Viewing Security as a "Process" Rather than as a "Product"

We still have not decided whether foolproof security is possible for computer systems, even if we are willing to pay the price of increased cost, less convenience, and less flexibility. Bruce Schneier (2004) claims that anyone who promises a totally secure, or "hackerproof," system is selling snake oil, because there is no magic wand to make a system secure. Schneier points out that many security experts mistakenly assume that security solutions are simply a question of finding the right technology or the foolproof mathematical combination for an encryption device. He also believes that traditional approaches to security have been ineffective because they have relied too heavily on technology itself; this is especially apparent in the case of conventional security countermeasures.

For Schneier, the thesis that *security is a process, not a product* has become a mantra. Schneier also believes that an important element in that process is one involving risk assessment. He argues that seeking perfect security would make a system useless, because "anything worth doing requires some risk."

▶ 6.8 CYBERSECURITY AND RISK ANALYSIS

Schneier argues that security, at bottom, is an ongoing *process*, which is essentially about assessing and managing risk. (Recall that we briefly considered the concept of risk analysis in Section 4.6, where we examined a model for analyzing risk in the development of safety-critical software systems.) Perhaps it is important to note that what we refer to here as *risk analysis* is sometimes further articulated in terms of two distinct categories: risk assessment and risk management. For example, Epstein (2007) describes risk assessment as an activity that falls under a more general heading or rubric called risk management. While this distinction may be important to those conducting full-fledged studies of risk, we do not need to worry about these differences here, since our focus is on an analysis of ethical issues affecting cybersecurity per se and not on subtle distinctions involved in the formal processes used in assessing and managing risk. So, we use the expression "risk analysis" to cover both the assessment and management aspects of risk.

6.8.1 Criteria for Analyzing Risk

Risk analysis is one of several methodologies used to reach an informed decision about the most cost-effective way to limit the risks to your assets. Consider that banks and credit card companies can tolerate a considerable amount of credit risk and fraud because they know how to anticipate losses and price their services accordingly. But what exactly is the level of risk that can be acceptable in computer systems?

Consider how risk analysis could be applied in the following scenario involving an older automobile.

▶ SCENARIO 6–5: Risk Analysis

Karen lives in an urban area where there is a high degree of automobile theft, but she decides to purchase a 1995 Toyota Corolla. Even though 1995 Corollas have a low Blue-Book value (say, for example, $800), they are valued for their parts that can be sold once the stolen vehicle has been "stripped." So Karen wants to take the appropriate measures to make her car secure against theft and vandalism. She learns that purchasing a security system for her car would cost approximately $1100. Is Karen's asset (the 1995 Toyota) worth the price she must pay to secure it? ■

According to most risk analysis models, including Schneier's, it would be advisable for Karen to find some alternative means to secure her car. Schneier believes that risk can be understood and assessed in terms of the net result of the impacts of five elements: assets, threats, vulnerabilities, impact, and safeguards. Although we will not analyze Schneier's model of risk analysis in detail, you can, on your own, consider how these five elements apply in the scenario above.

We will try to determine whether Schneier's model can help us to frame an adequate security policy that also addresses ethical challenges; for example, we can ask whether we can apply a cost-benefits analysis to computer security issues that impact the safety and lives of individuals. Financial considerations alone might be adequate for determining the "bottom line" when most corporations and organizations decide how to increase their computer security. But should all decisions involving cybersecurity be market driven—that is, determined by how much consumers are willing to spend and how much businesses are willing to invest? Recall our discussion in Chapter 4 where Don Gotterbarn (2004) claimed that an expanded sense of both "ethical risks" and "system stakeholder" should be taken into account in models of risk analysis for software development. There, we also saw how the SoDIS Inspection mechanism functions as a practical scheme for assessing ethical risk in software development.

Should the results of a procedure based on conventional risk analysis be used to determine security policies involving our national infrastructure, which has implications for the safety and well being of millions of people? And if the private sector is not willing to pay for enhanced security, does the government have an obligation to do so? The ethical issues surrounding cybersecurity are not trivial; as noted, they have implications for public safety that can result in the deaths of significant numbers of persons. So it is not clear that all cybersecurity issues can be understood simply in terms of the risk-analysis model advocated by Schneier. On the contrary, it is also not clear where the moral responsibility for ensuring greater cybersecurity lies.

6.8.2 The "De-perimeterization" of Information Security

One reason why it is difficult to determine who is responsible for securing cyberspace may have to do with a factor that Wolter Pieters and Andre van Cleeff (2009) call the "de-perimeterization of information security." They point out that IT systems now "span the boundaries of multiple parties" and they "cross the security perimeters" that these parties have put in place for themselves. As a result, we can no longer achieve adequate cybersecurity by simply building a "digital fence" around a single organization. In their view, IT security has become de-perimeterized because of the following trends:

- Many organizations now outsource their information technology processes.
- Many employees expect to be able to work from home.
- Mobile devices make it possible to access data from anywhere.
- "Smart buildings" are being equipped with small microchips that allow for constant communication between buildings and their headquarters.[28]

To illustrate some of the security concerns that arise because of de-perimeterization, especially with respect to the interdependencies that now exist between two or more organizations or parties, Pieters and van Cleeff cite an example involving Skype, a popular voice over Internet protocol (VOIP) system, and Microsoft. They note that in 2007 Skype had to go offline for a period of time, following an automatic software update from Microsoft. As a result, Skype users had to log back in once the service was available again online. Because many users decided to log back on at the same time, they experienced a denial-of-service condition. Pieters and van Cleeff point out that before the incident, neither Microsoft nor Skype realized the extent of the dependency that existed between their two applications.

Pieters and van Cleeff believe that de-perimeterization leads to concerns affecting "uncertain risk" for IT security. As a result, they argue that an adequate analysis of security-related risks now requires a "new paradigm" that integrates elements of the *precautionary principle*—a principle that incorporates "the unknown" into the ethics of risk analysis. Pieters and van Cleeff also note that the precautionary principle is closely related to the legal concept "duty of care" in that it implies that failure to "exercise care" can result in liabilities for damages. We examine the precautionary principle in detail in Chapter 12 in connection with our discussion of whether computing/IT professionals should engage in nanotechnology research.

We conclude this section by noting that if Pieters and van Cleeff are correct, the de-perimeterization of IT security indeed poses a significant challenge for measuring security-related risk and for achieving adequate security in cyberspace. But in responding to this challenge with an alternative framework for analyzing risk, they also make an important contribution to achieving a security-related objective that Rashid, Weckert, and Lucas (2009) call *ethics-aware software engineering*—i.e., a model where "ethical considerations are explicitly taken into account across the software development cycle and are an integral part of the risk assessment and acceptance criteria."[29]

▶ 6.9 CHAPTER SUMMARY

In this chapter we examined the ethical implications of a wide range of cybersecurity issues, including the question whether unauthorized computer break-ins can ever be ethically justified. We argued that it is useful to draw distinctions involving data, system, and network security, and distinctions between concepts such as hacking and hacktivism, and information warfare and cyberterrorism. We also considered arguments for the view that foolproof security for computer systems may be neither possible nor desirable. Finally, we described some ethical challenges involved in trying to understand cybersecurity issues in terms of models for risk analysis.

We also drew some distinctions between the traditional and the current meanings of "hacker," in our discussion of the "hacker ethic." In Chapter 7 we will focus on legal and criminal aspects of malicious hacking and related behavior in cyberspace.

▶ REVIEW QUESTIONS

1. What do we mean by "computer security" or "cybersecurity"?
2. How can cybersecurity concerns be differentiated from issues in cybercrime?
3. How are cybersecurity issues similar to and different from privacy issues affecting cybertechnology?
4. Identify and briefly describe the key distinguishing features separating data security, system security, and network security.
5. How do security issues in cyberspace raise ethical concerns?
6. Who are computer hackers, and how has the term "hacker" evolved?
7. What is meant by the expression "hacker code of ethics"?
8. According to Steve Levy, what are the six "principles" of this code?
9. Describe and briefly evaluate the argument used by some hackers, who assert that "information wants to be free."

10. Assess the argument that (nonmalicious) hackers can provide society with a valuable service. Is it a plausible argument?
11. Describe the argument that some hackers use to show that hacking causes only virtual harm, not real harm.
12. What, exactly, is cyberterrorism?
13. What is meant by "hacktivism"? How is it distinguished from traditional computer hacking?
14. Can "hacktivist activities" be justified on the grounds of civil disobedience toward unjust laws?
15. What is meant by "information warfare"? How can information warfare be distinguished from cyberterrorism?
16. Identify and briefly describe four types of countermeasures that can be used to enhance computer security: firewalls, antivirus software/spyware, encryption, and anonymity tools.
17. If complete security in cyberspace were possible, would it also be desirable? Explain.
18. Is total security in cyberspace a reasonable goal? Why or why not?
19. What is meant by the expression, "Security is a process, not a product"?
20. How might our understanding of cybersecurity be enhanced by using models of risk analysis?

▶ DISCUSSION QUESTIONS

1. Because hacking activities are carried out in cyberspace, or virtual (as opposed) to real space, does it follow that any harms resulting from these activities are only virtual harms as opposed to real harms? Assess the arguments used to defend this position. Why does James Moor believe that those who support this view use a fallacious line of reasoning that he calls the *virtuality fallacy*?
2. Consider some of the trade-offs regarding security and convenience that we examined in this chapter. Is it possible to strike an appropriate or reasonable balance? For example, suppose that in the United States, 20,000 lives could be saved each year if the speed limit were reduced from fifty-five to thirty miles per hour. Is reducing the speed limit that drastically plausible? What implications does your answer have for trade-offs involving computer security and considerations of convenience?
3. Is the expression "ethical hacker" an oxymoron? Do you agree that some individuals should be allowed to be "certified" as hackers to work on behalf of industry or for the interests of other organizations? Do the kinds of activities permitted by certified hackers in the CEH Program raise any moral issues? Explain.
4. Revisit the GhostNet controversy described in Scenario 6–3. What kinds of actions should sovereign nations take against countries that engage in cyberespionage? Should they directly confront China, which is implicated only by circumstantial evidence in the IMW Report? Does President Obama's decision to create a Cyber Security Coordinator, and possibly also to create a new military command in the United States on cyberwar, go far enough? If not, what additional steps should be taken? Explain.

▶ ESSAY/PRESENTATION QUESTIONS

1. In Section 6.3.1, we examined some issues surrounding a "hacker code of ethics." We also saw why this code, containing the six principles described by Steven Levy, has been controversial. Is it possible to establish an *appropriate* set of guidelines for a hacker code of ethics, i.e., for nonmalicious hackers, without becoming a moral relativist? You may want to revisit our discussion of moral relativism in Chapter 2 in deciding your answer to this question.
2. Recall Eugene Spafford's argument as to why computer break-ins can be justified under extraordinary circumstances. Apply Spafford's rationale to the following case. Imagine that you will have to break into a neighbor's car in order to drive a friend, who will otherwise die, to the hospital. You are morally obligated to save a person's life when it is in your power to do so. You are also obligated to obey the law, which forbids breaking into someone's motor vehicle. How would your decision in this case be similar to or different from the one Spafford uses when determining whether to break into the computer database containing the medical information needed to save someone's life?

3. In our discussion of Internet anonymity, we saw how some forms of anonymous behavior in cyberspace can have profound ethical implications. Imagine that there is a very close political election involving two candidates who are running for a seat in a state legislature. The weekend before citizens will cast their votes, one candidate decides to defame his opponent by using an anonymous re-mailer service (which strips away the original address of the sender of the e-mail) to send a message of questionable truth to an electronic distribution list of his opponent's supporters. The information included in this email is so defamatory that it may threaten the outcome of the election by influencing many undecided voters, as well as the libeled candidate's regular supporters, to vote against her. Does the "injured" candidate in this instance have the right to demand that the identity of the person using the anonymous re-mailer (whom she suspects for good reasons to be her opponent in this election) be revealed?[30]

4. Assess the claims made by Wolter Pieters and Andre van Cleeff regarding the "de-perimeterization" of information security. Are their claims plausible? Can you think of any other factors that can contribute to the de-perimitization process? What implications does this process have for our ability to assess the risks involved in adequately securing our national infrastructure? Explain.

▶ ENDNOTES

1. Epstein (2007), p. 176. Kizza (2008), who has a similar three-fold distinction regarding the key elements of cybersecurity, describes the third element as *availability* rather than *accessibility*.
2. See Neumann (2004), pp. 208–09, for more examples of how security can be viewed as a double-edged sword that "cuts both ways."
3. Some of the distinctions I draw between privacy and security are adapted from Tavani (2000).
4. My analysis of cybersecurity in terms of these three categories is adapted from Spinello and Tavani (2004) and Tavani (2007).
5. Spinello (2000), p. 158.
6. For more detail about the effects of the Code Red worm, see Meinel (2005) and Bottis (2007).
7. This scenario is based on the account of the Conficker Worm in Lawton (2009).
8. See the account of the "Internet worm," also referred to by some as the "Cornell virus," in Spafford (2007).
9. See Maidment (2009) and the Information Warfare Monitor Report (2009).
10. See Levy (2001) for a full explanation of these principles.
11. I am grateful to Mason Cash for pointing out this distinction to me.
12. Spafford (2007), p. 57.
13. See www.eccouncil.org/ceh.htm. I am grateful to Hien Nguyen for pointing out this Web site to me.
14. See http://edition.cnn.com/2009/POLITICS/05/29/cyber.czar.obama/index.html.
15. Denning (2004), p. 536.
16. See http://catless.ncl.ac.uk/Risks/12.43.html. Although the incident has generated some controversy with regard to what actually caused the disruption, it is not clear that it qualifies as an instance of cyberterrorism.
17. Himma (2007), pp. 73–74. Here, Himma's original text has been transposed into the form of a logical argument (with the author's permission).
18. Manion and Goodrum (2004), p. 528.
19. Denning (2008), p. 421.
20. Denning (2007), p. 136.
21. See, for example, Arquilla (2002), De George (2003), and Denning (2008) for some excellent discussions of just warfare in the cyber era.
22. Power (2000), p. 329.
23. Ibid., p. 331.
24. My discussion of encryption in this section draws from material in Tavani (1999).
25. For more information on digital signatures and digital certificates, see http://searchsecurity.techtarget.com/sDefinition/0,,sid14_gci211953,00.html.
26. Wallace (1999, p. 23) defines anonymity as "noncordinability of traits in a given respect respect."
27. Nissenbaum (2004), p. 555.
28. Pieters and van Cleeff (2009), p. 50.
29. Rashid, Weckert, and Lucas (2009), p. 36.
30. I am grateful to an anonymous reviewer who suggested this hypothetical scenario, illustrating an ethical dilemma involving Internet anonymity, that is included here.

▶ REFERENCES

Arquilla, John. 2002. "Can Information Warfare Ever Be Just?" In J. Rudinow and A. Graybosch, eds. *Ethics and Values in the Information Age*. Belmont CA: Wadsworth, pp. 403–14.

Bottis, Maria Canellopoulu. 2007. "Disclosing Software Vulnerabilities." In K. E. Himma, ed. *Internet Security: Hacking, Counterhacking, and Society*. Sudbury MA: Jones and Bartlett, pp. 255–68.

De George, Richard T. 2003. "Post-September 11: Computers, Ethics, and War." *Ethics and Information Technology* 5, no. 4: 183–90.

Denning, Dorothy E. 1999. *Information Warfare and Security*. New York: ACM Press, and Reading MA: Addison Wesley.

Denning, Dorothy E. 2001. "Activism, Hacktivism, and Cyberterrorism: The Internet as a Tool for Influencing Foreign Policy." In J. Arquilla and D. Ronfelt, eds. *Networks and Netwars*. Santa Monica CA: Rand Corp., pp. 229–88.

Denning, Dorothy E. 2004. "Cyberterrorism." In R. A. Spinello and H. T. Tavani, eds. *Readings in CyberEthics*. 2nd ed. Sudbury MA: Jones and Bartlett, pp. 536–41.

Denning, Dorothy E. 2007. "A View of Cyberterrorism Five Years Later." In K. E. Himma, ed. *Internet Security: Hacking, Counter-Hacking, and Society*. Sudbury MA: Jones and Bartlett, pp. 123–29.

Denning, Dorothy E. 2008. "The Ethics of Cyber Conflict." In K. E. Himma and H. T. Tavani, eds. *The Handbook of Information and Computer Ethics*. Hoboken NJ: John Wiley & Sons, pp. 407–28.

Epstein, Richard G. 2007. "The Impact of Computer Security Concerns on Software Development." In K. Himma, ed. *Internet Security: Hacking, Counter-Hacking, and Society*. Sudbury MA: Jones and Bartlett, pp. 171–202.

Garber, Lee, and Richard Raucci. 2001. "Antivirus Technology Offers New Cures." In K. W. Bowyer, ed. *Ethics and Computing: Living Responsibly in a Computerized World*. 2nd ed. New York: IEEE Press, pp. 105–10.

Gotterbarn, Don. 2004. "Reducing Software Failures: Address Ethical Risks with Software Development Impact Statements." In R. A. Spinello and H. T. Tavani, eds. *Readings in CyberEthics*. 2nd ed. Sudbury MA: Jones and Bartlett Publishers, pp. 674–89.

Himanen, Pekka. 2001. *The Hacker Ethic: A Radical Approach to the Philosophy of Business*. New York: Random House.

Himma, Kenneth Einar. 2007. "Hacking as Politically Motivated Digital Civil Disobedience: Is Hacktivism Morally Justified?" In K. E. Himma, ed. *Internet Security: Hacking, Counter-Hacking, and Society*. Sudbury MA: Jones and Bartlett, pp. 61–71.

Kaufman, Charlie, Radia Perlman, and Mike Speciner. 2002. *Network Security: Private Communication in a Public World*. 2nd ed. Upper Saddle River NJ: Prentice Hall.

Kizza, Joseph M. 2008. *Ethical and Social Issues in the Information Age*. 3rd ed. New York: Springer-Verlag.

Lawton, George. 2009. "On the Trail of the Conficker Worm." *IEEE Computer* 42, no. 6: 19–22.

Levy, Steve. 2001. *Hackers: Heroes of the Computer Revolution*. Rev. ed. New York: Penguin.

Lodin, Steven W., and Christopher L. Schuba. 2001. "Firewalls Fend Off Invasions from the Net." In K. W. Bowyer, ed. *Ethics and Computing: Living Responsibly in a Computerized World*. 2nd ed. New York: IEEE Press, pp. 128–29.

Maidment, Paul. 2009. "GhostNet in the Machine." *Forbes.com*. Available at http://www.forbes.com/2009/03/29/ghostnet-computer-security-internet-technology-ghostnet.html (accessed April 3, 2009).

Manion, Mark, and Abby Goodrum. 2004. "Terrorism or Civil Disobedience: Toward a Hacktivist Ethic." In R. A. Spinello and H. T. Tavani, eds. *Readings in CyberEthics*. 2nd ed. Sudbury MA: Jones and Bartlett, pp. 525–35. Reprinted from *Computers and Society* 30, no. 2 (2000): 14–19.

Matthews, William. 2008. "Seeking Virtual Protection." *Defense News*. Available at http://www.defensenews.com/story.php?i=3651423 (accessed May 19, 2009).

Meinel, Carolyn. 2005. "Code Red for the Web." In P. De Palma, ed. *Computers in Society 05/06*. Dubuque IA: McGraw-Hill/Dushkin, pp. 132–38. Reprinted from *Scientific American* (October 2001): 42–51.

Moor, James H. 2000. "Towards a Theory of Privacy for the Information Age." In R. M. Baird, R. Ramsower, and S. E. Rosenbaum, eds. *Cyberethics: Social and Moral Issues in the Computer Age*. Amherst NY: Prometheus Books, pp. 200–12.

Moor, James H. 2001. "Just Consequentialism and Computing." Paper presented at the Humanities Lecture Series, Rivier College, Nashua, NH, February.

Moor, James H. 2004. "Reason, Relativity, and Responsibility in Computer Ethics." In R. A. Spinello and H. T. Tavani, eds. *Readings in CyberEthics*. 2nd ed. Sudbury MA: Jones and Bartlett, pp. 40–54.

Neumann, Peter G. 2004. "Computer Security and Human Values." In T. W. Bynum and S. Rogerson, eds. *Computer Ethics and Professional Responsibility*. Malden MA: Blackwell, pp. 208–26.

Nissenbaum, Helen. 2004. "The Meaning of Anonymity in an Information Age." In R. A. Spinello and H. T. Tavani, eds. *Readings in CyberEthics*. 2nd ed. Sudbury MA: Jones and Bartlett, pp. 555–60. Reprinted from *The Information Society* 15 (1999): 41–44.

Pieters, Wolter, and Andre van Cleeff. 2009. "The Precautionary Principle in a World of Digital Dependencies." *IEEE Computer Society* 42, no. 8: 50–56.

Power, Richard. 2000. *Tangled Web: Tales of Digital Crime from the Shadows of Cyberspace*. Indianapolis IN: Que Corp.

Rashid, Awais, John Weckert, and Richard Lucas. 2009. "Software Engineering Ethics in a Digital World." *IEEE Computer* 42, no. 8: 34–41.

Sang-Hun, Choe, and John Markoff. 2009. "Cyberattacks Jam Government and Commercial Web Sites in U.S. and South Korea." *New York Times*, July 9. Available at http://www.nytimes.com/2009/07/09/technology/09cyber.html.

Schneier, Bruce. 2004. *Secrets and Lies: Digital Security in a Networked World*. Rev. ed. New York: John Wiley and Sons.

Simpson, Michael T. 2006. *Hands-On Ethical Hacking and Network Defense*. Boston MA: Thomson.

Skoudis, Ed. 2004. *Malware: Fighting Malicious Code*. Upper Saddle River NJ: Prentice Hall.

Spafford, Eugene H. 2007. "Are Computer Hacker Break-Ins Ethical?" In K. Himma, ed. *Internet Security: Hacking, Counter-Hacking, and Society*. Sudbury MA: Jones and Bartlett, pp. 49–59. Reprinted from *Journal of Systems Software*, 17: 41–47.

Spinello, Richard A. 2000. "Information Integrity." In D. Langford, ed. *Internet Ethics*. London UK: Macmillan Publishers, pp. 158–80.

Spinello, Richard A., and Herman T. Tavani. 2004. "Introduction: Security and Crime in Cyberspace." In R. A. Spinello and H. T. Tavani, eds. *Readings in Cyberethics*. 2nd ed. Sudbury MA: Jones and Bartlett Publishers, pp. 501–12.

Tavani, Herman T. 1999. "Social and Ethical Aspects of Information Technology." In J. Webster, ed. *Wiley Encyclopedia of Electrical and Electronics Engineering*. Vol. 19. New York: John Wiley and Sons, pp. 413–25.

Tavani, Herman T. 2000. "Privacy and Security." In D. Langford, ed. *Internet Ethics*. London UK: Macmillan, and New York: St. Martin's Press, pp. 65–95.

Tavani, Herman T. 2007. "The Conceptual and Moral Landscape of Computer Security." In K. E. Himma, ed. *Internet Security: Hacking, Counter-Hacking, and Society*. Sudbury MA: Jones and Bartlett, pp. 29–45.

Thompson, Paul B. 2001. "Privacy, Secrecy, and Security." *Ethics and Information Technology* 3, no. 1: 13–19.

"Tracking GhostNet: Investigating a Cyber Espionage Network (2009)." Report in the *Information Warfare Monitor*. Available at http://www.scribd.com/doc/13731776/Tracking-GhostNet-Investigating-a-Cyber-Espionage-Network (accessed April 3, 2009).

Wallace, Kathleen A. 1999. "Anonymity." *Ethics and Information Technology* 1, no. 1: 22–35.

Wallace, Kathleen A. 2008. "Online Anonymity." In K. E. Himma and H. T. Tavani, eds. *The Handbook of Information and Computer Ethics*. Hoboken NJ: John Wiley and Sons, pp. 165–89.

▶ FURTHER READINGS

Bowyer, Kevin. "Face Recognition Technology: Security vs. Privacy." *IEEE Technology and Society Magazine* 23, no. 1 (2004): 9–20.

Brey, Philip. "Ethical Aspects of Facial Recognition Systems in Public Places." *Journal of Information, Communication and Ethics in Society* 2, no. 2 (2004): 97–109.

Birrer, Frans. "Data Mining to Combat Terrorism: What Exactly Is the Issue?" *Ethics and Information Technology* 7, no. 4 (2005): 211–20.

Diettrich, David, and Kenneth E. Himma. "Active Response to Computer Intrusion." In H. Bidgoli, ed. *The Handbook of Information Security*. Hoboken NJ: John Wiley and Sons, 2005.

Gotterbarn, Don, and Keith W. Miller. "The Public is the Priority: Making Decisions Using the Software Engineering Code of Ethics." *IEEE Computer* 42, no. 8 (2009): 66–73.

Himma, Kenneth Einar. "The Ethics of Hacking Back: Active Response to Computer Intrusions." In K. E. Himma, ed. *Internet Security: Hacking, Counter-Hacking, and Society*. Sudbury MA: Jones and Bartlett, 2007, pp. 99–122.

Jordan, Tim. *Hacking*. Cambridge, UK: Polity Press, 2008.

Klang, Mathias. "Spyware—The Ethics of Covert Software." *Ethics and Information Technology* 6, no. 3 (2004): 193–202.

Nissenbaum, Helen. "Hackers and the Contested Ontology of Cyberspace." In R. Cavalier, ed. *The Impact of the Internet on Our Moral Lives*. Albany NY: State University of New York Press, 2005, pp. 139–60.

Oppliger, Rolf, Ruedi Rytz, and Thomas Holderegger. "Internet Banking: Client-Side Attacks and Protection Mechanisms." *IEEE Computer* 42, no. 8 (2009): 27–33.

CHAPTER

7

Cybercrime and Cyber-related Crimes

In Chapter 6, we examined cybersecurity issues independent of their implications for crime, even though issues involving crime and security in cyberspace sometimes overlap. In Chapter 7, we focus specifically on criminal activities involving cybertechnology. Among the questions examined in this chapter are:

- What is cybercrime, and how can it be distinguished from cyber-related crimes?
- Is there a typical cybercriminal?
- Can a meaningful distinction be drawn between hacking and "cracking" in the context of cybertechnology?
- What is "active defense hacking" or counter hacking, and is it morally permissible?
- How do some uses of encryption technology pose an ethical challenge for law enforcement agencies?
- Can biometric technologies be used to assist law enforcement groups in identifying criminals and terrorists in ways that are ethically permissible?
- Why are jurisdictional issues problematic for prosecuting some cybercrimes?

We begin our examination with a brief look at some classic cybercrimes that have received worldwide media attention.

▶ 7.1 CYBERCRIMES AND CYBERCRIMINALS

Reports of criminal activities involving cybertechnology have appeared as cover stories in periodicals, as headlines in major newspapers, and as lead stories on television news programs in the United States and around the globe. In the 1970s and 1980s, we heard about numerous crimes that involved the use of computers to launch viruses and to break into financial and government institutions. In the 1990s, as the Internet insinuated itself into mainstream society, we heard stories about crimes involving digital piracy, cyberstalking, cyberpornography, and Internet pedophilia. In the first decade of this century, high-profile cyber-related crimes have expanded to include cyberbullying, sexting, phishing, and so forth. In light of the evolutionary aspects of crimes involving cyber-technology, David Wall (2007) differentiates "three generations" of computer crimes.

In 2008 and 2009, there were reports of "hacks" into Facebook user accounts, into people's pacemakers, and even into a person's genome.[1] It seems as if novel types of cyber-related crimes continue to arise as new cyber-related technologies are developed and implemented. But we will see that despite the increase in the number and kinds of cyber-related crimes in recent years, the use of computers and cybertechnology to carry out criminal activities is not exactly new.

7.1.1 Background Events: A Brief Sketch

In our analysis of cybercrime, it is useful to trace the developments of some key criminal activities involving computers and cyberspace. As noted above, some of the earliest incidents occurred in the 1970s. During that period, stories surfaced about disgruntled employees who altered files in computer databases or who sabotaged computer systems to seek revenge against employers. Other highly publicized news stories described computer-savvy teenagers, sometimes described in the media as "hackers," breaking into computer systems, either as a prank or for malicious purposes. There were also reports, frequently sensationalized and occasionally glamorized by some members of the press, involving "hackers" who used computers to transfer money from wealthy individuals and corporations to poorer individuals and organizations.

In Chapter 6 we saw that malicious hackers have engaged in a wide range of illicit, or at least questionable, activities. As a society, our attitude toward activities associated with hacking, as that concept has been used in the media, has changed. In the past, young computer enthusiasts who figured out ways of gaining unauthorized access to computer systems were sometimes portrayed as countercultural heroes who single-handedly took on the establishment, like David taking down Goliath (i.e., big government or big business) or Robin Hood robbing the rich to give to the poor. By the turn of the twenty-first century, however, there was a growing concern in both the private and the public sectors that no types of activities leading to unauthorized access should be tolerated. The media, which itself had become a victim of cyberattacks (e.g., denial-of-service attacks on the *New York Times* and the CNN Web sites), as well as ordinary computer users shifted their attitude considerably. Perhaps this change in sentiment is due to our society's increased dependence on networked computers and the Internet, as we noted in Chapter 6.

Of course, unauthorized break-ins are only one of the many kinds of crimes made possible by computers and cybertechnology. Richard Power (2000), who believes that most computer crimes involve either fraud or abuse, or both, distinguishes between the two notions in the following way. He identifies *computer fraud* as computer-related crimes involving "deliberate misrepresentation or alteration of data in order to get something of value"; he defines *computer abuse*, on the contrary, as "willful or negligent unauthorized activity that affects the availability, confidentiality, or integrity of computer resources." Power notes that these abuses can include "fraud, embezzlement, theft, malicious damage, unauthorized use, denial of service, and misappropriation."[2]

Analysts believe that many cybercrimes go unreported. Wall (2007) notes that in at least some cases, organizations are reluctant to report cybercrimes because of the embarrassment it might cause them. Other analysts believe that many of these crimes go unreported because the victims fear the negative repercussions: reporting the crimes would be tantamount to admitting that their computer security practices are inadequate. Consider, for example, what might happen if a customer discovered that the bank where she deposits and saves money had been broken into—she might decide to transfer her funds to a bank that she perceives to be more secure. And if cyber-related crimes committed by employees working inside a financial institution were reported and publicized, the institution could also suffer a loss of customer confidence.

7.1.2 A Typical Cybercriminal

Can we construct a profile for a typical cybercriminal? Some people associate cyber-criminals with "hackers," or what we described in Chapter 6 as "malicious hackers." Many people think of the typical computer hacker as the very bright, technically sophisticated, young white male in the popular movie *War Games*. Is such a portrayal accurate? Donn Parker, one of the first authors to write on the topic of computer crime, points out that a traditional hacker tended to perceive himself "as a problem solver rather than as a criminal."[3] Parker's classic study also suggested that we should carefully distinguish between hackers who commit crimes, i.e., as people who are primarily nonprofessional or amateur criminals, and "professional criminals." He believes that stereotypical computer hackers, unlike most professional criminals, are not generally motivated by greed; some seem to thrive on a kind of "joyriding" (the thrill experienced in figuring out how to break into unauthorized systems). Along somewhat similar lines, Sagiroglu and Canbek (2009) point out that in the early days of computing, "idealistic hackers" were inclined to attack computers merely to prove that they could or to "show off" to one another. Characteristics such as these would seem to differentiate many traditional hackers from professional criminals.

Although many malicious hackers are considered amateur criminals, some possess an expertise with computers comparable to that of the best technical experts in computer science. On the contrary, many malicious hackers do not possess outstanding technical skills but are savvy enough to locate sophisticated "hacking tools" that can be down-loaded from the Internet for free, and many of these individuals are sufficiently astute to take advantage of "holes" in computer systems and programs. Michael Simpson (2006) notes that these individuals, who tend to be young and inexperienced, are sometimes referred to by sophisticated computer programmers as "script kiddies" or "packet monkeys," because they copy code from knowledgeable programmers as opposed to creating the code themselves.

▶ 7.2 HACKING VS. CRACKING: CAN A LEGAL DISTINCTION BE DRAWN?

We have already noted that computer criminals are often referred to in the media as hackers, and that, as a result, "hacker" now has a negative connotation. In Chapter 6, we saw why this definition of "hacker" is controversial and why many believe it to be both an inaccurate and an unfortunate use of the term. Pekka Himanen (2001) notes that "hacker" originally meant anyone who "programmed enthusiastically" and who believed that "information sharing is a powerful positive good." The hacker Jargon File (maintained on the Web by Eric Raymond at www.tuxedo.org/esr/jargon) defines a hacker as "an expert or enthusiast of any kind." Note that, according to this definition, a person can be an astronomy hacker: a hacker need not be a computer enthusiast. In fact, a hacker, in the generic sense of the term, might have no interest in computers or cybertechnology at all.

As we saw in our examination of hacking activities vis-à-vis cybersecurity in Chapter 6, many traditional hackers believe that they have an ethical duty to share their expertise by writing free software and facilitating access to computer resources. This was the view of the "hacker ethic," as described by Steve Levy (2001), which emerged in the 1960s at institutions such as MIT. Himanen points out that this earlier understanding of a hacker began to change in the 1980s when the media started applying the term "hacker" to criminals. In order to avoid the confusion with virus writers and intruders into information systems, traditional hackers began calling these destructive computer users *crackers*. According to the hacker Jargon File, a cracker is one "who breaks security on a system." Crackers often engage in theft and vandalism once they have gained access to computer systems.

Some authors, including Wall (2007), also use the expressions *white hat* and *black hat* to distinguish between the two types of hacking behavior. The phrase "white hat hackers" is used to refer to those "innocent," or nonmalicious, forms of hacking, while "black hat hackers" refers roughly to what we described above as "cracking." Unfortunately, distinctions between hacking and cracking, and between white-hat and black-hat hackers, are generally not recognized and observed in the world beyond the computer community. So the media often refer to crackers, or "black hat hackers," simply as hackers. This, in turn, has perpetuated the negative image of hackers and hacking in society at large.

In this chapter, our uses of "hacker" sometimes reflect the broader societal (i.e., negative) meaning of the term. Because of the way "hacker" has been used in the media, it is difficult, if not impossible, to refer to some classic cases of cybercrime without invoking it. So it is important to keep in mind that many activities and crimes described in this chapter in terms of hacking would be better understood as instances of cracking.

7.2.1 Active Defense Hacking: Can Acts of "Hacking Back" or Counter Hacking Ever Be Morally Justified?

A more recent controversy associated with hacking activities has to do with *active defense hacking*, sometimes also referred to as "counter hacking" or "hacking back against hackers." Counter hacking activities have been carried out by both individuals and corporations; they are directed against those who are suspected of originating the hacker attacks. In some cases, counter hacking has been pre-emptive; in other cases, it has been reactive. Both forms are controversial, but pre-emptive counter hacking is arguably more difficult to defend. Is counter hacking an act of "self-defense," as some argue? Or is it simply another case of "two wrongs making a right"? Should counter hacking be legalized? Can it ever be ethically justified?

In Chapter 6, we saw that at least one organization offers a certification program to train "ethical hackers." Individuals who successfully complete this program—i.e.,

Certified Ethical Hackers—are trained and certified not only in the use of defensive measures to ensure security for their employers, but also appear to be authorized to engage in security-related activities that involve pre-emptive strikes as well. According to the Certified Ethical Hacker (CEH) Web site (www.eccouncil.org/ceh.htm),

> The goal of the ethical hacker is to help the organization take *preemptive measures* against malicious attacks by attacking the system himself; all the while staying within legal limits . . . an Ethical Hacker is very similar to a Penetration Tester . . . When it is done by request and under a contract between an Ethical Hacker and an organization, it is legal. [Italics added]

But is it, or should it be, legal to engage in pre-emptive hacking attacks? Some who defend pre-emptive acts of counter hacking believe that they can be justified on utilitarian, or consequentialist, grounds. For example, they argue that less overall harm will likely result if pre-emptive strikes are allowed. However, it would seem that many of the same difficulties that arose in applying a utilitarian justification for computer break-ins in extraordinary cases (examined in Chapter 6) also arise in the case of extending a utilitarian argument to defend counter hacking in its pre-emptive form.

Because counter hacking can cause harm to innocent individuals, we can question whether this practice can be defended on moral grounds. Kenneth Himma (2004, 2008) points out that in the case of hacking back against those who launch distributed denial of service (DoS) attacks, many innocent persons are adversely affected because the attacks are routed through their computer systems. As we noted in Chapter 6, perpetrators of DoS attacks use "host computers," which often include the computers of innocent persons, to initiate their attacks (a technique sometimes referred to as "IP spoofing"). This gives the victims of these attacks the sense that the DoS attacks are originating from the host computer, as opposed to the computer of the initiator of the attack. So when victims hack back, they can unintentionally cause the intermediate computer to be assaulted.

So, even if utilitarian arguments showed that counter hacking resulted in more desirable outcomes for the majority of society, deontologists (and other nonconsequentialists) would argue that such practices are morally unacceptable if they do not respect the rights of innocent individuals. In this case, those individuals would be unfairly used as a means to an end, which, as we saw in Chapter 2, is not permissible in deontological ethical theories.

It is difficult to provide a moral justification for counter hacking; and from a legal perspective, it is not clear whether "hacking back" can be viewed in a way that is not criminal. For example, if hacking is illegal, then it would seem that hacking back would be no less illegal. However, until a case of counter hacking—especially one that involves a pre-emptive attack in the form of a DoS—is officially tried in court, it is difficult to say how our legal system will respond.

In Chapter 6, we considered whether at least some computer break-ins, under extraordinary conditions, might be ethically justifiable. In this chapter, we analyze computer break-ins and hacking-related issues mainly from a legal perspective. For example, we ask, Should all forms of computer hacking be declared illegal? Should every hacker be prosecuted as a criminal? Can some forms of hacking be viewed as an expression of individual freedoms and thus defended on constitutional grounds in the United States? Some advocates for "hacker's rights" note that traditional forms of hacking played an important role in computer developments and breakthroughs.[4] Others suggest that many of today's "computer heroes," including some successful entrepreneurs in the computer industry could also be accused of having been hackers in the past (see, for example, Jordan 2008).

7.2.2 Hackers and the Law

Even though nonmalicious hackers may enjoy some support for their activities from civil-liberties organizations and from members of the computer community, many in the government and business sectors view hacking activities in any form (even nonmalicious hacking) as a form of trespass. Current legislation against trespass in cyberspace has taken the side of business, government, and law enforcement agencies. Many on both sides of the debate, however, support legislation that would distinguish between the degrees of punishment handed to those who are found guilty of trespass in cyberspace. Earlier computer crime legislation did not always allow for such distinctions, because of some conceptual muddles surrounding the idea of trespass in cyberspace, i.e., determining which behaviors should and should not be considered trespass.

To see that some laws for prosecuting trespass and break-ins involving computers have not been adequate, we need only look at comparable laws that apply to analogous crimes in physical space. Courts and juries understand very well the distinctions in crimes involving breaking and entering into property in physical space; for example, a person who only picks the lock of a door handle or one who turns an unlocked door handle but does not enter someone's house would not likely receive the same punishment as someone who also turns the door handle and then enters the house. Similarly, a person who illegally enters someone's house only to snoop, and not to steal or vandalize, would probably not receive the same punishment as someone who illegally enters a person's house and then goes on to steal items or vandalize property, or both. Yet, in crimes committed in cyberspace, these distinctions have not always been made by judges and juries in determining sentences.

We describe some national and international laws involving cybercrime in Section 7.8. Before examining those laws, however, we examine some reasons why it is important to define what we mean by "cybercrime."

▶ 7.3 DEFINING CYBERCRIME

We have seen that crimes affecting cybertechnology, especially those involving teenage computer enthusiasts, have received considerable attention in the popular press. The criteria used for determining which kinds of crimes should be labeled "computer crimes" or "cybercrimes" have been neither clear nor consistent. Some news reporters and journalists seem to suggest that any crime involving the use, or even the presence, of a computer is a computer crime; others, however, have argued that there is nothing special about crimes that happen to involve computers. Don Gotterbarn has criticized much of the media hype surrounding computer-related crimes as "a new species of yellow journalism."[5] As we saw in Chapter 1, Gotterbarn argues that a crime in which an individual uses a surgeon's scalpel to commit a murder would not be considered an issue in medical ethics, even though a medical instrument was used in the criminal act; so, by analogy, Gotterbarn concludes that crimes involving computers are not necessarily issues in computer ethics.

Gotterbarn's position can be interpreted in a way to suggest that no distinct category of computer crime or cybercrime is needed. Stephane Leman-Langlois (2008) makes a similar suggestion in stating that cybercrime, or what she calls "technocrime," "does not exist." In Leman-Langlois' view, cybercrime "is simply a convenient way to refer to a set of concepts . . . shaping the ways we understand matters having to do with the impact of technology on crime, criminals and our reactions to crime — and vice versa."[6]

If Gotterbarn and Leman-Langlois are correct, we can reasonably ask whether a separate category, cybercrime, is necessary or even useful. Consider the crimes that have involved technologies other than computers. Do we have separate categories for them? People steal televisions, but we don't have a category, television crime. People also steal automobiles, and some people have used automobiles to assist criminals in "getaway" operations, but we don't have a category, automobile crime. So why do we need a separate category, cybercrime, for criminal acts involving cybertechnology? Yet law-makers have determined it necessary, or at least useful, to enact specific laws for crimes involving computers and cybertechnology. Have the criteria used by lawmakers to frame various categories of computer crime or cybercrime been coherent? We next take up the question of criteria for distinguishing computer crimes from other kinds of crimes.[7]

7.3.1 Determining the Criteria

Do any of the following three incidents, each of which illustrates criminal activity involving a computer lab, convincingly demonstrate the need for a distinct category of computer crime?

a. Sheila steals a computer device (e.g., a printer) from a computer lab.

b. Sheila breaks into a computer lab and then snoops around.

c. Sheila enters a computer lab that she is authorized to use and then places an explosive device, set to detonate a short time later, on a computer system in the lab.

Clearly, (a)–(c) are criminal acts, but should any of these acts necessarily be viewed as a computer crime or cybercrime? One could point out that it would not have been possible to commit any of them if computer technology had never existed, and this might initially influence some to believe that the three criminal acts are somehow unique to computer technology. Even though each act involves the presence of computer technology, they each can easily be understood and prosecuted as a specific example of ordinary crime involving theft, breaking and entering, and vandalism, respectively. So we might infer that there are no legitimate grounds for having a separate category of computer crime. Can we justify such an inference?

7.3.2 A Preliminary Definition of Cybercrime

A computer crime could, as Forester and Morrison suggest, be defined as "a criminal act in which a computer is used as the *principal tool*" [italics added].[8] According to this definition, the theft of a computer hardware device (or, for that matter, the theft of an automobile or a television which also happened to contain a computer component) would not qualify as a computer crime. If we apply the definition to incidents (b) and (c) above — i.e., breaking and entering into the computer lab and vandalizing a computer system in the lab, respectively—Forester and Morrison's definition eliminates these criminal acts as well. So their definition of computer crime might seem plausible. But is it adequate? Consider the following scenario.

▶ **SCENARIO 7–1:** Using a Computer to File a Fraudulent Tax Return

Sheila uses a computer to enter the data for her annual income tax forms, which she will submit electronically. In the process of completing her income tax forms, she decides to enter false information and thus files a fraudulent statement. Since income tax fraud is a crime and Sheila uses a computer in committing this crime, is this criminal act a computer crime? ▪

Arguably, Sheila has used a computer as the "principal tool" to commit fraud in this scenario. So according to Forester and Morrison's definition, it would seem that Sheila has committed a computer crime. But has she? Sheila could commit the same crime by manually filling out a hard-copy version of the income tax forms using a pencil or pen. Sheila's using a computer is coincident with, but by no means essential to, this particular criminal act, so Forester and Morrison's definition of computer crime, which fails to rule out Sheila's criminal act of income tax fraud as a computer crime, is not adequate.

Roy Girasa (2002) defines cybercrime as a crime that involves a "computer as a central component." Is this definition any more helpful than Forester and Morrison's? What does it mean for a crime to have a computer as its "central component"? Was a computer a central component in our example of Sheila's cheating on her income tax return? It is difficult to distinguish which crimes have and which do not have a computer as their central component, so Girasa's definition of computer crime is not much of an improvement over the one advanced by Forester and Morrison.

7.3.3 Framing a Coherent and Comprehensive Definition of Cybercrime

Recall our discussion in Chapter 1 of James Moor's insight that computer technology is "logically malleable" and thus creates "new possibilities for human action." We saw that these new possibilities, in turn, sometimes generate both "policy vacuums" and "conceptual muddles" (Moor 2007). By extension, these new possibilities for human action include new possibilities for crime. Many of these possibilities have resulted in criminal actions that have forced us to stretch traditional concepts and laws dealing with crime. Applying Moor's insight, we can further ask whether any new forms of crime have been made possible by cybertechnology. If we answer "yes," then some crimes may be unique to computers and cybertechnology.

By thinking about cybercrimes in terms of their unique or special features—i.e., conditions that separate them from ordinary crimes—we could distinguish authentic or "genuine" cybercrimes from other crimes that merely involve the use or the presence of cybertechnology. We propose a definition of a genuine cybercrime as a crime in which

the criminal act can be carried out only through the use of cybertechnology and can take place only in the cyberrealm.

Note that this definition would rule out the scenario where Sheila used a computer to file a fraudulent income tax return as an example of a genuine cybercrime. Of course, it also rules out the three examples of crimes involving a computer lab that we considered.

► 7.4 THREE CATEGORIES OF CYBERCRIME: PIRACY, TRESPASS, AND VANDALISM IN CYBERSPACE

Using our definition of cybercrime, we can further categorize genuine cybercrimes as follows:

1. *Cyberpiracy:* using cybertechnology in unauthorized ways to
   a. reproduce copies of proprietary information, or
   b. distribute proprietary information (in digital form) across a computer network.
2. *Cybertrespass:* using cybertechnology to gain unauthorized access to
   a. an individual's or an organization's computer system, or
   b. a password-protected Web site.
3. *Cybervandalism:* using cybertechnology to unleash one or more programs that
   a. disrupt the transmission of electronic information across one or more computer networks, including the Internet, or
   b. destroy data resident in a computer or damage a computer system's resources, or both.

Consider three incidents that can each illustrate one of the three categories: (a) the unleashing of the Conficker computer virus in 2009, which infected computers around the world; (b) the launching of cyberattacks on major e-commerce sites (including Yahoo, the *New York Times*, and eBay), in 2000, that resulted in "denial-of-service" to thousands of users wishing to access those sites; and (c) the unauthorized exchanging of copyrighted music files over the Internet (beginning with the original Napster site). Using our model of cybercrime, activities involving the unauthorized exchange of copyrighted music on the Internet via Napster and subsequent P2P-related file-sharing sites are examples of cyberpiracy (Category 1); the launching of the Conficker virus is an instance of cybervandalism (Category 3); and the denial-of-service attacks on the e-commerce Web sites illustrate an example of cybertrespass (Category 2), because they involved the breaking into, as well as the unauthorized use of, third-party computer systems to send spurious requests to commercial Web sites (as opposed to the kind of "genuine" requests sent by users who wish to access those sites for legitimate purposes). Since denial-of-service attacks also cause serious disruption of services for the targeted Web sites, they can also be classified as cybervandalism (Category 3); some cybercrimes will span more than one category.

If our model is correct, then many crimes that use cybertechnology are not genuine cybercrimes. For example, crimes involving pedophilia, stalking, and pornography can each be carried out with or without computers and cybertechnology; there is nothing about them that is unique to cybertechnology, so crimes such as Internet pedophilia, cyberstalking, and Internet pornography would not qualify as genuine cybercrimes. (We will see below that they are examples of *cyber-related* crimes.)

In Chapter 6, we saw that it was difficult to draw a coherent distinction between cyberterrorism and hacktivism. We now see that both can be understood as instances of cybertrespass, regardless of whether they were perpetrated by "electronic political activists" (called hacktivists) or by cyberterrorists. If, however, hacktivists and cyberterrorists also break into computer systems in order to disrupt or vandalize computer systems and networks, then they have committed cybervandalism as well. Using our definition of cybercrime, there is no need to consider motive, political cause, ideology, etc., when determining how the criminal acts best fit into one of our three categories. (However, motive or intention could influence the ways that cybercrimes are prosecuted and that convicted cybercriminals are sentenced.)

▶ 7.5 CYBER-RELATED CRIMES

Thus far we have differentiated genuine cybercrimes, i.e., crimes that are specific to cybertechnology, from crimes that are cyber-related. We next see that *cyber-related* crimes can, in turn, be divided into two subcategories: *cyberexacerbated* crimes and *cyberassisted* crimes. This distinction enables us to differentiate between a crime in which someone merely uses cybertechnology (e.g., a personal computer to file a fraudulent income tax return) from crimes such as Internet pedophilia and cyberstalking, which are significantly affected by computers and cybertechnology. The role that cybertechnology plays in the first example seems at best trivial and possibly altogether irrelevant, but in the latter two examples, cybertechnology does much more than merely *assist* someone in carrying out a crime—cybertechnology *exacerbates* it.

Certain kinds of crimes aided by cybertechnology can increase significantly because of that technology. For example, in the case of cyberexacerbated crimes, the scale on which crimes of a certain type can be carried out is significantly affected. Consider the potential increase in the number of stalking-, pornography-, and pedophilia-related crimes that can now occur because of cybertechnology, versus the likely increase in the number of income tax crimes, which are also assisted by computer technology.

Along lines that are somewhat similar to the distinctions we have drawn in separating three categories of cybercrime—cyberassisted, cyberexacerbated, and cyberspecific (or genuine cyber) crimes—Wall (2007) proposes the following scheme based on three "generations" of cybercrime. What we call cyberassisted crimes, he describes as "first generation" cybercrimes that are, in effect, "traditional" or "ordinary" crimes that happen to involve the use of a computer. Corresponding to our category of cyberexacerbated crimes is Wall's notion of second generation or "hybrid crimes." For this set of cyber-related crimes, Wall points out that network technology has "created entirely new global opportunities." His third generation of cybercrimes comprises a category that Wall calls "true cybercrimes," which corresponds to our category of genuine cybercrimes in that they are "solely the product of the Internet" (or, in our case, the product of cybertechnology).

Wall notes that in the case of cybercrimes involving the first two generations, individuals and organizations could still find ways of carrying out the criminal activities in the event that either the computer or the Internet was eliminated. In the case of true cybercrimes, however, Wall points out that if you eliminate the Internet, those crimes "vanish." He uses the examples of spamming and phishing to illustrate this point. These examples complement the set of crimes we identified above as genuine cybercrimes.

Figure 7.1 illustrates some ways in which crimes involving the use of cybertechnology can be catalogued according to this threefold scheme.

We should not underestimate the significance of many cyber-related crimes, even if they fail to qualify as genuine or true cybercrimes. Consider that many professional or

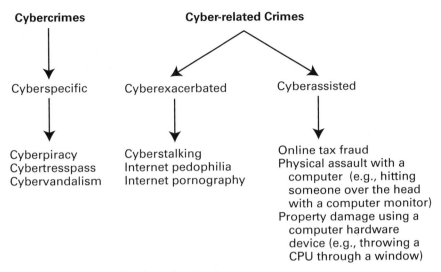

Figure 7-1 Cybercrimes and cyber-related crimes.

career criminals, including those involved in organized crime, are using cybertechnology to conduct illicit gambling, drug trafficking, and racketeering scams. When cybertechnology is used, these crimes can be viewed as cyber-related crimes. Yet these kinds of crimes, which some describe as "old-style" crimes, receive far less attention in the popular media than those perpetrated by malicious hackers, many of whom are young and could be viewed as "amateur criminals." Because stories about these amateur criminals tend to grab the headlines, our attention is diverted from crimes committed in cyberspace by professionals. Power (2000) believes that youthful hacker stereotypes provide a "convenient foil" for both professional criminals and foreign intelligence agents. In Section 7.1.2 we saw that unlike many individuals who are described in the media as "hackers," and who are amateurs, professionals do not seek technological adventure; rather they hope to gain a financial advantage. But Power points out that since professional criminals have superior skills, they are less likely than amateurs to get caught in carrying out their criminal acts.

Also consider that some cyber-related crimes, including cyberstalking and cyberbullying, have resulted in deaths.[9] Paul Bocij (2004) describes the wide range of criminal activities made possible by cyberstalking in a book dedicated to that topic.[10] And Kowalski, Limber, and Agatston (2008), in their book on cyberbullying, identify many of the ways that cybertechnology has provided new opportunities for traditional bullying.[11] Although the authors of both books suggest that there may be some aspects of cyberstalking (vs. offline stalking) crimes and of cyberbullying (vs. traditional bullying) crimes, respectively, that challenge our conventional laws, neither succeeds in making a convincing case for why those criminal acts should qualify as examples of what we call genuine cybercrimes. But, in describing the many ways that stalking and bullying crimes have increased significantly because of cybertechnology, the authors make a very strong case for why those cyber-related crimes qualify as cyberexacerbated crimes rather than merely cyberassisted crimes.[12]

Next we examine two additional examples of cyber-related crimes: identify theft and corporate espionage: Both kinds of crimes have been exacerbated by cybertechnology, even though neither is dependent on that technology.

7.5.1 Identity Theft

What is identity theft, and how is it exacerbated by cybertechnology? Lininger and Vines (2005) define identity theft as

> a crime in which an imposter obtains key pieces of personal information, such as social security or driver's license numbers, in order to impersonate someone else. The information can be used to obtain credit, merchandise, and services in the name of the victim, or to provide the thief with false credentials.[13]

Identity-theft crimes can also include the taking of another person's identity through the fraudulent acquisition of personal information in credit card numbers. However, Wall (2007) notes that identity theft is often mistakenly used to describe crimes involving credit card theft. So, not all instances of the latter kind of theft qualify as identity theft.

Of course, identity theft, like other cyber-related crimes, does not require cyber-technology. In the past, identity thieves have combed through dumpsters (and some still do) looking for copies of bank statements and for papers containing account information on credit card bills that people dispose of in their trash. (This behavior is sometimes referred to as "dumpster diving.") But identity thieves have been very successful in scams involving cybertechnology in general (e.g., in recording credit card "swipes"), independent of the Internet per se.

Factors such as lax security and carelessness involving customer information contained in computer databases and in company-owned laptop computers has made it easy for some identity thieves to acquire personal information about their victims. Ellen Simon describes two examples that occurred in 2005: (a) the Bank of America lost computer tapes containing data on 1.2 million federal employees; and (b) ChoicePoint Inc. and Lexis-Nexis disclosed that the dossiers of more than 170,000 Americans on the companies' databases had been illegally accessed by criminals, and that at least 750 of them had their identities stolen. The information in these databases contained the addresses and social security numbers of individuals—all of the information that identity thieves needed to open up a credit card account. Simon points out that another incident linked to lax security and carelessness involved an MCI laptop computer containing the names of 165,000 current and former MCI employees. The computer was stolen from the car of an MCI employee, which was parked in front of his home garage.[14]

As we saw in Chapter 5, information merchants purchase and sell personal infor-mation, including social security numbers and credit card information. And many are willing to pay for this information. So information brokering has become a lucrative business, and this has not gone unnoticed by professional criminals as well as by some employees in organizations that have access to sensitive information about people's financial records. Simon describes an incident where a former bank employee of Wachovia Corporation allegedly sold information about account numbers and account balances to a person who then sold them to data collection agencies. Some data brokers, such as ChoicePoint, have tried to screen customers, to avoid selling information to criminals. But critics, especially privacy advocates, remain skeptical; many believe that for information brokers, concerns about privacy and security are more of an "after-thought" than a priority.[15]

Many kinds of identity-theft scams have also been carried out on the Internet. One common example is a scheme involving e-mail that appears to have been sent by a reputable business. For example, you may receive e-mail that looks as if it were sent by eBay, Amazon, or PayPal. Often these e-mail messages include the official logos of the companies they purport to represent; the message informs you that your account is about to expire and that you need to update it by verifying your credit card number. Although the e-mail may look legitimate, it may have been sent to you by identity thieves or other individuals whose objective is to get your credit card number as well as other kinds of personal information. How can a potential victim differentiate legitimate e-mail sent from businesses such as eBay or PayPal from that sent by identity thieves? Typically, e-mail from identity thieves will not address the potential victim by name; so this can be an indication that the e-mail is not from a legitimate source. Users wishing to verify the authenticity of the e-mail can contact the company by phone, or through the company's legitimate e-mail address, if they are in doubt.

Many e-mail messages sent from identity thieves are generated through spam (examined in Chapter 9). Using spam to gather personal information is sometimes referred to as *phishing*, which Lininger and Vines (2005) describe as "automated identity theft." They point out that phishing "combines the power of the Internet with human nature to defraud millions of people out of billions of dollars."[16] They also believe that phishing may soon overtake spam as "the main Internet headache." Lininger and Vines cite a study by the Anti-Phishing Working Group (APWG), which reports that the number of phishing incidents is increasing at a rate of about 56% per month.[17]

An automated version of phishing, sometimes called "pharming," automatically "redirects the victim to the offending site" (Wall 2007). Activities involving pharming and phishing, along with conventional e-mail spam, increase the amount of identity theft that can be accomplished over the Internet. And we have seen how other, non-networked uses of cybertechnology also exacerbate identity-theft crimes.

7.5.2 Corporate Espionage

Another crime that has been exacerbated by the use of cybertechnology is espionage in the corporate world. Power (2000) notes that corporate spies in Silicon Valley (California) — the high-tech capital — have intercepted cell phone conversations between corporate executives through which they were able to acquire highly sensitive and confidential information, including company secrets. He also describes a case in which an ingenious spy, posing as a consultant, visited a corporation at a time when he knew the senior manager was on vacation. The consultant cleverly managed to get the inside information he needed by claiming to be a close associate of the vacationing manager and by convincing employees of the corporation that the manager had given him permission to consult during the manager's absence; he was able to get the source code for a software product the company was developing and then deliver that product to market before that company could. Tales describing recent cases of economic espionage involving the high-tech industry abound, but there is no need to examine any of these incidents in detail to understand the severe harm caused by corporate spies.

Corporate espionage has been made easier because of cybertechnology, which has provided spies with data-gathering techniques that were not previously possible. Of course, crimes involving corporate espionage need not involve the use of cybertechnology, nor need they be directed at computer corporations; but there has been concern about the ways in which cybertechnology is increasingly used in economic espionage crimes in general.

The U.S. Congress passed the Economic Espionage Act in 1996, making it a federal crime to profit from misappropriating someone else's trade secret.[18] Power notes that although this act is not exclusively a computer-crime law, it specifically includes language about "downloads," "uploads," "e-mails," etc. Some economic analysts in the United States worry that economic espionage, especially in the high-tech industry, threatens the American position in a global market. Ironically, cybertechnology in general, and the Internet in particular, have made it much easier for spies to carry out their espionage operations against the very corporations that develop that technology.

In our analysis of cybercrime and cyber-related crimes thus far, we have examined some ways that individuals and organizations have used cybertechnology to carry out criminal activities. Some of these crimes were "genuine" cybercrimes because they could not have committed without the use of cybertechnology; others were crimes that were either assisted or exacerbated by the use of cybertechnology. Not only has this technology enabled criminals to carry out their crimes, it has also provided law enforcement agencies with new tools to track down criminals, including cybercriminals. We have already examined some ethical issues that arise because of the ways individuals can use cybertechnology to carry out criminal acts. Next, we consider some ways that the use of cybertechnology by law enforcement agencies to combat crime can also raise ethical concerns.

▶ 7.6 TECHNOLOGIES AND TOOLS FOR COMBATING CYBERCRIME

In our discussion of privacy in Chapter 5, we saw some examples of how the U.S. government has used cybertechnology to track down criminals via a technique called computerized record matching. We also saw why this technique was considered controversial when it was used to match records in databases containing the names of federal government employees against the records in databases with the names of welfare recipients in order to identify welfare cheats. There our analysis of computerized matching focused mainly on implications for personal privacy. But we also noted some of the concerns that practices involving record matching can raise when used to combat crime. One popular line of reasoning frequently used to defend computerized techniques (including record matching) in tracking down individuals suspected of committing crimes is: If you have done nothing wrong, you have nothing to worry about. Critics, however, argue that this line of reasoning misses an important point—one that is illustrated in the following scenario.

▶ **SCENARIO 7–2:** Intercepting Mail that Enters and Leaves Your Neighborhood

Imagine that local law enforcement authorities have heard rumors that members of an organized crime syndicate have been communicating via the United States Postal Service with someone living in your neighborhood. The authorities decide to intercept the mail sent to and from homes in your neighborhood and then compare the information included in the return and destination addresses on the envelopes against a list of names and addressees of suspected mobsters. When you discover what the authorities are doing and you protest against it, you are told, "If you have nothing to hide, you have nothing to worry about." Of course, you could respond that even though you have nothing to hide, you believe that you still have quite a bit to worry about; that is, you have to worry about how to retain your basic freedoms and civil liberties as a United States citizen under such conditions.[19]   ■

Computerized record matching is like the cross-checking procedures in the above scenario. Although many citizens might be inclined to view the kind of electronic surveillance implicit in computer matching as less intrusive, or at least less objectionable, than the physical surveillance techniques used in intercepting and cross-checking the mail sent to and from a particular neighborhood, both practices raise serious concerns for civil liberties. From a utilitarian perspective, it could be argued that the end (e.g., catching welfare cheats or "deadbeat" parents) justifies the means used (matching the records of many innocent citizens in the process). But we can also see why techniques involving the computerized record matching of ordinary citizens (who are presumed to be innocent) can raise concerns about basic civil liberties.

Civil liberties issues often lie at the heart of the controversies surrounding the use of cybertechnology by law enforcement agencies in tracking down criminals. Not surprisingly, law enforcement organizations desire to use the latest available technologies in pursuing criminals, including cybercriminals. We next consider some controversies surrounding a proposal for using a specific type of encryption technology (defined in Chapter 6).

7.6.1 Encryption Technologies

As we saw in Chapter 6, one virtue of encryption tools is that they help to ensure the integrity of electronic data exchanged between two or more computer systems. That same technology, however, has made it possible for criminals and terrorists to send and receive encrypted messages via electronic communications. Furthermore, electronic communications devices that employ strong encryption features threaten the ability of law enforcement agencies to carry out effective wiretap operations. As a result, many crime and security experts believe that encryption technologies can provide a communication shield for individuals involved in organized crime and terrorism. So, governments and law enforcement groups have argued for the need to develop and use strong encryption technologies in their efforts to combat crime and terrorism.

The following example illustrates many of the controversies surrounding the U.S. government's plan to use encryption technology in the 1990s. In early 1994, the Clinton administration proposed that an encryption system, which came to be known as the Clipper Chip, be installed in all electronic communication devices. This device was intended to support law enforcement agents in their attempts to "crack" encrypted messages sent by individuals and organizations suspected of violating the law. A highly controversial aspect of the proposal for Clipper, however, was that it required the keys to this encryption system to be held in escrow by the federal government.[20]

Critics of Clipper, including both liberals and conservatives, raised concerns that the use of Clipper could violate the Fourth Amendment of the U.S. Constitution, which protects against unwarranted search and seizure? Some critics also questioned whether the federal government could be trusted with a technology like Clipper. What were the chances, for example, that the government would abuse it by appealing to national security interests as a rationale for using Clipper in questionable political practices? Government officials and supporters of Clipper responded by noting that this particular encryption technology would help to better ensure legitimate, private communications among ordinary citizens while deterring criminals. However, Steven Levy (1995) pointed out that with Clipper, or with any similar type of government-controlled encryption system, we could be sure that our communications would be completely private—except, of course, from the government itself.

Clipper's defenders rejected the claim that Clipper threatened individual civil liberties. They argued that individual rights were no more threatened or compromised by Clipper than they were under existing laws, since government agencies were already permitted to eavesdrop on the communications of both private citizens and organizations, provided that they have a legal warrant to do so. In this case, Clipper could be viewed as only one more tool used in court-approved surveillance activities.

Perhaps the principal argument put forth by Clipper's proponents was that a strong encryption technology was essential for keeping tabs on organized crime members, international drug dealers, terrorists, and so forth. But because of the sustained efforts on the part of the anti-Clipper coalition, the Clinton administration formally withdrew its support for the chip in 2000. However, the events of September 11, 2001, may have caused some of Clipper's original critics to reassess their argument against a strong encryption standard for the federal government. The Clipper controversy can now be viewed as a classic dispute involving diametrically opposed interests in a democratic society; it gets at the heart of the basic tension between civil libertarians, who want to retain basic freedoms, and law enforcement groups who wish to use tools (such as encryption) to keep society safe from criminals and terrorists.

7.6.2 Biometric Technologies

Biometric technologies have also been used by law enforcement agencies to combat crime and terrorism. Power defines biometrics as "the biological identification of a person, which includes eyes, voice, hand prints, finger prints, retina patterns, and handwritten signatures."[21] Irma van der Ploeg (1999, 2004) points out that through biometric technologies, one's iris can be read in the same way that one's voice can be printed. She also notes that one's fingerprints can be read by a computer that, in turn, has become touch sensitive and endowed with hearing and seeing capacities. The digital representation of these biometric data is usually transformed via some algorithm to produce a template, which is stored in a central computer database.

In 2002 a biometric identification scheme was tested at London's Heathrow Airport; the iris-scanning device captures a digital image of one's iris, which is then stored in a database and can then be matched against images of the irises of other individuals entering and leaving public places such as airports.[22] As biometric technologies improve, security officials at airports such as Heathrow and elsewhere may consider adopting them for authenticating an individual's identity, in combination with (or possibly even in place of) passports.

Possibly you have heard the expression, "Eyes are the window to the soul." In an age of biometrics, however, one's eyes may become the window to one's identity in a much more tangible sense than the classic metaphor ever intended. While biometric devices are a highly accurate means for validating an individual's identity, they are also controversial. Recall our analysis of a scenario in Chapter 5 involving Super Bowl XXXV (in January 2001), where a biometric identification tool using face-recognition technology scanned the faces of people entering the football stadium. The scanned images were then instantly matched against the facial templates of suspected criminals and terrorists, which were contained in a central computer database.[23]

Initially, the use of this technology at Super Bowl XXXV drew scathing criticism from civil liberties groups and privacy advocates. In the post-September 11 world, however, practices that employ biometric technologies such as face-recognition devices have received overwhelming support from the American public; a poll conducted in October 2001, for example, indicated that more than 86% of Americans approved of using biometric technologies in public places, including sports stadiums and airports.[24]

Does the use of biometric technologies violate human rights? Do arguments against the government's traditional uses of computerized record matching apply equally in the case of biometric techniques? In nonbiometric-based computerized matching, including the traditional record-matching techniques used by the U.S. government in the 1970s, the databases that were used contained records of individuals all of whom were presumed to be innocent; for example, records of government workers were matched against records of welfare recipients to generate one or more hits. In matching practices involving biometric technology, such as the one used at Super Bowl XXXV, images of people who are presumed innocent are recorded and matched against a database of known or suspected criminals and terrorists. So, there is at least one critical difference involving these two practices.

But critics still raise questions regarding the use of biometric technologies by law enforcement agencies. Philip Brey (2004) notes that critics of face-recognition technologies in particular, and biometrics in general, point to at least three problems: error, abuse, and privacy. He notes that errors occur in matches resulting from biometrics technology, and the rate of error increases when the criteria used to determine what qualifies as an acceptable match is expanded. Second, the uses for which biometric technologies are originally authorized can expand significantly and can lead to possible abuses, such as those described by the critics of the Clipper Chip (in the preceding section). And finally, some privacy advocates argue that the net security gained in the use of biometrics is not commensurate with the loss of privacy and civil liberties for individuals. But those who favor using biometric technology appeal to many of the same arguments articulated by defenders of the Clipper Chip to make the case for increased security, even if using this technology undercuts some civil liberties for ordinary citizens.

7.6.3 Keystroke-Monitoring Software and Packet-Sniffing Programs

In addition to encryption and biometric technologies, law enforcement agencies have used other forms of cybertechnology to track the activities of criminals who themselves use cybertechnology. One such technique is *keystroke monitoring*, which Power describes as "a specialized form of audit-trail software . . . that records every key struck by a user and every character of the response that the system returns to the user."[25] This software can trace the text included in electronic messages back to the original sequence of keys and characters entered at a user's computer keyboard. So it is especially useful in tracking the activities of criminals who use encryption tools to encode their messages. Wall (2207) notes that "keystroke loggers" were originally designed to "identify errors in systems." The later use of this technology by law enforcement groups, however, has been controversial.

Government agencies such as the Federal Bureau of Investigation (FBI) have also tracked criminals and their activities via *Carnivore*, a "packet sniffing" program that monitors the data traveling between networked computers; a packet sniffer or "sniffer" is a program that captures data across a computer network. However, these kinds of software programs have also been used by malicious hackers to capture user IDs and passwords. So Carnivore became somewhat controversial, and because of the negative publicity it received in the media, the FBI officially changed the name from Carnivore to DCS1000. However, DCS (Digital Collection System) has functioned in much the same way as Carnivore.[26]

▶ 7.7 PROGRAMS AND TECHNIQUES DESIGNED TO COMBAT CYBERCRIME IN THE UNITED STATES

In the preceding section we saw that the government and law enforcement groups, in their efforts to track suspected criminals, have used a variety of technologies and tools—including encryption, biometrics, keystroke-monitoring software, and packet-sniffing programs—all of which were controversial from the perspective of civil liberties groups. Next, we examine some programs and practices, as well as some interpretations of controversial laws, that government and law enforcement agencies have also used to apprehend and catch individuals, including professional criminals who use cybertechnology to carry out their criminal activities. We begin with a look at the practice of entrapment on the Internet.

7.7.1 Entrapment and "Sting" Operations to Catch Internet Pedophiles

Police and federal agents have used "sting" operations and entrapment techniques to catch members of organized crime involved in drug dealing, gambling, pornography, and so forth. Consider a controversial case of entrapment involving cybertechnology that was intended to lure and catch a pedophile who used the Internet to solicit sex with an under-aged person.

▶ **SCENARIO 7–3:** Entrapment on the Internet

Under an alias, detective James McLaughlin of Keene, New Hampshire posed as a young boy in boy-love chat rooms, searching for adults using the Internet to seek sex with underage boys and gathering evidence from conversations recorded in the chat rooms. Philip Rankin, a British marine-insurance expert living in Norway, communicated with McLaughlin under the assumption that the police officer was a young boy. Rankin then agreed to travel to Keene to meet his online contact in person at a Dunkin' Donuts restaurant. Upon his arrival at the restaurant, Rankin was arrested by McLaughlin on the charge of using the Internet to solicit sex with an under-aged person.[27]   ■

Critics of Internet entrapment have questioned whether such practices for catching child molesters are ethically justifiable, even if they are legal. In the United States, numerous cases of child molestation have been investigated by the FBI where pedophiles have crossed over a state line to meet and molest children they met via an Internet forum such as a chat room. Sometimes police officers have entered chat rooms, posing as young girls to lure unsuspecting pedophiles. In 2003, a three-week sting operation was conducted in Spokane, Washington, where a policeman posing as a 13-year-old girl in an Internet chat room arrested a twenty-two-year-old man on charges of attempted (second-degree) rape of a child.[28]

Supporters of online entrapment operations argue that they can save many innocent lives and can significantly lessen the harm to individuals. For example, one could speculate about the outcome of the Amy Boyer stalking incident (described in Chapter 1) if an entrapment scheme, similar to the one used in the pedophile scenario we described, had been in place to catch cyberstalkers such as Liam Youens. Of course, a critical question from the point of view of many civil libertarians is whether the ends achieved by entrapment operations justify the means. Are such means morally acceptable? At the root of this question are some of the same issues involving civil liberties that we examined in our scenario involving computerized record matching above, where we saw that the end achieved, catching welfare cheats and deadbeat parents, was desirable, but the means used to accomplish this end were questionable.

7.7.2 Enhanced Government Surveillance Techniques and the Patriot Act

Another controversial practice involving government surveillance of criminal activities is supported by provisions in the USA (United and Strengthening America) PATRIOT (Provide Appropriate Tools Required to Intercept and Obstruct Terrorism) Act. This act, which was passed by the U.S. Congress in October 2001 and renewed (in a slightly modified form) in March 2006, provides law enforcement agencies with increased powers to track down suspected terrorists and criminals by allowing those agencies to closely monitor e-mail communications and cell phone conversations.

The Patriot Act works in conjunction with, and in some cases expands on, two related acts: the Foreign Intelligence Surveillance Act (FISA) of 1978, and the Electronic Communications Privacy Act (ECPA) of 1986. The original FISA, which was amended in 2008, established legal guidelines for federal investigations of foreign intelligence targets.[29] The Patriot Act amended FISA: whereas the original FISA applied only to "snooping" in foreign intelligence investigations, the Patriot Act permits "domestic surveillance" as well.

ECPA, which includes provisions for "access, use, disclosure, interception and privacy protections of electronic communications," allows the government to attach two kinds of devices to a criminal suspect's phone: "pen registers" and "trap-and-trace devices." When a suspect makes a phone call, a pen register displays the number being dialed, and when the suspect receives a phone call, the trap-and-trace device displays the caller's phone number.[30] A pen register used on the Internet can reveal the URLs of Web sites visited by a suspect. The Patriot Act allows police to install Internet pen registers without having to demonstrate probable cause and without having to demonstrate that the suspect is engaged in criminal activity.

In late 2005, reports began to surface that the Bush administration had been monitoring the e-mails and phone calls of U.S. citizens who were communicating with individuals outside the United States. Opponents of this practice, including many members of the U.S. Congress, argued that the administration's practices violated the law because no court order was requested in conducting the surveillance on U.S. citizens. Others, however, supported the Bush administration's decision because of the positive effect it could have for national security. Some supporters also noted that it is legal for the National Security Agency (NSA) to conduct wiretaps on non-U.S. citizens, because of the authority given to it by FISA. However, critics objected that NSA is not authorized to intercept the communications of American citizens without first getting a court order. But, in its defense, the Bush administration argued that it was acting within the law because its primary obligation was to protect the American public against terrorist attacks.

While many conservative organizations have supported the enhanced domestic surveillance provisions made possible by the Patriot Act, critics argue that this increased surveillance has eroded basic civil liberties. Some critics also worry that certain provisions in this act could be abused by those in power, under the convenient excuse of crime prevention and national defense, to achieve certain political ends. So, controversial aspects of the Patriot Act once again illustrate the classic tension between interests involving civil liberties and national security (as it affects terrorism and crime).

7.7.3 The Total Information Awareness Project

Another controversial government program, proposed by the Information Awareness Office (IAO) of the U.S. Defense Advanced Research Projects Agency (DARPA), was the Total Information Awareness (TIA) project. The objective of this program was not only to detect criminals but also to identify and monitor potential terrorists via sophisticated data-mining tools and techniques (described in Chapter 5), which can reveal terrorist-like patterns in the activities of individuals. The TIA database could look for patterns implicit in data that included financial, medical, travel, and other records. This information can then be matched against biometric data (described in Section 7.6.2), which include video images. In 2003, the U.S. Congress suspended funding of the domestic surveillance portion of TIA, and DARPA has since changed the name of the program to "Terrorist Information Awareness."[31]

To conclude this section, it is important to note that many, possibly even most, crimes involving cybertechnology have involved neither terrorists nor members of organized crime syndicates. So, one question that arises is whether the government should be permitted to use the same aggressive tactics that it claims are needed to counter terrorism and organized crime in catching lesser criminals who commit crimes that do not impact our security and safety as a nation. For example, should measures designed to detect and trap terrorists also be used to catch those who engage in nonmalicious hacking?

► 7.8 NATIONAL AND INTERNATIONAL LAWS TO COMBAT CYBERCRIME

Laws are typically limited in jurisdiction to nations where they are enacted. For example, the Economic Espionage Act of 1996 (described in Section 7.5.2) is enforceable only in the United States. Other laws involving cybercrime and also intended to have international reach have been enacted, but issues involving legal jurisdiction have impeded their prosecution in many instances.

7.8.1 The Problem of Jurisdiction in Cyberspace

Traditionally, crimes are prosecuted in the legal jurisdictions in which they were committed. In certain cases, suspected criminals have been extradited from one legal jurisdiction to another (and sometimes from one country to another) to stand trial for an accused crime. Girasa (2002) points out that jurisdiction is based on the concept of boundaries, and laws are based on "territorial sovereignty." Because cyberspace has no physical boundaries, it can be difficult to prosecute cybercrimes involving multiple nations, as well as multiple states within nations. So, some have questioned whether the concept of legal jurisdiction make any sense in cyberspace.

Enforcing Cybercrime Laws across States/Provinces within Nations

States and provinces within nations have often been challenged in determining how to enforce local laws when crimes are committed within their jurisdictional boundaries by criminals residing outside those boundaries. In the United States, for example, different states have different laws regarding gambling. How can those laws be prosecuted in the case of online gambling, which can span multiple states? Consider the following scenario.

▶ **SCENARIO 7–4:** A Virtual Casino

Phil, a resident of the state of Nevada, has decided to set up a Web site called "Virtual Casino" dedicated to online gambling. Because gambling is legal in Nevada, let us assume that online gambling is also legal there, provided that the owners and operators of an online gambling site comply with the state's overall gambling regulations and laws. Let us also assume that gambling in any form, either off- or online is illegal in the state of Texas. Sarah, who is a resident of Texas, decides to visit the Virtual Casino Web site physically located on a server in Nevada. She then places a bet at one of the virtual tables in the virtual casino.[32] ∎

When Sarah engages in gambling activities on the Web site in Nevada from her home computer, she has technically broken the law in Texas, but where, exactly, has the violation of the law taken place—in Texas, where the illegal gambling activities are carried out from Sarah's home, or in Nevada where the server for the Virtual Casino resides? And where should this "crime" be prosecuted? Can the state of Texas demand the extradition of the Nevada resident who owns and operates the online gambling site, on grounds that the Web site owner has assisted (or has made possible) the "crime" that was committed by the resident of Texas? Note that in this particular scenario, no interstate transmission of illegal material, in the strict legal sense of that definition, has occurred. Interstate statutes have been established to combat crimes of this type.

Our scenario is, of course, hypothetical. But there have been some actual jurisdictional quagmires. An Internet bulletin board system (BBS) located on a server in California contained pornographic material that was legal in that state, but the BBS's content was illegal in Tennessee, where it was viewed by a resident of that state. In our discussion of pornography laws in Chapter 9, we examine this case more closely, and we will also see why it is important to reach consensus about how cyberspace should be viewed in order to both regulate it and determine whether specific laws have been broken. There we consider whether cyberspace should be regarded as a "place" or public space, such as a bookstore, or whether it is better understood as a broadcast medium, such as television or radio.

Enforcing Cybercrime Laws Involving Multiple Nations

Not only have there been problems in prosecuting Internet crimes that span state borders within nations, but criminal enforcement has been hampered as well by a lack of international legal agreements and treaties. Consider the case of the ILOVEYOU virus that wreaked havoc worldwide in 2001 and which was allegedly launched by Onel de Guzman from the Philippines.

Where, exactly, did the crime take place? In the Philippines? In the United States? In Europe? Or in all of the above? Even though it originated in the Philippines, its effect was global. And if in the Philippines there is no explicit crime against launching computer viruses, did an actual crime even occur? Furthermore, if no crime was committed by Guzman in the Philippines, should he be extradited to nations that do have cyber-related crime laws, and should he be required to stand trial in those nations?

On the one hand, it might be argued that Guzman should stand trial in any country that was affected by the virus he launched; after all, individuals and institutions in those countries were harmed by Guzman's act. On the other hand, we might also wish to consider the flip side of that argument: Would we want all cases of crimes or controversial Internet practices that have a global reach prosecuted by multiple nations? Consider the following scenario.

▶ **SCENARIO 7–5:** Prosecuting a Corporation in Multiple Countries

XYZ Corporation, a major computer corporation in the United States, has developed and released a new software product that has been distributed globally. However, this product has a serious defect that causes computer systems using it to crash under certain conditions. These system crashes, in turn, result in both severe disruption and damage to system resources. A company in south Asia that purchased this product from XYZ has experienced multiple system crashes since installing it, which has also resulted in a severe loss of profits. ■

What recourse do those who purchase this product have in their complaint against XYZ Corporation? In America, there are strict liability laws, but there are also disclaimers and caveats issued by manufacturers to protect themselves against litigation. Suppose that several countries where XYZ Corporation has sold its new product also have strict liability laws but do not recognize disclaimers. Should XYZ Corporation be held legally liable and then be forced to stand trial in each of these countries? If XYZ were found guilty in their courts, the litigation costs alone could result in bankruptcy for that corporation. So, we need to think through the ramifications that broadening the sphere of legal jurisdiction could have for corporations, or any organizations, even if they are not overtly engaged in criminal activities involving cybertechnology.

In response to crimes committed in cyberspace, several laws have been enacted (and revised), but many critics claim that these laws have failed to keep pace with ever-changing technology. Table 7.1 includes a list of federal laws that address computer-related crimes. For more information about these laws, see the United States government's cybercrime Web site (http://www.cybercrime.gov).

7.8.2 Some International Laws and Conventions Affecting Cybercrime

The Council of Europe (COE) has considered ways to implement an international legal code that would apply to members of the European Union. Because cybercrimes can

TABLE 7.1   United States Criminal Laws Involving Computers and Cybertechnology

18 U.S.C. Sec. 1029.	Fraud and Related Activity in Connection with Access Device
18 U.S.C. Sec. 1030.	Fraud and Related Activity in Connection with Computers
18 U.S.C. Sec. 1362.	Communication Lines, Stations, or Systems
18 U.S.C. Sec. 2511.	Interception and Disclosure of Wire, Oral, or Electronic Communication Prohibited
18 U.S.C. Sec. 270.	Unlawful Access to Stored Communication
18 U.S.C. Sec. 2701.	Disclosure of Contents
18 U.S.C. Sec. 2703.	Requirements for Governmental Access

involve multiple law enforcement agencies and multiple ISPs in diverse countries under diverse rules of law, the G8 countries met in May 2000 to discuss an international treaty involving cybercrime. (The G8 is an informal group of eight countries: Canada, France, Germany, Italy, Japan, Russia, the United Kingdom, and the United States of America.) In conjunction with the G8 conference, the Council of Europe (COE) released its first draft of the COE Convention on Cybercrime on April 27, 2000 (http://conventions.coe. in/treaty/en/projects/cybercrime.htm).[33] It addresses four types of criminal activity in cyberspace:

- offenses against the confidentiality, availability, and integrity of data and computer systems
- computer-related offenses (such as fraud)
- content-related offenses (such as child pornography)
- copyright-related offenses

Crimes involving economic espionage are not considered in the COE draft. However, international crimes involving copyright offenses are included, and this may prove to be important because of the sheer volume of unauthorized file sharing at the global level.

Many crimes affecting digital intellectual property are international in scope. Beginning in the late 1990s, Internet users around the world downloaded proprietary music from the original Napster Web site, whose central servers resided in the United States. In subsequent years, many illicit file-sharing sites that built upon the Napster system have operated outside the United States. For example, the servers for KaZaA, a well-known P2P file-sharing site, resided in the Netherlands before it ceased operations in 2005. But other sites, including Limewire, have taken the place of earlier sites such as Napster and KaZaA and have enabled the illicit sharing of proprietary music internationally. Perhaps one of the most "successful" sites dedicated to the unauthorized sharing of proprietary music, videos, games, and other copyrighted materials was The Pirate Bay, which operated out of Sweden. In 2009, an international trial took place, which determined the fate of that site.

▶ **SCENARIO 7–6:** The Pirate Bay Web Site

Established in 2003 by a Swedish anti-copyright organization, Pirate Bay is a well-known Web site that tracks and indexes files known as BitTorrent or "torrent" files. (Torrents are small files that contain "metadata," which are required to download the data files from other users.) By late 2008, Pirate Bay announced that it had more than 25 million "unique peers" (unregistered users) and about 3,600,000 registered users. (Only users who wanted to download pornography from that site were required to register.) In May 2006, Pirate Bay's servers were raided by Swedish police. Since then, Pirate Bay has faced a series of legal battles. On April 17, 2009, the four cofounders of Pirate Bay were found guilty by a Swedish court of "assisting the distribution of illegal content online." The verdict has since been appealed.[34]   ■

The prosecution of Pirate Bay received international attention, and the verdict in this case no doubt pleased those who favor the strict international enforcement of intellectual property laws. In this case, there was no need to dispute jurisdictional boundaries and no need to extradite individuals across nationally sovereign borders to prosecute a cyber-related crime that was international in scope.

▶ 7.9 CHAPTER SUMMARY

In this chapter, we examined crimes involving cybertechnology. We considered arguments as to whether a profile for a typical cybercriminal could be constructed and whether a reasonable distinction could be drawn between hacking and cracking. We also questioned whether "hacking back" or counter hacking is ever morally permissible. We then drew a distinction between "genuine" cybercrimes and cyber-related crimes and considered some examples of each type. We also considered some roles that cybertechnology, especially encryption and biometric technologies, can play in assisting law enforcement to combat crime in cyberspace. Finally, we identified and briefly discussed some national and international laws that have been enacted to facilitate the prosecution of cybercrimes.

It is important to note that many cyber-related crimes were either not examined, or not discussed in the detail they would seem to deserve, in this chapter. Our intent here was not to provide an exhaustive analysis of cyber-related crimes, but rather to clear up some conceptual confusion about the way that many of the crimes involving cybertechnology are analyzed. As a result, very little was said about crimes affecting software piracy, spam, sexting, virtual child pornography, etc.—all of which use cybertechnology at some level. These topics are discussed in detail in appropriate sections of later chapters. For example, criminal aspects of software piracy are examined in our discussion of intellectual property in Chapter 8. Issues affecting spam, child pornography, and sexting are discussed in our examination of regulatory challenges affecting cyberspace in Chapter 9.

▶ REVIEW QUESTIONS

1. How did the popular media's portrayal of computer-related crimes carried out in the 1970s and 1980s romanticize the behavior of some individuals who engaged in these activities?
2. Can we construct a profile of a "typical cybercriminal"?
3. Why do many in the computer community oppose the use of "hacker" to describe cybercriminals?
4. Can a meaningful distinction be drawn between hacking and "cracking"?
5. What is meant by "active defense hacking" or "counter hacking"?
6. Can this kind of hacking be justified on either legal or ethical grounds?
7. Can certain kinds of hacking be protected on the grounds of free speech?

8. Would the past activities that some leaders in today's major computer companies engaged in qualify as hacking?
9. What, exactly, is cybercrime?
10. How can a coherent definition of cybercrime be framed?
11. Identify and briefly describe the three categories of "genuine cybercrime" that we examined.
12. How can we distinguish between genuine cybercrimes and "cyber-related" crimes?
13. How might we distinguish between cyber-related crimes that are "cyberexacerbated" and those that are "cyberassisted"?
14. What is identity theft, and how has it been exacerbated by cybertechnology?
15. What is phishing, and how is it related to identity theft?
16. How has corporate espionage been affected by cybertechnology?
17. What is "entrapment on the Internet," and why has is it been controversial?
18. How have packet-sniffing programs and keystroke-monitoring technologies assisted law enforcement authorities in fighting cybercrime?
19. What is the Patriot Act, and why is it controversial?
20. What problems do issues of jurisdiction pose for understanding and prosecuting crimes committed in cyberspace?

▶ DISCUSSION QUESTIONS

1. Recall the case of Internet entrapment involving pedophiles that we described in Section 7.7.1. Which arguments can be made in favor of entrapment and "sting operations" on the Internet? From a utilitarian perspective, entrapment might seem like a good thing because it may achieve desirable consequences. Should sting operations be used to lure pedophiles? Justify your position by appealing to one or more of the ethical theories described in Chapter 2.
2. Describe some of the international laws designed to combat crime in cyberspace. What are some problems in enforcing international crime laws and treaties? How can biometric technology be used to fight cybercrime and cyber-related crimes internationally? What controversies does the use of this technology raise?
3. What kinds of ethical questions does the use of encryption technology raise with respect to cybercrime and cybercriminals? Describe some of the controversies associated with strong encryption technologies, such as in the Clipper Chip controversy, in combating crime. How are the tensions underlying the classic Clipper debate still relevant today?
4. Recall the distinctions that we drew between cyberspecific and cyber-related crimes. Why would cyberstalking be classified as a cyber-related crime, according to this distinction? Among cyber-related crimes, is it useful to distinguish further between cyberexacerbated and cyberassisted crimes? Why would cyberstalking be categorized as a "cyberexacerbated" rather than a cyberassisted crime? Why not simply call every crime in which cybertechnology is either used or present a cybercrime? Would doing so pose any problems for drafting coherent cybercrime legislation?

▶ ESSAY/PRESENTATION QUESTIONS

1. Assess arguments for and against the use of biometric technologies for security, especially in airports and large stadiums. Should biometric technologies such as face-recognition programs and iris scanners be used in public places to catch criminals? In the post-September 11 world, there is much more support for these technologies than there was when biometrics were used at Super Bowl XXXV in January 2001. Granted that such technologies can help the government to catch criminals and suspected terrorists, what kinds of issues do they raise from a civil liberties perspective? Compare the arguments for and against the use of biometric technologies in tracking down criminals to arguments we examined for and against computerized record matching in our discussion of privacy in Chapter 5. Do you support the use of biometrics in large, public gathering places? Defend your answer.

2. What implications does the conviction of the four cofounders of the Pirate Bay Web site in 2009 have for international attempts to prosecute intellectual property crimes globally? Should the four men also have been required to stand trial in all of the countries in which copyrighted material had been downloaded from their Web site? Will the outcome of the Pirate Bay trial likely deter entrepreneurs, worldwide, from setting up future P2P sites that allow the illicit file sharing of copyrighted material?

▶ ENDNOTES

1. See, for example Ragan (2009), Feder (2008), and Aldhous and Reilly (2009).
2. Power (2000), p. 329.
3. Parker (1988), p. 142.
4. See Kapor (1995) for a discussion of this point.
5. Gotterbarn (1995), p. 19.
6. Leman-Langlois (2008), p. 1
7. My analysis of cybercrime in Sections 7.3 and 7.4 is adapted from Tavani (2004).
8. Forester and Morrison (1994), p. 29.
9. For example, Amy Boyer was murdered in 1999 by a cyberstalker, and Meghan Meier committed suicide in 2006 as a result of a cyberbullying incident.
10. Bocij (2004, p. 14) defines cyberstalking as a "group of behaviors in which an individual, group of individuals, or an organization uses information and communications technology to harass another individual, group of individuals, or organization."
11. Kowalski, Limber, and Agatston (2008, p. 1) define cyberbullying as "bullying through e-mail, instant messaging (IM), in a Chat Room, on a Web site, or through digital messages or images sent to a cellular phone."
12. See Grodzinsky and Tavani (2001) for why cyberstalking crimes are not genuine cybercrimes.
13. Lininger and Vines (2005), p. 268.
14. For more detail, see the account of these incidents in Simon (2005).
15. Ibid.
16. Lininger and Vines (2001), p. 5.
17. Ibid., p. xxi.
18. See http://www.usdoj.gov/criminal/cybercrime/eea.html (accessed May 21, 2009).
19. This scenario is adapted from Tavani (1996).
20. My analysis of the Clipper controversy in this section draws from material in Tavani (1999). See also the description of this controversy in Wikipedia. Available at http://en.wikipedia,org/wiki_Clipper_Chip.
21. Power (2000), p. 328.
22. See http://goliath.ecnext.com/coms2/gi_0199-657504/Protecting-the-zone-London-City.html.
23. See the account in Brey (2004).
24. See the Harris Interactive Poll taken in late September 2001.
25. Power (2000), p. 332.
26. See http://en.wikipedia.org/wiki/Carnivore_(FBI) (accessed May 21, 2009).
27. This scenario is based on an analysis of Internet entrapment issues in Sinnott-Armstrong (1999).
28. See the account of this in Michael Martinez, "To Catch a Predator: An Ethical Analysis of Sting Journalism." Available at http://www.michaelmartinez.org/document.pdf.
29. See http://www.fas.org/irp/agency/doj/fisa/.
30. See http://personalinfomediary.com/ECPAof1986_info.htm.
31. See http://epic.org/privacy/profiling/tia/.
32. For more information about online gambling, see Wikipedia. Available at http://en.wikipedia.org/wiki/Online_gambling.
33. The former G8 countries have since expanded to include Australia, Belgium, Spain, and Switzerland, and are often referred to as the G12.
34. See Jemima Kiss, http://www.guardian.co.uk/technology/2009/apr/17/the-pirate-bay-trial-guilty-verdict (accessed May 22, 2009).

▶ REFERENCES

Aldhous, Peter, and Michael Reilly. 2009. "Special Investigation: How my Genome was Hacked." *New Scientist.* Available at http://www.newscientist.com/article/mg20127013.800-special-investigation-how-my-genome-was-hacked.html.

Bocij, Paul. 2004. *Cyberstalking: Harassment in the Internet Age and How to Protect Your Family.* Westport CT: Praeger.

Brey, Philip. 2004. "Ethical Aspects of Facial Recognition Systems in Public Places." In R. A. Spinello and H. T. Tavani, eds. *Readings in CyberEthics.* 2nd ed. Sudbury MA: Jones and Bartlett, pp. 585–600.

Feder, Barnaby J. 2008. "A Heart Device Is Found Vulnerable to Hacker Attacks." *New York Times*, March 12. Available at http://www.nytimes.com/2008/03/12/business/12heart-web.html?_r=1.

Forester, Tom, and Perry Morrison. 1994. *Computer Ethics: Cautionary Tales and Ethical Dilemmas in Computing.* 2nd ed. Cambridge MA: MIT Press.

Girasa, Roy J. 2002. *Cyberlaw: National and International Perspectives.* Upper Saddle River NJ: Prentice Hall.

Gotterbarn, Don. 1995. "Computer Ethics: Responsibility Regained." In D. G. Johnson and H. Nissenbaum, eds. *Computers, Ethics, and Social Values.* Englewood Cliffs NJ: Prentice Hall, pp. 18–24.

Grodzinsky, Frances S., and Herman T. Tavani. 2001. "Is Cyberstalking a Special Type of Computer Crime?" In T. W. Bynum et al., eds. *Proceedings of the Fifth International Conference on the Social and Ethical Impacts of Information and Communications Technologies: Ethicomp 2001.* Vol. 2. Gdansk, Poland: Mikom Publishers, pp. 73–85.

Himanen, Pekka. 2001. *The Hacker Ethic: A Radical Approach to the Philosophy of Business.* New York: Random House.

Himma, Kenneth. 2004. "Targeting the Innocent: Active Defense and the Moral Immunity of Innocent Persons from Aggression." *Journal of Information, Communication, and Ethics in Society* 2, no. 1: 31–40.

Himma, Kenneth Einar. 2008. "Ethical Issues Involving Computer Security: Hacking, Hacktivism, and Counterhacking." In K. E. Himma and H. T. Tavani, eds. *The Handbook of Information and Computer Ethics.* Hoboken NJ: John Wiley & Sons, pp. 191–217.

Jordan, Tim. 2008. *Hacking. Digital Media and Technological Determinism.* Malden MA: Polity.

Kapor, Mitch. 1995. "Civil Liberties in Cyberspace." In D. G. Johnson and H. Nissenbaum, eds. *Computers, Ethics, and Social Values.* Englewood Cliffs NJ: Prentice Hall, pp. 644–50.

Kiss, Jemima. 2009. "The Pirate Bay Trial: Guilty Verdict." Available at http://www.guardian.co.uk/technology/2009/apr/17/the-pirate-bay-trial-guilty-verdict.

Kowalski, Robin M., Susan P. Limber, and Patricia W. Agatston. 2008. *Cyber Bullying.* Malden MA: Blackwell.

Leman-Langlois, Stephane, ed. 2008. *Technocrime: Technology, Crime, and Social Control.* Portland OR: Willan Publishing.

Levy, Steve. 1995. "The Battle Over the Clipper Chip." In D. G. Johnson and H. Nissenbaum, eds. *Computing, Ethics and Social Values*, Englewood Cliffs NJ: Prentice Hall, pp. 651–63.

Levy, Steve. 2001. *Hackers: Heroes of the Computer Revolution.* Rev. ed. New York: Penguin.

Lininger, Rachael, and Russell Dean Vines. 2005. *Phishing: Cutting the Identity Theft Line.* Indianapolis IN: John Wiley and Sons.

Moor, James H. 2007. "What Is Computer Ethics?" In J. Weckert, ed. *Computer Ethics.* Aldershot UK: Ashgate, pp. 31–40. Reprinted from *Metaphilosophy* 16, no. 4 (1985): 266–75.

Parker, Donn B. 1998. *Fighting Computer Crime: A Framework for Protecting Information.* New York: John Wiley and Sons.

Power, Richard. 2000. *Tangled Web: Tales of Digital Crime from the Shadows of Cyberspace.* Indianapolis IN: Que Corp.

Ragan, Steve. 2009. "Facebook Accounts Hacked for $100." *The Tech Herald.* Sep. 18. Available at http://www.thetechherald.com/article.php/200938/4468/Facebook-accounts-hacked-for-100.

Sagiroglu, Seref, and Gurol Canbek. 2009. "Keyloggers: Increasing Threats to Computer Security and Privacy." *IEEE Technology and Society Magazine* 28, no. 3: 11–17.

Simon, Ellen. 2005. "Identities Get Harder to Keep." *The Nashua Telegraph*, May 24, pp. 14–15.

Simpson, Michael. 2006. *Hands-On Ethical Hacking and Network Defense.* Boston MA: Thompson.

Sinnott-Armstrong, Walter. 1999. "Entrapment in the Net?" *Ethics and Information Technology* 1, no. 2: 95–104.

Spafford, Eugene H. 2007. "Are Computer Hacker Break-Ins Ethical?" In K. Himma, ed. *Internet Security: Hacking, Counter-Hacking, and Society.* Sudbury MA: Jones and Bartlett, pp. 49–59.

Tavani, Herman T. 1996. "Computer Matching and Personal Privacy: Can They Be Compatible?" In C. Huff, ed. *Proceedings of the Symposium on Computers and the Quality of Life.* New York: ACM Press, pp. 97–101.

Tavani, Herman T. 1999. "Social and Ethical Aspects of Information Technology." In J. Webster, ed. *Wiley Encyclopedia of Electrical and Electronics Engineering.* Vol. 19. New York: John Wiley and Sons, pp. 413–25.

Tavani, Herman T. 2004. "Defining the Boundaries of Computer Crime: Piracy, Trespass, and Vandalism in Cyberspace." In R. A. Spinello and H. T. Tavani, eds. *Readings in CyberEthics.* 2nd ed. Sudbury MA: Jones and Bartlett, pp. 513–24.

van der Ploeg, Irma. 1999. "The Illegal Body: Eurodac and the Politics of Biometric Identification." *Ethics and Information Technology* 1, no. 2, 295–302.

van der Ploeg, Irma. 2004. "Written on the Body: Biometrics and Identity." In R. A. Spinello and H. T. Tavani, eds. *Readings in CyberEthics.* 2nd ed. Sudbury MA: Jones and Bartlett, pp. 571–84.

Thomas, Douglas. 2002. *Hacker Culture.* Minneapolis: University of Minnesota Press.

Wall, David S. 2007. *Cybercrime: The Transformation of Crime in the Information Age.* Malden MA: Polity.

▶ FURTHER READINGS

Brin, David. "Crime and Lawfulness in an Age of All-Seeing Techno-Humanity." In S. Leman-Langlois, ed. *Technocrime: Technology, Crime, and Social Control.* Portland OR: Willan Publishing, 2008, pp. 14–26.

Camp, L. Jean. "Digital Identity." *IEEE Technology and Society Magazine* 23, no. 2 (2004): 21–27.

Diettrich, David, and Kenneth E. Himma. "Active Response to Computer Intrusion." In H. Bidgoli, ed. *The Handbook of Information Security.* Hoboken NJ: John Wiley and Sons, 2005.

Fairweather, N. Ben, and S. Rogerson. "Biometric Identification." *Journal of Information, Communication and Ethics in Society* 2, no. 1 (2004): 3–8.

Gagnon, Benoit. "Cyberwars and Cybercrimes." In S. Leman-Langlois, ed. *Technocrime: Technology, Crime, and Social Control.* Portland OR: Willan Publishing, 2008, pp. 46–65.

Nissenbaum, Helen. "Hackers and the Contested Ontology of Cyberspace." In R. Cavalier, ed. *The Impact of the Internet on Our Moral Lives.* Albany NY: State University of New York Press, 2005, pp. 139–60.

Singel, Ryan. "National ID: Biometrics Pinned to Social Security Cards." In P. De Palma, ed. *Computers in Society 08/09.* New York: McGraw Hill, 2008, pp. 48–49.

Willard, Nancy. *Cyber Bullying and Cyberthreats: Responding to the Challenge of Online Social Threats.* Eugene OR: Center for Safe and Responsible Internet Use, 2006.

CHAPTER

8

Intellectual Property
Disputes in Cyberspace

What, exactly, is intellectual property? And how should it be protected in cyberspace? These are two of the questions examined in Chapter 8. Other questions include:

- Should computer software be protected by copyright law as well as by patent law?
- How does the principle of fair use apply to proprietary information in digital format?
- What are the similarities and differences between the Free Software Movement and the Open Source Initiative?
- What kinds of philosophical and legal arguments are used to justify protecting intellectual property?
- Do current intellectual property laws sufficiently balance the interests of the public good against those of individuals and corporations who own copyrights and hold patents?

The debate over intellectual property rights in cyberspace has become one of the defining ethical issues of the Internet era. Deciding who should have ownership rights to, and thus control over, digitized information will ultimately determine who can and cannot access that form of information. Disputes about intellectual property rights in cyberspace range from claims pertaining to ownership of software programs to arguments about who has the right to distribute (or even make available for use) proprietary information on the Internet. Perhaps no property issue has been more contentious in the past decade than the question as to whether computer users should be able to freely download and exchange copyrighted music in the form of MP3 files. It is estimated that more than 60 million users share music online and that by the year 2012, 40% of the global music market will be digital music (Evans 2008).

▶ 8.1 WHAT IS INTELLECTUAL PROPERTY?

An adequate analysis of *intellectual property* issues requires that we first have an understanding of the concept of property in general. Like privacy, property is a complex notion that is neither easily defined nor clearly understood. Yet, as legal scholars and philosophers have pointed out, property laws and norms play a fundamental role in shaping a society and in preserving its legal order; that is, laws and norms involving property rights establish relationships between individuals, different sorts of objects, and the state. When discussing issues involving property, we tend to think of tangible items. Originally, property referred to land; however, it now also includes objects that an individual can own, such as an automobile, articles of clothing, or a stamp collection.[1]

However, many legal theorists and philosophers suggest that property should not be understood simply in terms of objects or things, but rather as a *relationship between individuals in reference to things*. Hence, there are three elements to consider:

1. an individual, X
2. an object, Y
3. X's relation to other individuals (A, B, C, etc.) in reference to Y.

In this sense, X (as the owner of property Y) can control Y relative to persons A, B, C, and so forth. So if Tom owns a Dell laptop computer, then he can control who has access to his computer and how it is used; for example, Tom has the right to exclude Mary from using the laptop computer, or, as its owner, he can grant her unlimited access to it. Ownership claims involving "intellectual objects" are similar in certain respects but are less straightforward than claims involving the ownership of tangible objects.

8.1.1 Intellectual Objects

Some philosophers use the expression *intellectual objects* when referring to forms of intellectual property.[2] Unlike physical property, intellectual property consists of objects that are not tangible. These nontangible, or intellectual, objects represent creative works and inventions, which are the manifestations or expressions of ideas. Unlike tangible objects, which are exclusionary in nature, intellectual objects (e.g., software programs) are *nonexclusionary*: Consider once again Tom's laptop computer, which is a physical object. If Tom owns it, then Mary cannot own it, and vice versa. Tom's laptop is an exclusionary object. Next consider a word processing program that resides in Tom's computer. If Tom makes a copy of that program, then both Mary and Tom have copies of it. The word processing program is nonexclusionary.

Note that scarcity (which often causes competition and rivalry when applied to physical objects) need not exist in the case of intellectual objects, which can be easily reproduced. Note also that there are practical limitations to the number of physical objects one can own and that there are natural as well as political limitations to the amount of land that can be owned, but that countless digital copies of a Microsoft Word program can be produced and each at a relatively low cost.

Another feature that distinguishes intellectual objects from physical objects has to do with exactly what it is that one can lay legal claim to. One cannot own an idea in the same sense that one can own a physical object; ideas themselves are not the kinds of things for which governments are willing to grant ownership rights to individuals. As Adam Moore (2008) points out, ownership rights do not apply to an intellectual object as an "abstract physical entity" but rather to the control of "physical manifestations or expressions" of that object. In other words, legal protection is given only to the tangible *expression* of an idea that is creative or original.

For a literary or artistic idea to be protected it must be expressed (or "fixed") in some tangible medium such as a physical book or a sheet of paper containing a musical score. If the idea is functional in nature, such as an invention, it must be expressed as a machine or a process. Whereas authors are granted copyright protections for expressions of their literary ideas, inventors are given an incentive, in the form of a patent protection, for expressions of their functional ideas. Both copyright law and patent law, along with other legal schemes for protecting intellectual property, are discussed in detail in Sections 8.2 and 8.3.

8.1.2 Why Protect Intellectual Objects?

What is our basis for saying that intellectual property, or for that matter any kind of property, ought to be protected? One answer lies in our current laws. Of course, we could then further ask, On what philosophical grounds are our laws themselves based? In Section 8.5 of this chapter, we will see that in Anglo-American law the philosophical justification for granting property rights is grounded in two different theories about property. One theory is based on the rationale that a property right is a type of "natural right" that should be granted to individuals for the products that result from the labor expended in producing a creative work or a practical invention. The other theory is based on the notion that property rights themselves are not natural rights but rather social constructs designed to encourage creators and inventors to better serve society in general by bringing forth their creative works and practical inventions into the marketplace. To encourage authors and inventors, utilitarians believe that it is necessary to grant them property rights in the form of limited monopolies that result in financial advantages.

In many continental European countries, neither individual labor nor social utility are used as a justification for granting intellectual property rights and corresponding protections. Instead, creative works and inventions represent the expressions and personalities of their creators and inventors, who should, it is argued, have the right to determine how their works are displayed and distributed. This view is sometimes referred to as the personality theory of intellectual property. In Section 8.5, where we consider examples of each kind of property theory, we will see that some critics reject the notion that intellectual property rights should be extended to computer software.

Philosophers and legal theorists point out that the introduction of computer software has created questions regarding intellectual property laws for which there are no easy answers. Innovations in computer hardware, on the contrary, have clearly qualified for patent protection, and in this sense, computer hardware inventions are no different than other kinds of inventions involving physical objects. But questions about whether and how software, as a kind of intellectual object, should be protected have been vehemently debated in the courts.

8.1.3 Software as Intellectual Property

Is computer software a special kind of intellectual object that deserves both copyright and patent protection? Software, which consists of lines of programming code (or codified thought), is not exactly expressed, or "fixed," in a tangible medium as literary works are. To complicate matters, a program's code takes many forms: source code, object code, and the final executable code. Because of conceptual muddles and confusions surrounding the nature of programming code, computer programs were not, initially, eligible for either copyright or patent protection. Eventually, however, they were granted both forms of legal protection. Although software programs seem to be like inventions that could be patented, they also resemble algorithms, which, like mathematical ideas or "mental steps," are not typically eligible for patent protection.

Initially, software was not conceived of as a distinct commodity, since computer corporations tended to bundle together their software and hardware offerings as part of a single package. But Grodzinsky, Miller, and Wolf (2004) note that in the late 1960s, IBM adopted a new marketing policy that separated software (and services) from hardware, which also suggested the need for "closed source software" so that its programming division could be profitable. The practice of separating these components became further entrenched when IBM contracted with Intel and Microsoft to develop the personal computer in 1981. However, in the early 1970s, AT&T Bell Laboratories in New Jersey decided to make the source code for one of its software products "open" or freely accessible. AT&T gave away the source code and licenses for its Unix operating system to universities.[3] So two very different strategies emerged in the 1970s with respect to whether software code should be protected as proprietary information.

As late as the 1970s and early 1980s, software programs and software code were often freely exchanged among computer enthusiasts without concern for copyright law. I worked in the software industry in the early 1980s, and I recall incidents where software developers freely exchanged with each other copies of programs on which they were working: A software developer might lend a fellow developer a copy of a database program in return for a copy of a word processing program. (As we will see in our discussion of the Free Software Movement and the Open Source Initiative in Section 8.6, some programmers believe that these kinds of exchanges actually improved the quality of the software products that eventually went to market.) By the mid-1980s, the cavalier attitude that once surrounded the exchange of software programs had changed considerably, and by the 1990s, software companies carefully guarded their proprietary software, sometimes to the point of encouraging law enforcement officials to raid private homes where they suspected that unauthorized software was being used.

Some people believe that a distinction should be drawn between an individual's unauthorized copying of a friend's software program for personal use and the pirating of software in a systematic way for profit by corporations and criminals. The economic impact of systematic software piracy by organizations is far more significant than the impact of a few individuals copying their friends' programs. From a moral point of view, however, if unauthorized copying of proprietary software is wrong, then it is just as wrong for individuals as it is for organizations interested in profiting from it.

8.1.4 Evaluating an Argument for Why It is Wrong to Copy Proprietary Software

Why, exactly, is the unauthorized copying of proprietary software morally wrong? The software industry has made the following kind of argument.

PREMISE 1. Stealing a tangible object is morally wrong.

PREMISE 2. Making an unauthorized copy of proprietary software is identical to stealing a tangible object.

CONCLUSION. Making unauthorized copies of proprietary software is morally wrong.

If we apply the rules for logical validity that we examined in Chapter 3, we see that this argument is valid because of its logical form—in other words, if Premises 1 and 2 are both assumed to be true, the conclusion cannot be false. Even though the argument's form is valid, however, we could still show the argument to be unsound if either or both of the premises are false. (You may want to review the rules for valid and sound arguments in Chapter 3.)

Premise 1 is fairly straightforward, and few would question its truth. But Premise 2 is more controversial and thus we can question whether it is empirically true. For example, is duplicating a software program *identical* to stealing a physical item? We noted that intellectual objects, such as software programs, are nonexclusionary, which means that my having a copy of Program X does not exclude you having a copy of that program, and vice versa. The computer hardware on which that software program runs—e.g., my laptop computer—is exclusionary in the sense that if I own it, you do not, and vice versa. So, the act of your making an unauthorized copy of the proprietary software program that resides on my computer is *not* identical to your stealing my (physical) laptop computer, in at least one important sense. Because the truth of Premise 2 is questionable, we cannot infer that the above argument (in its present form) is sound.

Even if the original argument turns out to be unsound, however, it does not follow that its conclusion is false. Note that the conclusion—"Making unauthorized copies of proprietary software is morally wrong"—could be true for reasons other than those stated in the original argument's premises. In fact, there could be several reasons why the conclusion can be true, despite the fact that the second premise may be false. For example, even if duplicating software is not identical to stealing physical property, we can show that it may cause harm. Consider that copying the proprietary software program, like the theft of someone's physical property, deprives the property owner of the legitimate use of his or her property. If someone steals my laptop, he deprives me of my right to use a device that I own; similarly, when someone makes an unauthorized copy of a proprietary program that I own (as the copyright holder), he deprives me of income to which I am entitled. Richard Spinello (2008) argues that unauthorized copying is harmful because it is a misuse, misappropriation, or "unfair taking" of another person's property against the property owner's will.

But some still might object by claiming that while an individual programmer, who is self-employed, may be harmed by the unauthorized copying of his program, most proprietary software programs are owned by wealthy corporations; for instance, they might argue that Microsoft is so well-off that it will not suffer if it loses the revenue from a few sales of its Word program. However, you can probably see the danger that might result if everyone used this line of reasoning. (Recall our discussion of the Slippery Slope Fallacy in Chapter 3.) Thus, the unauthorized copying of software can be shown to be morally wrong, independent of whether it has a negative financial impact for the company that has ownership rights to the program.

Many nations have enacted specific laws and statutes to protect the rights and interests of "owners" of computer software programs and applications (as forms of intellectual property). We examine four different types of schemes for protecting intellectual property rights: copyright law, patents, trademarks, and trade secrets.

▶ 8.2 COPYRIGHT LAW AND DIGITAL MEDIA

Legal scholars trace the development of Anglo-American copyright law to a response to the widespread publishing of pamphlets made possible by the printing press. On the one hand, the British monarchy wanted to control the spread of "subversive" and "heretical" works that were being printed. On the other hand, authors had a vested interest in protecting their works from unauthorized reproduction. The English Statute of Anne, enacted in 1710, was the first law to give protection to authors for works attributed to them. The American colonies followed English law regarding copyright; the Framers later included these ideas in Article 1, Section 8, of the United States Constitution:

> The congress shall have the power . . . to promote the Progress of Science and the useful Arts, by securing for limited Times to authors and inventors the exclusive Rights to their respective Writings and Discoveries.

8.2.1 The Evolution of Copyright Law in the United States

The first copyright law in the United States was enacted in 1790 and applied primarily to books, maps, and charts. As newer forms of media were developed, it was extended to include photography, movies, and audio recordings. In 1909 the copyright law was amended to include any form that could be seen and read visually by humans; this modification was motivated by a new technology (namely, the player piano) in which a song could be copied onto a perforated roll. Since the musical copy could not be read from the piano roll visually (by humans), the copy was not considered a violation of the song's copyright. The "machine readable" vs. "human readable" distinction has implications for decisions as to whether software programs qualify for copyright protection: Although a program's source code can be read by humans, its executable code, which runs on a computer, cannot. Beginning in the 1960s, arguments were made that computer programs, or at least parts of computer programs, should be eligible for copyright protection.

The Copyright Act of 1976 modified copyright law, but computer programs still did not clearly satisfy the requirements necessary for making them eligible for copyright protection. It was amended again in 1980 to address the status of software programs, and the concept of a literary work was extended to include programs, computers, and "databases that exhibit authorship." The amendment defined a computer program as "a set of statements or instructions to be used directly in a computer in order to bring about certain results." To obtain a copyright for a computer program, however, its author had to show that the program contained an original expression (or arrangement) of ideas and not simply the ideas themselves.[4]

The Copyright Act of 1976 has been amended several times because of changes in computers and digital technology; for example, it was amended in 1984 with the

Semiconductor Chip Protection Act. In 1998, two important amendments were made: the Sonny Bono Copyright Term Extension Act (SBCTEA), and the Digital Millennium Copyright Act (DMCA). The SBCTEA extended the length of copyright protection from the life of the author plus fifty years to the life of the author plus seventy years. Protection for works of hire produced before 1978 were extended from seventy-five years to ninety-five years. (When an author receives payment from a corporation or organization to produce a creative or artistic work, it can be considered a work of hire.) Critics of the SBCTEA noted that the law was passed just in time to keep Mickey Mouse from entering the public domain, and they also pointed out that the Disney Corporation lobbied very hard for the passage of this act.

The DMCA has also been severely criticized—not because it extends the amount of time that a copyrighted work is protected, but because of the manner in which copyrights are extended. For example, Henderson, Spinello, and Lipinski (2007) point out that DMCA's critics identify three areas of controversy that need to be addressed: its "chilling effect" on *fair use*, its suppression of *innovation*, and its *overreach*. (We examine each of these points in later sections of this chapter.) Many critics also believe that these controversies are, in turn, closely linked to DMCA's highly controversial anti-circumvention clause, which prohibits the development of any software or hardware technology that *circumvents* (or devises a technological workaround) to copyrighted digital media.

DMCA laws have also been passed at the state level. These laws, sometimes called "Super DMCA" or "S-DMCA," have been very controversial because some are interpreted as exceeding the conditions specified in the federal DMCA. Critics, including the Electronic Frontier Foundation (EFF), argue that the Motion Picture Association of America (MPAA) has been pressing states to pass S-DMCA-type legislation that is aimed at criminalizing the possession of what the MPAA calls "unlawful communication and access devices." EFF also believes that this legislation would constitute "an unprecedented attack on the rights of technologists, hobbyists, tinkerers and the public at large."[5]

8.2.2 The Fair-Use and First-Sale Provisions of Copyright Law

The set of exclusive rights given to copyright holders is described in Section 106 of the 1976 Copyright Act. In certain cases, however, exceptions have been made to the exclusive rights that copyright holders otherwise enjoy. For example, in the case of software programs, the purchaser is allowed to make one archival copy of the program.

To balance the exclusive controls given to copyright holders against the broader interests of society, two provisions have been developed: *fair use* and *first sale*. According to the fair-use principle, every author or publisher may make limited use of another person's copyrighted work for purposes such as criticism, comment, news, reporting, teaching, scholarship, and research. This principle is important to the computer industry in particular, and to engineering in general, because it supports the practice of "reverse engineering," which allows someone to buy a product for the purpose of taking it apart to see how it works.[6]

Another balancing scheme in copyright law is the first-sale provision, which applies once the original work has been sold for the first time. At this point, the original owner loses rights over the previously protected work. For example, once you purchase a copy of a (physical) book, you are free to give away, resell, or even destroy your copy. It is not clear, however, that one can give away media in digital format that is licensed for use but not, strictly speaking, owned by a user.

Critics believe that the fair-use provision of copyright law is threatened by both SBCTEA and DMCA. Some believe that SBCTEA threatens fair use because it has delayed many proprietary works from entering the public domain and being freely available for general use. Critics argue that the DMCA also has serious implications for the fair-use principle, mainly because its anti-circumvention clause makes it illegal to reverse engineer a competitor's product to see how it works. Innovators and competitors have depended on the use of reverse engineering, which has been protected by the Copyright Act's fair-use principle. The DMCA also has implications for the first-sale provision because works formatted in digital media are typically licensed by a user rather than purchased and owned by a consumer.

We next consider two scenarios that illustrate some concerns affecting the fair-use and first-sale provisions of the current copyright law. The first scenario demonstrates one way in which the SBCTEA threatens access to older books about to enter the public domain. The second scenario illustrates how the DMCA threatens our ability to use e-books in the same way that we have been able to use physical books.

▶ SCENARIO 8–1: Eric Eldred's Web Site for Sharing Classic Books

Eric Eldred of Derry NH operated a personal, nonprofit Web site on which he included electronic versions of classic books that are in the public domain. While helping his daughters locate some older and out-of-print books for a high school literature project, Eldred discovered that it was difficult to find electronic versions of books such as *The Scarlet Letter*, so he decided to set up a Web site (www.eldritchpress.org) dedicated to online versions of older books. He included on his site, for example, the complete works of Nathaniel Hawthorne. Legally, Eldred was allowed to include electronic versions of these books on his site because their copyright protection had expired. But with the passage of SBCTEA in 1998, some of the books that were about to enter the public domain (and would thus be eligible for inclusion on Eldred's site) would instead remain under copyright protection. Eldred decided to challenge the legality of the amended Copyright Act, which he argued is incompatible with the fair-use provision and in violation of Article 1, Section 8, Clause 8, of the U.S. Constitution (see the opening of Section 8.4). His court challenge (*Eldred v. Attorney General John Ashcroft*) was turned down by a lower circuit court.[7] ■

Eldred appealed his case to the Supreme Court, and some of his advocates believed that the circuit court's decision had a good chance of being overturned. In January 2003, however, the high court upheld the lower court's decision in a 7–2 ruling.

▶ SCENARIO 8–2: Dimitri Sklyarov's Controversial Decryption Program

In the summer of 2001, Dimitri Sklyarov, a Russian citizen, traveled to Las Vegas to attend the annual Def Con Computer Security Conference. While in Las Vegas, Sklyarov was arrested by United States federal agents for carrying a copy of a program he had written to decrypt the code for the book-reading software developed by Adobe. Adobe's Acrobat eBook Reader software enabled computer users to read digital books, available online for a fee. Adobe feared that with Sklyarov's program, users would be able to read e-books for free. It also turned out that the United States government was eager to test the DMCA, especially its anti-circumvention clause, which was passed in 1998 but was not enforceable until 2000.[8] ■

Sklyarov's arrest caused considerable controversy and protest, especially in the software engineering community, where there was concern that the principle of fair use was being threatened by Adobe's e-book-reading technology. This technology could also be seen as threatening the principle of first sale. Consider that in the case of a physical ("paper and glue") book, one can do whatever one wishes after purchasing it. For example, one can give the book to a friend. Also, one can resell that book, in compliance with the first-sale provision of copyright law. The same is not true, however, of e-books, because the digitized information contained in those books cannot be subsequently exchanged without permission of the copyright holder. Note, for example, that if you own a Kindle (or some competitor to this e-book reader) and you purchase an e-book, you have the right to read that book but not to legally exchange the book with a friend in the same way that you could a physical book.

8.2.3 Software Piracy as Copyright Infringement

With the proliferation of personal computers in the 1980s, many users discovered how easy it was to duplicate software, but as we saw in Chapter 1, there was some legitimate confusion during that period as to whether it was legal to make a copy of someone else's software program. A policy vacuum existed with respect to copying proprietary software for personal use; the vacuum arose, in large part, because of certain confusions or conceptual muddles in our understanding of software. Earlier in this chapter, we noted that in the 1970s and early 1980s, software developers sometimes shared and exchanged programs with one another, and that by the late 1980s, many software companies had become extremely zealous when it came to protecting their proprietary software.

Software manufacturers, who claim to have lost millions of dollars of potential revenue because of software piracy, seem justified in their concerns regarding the pirating of proprietary software by individuals and organizations, both nationally and globally. However, some critics have argued that claims made by American software manufacturers about their loss of revenue due to the use of pirated software in developing countries are either greatly exaggerated or altogether bogus. They point out that many people and organizations in those countries could not afford to pay the prices set by American software companies for their products, so the companies have not lost any (real) revenues, because their (expensive, by American standards) software would not sell on the open market in most developing countries.

Software companies also worry about revenues lost in developed nations, including the United States, due to the illegal copying of software. Corporations such as Microsoft have been far more concerned with piracy as a form of organized crime, both domestically and internationally, than they have been about individuals making occasional unauthorized copies of their proprietary software. From a financial point view, it would seem to make perfectly good sense for Microsoft to allow some illicit copying of its software by individuals rather than spend money to pursue their arrest and prosecution. However, many corporations have been quite willing to pursue those who engage in software piracy for commercial gain. And corporations have been especially concerned about the ways that their proprietary information can be pirated over a computer network. As we saw in Chapter 7, cyberpiracy applies to more than the mere unauthorized copying of software; it also covers the unauthorized distribution (or facilitation of the distribution) of digital information on a computer network. The software industry confronted this phenomenon for the first time in 1994.

▶ **SCENARIO 8–3:** Freely Distributing Proprietary Software on the Internet

In the spring of 1994, Robert LaMacchia, then a student at MIT, operated an Internet bulletin board system (BBS) called Cynosure. He invited its users to upload and download (for free) copyrighted software to and from an anonymous server that resided in Finland. LaMacchia was arrested on charges that he had pirated software, but since LaMacchia himself did not make unauthorized copies of the proprietary software, and since he did not receive a fee for his services, law enforcement authorities had a difficult time bringing piracy charges against him. In fact, they had a difficult time finding any clear criminal grounds for prosecuting LaMacchia—there were no explicit provisions in the 1986 Computer Fraud and Abuse Act (see Chapter 7) under which he could be prosecuted. Eventually, federal authorities decided to bring charges against him (*United States v. LaMacchia*) by appealing to the Wire Fraud Act, a federal statute. Charges against LaMacchia, were eventually dropped, however, and the indictment was officially struck down by District Judge Richard Stearns, who ruled that, for constitutional reasons, any criminal copyright charge must be brought under copyright laws and not under general federal criminal laws.[9] ■

The software industry followed the case closely, and, not surprisingly, was disappointed with the outcome. Some had hoped that a conviction in the LaMacchia case would have set a precedent. In the aftermath of the LaMacchia incident, however, the 1986 Computer Fraud and Abuse Act was amended to broaden the scope of criminal behavior that could be prosecuted under it, and the No Electronic Theft (NET) Act was passed in 1997, criminalizing the "dissemination" of copyrighted information by electronic means.

While many agree with the spirit of the NET Act, some also believe that it goes too far. Prior to the NET Act, a person had to "infringe a copyright willfully" and for "purposes of commercial or financial gain" in order to be punished under the criminal provisions of the Copyright Act. The NET Act, however, has made criminal the reproduction or distribution, including by electronic means, of one or more copyrighted works, which have a total retail value of more than $1,000.[10]

Andrew Grosso (2000) believes that the meaning of copyright infringement has been "expanded" under the Net Act. He points out that a copyright infringement can occur either in fixation (in print or paper) or in virtual space, that is, by means of a mere electronic distribution, regardless of whether the copyrighted work is ever printed on paper or downloaded on to a disk, etc. According to the NET Act, merely viewing a copyrighted work posted on the Internet can be interpreted as a criminal violation of copyright. One possible interpretation is that "fixation" occurs in online viewing, because a temporary copy is "fixed" in the memory (i.e., in RAM) of the host computer, no matter how briefly the information is stored there.

8.2.4 Napster and the Ongoing Battles over Sharing Digital Music

In some ways, the LaMacchia incident foreshadowed many issues in the highly publicized Napster controversy. Like LaMacchia's Cynosure BBS, Napster provided a distribution center for proprietary digital information. Unlike Cynosure, however, Napster did not facilitate the distribution of software. But both involved the unauthorized distribution and exchange of proprietary information online.

▶ **SCENARIO 8–4:** Shutting Down the Original Napster Web Site

Napster, a very popular site for sharing music online in the late 1990s, was founded by Shawn Fanning while he was a student at Northeastern University. Napster's users were able to exchange copyrighted music files, in MP3 format, with one another. In December 1999, the Recording Industry Association of America (RIAA) sued the Napster Web site for illegally distributing copyrighted music on the Internet. Napster responded by arguing that its activities were perfectly legal under the fair-use doctrine. However, the courts ultimately ruled against Napster.[11] Although the original Napster site ceased operations, it later reopened as a pay-per-song Web site, similar to iTunes, in cooperation with the RIAA. ◼

The Napster controversy was just the beginning of an ongoing battle involving the recording industry and file-sharing sites over the unauthorized exchange of proprietary music online. Internet music providers such as Morpheus, KaZaA, and LimeWire have also supported the online exchange of MP3 files containing copyrighted music. Initially, they were able to avoid the plight of Napster, which used a centralized distribution point consisting of a centralized server, index, and registry of names in the file-exchange process. The later file-sharing services used either decentralized or "supernode" systems, based on peer-to-peer (P2P) technologies developed by Gnutella. As P2P file-sharing sites have evolved, they have become more and more decentralized and distributed.

Spinello (2008) notes that the methods for indexing the files that are exchanged in P2P systems comprise three categories: (a) a centralized indexing system (such as in the original Napster site), (b) a decentralized indexing system, and (c) a supernode system (where a group of computers can act as indexing servers). Another P2P protocol is Bit Torrent, which enables large files, such entire music CDs, to be exchanged more efficiently through a system of networked computers designated as "peers" and "seeds." Whereas KaZaA used the supernode system, the Pirate Bay service used the Bit Torrent protocol. (We briefly examined the outcome of the trial involving the Pirate Bay site in Chapter 7.)

The recording industry, in its effort to crack down on illicit file sharing, has not been deterred by the fact that later P2P systems were able to avoid the legal pitfalls surrounding the centralized indexing method used by Napster. Alternatively, the recording industry employed some new strategies and techniques in the ongoing battle with file-sharing sites. For example, it began to track down individuals that it suspected of exchanging proprietary music online. As we saw in Chapter 1 in our brief discussion of the *Verizon v. RIAA* case (2003), the recording industry issued court subpoenas to Internet service providers (ISPs) such as Comcast and Verizon, as well as to major universities, for the names of users who it suspected of downloading and exchanging large volumes of copyrighted music via those online services. While many ISPs and universities complied with the recording industry's request, Verizon challenged the RIAA in court on the grounds that complying with such requests violated specific articles of the U.S. Constitution. However, many universities have since developed strict policies that prohibit the use of their networks to exchange copyrighted music; some have even disabled their P2P file-sharing systems altogether.[12]

The recording industry has also taken other tacks in its efforts to deter the unauthorized sharing of copyrighted music files online. For example, one way it fought back was by uploading "corrupted" music files onto the popular P2P sites, so that users downloading these files would be discouraged from downloading music from those sites.

And in what could be viewed as an even more aggressive attempt to control the downloading of music by students on university campuses, the RIAA has also tried to tie the unauthorized downloading of files by college students to a loss of financial aid. Legislation introduced in November 2007 to amend and extend the Higher Education Bill of 1965 included the controversial Section 494, entitled Campus-based digital theft prevention. Kalara (2007) points out that under this controversial section of the bill, eligible institutions that participate in the federal aid program would be required to provide "annual disclosure/warnings to the students applying for or receiving financial aid," which inform them that "P2P file sharing may subject them to civil and criminal liability." The bill also would require that the universities offer subscription services to their student bodies that will give them an alternative to illegal file sharing. This legislation has been opposed by the American Association of Universities, who worries that many innocent students could be deprived of financial aid, if universities do not comply.[13]

The debate over sharing copyrighted material in P2P systems has not been limited to copyrighted music files. The motion picture industry has also been concerned about the ease with which copyrighted movies can be freely exchanged in file-sharing systems. In 2003, Metro-Goldwyn-Mayer (MGM) Studies Inc. sued two P2P file-sharing services.

▶ **SCENARIO 8–5:** The "Napster Wars" Continued: *MGM v. Grokster*

MGM and several music and motion picture studios sued Grokster (and Morpheus, who was owned by Streamcast) for "contributory copyright infringement" through its file-sharing service. MGM claimed that over 90% of the material exchanged on Grokster was copyrighted material and that the P2P service was legally liable. A district court disagreed with MGM, ruling that Grokster could not be held liable for the distribution of copyrighted material for two reasons: (a) it lacked sufficient knowledge of the infringement, and (b) it did not "materially contribute" to it. MGM then appealed the decision to the Ninth Circuit Court of Appeals, which upheld the lower court's decision. Next, MGM appealed to the U.S. Supreme Court. In their deliberations, the justices deliberated over two key principles that seemed to be in conflict: (i) the need to "protect new technologies" (such as P2P networks), and (ii) the need to provide "remedies against copyright infringement." Although the Court was unable to reach consensus on whether Grokster should be protected from liability for copyright infringement, it unanimously confirmed that using Grokster's service for exchanging copyrighted material is illegal.[14]   ∎

A central argument made by Grokster in the MGM case involved a precedent from *Sony Corp of America v. Universal City Studios Inc.* (1984), which had to resolve whether it is legal to prohibit the use of technology merely because it *could* result in copyright infringement. In that case, Universal sued to ban the sale of video recorder (VCR) technology, claiming that Sony, who manufactured the Betamax home video recorder (a rival of later VHS-based recording devices), was liable for copyright infringement, either directly or indirectly, because the new technology could be used to make illegal copies of movies. Sony argued, however, that people who used VCR machines could record movies already being televised at a certain time and then view those movies at their own convenience.

By a very narrow decision—one decided by a 5–4 vote—the Supreme Court ruled in favor of Sony. (It is very difficult to imagine the consequences for both the entertainment industry and consumers if the decision had gone the other way.) The Court ruled that simply because VCR technology could be used to do something illegal is not sufficient grounds for banning that technology. In essence, it concluded that as long as the technology was capable of "substantial noninfringing uses" (SNIU), it could not be barred from sale and distribution. So, in effect, the Court also determined that VCRs did not violate copyright law merely because they were capable of substantial copyright infringement. (This interpretation has since come to be known as the "Sony Safe Harbor" precedent.) However, courts have since been reluctant to ban or limit the use of technological advances because of this precedent. And since P2P networks are considered a "technological advance" that is capable of SNIU, they would seem to fall under the Sony precedent (Samuelson 2004).

As previously noted, MGM argued that 90% of the material exchanged on Grokster's P2P system was copyrighted material; they also argued that this clearly met the threshold of substantial copyright infringement. In this sense, MGM seemed to be challenging the legitimacy of the Sony safe harbor precedent itself. But the Supreme Court justices were careful not to appeal to the Sony precedent in their ruling, which disagreed with the lower courts. Instead they found Grokster liable for "inducing" copyright infringement through their practices such as advertising; but the Court did not rule that P2P technology itself violated copyright law. So some legal analysts such as Pamela Samuelson (2005) believe that MGM did not get the victory in court that it sought, even though Grokster was forced to pay $50 million to the music and recording industries.

▶ 8.3 PATENTS, TRADEMARKS, AND TRADE SECRETS

We noted earlier that in addition to copyright law, three alternative legal frameworks have been devised to protect intellectual property: patents, trademarks, and trade secrets. We examine examples of each form of protection with respect to how each can be applied to cybertechnology.

8.3.1 Patent Protections

A patent is a form of legal protection given to individuals who create an invention or process. Unlike copyright protection, patents offer a twenty-year exclusive monopoly over an expression or implementation of a protected work. The current U.S. patent law is based on the Patent Act of 1952, which was amended in 1995. Patent protection can be applied to inventions and discoveries that include "utilitarian or functional" devices such as machines and "articles of manufacture." Patent law requires that inventions satisfy three conditions:

- usefulness
- novelty
- nonobviousness

First, an invention must have a certain *usefulness*, or utility, in order to be awarded a patent; inventing a machine or process that does nothing "useful" would not merit its inventor a patent. Also, the invention must be *novel*, or new, in order to qualify for a patent. One cannot simply modify an existing invention and expect to be granted a patent for it; the modification would have to be significant enough to make a qualified difference. Finally, the invention or process must be *nonobvious*.[15] For example, it is possible that no one has yet recorded directions for how to travel from Buffalo, New York, to Cleveland, Ohio, through Pittsburgh, Pennsylvania, but describing the route would not satisfy the condition of nonobviousness.

Although computer hardware inventions clearly satisfied the requirements of patent law, this was not initially the case with computer software. John Snapper (1995) points out that in the 1960s, most of the discussion involving the protection of software focused on patents. He also notes that in a series of decisions beginning with *Gotshalk v. Benson* (1972), the United States Patent Office and the courts established a strong opposition to patenting software. Benson applied for a patent for an algorithm that translated the representation of numbers from base 10 to base 2; such an algorithm is an important feature of all programs. So, critics worried that if Benson had been granted a patent for his algorithm, he would have controlled almost every computer in use for a number of years.

However, Benson was denied the patent because his algorithm was viewed as an abstract process or mathematical formula that could be performed by a series of mental steps with the aid of pencil and paper (Snapper 1995). But the goal of obtaining patents for computer programs did not end with Benson. And in 1981, the U.S. Supreme Court ruled in what many now consider a landmark case for patents affecting computer software.

▶ **SCENARIO 8–6:** A Pivotal Court Decision Involving Software Patents

In *Diamond v. Deihr*, the Supreme Court decided 5–4 that a patent could be awarded for a computer program under certain conditions; in this instance, the program assisted in converting rubber into tires. On the one hand, Deihr had developed a new process that physically transformed raw rubber into rubber tires; on the other hand, Deihr had only a new computer program, since every other part of the machinery used in the conversion process consisted of traditional technology. Initially, Deihr's request for a patent was denied by Diamond, the director of the Patent Office. But Deihr appealed, and his case was eventually heard by the Supreme Court, which ruled in Deihr's favor. However, in their ruling, the justices also continued to affirm the view that computer algorithms themselves are not patentable. They pointed out that the patent awarded to Deihr was not for the computer program but for the rubber tire transformation process as a whole.[16]   ■

Since the Deihr case, numerous patents have been granted to computer programs and software applications. Some fear that now patent protection has gone too far—the United States Patent and Trademark Office (PTO) issues about 20,000 new software patents every year. Gregory Aharonian (2001) points out that between 1990 and 1999 the number of patents increased from 1,300 to 22,500; and between 1993 and 1999, the number of patents issued increased tenfold. He also points out that between 1979 and 1999, more than 700,000 patents were issued for electronics inventions, including software products.

8.3.2 Trademarks

A trademark is a word, name, phrase, or symbol that identifies a product or service. In 1946 the Lanham Act, also referred to as the Trademark Act, was passed to provide protection for registered trademarks.[17] To qualify for a trademark, the "mark" is supposed to be distinctive. Consider, for example, the apple that has come to symbolize Apple and Macintosh computers and products. As Debora Halbert (1999) notes, however, a (not very distinctive) trademark for "uh-huh" was granted to Pepsi-Cola.

Because of decisions such as this, critics have argued that trademark protections are being expanded in ways that are inappropriate.

Consider the following example, involving the e-commerce sector, which may support the view that some entrepreneurs are trying to expand the scope of trademarks inappropriately.

▶ **SCENARIO 8–7:** A Trademark Dispute in Cyberspace

America Online (AOL) applied for trademarks for its expressions "You've Got Mail," "Buddy List," and "IM" (Instant Messenger). If AOL were allowed to own these trademarks, other ISPs that used these or very similar expressions could be sued for infringing on AOL's registered trademarks. So, AT&T decided to challenge AOL. In this case, the court ruled that the expressions were not unique to AOL.[18] ◼

We examine some controversies affecting trademarks in cyberspace in Chapter 9, where we consider the process used to register Internet domain names and the use of HTML metatags.

8.3.3 Trade Secrets

A *trade secret* consists of information that is highly valuable and considered crucial in the operation of a business or other enterprise. The "secret" is accessible to only a few select individuals within the organization. Trade secrets can be used to protect formulas (such as the one used by Coca-Cola) and blueprints for future projects. They can also protect chemical compounds and processes used in manufacturing. Owners of a trade secret have exclusive rights to make use of it, but they have this right only as long as the secret is maintained.[19]

One problem with protecting trade secrets is that trade secret law is difficult to enforce at the international level. Not only have corporate spies in the United States tried to steal secrets from their corporate rivals, but there is evidence to suggest that international industrial espionage has become a growing industry. The TRIPS (Trade Relationship Aspects of Intellectual Property Standards) agreement, which was part of the WIPO (World Intellectual Property Organization) agreements, includes a provision for protecting trade secrets at the international level; specifically, Article 39 of the TRIPS agreement protects trade secrets by stating explicitly that disclosure of trade secrets comes within the meaning of unfair competition in the global community.[20] (Both WIPO and TRIPS are described in detail in Section 8.4.)

Of course, protecting trade secrets is not something that is peculiar to the computer industry or to the high-tech industry. However, because of the considerable amount of research and development conducted in those industries, and the fortunes that can be made from computer-based products, they are highly vulnerable to trade secret violations.

▶ 8.4 JURISDICTIONAL ISSUES INVOLVING INTELLECTUAL PROPERTY LAWS

The specific intellectual property laws described in this chapter apply mostly to the United States even though their implications are global. Some international treaties pertaining to intellectual property in general, and copyright in particular, have also been signed; for example, the TRIPS agreement has implemented requirements from the Berne Convention for the Protection of Literary and Artistic Works.[21] This agreement is recognized by signatories to the WIPO.[22]

International intellectual property laws have been very difficult to enforce globally, in large part because of jurisdictional issues. In recent years, however, there has been considerable international cooperation in prosecuting digital piracy cases across juris-dictional lines. For example, in April 2009 the owners and operators of the internation-ally controversial (Sweden-based) Pirate Bay site, who were found guilty of "unlawful transfer" of copyrighted material, received both fines and jail sentences.[23]

In countries such as the United States, some laws affecting intellectual property also apply at the state level. These laws apply to the sale of goods, as well as to contracts involved in those sales, and they often vary from state to state. With regard to sales and contracts involving computers and electronic devices, two pieces of legislation have aimed at establishing uniformity across states: the Uniform Computer and Information Transactions Act (UCITA) and the Uniform Electronic Transactions Act (UETA).[24] Whereas UETA applies to electronic contracts in general, UCITA is designed to govern transactions, including contracts, involving the development, sale, licensing, mainte-nance, and support of computer software. It would also extend to all shrink-wrap licenses and "click-wrap" agreements. Roy Girasa (2002) points out that click-wrap agreements give the user an on-screen choice to agree or not agree with the product requirements, and a program might not open until a user consents by clicking on the words "I agree." Thus far, UCITA has been enacted into law in the states of Virginia and Maryland.

Even though UCITA is not law in most states, critics point out that its effects can be felt in all states because contracts involving electronic goods and services can span multiple states and thus potentially involve Virginia and Maryland law in the process. Although there is general agreement that a uniform law across states pertaining to electronic contracts would be desirable, critics worry about the effects that universal passage of UCITA would have for American consumers. While UCITA has been supported by major companies in the software industry, it has been criticized by the Software Engineering Ethics Research Institute and the American Library Association,

TABLE 8.1 **Acronyms Corresponding to Intellectual-Property Laws and Agreements**

DMCA	Digital Millennium Copyright Act (U.S. Public Law 304, 1998)
NET Act	No Electronic Theft Act
PLT	Patent Law Treaty
SBCTEA	Sonny Bono Copyright Term Extension Act
S-DMCA	Super-DMCA (DMCA legislation passed at the state level in the U.S.)
TLT	Trademark Law Treaty
TRIPS	Trade Relationship Aspects of Intellectual Property Standards
UCC	Uniform Commerce Code (for electronic contracts)
UCITA	Uniform Computer and Information Transactions Act
UETA	Uniform Electronic Transactions Act
UTSA	Uniform Trade Secrets Act
WIPO	World Intellectual Property Organization

as well as by many consumer advocacy groups. Some critics worry that UCITA would undermine existing consumer protection laws and threaten current copyright exceptions for fair use and first sale.

In our discussions involving copyright protection schemes, we have used several acronyms and abbreviations to describe and refer to national and international policies, treaties, and statutes. Table 8.1 contains a list of those acronyms.

► 8.5 PHILOSOPHICAL FOUNDATIONS FOR INTELLECTUAL PROPERTY RIGHTS

Even though some philosophers and political theorists have opposed the notion of private property rights, we will presume that property ownership is justifiable. We should note that some believe that property ownership rights make sense in the physical realm but are skeptical that property rights can be extended to intellectual objects in cyberspace. We will examine arguments for this position in Section 8.6.

In Section 8.1.2, we alluded to three philosophical theories—labor, utilitarian, and personality theories—that have been used to justify property rights. We next examine each of those theories in greater detail.

8.5.1 The Labor Theory of Property

The labor theory of property traces its origins to seventeenth-century philosopher John Locke. In his *Second Treatise on Civil Government*, Locke argues that when a person "mixes" his or her labor with the land, that person is entitled to the fruit of his or her labor. So if a person tills and plants crops on a section of land that is not already owned by another—an act which, Locke notes, requires considerable toil—that person has a right to claim ownership of the crops. Analogously, if a person cuts down a tree in the woods and saws it into several pieces, then the person is entitled to the pieces of wood that result from his or her labor. Hence, for Locke, a person's right to property is closely tied to that person's labor.

Locke also includes an important qualification with respect to the appropriation of property, which has come to be known as the "Lockean proviso." The proviso states that when someone either encloses a section of land from the commons or appropriates objects from it, "enough and as good" must be left for others. So, in Locke's account of property, a person has neither the right to cut down all of the trees in a "commons" nor the right to take the last tree. Even with this qualification, however, some argue that Locke's theory fails to provide an adequate account of property rights.

Locke's property theory has been attacked on several fronts. For example, some critics argue that even if Locke's labor theory makes sense for physical property, it does not follow that it can be extended to intellectual property. Noting that Locke associates labor with arduous physical work, these critics point out that the production of intellectual objects does not necessarily require the same kind of onerous toil (or "sweat of the brow") that goes into producing tangible goods. But we can see how an author might claim a right to the ownership of intellectual objects generated by his or her labor, because writing a book, a poem, or a software program does require a fair amount of toil.

Other critics of Locke's property theory point out that intellectual objects are nonexclusionary in nature (as we saw in Section 8.2.1) and thus are not scarce. From this, they go on to infer that there is no need to grant property rights for those objects in a way that would be strictly analogous to rights involving physical property.

Others dispute Locke's claim that a property right is a *natural right*. They ask, What evidence is there for Locke's assertion that an individual's right to own property is a natural right, as opposed to an artificial (or man-made) right? Also, Locke's theory of property presupposes that persons making property claims "own their own bodies." If the right to own property is indeed a natural right, then it should apply to all persons, but consider the example of slavery, a relevant issue in Locke's time. Slaves do not legally own their bodies and it would follow, on Locke's reasoning, that they have no claim to the fruits of their labor—that is, they do not have property rights. So property rights, according to Locke's labor theory, do not apply equally to all people; if they did, Native Americans who mixed their labor with the soil should have been granted property rights to their land in North and South America. It is not clear how Locke can claim that property ownership is a natural right, and yet at the same time imply that such a right could possibly be denied to some individuals who happen to be slaves or Native Americans.

Despite these objections, however, some believe that Locke's property theory can be used to justify the protection of intellectual objects. We next consider a scenario in which an appeal for copyright protection is made on the basis of the labor theory of property.

▶ **SCENARIO 8–8:** DEF Corporation vs. XYZ Inc.

DEF Corporation, a software company with eighty employees, has spent the last year developing a database program that it is about to release. Thirty software developers have been employed full time on this project, and each software developer worked an average of sixty hours per week. The company expects that it will take more than one year to recoup the investment of labor and time put into this project. DEF applies for a copyright for its product.

XYZ Inc., which also produces database software, files a suit against DEF Corporation for allegedly infringing on its copyright: XYZ claims that DEF has copied a feature used in the interface in one of XYZ's software products. DEF objects by arguing that the feature is, in fact, not original and thus XYZ Inc. should not be eligible for copyright protection. More importantly, DEF further argues that it has invested considerable labor and "sweat" in its database program, so it should be rewarded for its hard work. ∎

Does DEF's claim make sense in light of the labor theory of property? Is the labor expended on a particular project, in itself, sufficient to make the case for copyright protection? According to Locke's labor theory, DEF would seem to have a reasonable case, but XYZ sees the matter very differently. Do you agree with DEF's position or with the case made by XYZ?

8.5.2 The Utilitarian Theory of Property

Critics of the labor theory argue that a rationale for granting property rights should not be confused with an individual's labor or with a natural right; rather, property rights are better understood as artificial rights or conventions devised by the state to achieve certain practical ends. According to utilitarian theory, granting property rights will maximize the good for the greatest number of people in a given society. (Recall our Chapter 2 discussion of utilitarianism, and Jeremy Bentham and John Stuart Mill's arguments for it.) In many respects, utilitarian theory was used by the framers of the U.S. Constitution to justify the granting of property rights for intellectual objects (creative works and inventions) to individuals. The Founders believed that incentives in the form of copyrights and patents would motivate individuals to bring out their creative products and that, as a result, American society in general would benefit.

An advantage of the utilitarian theory is that it does not need to appeal to the abstract principle of a natural right to justify the granting of property rights to creators and inventors of intellectual objects. However, utilitarians have their critics as well. In Chapter 2, we saw some shortcomings of utilitarian theory with respect to protecting the interests of individuals who fall outside the scope of the greatest number in a given society. Also, utilitarians tend to appeal to an economic/financial incentive as a necessary motivation for bringing creative works into the marketplace. For these reasons, many critics find the utilitarian rationale for granting property rights to be inadequate. The following scenario considers some incentives one might have for bringing forth a creative work based on the utilitarian argument for property rights.

▶ **SCENARIO 8–9:** Sam's Multiple CD Loader/Reader

Sam is a very talented and creative person, but he is not terribly industrious when it comes to following through with his ideas. He has an idea for loading multiple CDs onto a desktop computer and then retrieving and playing them individually through a series of mouse clicks. Many of Sam's friends are interested in his idea, and some have strongly encouraged him to develop his CD loading device so that they can use it on their home computers. But Sam remains unconvinced and unmotivated. Then Sam's friend, Pat, tells him that an acquaintance of hers patented an analogous invention and parleyed it into a profit of several thousand dollars. Pat tries to persuade Sam that not only would his invention benefit his friends but also that he would stand to gain financially if he patents the product. After considering Pat's advice, Sam decides to work on his multiple CD-retrieval invention and apply for a patent for it. ■

Was a utilitarian incentive (i.e., in the form of a financial benefit) necessary to get Sam to follow through on his invention? Would he have brought his invention into the marketplace if there were not a financial enticement? Do people only produce creative works because of financial rewards they might receive? On the one hand, it would seem that financial incentives could motivate some individuals, such as Sam, to produce a creative work that benefits society in general. However, it is not clear that all great musical composers have written scores solely because of the prospects of becoming wealthy. It is possible, for example, that some gifted composer wrote music for the sheer enjoyment it brought him or her as a creator of artistic works. So there may be factors other than financial incentives that influence creators to bring forth their works.

8.5.3 The Personality Theory of Property

Critics of the labor and utilitarian theories believe that a theory that links the granting of property rights to either (a) an individual's onerous labor or (b) the notion of social utility misses an important point about the nature of the creative work involved in the production of intellectual objects. Both the labor and utilitarian theories appeal to criteria external to the individual himself as the rationale for granting a property right. Note that in each case, the criterion is a reward that is directly monetary in the case of utilitarian theory, and indirectly monetary in the case of labor theory. Both theories assume an extrinsic criterion – i.e., either one's labor or some economic incentive – for justifying property rights; neither considers the possibility that an internal criterion could justify these rights. In this sense, both theories underestimate the role of the persona or *personality* of the creator of the intellectual work. According to the personality theory of property, the intellectual object is an extension of the creator's personality (i.e., the person's being, or soul). And it is because of this relationship between the intellectual object and the creator's personality that advocates of the personality theory believe that creative works deserve legal protection.

The personality theory traces its origins to the writings of G. W. F. Hegel, a nineteenth-century philosopher, and it has served as a foundational element in intellectual property laws enacted by nations in continental Europe. In France, the personality account of property is sometimes referred to as the "moral rights" (*droits morals*) theory of property. The personality theory provides an interesting interpretation of *why* an author should have control over the ways in which his or her work can be displayed and distributed. To ensure this control, personality theorists suggest that authors should be given protection for their artistic work even if they have no legal claim to any monetary reward associated with it. Consider a scenario in which the personality theory of property can be applied.

▶ **SCENARIO 8–10:** Using a Beatles' Song in the Context of a TV Commercial

In mid-1987, the Nike Corporation aired a television commercial for its sneakers that featured the song "Revolution," composed by John Lennon in the late 1960s (when he was a member of the Beatles). Lennon was murdered in 1980, so when the Nike ad aired on commercial television, he could neither approve nor disapprove of how his song was being used. Many of Lennon's fans, however, were outraged that a song penned by Lennon to address the serious political and social concerns of the turbulent 1960s could be used so frivolously in a TV commercial. Critics argued that Lennon would not have approved of his song being used in this manner. However, even if Lennon had been alive, he may not have had any legal recourse when the TV commercial aired, because the entire Lennon-McCartney corpus of songs was purchased by Michael Jackson in the 1980s; Michael Jackson owned the copyright to "Revolution."[25] ■

By appealing to the personality theory, however, the case could be made that Lennon—or in this instance, his widow—should have some say in how his song was represented in a commercial forum. Next consider a hypothetical scenario in which we can also apply the personality theory of property.

▶ **SCENARIO 8–11:** Angela's B++ Programming Tool

Angela, a graduate student who has been struggling to make ends meet, has developed a new programming tool, called B++. This software application, which employs the notion of a "reduced instruction set" technique, can be used in conjunction with the standard C++ programming language to execute certain tasks more quickly than the C++ instruction set. Angela has recently published an article that describes, in detail, the reduced set of instructions, how they work, and why she was motivated to develop B++. She was delighted to have her article published in the prestigious journal *CyberTechnology*. As part of the conditions for publication, however, Angela had to agree to sign over the copyright for her article to CyberPress (the publisher of *CyberTechnology*).

TABLE 8.2 Three Philosophical Theories of Property

Labor Theory	Argues that a property right is a natural right and that property rights can be justified by the labor, or toil, that one invests in cultivating land or in creating a work of art.
Utilitarian Theory	Argues that property rights are not natural rights but rather artificial rights created by the state. Property rights are granted to individuals and to corporations because they result in greater overall social utility.
Personality Theory	Argues that a property right is a moral right and that property rights are justified not because of labor or social utility but because creative works express the personalities of the authors who create them.

Angela is then informed that a textbook publisher, CyberTextbooks Inc., wishes to include a portion of her article in a textbook. As the copyright holder for Angela's article, CyberPress is legally authorized to allow CyberTextbooks to reprint all or selected portions of her article. Suppose, however, that Angela protests that mere excerpts from her article neither truly convey the important features of her programming tool nor explain how it works. She further argues that the article is an extension of her persona and that only in total does the article reveal her creative talents as a programmer. ■

Does Angela have a legitimate objection in this case? Should she, the original author of the article and the creator of the new programming tool, have the right to prevent her article from being published in abridged form? Can her argument, based on the notion of intellectual property as an expression of one's personality, be defended on moral grounds? Because she signed over the copyright for her article to CyberPress, she has no legal grounds for objecting to how that article is subsequently used. However, on moral grounds, she could claim that the publication of her abridged article does not fairly present her creative work.

Table 8.2 summarizes the three philosophical theories of property.

▶ 8.6 THE FREE SOFTWARE AND THE OPEN SOURCE MOVEMENTS

We have examined three traditional theories that have been used to justify the protection of intellectual property from a philosophical perspective. In the introduction to Section 8.5, however, we also noted that some have argued for the view that no formal legal protection should be given to intellectual property even if we do grant such protection to physical property. One of the best known, and perhaps most controversial, arguments for why conventional intellectual property rights should not be granted to computer software has been made by Richard Stallman (2004), who views software ownership as a form of "hoarding" that disregards the general welfare of society. As an alternative to this trend, Stallman proposes that programmers work together to make software freely available for humankind rather than supporting efforts to restrict its use.

Although Stallman has been a staunch advocate for the view that software should be free, we should note that he intends "free" to refer to liberty, not to price (or "free" as in free speech versus free beer). Grodzinsky, Miller, and Wolf (2004) suggest that Stallman's position on why software should be free may have been influenced by the culture of the 1970s at the Massachusetts Institute of Technology, where source code could be freely exchanged. As we saw in Section 8.3, however, that practice began to change in the late 1970s and early 1980s. Also during that period, the burgeoning computer industry hired many of the best software developers and programmers from academic computing labs, and some of those individuals took the software they developed with them. As a result, some of that software eventually became proprietary. In response to these trends, Stallman began his GNU (Gnu's Not Unix) project in 1984. GNU's goal was to develop an entire Unix-like operating system, complete with system utilities, that was "open" and freely accessible.

8.6.1 GNU and the Free Software Foundation

As stronger intellectual property rights began to be granted to software "owners" in the early 1980s, and as more and more software became proprietary, some programmers were concerned about whether they would be able to exchange software programs with each other in the future. They also worried that someone other than themselves would "own" their creative works. In 1985, the Free Software Foundation (FSF) was formed in response to these concerns, as well as to support of Stallman's GNU project.

According to FSF, four "freedoms" are essential for free software. These include *freedom to*

1. run the program, for any purpose;
2. study how the program works, and adapt it for your needs;
3. redistribute copies so you can help your neighbor;
4. improve the program, and release your improvements to the public so that the whole community benefits.[26]

The software that is produced by programmers adhering to "free software" requirements is typically accompanied by a licensing agreement that is designed to keep it freely available to other users "downstream," who can continue to modify the source code. The best known of these is the GNU Public License (GPL). The kind of protection granted by this license is also known as *copyleft*. ("Copyleft" refers to a group of licenses that currently apply to documents, music, and art, as well as software.) Whereas copyright law is seen by FSF's proponents as a way to restrict the right to make and redistribute copies of a particular work, a copyleft license included in GPL uses an alternative scheme that "subverts" the traditional copyright mechanism in order to ensure that every person who receives a copy, or derived version of a work, can use, modify, and also redistribute both the work and the derived version of the work. All derivative works of GPL software must also be licensed under GPL. In this way, the four freedoms of FSF are propagated in future software developed under this agreement.[27]

By the early 1990s, the GNU project had produced many important software development tools in compliance with FSF guidelines and the specifications for Unix-like source code. Throughout the 1980s, however, there was some confusion as to just what "Unix" meant, since several versions of that operating system existed—some at universities such as Berkeley, and others in the private sector such as AT&T Bell Laboratories where Unix was originally developed. This resulted in lawsuits and counter lawsuits regarding which sections of Unix software source code could be freely distributed and which sections were proprietary. The legal problems created some difficulties for Stallman and the GNU project because GNU still lacked the core of its (Unix-like) operating system—that is, the kernel. However, this issue was finally resolved in the early 1990s, when Linus Torvalds developed the kernel for a Unix-like operating system that he called Linux. At this point, GNU realized its goal of having a complete, functional operating system with all of the source code freely available for inspection, modification, and improvement.[28] The GNU project and FSF significantly influenced another, related software development movement known as the Open Source Initiative.

8.6.2 The Open Source Movement

The Open Source Initiative (OSI), which began in 1988, shares many of the same goals as FSF—most notably, the ability of a software user to look at, understand, modify, and redistribute the source code for that software. Like FSF, OSI requires that the source code for "open source software" (OSS) be freely available. So, both movements are similar with respect to their requirements for source code in the software development process. And some authors, including Chopra and Dextra (2009), use the expression "FOSS" to describe "Free and Open Source Software." However, as Eric Raymond (2004) notes, there are significant differences in the "attitudes" or philosophies of these two groups. Whereas FSF continues to focus on promoting its philosophical position that software should be free, OSS has concentrated its efforts more on promoting the open source model as an alternative methodology to "closed-source" development for software. OSS and FSF also differ with respect to requirements for how the software is used downstream. For example, FSF requires that all derivative pieces of software be subject to the original requirements and thus remain "open" and nonproprietary. OSS, on the contrary, is more flexible with respect to its derivative software. Unlike FSF, which requires that users strictly adhere to its GPL license in all derivative uses of its software, OSS supports less restrictive licenses such as Berkeley's Software Distribution (BSD) and Netscape's Mozilla Public License (MPL). These licenses are considered more "lenient" than GPL because they permit programmers to alter the open source software and to release it as a proprietary product.[29]

Another difference between OSS and FSF can be found in their attitudes toward the business community. The former is less anticommercial than the latter. In fact, many in the open source community interact comfortably with members of the business community. Because of its success in the software world, OSS now poses a significant threat to companies that produce proprietary software, such as Microsoft Corp. In addition to the Linux operating system, other well-known open source products include the Apache Web server and the Perl programming language. Whereas Torvalds believes that OSS and commercial software can co-exist, Stallman does not believe that this is possible in the long run because of the profit incentives that drive investors in the commercial sector. Stallman also condemns the business community's practice of producing proprietary or "closed" code as unethical, and he claims that signing a typical software licensing agreement is like "betraying your neighbor." Richard Spinello (2003) notes that some of Stallman's followers have gone so far as to suggest that FSF is "morally superior" to proprietary software. However, we will not pursue that debate here. Instead, a more important question for our purposes is how the OSS and FSF movements can help us to think about at an issue at the heart of the contemporary intellectual property debate: Is the free flow of information still possible in a digital world?

As we saw in Chapter 6, some of Stallman's followers subscribe to the mantra *information wants to be free*. We should not assume that Stallman himself holds this view with respect to all information, however, because he focuses his arguments specifically on why computer software should be free. One point that Stallman makes in his discussion of software is particularly useful in helping us think about issues involving the concept of information (in general) vis-à-vis intellectual property from a radically different perspective—namely, information is something that humans desire to *share* with one another. Although this insight undergirds Stallman's view that software should be free, we do not need to embrace his position on software to appreciate the force of Stallman's insight with respect to the broader notion of information. In order to be shared, information must be communicated; so elaborate intellectual property structures and mechanisms that prohibit, or even discourage, the communication of information would seem to undermine its very purpose as something to be shared.

▶ 8.7 THE "COMMON GOOD" APPROACH: AN ALTERNATIVE FRAMEWORK FOR ANALYZING THE INTELLECTUAL PROPERTY DEBATE

In the preceding section we focused our discussion on the question whether software should be unrestricted and thus freely available to distribute and modify in conformance with certain "open" or "free" licensing agreements, as opposed to being legally protected in virtue of one or more philosophical theories. Although our discussion centered on computer software, in particular, we saw that a more general question that arises is whether the free flow of information itself, in digital form, should be restricted. While not everyone may agree with the claim that software should be free, we noted that some have found Stallman's insight about the nature and purpose of *information* (i.e., as something that humans naturally want to share and communicate) to be compelling.

Some authors writing on the topic of intellectual property have noted that Stallman's insights are compatible with key elements in virtue ethics, which we discussed in Chapter 2. Michael McFarland (2004, 2005), who suggests that we can draw from principles in virtue ethics in understanding and analyzing issues involving intellectual property, appeals to Stallman's insight that the essential purpose of information is to be shared. McFarland also notes how this insight supports the "common good" view of intellectual property.

McFarland's notion of a "common good" view of computer ethics incorporates aspects of Aristotle's *Nicomachean Ethics*. In Chapter 2, we saw that key elements of Aristotle's theory serve as the cornerstone for virtue ethics, but how can this view provide a framework for discussing intellectual property issues? McFarland suggests the following strategy. First, it is important to note that Aristotle believed that every object had a nature, end, or purpose, which he called its *good*. Following his method of inquiry, we begin any philosophical investigation by asking what the good, or purpose, of an object *is*. To investigate information as an intellectual object, we should aim at understanding its ultimate purpose.

Although information can certainly be understood as a form of self-expression (as the personality theory rightly suggests), and as a product that performs some useful functions (as utilitarians correctly suggest), it also has an even more fundamental purpose than personal expression and utility. Information, McFarland argues, is ultimately about communication; hence the nature and purpose of intellectual property in the form of information is communication, and thus an adequate account of the purpose of information (as something to be communicated) must take that into consideration.

McFarland believes that traditional concepts of property often overlook the ethically significant relationships that some kinds of property have with the rest of society. The three traditional theories of property that we examined in Section 8.6 focus on criteria such as an individual's (or a corporation's) labor, social utility (cost benefits), or the author's personality. But they fail to consider that the purpose of information is something whose essential nature is to be shared and communicated. Hence, McFarland believes that a common-good analysis of property, which examines the nature of information in terms of a broader social context, can provide us with an attractive alternative to the traditional property theories.

How is a common-good approach to intellectual property issues, which takes into account the overall good of society, different from a utilitarian theory? We noted earlier that a utilitarian system's primary concern is with maximizing the good for the majority, but utilitarianism does not always take individual rights into consideration in producing the greatest good for the greatest number. McFarland points out that a utilitarian analysis based solely on cost-benefits criteria might determine that it is desirable to publish a person's private diary because many people would enjoy reading it. Although the benefit to the overall majority would outweigh any embarrassment to the individual writer of the diary, such a practice is not morally correct, because it violates the basic right of humans to be respected.

McFarland also points out that if we begin our analysis of intellectual property issues simply by analyzing the notion of property itself, then the central point of debate tends to be about ownership and control; this is indeed how property issues are typically conceived and debated. McFarland believes that if we are willing to step outside that conventional framework, we can get a more complete view of the issues surrounding the intellectual property debate. In doing this, we gain the insight that an adequate theory of information must take into account its *social nature*, an important feature that we tend to overlook when we think of intellectual objects only in terms of rights and property.

8.7.1 *Information Wants to be Shared* versus Information Wants to be Free

Perhaps a new principle will emerge from the insights of Stallman, McFarland, and others: Information wants to be shared.[30] Note that this principle is very different from the claim "information wants to be free." We do not need to embrace the latter in order to defend the former. As we saw in Chapter 6, the view that all information should be free is not only naïve, it is conceptually flawed. For example, Eugene Spafford (2007) has described some of the undesirable consequences that such a principle would have for protecting individual privacy if all personal information were freely accessible. Also, Kenneth Himma (2005) has shown why the view that information should be free is problematic as a "normative principle" since it is not clear who, exactly, should be responsible for making it free. For example, is the government or the state obligated to make this information freely available to its citizens? So it is important to distinguish the principle we defend in this chapter from the more controversial view that all information should be free.

Not only is the principle *information wants to be shared* clearly compatible with McFarland's "common-good" approach to intellectual property, it is also compatible with positions that others have expressed with regard to the social benefits of being able to share information freely. For example, Richard De George (2003) points out that because technology now makes possible the sharing of information in ways that were not previously possible, it has provided us with greater opportunity to move from the level of individual to the level of community. Yet he also notes that, paradoxically, by focusing on information as a commodity, the software industry has highlighted its commercial value, and, as a result, policies and schemes have been constructed to control information for commercial purposes rather than to share it freely.

To see the force of De George's claim, consider that copyright laws, originally intended to cover print media, were designed to encourage the distribution of information. We have seen that these laws have since been extended to cover digital media, inhibiting the distribution of electronic information. The distribution of digitized information is now being discouraged, despite the fact that cybertechnology has made information exchange easy and inexpensive. To illustrate this point, consider the interlibrary loan policy used by many libraries—a practice that has helped expand the notion of a learning community. Physical books are exchanged between libraries so that individuals can borrow, for a limited time, books not physically available at their local library. When I was a graduate student, I would sometimes take advantage of my university's interlibrary loan policy: If the books that I so easily borrowed then were available only in digitized form now, it might no longer be possible to borrow them because the Digital Millennium Copyright Act discourages the sharing of electronic information by granting copyright holders of digital media the ability to prohibit their exchange.

Copyright laws were originally designed to encourage the flow of information in print media, via their fair-use provisions. Yet, for digital media they have been revised in a way that discourages the flow, and thus the sharing, of electronic information. What implications could this trend have for the future? Consider that the ability to share, not to hoard, information contributed to the development of the World Wide Web. Also consider what might have happened if the inventors of the Internet and the Web had been more entrepreneurial-minded and less concerned with sharing information. Tim Berners-Lee, who invented HTTP (the protocol used on the Web), never bothered to apply for a patent for his invention or for a copyright for his code. As a physicist working at CERN (a laboratory in Switzerland), he desired to develop a common protocol for Internet communication so that scientists could share information more easily with each other. Note that Berners-Lee's goal in developing the Web was to provide a forum where information could be *shared*. A person whose interest was more entrepreneurial could have sought intellectual property protection for his or her contribution, thereby reducing the amount of information that could be shared. Also consider that Doug Englebart, who invented the mouse, received no patent for his contribution, but virtually every major computer manufacturer, as well as every computer user who has used a graphical interface, has benefited by his seminal contribution to what came to be called the "windows interface" in computing.

Consider also how the sharing of information has benefited many of those entrepreneurs who now seek to control the flow of information in cyberspace. It has been argued that Microsoft benefited significantly from the work done by Apple Corporation on its graphical user interface (the system of icons that users can point to and click on to accomplish a task). And it is well known that when Steve Jobs was at Apple, he visited Xerox Park, where he discovered that a graphical interface had already been invented by researchers there. So it is reasonably accurate to say that current user interfaces have benefited from the sharing of information along the way. Would it be fair to credit any one company or person with exclusive rights to a graphical user interface? Would doing so not also eliminate, or certainly impede, the possibility of incremental development and innovation? And more importantly, would it not also prevent us from sharing that important information?

It is interesting to note that John Perry Barlow (1997) confidently predicted the end of intellectual property laws in cyberspace, arguing that such laws no longer made sense in the information age. Although he correctly noted that existing property laws were grossly inadequate in an age of digital media, his prediction that intellectual property laws in cyberspace would disappear has, so far at least, turned out to be mistaken. Instead, one could make a plausible case, given the recent trends affecting property protection examined in this chapter, that the opposite has happened. For example, Shelly Warwick (2004) argues that the original copyright framework, which valued the interests of the people as a whole over the interests of creators of intellectual property, is being "slowly dismantled" to give more weight to the interests of the latter group. And Dan Burk (2003) notes that "overreaching" in copyright licensing is now beginning to be recognized by some courts to "constitute a new form of misuse." In fact, many critics worry that digital information is now becoming less available and that we as a society are worse off because of it. Some also fear that if the public domain of ideas continues to shrink, our "intellectual commons" may eventually disappear.

8.7.2 Preserving the Intellectual Commons

What do we mean by *intellectual commons*? One way of understanding this concept is by comparing it to a "physical commons," a common area that has been set aside and is open to the general public or to residents of a community. Garret Hardin, in his classic account of the "tragedy of the commons," describes the disappearance of the public space, or commons, that farmers living in a certain community had once enjoyed. In Hardin's tale, a public plot of land is shared by many farmers but owned by none of them; by sharing the land in a reasonable and mutually agreed manner, the commons benefits all of the farmers. Suppose that they agree collectively that each is allowed to have no more than ten cows graze on the commons on a given day. Further suppose, however, one day a farmer decides to cheat a little by having eleven or twelve of his cattle graze on the commons, reasoning that having one or two additional cows graze will not deplete the land's resources and will also enable him to profit slightly.[31] If other farmers also use the same rationale, you can see that before long the entire commons would be depleted.

It is very easy to underestimate the importance of the commons, or the public domain. We often take for granted the public parks, public beaches, and public gathering places that have been set aside for general use. Imagine the quality of our lives without them, and consider that without proper foresight, planning, and management, our parks could easily have been turned over to entrepreneurs for private development. Imagine, for example, if early city planners in New York City had not had the wisdom to set aside the area of Manhattan called Central Park; yet there was nothing inevitable about this. An entrepreneurial-minded city council might have sold the land to developers and businesses on the grounds that doing so would bring revenue to the city. In the short term, the city might have realized significant financial gain, but they would have been very shortsighted, and it would likely have been economically disadvantageous in the long term as well. Although Central Park is a tourist attraction that draws many people to New York City, it is not valued simply as a tourist attraction—it is a gathering place for city residents as well as visitors—a place to hear a concert on a summer evening, have a picnic in the fall, or ice skate in the winter. Imagine if Central Park were to disappear from the New York City landscape.

We have briefly considered some ways in which the physical commons has been threatened, but how is this analogous to the current threat posed to the intellectual commons? We can conceive of the intellectual commons as a domain or (nongeographical) space comprised of intellectual objects that are accessible to everyone because they are not owned by anyone. Elizabeth Buchanan and James Campbell (2005), who use the phrase "information commons," capture the essence of this domain of intellectual objects when they describe it as

> a body of knowledge and information that is available to anyone to use without the need to ask for or receive permission from another, providing any conditions placed on its use are respected.[32]

Just as the physical commons in England began to vanish in the seventeenth and eighteenth centuries when property laws were passed by Parliament that prohibited peasants from fishing and hunting in newly enclosed territories that had previously been accessible to everyone, some now worry that the intellectual commons is now undergoing a similar fate.[33] James Boyle (2006), who describes this trend as the "second enclosure movement," draws some useful comparisons to the original enclosure movement that resulted in the "fencing off" of much of the "grassy commons of old England." In the current enclosure movement, of course, it is ideas and information that are being fenced off or enclosed. So, just as there is reason to be concerned about the tragedy of the physical commons, as described by Hardin, there would also seem to be good reason to worry about what Harlan Onsrud (1998) calls "the tragedy of the information commons." Buchanan and Campbell note that what is especially tragic is that the information commons is now

> . . . being enclosed or even destroyed by a combination of law and technology that is privatizing what had been public and may become public, and locking up and restricting access to ideas and information that have heretofore been shared resources.[34]

A different way of expressing the concern about what is being lost in this second enclosure movement is offered by Michael Heller (1998) in his description of the "tragedy of the anti-commons"—a phenomenon that occurs whenever resources are *under-consumed* or *underutilized*. As more and more of the intellectual commons is fenced off because of strong intellectual property laws, critics such as Heller fear that fewer and fewer intellectual resources will be available to ordinary individuals and that, as a result, our information resources will be underutilized.

8.7.3 The Fate of the Intellectual Commons: Could the Public Domain of Ideas Eventually Disappear?

Now imagine what it would be like if the public domain of ideas, which we have all enjoyed and benefited from, disappeared. In a book subtitled *The Fate of the Commons in a Connected World*, Lawrence Lessig (2002) raises some serious concerns about the future of ideas in a medium that is overly regulated and controlled by economic interests. Recall Section 8.4.3, where we discussed Eric Eldred's Web site, which included classic books from the public domain available in electronic form. We saw that the Sonny Bono Copyright Extension Term Act (SBCTEA), which extended copyright protection by twenty years, thwarted Eldred's plans to include on his site books that were about to enter the public domain. Siva Vadhyanathan (2003) believes that recent "trends and changes" to copyright law threaten not only scholarly research but the "free flow of information." These legislative changes also seem to run counter to the notion in which the public domain of ideas has traditionally become populated—i.e., intellectual objects are supposed to enter the public domain after a reasonable period of time. Wolfgang Coy (2007) notes that this factor distinguishes intellectual property from physical property, which can always remain proprietary.

Of course, governments could continue to pass laws extending the term limits of copyright law (as in the case of SBCTEA in the United States) to the point where precious little, if anything, remains in the public domain. We have already seen how the Digital Millennium Copyright Act, with its controversial anti-circumvention clause, contributes to the erosion, and possible future elimination, of the intellectual commons. We may wish to consider the short-term versus long-term gains and losses that can result from current trends in information policy. In the near term, corporations and some individuals will profit handsomely from privatization of information policy. In the long term, however, our society may be worse off intellectually, spiritually, and even economically if the short-term goals of privatization are not balanced against the interests of the greater public.

Imagine if more of the information that we have traditionally shared freely were to disappear from the public domain and enter the world of copyright protection. Suppose, for example, that beginning tomorrow every recipe will be copyrighted and thus not be able to be disseminated without the permission of the new rights holder (i.e., the legal owner of that recipe). We would not even be permitted to use, let alone improve on, a particular recipe without first getting permission from the copyright holder. In the past, chefs could use recipes freely and improve upon them. Would it be fair if those chefs who had previously benefited from the sharing of recipes were all of a sudden awarded exclusive rights to them? And would it be fair if they were awarded the exclusive rights simply because they just happened to be experimenting with food at a time when the legal system favored the privatizing of information for commercial interests? Does it matter that society would be deprived of communicating freely the kind of information it has always had the luxury to share? What would this mean for the public domain of ideas and for ordinary discourse and information exchange?

Writing in response to worries about the disappearance of the public domain of ideas, Boyle (2004) advocated for the formation of a political movement similar to the environmental movement that arose in the 1970s. Just as a political movement was essential to save the environment from further erosion, so is a similar kind of movement needed to preserve the intellectual commons. Boyle points out that the environment could have disappeared because of simplistic claims based on (highly individualistic) property rights, and in a similar way the public domain of information is disappearing under an intellectual property system built around the interests of the current stakeholders. As the environmental movement invented the concept of "the environment" so that farmers, consumers, hunters, and bird watchers could all "discover themselves as environmentalists," Boyle suggests that we need to frame the concept of the public domain to call into being the coalition of interested parties to protect it. Boyle is optimistic that we might still be able to reclaim the public domain of ideas if we act responsibly.

In defending the view that the ultimate purpose of information is something to be shared and communicated, we have made the case that the public domain of ideas should be preserved. Of course, the rights and interests of both software manufacturers and individual creators of literary and artistic works also deserve serious consideration in any debate about intellectual property rights in cyberspace. And we do not need to advocate for the controversial view that all information should be absolutely free to move the debate forward. Indeed, companies and individuals need fair compensation for both their costs and the risks they undertake in developing their creative products and bringing them to market. The key phrase here, of course, is "fair compensation"; a fair intellectual property system is one that would enable us to achieve a proper balance. In reaching that state of equilibrium, however, we must not lose sight of the fact that information is more than merely a commodity that has commercial value.

If we defend the principle that information wants to be shared (but not totally free), then perhaps it will be possible to frame reasonable intellectual property policies that would both encourage the flow of information in digital form *and* reward fairly the creators of intellectual objects, including software manufacturers. One promising scheme for accomplishing these objectives can be found in the kind of licensing agreements currently issued in the Creative Commons initiative.

8.7.4 The Creative Commons

The Creative Commons (CC), a nonprofit organization launched in 2001, was founded by Lawrence Lessig, along with Eric Eldred, James Boyle, and others. The principal aim of this organization is to provide creative solutions to problems that current copyright laws pose for sharing information. One of CC's goals is to expand the range of creative work available to others legally to build upon and share. To accomplish this objective, CC provides a set of licensing options that help artists and authors give others the freedom and creativity to build upon their creativity. Lessig (2004) points out that such a "creative" scheme for licensing is needed because many people now realize that the current intellectual property rights regime does not make sense in the digital world.

We should note that CC does not aim to undermine the principle of copyright. Lessig concedes that copyrights protect important values and are essential to creativity, even in a digital age. He also believes that if the essence of copyright law is to allow creators to have control, then there should be a way to maintain ownership of copyrighted works and still make it possible for the average person to license the use of those works. Lessig notes that, unfortunately, the current version of copyright, which was not written for a world of digital creativity, "restricts more than it inspires." Traditional copyright regimes tend to promote an "all or nothing" kind of protection scheme with their "exclusive rights" clauses. According to Thomas Goetz (2004), CC provides a "middle ground" with respect to copyright protection because it makes possible a "some rights reserved" approach versus an "all rights reserved" policy.

Lessig believes that the Internet allows for an "innovation commons" and that the CC licensing schemes help to promote this vision. CC provides a menu of options in its licensing and contract schemes, available on its Web site (http://creativecommons.org) free of charge, that enable copyright holders to grant some of their rights to the public while retaining others. Each CC license is available in three forms: human-readable, lawyer-readable, and computer-readable. The following options are provided:

- Attribution—permit others to copy, distribute, display, and perform the work and derivative works based upon it only if they give you credit;
- Noncommercial—permit others to copy, distribute, display, and perform the work and derivative works based upon it only for noncommercial purposes;
- Derivative—permit others to copy, distribute, display, and perform only verbatim copies of the work, not derivative works based upon it;
- Share alike—permit others to distribute derivative works only under a license identical to the license that governs your work.

By specifying one or more of these options, you can retain the copyright for your creative work while also allowing for uses of it under some circumstances.

Suppose you have composed a musical score. If you wish to protect that musical composition under a CC license, you choose the combination of options from the above menu. You may want to allow your musical composition to be used at certain kinds of noncommercial functions—for example, concerts or political rallies supporting some social or environmental cause—but not used for commercial purposes. You may also allow that, in certain cases, derivative works from your composition can be made, provided that you are given credit. Perhaps an accomplished musical group, which is also commercially successful, would like to include a variation of your work in a forthcoming CD. That group could consult the terms of your CC license to see whether they are permitted to do so. Assuming that you have granted such permission, you could receive increased exposure as a musical composer, and at the same time still retain control over your composition.

Lessig believes that artists, authors, and other creators who use the CC license are, in effect, saying,

> We have built upon the work of others. Let others build upon ours.

Building on the notion that every author "stands on the shoulders of giants," CC's proponents believe that musicians and artists who use the CC license are, in effect, "standing on the shoulders of peers" and allowing peers to "stand on their shoulders."

Goetz points out that because CC grants musicians, authors, and other creators a flexible "opt-in" licensing system that lets them determine what secondary uses are allowed and under what conditions, a musician or artist will not have to call a lawyer before building on or sharing a CC-licensed work. A work released under that license grants (or denies) "before-the-fact" permission, which explicitly specifies under what circumstances and under which conditions that work may be used by others. Pointing out that John Coltrane did not need a lawyer to create his immortal version of *The Sound* of Music's "My Favorite Things," Lessig asks: Why should today's young musicians need one?

Hilary Rosen (2004), a former CEO for the RIAA, recognizes some of the effects that CC will likely have for the music industry. Rosen notes that in the past, many musicians feared reusing others' songs (even if only for noncommercial purposes). Licenses from the CC, however, allow musicians to dictate how their music will be used—even if they sign with a record label (as long as the CC terms are part of the contract). Many believe that both artists and fans will benefit from the kinds of licenses made available through CC. The RIAA, as well as other organizations that have benefited significantly from the traditional copyright regime, however, stand to lose some influence, power, and control because of the new licensing schemes made possible by CC.

We can see how CC, via its creative and flexible licensing schemes, both encourages the flow of information in digital form and protects the legal rights and interests of artists and authors. Artists and authors can be recognized and rewarded, financially and otherwise, for their creative contributions, yet still share their works (or portions of their works) with others. This, in turn, enables us to realize Lessig's notion of an "innovation commons" because it allows authors and artists to build upon the works of others. It also contributes to the future of the commons, and it promotes the kind of spirit of cooperation and sharing among creators that Stallman and the FSF movement advocate for software development (although FSF does not endorse CC's licensing scheme). In promoting these and related goals, CC provides an implementation scheme for the presumptive principle defended in this chapter—viz., "information wants to be shared." Implementing our presumptive principle through a mechanism such as CC enables us to frame intellectual property policies that avoid the kinds of problems inherent in both: (a) the claim that information should be absolutely free, and (b) overly strong copyright laws that discourage sharing and innovation and also diminish the intellectual commons.

▶ 8.8 CHAPTER SUMMARY

In this chapter we have examined disputes involving intellectual-property-right claims affecting digital information. In particular, we considered how current intellectual property laws, especially those involving copyright and patents, can be applied to software and other forms of digital media. We saw that various philosophical theories of property underpin much of the rationale for our current schemes of legal protection, and we examined the rationales behind the Free Software and Open Source movements. We also saw that an alternative framework for analyzing property disputes affecting digital media, based on the "common good" approach, suggests that we need to take into account the fact that an essential purpose of information is to be shared. Ironically, however, we noted that recent copyright laws, such as the DMCA and SBCTEA, restrict the distribution, and thus the sharing, of information. We defended the view that *information wants to be shared*, as a guiding principle that can inform the contemporary debate about intellectual property rights affecting digitized information. Finally, we saw how the Creative Commons initiative provides a scheme that enables us to implement our principle in the digital world.

▶ REVIEW QUESTIONS

1. What is intellectual property?
2. How is intellectual property different from tangible property?
3. What is meant by the expression "intellectual object"?
4. Describe the difficulties that arose in determining whether computer software (as a kind of intellectual object) should be eligible for the kinds of legal protection (i.e., copyrights and patents) that are typically granted to authors and inventors of creative works.
5. Describe some of the key differences in the four legal schemes designed to protect intellectual property: copyrights, patents, trademarks, and trade secrets.
6. What is the Sonny Bono Copyright Term Extension Act (SBCTEA), and why is it controversial?
7. What is the Digital Millennium Copyright Act (DMCA), and why is it controversial?
8. What is the principle of fair use?
9. What is the principle of "first sale" with respect to copyright law?
10. How is the principle of fair use, as illustrated in the Eldred and Sklyarov scenarios, threatened by recent changes to copyright law?
11. How were the controversies involving the Napster dispute anticipated by the case involving the Cynosure BBS at MIT in 1990s?
12. What are the arguments for and against protecting software with patents?
13. Describe the rationale behind the labor theory of property. Is it a plausible philosophical theory when used to justify intellectual property rights?
14. What is the utilitarian theory of property? Can it justify the protection of software?
15. How does the personality theory of property differ from both the labor and the utilitarian property theories?
16. What is the Free Software Foundation, and what does it advocate?
17. What is GNU?
18. What is the Open Source Initiative, and how is it different from the Free Software Movement?
19. What is meant by the expression "intellectual commons"?
20. What is the Creative Commons (CC) Initiative?

▶ DISCUSSION QUESTIONS

1. Why does Richard Stallman believe that software should be free? How is Stallman's view about the ownership of computer programs both similar to and different from that advocated by the Open Source Initiative? What do we mean by the expression "Information wants to be shared"? How is it different from the position "Information wants to be free"?
2. Recall Michael McFarland's argument for an alternative way of looking at the current intellectual property dispute about digital information. How can we use his "common-good" approach to analyze that debate from a novel perspective? In which ways does McFarland appeal to the insights of Aristotle and virtue ethics to make his argument? Explain.
3. What is the public domain of ideas, or what some also call the "intellectual commons"? Can the Creative Commons (CC) initiative help to preserve the intellectual commons? Are CC's objectives compatible with the principle *information wants to be shared*? What are CC's strengths, and what are some of its challenges?
4. Why does Lawrence Lessig believe that the "intellectual commons" is disappearing? Examine James Boyle's suggestion that a political movement, similar to the environmental movement in the 1970s, may be needed to save the intellectual commons. Does his suggestion merit further consideration? Explain.

▶ ESSAY/PRESENTATION QUESTIONS

1. Critics argue that more and more information in digital form is being "fenced off" because of recent copyright legislation. Yet owners of proprietary information fear that they could lose control of their property without those laws. How can we achieve an appropriate balance between those who hold legal

rights to proprietary information and ordinary users who wish to access, share, and communicate that information?

2. Recall the arguments we examined in Section 8.1.3 to show how the software industry has tried to make its case for strong legal protection for software. Has protection for proprietary software gone too far, as some critics suggest? If so, what are the implications for innovation and competition in the computer industry?

3. In Chapter 5 we saw that privacy advocates argue for greater control of personal information by individuals, while many in the commercial sector argue for increased access to that information. In this chapter, we saw that those positions have become reversed—entrepreneurs argue for control of the flow of information on the Internet, while ordinary users argue for access to that information. Is there an irony, perhaps even an inconsistency, here? Can this inconsistency be resolved in a logically coherent manner? How? Explain.

4. In examining the evolution of the ongoing battle between the recording industry and P2P file-sharing sites, from the original Napster site to the demise of the Pirate Bat site in 2009, we have seen how different technologies were used by the various sites to circumvent prosecution under copyright law. For example, we saw that since Napster, file-sharing sites have become increasingly more decentralized and distributed—i.e., evolving from centralized indexes to super nodes to Bit Torrent technology, etc. While these technologies may make a legal difference with regard to whether and how the proprietors of unauthorized file-sharing sites can be prosecuted, have they made a moral difference? Explain.

▶ ENDNOTES

1. My analysis of intellectual property issues in this chapter draws from material in Tavani (2002, 2005, 2007).
2. See, for example, Hettinger (1997) and Spinello and Tavani (2005).
3. See Grodzinsky, Miller, and Wolf (2004) for more detail.
4. See http://www.austlii.edu.au/au/legis/cth/num_act/caa1980213/.
5. See http://w2.eff.org/IP/DMCA/states/200304_sdmca_eff_analysis.php. (accessed January 17, 2009).
6. Http://w2.eff.org/IP/eff_fair_use_faq.php.
7. For more information about the Eldred case, see Lessig (2002).
8. For more detail, see Jennifer Lee (2001). "Technology; U.S. Arrests Russian Cryptographer as Copyright Violator." *New York Times*, July 18. Available at http://query.nytimes.com/gst/fullpage.html?res=9901EED91F3BF93BA25754C0A9679C 8B63 (accessed on August 11, 2008).
9. See *United States v. Lamachia*. (1994). 871 F Supp 535.
10. See http://www.gseis.ucla.edu/iclp/hr2265.html.
11. See *A&M Records Inc. v. Napster Inc.* (2001). 239 F 3d 1004.
12. See Grodzinsky and Tavani (2005).
13. See Grodzinsky and Tavani (2008).
14. *MGM Studios Inc. v. Grokster Ltd.* (2005). 545 US 913.
15. See http://www.uspto.gov/.
16. See *Diamond v. Diehr* (1981). 45 U.S. 175.
17. See http://www.uspto.gov/#.
18. See *America Online Inc. v. AT&T Corp.* 243 F. 3d 812.
19. See http://www.wipo.int/sme/en/ip_business/trade_secrets/trade_secrets.htm.
20. See http://www.wto.org/english/tratop_E/trips_e/trips_e.htm.
21. See http://www.wipo.int/treaties/en/ip/berne/trtdocs_wo001.html.
22. See http://www.wipo.int/portal/index.html.en.
23. See http://torrentfreak.com/the-pirate-bay-trial-the-verdict-090417/.
24. See http://www.law.cornell.edu/ucc/; http://www.law.upenn.edu/bll/archives/ulc/ucita/ucita200.htm; and http://www.law.upenn.edu/bll/archives/ulc/ecom/ueta_final.pdf.
25. See http://www.pophistorydig.com/?tag=the-beatles-revolution.
26. See http://www.gnu.org/philosophy/free-sw.html.
27. See http://www.gnu.org/copyleft/gpl.html.
28. See Grodzinsky, Miller, and Wolf (2004).
29. See http://www.opensource.org/.
30. See Tavani (2002).

31. See Hardin (1968) for more detail.
32. Buchanan and Campbell (2005), p. 229.
33. See the account of the "fencing off" of the original commons in Rose (1993).
34. Buchanan and Campbell, p. 226.

▶ REFERENCES

Aharonian, Gregory. 2001. "Does the Patent Office Respect the Software Community?" In K. W. Bowyer, ed. *Ethics and Computing: Living Responsibly in a Computerized World*. 2nd ed. New York: IEEE Press, pp. 296–98.

Barlow, John Perry. 1997. "The Economy of Ideas: A Framework for Copyrights and Patents (Everything You Know About Intellectual Property is Wrong)." In A. D. Moore, ed. *Intellectual Property: Moral, Legal, and International Dilemmas*. Lanham MD: Rowman and Littlefield, pp. 349–72.

Boyle, James. 2004. "A Politics of Intellectual Property: Environmentalism for the Net." In R. A. Spinello and H. T. Tavani, eds. *Readings in CyberEthics*. 2nd ed. Sudbury MA: Jones and Bartlett Publishers, pp. 273–93.

Boyle, James. 2006. "Enclosing the Human Genome: What Squabbles Over Genetic Patents Can Teach Us." In H. T. Tavani, ed. *Ethics, Computing, and Genomics*. Sudbury MA: Jones and Bartlett, pp. 255–77.

Burk, Dan L. 2003. "Anti-Circumvention Misuse: How I Stopped Worrying and Love the DMCA." *IEEE Technology and Society Magazine* 22, no. 3: 40–47.

Buchanan, Elizabeth A., and James Campbell. 2005. "New Threats to Intellectual Freedom: The Loss of the Information Commons Through Law and Technology in the U.S." In R. A. Spinello and H. T. Tavani, eds. *Intellectual Property Rights in a Networked World: Theory and Practice*. Hershey PA: Idea Group/Information Science Publishing, pp. 225–42.

Chopra, Samir, and Scott D. Dexter. 2009. "Free Software, Economic 'Realities,' and Information Justice." *Computers and Society* 39, no. 3: 12–26.

Coy, Wolfgang. 2007. "On Sharing Intellectual Properties in Global Communities." In J. Fruhbauer, R. Capurro, and T. Hassmanninger, eds. *Localizing the Internet: Ethical Issues in Intercultural Perspective*. Munich: Fink Verlag.

De George, Richard T. 2003. *The Ethics of Information Technology and Business*. Malden MA: Blackwell.

Evans, Jonny. 2008. "Forty Percent of Global Music Sales to Be Digital." *PC World* (April). Available at http://www.pcworld.com/businesscenter/article/144392/forty_percent_of_global_music_sales_to_be_digital.html (accessed June 1, 2009).

Girasa, Roy J. 2002. *Cyberlaw: National and International Perspectives*. Upper Saddle River NJ: Prentice Hall.

Goetz, Thomas. 2004. "Rip, Mix, Burn. Swap till You Drop. The Music Cops Can't Do a Thing — It's 100% Legal, Licensed By the Bands" *Wired* (November): 181–83.

Grodzinsky, Frances S., Keith Miller, and Marty J. Wolf. 2004. "Ethical Issues in Open Source Software." In R. A. Spinello and H. T. Tavani, eds. *Readings in CyberEthics*. 2nd ed. Sudbury MA: Jones and Bartlett, pp. 305–21.

Grodzinsky, Frances S., and Herman T. Tavani. 2005. "P2P Networks and the *Verizon v. RIAA* Case: Implications for Personal Privacy and Intellectual Property." *Ethics and Information Technology* 7, no. 4: 243–50.

Grodzinsky, Frances S., and Herman T. Tavani. 2008. "Online File Sharing: Resolving the Tensions between Privacy and Property Interests." *Computers and Society* 38, no. 4: 28–39.

Grosso, Andrew. 2000. "The Promise and the Problems of the No Electronic Theft Act." *Communications of the ACM* 43, no. 2 (February): 23–26.

Halbert, Debora J. 1999. *Intellectual Property in the Information Age: The Politics of Expanding Ownership Rights*. Westport CT: Quorum Books.

Hardin, Garret. 1968. "The Tragedy of the Commons." *Science* 162: 1243–48.

Heller, Michael. 1998. "The Tragedy of the Anticommons: From Marx to Markets." *Harvard Law Review* 111: 611–28.

Henderson, Katherine A, Richard A. Spinello, and Tomas A. Lipinski. 2007. "Prudent Policy? Reassessing the Digital Millennium Copyright Act." *Computers and Society* 37, no. 4: 25–40.

Hettinger, Edwin. 1997. "Justifying Intellectual Property." In A. D. Moore, ed. *Intellectual Property: Moral, Legal, and International Dilemmas*. Lanham MD: Rowman and Littlefield, pp. 57–80.

Himma, Kenneth Einar. 2005. "Information and Intellectual Property Protection: Evaluating the Claim That Information Should Be Free." *APA (American Philosophical Newsletter) on Philosophy and Law* 4, no. 2: 3–8.

Lessig, Lawrence. 2002. *The Future of Ideas: The Fate of the Commons in a Connected World*. New York: Random House.

Lessig, Lawrence. 2004. "Creative Freedom for All: Done Right, Copyrights can Inspire the Next Digital Revolution." *Wired* (November): 188–89.

Moore, Adam. 2008. "Personality-Based, Rule-Utilitarian, and Lockean Justifications of Intellectual Property." In K. E. Himma and H. T. Tavani, eds. *The Handbook of Information and Computer Ethics*. Hoboken NJ: John Wiley and Sons, pp. 105–30.

McFarland, Michael C. 2004. "Intellectual Property, Information, and the Common Good." In R. A. Spinello and H. T. Tavani, eds. *Readings in CyberEthics*. 2nd ed. Sudbury MA: Jones and Bartlett Publishers, pp. 294–304.

McFarland, Michael C. 2005. "Whose Bytes? A Common Good View of Computer Ethics." Presented at the 2005–2006 *Humanities Lecture Series*, Rivier College, Nashua NH, November 10.

Onsrud, Harlan. 1998. "The Tragedy of the Information Commons." In D. Taylor, ed. *Policy Issues in Modern Cartography*. Oxford UK: Pergamon, pp. 141–58.

Raymond, Eric. 2004. "The Cathedral and the Bazaar." In R. A. Spinello and H. T. Tavani, eds. *Readings in CyberEthics*. 2nd ed. Sudbury MA: Jones and Bartlett Publishers, pp. 367–96.

Rose, Mark. 1993. *Authors and Owners: The Invention of Copyright*. Cambridge MA: Harvard University Press.

Rosen, Hilary. 2004. "How I learned to Love Larry: She Was the Champion of the Music Industry—He Was the Champion of the People." *Wired* (November): 188–89.

Samuelson, Pamela. 2004. "What's at Stake in *MGM v. Grokster*? Seeking to Balance the Needs of Copyright Holders and Technology Developers." *Communication of the ACM* 47, no. 2: 15–20.

Samuelson, Pamela. 2005. "Legally Speaking: Did MGM Really Win the *Grokster* Case?" *Communication of the ACM* 48, no. 10: 19–24.

Snapper, John W. 1995. "Intellectual Property Protections for Computer Software." In D. G. Johnson and H. Nissenbaum, eds. *Computing, Ethics, and Social Values*. Englewood Cliffs NJ: Prentice Hall, pp. 181–89.

Spinello, Richard A. 2003. "The Future of Open Source Software: Let the Market Decide." *Journal of Information, Communication, and Ethics in Society* 1, no. 4: 217–34.

Spinello, Richard. 2008. "Intellectual Property: Intellectual and Moral Challenges of Online File Sharing." In K. E. Himma and H. T. Tavani, eds. *The Handbook of Information and Computer Ethics*. Hoboken NJ: John Wiley and Sons, pp. 553–69.

Spinello, Richard A., and Herman T. Tavani. 2005. "Intellectual Property Rights from Theory to Practical Implementation." In R. A. Spinello and H. T. Tavani, eds. *Intellectual Property Rights in a Networked World: Theory and Practice*. Hershey PA: Idea Group, pp. 1–66.

Stallman, Richard. 2004. "Why Software Should Be Free." In T. W. Bynum and S. Rogerson, eds. *Computer Ethics and Professional Responsibility*. Malden MA: Blackwell, pp. 294–310.

Tavani, Herman T. 2002. "'Information Wants to Be Shared': An Alternative Framework for Approaching Intellectual Property Disputes in an Information Age." *Catholic Library World* 73, no. 2: 94–104.

Tavani, Herman T. 2005. "Recent Copyright Protection Schemes: Implications for Sharing Digital Information." In R. A. Spinello and H. T. Tavani, eds. *Intellectual Property Rights in a Networked World: Theory and Practice*. Hershey, PA: Idea Group, pp. 182–204.

Tavani, Herman T. 2007. "Balancing Intellectual Property Rights and the Information Commons: A Lockean Analysis." In J. Weckert, ed. *Computer Ethics*. Aldershot, UK: Ashgate, pp. 85–94. Reprinted from *Journal of Information, Communication and Ethics in Society* 2, Supplement, 2004: S5–S14.

Vaidhyanathan, Siva. 2003. *Copyrights and Copywrongs: The Rise of Intellectual Property and How it Threatens Creativity*. New York: New York University Press.

Warwick, Shelly. 2004. "Is Copyright Ethical? An Examination of the Theories, Laws, and Practices Regarding the Private Ownership of Intellectual Work in the United States." In R. A. Spinello and H. T. Tavani, eds. *Readings in CyberEthics*. 2nd ed. Sudbury MA: Jones and Bartlett Publishers, pp. 305–21.

▶ FURTHER READINGS

Barrett, William, Christopher Price, and Thomas Hunt. *iProperty: Profiting from Ideas in an Age of Global Information*. Hoboken, NJ: John Wiley and Sons. 2008.

Chopra, Samir, and Scott D. Dexter. *Decoding Liberation: The Promise of Free and Open Source Software*. New York: Routledge, 2008.

Coles, A. M., Lisa Harris, and R. Davis. "Is the Party Over? Innovation and Music on the Web." *Journal of Information, Communication, and Ethics in Society* 4, no. 1 (2004): 21–29.

Gordon, Wendy. "Moral Philosophy, Information Technology, and Copyright: The Grokster Case." In J. van den Hoven and J. Weckert, eds. *Information Technology and Moral Philosophy*. New York: Cambridge University Press, 2008.

Grodzinsky, Frances S., and Maria C. Bottis. "Private Use as Fair Use: Is it Fair?" *Computers and Society* 37, no. 4 (2007): 11–24.

Grodzinsky, Frances S., and Marty J. Wolf. "Ethical Interest in Free and Open Source Software." In K. E. Himma and H. T. Tavani, eds. *The Handbook of Information and Computer Ethics*. Hoboken NJ: John Wiley and Sons, 2008, pp. 245–72.

Lanier, Clinton R. "Linux and the Appeal to Cultural Values." *IEEE Technology and Society Magazine* 24, no. 4 (2005): 12–17.

Moore, Adam D. *Intellectual Property and Information Control*. Rev. ed. New Brunswick NJ: Transaction Publishers, 2004.

Samuelson, Pamela. "The Supreme Court Revisits the Sony Safe Harbor." *Communication of the ACM* 48, no. 6 (2005): 21–25.

CHAPTER

9

Regulating Commerce and Speech in Cyberspace

Should cyberspace be regulated? Can it be regulated? If the answer to both questions is "yes," which aspects of it should be regulated? Who should be responsible for carrying out the regulatory functions—the government? Private organizations? Or perhaps Internet users themselves? In this chapter, we examine issues that have led to a call for strong regulatory proposals in cyberspace by considering the following questions:

- What is "regulation by code"?
- What is Digital Rights Management (DRM) technology, and why is it controversial?
- Can the distribution of some forms of e-mail spam be defended?
- Should online pornography, especially pornographic images involving minors, be censored?
- Can existing child pornography laws be applied in cases of "sexting" (where young teenagers use cell phones, and similar kinds of electronic hand-held devices, to send nude or seminude photos to one another)?
- Can software filters provide a satisfactory alternative to censorship and government regulation of speech on the Internet?
- Should hate speech, as well as speech that can cause physical harm to others, be tolerated on the Internet?
- Who should be held responsible for incidents involving online defamation?

Many conservative organizations have argued for censorship of certain kinds of speech in cyberspace. Some liberal groups, on the contrary, who oppose any restrictions on free speech in cyberspace, argue that e-commerce, not speech, needs to be regulated. We consider "speech" to include issues involving pornography, hate speech, and defamation. And somewhat more loosely we consider e-commerce regulation issues to include concerns involving electronic spam, the assignment of Internet domain names, and practices affecting hyperlinking and the misuse of HTML metatags on the Web.

We will also see why we should be concerned about cyberspace regulation that can be implemented with technology itself, by means of "regulation by code." Some critics worry that regulation by code is becoming the default regulatory scheme in cyberspace. We begin with background issues.

▶ 9.1 BACKGROUND ISSUES AND SOME PRELIMINARY DISTINCTIONS

John Weckert (2007) believes that when discussing cyberspace regulation, we need to ask two separate questions:

(A) *Can* it be regulated?

(B) *Should* it be regulated?

Asking question (A) implies that it is not clear whether cyberspace can be effectively regulated, but we will operate on the assumption that it can, in fact, be, regulated. We also acknowledge, however, that regulation schemes can be difficult to implement and enforce, and we concede that regulation can have undesirable side effects in terms of both cost and efficiency. We will focus on question (B), that is, the normative question as to whether cyberspace *ought* to be regulated. This question also can be broken down into two separate questions, as Weckert points out when he asks: "Should it be regulated in general, and should it be regulated in any one country in the absence of cooperation by others?"[1] In a later section of this chapter, we examine some controversies affecting consensus at the international level with regard to regulatory schemes and practices.

Despite some of the controversies and challenges that arise in schemes for regulating cyberspace, Weckert and Al-Saggaf (2008) note that we should not presume against Internet regulation. In fact, they believe that a "strong moral case can be made for regulating the content of the Internet."[2] Before proceeding with specific issues affecting the regulation of cyberspace, it is useful to consider two additional questions:

1. What do we mean by *cyberspace*?

2. What do we mean by *regulation*, particularly as it applies to cyberspace?

9.1.1 The Ontology of Cyberspace: Is the Internet a Medium or a Place?

In Chapter 1, we loosely defined the Internet as the network of interconnected computers, and we suggested that the terms "Internet" and "cyberspace" were roughly equivalent. In this chapter, we use the two terms interchangeably. But we have not yet described the ontology of cyberspace, that is, we have not said what, exactly, cyberspace *is*. For example, is it a *place*, that is, a virtual space that consists of all the data and information that resides in the connected servers and databases that make up the Internet? Or is cyberspace a *medium* of some sort?

Some believe that the Internet is best understood as a new kind of medium, significantly different from earlier media, such as the telephone or television. Whereas the telephone is a "one-to-one medium," and television is a "one-to-many medium," Mike Goodwin (1995, 2003) describes the Internet is a "many-to-many medium." He also notes that one does not need to be wealthy to have access to this medium; nor does one need to win the approval of an editor or a publisher to speak his or her mind there. But is the Internet a medium, or can it be better understood as a public space?

Jean Camp and Y. T. Chien (2000) differentiate four types of media: *publisher*, *broadcast*, *distributor*, and *common carrier*. An example of a publisher is a newspaper or a magazine, and broadcast media include television and radio. Telephone companies and cable companies are instances of common carriers, conduits for the distribution of information. Camp and Chien argue that none of the media models are appropriate for understanding the Internet. Instead, they believe that a spatial model—one in which cyberspace is viewed as a public space with certain digital characteristics—is more plausible.

But can we model the Internet accurately as a public space, as Camp and Chien suggest? Or is it better understood as a new kind of *medium*, as Goodwin and others have argued? We are making more than a mere semantic distinction, because, as Camp and Chien believe, the model we use can influence our decisions about public policies on the Internet. If the Internet is viewed as a public space, for example, then there are good legal and moral reasons for ensuring that everyone has access to it. The ontology of cyberspace will ultimately determine whether and how we should (or perhaps should not) regulate it.

Consider the rules used to regulate the distribution and sale of "adult" magazines and videos in physical space. Bookstores and video rental stores are permitted to carry and sell such merchandise, and because a store is a physical place, certain sections can be partitioned so that adults can visit them but individuals under a certain age cannot. The rules are drastically different, however, for broadcast media such as television, where the Federal Communications Commission (FCC) regulates which kinds of content can be broadcast over the airwaves. Movies that can be rented and sold only to adults in stores can also be deemed inappropriate (by the FCC) for general television viewers. So before we can successfully resolve questions about Internet regulation, we need to keep in mind that the model we use to understand cyberspace will also strongly influence which regulatory schemes are appropriate.

Figure 9.1 illustrates our two models of cyberspace.

9.1.2 Two Categories of Cyberspace Regulation

To "regulate" means to monitor or control a product, process, or set of behaviors according to certain requirements, standards, or protocols. Sometimes regulatory discussions about cyberspace have centered on its *content*, for example, whether online pornography and hate speech should be censored. And sometimes the regulatory

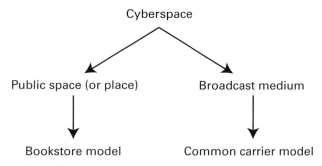

Figure 9-1 The ontology of cyberspace.

discussions have focused on which kinds of processes, that is, rules and policies, should be implemented and enforced in commercial transactions in cyberspace. Physical space is regulated in both ways.

Some regulatory agencies monitor the content, and others the process, of items in physical space. The Food and Drug Administration (FDA) monitors food products on the shelves of supermarkets to ensure that they meet health and nutrition standards; FDA regulations ensure that the contents of each food item both matches and is accurately described by its label. Unlike the FDA, state public health boards do not regulate content; their regulations apply to conditions for compliance with community health standards. For example, public health officials inspect restaurants and grocery stores to ensure that they meet sanitation standards in their preparation and sale of food. So an agency can regulate for content or process, or both.

In the commerce sector, federal and state agencies, such as the Federal Trade Commission (FTC) and the Securities and Exchange Commission (SEC), enforce laws and policies that apply to commercial activities and transactions; for example, they regulate against monopolies and other unfair business practices, such as those alleged in the Microsoft antitrust case in the late 1990s. Regulatory principles in the commerce sector also determine whether to permit mergers, such as the one between America Online (AOL) and Time Warner. Some believe that in cyberspace an additional set of criteria is needed to regulate the e-commerce, or so-called *dot.com*, sector.

Figure 9.2 illustrates the ways in which cyberspace can be regulated.

It is not difficult to point out positive effects that regulatory practices in physical space have for health and safety. Consider, for example, the role that state liquor boards play in regulating the distribution and sale of liquor: they determine who is and is not eligible for a license to distribute liquor in their state, and if a board determines that a licensed distributor has violated its licensing agreement with the state, its license can be revoked. And boards that regulate liquor can help to keep liquor out of the hands of minors and help to discourage an underground, or black market, for the sale of bootleg liquor, which is not tested and certified as meeting standards of quality and authenticity. State liquor boards also help determine fair pricing to prevent unscrupulous merchants from price gouging. So there are many good reasons for regulating the distribution and sale of liquor. But how can we extend this analogy to the Internet?

First, we can ask how we can possibly regulate cyberspace, which is inherently decentralized. Cyberspace is not compartmentalized neatly into state jurisdictions that

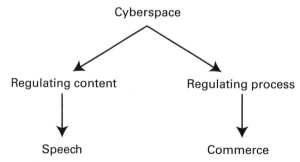

Figure 9-2 Two categories of cyberspace regulation.

can set up their own control boards. Does this mean that effective regulation of any type is impossible in cyberspace? Not according to Lawrence Lessig (2000) and Philip Agre (2005), who suggest that a decentralized cyberspace does not preclude Internet regulation from being carried out quite effectively. In describing the architecture of P2P (peer-to-peer) networks in cyberspace, Agre notes that decentralized institutions do not imply decentralized architectures, and vice versa. Lessig believes that in cyberspace, understanding architecture, or what he calls *code*, is the key to understanding how regulation works.

▶ 9.2 FOUR MODES OF REGULATION: THE LESSIG MODEL

Lessig describes four distinct but interdependent constraints, which he calls "modalities," for regulating behavior: *laws*, social *norms*, *market* pressures, and *architecture*. Before we apply each modality to cyberspace, consider how each can be applied in regulating behaviors in the physical world.

Cigarette smoking can be regulated through the passage and enforcement of explicit laws that make it illegal to smoke in public buildings. And we have specific laws that prohibit cigarette manufacturers from advertising on television or in magazines targeted at teenage audiences. Independent of explicit laws, however, social norms can also discourage cigarette smoking in public; for example, it is socially acceptable for homeowners to place "Thank you for not smoking in our house" signs on their front doors. And restaurant owners can, under social pressure from patrons, partition smoking and nonsmoking sections of their establishments even when there is no explicit law requiring them to do so.

Market pressures can also affect smoking behavior. Cigarettes can be priced so that only the wealthiest people can afford to buy them. Finally, merchants can impose an "architecture of control" on cigarettes by using physical constraints. All cigarettes sold in grocery stores could be located behind locked doors, causing interruptions in checkout transactions. A cashier might have to temporarily suspend the transaction, locate the store's manager, and get the proper authorization and the key to open the locked doors to remove the cigarettes. Contrast this architecture with one in which cigarettes are available in vending machines easily accessible to everyone, including minors.

To apply Lessig's four-fold distinction to cyberspace, we replace architecture, which is in physical or geographic space, with *code*. Code, for Lessig, consists of programs, devices, and protocols—that is, the sum total of the software and hardware—that constitute cyberspace. Like physical architecture in geographic space, code sets the terms upon which one can enter or exit cyberspace. Also like architecture, code is not optional. Lessig notes that we do not choose to obey the structures that architecture establishes. Just as we are subject to architectures of physical space, so we are subject to code in cyberspace; a physical door can block you from entering a physical building, and a password requirement can prevent you entering a Web site. And code can be used to limit access to Web sites by requiring that users accept cookies (see Chapter 5) if they wish to visit those sites. Lessig believes that code can either facilitate or deter access to, or transfer of, information in cyberspace.

In Chapter 1, we saw that James Moor (2007) described computer technology as "logically malleable" because, unlike most other technologies that are dedicated to performing specific tasks, computers can be instructed through software to perform an indefinite number of diverse functions. Lessig (2004) also recognizes that computer technology is not fixed, noting that different computer architectures create very different kinds of environments. He compares the Internet of 1995, which he calls NET 95 and which he believes has a "libertarian architecture," to the Internet of 1999 (and later). To illustrate differences between these two architectures, Lessig offers a comparison of the computer network systems at the University of Chicago and Harvard University. The University of Chicago's network was like NET 95, because anyone could connect his or her machine to jacks on the campus. As such, the code at Chicago favored freedom, or free speech. At Harvard, on the other hand, one first had to register his or her machine before getting on the Harvard's network. Once registered, all interactions with the network could be monitored and identified by Harvard's network administrators. Lessig points out that at the University of Chicago, facilitating access was the ideal; at Harvard, controlling access is the ideal. The University of Chicago's network had the architecture of NET 95, whereas the architecture of Harvard's system is a contemporary "intranet architecture."

Note that the underlying network protocols (i.e., TCP/IP) were the same for the computer systems at both Harvard and the University of Chicago. But layered on top of Harvard's TCP/IP protocol was an additional set of protocols, or *code*, which Lessig says "facilitates control." Why should we care about the differences between the two kinds of architectures? Lessig notes that in the NET 95 environment, one could roam the Internet freely and anonymously. Today, one cannot. Lessig concludes from this that we have moved from an "architecture of freedom" to an "architecture of control." He also concludes that in cyberspace, code is a more effective regulator than law. In fact, Lessig claims that in cyberspace, *code is the law*.

▶ 9.3 DIGITAL RIGHTS MANAGEMENT AND THE PRIVATIZATION OF INFORMATION POLICY

To understand the force of Lessig's claim that code is regulating cyberspace, consider the role that software code in the form of digital rights management (DRM) technologies play in regulating digital media. DRM technologies allow content owners to regulate the flow of information in digital media by blocking access to it via encryption mechanisms, and by enabling access to it through the use of passwords. The combination of DRM technology and copyright protection laws, such as the Digital Millennium Copyright Act (DMCA), has made possible the regulation and enforcement of policies and laws in cyberspace to a degree that never existed in the physical realm. As we saw in Chapter 8, the DMCA prohibits the development and use of technologies designed to circumvent copyright management systems. As a result, the DMCA works hand in hand with DRM technology to control the flow of information in digitized form; any programs designed to circumvent DRM controls are in violation of Section 1201 of the DMCA.

9.3.1 DRM Technology: Implications for Public Debate on Copyright Issues

Critics worry about the ways in which DRM technology can be used to enforce copyright law. Because software code in DRM systems is being developed and used with the express purpose of precluding the possibility of copyright infringement, Niva Elkin-Koren (2000) fears that the traditional mechanism for debating public policy may now be closed to us. She notes that if computer manufacturers can decide what the copyright rules should be, and if they are permitted to embed code in their products that enforces those rules, then there is no longer a need for, or even the possibility of, public policy debate about copyright issues.

In the past, when individuals duplicated proprietary information by using the latest available technologies, we were often forced to question the viability of existing copyright laws in light of those new technologies vis-à-vis principles such as fair use and first sale (described in Chapter 8.) Elkin-Koren notes that we could then engage in meaningful public policy debates about whether traditional copyright laws should apply or whether some new laws are needed. Most importantly, we could challenge the viability and constitutionality of such laws through the judicial process.

Elkin-Koren worries that a framework for *balancing* the interests of individuals and the public, which in the past had been supported by "spirited policy debates" and judicial review, will no longer be possible in a world in which copyright policies are predetermined by code. As Richard Spinello (2003) notes, restrictions embedded into computer code end up having the force of law without the checks and balances provided by the legal system.

Pamela Samuelson (2003), who also has been critical of technologies that regulate through embedded code, believes that DRM systems may violate the fair-use provision of copyright law. She notes that DRM technology allows content owners to exercise far more control over uses of copyrighted works in digital media than what is provided by conventional copyright law. Frances Grodzinsky and Maria Bottis (2007) also argue that DRM threatens the fair-use provision of copyright law. They believe that because of the way DRM is designed to protect digital content, our conventional understanding of "private use as fair use" has changed.

DRM and the Music Industry

Other critics worry about the ways DRM systems can be abused by content owners to control users' computers and to spy on unsuspecting users. Because of these and related factors, some now believe that DRM technology has gone too far. Consider a controversial incident involving a DRM system used by Sony BMG that would seem to support this view.

▶ **SCENARIO 9–1:** The Sony Rootkit Controversy

Sony BMG Music Entertainment used a DRM system called Extended Copy Protection (XCP) to protect its music CDs. In October 2005, a Web blogger named Mark Russinovich posted an article that described the characteristics of the software protection scheme used by Sony. In that article, Russinovich (2005) disclosed certain flaws in the design of Sony's software that manifested themselves as security holes that could be exploited by malicious software such as viruses or worms. He also noted that Sony provided no "uninstall" program to remove XCP. Sony responded to this criticism by releasing a software removal utility.

But Russinovich, in a follow-up blog article, noted that Sony's removal utility had only exacerbated privacy-and-security concerns about the software. For example, he pointed out that the program merely "unmasked" the hidden files in the "rootkit" component of XCP, but did not actually remove the rootkit itself. In November 2005, Sony provided a "new and improved" removal tool to uninstall the rootkit from affected Microsoft Windows computers.

Some of Sony's critics accused Sony of violating the privacy of its customers by using code that created a "backdoor" into their customers' machines. Other critics also claimed that Sony's DRM program, which gave the company control over its customers' machines in the name of copyright protection, itself infringed copyright law. And some critics argued that Sony violated the open source license agreement (see Chapter 8) because of the way in which it used some open source software code to build its protection system. In late 2005, Sony decided to back out of its copy protection software, recalling unsold CDs from all stores, and allowing customers to exchange their CDs for versions that did not include the controversial software.[3] ■

Sony's critics were still not satisfied by the company's concessions. In fact, class action lawsuits were filed against Sony BMG in California and New York.

The DRM-related controversies in the Sony rootkit scenario raise the following kinds of questions: Can users trust content owners, such as Sony BMG, who are easily able to spy on them and able to control aspects of their computers via the use of DRM technology? Are Sony's actions justified on grounds that companies need DRM systems to protect their intellectual property rights?

Another area of tension involving DRM and the music industry has to do with "interoperability" across the devices on which music can be played. Interoperability enables users to download and play music on a variety of devices. However, it also challenges the notion that downloadable content can and should be restricted to proprietary devices controlled by the company that owns an "online store," such as iPods in the iTunes store. Internationally, there have been some efforts to promote interoperability. For example, in 2006, France's National Assembly passed a law that would force distributors of online music in France to remove DRM so that music can be played on any device. Some believe that this move could pave the way for other EU countries to follow (Hesseldahl 2006). However, many owners and distributors of music content believe that removing DRM to support interoperability could also result in opening the door to file sharing of copyrighted material without compensation for the content owners and distributors.

In April 2007, EMI announced that it would sell its music without DRM on Apple Corporation's iTunes music store. However, non-DRM-formatted music will cost slightly more than DRM versions. Steve Jobs (2007) believes that if DRM restrictions were lifted on music, there might be an influx of new stores and players. But the debate about DRM in the contexts of online music and interoperability is ongoing.[4]

9.3.2 Privatizing Information Policy: Implications for the Internet

We have seen that DRM schemes tip the balance in favor of the copyright owner who can determine how and by whom his/her content may be used. For that reason, DRM has become an obstacle to fair use because it limits the user's freedom by allowing private interests to define the parameters of the law. Elkin-Koren argues that because of the technological controls embedded in software code (such as in DRM systems), our policies affecting information and digital media are becoming increasingly *privatized*. She also notes that this trend toward privatization has enabled software companies to design code that reflects their own interests and values, without having to worry about any adverse effects that code can have for the public's interests.

Jessica Litman (2002) is also concerned about efforts that have been made to privatize information policies in cyberspace via the use of technology and law. She describes how the Recording Industry of America (RIAA) tried to pressure computer manufacturers to embed code in their computer systems that would make it impossible to use personal computers to download MP3 files and to burn CDs. Litman also notes that, in the late 1990s, the recording industry sought legislation that would ban the manufacture of portable MP3 players on grounds that such devices *could* be used to play pirated music, even though the MP3 file format is perfectly legal and even though many MP3 files do not contain copyrighted music.

Some critics worry about potential conflicts of interest that arise in the e-commerce sector in connection with the trend toward privatization. These critics note that lines have begun to blur between common carriers (such as telephone companies) and commercial content providers, which in the past were closely regulated and monitored by the FCC. For example, consider that the business merger involving AOL (America Online Inc.) and the Time Warner Corporation in 2001 brought together a carrier and a content provider under the umbrella of one major corporation. Mergers of this type have created conflicts of interest because the content provided by a company such as Time Warner could receive preferential consideration in offerings provided to AOL subscribers.

Noting some other ways in which the privatization of information policy has affected cyberspace, Litman points out that in 1998 the Internet was transformed into a "giant American shopping mall." That year, the U.S. Congress passed three copyright-related acts that strongly favored commercial interests: the DMCA, SBCTEA, and the NET Act (each discussed in Chapter 8). Also in 1998, responsibility for the assignment of Internet domain names was transferred from the National Science Foundation (NSF), an independent organization, to the Internet Corporation for Assigned Names and Numbers (ICANN). This move was controversial because ICANN is viewed by its critics as being "business friendly" in its policies for registering domain names.

Assigning Internet Domain Names

A *domain name* is a string of letters or words used to identify a Web page; it is included in a URL (universal resource locator) such as http://www.myuniversity.edu. The domain name (in this case, *myuniversity.edu*) immediately follows the Hypertext Transfer Protocol (http://) and the World Wide Web (www) portions of the URL. The ".edu," ".com," ".net," and ".org" sections of the domain name are also referred to as *generic top-level domain names* (gTLDs). The gTLDs identify sites that are educational (.edu), commercial (.com), network-related (.net), governmental (.gov), and organizational (.org). Country-code top-level domain names (ccTLDs) are used to indicate various countries, such as Australia (.au), Germany (.de), Japan (.jp), and so forth.[5]

When NSF had been responsible for registering domain names, there was no clear or systematic policy for deciding which domain names one was eligible or ineligible to register. Anyone could, in principle, register domain names that contain "Budweiser" or "RedSox," and a serious issue arose when certain individuals registered domain names containing such key phrases and symbols that were previously registered as legal trademarks in physical space. Consequently, some trademark owners filed lawsuits against proprietors of Web sites whose domain names included symbols identical to their registered trademarks.[6] Many trademark owners viewed those who registered domain names that infringed on their trademarks as "cybersquatters," and they pressured the U.S. Congress for legislation that would protect their trademarks. In 1999, Congress passed the Anticybersquatting Consumer Protection Act.[7]

Litman suggests that ICANN could have devised alternative or compromise strategies to resolve trademark disputes in cyberspace, but she also believes that such strategies were never seriously explored. For example, the number of gTLDs could have been expanded in ways that would have satisfied both parties in a dispute involving domain names. Critics believe that a policy to include extensions such as ".biz" could have resolved some trademark disputes, including a classic case involving Amazon.com and a (bricks-and-mortar) bookstore by the name of Amazon located in Minnesota. That bookstore, which had been in business before Amazon.com, could have registered a trademark such as "Amazon.biz" to distinguish itself from the well-known (online) Amazon site. In 2002, ICANN decided to expand the number of gTLDs, approving extensions such as ".aero" for the air transport industry, ".biz," ".museum," and ".travel."[8] Even with the addition of these gTLDs, however, critics still see ICANN's policies as favoring the interests of commerce and thus contributing further to the privatization of the Internet.

▶ 9.4 (HYPERTEXT MARKUP LANGUAGE) METATAGS AND HYPERLINKING ON THE WEB

We have seen how some information policies, in conjunction with technologies such as DRM, increasingly privatize cyberspace. And we have seen how policies involving the assignment of Internet domain names, in particular, can favorably affect trademark holders as well as the interests of others in the e-commerce sector. Another controversy that has implications for trademarks involves the use (and abuse) of hypertext markup language (HTML) metatags in software code. And another code-related controversy that affects property rights for Web site owners is "deep linking," a form of hyperlinking. We examine both issues in this section.

9.4.1 Issues Surrounding the Use and Abuse of HTML Metatags

What are HTML metatags, and why are they controversial? A *metatag* is a string of text that is embedded in HTML code. To see which metatags have been included in a Web site, one can "view" the HTML source code used to construct the site, and most Web browsers enable users to do this. Metatags can be either *keyword metatags* or *descriptive metatags*. Keyword metatags, such as <football> and <Peyton Manning> enable Web-page designers to identify terms that can be used by search engines. Descriptive metatags, on the contrary, enable the designer of a Web page to describe the page contents. For example, the description of a Web site for Peyton Manning might read: "Peyton Manning . . . quarterback for the Indianapolis Colts . . . received the NFL's Most Valuable Player award for the 2008–2009 season . . ." The description typically appears as one or more sentence fragments, directly beneath the Web page's listing in an Internet search result.

Search engines examine keyword metatags to help determine how best to organize the listings of Web sites they return to queries, according to meaningful categories that a user might request. For example, if I were constructing a Web site on cyberethics that I wanted students to visit, I might include the following keyword metatags in my HTML source code: <cyberethics>, <cyberethics courses>, <computer ethics instruction>, and <issues in Internet ethics>. In doing this, my objective is to make the contents of my Web site known to search engines so that they can direct Internet users who request cyberethics-related information to my Web site.

Metatags hardly seem controversial; however, they can be used for deceptive purposes. Consider the following scenario illustrating a sinister way that metatags might be used.

▶ **SCENARIO 9–2:** A Misuse of HTML Metatags

Keith, a student at Technical University, recently completed a cyberethics course taught by Professor Bright. But Keith did not do well in the class, and he wishes to express his opinion about Professor Bright to anyone who will listen. Keith decides to construct a Web site called Cyberethics Review, where he intends to comment on the course and its instructor. Note that his Web site, despite its title, has nothing at all to do with cyberethics per se. In the HTML code for his site, Keith includes the keyword metatag <cyberethics> as well as the following descriptive metatag: "Professor Bright is a jerk . . . unfair to students . . . terrible instructor . . . " Now if someone enters the keyword "cyberethics" in a search engine's entry box, that person may receive information about the Cyberethics Review site in the list of entries returned by the search. Directly under that site's name and corresponding URL, the user will also find the (summary) descriptive sentence fragments containing the disparaging remarks about Professor Bright.

Keith could also accomplish his goal by using only a series of keyword metatags. Suppose he decides to call his Web site "Professor Bright." Of course, no search engine responding to a query about cyberethics would ordinarily return in its list (of relevant sites) information about Keith's Professor Bright site. Keith, however, is very shrewd when it comes to writing the code for his Web site. He decides to embed keyword metatags such as <Professor Bright>, <cyberethics>, and <computer ethics instructors> in the HTML source code. Suppose also that he decides not to use any descriptive metatags that might give away the true nature of the site he has constructed. Now a search engine will likely determine that Keith's site does pertain to cyberethics and will return its URL (as part of a list) to a user who has conducted a search query for the keyword cyberethics. Unsuspecting users who may be interested in visiting a site that they assume was constructed by Professor Bright for the purposes of discussing cyberethics issues, will be surprised when they click on the URL for Keith's site. Users will receive no information pertaining to cyberethics but instead find a Web page whose content includes derogatory, and possibly defamatory, remarks about Professor Bright. ■

The scenario involving Keith and Professor Bright is, of course, hypothetical; however, there have been actual cases involving the deceptive use of metatags, which have been contested in court. One such incident resulted in the *Bihari v. Gross* (2000) case, involving a former associate of Bahari Interiors who registered two domain names, "designscam.com" and "manhattaninteriordesign.com." On both sites, Gross included derogatory remarks about Bahari; he also used HTML metatags that would likely direct responses to search queries about Bahari Interiors to one or both of his Web sites, as well.[9] This case also raises questions of "defamation" in cyberspace, which we examine in Section 9.7.

9.4.2 Hyperlinking and Deep Linking

Users can navigate the Web from one site to another via direct connections called *hyperlinks*. Clicking on a hyperlink takes the user directly to the target Web site. Without hyperlinks, users have to either use search engines to locate and access related Web sites before being able to link to them or enter by hand (i.e., key in) the complete URL of a site in order to access it.

Before electronic commerce, the practice of including direct links to related Web pages had become the default mode of operation on the Web; Internet users gave little thought as to whether they needed permission to include a hyperlink to a target Web site (or to any particular section of that targeted site). They did not consider, from a legal perspective, whether they had an explicit right to link directly to another person's Web site, or to any portion of it, without first acquiring the express consent of its owner.

Consider a scenario where Professor Jones has, as part of her Web site, a sub-page devoted to bibliographic material on environmental ethics. Should Internet users be able to link directly to the bibliographic portion of her site? Or, if Professor Jones prefers, should they be required to first access her (top-level) home page and then click down to the bibliography page? Jones may not care whether visitors to her site access the top level of her site before going to the bibliography section, but the operators of some commercial Web sites have objected to visitors linking "deep" into their sites, thus bypassing the top-level pages. They point out that online advertisers, who typically place ad banners on the top-level pages of Web sites, want their ads to be seen by all visitors to the sites they are sponsoring.

Also, counter mechanisms (which track both the number of users who visit a site over a certain period and information about the time of day most visitors connect to that site) often appear on a commercial Web site's top-level page, and this kind of information can be a key factor in determining whether advertisers will sponsor a particular site. Commercial Web-site owners, especially those who depend on advertisers, have been concerned about how users access their sites.

Those who operate noncommercial Web sites might also want to be able to exercise control over how visitors enter their sites, just as a homeowner may prefer that guests enter his house by way of the front door instead of the side or back door. We next consider two examples of deep linking: one in a commercial context, and the other in a personal Web site.

▶ **SCENARIO 9–3:** Deep Linking on the Ticketmaster Web Site

Ticketmaster is a Web site that operates in Seattle, Washington; it lists cultural events in the Seattle area and enables users to purchase tickets for those events. Microsoft, as a service to its employees, included a link from its Web site directly to a page on the Ticketmaster site that described information about cultural events in the Seattle area. But Ticketmaster objected to Microsoft's use of this direct link to their sub-page, arguing that it should have a right to determine how information on its site is viewed. Ticketmaster also worried about revenue that might be lost from its advertisers, if the site's visitors systematically bypassed its top-level page, which contained various advertising banners. Ticketmaster sued Microsoft.[10] ■

Microsoft eventually settled out of court. So we have no court ruling on the legality of deep linking, but many legal observers believe that Microsoft had a strong case and would have prevailed. From the standpoint of commercial interests, Ticketmaster's position seems reasonable: Ticketmaster stood to lose valuable revenue from advertisers, which could eventually have resulted in Ticketmaster's going out of business altogether. But what about our earlier example involving Professor Jones who seemed indifferent as to whether visitors entered her site via the top-level Web page before accessing the bibliography on that site's sub-page? In this case, there would be no concern about lost revenue from advertisers. But could Jones insist, as Ticketmaster did, that visitors access her site through the top-level page? What grounds would she have for doing so? Perhaps Jones believes that her Web site reflects her work as a scholar and that the bibliography section can be more fully appreciated in the context of the overall site. Recall our analysis of the personality theory of property in Chapter 8. There, we considered a scenario where Angela, the author of a scholarly journal article, wanted her article reprinted only in its entirety in a textbook, because she believed that an excerpted form of the article did not truly represent her work. Is Professor Jones' position regarding how the bibliography on her Web site should be accessed similar to Angela's position about how her article should be read?

Richard Spinello (2004) describes a scenario where an imaginary artist named Maria has set up an online exhibit of her paintings on her personal Web site. One of Maria's paintings is highly controversial and has generated considerable interest both within and outside the art community, so many people would like to link directly to the image of that painting on Maria's Web site. But Maria argues that the artist should be able to determine the sequential arrangement of paintings in a physical art gallery, and thus how the visitors to her online gallery are required to view the images of her paintings there. The controversial painting in question, she further argues, is best understood within the context of other paintings that both precede and follow it in the online exhibit.

Is Maria's position reasonable? If a Web site is viewed as a form of (intellectual) property, then she may have a strong case. Consider that Maria, as a property owner, could determine how people enter her site in the same way that a home owner in physical space can require that visitors enter the house only through either the front door or a side door. If a Web site is considered private property, however, another controversial issue also arises: an unwelcome visitor to a Web site could be accused of trespassing. The notion of trespass in cyberspace is far from clear; however, some believe that the practice of sending unsolicited e-mail, which is now commonly referred to as spam, qualifies as a form of trespass in cyberspace.

▶ 9.5 E-MAIL SPAM

What is *spam*, and why is it problematic from a social and moral perspective? Keith Miller and James Moor (2008) point out that according to some estimates, as much as 80% of e-mail sent could qualify as spam. But they also note that there are "dramatically different definitions" of what can count as spam.

9.5.1 Defining Spam

While there is no universally agreed-upon definition of spam, it is typically viewed as e-mail that is *unsolicited*, *commercial*, and sent in *bulk* to multiple users. Is this definition adequate? Because spam is *unsolicited*, it is also nonconsensual. However, not all nonconsensual e-mail is spam. If you have an e-mail account, you have probably received unsolicited e-mail messages requesting information from you or informing you about an upcoming event; they may have been sent to you because you are a member of a particular social networking service (SNS) or because you have an e-mail address associated with an academic institution, government organization, and so forth. You may have considered some of these messages annoying, but are they necessarily spam?

Another feature of our working definition of spam is that it is *commercial*. However, some commercial e-mail you receive can be in the form of advertisements that you have authorized a commercial Web site to e-mail you. For example, you could have registered on an e-mail distribution list for a department store at which you frequently shop, requesting to be informed about upcoming sales and discount items. The e-mails you receive from this site, while commercial or promotional in nature, would not qualify as spam.

Spam is distributed in *bulk*, but not all e-mail distributed in that form necessarily qualify as spam. For example, some messages sent in bulk form (i.e., to an e-mail list) might have been directed to people in the group who are known by the sender; there could be some personal or professional connection between the sender and receiver of the e-mail message. So, our initial working definition of spam as e-mail that is "unsolicited, promotional, and sent in bulk" to multiple users would not seem adequate.

Miller and Moor believe that much of the popular discussion about spam in terms of what they describe as unsolicited commercial bulk e-mail (UCBE) is both "confused and degraded" because it fails to distinguish between UCBE that is "deceptive" and "intended to harm" and UCBE that is not. They also believe that the problems affecting e-mail spam can be better analyzed by focusing on a series of distinct, but interrelated, criteria such as the

- content of the e-mail
- intent of the sender
- consequences of the receiver
- consent of the receiver
- relationship between the sender and the receiver
- accountability of the sender and the degree of deception
- number of identical e-mails sent.[11]

Miller and Moor disagree with many critics of spam who tend to assume that all e-mail advertisements are deceptive. Alternatively, they believe that it is possible to distinguish between UCBE advertisements that (a) "misrepresent and are fraudulent" and (b) "present information in a favorable light." They refer to the former as *F-UCBE* and distinguish it from the nonfraudulent version they call *NF-UCBE*. They also believe that NF-UCBE requires a more complex ethical analysis than F-UCBE.

9.5.2 Why Is Spam Morally Objectionable?

Richard Spinello (2006) believes that spam is morally objectionable for two reasons— one based on utilitarian grounds and the other on deontological considerations. Spam not only has harmful consequences, but it also violates the individual autonomy of Internet users. First, consider some of the harmful consequences of spam—e.g., its financial impacts, such as cost shifting and the consumption of valuable network resources. For example, spam consumes and strains valuable computing resources and thus contributes to the degradation of what Spinello describes as the "fragile ecology of the Internet." Miller and Moor describe these kinds of abuses of the Internet as one more instance of "spoiling of the commons." (Recall our discussion of the "tragedy of the commons" in Chapter 8.)

Spinello argues that even if Internet resources were infinite and there were no negative utilitarian consequences, spam would still be morally objectionable because it does not respect individual users as persons. He believes that deontological arguments, such as Kant's (see Chapter 2), can be used to show why this so. Recall that Kant argues that a practice has moral worth only if it can be universalizable. And, in Kant's system, a practice is universalizable only if it can coherently apply to all persons without exception. So, we need to ask: Could we universalize a coherent practice in which each e-mail user would allow spam to be sent and received by every other user? Could such a practice, if instituted, be logically coherent? On Kantian grounds, if spammers did not accept the principle that everyone should be able to send and receive spam, then they would be inconsistent. If spammers believed that only they should be permitted to send spam, then they would be making an exception for themselves. And if they granted themselves this exception, while relying on the good will of ordinary users not to engage in the practice of spamming others, then spammers would be treating ordinary users as a means to their ends. So, Spinello makes a plausible case for why spam can be considered morally objectionable on deontological as well as on utilitarian grounds.

Miller and Moor believe that an adequate ethical analysis of spam also needs to take into consideration criteria such as accountability and deception—generally, the "more deceptive the content and the less accountable the sender, the more blameworthy the sender becomes." Employing their distinction between NF-UCBE and F-UCBE, they argue that fraudulent UCBE should always be condemned, whereas some cases of NF-UCBE can be justifiable from a moral point of view. For example, they point out that a whistle-blower might send a message to a large commercial mailing list to alert recipients of an injustice or a danger. Here, the whistle-blower may have justifiable reasons for sending the e-mail broadly and for wishing to be anonymous. Miller and Moor believe that in this whistle-blowing scenario, the "intent" of the sender needs to be taken into consideration. So, there can be some cases where sending spam in the form of NF-UCBE would be justifiable.

It is one thing to say that spam, at least in its F-UCBE form, is morally objectionable, but it is another to ask what can be done about it from a legal and a public policy perspective. Because spam is very similar to the "junk mail" that we receive via the postal delivery system, we might ask why the same laws that apply to physical junk mail do not also apply to electronic spam. Although there are similarities between the two forms of junk mail, there are also relevant differences; practical and financial constraints determine how much physical junk mail merchants can send, but the same kinds of constraints do not apply in the case of electronic spam.

Miller and Moor believe that e-mail spam is also analogous to unsolicited commercial phone calls. And they point out that the latter have been significantly reduced in the United States through legislation, even though they have not been altogether eliminated. But they also note that because of the "open" nature of Internet architectures and protocols, spam has been far more resistant to the kinds of legislative and technological solutions used to discourage unsolicited commercial phone calls.

Various state laws against spam have been enacted in the United States, and in 2003, Congress passed the CAN SPAM (Controlling the Assault of Non-Solicited

Pornography and Marketing) Act. That law, which went into effect in January 2004, specifies criminal penalties that include a fine of $250 for each spam e-mail. However, critics of the CAN SPAM Act note that spammers who use ISPs outside the United States to send their spam e-mail cannot be prosecuted under this act, which cannot be enforced internationally. Some critics are also skeptical as to whether any kind of legislation, even international laws, can solve the problem of spam.

▶ 9.6 FREE SPEECH VS. CENSORSHIP AND CONTENT CONTROL IN CYBERSPACE

We have examined a set of regulatory issues that either involved, or had implications for, electronic commerce. In this section we turn our attention to regulatory issues involving the *content* of cyberspace. Such issues center on the question as to whether all forms of online speech should be tolerated. Some issues concerning the regulation of online speech and online commerce overlap. For example, questions concerning spam, considered in the preceding section, straddle the divide. Some purveyors of spam have defended their practice on the grounds of free speech.

Should certain forms of speech on the Internet be censored? Or do they deserve to be protected under the U.S. Constitutional guarantee of free speech? According to the First Amendment of the United States Constitution, "Congress shall make no law . . . abridging the freedom of speech, or of the press." This passage, consisting of merely fourteen words, has often been quoted by libertarians who strongly believe that the government should not intrude in matters involving our constitutionally guaranteed right to free speech. We should note, however, that free speech is not an absolute right. As in the case of other rights contained in the Bill of Rights, which comprise the first ten amendments to the Constitution, the right to free speech is *conditional* in the sense that it is only a right if all things are equal. While your right to free speech protects your freedom to express controversial ideas concerning politics, religion, and so forth, it does not grant you the right to shout "Fire!" in a crowded shopping mall or in a movie theater.

Also, during times of war, one's ability to speak freely is sometimes constrained. For example, in the period immediately following the attacks of September 11, 2001, some labeled the news commentators, reporters, and talk show hosts who criticized the Bush White House as "unpatriotic." Ordinarily, such criticisms are considered normal and in accordance with the principle of free speech accorded to the press. But at other times, social norms and market forces rather than law itself can regulate free speech. Television viewers who were offended by remarks they perceived as either anti-Bush or antigovernment pressured advertisers not to sponsor programs that expressed viewpoints that could be considered unpatriotic. This, in turn, caused television networks either to cancel some programs or not to broadcast them in certain areas of the country. (Note that this is an example of Lessig's claim that, in certain cases, social norms and market forces can be more effective regulators than laws themselves.) Nonetheless, free speech is a broad right, cited time and again by publishers of unpopular tabloids and also appealed to by many who distribute pornography. Many believe, however, that some forms of speech on the Internet, including pornography, should be censored.

What, exactly, is censorship? Kay Mathisien (2008) characterizes censorship as limiting access to content by deterring either (a) the speaker from speaking or (b) the hearer from receiving the speech. She also advances a more formal definition of censorship, claiming that to censor is to

> restrict or limit access to an expression, portion of an expression, or category of expression, which has been made public by its author, based on the belief that it will be a bad thing if people access the content of that expression.[12] [Italics Mathiasen]

Jacques Catudal (2004) points out that an important distinction can be drawn between two types of censorship that he describes as "censorship by suppression" and "censorship by deterrence." Both forms presuppose that some "authorized person or group of persons" has judged some text or "type of text" objectionable on moral, political, or other grounds.

Censorship by suppression prohibits the objectionable text or material from being published, displayed, or circulated. Banning certain books from being published or prohibiting certain kinds of movies from being made are both examples of censorship by suppression. In this scheme, pornography and other objectionable forms of speech would not be allowed on the Internet.

Censorship by deterrence, on the contrary, is less drastic. It neither suppresses nor blocks out objectionable material, nor does it forbid such material from being published. Rather, it depends on threats of arrest, prosecution, conviction, and punishment of both those who make an objectionable text available and those who acquire it. Heavy fines and possible imprisonment can deter the publication and acquisition of objectionable content. Again, using Lessig's regulatory model, social norms, such as social disenfranchisement, personal disgrace, and public censure, can also work to deter individuals from engaging in the publication, display, and transmission of objectionable speech.

9.6.1 Pornography in Cyberspace

Before examining the issue of pornography on the Internet, it is instructive to understand what legally qualifies as pornography. It is often debated in terms of notions such as obscenity and indecent speech. In *Miller v. California* (1973), the court established a three-part guideline for determining whether material is obscene under the law and thus not protected by the First Amendment. According to this criteria, something is obscene if it

1. depicts sexual (or excretory) acts whose depiction is specifically prohibited by law;
2. depicts these acts in a patently offensive manner, appealing to prurient interest as judged by a reasonable person using community standards;
3. has no serious literary, artistic, social, political, or scientific value.[13]

These criteria have proved problematic in attempts to enforce pornography laws. For example, the second criterion includes three controversial notions: "prurient interest," "reasonable person," and "community standards." *Prurient* is usually defined as having to do with lust and lewd behavior, concepts that, in turn, have been challenged as being vague and arbitrary. Also, many ask who, exactly, counts as a reasonable person. Until the advent of cybertechnology, we might have assumed a fairly straightforward notion of "community standard" because traditionally a community has been defined in terms of geographical space. But what, exactly, is a community in cyberspace? And when more than one community is involved in a dispute involving pornography, whose community standards should apply?

Interpreting "Community Standards" in Cyberspace

Interpretations of "community" and "community standards" were among the issues debated in a court case involving pornography and the Amateur Action (Electronic) Bulletin Board System. This particular bulletin board system (BBS), which made sexually explicit images available to its members, was operated by a couple who lived in California. Because it was an online forum, its contents were available not only to residents of California but to users who had Internet access in other states and countries. A resident of Memphis, Tennessee, became a member of the BBS and then downloaded sexually explicit pictures onto his computer in Tennessee. Although including sexually explicit images on a BBS may not have been illegal in California, viewing such images was illegal under Tennessee state law, and criminal charges were brought against the California operators of the BBS, who were prosecuted in Tennessee.[14]

The California couple was found guilty under Tennessee law of distributing obscenity as defined under the local community standards that applied in Memphis. Not surprisingly, this case raised issues of what was meant by "community standards" on the Internet. Can a community in cyberspace be defined simply in terms of geography? Or in an era of Internet-based social networking sites such as Facebook and MySpace, should "community" be defined by other criteria? For example, can an online community be better understood as a computer-mediated forum where individuals who share common interests come together? (We examine online communities in detail in Chapter 11.)

The Amateur Action case also raised another important issue: Were the pornographic files *distributed* over the Internet by the operators of the BBS in California, as alleged? Or, instead, did the resident in Tennessee who actually downloaded them via the interstate telephone lines that transmit information between the two states *retrieve* those controversial files from the Internet? Questions involving distribution and community standards in cyberspace contribute to the difficulty of interpreting and enforcing pornography laws online.

Many people first became aware of the amount of pornographic material available on the Internet through a news story, entitled "CyberPorn," which appeared in *TIME* magazine in the summer of 1995. *TIME* reported that there were 900,000 sexually explicit pornographic materials (pictures, film clips, etc.) available on the Internet. Many people, including most lawmakers, were outraged when they learned about the amount of pornographic material that was so easily accessible to Internet users, including minors. Later, however, the *TIME* magazine story, based on an Internet study that had been conducted by a researcher at Carnegie Mellon University, was shown to be seriously flawed.

Although the Carnegie Mellon study accurately reported the number of pornographic images and pornographic Web sites that were available, it failed to put this information into proper perspective—it made no mention of the fact that the percentage of pornographic sites relative to other sites on the Web was very low. However, the report caught the attention of many influential politicians, some of whom drafted legislation in response to what they saw as the growth of the "pornography industry" on the Internet. The result was the passage of the Communications Decency Act (CDA) in early 1996.

Internet Pornography Laws and Protecting Children Online

The CDA caused controversy from the outset, especially the section referred to as the Exon Amendment, which dealt specifically with online pornography. The American Civil Liberties Union (ACLU) and other organizations soon challenged the constitutionality of CDA. In the summer of 1996, a court in Philadelphia struck down CDA on grounds that it was too broad and that it violated the United States Constitution; in the summer of 1997 the Supreme Court upheld the lower court's ruling.[15] A portion of the CDA, known as the Child Pornography Protection Act (CPPA) of 1996, was determined to be constitutional. According to the CPPA, it was a crime to "knowingly send, receive, distribute, reproduce, sell, or possess more than three child pornographic images."[16] So even though CDA itself was overturned, supporters of that legislation were pleased that the section on child pornography still held.

In June 1998, Congress passed the Child Online Pornography Act (COPA). (We should note that COPA is sometimes confused with COPPA, the Children's Online Privacy Protection Act of 2000, which was designed to reduce the amount of information that could be collected from children under the age of 12 who use the Internet.) Many of COPA's proponents believed that this act would be upheld by the courts, but as in the case of CDA, COPA was ill-fated. In February 1999, the Supreme Court ruled that COPA was unconstitutional.[17] The only remaining federal law in 1999 that was specifically directed at online pornography and that had managed to withstand constitutional scrutiny was the CPPA of 1996, a section of the original CDA. Although it appeared that CPPA would remain intact, many critics argued that provisions of this act also conflicted with the U.S. Constitution. On April 16, 2002, the Supreme Court, in a ruling of 6–3, struck down portions of CPPA as unconstitutional.[18]

In December 2000 the U.S. Congress enacted into law the Children's Internet Protection Act (CIPA), designed to address concerns about children's access to "offensive content" over the Internet on school and library computers. CIPA was targeted specifically to schools and libraries, where federal and local governments have greater control. This law affects any schools or public libraries that receive federal funding in the form of "E-Rate" discounts (described in Chapter 10), which make certain technologies more affordable for eligible schools and libraries. According to CIPA requirements, schools and libraries may not receive the discounts offered by the E-Rate Program unless they certify that they have an "Internet safety policy" in place. This policy includes technology protection measures to block or filter Internet access by minors to pictures that are (a) obscene, (b) child pornography, and (c) harmful to minors.[19]

As in the case of CPPA and COPA, CIPA was eventually challenged in the courts. In March 2001 several groups, including the American Library Association (ALA) and the ACLU, filed suit to prevent the enforcement of CIPA's filtering requirement in public libraries. On May 31, 2002, the U.S. District Court for the eastern district of Pennsylvania ruled that the CIPA filtering mandate was unconstitutional. However, the District Court's decision was overturned by the U.S. Supreme Court, which upheld CIPA in a 6–3 decision on June 23, 2003 (*United States v. American Library Assn. Inc.*, 2003).

Legal analysts who have closely followed the Supreme Court's ruling in CIPA note that no clear precedent had been established with respect to how online child pornography laws will be interpreted in the future. This is especially apparent in legal precedents for interpreting an appropriate scope of filtering in public libraries. The Supreme Court's ruling in CIPA is considered a "plurality decision" because there was

TABLE 9.1   Internet-specific Child Pornography Laws

CDA (Communications Decency Act)	Passed in January 1996 and declared unconstitutional in July 1996. The Supreme Court upheld the lower court's decision in 1997.
CPPA (Child Pornography Protection Act)	Passed as part of the larger CDA, but not initially struck down in 1997 with the CDA. It was declared unconstitutional in April 2002.
COPA (Child online Pornography Act)	Passed in June 1998 and (portions) declared unconstitutional by the Supreme Court in February 1999.
CIPA (Children's Internet Protection Act)	Passed in December 2000 and declared unconstitutional by a U.S. district court in 2002. The Supreme Court overturned the lower court's ruling in June 2003.

less than a clear majority in the justices' written opinions. Justices Kennedy and Breyer, who sided with the majority, did not concur with the rationales stated in Justice Reinquist's "majority opinion." Although they agreed with Reinquist's conclusion, they wrote a separate opinion supporting the majority decision only to the extent that it provides filtering for children, but Kennedy and Breyer also sated that filtering must be easily disabled for adults who request it in public libraries.[20]

Although CIPA provides protection for children in school and library settings, proponents of broad-based pornography legislation are concerned that CIPA falls short because it does not provide the kind of protection children need outside those contexts. However, critics of CIPA argue that too much nonpornographic content is blocked in the process of protecting children. We will see why this concern is problematic in our discussion of Internet filters and libraries in Section 9.6.2.

Table 9.1 identifies the four online child pornography laws that have been enacted at the federal level, including when the laws were passed and when three of them were eventually struck down.

Child Pornography Laws and Sexting

What is sexting, and what challenges does it pose for current child pornography laws? Sexting is typically defined as the use of cell phones (or similar handheld electronic devices) to send nude or seminude photos of oneself to others. In some cases these photos become widely distributed and can eventually end up on the Internet.

► **SCENARIO 9–4:** A Sexting Incident Involving Greensburg Salem High School

In early 2009, six teenagers—three girls and three boys—at the Greensburg Salem High School in Pennsylvania were charged under child pornography laws in a sexting incident. The three girls, ages 14 and 15, who took nude or seminude photos of themselves on their cell phones and sent them to male classmates, faced charges involving the "manufacturing and dissemination of child pornography." The boys, who were ages 16 and 17, faced charges of possession of child pornography. The nude pictures were discovered by Greenburg High School officials in October 2008, when they seized a cell phone from a male student who was using it in violation of school policy.[21] The charges were later reduced to misdemeanors. ■

Should the six teenagers have been charged with either dissemination or possession of child pornography? Were the original felony charges brought against them too harsh? Alternatively, are misdemeanor charges too lenient in cases such as this one? There does not yet seem to be any clear consensus on the answer to this question. Yet, the number of reported sexting incidents involving teenagers has increased sharply in recent years.

Next consider two sexting incidents that each had very unfortunate outcomes—one resulting in the suicide of an 18-year-old female, and one resulting in a felony charge brought against a male who had just turned 18. An Ohio resident—we will call her "Jill"—sent nude photos of herself via her cell phone to a boy, who then forwarded the pictures to others. The nude pictures of Jill were seen by some of her classmates at school and as well as by others who lived in her community. As the photos became more widely distributed, Jill was taunted by some of her classmates as well as by others in her community. In May 2008, Jill took her life by hanging herself in her bedroom.[22]

A Florida resident, whom we will call "Phil," sent a nude cell phone picture of his girlfriend to his friends and family, following the couple's break-up. His girlfriend was 16, and Phil had recently turned 18. He was arrested by police in Florida who charged Phil with sending child pornography, and he was later convicted of a felony offense. Consequently, Phil was required to register as a sex offender, which means that his name will appear on an Internet registry of sex offenders in Florida until he is 43. Phil was also expelled from college and was unable to find employment. Additionally, he is required to check with his probation officer if he plans to travel outside of the United States.[23]

How should sexting be understood in a manner consistent with our legal framework? It would seem that sexting incidents have once again generated what James Moor (2007) describes as a "conceptual muddle." This, in turn, complicates the question of how these incidents should be punished. Legal analysts point out that the current laws are inconsistent in their application from state to state. We have seen that states such as Pennsylvania and Florida have prosecuted, or have tried to prosecute, sexting cases as a felony offense. However, in other states, including Vermont, lawmakers have introduced legislation that would exclude teenagers who engage in sexting from being tried under child pornography laws and would instead make sexting a misdemeanor.[24] Advocates on both sides of this view, however, can agree on one thing: more consistent laws are needed.

Can "Exceptions" be applied to Child Pornography Laws in Sexting Cases?

Julie Hilden (2009) believes that instead of applying older child pornography laws that were designed for "graver and much more exploitative contexts," we should "craft new laws designed specifically for sexting." She agrees with critics of the Greenburg case, including the ACLU, that the initial charges brought against the six Pennsylvania teenagers were "ill-grounded," because the child pornography laws under which the teenagers were first charged were intended to cover "lascivious displays of the genitals and/or sexual activity." Hilden believes that the teenagers involved in the Greensburg High School incident were not guilty of this kind of behavior, especially since two of the girls were wearing bras and one was topless in the photos sent to the three boys. So prosecuting the three girls under strict child pornography laws would be inappropriate.

Hilden also believes, however, that the prosecution of some teenagers under such laws would be appropriate in future cases of sexting that might involve "underage teens having sex, displaying their genitals in a lascivious way, or both." In these cases, she suggests that the behavior of the teenagers could validly "form the basis of child-pornography charges." Hilden also suggests that lawmakers should consider two kinds of "exceptions" to child pornography laws in sexting cases: (1) a "Romeo and Juliet" exception (which is sometimes used in statutory rape laws where consensus is involved), and (2) an "age-specific" exception. She believes that the Romeo and Juliet exception could apply when the two parties to an act of sex are close in age (say 18 and 16, or 15 and 17). She notes, for example, that a 16-year-old sexting a nude photo of herself or himself to someone roughly the same age is far less disturbing than a 16-year-old doing so at the invitation of a 40-year-old. Hilden asks us to imagine a 16-year-old, named Jane, who sends a nude photo of herself to her 18-year-old boyfriend, Bill. Here Jane might be protected under the Romeo and Juliet exception (and thus be immune from prosecution).

But Hilden also points out that if Bill forwards the photo to one or more persons without Jane's consent, he should not be immune from prosecution. Although these exceptions do not provide a "bright line," Hilden believes that they at least allow authorities to differentiate between a high school senior who takes and "sexts" a photo of a 13-year-old eighth grader, and is truly engaging in child pornography, and a sexting incident involving two teenagers in the same age category. In this way, the exceptions would avoid the need to impose severe criminal penalties on more-or-less same-age kids for what Hilden describes as "ugly immaturity," not crime.

One question that Hilden does not consider, however, is what would happen in the case where a teenage girl sends an uninvited nude photo of herself to an older man. In this case, would the man receiving the unsolicited photo be liable for prosecution under child pornography laws merely for having (or having had at some point) the nude photo of the teenager on his cell phone? An actual case involving sexting between a 52-year-old man and a 14-year-old female occurred in Georgia (Bunker 2009). In this incident the older man was trying to set up a "sexual rendezvous" with the young female. The girl sent him nude photos that she had taken of herself on her cell phone. Here, of course, the controversies raised go well beyond sexting—for example, they also include questions of intended child molestation or pedophilia. But what if this man had made no sexual advances toward the 14-year-old girl and still received the pictures? It is not clear if he would still be culpable of possessing child pornography on his cell phone. So it would seem that answers to questions of this type would also need to be spelled out more clearly and explicitly in any future legislation drafted for sexting that incorporates age-specific exceptions.

What can we conclude about sexting as it relates to our examination of child pornography in this section? We can agree with critics that most teenagers who have been prosecuted thus far for sexting have not engaged in behavior that meets the threshold of crimes intended for prosecution as felonies under child pornography laws. Yet, sexting is a serious offense and thus needs to be dealt with appropriately in the legal and judicial systems. In the meantime, it seems that drafting some kind of federal standard that could be applied to sexting cases occurring in all states would be the best short-term solution.

Virtual Child Pornography

Critics have argued that online pornography laws, especially CPPA, broaden the definition of child pornography to include entire categories of images that many would not judge to be "child pornographic." Catudal (2004) notes that visual depictions of sexually explicit conduct that do not involve *actual* minors would be included as child pornography under CPPA. In fact, Catudal believes that the CPPA's definition of child pornography includes categories of images that some would judge not pornographic at all.

Child pornography, according to CPPA, is "any depiction, including a photograph, film, video, picture, or computer or computer-generated image or picture, whether made or produced by electronic, mechanical, or other means, of sexually explicit conduct." The definition goes on to list four categories of such depictions:

A. the production of such visual depiction involves the use of a minor engaging in sexually explicit conduct;

B. such visual depiction is, or appears to be, of a minor engaging in sexually explicit conduct; or

C. such visual depiction has been created, adapted, or modified to appear that an identifiable minor is engaging in sexually explicit conduct; or

D. such visual depiction is advertised, promoted, presented, described, or distributed in such a manner that conveys the impression that the material is or contains a visual depiction of a minor engaging in sexually explicit conduct.[25]

Whereas category (A) images represent depictions of what has been traditionally regarded as child pornography, Catudal argues that the same is not true of category (B) images. For example, he considers the case of a 19-year-old girl who appears in a pornographic image in which she looks much younger. Sexual depictions of this sort are sometimes referred to as the "little girl" genre; they have been used in many artistic works. (The "little girl" type does not, by definition, actually involve little girls or minors of any age.) In the United States, the sexually explicit depiction of a "young looking" 19-year-old would be considered child pornography under CPPA, but in some other countries, such as Norway, it would not. Catudal believes that CPPA fails to note that category (A) and category (B) depictions represent two different types of prurient images.

Note also that in categories (C) and (D), the pornographic image can consist of a depiction of someone who *appears* to be a minor engaging in sexual activity, or a depiction that *conveys the impression* of a minor engaging in such an activity. So, a computer-generated image that does not refer to an actual human being would also qualify as a child pornography image under CPPA. In its decision to strike down portions of the CPPA, the Supreme Court reasoned that a distinction needed to be made between a pornographic image of an actual child and that of a "virtual," or computer-generated, image of a minor.

Some argue that because no real children are used in the production of virtual child pornography, no children are harmed in the process. However, Per Sandin (2004) argues that even if the production of virtual child pornography does not harm real children, it doesn't follow that the *use* of virtual child pornography causes no harm to real children. Sandin suggests that a utilitarian argument could be made against allowing virtual child pornography if it is shown to have harmful consequences for real children. In our discussion of virtual reality in Chapter 11, we will see that "objectionable behavior" performed in virtual environments such as VR games, which portray only virtual or computer-generated images, can nonetheless cause real harm to real people. However, we will not continue with the debate about real vs. virtual harm here. Our purpose in this section has been to describe Internet pornography legislation that has been enacted to protect children online and to show why that legislation has been controversial, especially when it is extended to include virtual child pornographic images.

9.6.2 Software Filtering Programs as an Alternative to Censoring Speech

Does pornography qualify as a form of speech, even if it is often classified as "obscene speech"? If so, should all forms of pornography be censored on the Internet? Some believe that filtering programs can provide a reasonable alternative to censoring objectionable forms of online speech. Others, however, are less convinced that software filters can resolve the censorship-free speech debate in cyberspace. Essentially, software filters are programs that screen Internet content and block access to unacceptable Web sites. Some filters have been criticized because they screen too much. Consider that filtering out objectionable material through the use of the keyword "sex" could block out important literary and scientific works, precluding the ability to access works by Shakespeare as well as books on biology and health. Other filters are criticized because they screen too little; such schemes might not successfully block nonobvious pornographic Web sites, such as www.whitehouse.com. A number of software filtering programs, such as Net Nanny, have been available to parents who wish to block access to certain sites on their home computers.

Not everyone, however, has been impressed with the use of software filters for self-regulatory purposes. Lessig (2000) believes that architectures designed for filtering are also a form of regulation by code, which is why he is skeptical of filtering schemes in cyberspace. He argues that some filtering architectures such as the Platform for Independent Content Selection (PICS) are, in effect, universal censorship systems, which can censor any kind of material, not just pornography. For example, software filters can be used to block unpopular political speech or dissenting points of view. Richard Rosenberg (2001), whose position is similar to Lessig's, points out that filters could also be used by conservative school boards to block out information about evolutionary theory. The ACLU (2004) has also taken a similar position on the use of filtering. The ACLU report expressed the fear that using censoring mechanisms such as filters may "burn the global village to roast the pig."

Whereas proponents of filtering on architectures such as PICS assume that the labeling schemes and protocols used are neutral or value-free, Lessig argues that such schemes and protocols will always reflect the biases of those who are the content labelers. For Lessig, the fundamental flaw of rating systems for software filters is that we, as citizens, will be turning over to those who rate content (e.g., private industry, public interest groups, etc.) the government's role as an arbiter of speech rights. Thus privately owned corporations and their computer programmers will ultimately make decisions about which Web sites children should and should not see.

Software filters can be used at two different levels: downstream and upstream. We have already noted one example of "downstream filtering," in pointing out that parents can use filters to control what their children see in the home; however, "upstream filtering," done at the ISP level, or at the government level, is more controversial. Some argue that upstream filtering is repressive because it "fences out" many legitimate voices in the act of filtering. These critics also believe that filtering upstream prevents the free flow of information, which can also threaten the democratizing aspects of the Internet.

A classic court case that illustrates the key controversies involved in upstream filtering is *Mainstream Loudon v. Board of Trustees*. The Loudon County Public Library in Virginia used filtering software to block out obscene material, including child pornography. In 1998, the library was sued by an association called Mainstream Loudon, whose members consisted of patrons of the Loudon County Public Library, because the filtering devices used by the library also blocked access to nonpornographic sites such as the Quaker Home Page and the American Association of University Women. In this case, the district court ruled that the installation of filtering software on public-access computers in libraries violated the First Amendment.[26] Unfortunately, however, the court did not provide any clear direction on how to resolve future cases affecting the use of filters in libraries to protect children from online pornography.

We noted earlier that the U.S. Congress passed CIPA in 2000 and that this act was upheld by the U.S. Supreme Court in a split decision in June 2003. Although CIPA supports filtering in school libraries, the justices were not in agreement on how it should be implemented. For example, Justices Kennedy and Breyer, emphasized in their opinions that a librarian should upon the request of an adult, remove blocking on specific sites, or entirely disable filtering for that user.[27] So, it would seem that the battle over Internet filtering in libraries vis-à-vis protecting children online is far from settled and will likely continue to be debated in the courts.

9.6.3 Hate Speech and Speech That Can Cause Physical Harm to Others

In addition to pornography, which is sometimes viewed as "obscene" speech, *hate speech* and forms of *speech that can cause physical harm* to individuals and communities have both caused controversy in cyberspace. Hate speech on the Internet often targets racial and ethnic groups. For example, white supremacist organizations such as the Ku Klux Klan (KKK) can include offensive remarks about African Americans and Jews on their Web pages. Because of the Internet, international hate groups, such as "skin heads" in America, Europe, and Russia, can spread their messages of hate in ways that were not previously possible.

Hate Speech

Whereas the United States has focused its attention on controversial Internet speech issues that involve online pornography, European countries such as France and Germany have been more concerned about online hate speech. For example, Germany's Information and Communications Act was designed to censor neo-Nazi propaganda. But the law applies only to people who live in Germany; it cannot regulate the speech transmitted by ISPs outside that country. Roy Girasa (2002) believes that if the German government had tried to enforce this law, countries such as the United States would likely have refused to extradite individuals to Germany.

In France, it is illegal to sell anything that incites hate and racism. However, Nazi and KKK memorabilia are auctioned daily on Web sites such as Yahoo that have an international reach. In 2000, a French judge ruled that Yahoo must "make it impossible" for people in France to access sites selling that kind of material. Yahoo complied, and as a result, Nazi-related items are no longer available on Yahoo's French site (www.yahoo.fr). But French citizens who use an ISP outside France could potentially access the sites that are banned in France.[28]

In the United States, some "hate-watch" Web sites, such as the Southern Poverty Law Center's (SPLC) "Intelligence Project" (http://www.splcenter.org), monitor online hate speech aimed at racial minorities. In an effort to counter the effectiveness of "hate sites," these hate-watch Web sites have exposed the existence of various hate organizations to the public. The SPLC site also features a Hate Watch blog and it includes a detailed map with physical locations of various hate groups, which it identifies under categories such as Ku Klux Klan, Neo-Nazi, Racist Skinhead, and so forth. Ironically, perhaps, the information available on these sites also provides an easy way for consumers of hate speech to locate and visit particular hate sites that serve their interests.

Some hate sites use deceptive metatags (described in Section 9.4.2) to lure unsuspecting users to their sites. For example, a hate site directed against African Americans could use a keyword metatag such as "Martin Luther King, Jr." to intentionally mislead persons interested in acquiring information about Dr. King by directing them instead to its racist Web site.

Another form of hate speech has involved radical elements of conservative organizations; for example, right-wing militia groups, whose ideology is often anti-federal government, can broadcast information on the Internet about how to harm or even kill agents of the government. Some critics believe that the kind of antigovernment rhetoric that emanated from militia movements in the United States in the 1990s influenced the two individuals that carried out the Oklahoma City bombing in April 1995.

Web sites have also been established to promote white supremacist hate speech. One such site was operated by James von Brunn who fatally shot an African American museum guard at the Holocaust Museum in Washington DC in June 2009. On his site (holywesternempire.com), von Brunn included hate speech aimed at Jews and African Americans. In fact, his site was listed on the Southern Poverty Law Center's notorious hate sites. A few days before von Brunn shot his victim, he transferred control of his Web site to Steve Reimink who described the 88-year-old von Brunn as a "sick individual." But Rimink's message also included "code," familiar to many white supremacists, suggesting that Rimink's remarks were not sincere.[29]

Some antiabortion groups in the United States have set up Web sites dedicated to distributing hate-related information about doctors who perform abortions. Some of these sites have included information about where these doctors live, what times they travel to and from abortion clinics, where they go in their free time, etc. As in the case of the antigovernment and white-supremacist rhetoric used by radical groups in the United States, this type of (hate) speech can also result in physical harm to others. Some information made available on antiabortion Web sites has been linked to the murder of doctors who perform abortions. In May 2009, for example, Dr. George Tiller, who performed late-term abortions in Kansas, was murdered by an antiabortionist. Information about Tiller was available to Tiller's murderer via a Web site set up by an antiabortionist group (http://www.dr-tiller.com/), which described Tiller as "America's most notorious abortionist" and as "Tiller the Killer." This site also included information about Tiller's employees and assistant abortionists.

Speech That Can Cause Physical Harm to Others

Some forms of hate speech on the Internet are such that they *might* also result in physical harm being caused to individuals. Other forms of this speech, however, are by the very nature of their content, biased toward violence and physical harm to others. Consider two examples of how of speech communicated on the Internet can result in serious physical harm: one involving information on how to construct bombs, and another that provides information on how to abduct children for the purpose of molesting them. Should this information be censored in cyberspace? This kind of information was available before the Internet era and it may even have been (and still may be) available in public libraries. If it is available elsewhere, should it be censored on the Internet?

Critics point out that Internet access now makes it much easier to acquire all kinds of information, including information about how to make and do things that cause physical harm. They also note that it is possible to access and read this information in the privacy and comfort of one's home. Even more disturbing is that it is now far easier for international and domestic terrorists to obtain information about how to construct bombs. Some believe that these are good enough reasons for censoring this kind of speech on the Internet.

Recall our discussion in Section 9.1.1 about whether the Internet should be conceived as a broadcast medium, like television or radio, or as a place, like a bookstore. We saw that the rules that apply in each are significantly different. Viewing the Internet as a medium of some sort makes it far easier to control the dissemination (or broadcast) of certain kinds of information than viewing it as a public place, such as a bookstore or library.

Also recall our example in Chapter 1 of the cyberstalking case of Amy Boyer. Was the posting on Liam Youen's Web site describing his plans to murder Boyer an example of hate speech? Consider that it resulted in physical harm to Boyer—viz., her death. Should the ISPs that enable users to construct Web sites containing such speech be held legally liable? Are they morally accountable? We take up the question of the legal liability/moral responsibility of ISPs in the final section of this chapter.

▶ 9.7 DEFAMATION IN CYBERSPACE

We have described some instances of online speech that border on defamation. For example, we saw how certain racial and ethnic groups have been harassed on the Internet through the posting of offensive remarks. And in our discussion of HTML metatags in Section 9.4.1, we saw how HTML code could be used deceptively to demean and insult individuals, organizations, or corporations. Recall our scenario in which a student included derogatory remarks about his professor on the student's Web site.

Which kinds of speech actually constitute legal defamation? Who should be held legally liable and morally accountable for defamatory remarks that occur in cyberspace? We address both questions in the following sections.

9.7.1 Defining Defamation

Richard Spinello defines *defamation* as "communication that harms the reputation of another and lowers that person's self esteem in the eyes of the community."[30] Defamatory remarks can take two forms: *libel*, which refers to written or printed defamation, and *slander*, which refers to oral defamation. But defamation can also occur through pictures, images, gestures, and other methods of signifying meaning. For example, Mawhood and Tysver (2000) note both that a picture of a person that has been scanned and changed by merging with another image can suggest something defamatory and that anyone passing on such an image can also be held liable by the person filing defamation charges. Our concern, however, is primarily with defamatory speech in the form of written words on the Internet.

We should also point out that libelous speech on the Internet can be distinguished from certain kinds of inflammatory speech. Inflammatory remarks made in online forums are sometimes referred to as "flames," and the person who is the victim of such a remark has been "flamed." A flame need not meet the legal standards of defamation; nonetheless, flames, as in the case of genuine defamatory remarks, are problematic. In response to exchanges of inflammatory remarks, some online user communities have developed their own rules of behavior, or netiquette (etiquette on the Internet), to deal with this problem. Some online forums, for example, have instituted the rule that any individual who flames another member of the group will be banned from the forum. Although informal schemes based on netiquette might work well in regulating certain kinds of unwelcome speech in some online forums, they are not effective in regulating speech on the Internet in general. Hence, many believe we need more explicit laws involving online defamation.

In U.S. law, distinctions have been drawn between a "true publisher" of a defamatory statement and a "mere distributor" of a defamatory statement.[31] Under the standard of publisher liability, one who repeats or otherwise publishes defamatory material is subject to liability as if he had originally published it. Thus publishers of periodicals, such as newspapers and magazines, are held liable and accountable for the defamation that appears on their pages, since they exercise editorial control over those publications. With regard to distributing defamatory information, legal analysts point out that there are different standards of liability depending on the role that an individual or organization plays in the process.

Can the rules that apply to defamation in physical space be extended to cyberspace? Is there an instructive analogy that can link our understanding of defamation in the two realms? If an individual is defamed in print, he or she can hold the publisher of the periodical (newspaper, magazine, etc.) legally liable. Would it follow that if an individual is defamed in an online forum, he or she should be able to hold the Internet service provider, or ISP, legally liable? To consider this question, we briefly examine the evolution of rulings in three classic court cases: *Cubby Inc. v. CompuServe Inc*, 1991; *Stratton Oakmont Inc. v. Prodigy Services Company*, 1995; and *Zeran v. America Online Inc.*, 1997.

9.7.2 ISPs, Defamation Suits, and Legal Liability

In the case of *Cubby Inc. v. CompuServe Inc.*, the court ruled that CompuServe was not liable for disseminating an electronic newsletter with libelous content. The court determined that CompuServe had acted as a distributor, and not as a publisher, since the service provider did not exercise editorial control over the contents of its bulletin boards or other online publications. However, a different interpretation of the role of ISPs was rendered in the 1995 case of *Stratton Oakmont Inc. v. Prodigy Services Company*. There, a court found that Prodigy was legally liable since it had advertised that it had "editorial control" over the computer bulletin board system it hosted.

The court noted that Prodigy had positioned itself as a proprietary, family-oriented, electronic network that screened out objectionable content, thereby making the network more suitable for children. In the eyes of the court, Prodigy's claim to have editorial control over its electronic forums made it seem much like a newspaper, in which case the standard of strict legal liability used for original publishers would apply. In light of the Prodigy case, many ISPs have since argued that they should be understood not as "original publishers," but rather as "common carriers," similar to telephone companies. Their argument rested, in part, on the notion that ISPs provide the "conduits for communication but not the content." This view of ISPs was used in the *Zeran v. America Online Inc.* case in 1997, where AOL was found not to be legally liable for content disseminated in its electronic forums.

The Zeran case was the first to test the new provisions for ISPs included in Section 230(c) of the Communications Decency Act of 1996, which we examined in our discussion of online pornography in Section 9.6.1. Although, as we noted, portions of the CDA were struck down as unconstitutional, Section 230 remained intact; the 1996 law protects ISPs from lawsuits similar to the one filed against Prodigy. According to the relevant section of the CDA, "[n]o provider or user of an interactive computer service shall be treated as the publisher or speaker of any information provided by another information content provider."[32] Some refer to this policy as the "Good Samaritan immunity for ISPs."

Although ISPs cannot, at the present time, be held legally liable for content that is communicated in their electronic forums, they have been encouraged to monitor and filter that content to the extent that they can. But this has presented a thorny legal problem: The more an ISP edits content, the more it becomes like a publisher (such as a newspaper). And the more it becomes like a publisher, with editorial control, the more it becomes legally liable. So there may be an unintended disincentive for ISPs to monitor and filter content, and this, in turn, raises a moral dilemma for ISPs.[33]

Another dilemma arises because ISPs seeking immunity from lawsuits might be inclined to cooperate with organizations in ways that threaten the privacy and anonymity of their subscribers. For example, we saw in Chapter 1 that some ISPs cooperated with the RIAA in 2003 by turning over the names of subscribers suspected of exchanging proprietary music files via their online services. However, we also noted that one ISP, Verizon, refused to comply with subpoenas issued on behalf of the RIAA and instead challenged the recording industry in court on grounds that it would be required to violate the privacy of its subscribers.[34] So we can see some of the dilemmas that ISPs face with respect to trying to avoid legal liability through compliance with the "Good Samaritan" principle (i.e., Section 230c) of the CDA.

9.7.3 Moral Accountability vs. Legal Liability for ISPs

Even if ISPs are exempt from legal liability in defamation cases, we can ask whether they can still be held accountable in a moral sense. Spinello (2001) argues that they can. However, he also notes that we must first distinguish between "moral responsibility" and "moral accountability," and he uses a framework articulated by Helen Nissenbaum to draw this distinction.[35] In Nissenbaum's scheme, accountability, unlike responsibility, does not require *causality*, or a causal connection. Spinello points out that because ISPs do not cause defamation, they cannot be held responsible in the strict or narrow sense of the term. But he also believes that they could be held accountable in the sense that they "provide an occasion or forum" for defamation.

However, Spinello is careful to point out that simply because an ISP presents an occasion for defamation, this does not necessarily imply that the ISP is accountable. Rather, for an ISP to be accountable, two conditions are required:

A. the ISP must have had the *capability* to do something about the defamation, and

B. the ISP failed to take action once it was informed that a victim had been defamed.

Spinello believes that this standard of accountability takes into consideration what ISPs can reasonably do—that is, what they are *capable* of doing—to prevent defamation or at least to limit its damage. So the fact that an ISP might not have caused the defamation does not rule out the possibility that the ISP can be held accountable in some sense for defamatory remarks.

Spinello concedes that technical and economic factors make it virtually impossible for ISPs to take preventive, or what he calls "pre-screening," measures that would detect or filter out defamatory messages. Thus we cannot hold ISPs responsible in a causal sense for defamation. Assuming that Spinello's overall argument is correct, however, we might hold them accountable if they failed to take certain actions (i.e., "post-screening measures") once they are informed that a victim has been defamed. For Spinello, these steps would include

1. prompt removal of the defamatory remarks,

2. the issuance of a retraction on behalf of the victim,

3. the initiation of a good faith effort to track down the originator so that the defamation does not reoccur.[36]

Does this threefold requirement provide us with a standard of accountability that is, as Spinello suggests, a "reasonable middle ground"? That is, does it lie between the extremes of strict legal liability (as in the Prodigy case) and immunity from all responsibility (as in the Zeran case)? Or is this an unreasonable expectation for ISPs? Spinello notes that in the current system, a victim of defamation has no legal recourse because of the absolute immunity given to ISPs. On the other hand, the strict legal liability that was applied in the Prodigy case seems unduly harsh. So Spinello believes that his alternative scheme, based on the pre-screening/post-screening distinction, provides the appropriate middle ground because it grants some protection to victims of defamation without burdening the ISP.

An interesting question is whether Spinello's model for analyzing moral accountability regarding defamation for ISPs could be extended to cover other kinds of harm that occur in ISPs—even where there may be no legal liability. For example, could we apply that model to the Amy Boyer cyberstalking case, described in Chapter 1? If so, we might be able to determine whether the two ISPs—Tripod and Geocities—that enabled Liam Youens to set up a Web site that posted life-threatening remarks about Boyer are morally accountable in some sense for the harm caused to Boyer, even if the law did not require those ISPs to take any action. We can also see whether that model could be applied to cyberbullying incidents that have occurred in social networking sites such as MySpace, which in the case of Megan Meier resulted in her committing suicide in 2006. (We examine this case of cyberbullying in Chapter 11.)

Of course, one might ask what the purpose would be in attributing moral responsibility to ISPs if no legal action could be taken against them. There are two replies that can be given, both of which might also cause us to be more careful in our thinking about moral issues involving cyberspace. First, analyzing moral issues in this light could help us to distinguish further between moral and legal aspects of controversial cyberspace issues. Second, such an analysis can also help us consider ways that moral responsibility can be applied at the collective, as well as at the individual, level.

▶ 9.8 CHAPTER SUMMARY

In this chapter we have considered some challenges to regulating cyberspace. Specifically, we considered Internet regulation issues from two different perspectives: the regulation of commercial activities on the Internet and the regulation of content in cyberspace. We saw that decisions to view cyberspace as a medium rather than as a public place or space, or vice versa, are significant, because they determine which kinds of rules apply to regulating speech on the Internet. We also saw that the enactment of formal or explicit laws is only one way to regulate cyberspace. As Lessig and others have noted, much regulation of the Internet is being accomplished through technology or "code."

Some legal issues examined in this chapter overlap with concerns affecting intellectual property rights that we examined in Chapter 8. For example, issues involving DRM technology, HTML metatags, Web hyperlinking, and e-mail spam each impact property-related concerns in cyberspace. Other issues, such as child pornography, hate speech, and speech that can cause physical harm to others, raise concerns in the ongoing dispute between censorship and free speech. Finally, we considered some issues affecting online defamation.

▶ REVIEW QUESTIONS

1. In discussing "cyberspace regulation," why is it useful to distinguish the question "Can cyberspace be regulated?" from the question "Should cyberspace be regulated?"
2. Describe the arguments for why cyberspace should be viewed as a medium, and why it should be viewed as a "place."
3. How does the way we interpret cyberspace affect the kinds of policies that can be used to regulate it?
4. What are the two different senses of "regulation" we examined, and how can they be applied to the regulatory issues involving cyberspace?
5. Identify the four modalities that Lawrence Lessig believes can be used to regulate behavior, and give an example of how each can be applied to regulating behavior on the Internet.
6. What does Lessig mean by the following claim: "In cyberspace, *code is the law*"?
7. What is Digital Rights Management (DRM) technology, and why is it controversial?
8. What does Niva Elkin-Koren mean when she asserts that information policy is becoming increasingly "privatized"? Why does she believe this is a problem?
9. In which ways does Jessica Litman's analysis of the activities of the RIAA, and of the emergence of e-commerce in the late 1990s, support Elkin-Koren's position regarding the privatization of information policy?
10. How can policies affecting the registration of Internet domain names contribute to the further privatization of cyberspace?
11. What are (HTML) metatags, and why can they be controversial?
12. What do we mean by hyperlinking on the Web? Should proprietors of Web sites have a right to include on their sites links to other Web sites?

13. What is e-mail spam, and why is it controversial from a moral point of view?
14. What is censorship? Describe the differences between "censorship by suppression" and "censorship by deterrence."
15. What is pornography? Why is interpreting what is meant by "community standards" especially difficult in establishing pornography laws for cyberspace?
16. Describe the three Internet-specific child pornography laws that were passed in the 1990s but later struck down by the U.S. Supreme Court.
17. How is the Child Internet Protection Act (CIPA) of 2000 both similar to and different from earlier laws affecting child pornography online?
18. What is "virtual child pornography"?
19. What do we mean by "hate speech"? Give some examples of hate speech in cyberspace.
20. What is defamation, and why is it problematic in cyberspace?

▶ DISCUSSION QUESTIONS

1. What do we mean by "speech that can cause physical harm to others"? How is this form of speech different from hate speech in general? How are problems concerned with both kinds of hate speech exacerbated by the Internet?
2. What is "deep linking," and why can it be controversial? Recall our discussion of the Microsoft vs. Ticketmaster dispute involving deep linking. Which side would you take in this dispute? Defend your answer by appealing to one or more of the ethical theories we considered in Chapter 2.
3. Assess the arguments that Richard Spinello uses to show that e-mail spam is morally objectionable. Are his arguments convincing? How does the distinction that Keith Miller and James Moor draw between F-UCBE and NF-UCBE inform the debate about the moral implications of spam?
4. What is sexting, and what challenges does it pose for applying current child pornography laws? Recall our examination of the sexting incident at Greensburg Salem High School, PA. Should the teens involved in that case be subject to felony charges under existing child pornography laws? Explain.

▶ ESSAY/PRESENTATION QUESTIONS

1. Have Digital Rights Management (DRM) systems gone too far, as some critics claim? Recall the 2005 Sony BMG Copy Protection case involving the controversial "rootkit" problem that we described in Section 9.3.1. Should Sony be allowed to use a DRM system that cannot easily be uninstalled when circumstances warrant it? Do companies such as Sony need strong DRM systems to ensure the protection of their intellectual property rights? What kind of compromise position could be reached between users and content owners in the ongoing debate about DRM systems?
2. Why was the Communications Decency Act (CDA), sections of which were designed to protect children from concerns about pornography on the Internet, so controversial? Why was it eventually stuck down by the U.S. Supreme Court? Why were both COPA and (portions of) CPPA also struck down as being unconstitutional? Should they have been declared unconstitutional? If so, then why was the Children's Internet Protection Act (CIPA) upheld as constitutional? Has the U.S. Supreme Court been consistent in its decisions involving Internet pornography?
3. Review Julie Hilden's arguments for why some "exceptions" should be made in cases of prosecuting sexting crimes under current child pornography laws. What does she mean by the "Romeo and Juliet" exception and by the "age-specific" exception? Are these exceptions plausible in the kinds of sexting cases that we examined? Describe some of the challenges posed by the age-specific exception. For example, what would happen if a middle-aged man received an unsolicited nude photo from a teenage girl on his cell phone? Should he be prosecuted for possessing a pornographic image of a minor? Should the teenage girl who sent this photo to him be prosecuted for transmitting the image? Defend your answer.
4. Examine Richard Spinello's argument for why ISPs can, in certain instances, be held morally accountable for defamatory remarks made in their forums even if they are immune from legal liability (under the "Good

Samaritan" provision of the CDA). How might Spinello's argument be extended to include other kinds of harm (i.e., in addition to defamation) that occur in ISPs? For example, consider the Amy Boyer case of cyberstalking that we briefly described in Chapter 1. Could the two ISPs involved, Tripod and Geocities, be morally accountable for what happened to Boyer, using Spinello's model? Can that model also help us to analyze moral accountability for cyberbullying incidents that have occurred on social networking services such as MySpace? Explain.

▶ ENDNOTES

1. Weckert (2007), p. 95.
2. Weckert and Al-Saggaf (2008), p. 491.
3. This scenario is based on the account of the Sony Rootkit controversy in *Wikipedia*. Available at http://en.wikipedia.org/wiki/2005_Sony_BMG_CD_copy_protection_scandal (accessed August 12, 2008).
4. This section draws from material in Grodzinsky and Tavani (2008).
5. For more information, see http://www.wipo.int/amc/en/center/faq/domains.html#1.
6. See "History of ICANN." Available at http://www.buydomains.com/domain-resources/domain-information/history-of-icann.jsp.
7. See http://www.wipo.int/amc/en/center/faq/domains.html#1
8. Ibid.
9. See *Bahari v Gross* (2001). 263 F.3d 359.
10. For more detail, see Larry Armstrong and Amy E. Cortese (1997). "Ticketmaster vs. Microsoft," *BusinessWeek*, May 12. Available at http://www.businessweek.com/1997/19/b352659.htm (accessed August 12, 2008).
11. Miller and Moor (2008), pp. 518-20.
12. Mathiesen (2008), p. 576.
13. See http://www.oyez.org/cases/1970-1979/1971/1971_70_73.
14. See http://www.spectacle.org/795/amateur.html.
15. See http://www.cdt.org/speech/cda/.
16. See http://faculty-web.at.northwestern.edu/commstud/freespeech/cont/cases/morphed.html.
17. See http://74.125.47.132/search?q=cache:sltTkgMAUmMJ:www.lc.org/profamily/copa.pdf+COPA+History&cd=1&hl=en&ct=clnk&gl=us.
18. See http://www.ala.org/ala/aboutala/offices/oif/ifissues/issuesrelatedlinks/cppacopacipa.cfm.
19. See http://www.universalservice.org/sl/applicants/step10/cipa.aspx.
20. See http://www.oyez.org/cases/2000-2009/2002/2002_02_361.
21. See Bunker (2009) for a detailed account of this incident.
22. For more detail, see Stiles (2009).
23. See Szustek (2009).
24. Ibid.
25. Cited in Catudal (2004, p. 201).
26. See *Mainstream Loudoun v. Board of Trustees of the Loudon County Library* (1998). 24 F. Supp. 2d 552.
27. See http://www.oyez.org/cases/2000-2009/2002/2002_02_361.
28. See http://news.bbc.co.uk/2/hi/europe/760782.stm.
29. See http://www.dailykos.com/storyonly/2009/6/12/741537/-von-Brunns-website-attacks-von-Brunn!
30. Spinello (2001), p. 199.
31. See Lipinski, Buchanan, and Britz (2002, 2004) for more detail.
32. See http://www.cdt.org/speech/cda/.
33. See Grodzinsky and Tavani (2006).
34. For more detail, see Grodzinsky and Tavani (2005).
35. See Nissenbaum (1994) for more detail on this distinction.
36. Spinello (2001, p. 209).

▶ REFERENCES

Agre, Philip E. 2005. "P2P and the Promise of Internet Equality." In P. De Palma, ed. *Computers in Society 05/06*. Dubuque IA: McGraw-Hill/Dushkin, pp. 12–15. Reprinted from *Communications of the ACM* 46, no. 2 (2003): 39–42.

American Civil Liberties Union. 2004. "Fahrenheit 451.2: Is Cyberspace Burning? (How Rating and Blocking Proposals May Torch Free Speech on the Internet)." In R. A. Spinello and H. T. Tavani, eds. *Readings in CyberEthics.* 2nd ed. Sudbury MA: Jones and Bartlett Publishers, pp. 159–72.

Bunker, Mike. 2009. "Sexting Surprise: Teens Face Child Porn Charges," MSNBC. Available at http://www.msnbc.msn.com/1d/28679588/ (accessed May 6, 2009).

Camp, L. Jean, and Y. T. Chien. 2000. "The Internet as Public Space: Concepts, Issues, and Implications in Public Policy." *Computers and Society* 30, no. 3: 13–19.

Catudal, Jacques. 2004. "Censorship, the Internet, and the Child Pornography Law of 1996: A Critique." In R. A. Spinello and H. T. Tavani, eds. *Readings in CyberEthics.* 2nd ed. Sudbury MA: Jones and Bartlett Publishers, pp. 196–213. Reprinted from *Ethics and Information Technology* 1, no. 2 (1999): 105–116.

Elkin-Koren, Niva. 2000. "The Privatization of Information Policy." *Ethics and Information Technology* 2, no. 4: 201–09.

Girasa, Roy J. 2002. *Cyberlaw: National and International Perspectives.* Upper Saddle River NJ: Prentice Hall.

Goodwin, Mike. 1995. "Alt.sex.academic.freedom." *Wired* 3, no. 2: 72. Available at http://www.wired.com/wired/archive/3.02/cyber_rights_pr.html (accessed September 25, 2009).

Goodwin, Mike. 2003. *CyberRights: Defending Free Speech in the Digital Age.* Rev. ed. Cambridge MA: MIT Press.

Grodzinsky, Frances S., and Maria C. Bottis. 2007. "Private Use as Fair Use: Is it Fair?" *Computers and Society* 37, no. 4: 11–24.

Grodzinsky, Frances S., and Herman T. Tavani. 2005. "P2P Networks and the *Verizon v. RIAA* Case: Implications for Personal Privacy and Intellectual Property." *Ethics and Information Technology* 7, no. 4: 243–50.

Grodzinsky, Frances S., and Herman T. Tavani. 2006. "Ethical Reflections on Cyberstalking." In L. Hinman, ed. *Contemporary Moral Issues: Diversity and Consensus.* 3rd ed. Upper Saddle River NJ: Prentice Hall, pp. 492–501.

Grodzinsky, Frances S. and Herman T. Tavani. 2008. "Online File Sharing: Resolving the Tensions between Privacy and Property." *Computers and Society* 38, no. 4: 28–39.

Hesseldahl, Arik. 2006. "Apple vs. France." http://www.businessweek.com/technology/content/mar2006/tc20060321_144066.htm.

Hilden, Julie. 2009. "How Should Teens' 'Sexting'—the Sending of Revealing Photos—Be Regulated?" *Find Law.* Available at http//writ.news.findlaw.com/hilden/20090428.html (accessed May 6, 2009).

Jobs, Steve. 2007. "Thoughts on Music." Available at http://www.apple.com/hotnews/thoughtsonmusic/.

Kalara, Sunny. 2007. "Now the RIAA wants Universities to get campus-wide Napster subscription or 'lose all federal aid.'" Available at http://www.bizorigin.com/2007/riaa_nuclear_option.

Lessig, Lawrence. 2000. *Code and Other Laws of Cyberspace.* New York: Basic Books.

Lessig, Lawrence. 2004. The Laws of Cyberspace. In R. A. Spinello and H. T. Tavani, eds. *Readings in CyberEthics.* 2nd ed. Sudbury MA: Jones and Bartlett Publishers, pp. 134–44.

Lipinski, Tomas A., Elizabeth A. Buchanan, and Johannes J. Britz. 2002. "Sticks and Stones and Words that Harm: Liability vs. Responsibility, Section 230 and Defamatory Speech in Cyberspace." *Ethics and Information Technology* 4, no. 1: 143–58.

Lipinski, Tomas A., Elizabeth A. Buchanan, and Johannes J. Britz. 2004. "Agents of Harm or Agents of Grace: The Legal and Ethical Aspects of Identifying Harm and Assigning Responsibility in a Networked World." In R. A. Spinello and H. T. Tavani, eds. *Readings in Cyberethics.* 2nd ed. Sudbury MA: Jones and Bartlett, pp. 214–46.

Litman, Jessica. 2002. "Electronic Commerce and Free Speech." In N. Elkin-Koren and N. W. Netanel, eds. *The Commodification of Information.* The Hague, The Netherlands: Kluwer Academic Publishers, pp. 23–42.

Mawhood, John, and Daniel Tysver. 2000. "Law and the Internet." In D. Langford, ed. *Internet Ethics.* London: Macmillan, pp. 96–126.

Miller, Keith, and James H. Moor. 2008. "Email Spam." In K. E. Himma and H. T. Tavani, eds. *The Handbook of Information and Computer Ethics.* Hoboken NJ: John Wiley and Sons, pp. 517–31.

Moor, James H. 2007. "What Is Computer Ethics?" In J. Weckert, ed. *Computer Ethics.* Aldershot UK: Ashgate, pp. 31–40. Reprinted from *Metaphilosophy* 16, no. 4 (1985): 266–75.

Nissenbaum, Helen. 1994. "Computing and Accountability." *Communications of the ACM* 37, no. 1: 73–80.

Rosenberg, Richard S. 2001. "Controlling Access to the Internet: The Role of Filtering." *Ethics and Information Technology* 3, no. 1: 35–54.

Rosenberg, Richard S. 2004. Filtering the Internet in the USA: Free Speech Denied. In R. A. Spinello and H. T. Tavani, eds. *Readings in CyberEthics.* 2nd ed. Sudbury MA: Jones and Bartlett, pp. 173–79.

Russinovich, Mark. 2005. "Sony, Rootkits, and Digital Rights Management Gone Too Far." Available at http://www.sysinternals.com/blog/2005/10sony-rootkits-and-digital-rights.html (accessed February 11, 2006).

Samuelson, Pamela. 2003. "DRM {and, or, vs.} the Law." *Communications of the ACM* 46, no. 4: 41–45.

Sandin, Per. 2004. "Virtual Child Pornography and Utilitarianism." *Journal of Information, Communication and Ethics in Society* 2, no. 4: 217–23.

Spinello, Richard A. 2001. "Internet Service Providers and Defamation: New Standards of Liability." In R. A. Spinello and H. T. Tavani, eds. *Readings in CyberEthics*. Sudbury MA: Jones and Bartlett, pp. 198–209.

Spinello, Richard A. 2002. "The Use and Abuse of Metatags." *Ethics and Information Technology* 4, no. 1: 22–30.

Spinello, Richard A. 2003. *Cyberethics: Morality and Law in Cyberspace*. 2nd ed. Sudbury MA: Jones and Bartlett.

Spinello, Richard A. 2004. "An Ethical Evaluation of Web-Site Linking." In R. A. Spinello and H. T. Tavani, eds. *Readings in CyberEthics*. 2nd ed. Sudbury MA: Jones and Bartlett. pp. 337–50.

Spinello, Richard A. 2006. "Ethical Reflections on the Problem of Spam." In L. Hinman, ed. *Contemporary Moral Issues: Diversity and Consensus*. 3rd ed. Upper Saddle River NJ: Prentice Hall, pp. 502–10. Reprinted from *Ethics and Information Technology* 1, no. 3 (1999): 185–91.

Stiles, Bob. 2008. "Effort Begins to Standardize Sexting Penalty." *Tribune-Review*, April. Available at http://m.triblive.com/triblive/db_7240/contentdetail.htm;jsessionid=198F0CC68FFC5176D6581C1E539F8C62?contentguid=tScPcIMY&full=true (accessed May 9, 2009).

Szustek, Anne. 2009. "Authorities Treat Those Accused of 'Sexting' as Sex Offenders." *Finding Dulcinea*, April. Available at http://www.findingdulcinea.com/news/Americas/2009/April/Authorities-Treat-Those-Accused-of-Sexting-as-Sex-Offenders.html (accessed May 9, 2009).

Weckert, John. 2007. "What Is So Bad about Internet Content Regulation?" In J. Weckert, ed. *Computer Ethics*. Aldershot UK: Ashgate, pp. 95–102. Reprinted from *Ethics and Information Technology* 2, no. 2 (2000): 105–11.

Weckert, John, and Yeslam Al-Saggaf. 2008. "Regulation and Governance of the Internet." In K. E. Himma and H. T. Tavani, eds. *The Handbook of Information and Computer Ethics*. Hoboken NJ: John Wiley & Sons, pp. 475–95.

▶ FURTHER READINGS

Armstrong Timothy K. "Digital Rights Management and the Process of Fair Use," *Harvard Journal of Law & Technology* 20 (2006). Available at http://ssrn.com/abstract=885371.

Bohman, James. "The Transformation of the Public Sphere: Political Authority, Communicative Freedom, and Internet Publics." In J. van den Hoven and J. Weckert, eds. *Information Technology and Moral Philosophy*. New York: Cambridge University Press, 2008, pp. 66–92.

Grossman, Wendy M. "The Spam Wars." In. P. DePalma, ed. *Annual Editions: Computers in Society 05/06*. Dubuque IA: McGraw-Hill/Dushkin, 2005, pp. 147–51.

Koepsell, David R. *The Ontology of Cyberspace*. Chicago, IL: Open Court, 2000.

Levy, David M. "Information Overload." In K. E. Himma and H. T. Tavani, eds. *The Handbook of Information and Computer Ethics*. Hoboken NJ, 2008, pp. 497–515.

Levy, Neil. "Virtual Child Pornography: The Eroticization of Inequality." *Ethics and Information Technology* 4, no. 4 (2002): 319–23.

White, A. "The Obscenity of Internet Regulation in the United States." *Ethics and Information Technology* 6, no. 2 (2004): 111–19.

Zittrain, Jonathan. *The Future of the Internet—And How to Stop It*. New Haven CT: Yale University Press, 2008.

10

The Digital Divide and the Transformation of Work

The moral, legal, and social problems we examined in Chapters 5–9 typically centered on specific issues such as privacy, security, crime, or intellectual property. In Chapter 10, we instead consider issues that cut across broader social categories, ranging from concerns about social equity and inclusion to issues affecting employment and work. We pay particular attention to the impacts these issues have for

- *sociodemographic groups* (involving social class, race, and gender),
- *social and political institutions* (such as education and government),
- *social sectors* (such as the workplace).

Specific questions examined in this chapter include:

- What do we mean by "digital divide"?
- What obligations do we have to make cybertechnology accessible to disabled persons?
- Has the widespread use of cybertechnology helped reduce racism, or does it exacerbate it?
- What implications does cybertechnology have for gender issues?
- How has cybertechnology transformed the nature of work?
- How has the use of cybertechnology affected the quality of work life?
- What kinds of social and ethical issues have been raised by computerized monitoring and surveillance in the workplace?

A common characteristic unifies these otherwise disparate issues; they are often approached from the perspective of *sociological/descriptive ethics*. In Chapter 1 we drew a distinction between descriptive and normative approaches to the study of moral issues, noting that while social scientists conduct research that is essentially designed to report (or describe) sociological aspects of cybertechnology, those aspects often have normative implications as well. In this chapter we examine some issues primarily from the vantage point of descriptive ethics. In other cases, we also examine normative aspects of those issues. We begin by looking at access and equity issues associated with the digital divide.

► 10.1 THE DIGITAL DIVIDE

What, exactly, is the digital divide? Emma Rooksby and John Weckert (2007) note that it is a "notoriously muddy term." So it is important to begin our analysis with a working definition. Benjamin Compaine (2001) suggests that the phrase *digital divide* is basically a new label for an earlier expression used to describe the "information haves and have-nots." He defines the digital divide as the gap, or "perceived gap," between those who have and do not have access to "information tools" *and* between those who have and do not have the ability to use those tools. So, in Compaine's view, merely having access to cybertechnology is not sufficient; one must also possess the knowledge and ability to use that technology.

First, we should note that an analysis of *the* digital divide might suggest that there is one overall divide—that is, a single divide as opposed to many "divides," or divisions. Actually, there are multiple divisions involving access to cybertechnology. Keiron O'Hara and David Stevens (2006) note that there are divides involving rich and poor people, rich and poor regions, and rich and poor nations. For our purposes, issues affecting the digital divide can be organized into two broad categories: a divide *between* nations and a divide *within* nations. The division between information-rich and information-poor nations is sometimes referred to as the "global digital divide"; the technological divides within nations, on the contrary, exist between rich and poor persons, racial majority and minority groups, men and women, disabled and nondisabled persons, and so forth. We examine issues affecting the disabled population in Section 10.2, and we examine issues involving race and gender in Sections 10.3 and 10.4, respectively. We begin with a look at the global digital divide.

10.1.1 The Global Digital Divide

Consider some statistics ranging from 2000 to 2008. In 2000, it was estimated that 361 million people, approximately 5.8% of the world's population, were online; the vast majority of those users lived in North America and Europe.[1] Since then, global Internet usage has more than quadrupled. In June 2008, it was estimated that there were more than 1,463 million Internet users.[2] A significant shift had already occurred by 2005, when the list of countries or regions where more than 50% of the population used the Internet had grown to 30.[3] That year, seven nations—Australia, Canada, Japan, South Korea, Taiwan, the United Kingdom, and the United States—had an Internet penetration rate of higher than 60%.

Yet, as of 2008, the disparity between the percentage of Internet users in developed and developing countries continues to be significant. In countries such as Niger, Ethiopia, and the Congo, approximately two people per thousand are Internet users, while the percentage of Internet users in Iceland and Norway is greater than 700 persons per thousand.[4] The disparity is especially apparent when viewed from the perspective of continents or world regions. For example, in Africa (which includes approximately 14% of the world's population) the Internet penetration rate is 5.3%, whereas in North America, the Internet penetration rate is 73.6% (Internet World Stats, 2008). On a positive note, however, the Internet usage growth in Africa was 1,031.2% between 2000 and 2008.[5] So it would seem that considerable progress has been made in bridging the global divide regarding Internet usage. O'Hara and Stevens note that regardless of whatever explanation we give for the "existence of a global digital divide, one thing is abundantly clear: inequalities in access to ICT [information and communication technologies] is tied closely to economic inequality."[6]

One obstacle to eliminating the global digital divide is that developing countries struggle with low literacy rates; many people in developing nations cannot read and write in their native language, let alone in English. Yet, much of the material on the Internet is in English. This has influenced advocates for improved Internet service for global users to lobby for the development of Web applications that include more graphics and images that can serve as universal symbols.

10.1.2 The Digital Divide within Nations

Many developed nations still have significant divides within them regarding access to cybertechnology. For example, O'Hara and Stevens point out a discrepancy in the UK. They note that in 2004, approximately one half of all households were online, while only 3% of the poorest households were included in this number. There are also significant disparities within some developing nations as well. And in rapidly developing countries like India, the divisions that currently exist may eventually deepen. Consider that a growing segment of India's population is fluent in English and has the technical literacy required to work in many of the highly-skilled jobs outsourced there; those on the other side of the divide, comprising the majority of the population of India, tend to have a low level of literacy and little or no access to cybertechnology.

Some countries, including the United States, have instituted specific strategies to bridge the divide within their national borders. In response to concerns about the gap that existed in America between those with and without access to computers, the Clinton administration initiated the National Information Infrastructure (NII) in 1993 to ensure that all Americans would have access to information technology. To accomplish this objective, the National Telecommunications and Information Administration (NTIA) conducted a series of studies that investigated computer use among various groups.

One question that arose from the NTIA reports was whether a *universal service* policy was needed to ensure that all Americans have an appropriate level of access to Internet technology. Universal service policies have been controversial because they require subsidies, which often result either in user fees or higher taxes. However, proponents of a universal service policy for the Internet pointed to the model that was used to subsidize telephone technology when that became available in the early part of the twentieth century. Without some kind of government-supported subsidy, people living in less-populated rural areas would not have been able to afford this new technology. So the U.S. Congress passed the Communications Act of 1934, which distributed the cost for telephone service in a way to make it affordable to all Americans. Today, the question is whether Internet access should be subsidized in a similar manner. In the case of telephone technology, arguments were made that having a telephone was necessary for one's well-being. Can the same argument be made in the case of cybertechnology?

As we saw in Chapter 9, subsidies in the form of "E-rates" (that is, federal technology discounts) have helped to defray the cost of Internet access for public schools and libraries. Unlike universal service policies involving telephones, which are aimed at subsidizing residential telephone service, E-rates for Internet access apply only to "community points of access" such as public libraries. While E-rates may support universal Internet *access*, they do not provide universal Internet *service*. So, critics such as Chapman and Rotenberg (1995) have argued that merely providing community points of access to the Internet would be similar to a policy that simply placed telephones in public locations rather than making telephone service affordable for all Americans. O'Hara and Stevens (2006) point out that the notion of "access" needs to be expanded to include more than *mere* access; it needs to be understood as "effective access." So, just as mere access points located in the community would not have met the requirements for a universal service policy for telephones, the current system of E-rates does not provide the kind of universal service required for "effective access" for the Internet.

10.1.3 Reconceptualizing the Digital Divide as an "Analog Divide"

Torin Monahan (2001, 2005) questions whether discussing disparities regarding access to Internet technology in terms of a *digital* divide accurately captures the essential issues at stake. He suggests instead that we describe the problem as an *analog* divide, referring to divisions or inequalities that already existed prior to digital technology and that continue to exist independently of that technology. Monahan argues that the educational system in the United States generates and perpetuates divisions affecting computers and Internet technology, and that the existing divisions cannot be understood simply in terms of access to digital technology, because these divisions are not ultimately about access to material resources.

Others, such as A. Rhae Adams (2001) and Mark Warschauer (2003), have presented similar arguments for the view that the problems creating the digital divide cannot be understood simply in terms of material resources, numbers, and other modes of quantitative measurement. Adams believes that focusing merely on numbers can actually mask other ongoing social inequalities relevant to understanding how the divide arises and is sustained. And Warschauer believes that technology projects around the world, which have focused too much on providing hardware and software, have failed to pay sufficient attention to the human and social systems that must also change for technology to make a difference.

These arguments for reconceptualizing the digital divide might initially seem appealing. However, they also tend to underestimate the significant role that technology itself plays in understanding (and potentially resolving) problems associated with unequal access to cybertechnology.[7] There are good reasons, therefore, for retaining a technological metaphor when analyzing these problems.

10.1.4 Is the Digital Divide an Ethical Issue?

We have examined sociological aspects of the digital divide and have seen how statistical data confirm unequal access to digital technology due to socioeconomic differences both between nations and between groups within nations. Granted that there are significant divisions between those who have and do not have access to cybertechnology, we can still ask whether these divisions also raise ethical issues.

What does it mean to say that the digital divide is an *ethical* issue? Is every kind of divide regarding unequal access to goods necessarily an ethical problem? A skeptic might note the divide between those who have and do not have Mercedes-Benz automobiles, arguing that there is a "Mercedes-Benz divide" and many of us fall on the "wrong side" of it, but that this is not an ethical issue. We could respond by pointing to the divisions between those who do and those who do not have access to vital resources such as food and healthcare, divisions that many ethicists believe raise questions affecting the just distribution of primary goods and resources in populations. But what about unequal access to cybertechnology? Is it closer to the Mercedes-Benz divide, or is it closer to divisions involving access to food and healthcare?

Distributive Justice and Access to Vital Human Resources

As suggested above, some question whether the digital divide raises concerns affecting distributive justice. But what do we mean by "distributive justice," especially in the context of cybertechnology? According to Jeroen van den Hoven and Emma Rooksby (2008),

> Distributive justice in contemporary information societies concerns, among other issues, the distribution of information, information services, and information infrastructures.[8]

The authors note that while there has been much enthusiasm about the emergence of new technologies, there is also concern over "the uneven distribution of the new information wealth, both within nations and internationally."[9] To argue that the unequal distribution of information wealth is a moral issue would require that we show that information is a kind of "primary good" that is vital for human flourishing. So, we need to consider whether information (made possible by cybertechnology) meets the criteria of a kind of good or resource that is *vital* for one's well-being. Additionally, if we can show that not having access to cybertechnology either denies or unfairly limits access to vital resources or to certain kinds of basic goods—what James Moor (2004) calls "core goods" (or "core values"), such as knowledge, ability, freedom, and so forth—then we can make a fairly strong case that unequal access to cybertechnology is a moral issue affecting distributive justice.

In his classic work, *A Theory of Justice*, philosopher John Rawls introduces the notion of *primary social goods*, which are resources that satisfy basic human needs and thus have a special value or moral weight in society. Rawls notes that with these goods, humans "can generally be assured of greater success in carrying out their intentions and in advancing their needs."[10] Van den Hoven and Rooksby argue that Rawls' theory of justice in general, and his notion of a primary social good in particular, can be extended to include "information goods." They further argue, however that a "fully-fledged theory of justice that takes adequate account of the new information goods . . . is still some way off."[11] But we can nonetheless examine some models that have been advanced for showing why the digital divide is indeed a moral issue affecting distributive justice.

One model has been articulated by Jeremy Moss (2002), who argues that persons lacking access to cybertechnology are deprived of resources that are vital for their well-being. He points out that without access to cybertechnology, people are unfairly disadvantaged because their

1. access to knowledge is significantly lessened or prevented,
2. ability to participate fully in the political decision-making process and to receive important information is greatly diminished, and
3. economic prospects are severely hindered.[12]

First, Moss claims that people who are deprived of access to cybertechnology are not able to benefit from the increasing range of information available on the Internet and thus are falling further behind in the information era. Second, because of political barriers to participation in the decision-making processes in developing countries, people in remote areas without access to the Internet may have no means at all of participating in national debates or of receiving information about important developmental matters and policies that can significantly affect them. Third, Moss believes that because so much economic growth is driven by the information and communication sector, people living in countries that are not part of this sector are disadvantaged. With regard to Moss's third point, Pippa Norris (2001) makes a similar observation by noting that "the underclass" of information poor may become "further marginalized in societies where basic computer skills are becoming essential for economic success and personal advancement." Norris notes these can include "entry to good career and educational opportunities," as well as "full access to social networks . . . and opportunities for civic engagement."[13]

In response to Moss and Norris, one could argue that some people (and some nations) have always been disadvantaged in access to new technologies such as automobiles, household appliances, and so forth. But this criticism misses a crucial point. As we have noted, disparities in access to certain technologies, such as Mercedes-Benz automobiles, do not in themselves constitute an ethical issue. We should also note that divisions of this type are generally accepted in capitalist societies. However, if Moss's thesis about why cybertechnology is important is correct, then having access to cybertechnology is essential for one's well-being in ways that having access to other kinds of technologies—for example, "discretionary technologies" that provide convenience and entertainment—is not. So, one question that arises is: Do we have a moral obligation to bridge the digital divide? If so, are affluent nations the ones responsible for doing this?

Making the Case for a Moral Obligation to Bridge the Digital Divide

Maria Bottis and Kenneth Himma (2008) note that in making the case that "affluent nations" have a moral obligation to do bridge the divide, some important points of clarification first need to be made. For one thing, we need to draw an important distinction between saying that "X is a good thing to do" and saying that "we are obligated to do X." Most people would likely agree that eliminating the digital divide would be a good thing to do, but there would also likely be far less consensus as to whether we (i.e., some affluent nations) have an obligation to do it.

Bottis and Himma note that failing to do something morally good is not necessarily morally wrong; they use the example of someone's risking his or life to save a person caught in a fire in a building. Failure to risk one's life to save another here, they correctly point out, is not something that necessarily merits either blame or punishment. Of course, the act of attempting to save someone's life in the fire would be a good thing, but (assuming that you and I are not firefighters) we are not morally obligated to do it. Doing such an act crosses over to a category that philosophers and ethicists call "supererogatory." That is, the act of risking one's life in a fire to save another is morally good but is also "beyond the call of moral obligation." Bottis and Himma note that we "praise supererogatory acts, but not obligatory acts" and we "blame nonperformance of obligatory acts, but not supererogatory acts."[14] So in this scheme, should bridging the digital divide be considered a supererogatory act, in which case we are not morally obligated to do anything?

Himma (2007) points out that because many people believe that we are morally obligated only to do no harm, they infer that we have no obligation to bridge the digital divide. But he also argues that such a view is "inconsistent with the ethics of every classically theistic religion as well as our ordinary intuitions, as well as classic theories of deontology and consequentialism." In the case of deontology, for example, Himma notes that deontological theories "almost universally hold that we have an obligation to help the poor."[15] For example, he points to the prima facie obligation of beneficence that we have to help the poor, as articulated in Ross' deontological theory. (You may want to review Ross' ethical theory of act deontology in Chapter 2.)

In Chapter 2, we saw that contract-based ethical theory holds that while we are morally obligated to "do no harm," we have no explicit obligation to do good—in this case, no moral obligation to bridge the digital divide. According to this view, we are behaving morally as long as we do nothing to prevent others from acquiring cybertechnology and Internet access. But is this minimalist view of morality adequate? Recall that in our discussion of contract-based ethical theories in Chapter 2, we saw that individuals and nations have a moral obligation to do good (to others) only in cases where individuals or nations have an express (legal) contract in which they are required to come to the aid of others. However, we also saw some compelling reasons to be skeptical about such a limited theory of moral obligation.

In our critique of contract-based ethical theories in Chapter 2, we saw that a more robust theory of morality requires that we come to the aid of those in harm's way, whenever it is in our power to do so. For one thing, this would help to make cyberspace a safer place, especially for those disadvantaged individuals and groups vulnerable to online harm. And we could construct an analogous argument to show why coming to the aid of other kinds of disadvantaged individuals and groups—that is, those without Internet access—would be the right thing to do. Also, if Moss is correct in claiming that the kind of access to information made possible by cybertechnology is a kind of access that is vital to one's well-being, then is it plausible to suggest that we have at least some obligation to provide access to those who are disadvantaged?

► 10.2 CYBERTECHNOLOGY AND THE DISABLED

In addition to its implications for developing nations and for low-income groups within developed nations, the digital divide has affected disabled people. There has been much discussion about implementing strategies and policies to make the Internet more accessible to this group. Tim Berners-Lee, director of the World Wide Web Consortium (W3C) and the inventor of the HTTP protocol that underlies the Web, has stated: "The power of the Web is in its universality. Access by everyone regardless of disability is an essential aspect." The W3C was formed, in large part, to promote standards that ensure universal Web access. It established a Web Accessibility Initiative (WAI), which has produced guidelines and protocols for developing software applications that improve access for disabled persons, ranging from software used in speech synthesizers and screen magnifiers to proposed software applications that will benefit people with visual, hearing, physical, cognitive, and neurological disabilities.[16]

WAI representatives have worked with industry groups and governmental organizations to establish guidelines for the design of "user agents," which are intended to lower barriers to Web accessibility for people with disabilities. These user agents include

Web browsers and other types of software that retrieve and render Web content; the agents are designed to conform and communicate with other technologies, especially "assistive technologies" such as screen readers (which perform a function similar to Braille applications in offline contexts). Frances Grodzinsky (2000) argues that computers equipped with assistive technologies and "adaptive devices" can be an "equalizer" in the era of information technology because they enable people with disabilities to participate in and compete for jobs that require computer access.

WAI's supporters point out that some measures taken for the disabled have had positive outcomes for other groups, especially poor people who often are forced to deal with literacy problems and inadequate equipment. Recall our earlier discussion of literacy problems in developing nations. It may well turn out that voice recognition technology designed to assist disabled persons who are unable to use keyboards may ultimately also benefit nondisabled persons with low literacy skills.

Consider an example of an accessibility-related initiative in the nondigital world that was intended to accommodate disabled persons but that has also benefited the public in general. Ramps designed for wheelchair accessibility have not only benefited people in wheelchairs, but have also been very useful to nondisabled persons as well, such as parents pushing baby carriages. Also consider some of the advantages that sloped curbs on street corners have provided to many nondisabled persons—bicyclists and skaters have benefited from these features, which were initially intended to serve disabled persons (Woodbury, 2002). It has been argued, analogously, that ordinary users will likely benefit from computer design enhancements to user interfaces that are initially intended to assist disabled persons.

Because improving access to cybertechnology for the disabled has potential benefits for society as a whole, we can formulate a utilitarian argument to advance this cause. However, we should also be cautious about extending this argument too far. What would happen if, in the future, the broader population did not realize any benefits from improving access to cybertechnology for the disabled? Would that provide for a utilitarian argument against investing in initiatives that improved access for the disabled? After considering this, you can better understand some of the possible dangers of relying too heavily on utilitarian principles when advancing a moral argument for improved access for the disabled.

In Section 10.5.3, in our discussion of remote work, we will return to issues involving the disabled. Next, we examine the impact of the digital divide on race.

► 10.3 RACE AND CYBERTECHNOLOGY

We have seen that in the United States many lower-income individuals and families, especially those in the inner cities, still do not have access to the Internet; many of these individuals also belong to racial and ethnic minority groups. Consider statistics that correlate income (social class) and race with the digital divide in the United States. In 2000, 51% of all homes had at least one computer, and 41.5% of all homes had Internet access. In terms of income, 86.3% of households earning more than $75,000 per year had Internet access, while of those households earning below $15,000 per year, only 12.7% had access. From the vantage point of race, 46.1% of white Americans and 56.8% of Asian Americans and Pacific Islanders had access, contrasted with only 23.5% of African Americans and 23.1% of Hispanics who did.[17] Table 10.1 summarizes these statistics.

TABLE 10.1   Internet Usage by Racial/Ethnic Groups in the United States in 2000

Whites	Asian Americans	African Americans	Hispanics
46.1%	56.8%	23.5%	23.1%

As of May 2008, 73% of adult men and women in the United States had Internet access at home, while 90% of young people between the ages of 18 and 29 used the Internet. However, the penetration rate for black Internet users in the United States in 2008 was 59%, which is still well below the penetration for the American population as a whole.[18]

We next focus our analysis on the impact of cybertechnology for African Americans by examining three kinds of concerns: Internet usage patterns vis-à-vis demographic statistics, technology policies and their implications for African Americans, and the Internet as a medium to spread racial prejudice.

10.3.1   Access Issues: Internet Usage Patterns and Demographic Statistics

Susan Kretchmer and Rod Karveth (2001) claim that African Americans who use the Internet differ from their white counterparts in two key respects: *usage patterns* and *demographic characteristics*. With respect to usage patterns, the authors describe four ways in which African Americans and whites differ. First, African American users are more likely to use the Internet for entertainment and for locating information about quality of life activities, such as job training, school, health care, and hobbies. Second, they are less likely to participate in Web-based auctions. Third, they are also less likely to feel that the Internet connects them with family and friends. Fourth, they are less likely to use e-mail to develop and sustain friendships.

Kretchmer and Karveth also cite relevant sociodemographic differences between African Americans and whites: the average age for African American users tends to be younger than for whites, African Americans typically access the Internet less frequently than whites, and adult African American Internet users are much more likely than their white counterparts to have modest incomes, no college degrees, and children under eighteen.

What factors contribute to these differences between African Americans and whites in levels and patterns of Internet access? Although it is difficult to identify the root causes, Kretchmer and Karveth provide two different explanations: (a) cultural attitudes of many African Americans toward technology, and (b) assumptions that those who control technology have about African Americans. Robert Johnson (1997) points out that many African Americans tend to view technology as something that is designed by white people for white people. For example, African Americans are aware that the culture that created and currently dominates the Internet is white. According to Kretchmer and Karveth, some African Americans believe that whites perceive them as not being very interested in computer technology.

A different set of explanations emerges from the perspective of the attitudes of whites, and in particular of those (whites) who control technology. Kretchmer and Karveth suggest that Web site developers see little value (economic or otherwise) in supplying and developing content that appeals to small groups on the Internet. Because

African American users constitute a relatively small percentage of the total user population, there is little incentive for non-African American e-vendors to develop Web content that would appeal primarily to African Americans. These factors could account for differences between African American and white Internet usage patterns.

10.3.2 Technology, Race, and Public Policy

Access and usage patterns are only one part of the overall problem concerning cyber-technology and race. Another important element involves public policy decisions. Historically, African Americans have not had a representative voice in policy decisions involving technologies that have affected them. Johnson argues that African Americans need to take a more active role in these decisions; he believes that if African Americans take up this challenge, they can help to reshape the course of technological development to better suit the needs and interests specific to their community. To illustrate his argument, Johnson describes policy decisions made in the development of the United States highway system.

▶ **SCENARIO 10–1:** A Technology-Related Public Policy Decision Affecting African Americans

Robert Johnson points out that when the federal government was developing plans for an interstate highway system, virtually no thought was given to the impact of the new highways on existing urban neighborhoods. He also notes that since "automobility" accelerated the exodus of both the middle class and businesses to suburbia, proportionately fewer white Americans were affected by the urban highway systems. African Americans who stayed behind in inner city neighborhoods, however, were adversely impacted. Many homogeneous African American neighborhoods were arbitrarily divided into segments that conveniently conformed to plans for the highway system, and African Americans who lived in the communities affected had no say in how the highway system would be developed. Consider that because of the highway policies that were implemented, proportionately more African Americans were subject to pollution generated by highway traffic; also consider that they were more vulnerable to injuries and deaths from automobile accidents.[19]   ■

African Americans also have much at stake in policies that involve the "information highway." To have a meaningful and effective voice in policy decisions that affect them, Johnson argues that African Americans need to become involved in the process during its early stages. Perhaps African Americans also need to see themselves as stakeholders in decisions involving cybertechnology policies affecting the information highway, just as they were (unknowingly at the time) stakeholders in policies that decided how the motor vehicle highway system would be constructed. Johnson believes that in order for African Americans to have an effective voice in those decisions, they must be willing to make technology an integral part of their socialization.

10.3.3 Rhetoric and Racism on the Internet

Has the Internet eliminated, or even helped to reduce, considerations of race in communication? Because Internet communication does not reveal users' physical attributes, we might assume that the answer is "yes." However, we need to question that assumption. Kretchmer and Karveth note that the study of race in cyberspace often leads to paradoxical inferences. On the one hand, cyberspace provides an opportunity and forum to discover and confront racial issues, but on the other, it can perpetuate, or perhaps even enhance, aspects of racism. For example, the Internet has introduced new tools for harassing members of certain groups. Thus Internet technology can be, and has been, used to magnify the *rhetoric* and significance of hate groups.

Lynn Theismeyer (1999) has pointed out the "rhetorical role" that the Internet can play with respect to race. She examines the rhetoric of racism, not as it applies specifically to racial and minority groups in the United States, such as African Americans and Hispanics, but rather as it has been used internationally in the rise of neo-Nazi propaganda. Theismeyer believes that there are two kinds of racist speech on the Internet:

a. *Hate speech*, including text, music, online radio broadcasts, and images that exhort users to act against target groups.

b. *Persuasive rhetoric* that does not directly enunciate but ultimately promotes or justifies violence.[20]

In Chapter 9, we saw that European countries, especially Germany and France, have made a greater effort than the United States to restrict online hate speech that has been targeted to racial groups, especially by neo-Nazi organizations. We also saw that the United States, on the contrary, has focused more on censoring pornography, which many also view as offensive speech. What Theismeyer refers to as "persuasive rhetoric" would seem to be protected in the United States under the First Amendment right to free speech. So it is not easy to control some forms of online racist rhetoric in the United States.

We also saw in Chapter 9 that designers and operators of Web sites can use misleading and deceptive (HTML) metatags and keywords to attract visitors. For example, we saw that a racist Web site can deceptively use a keyword such as "Martin Luther King Jr." to lure unsuspecting persons to its site. So, individuals who are interested in gaining information about Dr. King's life may instead be subjected to racist hate speech directed against African Americans.

Theismeyer asks us to consider two questions with respect to racial prejudice and cybertechnology:

1. Does information technology make the reemergence of prejudicial messages and attitudes swifter and more likely?

2. Does the Internet's wide range of distribution make for more followers and finally more persuasion?[21]

She concludes that it is impossible to know at this point whether cybertechnology has been the main cause of the rapid spread of racism, especially in the neo-Nazism movement, but she is convinced that cybertechnology has been its principal tool.

In Chapter 11, we examine some ways that blogs and the blogosphere also can either directly or indirectly contribute to the promotion of racial prejudice online. For example, some extreme right-wing political blogs have portrayed Barack Obama in ways that are generally considered to be offensive and demeaning to African Americans. On the one hand, these blogs include content that is protected by free speech; on the other hand, they can reinforce racial stereotypes and perpetuate racial prejudice.

► 10.4 GENDER AND CYBERTECHNOLOGY

Other equity and access concerns associated with cybertechnology in general, and with the digital divide in particular, can be analyzed with respect to gender. Feminist authors and others who advocate for women's issues proffer arguments similar to those advanced by or on behalf of African Americans, which we examined in the preceding section. Women, like certain racial and ethnic groups, have not been included in important decisions about technology policies and, until very recently, have not participated to the same degree as men in the use of cybertechnology.

We can begin by noting that the gap that has traditionally existed between the percentage of female and male Internet users in the United States has changed significantly since studies conducted in 2000. According to a report by the *Pew Internet & American Life Project* in 2005, young women were slightly more likely to be online than young men, and the number of black women online surged between 2002 and 2005 (black women who used the Internet outnumbered black men by about 10%). Pew Internet Project surveys conducted between January and June 2005 showed that in the United States, 66% of women went online, as opposed to 68% of men. But women Internet users slightly outnumbered men in the Internet population because they make up a greater share of the overall U.S. population. As of May 2008, however, the proportion of women who used the Internet was equal to that of men.[22]

Although the gap between female and male Internet users has narrowed considerably in the United States and in many Western countries, this has not been the case globally. Leslie Regan Shade (2002) has described how many women in the Philippines, Latin America, Africa, and Asia have developed "grass-roots" initiatives, which she refers to as "globalizing from below" to address the technology gap. She also notes that at the second Global Knowledge Conference, held in Malaysia in 2000, specific initiatives were introduced to support gender equity and women's empowerment using cybertechnology.

Global initiatives addressing gender equity and access, as well as recent statistics involving Internet use in the United States, would seem encouraging for those concerned with bridging the divide involving online access between women and men. However, Alison Adam (2004) argues that gender issues affecting cybertechnology are much more complex than mere concerns about access levels. Others point out that "access issues" for women can be better understood as concerns about access to jobs in technology, rather than merely access to the Internet.

In this section, we examine gender-related cybertechnology issues in terms of three broad categories: access to jobs in technology, gender bias in the design and development of software, and methodological frameworks.

10.4.1 Access to High-Technology Jobs

Some see the root of the gender and technology problem, at least as it applies to access issues involving jobs in computer science and engineering, in educational practices that contribute to the overall socialization process for women. For example, many social scientists point out that at an early age girls learn that science (and, by association, technology) is for boys; computers reinforce certain stereotypes regarding technology and gender. Many critics are willing to acknowledge that girls and young women have not literally been denied access to careers in computing, but they point out that socialization—for example, processes that encourage males and females to adopt particular gender-based roles—has perpetuated the gender imbalance.

Tracy Camp (1997) and others have conducted research on what they call "pipeline issues" by analyzing statistics involving the number of women entering the computer science and engineering professions; the data collected during the past twenty or so years suggest that proportionately few women elect to pursue degrees in either field. Michael Wesells (1990) pointed out that in 1989, fewer than 5% of those awarded PhD degrees in computer science were women. According to slightly later statistics provided by Camp (1997), this percentage increased to 15.4% (in 1993–1994), but Camp also noted that the percentage of women pursuing bachelor's and master's degrees in computer science declined slightly during those years.

Kirlidog, Aykol, and Gulscecen (2009) cite more recent evidence to support the ongoing concerns about the "pipeline," and they argue that computer science is still typically regarded as a "male profession," both in industry and academia. They also believe that women remain in the "margins" of a male-dominated profession, which is filled with highly gendered expressions such as "killing or aborting programs," "workbench," "toolkit," etc., that reflect the masculine culture of the field. The authors identify three "net results" of the male-dominated computing profession in which women

1. are underrepresented in computer-related jobs,
2. are more underrepresented in the managerial ranks in the computing field because of the "glass ceiling,"
3. earn less than men for doing the same jobs.[23]

To support (1), they cite a 2000 study showing that while 46% of the United States workforce was made up of women, only 28% of computer science and mathematics-related jobs were held by women. This problem is by no means unique to the United States or to Western nations, they argue, because a large discrepancy can also be found in the computing field in developing nations such as India. Not only are women there underrepresented in terms of the number of jobs and in the number of managerial positions in the computing field, but the "average Indian woman earns 60% of a man's pay for the same job, and only 3% of management jobs are occupied by women."[24]

So the "pipeline" concerns first articulated in the late 1980s regarding the low numbers of women entering the computer profession, as well as their limited career opportunities once in the profession, seem to have persisted well into the twenty-first century. What kinds of explanations can be given to account for this continued trend, especially in developed nations such as the United States? Admitting that no one really knows why this is the case, Paul De Palma (2005) proposes an alternative way of examining the question. First, he dismisses the view that women do not pursue computer science careers because of "math anxiety"—an explanation that has been advanced by some analysts. De Palma points out that, traditionally, many women pursued degrees in mathematics long before fields such as medicine and law were available to them. So he infers that mathematics programs in colleges and universities must have been doing something right in attracting and graduating women.

De Palma suggests that if computer science programs were more like mathematics programs than they currently are, then perhaps more women would be attracted to them. He also notes that much of the high-tech culture associated with the early days of computing was dominated by males, who tended to be fascinated with gadgetry and devices, as opposed to mathematics per se. This, in turn, affected how programming courses were conceived of and taught. De Palma speculates that if course instruction on how to program were designed to be as close as possible to pure logic, as opposed to "reliance on glitzy software packages and fancy graphical user interfaces," women might find programming courses and computer science programs more attractive. Although this explanation is based on speculation, as De Palma admits, it would be an interesting hypothesis to test.

While it is difficult to come up with a decisive and uncontroversial explanation as to why relatively few women have pursued careers in computer science, we need to consider some implications this will have for the future of the computing field. We should note that in addition to providing information used in projecting the number of women who will have access to jobs in the computer profession, analyses of "pipeline statistics" also provide projections of the proportion of women who will have access to important decision-making roles in the computing and high-tech industries. Because the decisions that women make could significantly impact future directions in cybertechnology development, it would seem that carefully monitoring statistics and trends affecting the "pipeline" is warranted.

10.4.2 Gender Bias and Educational Software

Design and development decisions involving educational software can not only influence whether women will elect to pursue degrees and careers in computer science and engineering, but can also affect the education that young girls and women receive. The following scenario illustrates one way that the design of computer software can have such an effect.

▶ **SCENARIO 10–2:** Designing Educational Software

Chuck Huff and Joel Cooper developed a study in the 1980s in which they had teachers design software for three categories of users: girls, boys, and (gender unspecified) children. They discovered that the programs the teachers designed for boys looked like games (with time pressure, hand-to-eye coordination, and competition the most important features). Programs the teachers designed for girls, on the contrary, looked like tools for learning (with conversation and goal-based learning features). And surprisingly, the programs the teachers designed for (gender unspecified) children looked just like the ones they designed for boys. So, the researchers concluded that when teachers designed programs for children, or students in general, they actually designed them for boys.[25] ■

It is worth noting that 80% of the program designers in Huff and Cooper's experiment were female, and, ironically, some of these women had originally expressed the concern that educational software was male biased. Huff and Cooper's research also points to a paradox: a software designer may be able to identify bias in a particular software application but may still not be able to design and develop software applications that avoid bias. At this point, you may find it useful to review our Chapter 1 discussion of bias and embedded values in technology.

Elizabeth Buchanan (2000) argues that gender bias can also be found in video game software and that this bias raises two ethical concerns: (1) video games tend to either misrepresent or exclude female characters, and (2) they tend to perpetuate traditional sexist stereotypes. With respect to (1), she argues that the representational politics of gender in video games needs greater evaluation, because many computer games, especially virtual sports games, include no female characters at all. And with respect to (2), Buchanan argues that video games such as Barbie Fashion Designer have reinforced traditional cultural stereotypes along gender lines.

Some might tend to dismiss concerns about gender bias in video games on the grounds that many women simply aren't interested in them. However, Philip Brey (2008) argues that the question of gender bias in these games is "morally significant." He points out, for example, that if

> computer games tend to be designed and marketed for men, then women are at an unfair advantage, as they consequently have less opportunity to enjoy computer games and their possible benefits. Among such benefits may be greater computer literacy, an important quality in today's market place.[26]

Brey also notes that many analysts believe that the computer industry is mainly to blame for the gender gap that exists. For example, most game developers are male; also, there has been little interest on the part of developers to design suitable games for women. Brey also points out that very few computer games include decent role models for women. He notes that a disproportionate number of the female characters in these games are strippers or prostitutes and that these characters tend to have "unrealistic body images. So, Brey and Buchanan each make a plausible case for how the design of video games contributes to gender bias and for why that bias is morally significant.

10.4.3 Methodological Frameworks for Understanding Gender Issues

A third perspective from which to view issues affecting cybertechnology and gender is one that questions the standard methodological framework used to identify and understand specific moral problems. Alison Adam (2004, 2005) notes that problems involving gender and cybertechnology are analyzed either by focusing on the low numbers of women in the computing profession, as in the case of the pipeline issues examined by Camp that we considered above, or by focusing on potential differences in moral decision making by males and females, as suggested in the research of Kreie and Cronin (1998). Adam acknowledges that the first approach is important because it reveals existing inequities in the field; however, she also believes that this approach tends to limit the study of gender to access-related concerns. She believes that research based on the second approach, which focuses on establishing differences in moral decision making between men and women, tends to reinforce behavioral stereotypes in males and females. According to Adam, both approaches miss the opportunity to use feminist ethical theory to analyze and understand contemporary cyberethics in light of the gender implications for broader issues such as privacy and power.

Adam argues that conventional methodological frameworks used to research gender, that is, gathering data via techniques based on student surveys, has prevented us from seeing larger issues. So she proposes an alternative strategy in which data are gathered via empirical observation and interviews and then tested against ethical theory. She argues that current computer ethics research involving gender is "under-theorized"; what little theory is being applied, Adam points out, is generally based on traditional schemes such as utilitarianism and deontology. She also believes that traditional ethical theories not only ignore gender, they also tend to emphasize the *result* of an ethical decision over the *process* used to reach the decision.

Adam suggests that we need a "gender informed ethics" to improve the process, based on a feminist ethics—in particular, on the "ethic of care" introduced in a seminal work on feminist ethics by Carol Gilligan.[27] According to this ethic, care and justice are part of a moral framework in which individuals are obligated to help one another when it is in their power to do so. An ethic based on care, therefore, is more robust than a mere "noninterference" notion of ethics (see Chapter 2). It contrasts with traditional ethical systems, which Adam believes tend to engender individualism and are often based on simply following formal rules.

Adam believes that a theoretical framework built on an ethic of care improves the understanding of gender issues. First, it shows why gender issues cannot be reduced to access issues and cannot be approached merely in terms of statistical studies based on quantitative analysis; second, and perhaps more importantly, it provides us with an insight for understanding many typical computer ethics issues that cannot be gained through the application of conventional ethical theories. For example, Adam argues that an ethic of care especially helps us both to see some of the relations of power involved in the development and use of computers and to see that the concept of privacy can be different for men and women and can vary according to age, class, ethnicity, etc. Adam (2005) has also argued that a gender-based ethics can also help us to understand issues involving cyberstalking and Internet pornography in a way that traditional ethical theories cannot.

So, Adam's methodological framework can do much more than simply help us to identify specific moral issues *as* gender issues (i.e., issues affecting women per se). It also helps us to analyze many standard computer ethics issues using a more robust theoretical framework than traditional ones that fail to show the impact of many technology-related issues on gender.

▶ 10.5 THE TRANSFORMATION OF WORK IN THE ERA OF CYBERTECHNOLOGY

Thus far, we have focused on equity and access issues, such as social inclusion and distributive justice concerns, as they pertain to specific sociodemographic groups. Some equity and access issues involving cybertechnology, however, affect a much broader segment of society: those in the contemporary workforce. Though still relatively new, cybertechnology already has had a profound effect on employment as well as on the nature of work itself. Computers and cybertechnology also significantly affect the quality of work life. Before considering this, we examine issues involving the transformation of the contemporary workplace.

Whether or not they believe that cybertechnology has benefited workers, few would seriously challenge the claim that it has significantly changed the workplace. Some have gone so far as to suggest that cybertechnology has *transformed* the nature of work itself. We examine this claim by way of social and ethical issues involving

- job displacement and remote work
- globalization and outsourcing.

10.5.1 Job Displacement and Remote Work

One question that frequently arises in discussions about the transformation of employment by cybertechnology is whether, on balance, it has created or eliminated more jobs. There are arguments to support both sides of this debate. Although cybertechnology has caused certain industries to eliminate human jobs, it has enabled other industries, such as computer support companies, to create jobs; social scientists often refer to this shift as *job displacement*.

Job displacement is associated with, and sometimes linked to, *automation*. Social issues associated with automation are by no means new, nor are they unique to cybertechnology. Social scientists note that the Industrial Revolution transformed jobs into smaller, discrete tasks that could be automated by machines, creating working conditions that adversely affected the lives of many workers. When new automated technology threatened to replace many workers, one group of disenchanted workers in England—later referred to as "Luddites"—smashed machines used to make textiles. ("Luddite" is derived from a nineteenth-century British worker, Ned Ludd, who reputedly led workers in destroying factory machinery.)

Just as the Luddites resisted factory technology in the nineteenth century because they thought it threatened their jobs and thus their livelihood, some workers oppose developments involving cybertechnology for similar reasons. In the 1970s, for example, workers tried to stall developments in microprocessor-based technology, fearing that it would lead to a loss of jobs. Workers as well individuals in general who have a pessimistic view of the impact of cybertechnology in the workplace are known as neo-Luddites.

Robotics and Expert Systems

Developments in *robotics* have also raised social concerns for job displacement. Robots, equipped with motor abilities that enable them to manipulate objects, can be programmed to perform tasks that are either (a) routine and mundane for humans, or (b) considered hazardous to humans. Although robots were once fairly unsophisticated, new-generation robotic systems are now able to perform a broad range of tasks.

Whereas (physical) robots have eliminated many blue-collar jobs, sophisticated programs called *expert systems* threaten many professional jobs. An expert system (ES) is a problem-solving computer program that is "expert" at performing one particular task. ESs use "inference engines" to capture the decision-making strategies of experts (usually professionals); they execute instructions that correspond to a set of rules an expert would use in performing a professional task. A "knowledge engineer" asks human experts in a given field a series of questions and then extracts rules and designs a program based on the responses to those questions.

Initially, expert systems were designed to perform jobs in chemical engineering and geology that both required the professional expertise of highly educated persons and were generally considered too hazardous for humans. More recently, expert systems have been developed for use in professional fields such as law, education, and finance. The following scenario illustrates one ethically controversial application of an ES.

▶ **SCENARIO 10–3:** Designing an "Expert Administrator" Program

Tom Forester and Perry Morrison ask whether an "expert administrator" should be designed in a way so that it is programmed to mislead or even to lie to human beings in cases where it might (generally, but unofficially) seem "appropriate" for human administrators to do so.[28] Consider that politicians and executives are sometimes put in situations where they are not permitted to be totally forthcoming. In these cases, being able to be deceptive with respect to answers to certain kinds of questions may be a requirement for being an "expert" (or at least successful) human administrator? If so, should the "skill" of "being able to deceive" be built into such a system? Is it morally permissible to design such a system? ■

The use of expert systems, much like the use of (physical) robotic systems, has raised some ethical and social issues having to do with "de-skilling" and "worker alienation." We noted the impact that automation had on some workers during the Industrial Revolution. Social scientists have suggested that prior to that period, workers generally felt connected to their labor and exhibited a strong sense of pride and craftsmanship. The relationship between worker and work began to change, however, when work became automated. Social scientists have used the term *alienation* to describe the effect that de-skilling had for workers whose skills were transferred to machines. Richard Mason (2007) cites as an example the introduction of Jacquard's loom and its effect on weavers during the Industrial Revolution, where skills were "disembodied" from weavers and craftsmen and then "re-embodied" into machines such as the loom.

Today, ES technology poses a similar threat to professional workers by allowing knowledge, in the form of knowledge-related skills, to be extracted from experts and then implanted into computer software. Mason points out that knowledge can now be "disemminded" from professional workers, or experts in a given field, and "emminded" into machines in the form of computer programs. Mason also believes that there is an interesting connection between the Industrial Revolution and the current era in that a proliferation of publications on ethics appears in each time period, and he suggests that working conditions during the Industrial Revolution may have been responsible for the greatest outpouring of moral philosophy since Plato and Aristotle. Works on ethics by Immanuel Kant, Jeremy Bentham, John Stuart Mill, and many others appeared during that era. Mason suggests that, similarly, contemporary workplace controversies associated with cybertechnology have contributed to the recent flurry of publications on ethics.[29]

Remote Work

Even though remote work, referred to by some as "telework," is a relatively recent practice, it has already raised social and ethical questions. One question has to do with whether all employees who perform remote work benefit from it equally. For example, are white-collar employees affected in the same way as those less-educated and less-skilled employees? It is one thing to be a white-collar professional with an option to work at home at your discretion and convenience. It is something altogether different, however, to be a clerical, or "pink collar," worker required to work remotely out of your home. Of course, some professional men and women may choose to work at home because of childcare considerations or because they wish to avoid a long and tedious daily commute, but employers may require other employees, especially those in lower-skilled and clerical jobs, to work at home.

Although concerns involving remote work can affect all employees, Ben Fairweather (1998) examines how disabled workers are particularly affected. He acknowledges that remote work has provided opportunities to some disabled workers who otherwise would be denied access to a job. But he also worries that for some disabled employees, especially those who are capable of working in both conventional and remote workplace settings, remote work can have unfortunate consequences.

Fairweather worries that a company's remote work policies might provide employers with a convenient scheme for keeping disabled workers out of the physical workplace. He finds this troubling for three reasons: First, it affects worker autonomy because it denies those disabled workers who could work *either* remotely or in a conventional workplace setting the choice of determining where they will work. Second, the practice of remote work can be used to "hide" disabled workers, keeping them out of sight and away from the physical workplace. Third, remote work provides employers with a convenient excuse not to make the physical workplace compatible with current laws affecting disabled employees, such as the ADA (Americans with Disabilities Act) guidelines and requirements. Frances Grodzinsky (2000) notes that because Section 508 of ADA applies only to organizations receiving government funds, those in the private sector can ignore the mandate on accessibility.

10.5.2 Globalization and Outsourcing

What is *globalization*, and what role does it play in the dynamic between work and cybertechnology? Torin Monahan (2005) defines globalization as "the blurring of boundaries previously held as stable and fixed . . . between local/global, public/private [and] nation/world."[30] Monahan notes that discussions of globalization tend to focus on concerns involving labor outsourcing, international trade agreements, immigration concerns, cultural homogenization, and so forth. So there are broad cultural issues, as well as economic controversies, underlying the debate about globalization. In this section, however, we focus on economic aspects of globalization, particularly as they impact cybertechnology and the workplace.

In a global economy where individual nations are protected less and less by tariffs, competition between countries for producing and exporting goods, as well as for providing services, has escalated. In the United States, considerable debate has focused on the NAFTA (North American Free Trade Association) initiatives during the past two decades. Those individuals and organizations that have been labeled "isolationists" and "protectionists" have opposed NAFTA, while proponents of "open" markets between countries have tended to support it. Do trade agreements such as NAFTA favor poorer countries that are part of the agreement, where the cost of labor is cheaper? Or do these trade agreements favor the majority of people in wealthier countries who are able to purchase more goods and services at lower prices? What is the net economic benefit of globalization for both richer and poorer countries? These questions are controversial, and proponents on each side have come up with drastically different statistical data to support their claims.

Trade agreements such as NAFTA and GATT (General Agreement on Tariffs and Trade) make possible a new global economy. On the one hand, these have encouraged greater competition between nations and, arguably, have resulted in greater efficiency for businesses. On the other hand, the economies of some nations have been severely impacted by the job loss that has resulted. For example, many traditional manufacturing jobs in the United States have been exported "offshore." Until recently, this phenomenon impacted mainly traditional "blue-collar" jobs; now it also affects many jobs in the service sector. Most recently, it has affected many highly skilled "white collar" jobs such as those in the computing/IT field. For example, programming jobs traditionally held by employees in American companies, such as IBM, are being "outsourced" to companies in India and China whose employees are willing to work for significantly lower wages than those paid to American programmers.

In one sense, cybertechnology has facilitated the process of *outsourcing*. We saw, in our analysis of remote work, how cybertechnology enabled the reallocation of work from traditional workplace settings to remote sites, including an employee's home. Before the globalization movement, however, most American jobs affected by remote work still remained in the United States. Ironically, perhaps, the jobs of the programmers who had the high-tech skills needed to make remote work a reality are now being outsourced to countries where programmers earn less money. Baker and Kripalani (2005) point out that the career prospects of American software programmers, which were "once dazzling," are now in doubt. In fact, the authors note that, because of this trend, the future of high-tech economy in the United States may also be at risk. Although it is still too soon to say with any confidence what the net effect of the outsourcing of programming jobs will mean, it raises concerns that warrant serious consideration (under the category of cybertechnology and the transformation of work).

▶ 10.6 THE QUALITY OF WORK LIFE

Thus far, we have focused on social and ethical issues surrounding the transformation of work, but many social scientists have also questioned how cybertechnology impacts the *quality* of work life. Quality issues address both health and safety concerns and employee stress. We begin with a brief examination of some health and safety issues in the computerized workplace.

10.6.1 Health and Safety Issues

Cybertechnology-related health and safety issues have been associated with the use of computer hardware. Keyboards and handheld pointing/tracking devices can cause arm, hand, and finger trauma leading to carpal tunnel syndrome (CTS), as well as other musculoskeletal conditions associated with cumulative trauma disorder (CTD); together these problems are called repetitive strain injury (RSI). Catherine Romano (1998) notes that complaints about RSI can be traced back to the eighteenth century, when Italian clerks and scribes reported ailments they believed to be caused by "repeated use of the hand." So RSI issues are by no means unique to computers and hand-held electronic devices, but, nevertheless, they have been greatly exacerbated by the increased use of these technologies, both within and outside the workplace.

Because of RSI-related litigation, employers, especially those who require employees to use computers extensively, now pay close attention to ergonomics. L. L. Bean, for instance, installed ergonomically adjustable workstations, and each worker's ergonomic measurements—that is, appropriate height level for keyboards and desktop work surfaces, proper eye-to-monitor distance, and measurements that ensure the employee's neck, back, and feet are properly aligned when the employee is seated at the computer—are recorded. At the beginning of each employee's shift, the workstation is automatically adjusted according to the individual's prerecorded ergonomic measurements. Other companies have also adopted similar ergonomic practices and policies.

10.6.2 Employee Stress, Workplace Surveillance, and Computer Monitoring

Another quality-of-work issue involves employee stress. Many workers experience stress because their activities are now monitored closely by an "invisible supervisor" — i.e., the computer, which can record information about work habits. The 2007 Electronic Monitoring and Surveillance Report, sponsored by the American Management Association (2008), noted that 43% of American companies monitor employee e-mail, and 96% of those companies "track external (incoming and outgoing messages)." The report also noted that 45% of companies track the amount of time an employee spends at the keyboard. An increasing number of these companies now also monitor the blogosphere (described in Chapter 11) to see what is being written about them in various blogs, and some also monitor social networking sites such as Facebook. As a result of increased monitoring, many employees have been fired for misusing a company's e-mail resources or its Internet connection, or both. So, the threats posed by computerized monitoring would clearly seem to contribute to employee stress.

Perhaps somewhat ironically, data entry clerks and so-called "information workers," whose work is dependent on the use of computer technology to process information, are among the groups of employees who have been most subjected to monitoring by that technology. Although computer monitoring techniques were initially used to track the activities of clerical workers such as data entry operators, they now also track and evaluate the performance of professionals, such as programmers, loan officers, investment brokers, and managers. And nurses are also frequently monitored to make sure that they do not spend too much time with one patient.

Why is employee monitoring via computerized surveillance tools increasing so dramatically? Kizza and Ssanyu (2005) identify multiple factors that have contributed to the recent expansion and growth of employee monitoring, two of which are worth highlighting:

1. the plummeting prices of both software and hardware
2. the miniaturization of monitoring products.[31]

The lower cost of cybertechnology has made monitoring tools available to many employers who, in the past, might not have been able to afford them. And the miniaturization of these tools has made it far easier to conceal them from employees. Lucas Introna (2004) points out that surveillance technology, in addition to becoming less expensive, has also become "less overt and more diffused." He also believes that current monitoring technologies have created the potential to build surveillance features into the "very fabric of organizational processes." Consider that monitoring tools are now being used to measure such things as the number of minutes an employee spends on the telephone completing a transaction (such as selling a product or booking a reservation) and the number and length of breaks he or she takes.

Monitoring software can even measure the number of computer keystrokes a worker enters per minute. John Weckert (2005) points out that an employee's keystrokes can be monitored for accuracy as well as for speed. He also notes that the contents of an employee's computer screen can easily be brought up on the screen of a supervisor "without the employee's knowledge."

Some companies also use monitoring tools and techniques to block out certain kinds of content. For example, Rudinow and Graybosch (2002) point out that Texas Health

Resources, a major hospital chain in the Southwest of the United States, uses software that scans employee e-mail for keywords that may indicate "inappropriate content." The authors also note that American Telephone and Telegraph, another major corporation, uses software that rejects incoming e-mail messages indicated as "having offensive content."

Distinguishing Between Two Different Aspects of Employee Monitoring

Thus far, we have talked about employee monitoring in fairly general terms, also noting some recent statistics. However, Weckert points out that it is crucial to draw some distinctions involving two areas of computerized monitoring:

1. the different *applications of monitoring*,
2. the different *kinds of work situations.*

Regarding (1), Weckert notes that employees could be monitored with respect to the following kinds of activities:

- e-mail usage,
- URLs visited while Web surfing,
- quality of their work,
- speed of their work,
- work practices (health and safety),
- employee interaction.[32]

He points out that the reasons given to justify the application of monitoring in activities involving employee e-mail and Internet use may be very different from the kinds of justifications needed to monitor an employee's speed of work or the quality of his or her work.

With regard to (2), some further distinctions also need to be made concerning which kinds of workers should be monitored. Weckert notes that while it may be appropriate to monitor the keystrokes of data entry workers to measure their performance in specific periods of time, it may not be appropriate to monitor the e-mail of workers in cases where client confidentially is expected. For example, he points out that a therapist employed in a health organization may receive highly sensitive and personal e-mail from one of her client's regarding the client's mental state or physical health.

Similarly, a teacher may receive e-mail from a student, or from an academic administrator communicating about a student, that contains sensitive information regarding the student. As a college professor, for example, I occasionally receive e-mail messages from students who may disclose to me, in confidence, personal details of their health or financial status, or an e-mail requesting information about a grade received for a paper. Arguably, these kinds of e-mails deserve more protection from monitoring than e-mails sent by other employees at my college who do not interact with students in ways that involve the communication of personal information that is sensitive and confidential. So, if my college were to institute an e-mail monitoring policy for its employees, factors such as these should be taken into consideration.

It is very useful to differentiate monitoring issues affecting an employee's activities in the workplace versus issues pertaining to the kinds of workers who should or should not be monitored. For purposes of this chapter, however, we will focus on employee monitoring with respect to questions affecting the former rather than the latter.

An additional distinction worth drawing at this point has to do with the kind of method or approach we use in understanding and analyzing monitoring controversies. According to Weckert, a comprehensive analysis of workplace monitoring should combine two separate approaches: one conceptual, and the other empirical. A conceptual analysis is needed to "enunciate and clarify" the relevant moral concepts such as privacy, autonomy, and trust. Empirical approaches, on the contrary, are needed to examine the technologies involved with respect to questions such as "what can be done?"; "how easily and at what cost can it be done?"; and "how intrusive will it be?"[33] Although the empirical questions are important in their own right, our analysis of workplace monitoring in this chapter focuses mainly on conceptual issues—especially as they pertain to moral concerns affecting privacy and autonomy.

Some Arguments for and Against Workplace Monitoring

As in the case of many controversies involving the use of cybertechnology, employee monitoring demonstrates a clash of legitimate interests and rights for the parties involved. While employees are concerned about protecting their rights to privacy and autonomy, employers want to protect their interests involving profit margin and overall efficiency. Forester and Morrison (1994) describe some classic arguments used in favor of, and in opposition to, computer monitoring. They note that some employers defend computer monitoring on the grounds that it is useful for training new employees who will work with the public. Others defend it by claiming it saves money, is essential for improving worker productivity, aids managers in motivating employees, or helps businesses to reduce industrial espionage and employee theft.

Opponents of monitoring have a very different perspective: Some see computer monitoring as a Big Brother tactic or as an "electronic whip" used unfairly by management, and they believe it creates a work environment tantamount to an "electronic sweatshop." Others claim that managers are motivated to use monitoring because they distrust their employees or that, because monitoring invades individual privacy, it disregards human rights. Some critics also charge that while monitoring may accurately measure the quantity of work an employee produces, it fails to measure the overall quality of that work. Others argue that computer monitoring is ultimately counter-productive, because employee morale generally declines along with overall workplace productivity. Table 10.2 summarizes arguments on both sides of the debate.

A Code of Ethics for Employee Monitoring

Although they do not endorse computer monitoring, Gary Marx and Sanford Sherizen (1991) have proposed a code of ethics that they believe would provide standards for determining when monitoring practices satisfy minimal criteria for fairness to workers. Their code has six guidelines:

1. Apply to monitoring the same protection that applies to pre-employment background checks—that is, permit only information directly related to the job to be collected. The burden of proof for the need to monitor should lie with the employer.

TABLE 10.2   Arguments Used to Support and to Oppose Computer Monitoring

Arguments in Favor of Monitoring	Arguments Against Monitoring
Helps to reduce employee theft	Increases employee stress
Helps to eliminate waste	Undermines employee trust
Helps employers to train new employees	Reduces individual autonomy
Provides employers with a motivational tool	Invades worker privacy
Improves competitiveness	Focuses on quantity rather than quality of work
Saves the company money	Creates an "electronic sweatshop"
Guards against industrial espionage	Provides employers with an "electronic whip"
Improves worker productivity and profits	Reduces employee morale and overall productivity

2. Require employers to provide employees with advanced notice of the introduction of monitoring as well as appropriate mechanisms for appeal.

3. Require people to verify machine-produced information before using it to evaluate employees.

4. Provide workers with access to the information on themselves.

5. Provide mechanisms for monetary redress for employees whose rights are violated or who are victims of erroneous information generated by a monitoring system.

6. Apply a "statute of limitations" on data from monitoring. The older the data, the less their potential relevance and the greater the difficulty employees have in challenging the information.[34]

Note that (2) requires that employees must be told in advance before computerized monitoring is used. This gives the employee a measure of autonomy because, once informed that a company plans to institute monitoring, he or she can elect not to work for that company. And according to (4), employees have the right to review information collected via monitoring and to determine whether that information is accurate; (3) allows them to challenge inaccurate information before it can be used against them. Another important feature of Marx and Sherizen's code is that (6) requires that a statute of limitations be set with respect to how long computer-gathered information about an employee could be used and kept on record in an employee's file.

Arguably, a code that protects at least some employees' interests in the monitoring process is better than no code at all. However, some critics believe that an alternative to the kind of code articulated by Marx and Sherizen is needed. For example, Introna (2004) believes that because of the "power differential" involving employer and employee, a workplace monitoring policy should "presume in favor of the employee," who is the weaker party in the relationship. Introna also believes that employees do not necessarily fear surveillance; they fear the choices that employers will likely make with respect to the information they collect. He claims that employees are concerned both that these choices will reflect only the interests of the employer and that the information will provide the employer with only part of the picture needed to make subsequent judgments about employees.

Employee Monitoring and Personal Autonomy

Emma Rooksby and Natasha Cica (2005) offer a perspective on workplace practices involving employee monitoring that takes into consideration a special interest or right for the employee—viz., the employee's right to personal autonomy. Although they do not argue that workplace monitoring is unjustified or "intrinsically wrong," the authors claim that this practice is wrong in cases where it used by employers or managers to

> facilitate *coercive* or *manipulative* changes to the workers' values insofar as this involves an attempt to undermine or distort their personal autonomy.[35]

Rooksby and Cica believe that it is important to analyze workplace monitoring from the perspective of psychological aspects of personal autonomy, which they refer to as "psychological autonomy," for the sake of convenience. They also argue that individuals have a "right to psychological autonomy" and that this right is analogous to other rights such as "freedom of opinion, expression, and association." To the extent that electronic surveillance in the workplace contributes to a "distortion or reduction of personal autonomy in the workplace by interfering with the workers' motivational attitudes," Rooksby and Cica believe that it undermines the workers' right to psychological autonomy.[36]

Is a compromise position possible in the debate over employee monitoring? Richard Spinello (2002) provides a very careful analysis of some of the key interests involved for both parties in this debate. He focuses his analysis on controversies surrounding the monitoring of employee e-mail. Spinello believes that an individual has a *prima facie* right to the confidentiality of his or her e-mail communications. He also believes, however, that this right must be carefully balanced with a corporation's "information requirements" and its "need to know." In Spinello's scheme, e-mail monitoring, which uses "extraordinary means" to acquire information about an employee, is intrusive and offensive; only "ordinary means," he argues, should be used to seek "relevant" knowledge about the employee.

Spinello acknowledges that some circumstances might warrant monitoring an employee's e-mail. But he also argues that, in general, employee communications should be free from routine monitoring because such a practice represents an "impertinent interference" in an employee's affairs. Thus Spinello favors a strong presumption for privacy rights in the workplace, which he believes is necessary to ensure the respect for the dignity of employees and for their autonomy. At the same time, however, he recognizes that monitoring employee e-mail can be legitimate under extraordinary circumstances.

In concluding our discussion of employee monitoring, we should note that there are additional aspects of this controversy that we have not considered in this chapter. For example, there are now many global and international dimensions to workplace monitoring, which raise controversial questions. Stephen Coleman (2005) points out that in the global workforce, a person's privacy could be violated by software monitoring programs that reside on a computer located in a country different from where that individual is working. This raises concerns about whether international agreements for employee monitoring policies may be needed. In fact, Coleman suggests that an

International Bill of Human Rights be adopted in response to concerns affecting global aspects of the employee monitoring. Unfortunately, an examination of this aspect of monitoring, as well as Coleman's proposed solution, is beyond the scope of this chapter.

▶ 10.7 CHAPTER SUMMARY

We have examined some issues involving social inclusion and distributive justice from the vantage point of access to cybertechnology. We have considered the implications of the digital divide at both the global and the local levels, and we have examined access and equity issues for demographic groups, affecting social class, race, gender, and disabled persons. We have also considered access and equity issues affecting employment in the computerized workplace. In particular, we examined these issues as they apply both to the transformation of work and to the quality of work in the computer era. Finally, we examined some of the challenges that contemporary workplace surveillance and computerized monitoring pose for our social values and our system of ethics, especially with respect to employee autonomy, privacy, and trust.

▶ REVIEW QUESTIONS

1. What is the "digital divide," and why is it significant?
2. What are the differences between the global digital divide and the divisions within nations affecting access to cybertechnology?
3. What is the "analog divide," and how can we distinguish it from the "digital divide"?
4. Are all "divides" or divisions regarding resources ethical problems? Is the digital divide an ethical issue?
5. According to Jeroen van den Hoven and Emma Rooksby, what is meant by "distributive justice" in the context of contemporary information societies?
6. Describe three ways, according to Jeremy Moss, that people in developing countries are currently disadvantaged because of lack of access to digital technology.
7. Do we have an obligation to bridge the digital divide? What kind of arguments have been put forth by Maria Bottis and Kenneth Himma for why affluent countries have an obligation to do so?
8. What are some of the special equity and access issues affecting disabled persons who use cybertechnology?
9. Identify and briefly describe three perspectives from which we can analyze issues involving race and cybertechnology.
10. Briefly describe three perspectives from which we can view issues involving gender and cybertechnology.
11. Why does Alison Adam believe that traditional schemes used to understand gender issues affecting cybertechnology are not adequate?
12. How has work been "transformed" in the computer age with respect to job displacement? Who were the Luddites, and what is meant by the expression "neo-Luddite"?
13. What are some of the ethical and social issues associated with the development and use of expert systems (ES) and robotics?
14. Describe some of the social issues affecting remote work.
15. What special implications does Ben Fairweather believe that remote work, or telework, has for disabled employees?
16. What is globalization? What impact could the outsourcing of highly skilled programming jobs, traditionally held by employees in American companies, to China and India have for the United States in the new global economy?
17. Describe some of the health and safety issues associated with computers in the workplace.
18. What is employee monitoring, and why is it controversial from an ethical perspective? What are some of the arguments used for and against the use of computers to monitor employees?

19. Describe the code of ethics for employee monitoring as suggested by Gary Marx and Sanford Scherizen. Is it adequate?

20. How can concerns about the monitoring of an employee's use of e-mail in the workplace be understood and analyzed in the context of issues affecting employee privacy and personal autonomy?

► DISCUSSION QUESTIONS

1. Some critics and skeptics suggest that the digital divide is not really an ethical issue, because there have always been divisions or "divides" between group. For example, we saw that some critics point out there is a "Mercedes-Benz Divide" and that most of us fall on the wrong side of this "divide." Is the division between those who have and do not have access to cybertechnology similar to or different from the division between those who own and do not own Mercedes-Benz automobiles? Explain.

2. Recall the kind of racist/hate Web sites described by Lynn Theismeyer in Section 10.3.3. Should Web sites that promote racist speech be allowed to thrive on the Internet? Has the proliferation of these sites increased the incidence of racism on a global scale? Or is the Internet, as some have suggested, a force that can help to reduce racism?

3. What obligations does the United States have, as a democratic nation concerned with guaranteeing equal opportunities for all it citizens, to ensure that all Americans have full access to the Internet? Does the United States also have obligations to developing countries to ensure that they have global access to the Internet? If so, what is the extent of those obligations? For example, should engineers working in the United States and other developed countries design applications to ensure that people living in remote areas with low connectivity and poor bandwidth have reasonable Internet access? If so, who should pay for the development of these software applications?

4. Do we, as a society, have a special obligation to disabled persons to ensure that they have full Internet access? Is the argument that by providing improved access and services for disabled persons, nondisabled users will benefit as well a reasonable one? Consider that it can be dangerous to reason along this line; for example, suppose that nondisabled persons did not benefit from software applications designed for the disabled. Would that be a reason for not investing in technological applications to assist disabled people?

► ESSAY/PRESENTATION QUESTIONS

1. Recall our discussion of expert systems (ESs) in Section 10.5.2. There, we saw that the increased use of ES technology in professional fields has generated some ethical and social concerns, and we also considered some ethical dilemmas that were raised in designing an "expert administrator." Other ethical controversies surrounding ES have to do with critical decisions, including life and death decisions; for example, should "expert doctors" be allowed to make decisions that could directly result in the death of, or cause serious harm to, a patient? If so, *who* is ultimately responsible for the ES's decision? Is the hospital that owns the particular ES responsible? Should the knowledge engineer who designed the ES be held responsible? Or is the ES itself responsible? In answering these questions, you may want to consult relevant sections of Chapter 4, where we discussed responsibility for software-related accidents such as the case involving the Therac-25 system.

2. We briefly noted that some controversies associated with workplace monitoring now have global and international implications. For example, Stephen Coleman points out that in the global workforce, an employee's privacy could be violated by software monitoring programs that reside on a computer located in a country different from where that employee works. Do we need new kinds of international agreements and policies for employee monitoring, as Coleman suggests? And do we need to adopt an "International Bill of Human Rights," as Coleman also suggests, in response to global challenges posed by workplace monitoring? If not, what kinds of alternative proposals might be suitable?

▶ ENDNOTES

1. *Human Development Report 2000.*
2. *Internet World Stats: Usage and Population Stats* (2008). Available at www.internetworldstats.com (accessed January 7, 2009).
3. *Internet World Stats: Usage and Population Studies* (2005). Available at http://www.internetworldstats.com/top20.htm (accessed January 11, 2006).
4. *Human Development Report 2007/2008: Internet Users (per 1,000 people).* Available at http://hdrstats.undp.org/indicators/124.html (accessed January 8, 2009). The report notes that Iceland has 869 users per 1,000 persons, whereas Norway has 735 users per thousand.
5. See *Internet World Stats: Usage and Population Stats* (2008). By contrast, Internet growth in North America increased by 129% during that same period.
6. O'Hara and Stevens (2006), p. 144.
7. I elaborate on this point in Tavani (2003).
8. Van den Hoven and Rooksby (2008), p. 376.
9. Ibid.
10. Rawls (1972), p. 92.
11. Van den Hoven and Rooksby, p. 395.
12. Moss (2002), p. 162.
13. Norris (2001), p. 168.
14. Bottis and Himma (2008), p. 623.
15. Himma (2007), p. 10.
16. See http://www.w3.org/WAI/.
17. *Digital Divide Network 2000.*
18. *Pew Internet & American Life Project, April 8–May 11, 2008 Tracking Report.*
19. This scenario is based on material in Johnson (1997).
20. Theismeyer (1999), p. 117.
21. Ibid.
22. The April/May 2008 *Pew Internet & American Life Project* reported that 73% of women and 73% of men used the Internet.
23. Kirlidog, Aykol, and Gulscecen (2009), p. 51.
24. Ibid.
25. See Huff and Cooper (1987).
26. Brey (2008), p. 381.
27. See Gilligan (1982).
28. See Forester and Morrison (1994).
29. Mason (2007), pp. 9–10.
30. Monahan (2005), p. 4.
31. Kizza and Ssanyu (2005), p. 3.
32. Weckert (2005), p. viii.
33. Ibid.
34. Marx and Sherizen (1991), p. 405.
35. Rooksby and Cica (2005), p. 243.
36. Ibid., p. 252.

▶ REFERENCES

Adam, Alison. 2004. "Gender and Computer Ethics." In R. A. Spinello and H. T. Tavanieds. *Readings in CyberEthics.* 2nd ed. Sudbury MA: Jones and Bartlett Publishers. Reprinted from *Computers and Society* 30, no. 4 (2000): 17–24.

Adam, Alison. 2005. *Gender, Ethics and Information Technology.* London, UK: Palgrave Macmillan.

Adams, A. Rhae. 2001. "Beyond Numbers and Demographics: Experience near Explorations of the Digital Divide." *Computers and Society* 31, no. 3: 5–8.

AMA/ePolicy Institute Research (2008). *Executive Summary: 2007 Electronic Monitoring & Surveillance Survey.* Http://press.amanet.orgpress-releases/177/2077-electronic-monitoring-surveillance-survey.

Baker, Stephen, and Manjeet Kripalani. 2005. "Software: Programming Jobs Are Heading Overseas by the Thousands: Is There a Way for the U.S. to Stay on Top." In P. De Palma, ed. *Computers in Society 05/06.* Dubuque IA: McGraw-Hill/Dushkin, pp. 47–51.

Bottis, Maria Cannellopulou, and Kenneth Einar Himma. 2008. "The Digital Divide: A Perspective for the Future." In K. E. Himma and H. T. Tavani, eds. *The Handbook of Information and Computer Ethics*. Hoboken NJ, pp. 621–37.

Brey, Philip. 2008. "Virtual Reality and Computer Simulation." In K. E. Himma and H. T. Tavani, eds. *The Handbook of Information and Computer Ethics*. Hoboken NJ, pp. 361–84.

Buchanan, Elizabeth A. 2000. "Strangers in the 'Myst' of Video Gaming: Ethics and Representation." *CPSR Newsletter* 18, no. 1.

Camp, Tracy. 1997. "The Incredible Shrinking Pipeline." *Communications of the ACM* 40, no. 2 (October): 103–10.

Chapman, Gary, and Marc Rotenberg. 1995. "The National Information Infrastructure: A Public Interest Opportunity." In D. G. Johnson and H. Nissenbaum, eds. *Computers, Ethics, and Social Values*. Englewood Cliffs NJ: Prentice Hall, pp. 628–44.

Coleman, Stephen. 2005. "Universal Human Rights and Employee Privacy: Questioning Employer Monitoring and Computer Use." In J. Weckert, ed. *Electronic Monitoring in the Workplace: Controversies and Solutions*. Hershey PA: Idea Group, pp. 276–95.

Compaine, Benjamin. 2001. *The Digital Divide: Facing a Crisis or Creating a Myth*. Cambridge MA: MIT Press.

De Palma, Paul. 2005. "Why Women Avoid Computer Science." In P. De Palma, ed. *Computers in Society 05/06*. Dubuque IA: McGraw-Hill, pp. 104–06.

Fairweather, N. Ben. 1998. "Moral Dilemmas and Issues of Telework for Disabled People." In M. J.van den Hoven, ed. *Computer Ethics: Philosophical Enquiry*. Rotterdam, The Netherlands: Erasmus University Press, pp. 130–41.

Forester, Tom, and Perry Morrison. 1994. *Computer Ethics: Cautionary Tales and Ethical Dilemmas in Computing*. 2nd ed. Cambridge MA: MIT Press.

Gilligan, Carol. 1982. *In a Different Voice: Psychological Theory and Women's Development*. Cambridge MA: Harvard University Press.

Grodzinsky, Frances S. 2000. "Equity of Access: Adaptive Technology." *Science and Engineering Ethics* 6, no. 2: 221–34.

Himma, Kenneth E. 2007. "The Information Gap, the Digital Divide, and the Obligations of Affluent Nations." *International Review of Information Ethics* 7: 1–11.

Huff, Chuck, and Joel Cooper. 1987. "Sex Bias in Educational Software: The Effects of Designers' Stereotypes on the Software They Design." *Journal of Applied Social Psychology* 17: 519–32.

Human Development Report 2000. Published for the United Nations Development Program (UNDP). New York: Oxford University Press.

Human Development Report 2007/2008. Available at http://hdrstats.undp.org/indicators/124.html (accessed January 8, 2009).

Internet Growth Statistics: Internet Usage Stats. 2008. Available at http://www.allaboutmarketresearch.com/internet.com/internet.htm (accessed January 8, 2009).

Internet World Stats: Usage and Population Studies. 2005. Available at http://www.internetworldstats.com/top20.htm (accessed January 11, 2006).

Internet World Stats: Usage and Population Studies. 2008. Available at http://www.internet worldstats.com/stats.htm (accessed January 8, 2009).

Internet World Stats News: Internet Usage Research. 2005. Available at http://www.internetworldstats.com/pr/edi012.htm (accessed January 11, 2006).

Introna, Lucas. 2004. "Workplace Surveillance, Privacy, and Distributive Justice." In R. A. Spinello and H. T. Tavani, eds. *Readings in CyberEthics*. 2nd ed. Sudbury MA: Jones and Bartlett Publishers.

Johnson, Robert C. 1997. "Science, Technology, and Black Community Development." In A. H. Teich, ed. *Technology and the Future*. 7th ed. New York: St. Martin's Press, pp. 270–83.

Kizza, Joseph M., and Jackline Ssanyu. 2005. "Workplace Surveillance." In J. Weckert, ed. *Electronic Monitoring in the Workplace: Controversies and Solutions*. Hershey PA: Idea Group, pp. 1–18.

Kreie, Jennifer, and Timothy Paul Cronan. 1998. "How Men and Women View Ethics." *Communications of the ACM* 41, no. 9: 70–76.

Kretchmer, Susan, and Rod Karveth. 2001. "The Color of the Net: African Americans, Race, and Cyberspace." *Computers and Society* 31, no. 3: 9–14.

Marx, Gary, and Sanford Sherizen. 1991. "Monitoring on the Job: How to Protect Privacy as well as Property." In T. Forester, ed. *Computers in the Human Context: Information Technology, Productivity, and People*. Cambridge MA: MIT Press, pp. 397–406.

Mason, Richard O. 2007. "Four Ethical Issues of the Information Age." In J. Weckert, ed. *Computer Ethics*. Aldershot UK: Ashgate, pp. 31–40. Reprinted from *MIS Quarterly* 10: 5–12.

Monahan, Torin. 2001. "The Analog Divide: Technology Practices in Public Education." *Computers and Society* 31, no. 3: 22–31.

Monahan, Torin. 2005. *Globalization, Technological Change, and Public Education*. New York: Routledge.

Moor, James H. 2004. "Reason, Relativity, and Responsibility in Computer Ethics." In R. A. Spinello and H. T. Tavani, eds. *Readings in CyberEthics*. 2nd ed. Sudbury MA: Jones and Bartlett, pp. 40–54.

Moss, Jeremy. 2002. "Power and the Digital Divide." *Ethics and Information Technology* 4, no. 2: 159–65.

Norris, Pippa. 2001. *Digital Divide? Civic Engagement, Information Poverty, and the Internet Worldwide*. Cambridge MA: Cambridge University Press.

O'Hara, Kieron, and David Stevens. 2006. *Inequality.com: Power, Poverty, and the Digital Divide*. Oxford UK: Oneworld.

Pew Internet & American Life Project. 2005. Washington DC. Available at http://www.pewinternet.org.

Pew Internet & American Life Project, April 8–May 11, 2008 Tracking Report. Available at http://www.pewinternet.org/trends/ User_Demo_7.22.08.htm (accessed January 9, 2009).

Rawls, John. 1972. *A Theory of Justice*. Cambridge MA: Harvard University Press.

Romano, Catherine. 1998. "Working Out the Kinks." In K. Schellenberg, ed. *Computers in Society*. 7th ed. New York: McGraw Hill, pp. 63–65.

Rooksby, Emma, and Natasha Cica. 2005. "Personal Autonomy and Electronic Surveillance in the Workplace." In J. Weckert, ed. *Electronic Monitoring in the Workplace: Controversies and Solutions*. Hershey PA: Idea Group, pp. 242–59.

Rudinow, Joel, and Anthony Graybosch, eds. 2002. *Ethics and Values in the Information Age*. Belmont CA: Wadsworth.

Shade, Leslie Regan. 2002. *Gender and Community in the Social Construction of the Internet*. New York: Peter Lang.

Spinello, Richard A. 2002. "Electronic Mail and Panoptic Power in the Workplace." In J. Rudinow and A. Graybosch, eds. *Ethics and Values in the Information Age*. Belmont CA: Wadsworth, pp. 303–11.

Tavani, Herman T. 2003. "Ethical Reflections on the Digital Divide." *Journal of Information, Communication, and Ethics in Society* 1, no. 2: 99–108.

Theismeyer, Lynn. 1999. "Racism on the Web: Its Rhetoric and its Marketing." *Ethics and Information Technology* 1, no. 2: 117–25.

Van den Hoven, Jeroen, and Emma Rooksby. 2008. "Distributive Justice and the Value of Information: A (broadly) Rawlsian Approach." In J. van den Hoven and J. Weckert, eds. *Information Technology and Moral Philosophy*. Cambridge UK: Cambridge University Press, pp. 376–96.

Warschauer, Mark. 2003. *Technology and Social Inclusion: Rethinking the Digital Divide*. Cambridge MA: MIT Press.

Weckert, John. 2005. "Preface." In J. Weckert, ed. *Electronic Monitoring in the Workplace: Controversies and Solutions*. Hershey PA: Idea Group.

Wessells, Michael G. 1990. *Computer, Self, and Society*. Englewood Cliffs NJ: Prentice Hall.

Woodbury, Marsha. 2002. *Computer and Information Ethics*. Champaign IL: Stipes Publishing.

▶ FURTHER READINGS

Al-Saggaf, Yeslam. "The Digital Divide within the Digital Community in Saudi Arabia." In E. Rooksby and J. Weckert, eds. *Information Technology and Social Justice*. Hershey PA: Information Science Publishing, 2007, pp. 262–82.

Chen. Jengchung V. "The Role of Control and Other Factors in the Electronic Surveillance Workplace." *Journal of Information, Communication and Ethics in Society* 3, no. 2 (2005): 79–91.

Dyson, Freeman. "Technology and Social Justice." In M. W. Winston and R. D. Edelbach, eds. *Society, Ethics, and Technology*. 3rd ed. Belmont CA: Wadsworth, 2006, pp. 130–39.

French, Sheila. "Discourses in Gender and Technology: Taking a Feminist Gaze." In E. Rooksby and J. Weckert, eds. *Information Technology and Social Justice*. Hershey PA: Information Science Publishing, 2007, pp. 171–88.

Gumbus, Andra, and Frances S. Grodzinsky. "Gender Bias in Internet Employment: A Study of Career Advancement Opportunities for Women in the Field of ICT." *Journal of Information, Communication and Ethics in Society* 2, no. 3 (2004): 133–42.

Rooksby, Emma, John Weckert, and Richard Lucas. "The Digital Divide in Australia: Is Rural Australia Losing Out?" In E. Rooksby and J. Weckert, eds. *Information Technology and Social Justice*. Hershey PA: Information Science Publishing, 2007, pp. 240–61.

Turner, Eva. *Women in Computing*. Special Issue of *Journal of Information, Communication and Ethics in Society* 3, no. 4 (2005). Leicester UK: Troubadour Publishing.

11

Community, Personal Identity, and our Sense of Self in Cyberspace

In Chapter 11, we examine the impact that cybertechnology has for our understanding of concepts such as *community* and *personal identity* by asking

- How have online communities, including social networking services (SNSs), affected our traditional notion of "community"?
- Do political blogs facilitate democracy, or do they threaten it?
- What implications do certain kinds of role playing in virtual environments have for our understanding of personal identity?
- Do some kinds of behaviors that have occurred in virtual reality (VR) technologies and massively multiplayer online role-playing games (MMORPGs) raise special ethical issues?
- How have developments in artificial intelligence (AI) affected our sense of self and our conception of what it means to be a human being?

▶ 11.1 COMMUNITY IN CYBERSPACE

What, exactly, is a *community*? Do we need to redefine our traditional notion of community in light of social interactions made possible by cybertechnology? Do online communities pose any special social and ethical challenges? We consider these and related questions in this section.

11.1.1 Online Communities versus Traditional Communities

Today, many people, both young and old, interact in Web-based social networking services (SNSs), such as MySpace and Facebook, as well as in professional-oriented networking services such as LinkedIn. Some also participate in one or more blogs (Web logs), while others send instantaneous "news feeds" to friends in the forms of "tweets" via a popular online service called Twitter. Many also continue to communicate with one another through electronic messenger services provided by Web-based organizations such as America Online's instant messaging (AIM), as well as messaging services that also include video, such as Skype. Assuming that you have an account on Facebook, do your "friends" on that SNS comprise a *community*? To answer this question, we first examine the meaning of "community" in the traditional sense of the term. *Webster's New World Dictionary of the American Language* defines a community as "people living in the same district, city, etc., under the same laws." Note that this traditional definition stresses the geographical aspects of community by associating it with concepts such as "district" and "city" that have typically constrained community life. So, for the most part, traditional communities are limited by geography.

Cybertechnology has made it possible to extend, or perhaps even ignore, the geographical boundaries of traditional community life. This, in turn, causes us to reexamine the concept of community; individuals physically separated by continents and oceans can now interact in SNSs and other online forums to discuss topics that bind them together as a community. Not surprisingly then, more recent definitions of "community" focus on the common interests of groups rather than on geographical and physical criteria.

What, exactly, do we mean by *online community*? Howard Rheingold (2001) defines online communities as "computer-mediated social groups"; he describes his experience in joining the WELL (Whole Earth 'Lectronic Link), an early electronic community, in 1985:

> The idea of a community accessible only via my computer screen sounded cold to me at first, but . . . [f]inding the WELL was like discovering a cozy little world that had been flourishing without me. . . . The WELL felt like an authentic community to me from the start, because it was grounded in my everyday physical world. WELLites who don't live within driving distance of the San Francisco Bay area are constrained in their ability to participate in the local networks of face-to-face acquaintances. . . . I've attended real-life WELL marriages, WELL births, and even a WELL funeral.[1]

Rheingold points out that because of the social contracts and collaborative negotiations that happened when members met online, the WELL became a *community* in that setting. He notes, for example, that in the WELL, norms were "established, challenged, changed, re-established, rechallenged, in a kind of speeded up social evolution." When the members decided to get together occasionally at physical locations in the greater San Francisco Bay area, the WELL became a "hybrid community," spanning both physical and virtual space. But some "pure" online communities also continue to thrive along side the hybrid communities. As Michelle White (2002) notes, these electronic-only forums seem like "real communities" because they offer their members "social exchange, emotional support, and learning environments."

Do users find as much enjoyment and satisfaction in participating in online communities as they do in traditional ones? Mitch Parsell (2008) cites a survey showing that 43% of members of online communities claimed to feel "as strong" about their online communities as their traditional or "real world" communities.[2] He also believes that this may be due to the enhanced nature of the Web—what some now refer to as "Web 2.0"—which is very different from the early Web, primarily because of the interactive aspects of the experiences it makes possible. Analysts disagree on exactly which criteria differentiate Web 2.0 from the original Web, but most agree that the kinds of services made possible by SNSs and blogging sites have significantly altered the way users interact in online communities.

11.1.2 Blogs as Online Communities

A very popular mode of online communication for both young and older Internet users is a forum called the blog (or Web log). According to the (online) *Merriam Webster Dictionary*, a blog is "a Web site that contains an online personal journal with reflections, comments, and often hyperlinks provided by the writer."[3] How do blogs facilitate interactions in, and function as, online communities? While some blogs function as online diaries, others provide commentary on a particular topic or news story. Based on their topics, blogs are often organized into categories such as personal blogs, political blogs, corporate blogs, health blogs, literary blogs, travel blogs, etc. Recall our discussion of the Washingtonienne scenario in Chapter 1, involving Jessica Cutler's blog; as a type of online personal dairy, her blog would fall under the category "personal blog."

Blogs can be maintained by either individuals or organizations. The community of blogs is often referred to as the "blogosphere." Online communities such as myBlogLog and Blog Catalog connect bloggers, whereas search engines such as Bloglines, Blog-Scope, and Technorati assist users in finding blogs. Blogging has become popular because it is an easy way to reach many people, but it has also generated some social and ethical controversies.[4] For example, we saw in our analysis of the Washingtonienne scenario (in Chapter 1) that a number of privacy-related concerns arose affecting Jessica Cutler and the six men implicated in her personal online diary. Other controversies arise in response to political blogs – for instance, some bloggers have been responsible for breaking news stories about political scandals and thus influencing public opinion. Some of these bloggers also had political agendas to advance and were eager to spread negative stories about politicians whose views they opposed, and in some cases these stories have not been accurate. We examine controversies affecting political blogs in detail in Section 11.2.3, in connection with our discussion of democracy and the Internet.

One question worth noting before we conclude this section is whether bloggers, especially those who write and maintain influential blogs, should be held to the same standards of accuracy, accountability, and liability as professional online journalists. Many bloggers claim that they are not journalists and thus should not be held to professional journalistic standards. Critics, however, argue that bloggers have certain "ethical obligations to their readers, the people they write about, and society in general" (A Bloggers' Code of Ethics, 2003). Unfortunately, an examination of this debate in the detail it deserves is beyond the scope of this chapter. Our analysis of blogs in this section has focused mainly on their role as online communities.

11.1.3 Assessing Pros and Cons of Online Communities

Have online communities had an overall positive effect on communication and interaction? Not surprisingly, arguments have been advanced on both sides of this question. Those who see these communities in a favorable light could point to the fact that on SNSs such as Facebook, users can make new "friends" and meet prospective college roommates before setting foot on campus; they can also possibly find future romantic partners in online dating services such as eHarmony. Additionally, users can join and form online medical support groups, as well as various blogs designed to disseminate material to like-minded colleagues. Through these online services and forums, users can communicate with people they might not otherwise communicate with by physical mail or telephone. Gordon Graham (1999) believes that online communities also promote individual freedom because members can more easily disregard personal attributes, such as gender and ethnicity, which are more obvious in traditional communities.

However, online communities have also had some negative effects. In addition to threatening traditional community life, they have

A. facilitated social polarization (because of the very narrow focus of some groups),

B. minimized the kind of face-to-face communications (that have defined traditional friendships),

C. facilitated anonymity and deception (thereby enabling some forms of socially and morally objectionable behavior that would not be tolerated in traditional communities).

We briefly examine each of these points.

Online Communities and Social Polarization

We have noted some ways cybertechnology provides us with choices about which kinds of online communities we wish to join; this would seem to contribute positively to human interaction by enabling us to come together with like-minded individuals we otherwise might not meet. However, some online communities, especially those whose focus tends to be on topics and issues that are divisive and narrow, can also contribute to social polarization. Mitch Parsell (2008) argues that "extremely narrowly focused" online communities can be dangerous because they "can polarize attitudes and prejudices," which can lead to increased division and "social cleavage." He worries that the narrow focus of many online communities presents us with cause for concern. Parsell expresses this concern in the form of the following argument:

1. People tend to be attracted to others with like opinions;

2. Being exposed to like opinions tends to increase our own prejudices;

3. This polarizing of attitudes can occur on socially significant issues . . . ;

4. Thus, where the possibility of narrowing focus on socially significant issues is available, increased community fracture is likely.[5]

So, even though online communities can empower individuals by providing them with greater freedom and choice in terms of their social interactions, they can also foster increased polarization in society. In Section 11.2.3, we will examine some issues affecting political and social polarization in the context of our discussion of democracy and the Internet.

Friendships in Online Communities

Does it matter that online communication has minimized the kinds of face-to-face interactions that define behavior in traditional communities? Is that necessarily a negative thing? On the one hand, being able to send an e-mail or a text message to someone, or to write on a Facebook user's Wall, is far more convenient than having to meet that person face to face in physical space to communicate with them. On the other hand, some worry that something is lost—possibly some critical interpersonal skills—in excessive online communications, at the expense of avoiding face-to-face interactions. A related, and very important, question that also arises has to do with the implications that online-only communication between individuals may have for our traditional under-standing of friendship. In other words, is it possible for people who interact only in virtual (or purely online) contexts to be "real friends"?

To what extent, if any, is physical interaction between individuals necessary for true friendships to develop and flourish? At one time, the notion of "disembodied friends" might have seemed strange. But today, we hear about so-called "friends" who commu-nicate regularly online but have never met in physical space. Dean Cocking and Steve Matthews (2000) argue that the kinds of close friendships we enjoy in physical space are not possible in pure virtual environments, i.e., in contexts that are solely computer-mediated, because online-only friendship occurs in

> a context of communication dominated by *voluntary* self disclosure, enabling and disposing me to construct a highly chosen and controlled self-presentation and world of interaction. I altogether miss the kind of interaction between friends that seems a striking and common-place feature of a close friendship.[6] [Italics Cocking and Matthews]

Cocking and Matthews' argument is complex and cannot be analyzed here in the detail that it deserves. But we will consider a few of their key points. The authors argue that it is not possible to realize close friendships in a "virtual world" because purely computer-mediated contexts (a) facilitate voluntary self disclosure, and (b) enable people to choose and construct a highly controlled "self-presentation" or identity. Because of these factors, essential elements of a person's character, as well as the "relational self ordinarily developed through those interactions in friendship" are distorted and lost. For example, they point out that in offline contexts, we involuntarily disclose aspects of ourselves through indicators or "cues" in our interactions with others. And because interactions in these contexts are acts of "nonvoluntary self disclosure," one has less control over the way one presents oneself to others. As a result, important aspects of our true personalities are involuntarily revealed, which makes close friendships possible in offline contexts but not in virtual ones.

Is the argument advanced by Cocking and Matthews convincing? Adam Briggle (2009) disagrees with their conclusion, but he uses different kinds of criteria—one based on "distance" and one on "deliberateness"—to make the case for why friend-ships in purely virtual contexts can be "initiated and flourish." First, he points out that communications among friends in offline contexts, which are based largely on "oral exchanges," are not always candid or sincere; consequently, important "dynamics and indicators" that are required to form close friendships can be distorted. But Briggle believes that the *distance* involved in typical computer-mediated communications can give friends the courage to be more candid with one another than in typical face-to-face interactions.

Second, Briggle points out that online friends depend on written correspondences (as opposed to oral exchanges), and he believes that the *deliberateness* required in composing those kinds of correspondences can lead to "deeper bonds and greater depth in friendships." He also notes that oral communication in offline contexts, on the contrary, is "often too shallow and hasty to promote deep bonds."[7] So, unlike Cocking and Matthews, Briggle concludes that it is possible to form close friendships in purely virtual contexts. He also concedes, however, that some purely virtual relationships can be "shallow relationships."

Deception Made Possible by Anonymity in Online Communities

Some critics believe that online communities reveal a "darker side" of the Internet because people can, under the shield of anonymity, engage in behavior that would not be tolerated in most physical communities. For instance, individuals can use aliases and screen names when they interact in online forums, which makes it easier to deceive about who actually is communicating with them. We briefly examine two scenarios—one relatively recent (involving the popular SNS, MySpace), and another that has become a classic case (involving an early online forum). Both illustrate how online anonymity, pseudonymity, and deception can contribute to the darker side of online communities.

First, consider a controversial incident that occurred in an online community called a MOO (multiuser object-oriented environment) that was reported by Julian Dibbell in the 1990s.

► **SCENARIO 11–1:** A Virtual Rape in Cyberspace

LambdaMOO was an early electronic forum in which participants had screen names, or virtual identities, to represent the characters they portrayed; for example, characters whose screen names were Mr. Bungle, Zippy, Legba, Starsinger, and Joe Feedback interacted in this online forum. Mr. Bungle designed a program called "voodoo doll" that enabled him to control the actions of other characters in the online forum and used it to take control of Legba and Starsinger to "perform" sexually offensive actions. When Bungle's program was "frozen" by Zippy, the incident ceased.[8] ∎

As you might imagine, the incident had a profound effect not only on the members of the Lambda community but also on many participants in other online communities who heard about it. Almost immediately, questions arose about how to deal with Bungle: Should he be evicted from Lambda community? Should the real person behind Bungle be prohibited from joining other online communities?

We examine the LambdaMOO case in more detail in Section 11.3, where we consider ethical aspects of virtual environments. We also discuss the effects that MOOs and MUDs (multiuser dimensions) have on personal identity in Section 11.4. Next, we briefly examine a scenario involving deception that took place in MySpace.

► **SCENARIO 11–2:** A Cyberbullying Incident on MySpace

Megan Meier was a 13-year-old resident of Dardenne Prairie, Missouri, who had an account on MySpace. There, she was "befriended" by a boy named "Josh Evans." Evans, who claimed to be a 16-year-old boy, told Meier that he lived near her and was being home-schooled by his parents. At first, "he" sent flattering e-mails to Meier, which also suggested that he might be romantically interested in her. Soon, however, Evans's remarks turned from compliments to insults, and Meier became a victim of cyberbullying (a form of online harassment). Meier, who was reported to have suffered from low self-esteem, became distressed by the insulting messages she continued to receive from Evans. On October 17, 2006, she decided to end her life by hanging herself in her room.

It turns out that Evans was not a teenage boy; she was Lori Drew, the 49-year-old mother of a former friend of Meier's. Drew was subsequently charged and prosecuted on three counts of computer fraud and one count of conspiracy. In November 2008, she was found guilty of three misdemeanor counts of computer fraud; however, the jury was deadlocked on a fourth charge, involving conspiracy.[9]   ■

Although this case could be examined from the vantage point of cyberullying, an offense that has affected numerous teenagers interacting in online communities, we consider it here from the perspective of deceptive behavior in online communities. How is the Meier case both similar to and different from the one involving LambdaMOO? Despite some significant differences, both incidents have one thing in common: they reveal a darker side of online communities that is made possible by anonymity and pseudonymity. One difference, however, is that no one was physically injured in the LambdaMOO incident. (But it could be argued that two Lambda members did experience some emotional or psychological harm, and in Section 11.3 we will see how emotional harm can occur to the real-life people whose characters are represented in virtual environments such as online communities.)

A second difference is that LambdaMOO was a "pure" online, or online-only, community, where the virtual characters that participated had screen names and acted out various roles in the game-like or role-playing context of that virtual environment. Also, it was appropriate for members of LambdaMOO to use names other than their actual ones because of the rules defining that Lambda community. In the Meier case, however, Lori Drew's use of an alias was deceptive by virtue of the rules, or at least the expected norms, in MySpace for initiating a request to befriend another. There, the expectation was that an individual using that SNS to seek out new "friends" would disclose his or her actual name and not use a fake name to intentionally deceive someone. However, one might also argue that such a rule was not sufficiently explicit at the time, because neither MySpace nor most other SNSs had clear policies when it came to individuals using actual names in setting up an account. (Typically, all that was required then to register for an account on MySpace was a legitimate e-mail address.)

Table 11.1 summarizes positive and negative features of online communities.

TABLE 11.1 Features of Online Communities

Positive Features	Negative Features
Empower individuals by giving them choices regarding community membership	Discourage face-to-face interaction between individuals
Enable people living in geographically remote locations to interact regularly as members of the same community	Facilitate anonymity, making it easier to perform morally objectionable acts that are not tolerated in physical communities
Tend to provide individuals with greater freedom	Tend to increase social and political fragmentation

► 11.2 DEMOCRACY AND THE INTERNET

In the preceding section we indirectly considered issues affecting governance, that is, which kinds of rules should apply in online communities and how those rules should be enforced. Consider once again the case of Bungle's behavior in the LambdaMOO community, which caused us to ask what kinds of decision-making powers its members had in determining whether and how Bungle should be punished. Can we simply extend existing rules that apply in physical communities to online communities? Or do we need at least some new rules? These questions broach the larger question as to what kind of political structure should be established in cyberspace. Many authors tend to assume that cyberspace should be governed in accordance with democratic principles and values.

What is the relationship between democracy and the Internet? Is the Internet an inherently democratic medium? Does it enhance democracy? Should it be used to spread democracy and democratic ideals? Deborah Johnson (2000) points out that claims involving the connection between the Internet and democracy tend to be made in three different ways. Some authors claim that the Internet is an inherently democratic technology, others claim that the Internet tends to facilitate or even enhance democracy, and still others claim that because democratic values are at stake in the cyberspace policies we adopt, we should develop the Internet along democratic principles.[10] Arguably, a fourth claim—namely, the Internet should be used to promote democracy and democratic ideals—also needs to be examined. We limit our discussion of the relationship between the Internet and democracy to two questions:

A. Does the Internet facilitate democracy and democratic ideals?

B. Should the Internet be used as a tool to promote democracy?

Notice that whereas question (A) is descriptive, (B) is normative. We begin with (A).

11.2.1 Does the Internet Facilitate Democracy?

Some authors who claim that cyberspace favors democracy and democratic ideals point to the Internet as an open forum in which ideas can generally be communicated freely and easily. But some countries have gone to great lengths to censor political speech in cyberspace. For example, China required Google to comply with strict rules for filtering information, which many nations in the West would view as unacceptable. Also, Saudi Arabia has censored political speech online. So, nondemocratic countries have found some ways around the "open" architecture of the Internet and its ability to spread information freely. However, we can still ask whether cybertechnology tends to facilitate democracy and democratic ideals.

Recall Gordon Graham's claim, in Section 11.1.3, that the Internet has provided individuals with greater choice and freedom in joining communities. Thus Graham can be interpreted as suggesting that Internet technology favors democratic values. But some authors have been skeptical about claims that technology, including Internet technology, has had a positive effect on democracy. For example, Richard Sclove (1997) argues that contemporary technologies tend to undermine, rather than facilitate, democracy and community life. Arguably, there is truth in both positions, and Cass Sunstein (2001, 2007) suggests that the Internet has both democracy-enhancing and democracy-threatening aspects.

Sunstein believes that the Internet enhances democracy by providing greater access to information at a lower cost, but at the same time he worries that *deliberative democracy*, the process of rationally debating issues in a public forum, may suffer irreparable harm because of the ways in which the Internet can filter information. People using software filters will not be inclined to gather new information that might broaden their views but will instead, Sunstein believes, use information available to them on the Internet to reinforce their existing prejudices.

We can construct a variation of Sunstein's argument in the following way:

PREMISE 1. On the Internet, people use filtering schemes that provide them with information that
(a) reinforces ideas that they already hold,
(b) screens out novel information and different points of view.

PREMISE 2. An increasing number of people get their information only from the Internet, which will likely
(c) insulate more and more people from exposure to new ideas as well as to ideas that may question or conflict with their own,
(d) lead to greater isolation and polarization among groups,
(e) encourage extremism and radicalism rather than foster compromise and moderation,
(f) reduce the need for the traditional give-and-take process in resolving differences in a public forum.

CONCLUSION. Behavior facilitated by the Internet tends to undermine deliberative democracy and corresponding democratic ideals.

Not everyone agrees with Sunstein's conclusion. Thomas Ulen (2001), for example, is not convinced that the "net effect" of the Internet on democracy is negative. Ulen also believes that even if Sunstein's analysis is correct so far, Sunstein fails to consider that the Internet is changing very rapidly and that, in the long term, these changes could have a positive impact for deliberative democracy. If Sunstein is correct, however, there are good reasons to be skeptical that the Internet necessarily facilitates democracy and democratic values. On the other hand, we have seen that it promotes democratic ideals such as openness, freedom, access to information, and so forth, and it facilitates communication in ways not possible in the pre-Internet era.

11.2.2 Should the Internet Be Used to Promote Democracy and Democratic Ideals?

We have considered whether the Internet facilitates, and possibly strengthens, democratic values and goals or whether it undermines them. We have seen that while certain aspects of Internet technology threaten democracy, at least in its deliberative sense, others enhance democratic ideals and goals. Now we can turn to our second question regarding democracy and the Internet: should the Internet be used as a tool to promote and spread democracy? And we can begin by noting that democracy, when compared to alternative forms of government, seems an attractive political structure and, arguably, one of the fairest.

Because of these assumptions, Graham points out that it is difficult to get people, especially in the Western world, to engage in a serious debate about the merits of democracy. He correctly notes that democracy, along with its corresponding notion of a "democratic ideal," has won almost universal and largely unquestioning acceptance in the West. Graham also points out, however, that political theorists and philosophers have not always regarded democracy as the best—or, in some cases, not even as an adequate—form of government. For example, in *The Republic*, Plato was highly critical of democratic government and viewed it as a form of mob rule in which important decisions could be made by a citizenry that typically was not well informed on matters involving the state. And in the nineteenth century, philosopher John Stuart Mill also questioned whether democracy was the ideal form of government.[11]

Let us assume, for the sake of argument, that democracy is superior to alternative political structures. We can still ask whether the Internet should be used to advance democracy and democratic ideals.

Sclove believes that all technological decisions should attend primarily to strengthening democracy. So, by extension, Sclove could be interpreted as making the case for the view that the Internet should be used to strengthen, and possibly also promote, democracy. He claims, for example, that "democracy provides the necessary circumstances for deciding freely and fairly which considerations must be taken into account in (technological and nontechnological) decision making."[12] So, there may be good reasons for using technologies such as the Internet to promote democracy. But we have also examined Sunstein's argument for how Internet technology poses a serious threat to deliberative democracy. Thus we may want to carefully assess the pros and cons of using the Internet as an instrument for promoting democracy.

Graham has suggested that the Internet might, perhaps unwittingly, strengthen the "worst aspects" of democracy, because Internet technology facilitates

  i.   political and social *fragmentation*
  ii. *irrationality* (i.e., irrational prejudice in direct democracies)
  iii. *powerlessness* (in representative democracies).

We briefly examine each point.

Political and Social Fragmentation

How does the Internet facilitate political fragmentation, and why is that problematic? We have already seen how the Internet can isolate individuals, insulate groups, and increase group polarization. (Recall Parsell's account of polarization in online communities that we examined in Section 11.1.3.) We also have seen how the Internet can filter information, entrenching existing ideas and reinforcing prejudice rather than encouraging exposure to new ideas. The Internet also fragments society by facilitating the formation of groups who depart from the mainstream perspectives of a cohesive society. An analogy involving television news programming in physical space might help us appreciate how easily political fragmentation can occur and why it can be problematic.

▶ **SCENARIO 11–3:** News Events Viewed from Multiple Ideological Perspectives

Until the advent of cable programming, American television viewers relied primarily on the three major networks for the evening news reports. Even though the program formats varied slightly and even though different anchors delivered the news to viewers, all three presented "mainstream" news reporting that satisfied certain standards of accuracy and credibility before the networks would broadcast it. At times, the members of political groups may have been annoyed with, or possibly even offended by, the way that a particular story was presented, but the news reports were generally descriptive, or factual. Some news programs also included commentaries, usually toward the end of the program, in which the commentator expressed an opinion, but there was a clear line between "factual" reporting and personal opinion.

Now you can select a news program that fits best with and reinforces your political ideology. For example, consider a news report of hostilities between Israelis and Palestinians. If supporters of Israel do not like the way the story is reported on an American news network, and if they have cable or satellite access to Israeli television, they can tune into an Israeli station for their news. Similarly, if Palestinian supporters dislike the American media's coverage, and if they have cable access to an Arab news network such as Al-Jazeera, they can choose to view the news story as an Arab station broadcasts it. On the one hand, these options provide supporters of both sides in this conflict with greater choices and seemingly greater freedom. On the other hand, these options increase fragmentation in American society, which already comprises so many diverse groups. ∎

We can apply a similar analogy to news reports of domestic political issues in the United States. Conservatives and liberals can each interact in online forums, including political blogs, and visit Web sites that exclusively promote the political views of these groups. Of course, we could object at this point by noting that prior to the Internet, people subscribed to newspapers and magazines that were labeled as either radically liberal or radically conservative and therefore filtered in their ideology. But it is more difficult to filter information in physical space because people in most physical communities encounter individuals with ideological perspectives different from their own, even when they seek out only those who share their belief systems. In online communities, however, it is possible for individuals to be in contact with only those people who share their ideological beliefs.

Richard Epstein (2000) worries that in the near future, the concept of the "public square," where ideas have been traditionally debated, could become fragmented into "thousands of highly specialized communities that do not communicate with one another." We next consider some ways that political and social fragmentation can contribute to what Graham calls the "problem of irrationality" in democracy.

Democracy and the Problem of Irrationality

In some respects, the problem of irrationality overlaps with and is reinforced by the problem of social fragmentation. We have seen that people can join extremist political groups, both in cyberspace and in physical space, and we have seen that these groups often filter information in ways not acceptable in "mainstream forums." On the one hand, to join these groups is to exercise one's democratic freedoms and choices. On the other hand, doing so can fragment democracy and undermine the possibility of larger group cohesiveness. Although a plurality of perspectives and values is consistent with democratic ideals, nonreflective and prejudiced views, endorsed by some groups, can also undermine conventional standards for separating rational perspectives from irrational ones.

While the Internet might help spread political opinions, Graham believes that it will not necessarily promote greater "rational evaluation" of these political opinions by people who are exposed to them. Sunstein has also suggested that the Internet, because of the kinds of insulation and polarization it facilitates, can encourage entrenched prejudices that are often irrational. Consider that, at least so far, there has been a much stronger tendency for Internet users to spread the opinions they already have rather than to use the Internet for debate with other users over which views are most rational and beneficial. From this, Graham concludes that the Internet may increase the problem of irrationality by putting the rational exercise of political judgment on a par with "prejudiced and irrational political choices."

The Problem of Powerlessness in Representative Democracies

Graham suggests using the Internet to promote representative democracy might concentrate more power in the hands of representatives instead of ordinary citizens. Consider that elected political leaders (and their staffs) tend to have both greater technological resources and the ability to use them more skillfully than many ordinary citizens. Does the following example illustrate Graham's point? In the 2004 U.S. presidential elections, Carl Rove, a member of the George W. Bush administration, used BlackBerry (smart phone) technology to coordinate with Republican officials across all of the voting precincts in Ohio, a "battleground state" that would determine the winner of that year's election; some political commentators suggested that Rove's coordinating a state-wide, get-out-the-vote effort to targeted voters via the use of BlackBerry technology helped to ensure victory in Ohio, which provided the necessary electoral votes for President Bush to remain in power for four more years. Although it is difficult to prove that Rove's use of this technology helped the incumbent president to remain in power in 2004, we can see how the use of the latest technology in a state or national election can influence the outcome of that election.

Next, consider that as Barack Obama prepared to run in the 2008 U.S. presidential elections, his staff organized a "grassroots" fund-raising strategy on the Internet through various SNSs to raise millions of dollars (mostly in small contributions from young people) to finance his presidential campaign. Now that Obama is in office, it will also be interesting to see whether his 2012 presidential reelection campaign—assuming that Obama runs for a second term—might take advantage of the latest technologies available at that time to win reelection and remain in power for four additional years.

It would seem that Graham's point that political parties in power can use the Internet and related technologies to maintain their power may have some merit, but it can also show why using these technologies to retain political power in democracies can be problematic. If Graham's contention that the Internet could easily be used to promote the worst aspects of democracy is accurate, we can seriously question whether the Internet should be used to spread democracy.

Table 11.2 summarizes advantages and disadvantages of using the Internet to promote democracy and democratic ideals.

11.2.3 Blogging and Democracy

We next consider the impact that online communication forums such as blogs will likely have for democracy. In Section 11.1.2, we briefly examined some aspects of blogging and the blogosphere vis-à-vis our analysis of online communities, and we noted that one type of blog was the "political blog." To what extent do political blogs reinforce democratic values and ideals, and how can they undermine them? Insofar as blogs function as instruments for communicating and disseminating information about important political issues, they would seem to have a positive effect for democracy. But we also saw that the standards for ensuring accuracy in political blogs are not always adequate.

TABLE 11.2   Considerations for Using the Internet to Promote Democracy

Advantages	Disadvantages
Empowers individuals by giving them choices regarding membership in online communities	Increases social fragmentation and discourages rational debate
Promotes individual freedom and decision making	Increases irrationality and prejudice (in direct democracies)
Gives individuals a voice in governance issues in cyberspace	Increases powerlessness for individuals (in representative democracies)

During the 2008 U.S. presidential elections, some extreme right-wing political bloggers reported that Barack Obama was a Muslim and that he was not born in the United States.[13] At the same time, some radical left-wing bloggers reported that (vice presidential candidate) Sara Palin's youngest child was really her grandchild and that Palin was protecting her unmarried daughter from embarrassment.[14] Neither story was vetted in the way that a report submitted by a professional journalist working for a reputable news organization would be, and neither story would likely have been published in a reputable newspaper. But these stories were read online by numerous people, many of whom may have assumed the reports about Obama and Palin to be true merely because they were published on the Internet.

As (hard copy) newspaper subscriptions continue to decline, and as more and more people get their news online, we may have to worry about the standards of accuracy that apply in the online political news media. A democracy depends on truthful information to flourish and survive. So perhaps we should be concerned about the lack of veracity in some political blogs and the implications that the mass dissemination of false information online may have for the future of democracy. However, some analysts do not seem concerned about the potentially negative effects of blogging for democracy. For example, Alvin Goldman (2008) points out that even if individual blogs are biased, it doesn't follow that the entire blogosphere is. (Recall our discussion of the Fallacy of Composition in Chapter 3, where we saw that attributes that apply to the part do not necessarily apply to the whole.) As Goldman aptly puts the matter, "the reliability of the blogosphere shouldn't be identified with the reliability of a single blog."[15]

Goldman suggests that the "zealous advocacy" of some political bloggers, as well as the "adversarial process" facilitated by blogs in general, may even turn out to be a good thing. For example, he believes the system of checks and balances, which are "collectively stronger than the kinds of filtering mechanisms used in the conventional media" may be a good mechanism for "truth-determination." If Goldman is correct on this point, the blogosphere may ultimately contribute to the preservation of democratic values in the Internet era.

In concluding this section, we note that many controversial issues affecting the Internet and democracy have not been examined. For example, there are controversies surrounding e-voting, as well as the selling of votes online, which are beyond the intended scope of this chapter. Our analysis of Internet and democracy issues here was not intended to be exhaustive; rather, our aim has been to analyze these issues mainly as they relate to concerns affecting online community life.

▶ 11.3 VIRTUAL ENVIRONMENTS AND VIRTUAL REALITY

We have examined some issues affecting online democracy and online communities; online communities are also often referred to as *virtual communities*. They are "virtual" in the sense that they exist in cyberspace, which is usually equated with *virtual space*. But what is virtual space? In contrast to physical space, or geographical space, virtual space can be viewed as a range of computer-generated environments that could not exist without computers and cybertechnology. These environments, in turn, include online or virtual communities, as well as virtual reality (VR) applications such as video games.

Although we now have a working definition of a virtual space or a virtual environment, we have yet to define "virtual." This term can be used in three senses. Sometimes it is contrasted with "real," as in distinguishing virtual objects from real ones. At other times the term is contrasted with "actual," as when a person says that she has "virtually finished" her project (i.e., she has not actually, or literally, finished it, but she believes that for practical purposes, she has finished it). The term "virtual" can also express feeling "as if" physically present in a situation, as when you are conversing with a friend online or on a telephone; even though you could be literally thousands of miles away from each other, the sense that you are interacting in real time makes you feel as if you are both in the same room. (Contrast this experience with radio and traditional broadcast communications, where messages can be transmitted in only one direction at a time.) We should keep these three different senses of "virtual" in mind as we examine ethical aspects of virtual environments, including VR applications.

11.3.1 Defining Virtual Reality

Philip Brey (1999, 2008) defines virtual reality, or VR, as "a three dimensional interactive computer generated environment that incorporates a first person perspective." Notice three important features in Brey's definition of VR:

- interactivity,
- a three-dimensional environment,
- a first-person perspective.

How does this distinguish VR from other computer-mediated environments? First, *interactivity* requires that users be able to navigate and manipulate the represented environment. Because a *three-dimensional environment* is required in VR, neither text-based computer-generated environments nor two-dimensional graphic environments will qualify. Brey also points out that a *first-person perspective* requires a single locus from which the environment is perceived and interacted with; the first-person perspective also requires an immersion in the virtual world rather than simply an "experience" of that world as an "object that can be (partially) controlled by the outside."

We can distinguish between Brey's notion of virtual reality, including VR applications that are three-dimensional, and a more broadly defined notion of "virtual environment." Recall our earlier discussion of online communities in Section 11.1, which included some two-dimensional virtual environments. For example, LambdaMOO would be considered a two-dimensional virtual environment (that was also a text-based forum). So LambdaMOO would not qualify as a virtual reality environment, or VR

Figure 11.1   Virtual environments.

application, as Brey defines it. As an online forum, however, it would qualify as a type of virtual environment.

Figure 11.1 illustrates some manifestations of virtual environments.

In Section 11.1.3 we noted that many actions that are considered morally objectionable in the physical world can be performed easily in online communities and forums. Virtual environments made possible in video games also enable users to engage in morally objectionable acts, including (virtual) prostitution, pornography, pedophilia, torture, mutilation, and murder. Brey argues that ethical concerns involving VR applications and virtual environments can be analyzed in terms of two broad categories: (A) *behavioral issues* affecting interactions between individuals, and (B) *representational issues* affecting the design of these applications. We begin with an analysis of (A); issues affecting (B) are examined in Section 11.3.3.

11.3.2   Ethical Aspects of Behavior in VR Applications and Games

Are ethical issues involving behavior in VR applications, including online games, different from those associated with morally controversial acts displayed on television or played out in board games? Consider that television programs sometimes display violent acts and some board games allow participants to act out morally controversial roles—how are VR applications different? Brey (1999) points out that in VR applications, users are actively engaged, whereas television viewers are passive. VR users are not spectators; rather, they are more like actors, as are board game players, who also act out roles in certain board games. This common feature suggests that there might not be much difference between the two kinds of games; however, Brey notes that VR applications, unlike board games, simulate the world in a way that gives it a much greater appearance of reality. And in VR, the player has a first-person perspective of what it is like to perform certain acts and roles, including some that are criminal or immoral, or both. We first examine some ethical aspects of online video games involving multiple players.

A distinction is sometimes made between single-player video games and multiplayer online games; the latter are commonly referred to either as MMOGS (massively multiplayer online games) or MMORPGS (massively multiplayer online role-playing games). An example of a MMOG is *Second Life* (designed by Linden Lab), which includes members called "Residents" who do not engage in some of the traditional role-playing activities available in many MMORPGs. (As of March 2008, Second Life had approximately 13 million registered accounts.[16]) Examples of MMORPGs include popular online games such as *World of Warcraft (WOW)*, *EVE Online*, and *Entropia Universe*. WOW is perhaps the most popular MMORPG, boasting over 11 million paying subscribers as of 2009.[17]

Many MMORPGs are organized around various "clans" or "guilds" that members join; if they wish, members can also pool their resources (Cooke 2006). Typically, these games are also developed around systems that are either "class-based" or "skill points-based." In the former scheme, a player's chosen division can determine his or her character's "strengths and weaknesses." So, players are encouraged to "interact with others and form teams to balance out strengths and weaknesses."[18] In Second Life, for example, "Residents" can socialize, participate in group activities, and create trade items (virtual property) and services with one another. The virtual currency used in that MMOG is the Linden Dollar (linden, or L$), which can also be traded for real currencies via a "resident to resident marketplace" that is facilitated by Linden Lab. Residents in Second Life, as well as players in other MMOGs and MMORPGs, often select an avatar (a graphical representation) to represent themselves.

Violent and Sexually Offensive Acts in MMORPGs and MMOGs

Why are MMORPGs and MMOGs controversial from an ethical perspective? In other words, which kinds of morally objectionable behavior do they make possible? Some critics claim that Second Life facilitates child pornography because virtual characters who are adults in real life can have sex with virtual characters who are children in that MMOG (Singer 2007). Cases of virtual prostitution on Second Life have also been reported—i.e., where some Residents were "paid to (use their avatar to) perform sex acts or to serve as escorts" (Brey 2008). So, if these reports are correct, there are clearly some forms of sexually offensive acts that take place in MMOGs and MMORPGs, which would not be tolerated outside these gaming environments.

In addition to concerns about sexually offensive behavior in online games, many worry about the kinds of violent acts that are also carried out in these environments. Monique Wonderly (2008) suggests that some forms of violence permitted in online games may be "more morally problematic" than pornography and other kinds of sexually offensive behavior in virtual environments. She points out, for example, that relatively few video games "permit sexual interaction between characters," and even fewer allow "deviant sexual conduct." But she notes that many popular games permit and that some "even *require* copious amounts of wanton graphic violence."[19]

Are violent acts in MMORPGs, including virtual murder, more morally problematic than the pornographic and sexually deviant acts that also have been carried out in these games? Or should violent acts such as virtual murder be tolerated as acceptable behavior? Morgan Luck (2009) notes that while most people agree that murder is wrong, they do not seem to be bothered by virtual murder in MMORPGs. He points out, for example, that some might see the virtual murder of a character in a video game as no different from the "taking of a pawn in a chess game." But Luck also notes that people have different intuitions about acts in virtual environments that involve morally objectionable sexual behavior, such as child pornography and pedophilia. And he worries that the kind of reasoning used to defend virtual murder in games could, unwittingly, be extended to defend virtual pedophilia. For example, he notes that the following line of reasoning, which for our purposes can be expressed in standard argument form, may unintentionally succeed in doing this.

1. Allowing acts of virtual murder will not likely increase the number of actual murders.

2. Allowing acts of virtual pedophilia may significantly increase the amount of actual pedophilia.

3. Therefore, virtual pedophilia is immoral, but virtual murder is not.[20]

While this kind of argument may appeal to some, Luck points out that it is difficult to defend because of the lack of empirical evidence needed to confirm both (1) and (2). More importantly, however, if (2) could be shown to be false, then virtual pedophilia, like virtual murder, would not be immoral (according to the reasoning used in this argument).

With respect to (2), Neil Levy (2002) has suggested that allowing virtual child pornography may even "reduce the harm to actual children" because it would provide an "acceptable outlet" for pedophiles and would encourage pornographers to seek an "alternative to real children." (But Levy does not believe that virtual child pornography should be acceptable; in fact, he opposes it for alternative reasons.)

A different kind of rationale for why virtual child pornography should be prohibited has been offered by Per Sandin (2004), who argues that it can cause significant harm to many people who find it revolting or offensive. But Brey (2008) points out that a problem with Sandin's argument is that it "gives too much weight to harm caused by offense." As Brey puts it, "If actions should be outlawed whenever they offend a large group of people, then individual rights would be drastically curtailed, and many things, ranging from homosexual behavior to interracial marriage, would still be illegal."[21] So none of the arguments considered thus far succeeds in showing why acts that are morally objectionable in physical space should not be allowed in virtual environments.

Assessing the Nature of "Harm" in Virtual Environments

Can a plausible argument be constructed to show why it is wrong to perform acts in virtual environments that would be considered immoral in real life? We have seen some difficulties with arguments that tried to show that allowing morally objectionable actions in virtual environments will likely lead to an increase (or decrease) in those actions in the real world. Other arguments have tried to link, or in some cases de-link, the kind of harm caused in virtual environments with the sense of harm one might experience in the real world. For example, some arguments have tried to show that sexually offensive acts in virtual environments can cause harm to vulnerable groups (such as children and women) in the real world.[22] (However, these arguments tend to lack sufficient empirical evidence to substantiate the claims they make.) On the contrary, some arguments claim that no one is physically harmed in virtual murder or, for that matter, in any act performed only in a virtual environment. But these arguments have also been criticized.

Does it follow that no one can be harmed in a virtual world? Can we infer that any harm that could be experienced in the virtual realm is not "real harm" but only *virtual harm*? In our discussion of logical fallacies in Chapter 3, we saw that using this line of reasoning commits the *virtuality fallacy*.

We saw that "virtual" is ambiguous in at least three ways, and we noted that sometimes virtual is contrasted with real in a way that might suggest that a "virtual harm" is equivalent to an "unreal harm." Because a harm caused in a virtual world might not result in physical harm to a "flesh-and-blood" person, however, it doesn't follow that the harm caused is not real. The LambdaMOO incident (described in Section 11.1.3), which involved a "virtual rape," can help us to see why harm caused in virtual environments is not itself limited to virtual characters in a virtual environment. We begin by asking why (the character) Bungle's behavior in LambdaMOO is morally objectionable. After all, it was not a "real rape," and it did not result in physical harm to any "flesh-and-blood" individuals. Brey (1999) believes that we can use two different kinds of arguments to show why it is wrong to engage in immoral acts in virtual environments:

a. the argument "from moral development,"

b. the argument from "psychological harm."

To illustrate the argument from *moral development,* Brey suggests that we can extend an argument advanced by Immanuel Kant for the treatment of animals to the treatment of virtual characters. Kant argued that even if we have no direct moral obligation to treat animals kindly, we should, because our treating animals kindly can influence our development of moral attitudes and behaviors for treating human beings. Similarly, then, the way we treat virtual characters may ultimately affect the way we treat real-life characters—raping virtual characters in virtual space, or even viewing such a rape, could desensitize us to the act of rape itself as it affects flesh-and-blood individuals in physical space.

The argument from *psychological harm* suggests that the way we refer to characters who represent a particular group can cause harm to actual members of the group. Consider a cartoon depicting a woman being raped: Actual (flesh-and-blood) women may suffer psychological harm from seeing, or possibly even knowing about, this cartoon image, even though none of them, as flesh-and-blood individuals, is being raped, either physically or as represented by the cartoon. Extending this analogy to virtual space, it would follow that the "rape" of a virtual woman in a virtual environment, such as a MOO, MMOG, MMORPG, etc., can also cause psychological harm to flesh-and-blood women.

Virtual Economies and "Gold Farming"

Thus far we have examined behavioral issues in virtual environments from the perspectives of violence and sexually offensive acts, as well as from the vantage point of the kind of harm that can result. But other behavior-related controversies involve some of the "virtual economies" that have arisen because of activities made possible in online games. We noted earlier that some MMORPGs and MMOGs have their own monetary currencies. For example, Second Life uses the Linden Dollar (linden, or L$), which its Residents can both use in in-game transactions and exchange outside the game for real currencies such as the U.S. dollar or the euro. As a result, virtual economies have emerged. Brey (2008) believes that their emergence can also increase the likelihood that moral controversies will arise in these environments—as Brey notes, people will be "more likely to act immorally if money is to be made or if valuable property is to be had."

Virtual property, as in the case of virtual money, can be acquired and exchanged with players in games. It can also be sold and exchanged outside the game to interested parties (in the physical world). In some cases, the virtual property has become so desirable that it has led to violent acts in the real world. Dorothy Warner and Mike Raiter (2005) describe an incident in China where a person who had stolen someone's virtual sword in a MMOG was murdered in real life by the "sword's" owner. So virtual economies can have real-life implications and can result in physical harm to individuals in the real world. One controversial activity associated with virtual economies in gaming environments is a form of labor and economic exchange called "gold farming."

Kai Kimppa and Andrew Bisset (2008) define gold farming as "playing an online computer game for the purpose of gaining items of value within the internal economy of the game and selling these to other players for real money."[23] These items can include "desirable items" as well as in-game money (where the rules defining the game's internal economy permit this); they can also include "highly developed" game characters. All of these items can also be sold via online auctions or designated Web sites. Kimppa and Bisset point out that the 2009 "in-game gold market" globally is estimated at 7 billion dollars; they also note that the practice of gold farming is most popular in countries such as China and Mexico that have both low-average income levels and "relatively good access to the Internet."[24]

Gold farming has also raised concerns about working conditions in the real world. For example, Warner and Raiter describe a situation in rural China where people who participate in World of Warcraft were paid to work 12-hour shifts of gold farming; the workers would acquire "virtual gold" within the game and then sell it outside the game to interested players. The business became profitable, Warner and Reiter point out, because many players who can afford to purchase the virtual gold preferred to buy it rather than to do the work necessary to earn it in the game.[25] It was also more advantageous to the "gold farmers" themselves, who could earn more money obtaining and selling virtual gold than they could in traditional agricultural work. But this practice has also led to reported cases of Chinese sweatshop laborers who work "day and night in conditions of practical slavery" to acquire the virtual gold and virtual resources (Brey 2008). If these reports are true, gold mining would seem to raise some serious ethical concerns. Brey believes that "many new ethical issues in virtual worlds" will likely arise because of the kind and the amount of "time, money, and social capital" people are willing to invest in virtual property and virtual economies.[26]

11.3.3 Ethical Concerns Affecting Misrepresentation, Bias, and Indecent Representations in VR Applications

Thus far, we have examined some *behavioral,* or what Brey (1999) also refers to as "interactive," controversies regarding ethical dimensions of VR applications. The other ethical aspect that needs to be considered, in Brey's VR model, has to do with the ways in which virtual characters and virtual objects are *represented* in these applications. Note that this set of ethical concerns includes not only virtual characters in games, but also features of VR applications used to simulate and model objects in the physical world.

Brey (2008) argues that representations can become morally problematic when they are

1. *misrepresentations* (that can cause harm by failing to uphold *standards of accuracy*),

2. *biased representations* (that fail to uphold *standards of fairness*),

3. *indecent representations* (that violate standards of decency and public morality).

Misrepresentation ranges from cases in which there is no correspondence between the virtual entity and its corresponding physical (or nonvirtual) entity to cases in which the correspondence is almost, but not fully, accurate. To illustrate this point, Brey uses examples of VR applications that have been developed to simulate visual features of buildings such as the Louvre or Taj Mahal, or to simulate the behavior of certain kinds of automobiles or airplanes. When a VR application does not accurately portray all of the characteristics or features of the physical (or nonvirtual) entities represented—whether by intention or as a result of an oversight—the application *mis*represents reality.

Misrepresenting entities with respect to descriptive features, however, can be distinguished from (otherwise accurate) representations that favor certain values or interests over others. Brey calls the latter "biased" representation; it can result from the choice of model. For example, *softbots* (or "bots") in the form of avatars, which often display human qualities, could be used in a VR application to represent members of a racial or minority group; even though the representation may be structurally accurate, if the bot is used in a way that suggests a racial stereotype, it can fail to accurately portray a member of the racial group. Paul Ford (2001) describes a scenario where a bot represents an African American "shoe-shine boy" in a video game. Although the bot does not misrepresent any physical characteristics of the particular African American represented, the depiction is a biased caricature of African Americans.

Brey describes *indecent* representations as representations that (a) are considered "shocking or offensive," (b) breach "established rules of good behavior or morality," or (c) are somehow "shocking to the senses or moral sensibilities." He also notes, however, that getting agreement on this category is difficult because standards of decency can vary widely across different individuals and cultures and thus may seem relativistic—i.e., "what is shocking or immoral to some will not be so to others."[27] For example, he points out that while some will find depictions of nudity or physical violence acceptable, others will deem such depictions to be unacceptable. So, there will often be disagreements about which representations qualify as indecent.

However, Brey also points out that the context in which a representation take place can also be a factor in determining whether it is considered decent. He uses the example of a representation of open heart surgery to illustrate this point, noting that a representation of this procedure in the context of a medical simulator may not be offensive to someone considering whether to undergo the surgery. However, it could be deemed offensive in other contexts, such as using the representation as a background in a music video.

Brey believes that VR model builders are morally obligated to avoid misrepresentation, biased representation, and indecent representation in designing VR applications. Extending an analytical scheme developed by Richard Mason (1994), Brey (1999) argues that developers of VR systems need to both recognize who the stakeholders are in those systems and take into account their values and interests as they develop VR models. He suggests that Mason's scheme works well for understanding and analyzing moral responsibility issues involved in developing VR systems that misrepresent or bias stakeholders.

Figure 11.2 Brey's scheme for analyzing ethical issues in virtual environments.

While Brey (2008) provides three useful distinctions in helping us to sort out representational issues affecting VR applications, he also suggests that identifying and evaluating the locus of moral responsibility for the harm caused by them may be more difficult to pinpoint. It would seem that the developers of VR systems, who design applications that incorporate inaccurate, biased, or indecent representations, should bear at least some of the moral responsibility for any harm caused by their applications. But it would also seem that users of VR applications who abuse or misuse representations in ways that are indecent or biased in virtual environments should also be held morally responsible for harm that results.

Figure 11.2 summarizes Brey's scheme.

Our analysis of controversial aspects of virtual environments thus far has focused mainly on their social impact and how they can affect community life. We next examine the implications of virtual environments in particular, and cybertechnology in general, for personal identity.

▶ 11.4 PERSONAL IDENTITY AND CYBERTECHNOLOGY

Social scientists have analyzed some effects that computers and cybertechnology have had on personal identity. One of the early cases that caught the attention of social scientists involved a male psychologist in an online forum; his alter ego (or "cyberego") was a woman who had become crippled as a result of an automobile accident. Under this alias, "she" joined an online forum for disabled persons and quickly struck up romantic exchanges with a few of the forum's members. When participants eventually learned "her" true identity, they were outraged. Some felt manipulated by the psychologist's use of a fraudulent identity, and others complained that they were victims of "gender fraud." Lindsy Van Gelder (1991) describes this incident as "the strange case of the electronic lover."

In one sense, the "electronic lover" incident could be examined under the category of online communities (discussed in Section 11.1) because of the impact of the psychologist's behavior on the online forum and its members. Yet we can also reflect on the implications this case has for personal identity; for example, was the male psychologist simply acting out his "would-be personality" in cyberspace instead of in physical space, as some might suggest? Or does cyberspace make a difference for understanding the identities that can emerge in different online communities?

Mitch Parsell (2008) describes the Internet as a "powerful new force" for what he calls "the manufacture of identity." He believes that this technology

> . . . offers an unparalleled ability to create ourselves in our own image. It gives users an unprecedented capacity to determine their initial presentations to others. . . . In short, it enables users to be masters of their identity.[28]

Are Parsell's remarks exaggerated or overstated? Or has cybertechnology indeed provided us with a "new force" for constructing our personal identities? This question has captured the interests of some psychologists and social scientists who have conducted research on the relationship between computer technology and personal identity.

11.4.1 The Computer as a Medium of Self-expression and Self-discovery

Sherry Turkle (2005) notes that by the mid-1980s, computers had become an "evocative object"—i.e., an object that "provoked self-reflection." In the first edition of her (now) classic book *The Second Self: Computers and the Human Spirit* (1985), Turkle suggested that a computer could be viewed as a model for analyzing and constructing one's identity. She also noted that the computer has become a medium through which people could discover their personal identity; for example, computers provide a context in which individuals can try out different cognitive styles and different methods of problem solving to ultimately discover which style or method they prefer. Because people develop their own unique style of computing, Turkle argues that the computational environment becomes an extension of themselves, in much the same way that their manner of dress is an extension of their personality. In this sense, she believes, the computer is a "medium of self-expression" as well as self-discovery.

Turkle's early studies focused mainly on the role that stand-alone, or non-networked, computers played in the relationship between personal identity and computers. Her subsequent research in this area has centered on interactions involving networked computers; in particular, her studies examine how behavior in networked environments significantly impacts our relationships with our "selves" as we conceive them. To illustrate several of her key points, Turkle (1995) uses examples involving MUDs (multiuser dimensions). MUDs are similar to MOOs (defined in Section 11.1.3) in that they are simulated or virtual environments in which members participate. Both forums enable users to construct "rooms" in cyberspace and to converse and interact with others in those rooms.

11.4.2 MUD Selves and Distributed Personal Identities

In MUDs and MOOs, participants can construct new identities and selves. Turkle maintains that as people participate, or "play characters," in MUDs, they "construct new selves" through social interaction. As Turkle also notes, however, "MUD selves" are constituted by and dependent upon interaction with machines; if the machine is taken away, "the Mud selves cease to exist."[29] Users participate in MUDs anonymously; they are known only by the names of their MUD character or characters. In MUDs, users can *be* (i.e., can represent themselves textually or graphically as) characters as different from their actual selves as they like; Turkle notes, for example, that the obese can be slender, and the old can be young. She points out that MUD users can also express multiple and often unexplored aspects of the self, and they can "play with their identity" by trying out new roles. In different MUDs the same physical person can represent himself as a seductive woman, a macho man, or even a creature of unspecified gender; so one's identity on the computer can be, Turkle suggests, the sum of one's "distributed presence."[30]

Acts in which individuals assume different identities or different gender roles are hardly unique to the world of MUDs and virtual environments; for example, transvestites in physical space can selectively represent themselves as member of the opposite sex in contexts of their choosing. Perhaps you are familiar with the movie and, later, Broadway musical *Victor, Victoria* in which a woman pretends to be a man playing the part of a woman. But gender role reversals in the physical world do not seem to have the same significant social impact as they do in cyberspace. Turkle notes that since traditional theater and role-playing games take place in physical space, they enable one to "step in and out of character." MUDs, on the contrary, offer parallel identities and parallel lives, and this parallelism encourages treating off-screen and on-screen lives as equally real.

Turkle notes that some of her research subjects experience their world through interactions in "multiple windows"; real life (or RL) is considered by some MUD participants as simply "one more window." One of Turkle's research subjects, whom she refers to as Doug, remarked that RL is not typically his "best" window. Turkle points out that in MUDs, we can "project ourselves into our own dramas in which we are producer, director, and star"; in this sense, Turkle believes that MUDs provide a "new location for acting out our fantasies."[31]

▶ 11.5 OUR SENSE OF SELF IN THE CYBERERA

We have considered arguments that behavior in virtual or computer-mediated environments can significantly affect, and possibly even alter, the personal identity of some individuals. In this section, we focus on the impact that cybertechnology has for our *sense of self*, especially in our relation to nature and the universe. We begin by noting that social scientists often describe three major epochs in human civilization: the agricultural age, the industrial age, and the information age. Each has been characterized by revolutionary technological breakthroughs in gaining control over nature.

At the dawn of the agricultural age, people who had previously led nomadic lives developed technology that enabled them to control the production of crops by controlling elements of nature rather than conforming to nature's seasonal rotations, which often required migrating to different locations. In the industrial age, humans harnessed steam power. With steam power, people were no longer compelled to set up communities close to large bodies of water that provided much of their energy. We have now entered a phase that social scientists call "the information age," the third great epoch. In this section, we consider the impact that this relatively recent shift has for the way we conceive of ourselves as human beings.

We should note that cybertechnology is not the first technology, or the first scientific discovery resulting from technological innovations, to have deeply affected our sense of self in relation to nature and the universe. Mary B. Williams describes three discoveries that have had such an impact on our sense of self:

> The first such milestone, a great (and greatly humbling) challenge to our sense of human beings as uniquely important, occurred when the Copernican revolution established that Earth, the human home, was not at the center of the universe. The second milestone was Charles Darwin's conclusion that emergence of Homo sapiens was . . . the result of evolution from lower species by the process of natural selection. The third milestone resulted from the work of Karl Marx and Sigmund Freud, which showed intellectual, social, and individual creativity to be the result of nonrational (unconscious) libidinal or economic forces—not, as has been believed, the products of the almost god-like powers of the human mind.[32]

Because of these three milestones, Williams suggests that we have a much humbler view of our place in the universe than our ancestors did. The interesting question for us, of course, is whether computerization and cybertechnology might join the other milestone events in deeply changing the way we see ourselves.

11.5.1 Cybertechnology as a "Defining Technology"

Although cybertechnology may be the latest in a series of technologies to have a significant influence on the way human beings have come to see themselves, it is not, as we have noted, the first technology to do so. J. David Bolter (1984) claims that many people in Western cultures have come to see themselves in terms of what he calls a *defining technology*, which "develops links, metaphorical or otherwise, with a culture's science, philosophy, or literature."[33] As such, "defining technologies" have been used by philosophers and humanists to define both human beings and their universe in a given age or time period. Bolter describes three ages in Western culture when humans have used a defining technology: the ancient Greek world, the Renaissance, and the contemporary computer age.

In the twentieth century we became fascinated with computer technology. Even though other technologies such as electricity, indoor plumbing, automobiles, etc., were arguably more important for day-to-day living than computers in the mid-twentieth century, Bolter notes that many philosophers and scientists used computer and computing metaphors to describe humans and their relationship to the universe. Twentieth-century computer science pioneer Alan Turing was one of the first to articulate interesting connections between the computer and the human mind as a manipulator of logical symbols. Acknowledging Turing's insight, Bolter uses the phrase "Turing's man" to depict those who view humans via the defining metaphor of computer technology. (Bolter contrasts "Turing's man" with "Plato's man" and "Descartes' man," both of which are expressions he uses to describe the representatives of two previous eras in which a "defining technology" was also highly influential.) Turing's man sees nature as *information*, and humans (or human brains) as *information processing engines*. We examine Turing's contribution to the field of artificial intelligence in Section 11.5.2.

To support Bolter's thesis that we see ourselves more and more in terms of the computer, we have only to reflect on the language we use to describe ourselves. For example, Bolter points out that when psychologists speak of "input and output states of the brain," or of the brain's hardware and software, they exemplify Turing's men. And when cognitive psychologists study the "mind's algorithm for searching long-term memory," or when linguists treat human language as if it were a programming code, they, too, are "Turing's men." Psychologists and cognitive scientists who suggest that the human mind is like a computer in that it "encodes, stores, retrieves, and processes information" are also, in Bolter's view, Turing's men.[34]

Describing some contemporary uses of language that would seem to support Bolter's insight that we have come to see ourselves in terms of computer metaphors, Turkle (2005) points out that one of her students had recast the idea of Freudian slips as "information processing errors." Turkle also notes that by the mid-1980s, people in their everyday conversations began to describe human mental activity in "computational terms"—for example, when uttering expressions such as "Excuse me, I need to clear my buffer" and "I won't be happy until I debug this problem."

Not only do we think of ourselves in computer-like terms, but we also now describe many objects and events in our environment in the language of computer technology. Bolter asks us to consider the economist who describes his work in terms of drawing up "input-output diagrams of the nation's business." We might also consider the person who describes her automobile, which cannot be used because it is in the repair shop, as being "down"; the manager running a business meeting who requests that a certain discussion should be taken "off-line"; and a cartoon portraying an expectant mother impatiently complaining that she has to wait nine months to "download her baby." These uses of computer language would seem to confirm Bolter's point that we increasingly see our world in terms of computer metaphors.

11.5.2 Artificial Intelligence and Implications for our Sense of Self

The view that only humans have intelligence and are rational can be challenged on two fronts. First, research in animal intelligence suggests that many primates, dolphins, and whales demonstrate skills we typically count as rational while many humans cannot demonstrate these same skills. Second, work in artificial intelligence (AI) and cognitive science shows that computers can exhibit certain forms of rational activity. In fact, questions that have surfaced in AI research cause some philosophers and scientists to reconsider our definitions of rationality, intelligence, knowledge, and learning.

Research and development in AI also question the nature of consciousness; for example, cognitive scientists now ask whether consciousness is a uniquely human attribute or whether it might be an *emergent property*—that is, capable of "emerging" in "highly intelligent" AI systems. Stanley Kubrick's classic 1967 film *2001: A Space Odyssey* portrays a computer named HAL with higher-order thinking functions resembling human consciousness. In addition to performing ordinary computational tasks, HAL engages in sophisticated conversations with members of the spaceship's crew, plays chess, and criticizes art. To take control of the spaceship from HAL, the sole surviving member of the crew removes the logic components of HAL's higher-order ("mental") functions: HAL is forced to undergo a sort of "lobotomy." Of course, HAL is merely science fiction, but then AI has progressed considerably since HAL's film debut in 1967.

Today, cognitive scientists and AI researchers working with computer systems called *neural networks* are on the verge of modeling higher-order thinking in these systems. Suppose that we reach general agreement that human consciousness can be understood as an emergent property and that conscious activity—similar to that of humans—emerges whenever a sufficient number of neurons (or "connection strengths" in neural networks) are present. If this were to happen, consider the implications for our sense of self.

Are computers indeed capable of exhibiting human-like intelligence? In 1950, computer science pioneer Alan Turing confidently predicted that by the year 2000 computers would be able to pass a test, which has come to be called the *Turing Test*, demonstrating their intelligence. Turing envisioned a person engaged in a conversation with a computer (located in a room not visible to the human), unable to tell whether he or she was conversing with another human or with a machine. And while most AI experts would concede that Turing's prophecy has not yet been fully realized, few working in AI doubt that sophisticated computers can now exhibit some form of intelligence and, in some cases, emulate aspects of human rationality. In 1997 an IBM computer program called *Deep Blue* defeated Gary Kasparov, then reigning champion, in the competition for the world chess title.

Unfortunately, an in-depth discussion of the current debate in AI regarding the question of machine intelligence is beyond the scope of this chapter; however, let us assume that at least some current computers do possess some degree of intelligence. Because historically many people have believed that intelligence is a distinguishing characteristic for humans, we can see how developments in AI raise profound questions for our notions of self and what it means to be human.

Before concluding this section, we briefly consider some implications of softbot, or "bot," technology (based on developments in AI) can have for our sense of self. Bots in the form of avatars (described in Section 11.3.3) and personal digital assistants have already begun to appear on computer screens and are designed to assist users in organizing their work schedules, reminding them of important scheduled meetings, arranging travel, and so forth. Even though they are virtual entities, some bots exhibit human-like features when viewed on computer screens and they can easily be confused with virtual representations of actual flesh-and-blood characters that can also appear on these screens. Can we tell the difference between them? Consider that some bots exhibit characteristics and stereotypic traits associated with certain professions. For example, a bot designed to interact with other bots, as well as with humans, as a "negotiation agent" may have the persona of a broker, and after interacting with your personal bot (or human-like, digital agent) over a period of time, you may sense that you are dealing with (the screen representation of) an actual person.

Andrew Clark (2003) examines some potential implications that recent technologies (enhanced by AI) can have for our sense of self. For example, suppose you use a PDA (personal digital assistant). Is your PDA part of your "extended self" that "knows" your friend's telephone numbers and your appointments for the next month? If I use "telepresence" technology, where am "I"? Also, who is responsible for "my" actions when my computer (as an extended system) and I make a decision to act?[35]

At present, we can only speculate about the implications that AI bots, as well as other "intelligent entities" of the future, will have for our sense of what it means to be a human being. Should we proceed with developments in AI, realizing that we may create intelligences vastly superior to our own? Perhaps John Weckert (2004) articulates this concern best when he asks:

> Can we, and do we want to, live with artificial *intelligences*? We can happily live with fish that swim better than we do, with dogs that hear better, hawks that see and fly better, and so on, but things that can reason better seem to be in a different and altogether more worrying category . . . What would such [developments mean for] our view of what it is to be human?[36] [Italics Weckert]

We examine some additional issues affecting AI in Chapter 12, where we consider some controversial questions involving bionic chip implants, cyborgs, and whether (at least some) AI entities deserve moral consideration. Our analysis of AI is this chapter has focused on its implications for our sense of self and what it means to be human in the age of cybertechnology.

▶ 11.6 CHAPTER SUMMARY

In this chapter we have examined some social and ethical issues that relate to community and personal identity in cyberspace. In particular, we have seen how cybertechnology has affected our traditional notion of community, and we considered arguments for the pros and cons of online communities vs. traditional communities. We also examined some implications of online communities in general, and political blogs in particular, for democracy and democratic ideals in cyberspace. We then looked at virtual reality (VR) applications, including online video games, and considered their implications for community and personal identity. Finally, we considered the impact that cybertechnology in general, and developments in artificial intelligence (AI) in particular, have had thus far for our sense of self and what it means to be human.

▶ REVIEW QUESTIONS

1. What are online communities?
2. How do online communities differ from traditional communities?
3. In what ways do blogs function as online communities.
4. Does the Internet facilitate democracy? Explain.
5. Why does Cass Sunstein believe that the Internet has both democracy-enhancing and democracy-threatening features?
6. What does Sunstein mean by "deliberative democracy"?
7. Why does he believe that Internet filters "undermine deliberative democracy"?
8. According to Graham, how does the Internet contribute to political and social fragmentation?
9. Why does Graham believe that the Internet poses a "problem of irrationality" in direct democracies?
10. What does he mean when he says that the Internet contributes to the "problem of powerlessness" in indirect democracies?
11. What implications do political blogs have for democracy and democratic values?
12. What is a virtual environment?
13. Describe three senses in which "virtual" is often used ambiguously.
14. How does Philip Brey define *virtual reality* (VR)?

15. How are VR applications distinguishable from other kinds of applications and forums that also comprise virtual environments?
16. What does Sherry Turkle mean when she says that the computer is a medium for self-discovery and self-expression?
17. What are MUDs, and what implications can they have for our understanding of personal identity?
18. Describe some of the implications that cybertechnology has had thus far for our sense of self.
19. What does J. David Bolter mean by a "defining technology" and by the expression "Turing's man"?
20. What is artificial intelligence (or AI)?

▶ DISCUSSION QUESTIONS

1. Identify and briefly describe some of the pros and cons of online communities. What does Mitch Parsell mean when says that online communities with an "extremely narrow focus" contribute to social polarization. Assess his arguments for that claim. Do you agree with Parsell? On balance, have online communities enhanced or threatened community life? Explain.
2. Evaluate the argument by Cocking and Matthews for why true friendships in pure virtual (or online-only) contexts are not possible. Assess the counter argument by Briggle. Does Briggle succeed in making the case for the possibility of genuine friendships in virtual contexts? Whose argument do you find more convincing?
3. Do political blogs enhance or undermine democracy and its corresponding values? Examine Alvin Goldman's views about the implication of the blogosphere for the dissemination of information in a democracy. Why he is not concerned about the impact that extremely partisan blogs will have, overall, for democracy? Do you agree? Explain.
4. What does Philip Brey mean when he suggests that ethical aspects of VR involve two distinct categories: (virtual) interaction and behavior, and misrepresentation and bias? How does Brey propose that the argument "from moral development" and the argument from "psychological harm" can both be applied to ethical issues involving "harm" in VR environments?

▶ ESSAY/PRESENTATION QUESTIONS

1. Howard Rheingold (1991), who speculates about what VR may mean for the future of social relationships, raises an interesting questions involving *teledildonics* (or simulated sex at a distance). Though not yet a marketable technology, current work in *interactive tactile presence* (or touch feedback) will, Rheingold believes, make it possible for computer users to have sex at a distance. Inviting us to imagine this not-too-distant phenomenon, Rheingold asks us to picture ourselves "dressing for a hot night in the virtual village," where people wear a "cybersuit" made of "smart skin." Whether Rheingold's account turns out to be cyberfiction or whether it turns out to be factual, it is difficult to avoid considering the implications that teledildonics-related technology could have for future social relationships. Apply Philip Brey's model for analyzing ethical issues in virtual environments, described in Section 11.3, to Rheingold's scenario.
2. Gordon Graham argues that experiences in virtual reality (VR) will never have the same character as everyday experiences. He believes that one disadvantage of VR is that we will miss the joys of comparable "real experiences," such as falling in love; he concludes that VR is an "impoverished reality" relative to life in the real world. Douglas Birsch (2002) critiques Graham's views and suggests that Graham seriously shortchanges VR. Birsch acknowledges that VR experience may be inferior to the "real life" one, but he points out that a VR experience is far superior to not having the experience at all. Birsch claims that he would rather ski the Alps in Switzerland than ski in a VR application, but he would rather have the virtual experience than none at all. He also points out that the virtual experience may be the only one available to physically challenged people. If Birsch is correct, then VR may not be as impoverished a form of reality as Graham suggests. Do you agree with Birsch or with Graham? Explain.
3. Consider again the incident of cyberbullying on MySpace that we examined in Section 11.1.3, which resulted in Megan Meier's suicide in 2006. To what extent can social networking sites control cyberbullying and other

forms of harassment that occur in their forums? In the case of MySpace, would a more explicit policy about the rules required to get a legitimate account on that SNS have prevented Lori Drew, the woman who harassed Meier under the alias Josh Evans, from succeeding in bullying Meier online? What implications does the Meier incident have for trust in cyberspace, especially for young teenagers who participate in social networking services?

4. We saw that MMOGs and MMORPGs have become very popular around the world. Some critics are concerned about the level of violence that occurs in these games, while others worry more about the effects that virtual pornography and pedophilia in those games will have for real-life children. Evaluate Morgan Luck's claim that arguments used to defend murder (and other violent acts) in these games may, unintentionally, also defend pedophilia in virtual environments. Do you agree with Luck's view on this matter?

▶ ENDNOTES

1. Rheingold (2001), pp. 1–2.
2. The survey cited by Parsell was conducted by the United States-based Center for the Digital Future.
3. See http://www.merriam-webster.com/dictionary/blog.
4. See Grodzinsky and Tavani (2009).
5. Parsell (2008), p. 44.
6. Cocking and Matthews (2000), p. 231.
7. Briggle (2009), p. 71.
8. See Dibbell (2001) for more detail.
9. See http://abcnews.go.com/GMA/Story?id=3882520.
10. Johnson (2000), p. 181.
11. See Graham (1999), p. 71.
12. Sclove (1997), p. 226.
13. See, for example, http://worldwideliberty.blogspot.com/2009/01/barack-obama-not-born-in-us-no-us-state.html.
14. See, for example, http://www.politicalbase.com/profile/jnail/blog/&blogId=3482.
15. Goldman (2008), p. 119.
16. Http://en.wikipedia.org/wiki/Second_Life.
17. Http://en.wikipedia.org/wiki/MMORPG.
18. Http://en.wikipedia.org/wiki/Social_Interaction_via_MMORPGs.
19. Wonderly (2008), p. 2. [Italics Wonderly]
20. Luck (2009), p. 33. Note that the argument as presented here is adapted from Luck's original text. Luck does not himself express the argument in this precise form, but I believe that the argument form used here is compatible with his position.
21. Brey (2008), pp. 371–372.
22. See, for example, Levy (2002).
23. Kimppa and Bisset (2008), p. 470.
24. Ibid.
25. Warner and Raiter (2005), pp. 49–50.
26. Brey, pp. 376–377.
27. Ibid., p. 370.
28. Parsell, p. 41.
29. Turkle (1995), p. 12.
30. Ibid., p. 13.
31. Ibid., p. 26.
32. Williams (1997), p. 16.
33. Bolter (1984), p. 11.
34. Ibid., p. 13.
35. I am indebted to Mason Cash for this example.
36. Weckert (2004), p. 697.

▶ REFERENCES

Birsch, Douglas. 2002. "Gordon Graham's *The Internet: A Philosophical Inquiry.*" *Ethics and Information Technology* 4, no. 4: 325–28.

Bolter, J. David. 1984. *Turing's Man: Western Culture in the Computer Age.* Chapel Hill NC: University of North Carolina Press.

Brey, Philip. 1999. "The Ethics of Representation and Action in Virtual Reality." *Ethics and Information Technology* 1, no. 1: 5–14.

Brey, Philip. 2008. "Virtual Reality and Computer Simulation." In K. E. Himma and H. T. Tavani, eds. *The Handbook of Information and Computer Ethics.* Hoboken NJ: John Wiley and Sons, pp. 361–84.

Briggle, Adam. 2008. "Real Friends: How the Internet Can Foster Friendship." *Ethics and Information Technology* 10, no. 1: 71–79.

Clark, Andrew J. 2003. *Natural-Born Cyborgs: Minds, Technologies, and the Future of Human Intelligences.* New York: Oxford University Press.

Cocking, Dean, and Steve Matthews. 2000. "Unreal Friends." *Ethics and Information Technology* 2, no. 4: 223–31.

Cook, Brad. 2006. "Traverse Near-Infinite Possibilities with MMORPGs." Available at http://www.apple.com/games/articles/2006/04/mmorpgs/ (accessed May 27, 2009).

Dibbell, Julian. 2001. "A Rape in Cyberspace." In D. M. Hester and P. Ford, eds. *Computers and Ethics in the Cyberage.* Upper Saddle River NJ: Prentice Hall, pp. 439–51. [Reprinted from *The Village Voice* (December 1993): 36–42.]

Epstein, Richard G. 2000. "The Fragmented Public Square." *Computers and Society.* Available at http://www.cs.wcupa.edu/~epstein.fragmented.htm.

Ford, Paul J. 2001. "A Further Analysis of the Ethics of Representation in Virtual Reality: Multi-User Environments." *Ethics and Information Technology* 3, no. 2: 113–21.

Goldman, Alvin I. 2008. "The Social Epistemology of Blogging." In. J. van den Hoven and J. Weckert, eds. *Information Technology and Moral Philosophy.* Cambridge UK: Cambridge University Press, pp. 111–22.

Graham, Gordon. 1999. *The Internet: A Philosophical Inquiry.* New York: Routledge.

Grodzinsky, Frances S., and Herman, T. Tavani. 2009. "Applying the Model of 'Privacy as Contextual Integrity' to Personal Blogs." In M. Bottis, ed. *Proceedings of the Seventh International Conference on Computer Ethics—Philosophical Enquiry.* Athens, Greece: Nomiki Bibliothiki, pp. 254–62.

Johnson, Deborah G. 2000. "Democratic Values and the Internet." In D. Langford, ed. *Internet Ethics.* New York: St. Martin's Press, pp. 180–99.

Kimppa, Kai, and Andrew Bisset. 2008. "Gold Farming." In T. Bynum, et al., eds. *Proceedings of the Tenth ETHICOMP international Conference on the Social and Ethical Impacts of Information and Communication Technology.* University of Pavia, Mantua, Italy (September 24–26, 2008), pp. 470–79.

Luck, Morgan. 2009. "The Gamer's Dilemma: An Analysis of the Arguments for the Moral Distinction Between Virtual Murder and Virtual Pedophilia." *Ethics and Information Technology* 11, no. 1: 31–36.

Mason, Richard O. 1994. "Morality and Models." In W. Wallace, ed. *Ethics in Modeling.* Oxford UK: Elsevier Science.

Mill, John Stuart. 1989. *On Liberty and Other Writings.* Cambridge UK: Cambridge University Press.

Parsell, Mitch. 2008. "Pernicious Virtual Communities: Identity, Polarization, and the Web 2.0." *Ethics and Information Technology* 10, no. 1: 41–56.

Rheingold, Harold. 1991. *Virtual Reality.* New York: Touchstone Books.

Rheingold, Harold. 2001. *The Virtual Community: Homesteading ón the Electronic Frontier.* Rev. ed. Cambridge MA: MIT Press.

Sclove, Richard E. 1997. "Technological Politics as if Democracy Really Mattered." In A. E. Teich, ed. *Technology and the Future.* 7th ed. New York: St. Martin's Press, pp. 223–45.

Singer, Peter. 2007. "Video Crime Peril vs. Virtual Pedophilia." *The Japan Times Online,* June 22. Available at http://search.japantimes.co.jp/cgi.bineo20070722a1.html.

Sunstein, Cass R. 2001. *Republic.com.* Princeton NJ: Princeton University Press.

Sunstein, Cass R. 2007. *Republic.com. 2.0.* Princeton NJ: Princeton University Press.

Turkle, Sherry. 1984. *The Second Self: Computers and the Human Spirit.* New York: Simon and Schuster.

Turkle, Sherry. 1995. *Life on the Screen: Identity in the Age of the Internet.* New York: Simon and Schuster.

Turkle, Sherry. 2005. *The Second Self: Computers and the Human Spirit.* Rev. ed. Cambridge MA: MIT Press.

Ulen, Thomas S. 2001. "Democracy on the Line: A Review of *Republic.com* by Cass Sunstein." *Journal of Law, Technology and Policy* 2001, no. 2: 317–46.

Van Gelder, Lindsy. 1991. "The Strange Case of the Electronic Lover." In C. Dunlop and R. Kling, eds. *Computerization and Controversy: Value Conflicts and Social Choices.* San Diego CA, pp. 364–75.

Weckert, John. 2004. "Lilliputian Computer Ethics." In R. A. Spinello and H. T. Tavani, eds. *Readings in CyberEthics*. 2nd ed. Sudbury MA: Jones and Bartlett, pp. 601–07.

White, Michelle. 2002. "Regulating Research: The Problem of Theorizing Research in LambdaMOO." *Ethics and Information Technology* 4, no. 1: 55–70.

Williams, Mary B. 1997. "Ethical Issues in Computing: Work, Privacy, and Justice." In M. D. Ermann, M. B. Williams, and M. S. Shauf, eds. *Computers, Ethics, and Society*. 2nd ed. New York: Oxford University Press, pp. 3–19.

Warner, Dorothy E., and Mike Raiter. 2005. "Social Context in Massively-Multiplayer Online Games (MMOGs): Ethical Questions in Shared Space." *International Review of Information Ethics* 4: 47–52.

Wonderly, Monique. 2008. "A Humean Approach to Assessing the Moral Significance of Ultra-Violent Video Games." *Ethics and Information Technology* 10, no. 1: 1–10.

▶ FURTHER READINGS

Al-Saggaf, Yeslam, and Mohamed M. Begg. "Online Communities versus Offline Communities in the Arab/Muslim World." *Journal of Information, Communication and Ethics in Society* 2, no. 1 (2004): 41–54.

Bohman, James. "The Transformation of the Public Sphere: Political Authority, Communicative Freedom, and Internet Publics." In J. van den Hoven and J. Weckert, eds. *Information Technology and Moral Philosophy*. Cambridge UK: Cambridge University Press, 2008, pp. 66–92.

Fagan, Barry. "Liberty and Community Online." In R. M. Baird, R. Ramsower, and S. E. Rosenbaum, eds. *Cyberethics: Social and Moral Issues in the Computer Age*. Amherst NY: Prometheus Books, 2000, pp. 332–52.

Huff, Chuck, Deborah G. Johnson, and Keith Miller. "Virtual Harms and Real Responsibility." *IEEE Technology and Society Magazine* 22, no. 4 (2003): 12–19.

Mathews, Steve. 2008. "Identity and Information Technology." In J. van den Hoven and J. Weckert, eds. *Information Technology and Moral Philosophy*. Cambridge UK: Cambridge University Press, pp. 142–60.

Noam, Eli. "Why the Internet is Bad for Democracy." *Communications of the ACM* 48, no. 10 (2005): 57–58.

Powers, Thomas M. "Real Wrongs in Virtual Communities." *Ethics and Information Technology* 5, no. 4 (2003): 191–98.

Wellman, Barry. "Community: From Neighborhood to Network." *Communications of the ACM* 48, no. 10 (2005): 53–56.

White, Michelle. "Representations or People." *Ethics and Information Technology* 4, no. 3 (2002): 249–66.

CHAPTER

▼

12

Ethical Aspects of Emerging and Converging Technologies

In Chapter 12, the final chapter of *Ethics and Technology*, we examine some ethical and social issues that arise in connection with emerging and converging technologies. In particular, we analyze the following questions:

- What do we mean by "technological convergence" in the context of cybertechnology, and what kinds of ethical challenges do converging technologies pose?
- What is ambient intelligence (AmI), and which kinds of social and ethical concerns does it raise?
- Do ethical concerns affecting bioinformatics deserve special consideration?
- What is nanotechnology, and why are certain aspects of this technology controversial from an ethical perspective?
- How should computer professionals proceed with research and development in nanocomputing?
- Do at least some artificial intelligence (AI) entities warrant moral consideration?

Our analysis in this chapter focuses on key social and ethical issues that arise in connection with three relatively recent technologies that have emerged because of technological convergence: ambient intelligence, bioinformatics, and nanocomputing. We also briefly examine some implications that ongoing developments in AI have for our conventional moral framework, and we conclude by asking whether our traditional sphere of moral consideration needs to be expanded to include some AI entities.

▶ 12.1 CONVERGING TECHNOLOGIES AND
TECHNOLOGICAL CONVERGENCE

What, exactly, do we mean by "convergence" in the context of cybertechnology? Howard Rheingold describes technological convergence as a phenomenon that occurs when "apparently unrelated scientific and technological paths" cross or intersect "unexpectedly to create an entirely new field."[1] As we move forward into the twenty-first century, cyber and noncyber technologies are converging at a pace that is unprecedented. However, we saw in Chapter 1 that technological convergence as it pertains to cybertechnology is hardly new. We also saw that many of the ethical issues we examined in the preceding chapters of this textbook arose because of convergent aspects of computing/information and communication technologies. One example is virtual reality technology (or VR), which, as Rheingold notes, resulted from the convergence of video technology and computer hardware in the 1980s. (Recall our discussion of ethical aspects of VR in Chapter 11.)

Arguably, convergence involving computing- and information-based technologies has been continuous and ongoing in the development and evolution of cybertechnology. However, cyber and cyber-related technologies are now converging with non-cyber technologies in ways that challenge our ability to articulate many of the social and ethical issues that also arise either because of, or in connection with, this increased level of convergence.

One kind of ethical/social concern that cuts across the converging technologies examined in this chapter has to do with new threats to personal privacy. Because Chapter 5 was devoted to privacy concerns pertaining to cybertechnology, you might assume that the appropriate place to discuss these privacy issues would have been in that chapter. There, however, we examined privacy concerns that tend to fit mainly within the category of "informational privacy." For example, those privacy issues typically involve concerns that have resulted from exchanging electronic records (of personal information in databases), which were acquired through explicit transactions on the part of users. Although some privacy concerns affecting the converging technologies that we examine in this chapter also fall within the category of informational privacy, many do not. The reason for this is not simply because these privacy issues are associated with newer technologies, but because they introduce different kinds of privacy concerns than those examined in Chapter 5. For example, some privacy issues affecting research in bio-informatics tend to fall under the category of medical/genetic privacy; these issues, as a result of the computational tools and techniques used, also sometimes stretch and strain the traditional boundaries of medical privacy and genetic privacy.

We will also see that some privacy issues generated by developments in ambient intelligence technology and nanotechnology introduce a relatively new category of privacy concern called "location privacy," because these technologies can disclose the precise spatial location of an individual at a particular point in time. Thus, many of the privacy concerns identified and analyzed in this chapter are sufficiently different from those examined in Chapter 5 to warrant a separate context for analysis. However, as you examine the privacy-related issues discussed in this chapter, especially those affected by data mining technology, you may find it helpful to refer back to relevant sections of Chapter 5.

▶ 12.2 AMBIENT INTELLIGENCE AND UBIQUITOUS COMPUTING

We begin our examination of social and ethical aspects of converging technologies in the twenty-first century with a look at some controversies associated with *ambient intelligence* (or *AmI*)—a technology that enables people to live and work in environments that respond to them in "intelligent ways."[2] Before describing the technological components that comprise AmI, we briefly consider a scenario in which a young mother and her baby arrive at their "intelligent home." Illustrating some of the promises that AmI's proponents envision for the near future, Raisinghani et al. (2004) describe a situation that we could call "a day in the life of a smart home":

> Arriving home, a surveillance camera recognizes the young mother, automatically disables the alarm, unlocks the front door as she approaches it and turns on the lights to a level of brightness that the home control system has learned she likes. After dropping off her daughter, the young mother gets ready for grocery shopping. The intelligent refrigerator has studied the family's food consumption over time and knows their preferences as well as what has been consumed since the last time she went shopping. This information has been recorded by an internal tracking system and wireless communication with the intelligent kitchen cabinets. Based on this information, the refrigerator automatically composes a shopping list, retrieves quotations for the items on the list from five different supermarkets in the neighborhood through an Internet link, sends an order to the one with the lowest offer and directs the young mother there. When arriving at the supermarket, the shopping cart has already been filled with the items on her shopping list. Spontaneously, she decides to add three more items to her cart and walks to the check-out. Instead of putting the goods on a belt, the entire cart gets checked out simply by running it past an RFID transponder that detects all items in the cart at once and sends that information to the cash register for processing.[3]

Is the scenario described by Raisinghani et al. based on science fiction? Or does it portray a real-world situation in the not-too-distant future? Consider that a 5040-square-foot "aware home" that was developed at the Georgia Institute of Technology is currently being used as a laboratory for AmI research. Research and development in ambient intelligence is also being conducted at other academic institutions such as the Massachusetts Institute of Technology, as well as at companies in the private sector such as Philips Electronics. AmI's optimists predict that intelligent homes will be available to consumers within the next ten years. Whereas proponents of AmI are enthusiastic about many of the conveniences made possible by this technology, critics worry about AmI's dark side.

We should note that some analysts use the expression "ubiquitous computing," or *ubicomp*, to describe the technological phenomenon we refer to in this chapter as AmI. However, ubicomp can easily be confused with "ubiquitous communication," a technological component of AmI, which we describe in Section 12.2.2. So we use the expression AmI in this chapter to avoid any confusion between the two terms.

To better understand ambient intelligence, including the ethical and social challenges it poses, we briefly describe three key technological components that make AmI possible:

- pervasive computing,
- ubiquitous communication,
- intelligent user interfaces (IUIs).

12.2.1 Pervasive Computing

According to the Centre for Pervasive Computing, *pervasive computing* can be viewed as a computing environment where information and communication technology are "everywhere, for everyone, at all times." In this scheme, computing technology is integrated into our environments—from "toys, milk cartons, and desktops to cars, factories, and whole city areas." Pervasive computing is made possible, in part, because of the increasing ease with which circuits can be printed or embedded into objects, including wearable, even disposable items. Pervasive computing goes beyond the traditional scheme of user interfaces—on the one hand, it "implodes them into small devices and appliances"; on the other hand, it "explodes them onto large scale walls, buildings and furniture" (Centre for Pervasive Computing). Bütschi, Courant, and Hilty (2005) note that computing has already begun to pervade many dimensions of our lives, including "the work sphere, cars, public transportation systems, the health sector, the leisure market, our homes, and so forth."

Pervasive computing, like AmI, is also sometimes referred to in the computer science literature as *ubiquitous computing* (or *ubicomp*). The expression "ubiquitous computing" was coined by Mark Weiser,[4] who envisioned "omnipresent computers" that serve people in their everyday lives, both at home and at work. He also envisioned ubiquitous computing as something that would function "invisibly and unobtrusively" in the background and that would free people to a considerable degree from tedious routine tasks. Adam Greenfield (2005) believes that ubiquitous or pervasive computing, because of the way it is designed, will insinuate itself much more thoroughly into our day-to-day activities than current Internet- and Web-based technologies. For pervasive computing to operate at its full potential, however, continuous and ubiquitous communication between devices is also needed.

12.2.2 Ubiquitous Communication

Ubiquitous communication aims at ensuring flexible and omnipresent communication possibilities between interlinked computer devices that can be stationed in various locations. Greenfield notes that ubiquitous communication is already occurring through the "slow fusion" of our mobile phones and wireless networks. Several different kinds of wireless technologies that make ubiquitous communication possible are now available or are in progress. According to Raisinghani et al. (2004), these include

- wireless local area networks (W-LANs),
- wireless personal area networks (W-PANs),
- wireless body area networks (W-BANs) interlinking various wearable devices and connecting them to outside networks,
- radio frequency identification (RFID).

Perhaps the most controversial of these technologies thus far—at least from the perspective of personal privacy—is RFID. Andreas Koehler and Claudia Som (2005) suggest that RFID transponders in the form of "smart labels" will probably become the most widespread example of ubiquitous computing/communication. Recall our discussion of RFID technology in Chapter 5, where we examined some implications of RFID for personal privacy. We will see that RFID technology, when used in AmI environments, can facilitate the tracking of an individual's location at any given point in time and thus make possible a form of "pervasive surveillance."

12.2.3 Intelligent User Interfaces

In addition to pervasive computing and ubiquitous communication technologies, AmI has another key component: *Intelligent User Interfaces* (or *IUIs*). This technology has been made possible by developments in the field of artificial intelligence (AI). In Chapter 11, we examined AI from the perspective of concerns about our "sense of self" and about what it means to be a human being in the era of cybertechnology. There we also saw that AI, in addition to raising some interesting conceptual and theoretical questions, has many practical applications as well—including the implementation of AI-based algorithms in various expert system technologies. (We examine some additional AI issues affecting converging technologies in the concluding section of this chapter.) AI-based applications also are at the core of the "intelligent" user interfaces needed to realize the full potential of AmI.

Brey (2005) notes that IUIs, which are also sometimes called "user adaptive interfaces" because of the way they can adapt to a user's preferences, go beyond traditional interfaces such as a keyboard, mouse, and monitor. As a result, they improve human interaction with technology by making it more intuitive and more efficient than was previously possible with traditional interfaces. With IUIs, for example, computers can "know" and sense far more about a person than was possible with traditional interfaces, including information about that person's situation, context, or environment. Because IUIs respond to input such as human gestures as well as to an individual's preferences within various contexts, they enable inhabitants of AmI environments to interact with their environment in a personalized way. Unlike traditional user interfaces, however, IUIs in AmI environments also enable *profiling*, which Brey describes as "the ability to personalize and automatically adapt to particular user's behavior patterns."

While AmI technology is able to sense changes in an environment, and while this technology can automatically adapt and act based on these changes—e.g., in response to the needs and preferences of users—AmI remains in the background and is virtually invisible to the user. As Brey notes, people are "surrounded with possibly hundreds of intelligent networked computers that are aware of their presence, personality, and needs." But users themselves may not be aware of the existence of this technology in their environments.

So far we have described three key technological components that make AmI environments possible: pervasive computing, ubiquitous communication, and IUIs. Next, we examine some of the ethical and social challenges posed by AmI environments and the technologies that comprise them.

12.2.4 Some Ethical and Social Issues Affecting AmI

Social and ethical concerns affecting AmI environments include worries about the loss of freedom and autonomy. These are sometimes closely related to concerns about humans becoming overly dependent on technology. Other ethical concerns involving AmI include threats associated with privacy and surveillance. We begin with a look at some issues affecting freedom and autonomy.

Freedom and Autonomy

Will human autonomy and freedom be enhanced or diminished as a result of AmI technology? AmI's supporters suggest that humans will gain more control over the environments with which they interact because technology will be more responsive to their needs. However, Brey notes a paradoxical aspect of this claim, pointing out that "greater control" is presumed to be gained through a "delegation of control to machines." But this, he suggests, is tantamount to the notion of "gaining control by giving it away." Brey considers some ways in which control can be gained in one sense, and lost in another. With respect to humans gaining control as a result of this technology, he notes that three different kinds of arguments can be made, where AmI may make the human environment more controllable because it can

1. become more responsive to the voluntary actions, intentions, and needs of users;
2. supply humans with detailed and personal information about their environment;
3. do what people want without having to engage in any cognitive or physical effort.

On the other hand, Brey considers some ways that AmI can diminish the amount of control that humans have over their environments. These also are organized into three arguments, where users may lose control because a smart object can

1. make incorrect inferences about the user, the user's actions, or the situation;
2. require corrective actions on the part of the user;
3. represent the needs and interests of parties other than the user.[5]

So, as Brey notes, AmI has the potential to enhance freedom through its ability to expand certain aspects of our control over the environment — e.g., in responding to our voluntary actions, intentions, and needs, and by freeing us from many routine and tedious tasks that require either cognitive or physical effort. But he also notes that AmI has the potential to limit freedom because it can make incorrect inferences about a user's intentions and needs. Even when AmI does what a user wants, it can still reduce control by requiring "corrective actions" on the part of the user. Brey also notes that users can lose control when smart objects perform autonomous actions that do not solely represent the user's interests. For example, the smart object could include a user profile or knowledge base that also is designed to take into account the interests of third parties (such as commercial interests). Additionally, Brey believes that AmI could undermine human freedom and autonomy if humans become too dependent on machines for their judgments and decisions.

Technological Dependency

We have come to depend a great deal on technology, especially on cybertechnology, in conducting many activities in our day-to-day lives. In the future, will humans depend on the kind of smart objects and smart environments made possible by AmI technology in ways that exceed our current dependency on computing devices? We noted above that IUIs could relieve us of having to worry about performing many of our routine day-to-day tasks, which can be considered tedious and boring. But we also noted that these interfaces could relieve us of much of the cognitive effort that has, in the past, enabled us to be fulfilled and to flourish as humans. What would happen to us if we were to lose this capacity because of an increased dependency on technology? Perhaps a brief look at a scenario envisioned by E. M. Forster in one of his classic works would be instructive at this point.

▶ **SCENARIO 12–1:** E. M. Forster's Precautionary Tale

In his classic work *The Machine Stops*, first published in 1909, E. M. Forster portrays a futuristic society that, initially at least, might seem like an ideal or utopian world. In fact, Forster's story anticipated many yet-to-be-developed technologies such as television and videoconferencing. But it also illustrates how humans have transferred control of much of their lives to a global Machine, which is capable of satisfying their physical and spiritual needs and desires. In surrendering so much control to the Machine, however, people begin to lose touch with the natural world. After a while, defects appear in the Machine, and eventually it breaks down. Unfortunately, no one remembers how to repair it. In Forster's tale, some of the characters begin to realize just how dependent they have become on this machine. [6] We could easily imagine Forster's scenario playing out in AmI environments of the future where individuals no longer are required to perform routine cognitive acts, and instead depend on IUIs to make decisions for them. ∎

Continuing with the analogy involving Forster's (futuristic) scenario, we could ask what would happen if the energy sources that powered the AmI environments were suddenly lost. Could we respond successfully if this happened to us? If not, it would seem that we have let ourselves become too dependent on this technology. Hypothetical questions of this kind are worth keeping in mind as we proceed with development of AmI and related technologies.

Privacy, Surveillance, and the Panopticon

Some of AmI's critics worry that a kind of "Big Brother" society may emerge. For example, Bohn et al. (2005) note that in AmI environments, all of our moves, actions, and decisions will be recorded by "tireless electronic devices, from the kitchen and living room of our homes to our weekend trips in cars." As Marc Langheinrich (2001) points out, no aspect of our life will be secluded from "digitization," because virtually anything we say, do, or even feel, could be "digitized, stored, and retrieved anytime later." But how are the privacy concerns associated with AmI different, in relevant ways, from privacy issues generated by earlier uses of computer technology? Langheinrich believes that with respect to privacy and surveillance, four features differentiate AmI from other kinds of computing applications:

- ubiquity
- invisibility
- sensing
- memory application

First, Langheinrich believes that because computing devices are *ubiquitous* or omnipresent in AmI environments, privacy threats involving AmI are more pervasive in scope and can affect us more deeply. Second, because computers are virtually *invisible* in AmI environments (in the sense that they easily "disappear" from view), it is likely that users will not always realize that computing devices are present and are being used to collect and disseminate personal data. Third, *sensing* devices associated with the intelligent user interfaces (IUIs) in AmI environments may become so sophisticated that, unlike conventional forms of cybertechnology, they will be able to sense (private and intimate) human emotions such as fear, stress, and excitement. Fourth, AmI has the potential to create a *memory* or "life-log"—i.e., a complete record of someone's past. So, Langheinrich concludes that AmI poses a more significant threat to privacy than earlier computing technologies.

In AmI environments, the sheer scale or amount of information that can be collected without our awareness is also problematic. Bohn et al. (2005) note that AmI has the potential to create a comprehensive surveillance network, because it can disclose an "unprecedented share of our public and private life." We saw that AmI environments are equipped with sensors that facilitate the collection of data about an individual from his or her surroundings without that individual's active intervention. As Johann Čas (2004) points out, "ubiquitous services" are provided by the "omnipresence of countless little helpers, invisibly embedded in the environment where one works or spends his or her private time." For example, this kind of ubiquitous observation, which some now refer to as "pervasive surveillance," can expose much about an individual's habits and preferences.

Čas notes that no one can be sure that his or her actions are not being observed; nor can one be sure that his or her words are not being recorded. Furthermore, individuals cannot be sure whether information about their presence at any location is being recorded. So, he believes that the only realistic attitude of human beings living in such environments is to assume that any activity or inactivity is being monitored, analyzed, transferred, and stored, and that this information may be used in any context in the future. In this sense, people in AmI environments would be subject to a virtual "panopticon."

▶ **SCENARIO 12–2:** Jeremy Bentham's Panopticon

Jeremy Bentham, an eighteenth-century philosopher and social reformer, conceived of the idea for managing a prison environment based on the notion of the *Panopticon*. Imagine a prison comprised of glass cells, all arranged in a circle, where prisoners could be observed at any moment by a prison guard who sits at a rotating desk facing the prisoner's cells. Further imagine that the inmates cannot see outside their cells, even though they can be observed by the prison guard at any time. Although a prisoner cannot be certain that he is being observed at any given moment, it would be prudent for him to assume that he is being observed at every moment. The prisoner's realization that he could be observed continuously, and his fear about what could happen to him if he is observed doing something that is not permitted in the cell, would likely be sufficient to control the prisoner's behavior.[7]   ■

Suppose Bentham's model of the Panopticon or "inspection house" were to be extended to public spaces such as the workplace and public buildings. Further suppose that it is extended to private and intimate environments as well. What effect could this have on social control? As Bentham and the supporters of the Panopticon realized, the possibility of being permanently observed is sufficient to create strict disciplines and uniformity within societies. In Bentham's classical Panopticon, however, one could not be certain whether he or she was actually being monitored at a given point in time. Persons living in AmI environments, on the other hand, can, with almost 100% certainty, know that they are being observed. Classical forms of surveillance, from Bentham's time to the period preceding AmI technology, were limited to time and place. But data captured in AmI environments will, as Čas notes, persist across space and time.

Thus far we have examined some key social and ethical concerns affecting AmI environments. Table 12.1 lists the technological components of AmI and the corresponding ethical and social issues associated with them.

We have seen that some of these ethical and social issues arise because of the pervasive aspects of AmI technology, while others reflect concerns pertaining to convergent features of its component technologies. In the next section, we examine

TABLE 12.1   Ambient Intelligence

Technological Components	Ethical and Social Issues Generated
Pervasive Computing	Freedom and Autonomy
Ubiquitous Communication	Privacy and Surveillance
Intelligent User Interfaces	Technological Dependence

ethical concerns that arise from a different set of converging technologies: cybertechnology and biotechnology.

▶ 12.3 BIOINFORMATICS AND COMPUTATIONAL GENOMICS

Recent discoveries in the life sciences, particularly in the fields of cell biology and genetics/genomics, have depended significantly on the application of computers and computational techniques and methodologies. This dependency has influenced the development of two relatively new fields at the intersection of computer science and biology: *bioinformatics* and *computational genomics*. Bioinformatics is a branch of *informatics*, which involves the acquisition, storage, manipulation, analyses, transmission, sharing, visualization, and simulation of information on a computer.[8] In particular, *bio*informatics is the application of the informatics model to the management of biological information, with the objective of making that information more understandable and useful. Computational genomics, like bioinformatics, uses computerized techniques, tools, and approaches to acquire, store, organize, analyze, synthesize, visualize, and simulate data. However, the data it analyzes are limited to genetic/genomic information, as opposed to broader biological data that can include biological systems as well as medical and health data.[9]

Before examining specific ethical and social issues that arise in connection with the convergence of computing and genetic/genomic technologies, it is helpful to consider some connections that link the fields of computer science and genetics. James Moor (2006) points out that computing provides a "conceptual model" for the function and malfunction of our genetic machinery. He also notes that researchers sometimes describe the computation of genes as straightforward computational programs in which the sequence of nucleotides can be regarded as a kind of "computer program for constructing an organism."[10] Consider that some geneticists describe their work in terms of "decoding" and "reprogramming" DNA. Also consider some ways that computational tools and techniques have significantly influenced developments in genetic/genomic research.

Computing technology has played an important practical role in the "new genetics" by providing critical tools and methods. For example, Antonio Marturano (2006) notes that a computerized technique called the "shotgun method" accelerated work on the Human Genome Project, enabling researchers to accomplish their objective of mapping the entire human genome ahead of schedule. Kenneth Goodman (1998) describes an incident in the early 1990s that aptly illustrates some of key roles that computer technology in general, and computational tools in particular, have played in genetic research. Goodman notes that scientists working in Cambridge, England, and St. Louis, Missouri, used computer technology to make 900,000 nucleotide bases available to colleagues around the world, who could then join their effort in locating the gene for breast cancer. He points out that in the pre-computer era, these scientists would have had to mail parcels of human tissue to their colleagues in order to accomplish this objective. They also would have had to publish a book or write a paper to describe the results of their research to colleagues. But in this case, the scientists, working at geographically distant sites, were able to make the information available to colleagues simply by placing information about the sequenced genetic data on two publicly accessible sites on the Internet. More importantly, however, the gene sequences represented in these data had already been identified *computationally*—i.e., the genes had been discovered, sequenced, and analyzed, via computers—before the data were shared electronically among an international group of scientists. [11]

Goodman's example nicely illustrates how the information about the gene sequences was not only able to be communicated and shared with colleagues via computer networks, but that the information itself had become available *only as a result of* certain computational techniques and methods that were used. Goodman also points out that the evolution of genetic databases, as well as the tools used for searching them, has developed so rapidly that scientists now build "computational toolkits" to hold their computational tools.

12.3.1 Ethical Aspects of Bioinformatics

Because of its special dependency on the computational techniques and analyses used by genetics/genomics researchers, the outcomes of that research can be very difficult to anticipate with respect to ethical implications. As a result, some ethical issues generated by this research are not always easy to identify, let alone analyze. Yet, ethical issues affecting bioinformatics are significant: in some cases, they involve psycho/social harm, including discrimination and stigmatization for certain individuals and groups; in other cases, they can affect broader social policies such as questions concerning the ownership of personal genetic data that are stored in electronic databases. The following scenario illustrates some of these concerns.

▶ **SCENARIO 12–3:** deCODE Genetics Inc.

DeCODE Genetics was founded in 1996 by Kari Stefansson, a former professor of neurology at Harvard University, when he returned to Iceland, his native country. Stefansson negotiated with the Icelandic government for access to the nation's medical and health care records, which date back to 1915. Iceland's rich genealogical data, which included records (that date back more than 1,000 years) were already freely available, and Iceland's Parliament promised Stefansson access to any government-owned medical information that he would need to conduct his research. With these and other agreements in hand, Stefansson officially formed deCODE Genetics Inc. and immediately began to construct a genetics database consisting of information based on DNA samples that would eventually be acquired from 70,000 volunteers. DeCODE was then able to link together and cross reference medical/healthcare records, genealogical records, and genetic information included in the three databases.[12] ■

Why are the practices used by deCODE Genetics Inc. so controversial from an ethical perspective? The ethical and social concerns that arise can be described in terms of three distinct but related kinds of issues:

- privacy and confidentiality
- autonomy and informed consent
- information ownership and property rights[13]

Privacy, Confidentiality, and the Role of Data Mining Technology

Should Icelandic citizens who voluntarily provided DNA samples to deCODE have assumed that their personal genetic data were confidential information, which would be protected by the company's privacy policies and by Icelandic privacy laws, even after it had been collected and aggregated? Anton Vedder (2004) points out that the kind of privacy protection that applies to personal information about individuals *as individuals* does not necessarily apply to that information once it is aggregated and cross-referenced with other information. So the aggregated personal genetic information stored in deCODE's genetic databases, which was cross-referenced with information in deCODE's nongenetic databases (i.e., databases containing medical and genealogical information), does not enjoy the kind of legal protection generally accorded to "personal information."

In the process of aggregating and cross-referencing data, deCODE used data mining techniques to find correlated genes and gene variations, simply by comparing databases of genetic samples and disease records. In Chapter 5, we saw that data mining tools can "discover" information based on patterns that are implicit in data. As such, no prior hypothesis about the possible relationship between a particular gene and a certain disease is necessary when data mining is used. Although this technology has helped researchers to identify disease genes that affect populations, data mining can also be controversial. For example, new categories or groups (of individuals) can be generated by the use of one or more *profiles* made possible by data mining technology.

Data mining also generates *group profiles*. Bart Custers (2006) describes a group profile as a set of properties or characteristics that serve as the basis for identifying an individual as a member of a particular group. Why is this kind of profile controversial? Some of the characteristics or attributes used in defining groups are commonly known and easily identifiable. For example, an individual might be identified as belonging to multiple groups—i.e., the group of females, the group of insurance executives, the group of BMW owners, and so forth. For the most part, people who are assigned to these kinds of groups would not be surprised to learn of their association with them. However, other kinds of groups can be constructed on the basis of profiles that are not obvious to the individuals who comprise them. As Custers notes, a person who owns a red car may have no idea that he belongs to a group of individuals likely to have or to contract colon cancer (merely because of a statistical correlation that associates people who own red cars with colon cancer). So the same technology used to discover patterns and relations that aid genetic researchers can also be used to generate new groups, which in turn can suggest "new facts" about the individuals assigned to them.

Why are the "new facts" about individuals that can be generated via data mining so controversial? For one thing, decisions can be made about people on the basis of certain kinds of information pertaining to them *as members of a group*. Custers points out that a decision could be made about whether to grant someone, X, life insurance based on the new fact that X owns a red car and would thus likely have a higher-than-average probability of contracting colon cancer. Financial decisions may also be made about an individual based on facts pertaining to his or association with a "newly discovered" group, even though this individual may have had no knowledge that such a group exists. For example, we saw in Chapter 5 that an individual might be denied a loan based solely on a coincidental statistical association with a "new group" rather than on his individual credit scoring. So, the person can be denied the loan for reasons that are unfair, irrelevant, or inaccurate.

Analogously, a person could be denied employment, health insurance, or life insurance based on similar uses of data mining technology. For example, a person could be placed into a risky category based on arbitrary associations and correlations (generated by data mining) that associate trivial nongenetic information (such as the color of one's car) with sensitive information about one's genetic data. We have also seen that many, if not most, individuals who eventually become identified or associated with the newly created groups may have no knowledge that the groups to which they have been assigned actually exist. (Also, these individuals will have no chance to correct any inaccuracies or errors in the information about them that is generated from their association with that group).

Autonomy and Informed Consent: Challenges from Secondary Uses of Information

Another concern that arises in the deCODE scenario involves individual autonomy—in particular, the process of *informed consent* used in getting permissions from human research subjects who participate in genetic studies. The genetic information that deCODE acquired from "informed" volunteers may not meet the required conditions for what some ethicists describe as *valid* informed consent. According to the requirements for valid informed consent included in the 1993 Office of Technology Assessment (OTA) Report, entitled *Protecting Privacy in Computerized Medical Information*, individuals must

   i. have adequate disclosure of information about the data dissemination process,

   ii. be able to fully comprehend what they are being told about the procedure or treatment.

Applying OTA's criteria to the deCODE scenario, individuals consenting to provide their genetic data are required to have both "adequate disclosure" of information and "full comprehension" of the process in which their data will be used. However, consider that even if the human subjects agreed to have their data used in a specific context by deCODE, it is not clear that they fully comprehended the process of how their genetic data could be used in secondary or subsequent contexts (where it could be cross-referenced with information in nongenetic databases). Also, it is not clear that these individuals were given "adequate" disclosure about the data dissemination process used by deCODE. Furthermore, it might not even be possible for deCODE to disclose this information to them because all of the *potential* secondary uses of their genetic information have not yet been determined.

If individuals who provided their genetic data to deCODE Genetics did not make choices that were "validly informed," was the consent process used in this research ethical? If not, why is that important? Onora O'Neill (2002) believes that the principle of informed consent is important from an ethical point of view because it enables individuals to protect themselves against both coercion and deception. In this sense, she believes that the consent process must be open or *transparent*. Can the transparency requirement be satisfied in research practices that use data mining techniques? We have seen that the data mining practices used by deCODE aggregate information, which can then be used for secondary purposes. Unless specific information about how this is done is adequately disclosed to research subjects in a way that is comprehensible to them, it would seem that O'Neill's transparency guidelines (essential for the consent process) are violated in the practices used by deCODE Genetics.

Because of the way data mining technology can be used to manipulate personal information that had been authorized for use in one context only, it would seem that the process of informed consent has increasingly become nontransparent or *opaque*. It would also seem that the kind of conditions required for "valid" informed consent are extremely difficult, if not impossible, to achieve in cases that involve secondary uses of personal genetic information via data mining technology.

Intellectual Property Rights and Ownership Issues

A third area of ethical concern in the deCODE scenario involves the question of property rights and ownership of genetic data. Some critics believe the Icelandic parliament's decision to grant deCODE exclusive rights (for 12 years) to the information included in the nation's health records database raises property right issues that also affect access to personal genetic information. Who should (and who should not) have access to those data? Should deCODE hold exclusive ownership rights to all of the personal genetic information that resides in its databases? Alternatively, should individuals retain (at least some) ownership rights over their personal genetic data, even though the data are stored in a privately owned database? Or is a different strategy needed—e.g., should the Icelandic government be granted custodial rights to the personal genetic information in deCODE's databases, in order to protect the interests of Iceland's citizens?

Have those individuals who donated samples of their DNA to deCODE necessarily lost all rights to their personal genetic data, once the data were stored in that company's databases? If so, should deCODE hold rights to these data in perpetuity, and should deCODE be permitted to do whatever it wishes with those data? Why, exactly, are these questions so controversial from an ethical point of view? Recall our discussion in Chapter 5 of a commercial database containing personal data that was owned by Toysmart.com, a now defunct online business. There we saw that customers who dealt with Toysmart were given assurances that any personal information they disclosed would be protected under the company's privacy policy. We also saw that when Toysmart filed for bankruptcy, however, it was required by law to list all of its assets. These included its database of customer information, the specific contents of which were presumably protected under Toysmart's privacy policy.

Perhaps an appropriate analogy can be drawn between deCODE and Toysmart. For example, we can ask what would happen to the information in deCODE's databases if deCODE were forced to file for bankruptcy. We can also ask what would happen if deCODE's databases were sold to, or otherwise acquired by, a different organization. Could what happened at Toysmart.com also happen to a privately owned genetics company in the commercial sector, such as deCODE Genetics? If so, should the Icelandic government intervene? Because the answers to these questions are not entirely clear, we need laws and policies that explicitly describe the ownership rights of the highly sensitive personal data stored in genetic databases.

12.3.2 Legislation and Ethical Guidelines

We have seen how ethical issues involving privacy and confidentiality, informed consent and autonomy, and property rights/ownership issues each arise in bioinformatics-related research in the deCODE scenario. These concerns also illustrate the need for clear ethical guidelines as well as adequate legislation to protect human research subjects. In the United States, government-funded genomic research is currently guided by a policy that requires researchers to take specific ethical, legal, and social implications (ELSI) into account. The ELSI program includes explicit guidelines affecting criteria such as privacy and fairness for research subjects. However, some question whether the original ELSI guidelines, developed in the late 1980s and early 1990s, are still adequate in an era when advanced computerized techniques such as data mining are used.[14] It is also important to note that the ELSI requirements do not apply to genetic research conducted in the commercial sector.

Because of concerns about potential misuses of personal genetic data, some genetic-specific privacy laws and policies have been proposed and enacted into law. In the United States, these laws have been enacted primarily at the state level. Prior to 2008, no federal laws in the United States protected personal genetic data per se. The Health Insurance Portability and Accountability Act (HIPAA) of 1996, enacted into law in April 2003, provides broad protection for personal medical information. That is, HIPAA includes standards for protecting the privacy of "individually identifiable health information" from "inappropriate use and disclosure." However, critics point out that HIPAA does not provide any special privacy protection for personal genetic information. Also, Baumer, Earp, and Payton (2006) note that it is not clear whether HIPAA adequately addresses concerns affecting nonconsensual, secondary uses of personal medical and genetic information (of the kind made possible by data mining).

In May 2008, George W. Bush signed into law the Genetic Information Non-discrimination Act (GINA). The aim of GINA is to protect Americans against forms of discrimination based on their genetic information; it is especially designed to protect an individual's interests with respect to employment and health insurance.[15] Some of GINA's detractors believe that this particular legislation is "overly broad" and that it will most likely not succeed in rectifying many of the existing state laws that tend to be inconsistent regarding genetic discrimination. GINA's advocates, on the contrary, believe that this measure will provide a comprehensive (and nation-wide) form of protection against virtually all forms of genetic discrimination.[16] It is still not clear at this point, however, whether GINA can respond to some of the potential problems we identified above regarding the use of data mining technology in genetic and genomic research.

Thus far, we examined some social and ethical aspects of two different kinds of converging technologies: ambient intelligence (AmI) and bioinformatics. We saw that both kinds of technologies introduce special concerns for personal privacy. We also saw that bioinformatics research has introduced some new challenges for policies affecting informed-consent practices and intellectual property rights. Table 12.2 lists, in summary form, the three kinds of ethical issues we examined in connection with bioinformatics.

The third area of technological convergence that we consider is nanocomputing, i.e., the intersection of cybertechnology and nanotechnology. Ruth Chadwick and Antonio

TABLE 12.2   Ethical Issues Associated with Bioinformatics

Personal privacy and confidentiality	The aggregation of personal genetic data, via data mining, can generate privacy issues affecting "new groups" and "new facts" about individuals.
Informed consent and autonomy	The nontransparent (or "opaque") consent process can preclude "valid" or "fully informed" consent, thereby threatening individual autonomy.
Intellectual property rights/ownership	The storage of personal genetic data in electronic databases raises questions about who should have ownership rights and access to the data.

Marturano (2006) argue that nanotechnology provides the "key" to convergence because it enables the bringing together of computer/information technologies and biotechnologies.

▶ 12.4 NANOTECHNOLOGY AND NANOCOMPUTING

What, exactly, is nanotechnology? Why is research at the nano level controversial from an ethical perspective? Should computer scientists and computer professionals participate in research and development in nanocomputing? We examine each of these questions.

12.4.1   What is Nanotechnology?

Rosalyn Berne (2005) describes *nanotechnology* as "the study, design, and manipulation of natural phenomena, artificial phenomena, and technological phenomena at the nanometer level." We should note, however, that, at this time, there is no universally agreed upon definition or conception of the field. One common or unifying feature of nanotechnology, regardless of how narrowly or broadly it is defined, is that it operates on matter on a scale of *nanometers*.

James Moor and John Weckert (2004) note that a nanometer, which is one billionth of a meter, is very close to the dimensions of individual atoms whose diameters range from 0.1 to 0.5 nanometers. K. Eric Drexler, who coined the term "nanotechnology" in the 1980s, conceived of the field as a branch of engineering dedicated to the development of electronic circuits and mechanical devices built at the molecular level of matter. Although such nano-level devices do not yet exist, current microelectricomechanical systems (or MEMS), tiny devices such as sensors embedded in conductor chips used in airbag systems to detect collisions, are one step away from the molecular machines envisioned by Drexler.

The origin of nanotechnology as a distinct field is generally traced to a 1959 talk by physicist and Nobel laureate Richard Feynman, who encouraged scientists to develop tools that could manipulate matter at the atomic level. In 1990, Eigler and Schweitzer, two scientists working at the IBM Almaden laboratory, succeeded in manipulating 35 individual xenon atoms to shape the three initials of their employer's logo. Since then, more practical kinds of applications have been carried out at the nano level. Drexler has proposed the idea of a nano-scale *assembler*—i.e., a molecular machine that could be programmed to build virtually any molecular structure or device from simpler chemical building blocks. He believes that the development of universally applicable assemblers, which could be programmed to replicate themselves, is essential for the full realization of nanotechnology's potential.

Although some critics argue that nanotechnology has generated more hype than substance, there are signs that important breakthroughs are beginning to occur at the nano level. For example, Ed Regis (2009) describes some of the implications of the nanotube radio that was invented by Alex Zettl and his colleagues in 2007. Regis notes that a "single carbon nanotube tunes in a broadcast signal, amplifies it, converts it to an audio signal and then sends it to an external speaker in a form that the human ear can readily hear." He also notes that this could be the "basis for a new range of applications: hearing aids, cell phones, and iPods small enough to fit completely within the ear canal."[17]

12.4.2 Nanocomputers and Nanocomputing

In the 1980s, Drexler predicted that developments in nanotechnology would result in computers at the nanoscale—that is, *nanocomputers.* Ralph Merkle (1997) believes that future nanocomputers will have mass storage devices capable of storing more than 100 billion bytes in a volume the size of a sugar cube and that these devices will be able to "deliver a billion billion instructions per second." Drexler (1991) suggests that nanocomputers will be designed using various types of architectures. For example, an electronic nanocomputer would operate in a manner similar to present-day computers, differing primarily in terms of size and scale. A quantum nanocomputer, on the contrary, would work by storing data in the form of atomic quantum states or spin. Weckert (2006) points out that quantum computers would be much more powerful than any computing systems available today.

Some predict that future nanocomputers will also be built from biological material such as DNA. For example, Nadrian Seeman (2004) believes that DNA is an ideal molecule for building nanometer-scale structures because strands of DNA can be "programmed to self assemble into complex arrangements" that bond together. Drexler, who believes that biology shows us how molecular machinery can construct complex organisms from the bottom up, suggests that biological computers are already a reality.

Whether biological and quantum computers will be available at the nano level is still a matter of speculation and dispute. However, more conventional notions of computing at the nanoscale are currently under development, and standard computing chips have already been constructed on the nanoscale. At Hewlett Packard, for example, Stan Williams and researchers have made computer memory devices by creating eight platinum wires 40 nanometers wide on a silicon wafer. Moor and Weckert note that it would take more than one thousand of these chips to be the width of a human hair.

As noted earlier, our main goal in this section of Chapter 12 is to identify and analyze ethical and social concerns that arise because of developments in nanocomputing and nanotechnology. To accomplish that objective, we first describe some predictions about the societal advantages and disadvantages that could result from continued nanotechnology research and development.

12.4.3 The Promises and Perils of Nanotechnology: Utopian Dream or Apocalyptic Nightmare?

Nanotechnology's optimists are quick to point out many of the advantages that would likely result from nano-level developments, especially for the medical field and for the environment in general. Those who worry about future developments in nanotechnology and nanocomputing, however, see things quite differently. Bert Gordijn (2003) describes the nanotechnology debate between the optimists and the pessimists as one that represents the views of "utopian dreams" vs. "apocalyptic nightmares," respectively. He uses "utopian" to refer to the seventeenth-century idea of being able to ideally control a natural environment in order to create a perfect society, i.e., one where life is prolonged, enhanced, and without pain and suffering.

The Optimistic View

For our purposes, the examples Gordijn cites for how nanotechnology could help bring about the utopian dream can be understood in terms of six categories, where "molecule by molecule manufacturing" would

1. be self-sufficient and "dirt-free,"
2. create unprecedented objects and materials,
3. enable the production of inexpensive high-quality products,
4. be used to fabricate food rather than having to grow it,
5. provide low-priced and superior equipment for healthcare,
6. enable us to enhance our human capabilities and properties.[18]

First, optimists believe that molecular manufacturing would be "dirt free" because molecular manufacturing techniques would not result in any chemical pollution. Also, because unwanted chemicals could be detected and inactivated, existing environmental degradation could be reversed by nanomachines (or *nanites*) that could be used to clean up toxic spills, as well as to eliminate other kinds of environmental hazards. Second, nanotechnology could create unprecedented objects and materials such as strong, lightweight materials that would enable easier access to (outer) space and space resources. Third, molecular manufacturing would enable the production of inexpensive, high-quality products. For example, nanotechnology's advocates point to the production of items that include dramatically inexpensive storage batteries, processors, personal computers, laptops, cell phones, and so forth.

Fourth, molecular manufacturing could be used to "fabricate food" rather than having to grow it; for example, nanotechnology's proponents point out that food is simply a combination of molecules in certain configurations. Hence, the problem of hunger could be effectively solved by efficient molecule-by-molecule mass production of food. Additionally, nanomachines (or nanite assemblers) could dismantle or "disassemble" garbage at the molecular level and recycle it again at the molecular level.

Fifth, molecular manufacturing could provide low-priced and superior equipment for healthcare because "medical nanites" could be programmed to travel through our bloodstream to clean out fatty deposits, thereby reducing the probability of cardio-vascular diseases. Also, nanoparticles inserted into bodies could diagnose diseases and directly treat diseased cells. Doctors could use nanites to make microscopic repairs on areas of the body that are difficult to operate on with conventional surgical tools (Weckert, 2006). And with nanotechnology tools, the life signs of a patient could be better monitored. Additionally, preventive medicine could be greatly improved by having nanorobots within our bodies that could provide a defense against viruses. Sixth, molecular manufacturing would facilitate the enhancement of our human capabilities and properties, thereby enabling us to overcome contemporary diseases, pain, and other unpleasant bodily symptoms.

So, if the optimists are correct, we have much to be excited about as developments in nanotechnology and nanocomputing proceed. However, Gordijn also describes some of the catastrophes or "apocalyptic nightmares" that nanotechnology's pessimists envision occurring if research and development in this area is allowed to continue.

The Pessimistic View

For our purposes, Gordijn's description of the arguments for the pessimistic view can once again be organized into six categories, where developments in molecular manufacturing could result in

1. severe economic disruption,
2. premeditated misuse in warfare and terrorism,
3. surveillance with nano-level tracking devices,
4. extensive environmental damage,
5. uncontrolled self-replication,
6. misuse by criminals and terrorists.[19]

First, some pessimists believe that rapid developments in molecular manufacturing could cause severe economic disruption that might result from the sudden abundance of low-priced products and rapidly changing employment problems. Second, molecular manufacturing could facilitate premeditated misuse in warfare and terrorism because nanite assemblers and disassemblers might be used to create weapons that could result in both (a) conventional weapons being constructed more rapidly, and (b) new weaponry being made in large numbers, becoming low-priced, and becoming extremely powerful. As Chen (2002) points out, guns, explosives, and electronic components of weapons could all be miniaturized. It is also possible that nanites themselves could be used as weapons.

Third, critics point out that infinitesimally small surveillance devices such as nanoscale tracking devices, sensors, nanocameras, and microphones could enable observation and control of subjects in a way that is unprecedented. For example, governments, businesses, and ordinary people could use molecular-sized microphones, cameras, and homing beacons to track and monitor people. Weckert (2006) notes that people with microscopic implants would be able to be tracked using Global Positioning Systems (GPS), just as cars can be now.

Fourth, nanotechnology could potentially cause extensive environmental damage because destructive nanite assemblers might enter the food chain thereby disturbing entire ecological systems. Also, nanoparticles could escape into the air and turn out to pose asbestos-like health threats.

Fifth, critics worry about nanomachines having the capacity of self-replication. Consider that technical malfunctions could cause unbridled self-replication in which the total number of nanite assemblers would grow exponentially. Some critics also note that all matter (objects and organisms) could theoretically be disassembled and reassembled by these nanite assemblers and disassemblers, if strict "limiting mechanisms" are not built into them. In this case, self-replicating nanites could multiply endlessly like viruses. If the uncontrolled assemblers used a variety of raw materials as resources for self-replication, they could devour the entire biosphere in a very short time. (This is sometimes referred to as the *grey-goo scenario.*)

Sixth, some pessimists worry that private companies, which are not subject to strict government regulation, might be motivated by profit incentives to try to develop and produce nanite assemblers as quickly as possibly and sell them on the "black market." So there is the danger of these assemblers being acquired by criminals and terrorists who could use them for devious means, including the creation of weapons of mass destruction. (Some refer to this possibility as the *black-goo scenario*).

So, nanotechnology's pessimists and critics present a variety of concerns that would seem to counter many of the enthusiastic predictions offered by optimists. Are the claims and predictions made by nanotechnology's optimists and pessimists plausible? Weckert (2006) believes that because many predictions about nanotechnology seem reasonable, it would be prudent for us to consider some of the ethical implications now while there is still time to anticipate them. Will a separate field of "nanoethics" be needed to analyze these implications?

12.4.4 Nanoethics: Identifying and Analyzing Ethical Issues in Nanotechnology

Moor and Weckert (2004) believe that assessing ethical issues that arise at the nanoscale is important because of the kinds of "policy vacuums" (Moor 2001) that can arise. (Recall our discussion of Moor's notion of policy vacuums in Chapter 1.) Although Moor and Weckert do not explicitly argue that a separate field of applied ethics called *nanoethics* is necessary, they make a convincing case for why an analysis of ethical issues at the nano level is now critical. In particular, they identify three distinct kinds of ethical concerns that warrant analysis:

1. privacy and control
2. longevity
3. runaway nanobots

With respect to (1), the authors note that as we construct nanoscale information gathering systems, it will become extremely easy to put a nanoscale transmitter in a room or onto someone's clothing in such a way that he or she will have no idea that the device is present or that he or she is being monitored and tracked. Implanting tracking mechanisms within someone's body would also become easier with nanotech devices. Consider that a tracking mechanism might be put into someone's food so that, when swallowed, it would be absorbed into the body, possibly migrating to a desired location. Moor and Weckert further note that in addition to privacy threats made possible by nanotechnolgy, individuals may also lose some degree of control. Because other people could know more about each other, for example, we might be less capable of controlling the outcomes of our choices. How these tracking devices will be developed and used is still a matter of some speculation. But Moor and Weckert argue that with the advent of nanotechnology, invasions of privacy and unjustified control over others will most likely increase.

Regarding (2), ethical concerns involving longevity, Moor and Weckert argue that developments in nanotechnology could have a dramatic effect on human life spans in three ways:

> First, and least controversially, nanotechnology will almost certainly have medical benefits. Early diagnosis and new cures will have an effect on longevity. A more spectacular, but more distant possibility is the development of cell repair devices. If these are developed, it will be possible to reverse or prevent aging, so life spans could be increased enormously. A third way that nanotechnology might contribute to longevity is through the development, by growth or construction, of body parts to replace those worn out or otherwise damaged. Particularly significant could [be] the development of tissue that the body would not reject.[20]

While many see longevity as a good thing, there could be negative consequences as well. For one thing, there could be a population problem if the life expectancy of individuals were to change dramatically. Moor and Weckert note that if fewer children are born relative to adults, there could be a concern about the lack of new ideas and "new blood." Also, questions could arise with regard to how many "family sets" couples, whose lives could be extended significantly, would be allowed to have during their expanded lifetime. Other questions might be conceptually confusing—e.g., would the (already) old stay older longer, and would the young remain young longer? So, in Moor and Weckert's analysis, longevity-related questions introduce some policy vacuums, as well as conceptual muddles, that will need to be resolved.

With regard to (3), Moor and Weckert argue that we need to consider the potential problem of "runaway nanobots." The authors note that when nanobots work to our benefit, they build what we desire. But when they work incorrectly, they build what we don't want. Moreover, the replication of these bots could get out of hand. As we saw earlier, the problem of runaway replication is often referred to as the "grey-goo scenario." Some critics, including Smalley (2001), have challenged the possibility of replicators, because of the way these assemblers would have to be constructed. Drexler, however, responds to Smalley's challenges by noting that biological assemblers such as ribosomes already do the kind of assembly at the molecular level needed for nanobots. Many believe that as long as it may be possible to construct nano-level robots that are capable of self-assembly and replication, it would be prudent to try to anticipate ethical outcomes that could arise. Woodhouse (2004) notes that important choices about how to proceed with nanotechnology will have to be made before it is determined whose prediction—Drexler's or Smalley's—is correct.

Thus far we have examined some of nanotechnology's potential advantages and disadvantages, as well as three kinds of ethical concerns that arise at the nano level. An important concern that we have not yet directly addressed, however, involves the implications that nanocomputing development could have for professionals in the computing/IT fields. In Chapter 4, we examined some specific challenges that these professionals currently face. However, we did not explicitly discuss nanocomputing issues in that chapter. We take up this question in the following section.

12.4.5 Should Computer Scientists and Computer Professionals Participate in Nanocomputing Research and Development?

Given some potential controversies involving nanocomputing, we might reasonably ask whether research and development in this area by computer professionals should be banned altogether or at least put on hold temporarily. For example, Joseph Weizenbaum (1984) argued that there are certain kinds of computer science research that should not be undertaken—specifically, research that can easily be seen to have "irreversible and not entirely unforeseeable side effects." And Bill Joy (2006), cofounder of Sun Microsystems, has suggested that because developments in nanocomputing are threatening to make us an "endangered species," the only realistic alternative is to limit the development of that technology. Others, however, such as Ralph Merkle (2001) disagree with Joy. Merkle argues that if research in nanocomputing and nanotechnology is prohibited, or even restricted, it will be done underground. If that happens, Merkle worries that nanotechnology research would not be regulated by governments and professional agencies concerned with social responsibility.

If Joy and others are correct about the dangers of nanotechnology, we must seriously consider whether research in this area should be limited and whether computer scientists should participate in developments in nanocomputing. Major computing associations such as the ACM and IEEE have taken no stance on questions involving the ethics of nanocomputing research and development, apart from providing standard codes of ethics/conduct for their members (see Chapter 4) which do not mention nanotechnology per se. Should research in this area be sanctioned by professional computing associations? If not, should computer professionals participate in it? Which criteria should be used to make decisions of this type? We next examine a scheme that could be used to guide the computer profession in assessing some of the risks associated with nanotechnology development.

Assessing Nanotechnology Risks: Applying the Precautionary Principle?

Initially, we might assume that because nanotechnology could be abused—e.g., used to invade privacy, produce weapons, etc.—nanocomputers should not be developed, or at least their development should not be sanctioned by professional computer associations. However, we would commit a logical fallacy (see the slippery slope fallacy in Chapter 3) if we used the following kind of reasoning: because some technology, say Technology X, could be abused, or because using Technology X could result in unintended tragedies, that technology should not be allowed to be developed. Consider some examples of why this form of reasoning is fallacious. Automobiles and medical drugs can both be abused, and each can contribute to the number of unintended deaths in a given year, even when used appropriately. In the United States, more than 40,000 deaths result each year from automobile accidents. And medical drugs (designed to save lives) have also been abused by some individuals, which has resulted in many deaths each year. Should the development of automobiles have been banned? Should we stop research on medical drugs? It would be fallacious to conclude that we should ban the development of these products merely because they could be abused and because they will inevitably lead to unintended deaths.

Arguments for how best to proceed in scientific research when there are concerns about harm to the public good, especially harms affecting the environmental and health areas, are often examined in terms of a scheme known as the *precautionary principle*. (Recall our brief discussion of this principle in Chapter 6, in connection with risk-analysis models for assessing cybersecurity.) We should note, however, that many formulations of this principle have been used in the scientific community (Clarke 2005). But according to Weckert and Moor (2004), the essence of the precautionary principle can be expressed in the following way:

> If some action has a possibility of causing harm, then that action should not be undertaken or some measure should be put in its place to minimize or eliminate the potential harms.[21]

Weckert and Moor believe that when this principle is applied to questions about nanotechnology research and development, it needs to be analyzed in terms of three different categories of harm: "direct harm," "harm by misuse," and "harm by mistake or accident." With respect to direct harm, they analyze a scenario in which the use of nanoparticles in products could be damaging to the health of some people. Weckert and Moor note that the kinds of risks in this scenario are very different from those used in the example they select to illustrate harm by misuse—viz., that developments in nano-electronics could endanger personal privacy. Here, it is neither the new technology nor the product itself that could cause the problem, but rather the way that new technology/product is used. Weckert and Moor also note that in this scenario, preventing certain uses of the technology would avoid the problem, without stopping the development of nanotechnology itself.

Regarding the third category, harm by mistake or accident, Weckert and Moor describe a scenario in which nanotechnology could lead to the development of self-replicating, and thus "runaway," nanobots. The authors note that harm will occur in this scenario *only if* mistakes are made or accidents occur. But this kind of potential harm is very different from the kind that results from the development of products that will damage health or from technologies that can be deliberately misused. Whereas legislation can be enacted to stop inappropriate uses of a technology or to prevent the development of products known in advance to be harmful to one's health, it is more difficult to draft legislation that will control mistakes and accidents.

Weckert and Moor conclude that when assessing the risks of nanotechnology via the precautionary principle, we need to look at not only potential harms and benefits of nanotechnology per se, but also at the "relationship between the initial action and the potential harm." In their scenario involving direct harm, e.g., nanoparticles damaging health, the relationship is fairly clear and straightforward: we simply need to know more about the scientific evidence for nanoparticles causing harm. In their scenario involving potential misuse of nanotechnology, e.g., in endangering personal privacy, the relationship is less clear. Here, we need scientific evidence that certain kinds of devices can be developed, and we need evidence about whether effective legislation could be implemented to control the uses of the devices. In their third scenario, we need evidence regarding the propensity of humans to make mistakes or the propensity of accidents to happen.

Presuming in Favor of Freedom in Scientific Research

Weckert (2006) believes that, all things being equal, potential disadvantages that can result from research in a particular field are not in themselves sufficient grounds for halting research altogether. Rather, Weckert suggests that there should be a "presumption in favor of freedom in research." However, he also argues that it should be permissible to restrict or even forbid research where it can be clearly shown that significant harm is more likely than not to result from that research. Weckert offers us the following strategy:

If a prima facie case can be made that some particular research will likely cause harm . . . then the burden of proof should be on those who want the research carried out to demonstrate that it is safe.[22]

Of course, we can understand the sense of "harm" described by Weckert in this passage to mean "serious" or "significant" harm.

Weckert also claims, however, that there should be

. . . a presumption in favour of freedom until such time a *prima facie* case is made that the research is dangerous. The burden of proof then shifts from those opposing the research to those supporting it. At that stage the research should not begin or be continued until a good case can be made that it is safe.[23]

So if Weckert is correct, it would seem that until a *prima facie* or self-evident case can be made to show that nanocomputers pose a dangerous threat, there are no compelling grounds for halting research in nanocomputing at the present time. Of course, we would need to reassess that position if future evidence were to suggest otherwise.

12.4.6 The Need for Clear Ethical Guidelines for Nanocomputing and Nanotechnology Research

We have seen some of the challenges that nanocomputing research and development poses for computer/IT professionals. We should also note that the ethical and social concerns that arise because of research in nanotechnology and nanocomputing are not limited to concerns that affect only scientists and computer/IT professionals. All humans will eventually be affected by this technology; thus everyone would benefit from clear guidelines that address social and ethical issues involving future developments in nanotechnology.

Perhaps we can look to the ELSI model, described in Section 12.3.2 in our discussion of bioinformatics, for some guidance on how to construct an ideal ethical framework for nanotechnology research. We saw that before work was able to proceed on the Human Genome Project, the anticipated ethical, legal, and social implications had to be addressed. Recall some of the salient features of the ELSI model—requirements that addressed concerns affecting privacy, confidentiality, fairness, etc.—were "built into" the scientific research methodology. Ray Kurzweil (2005) has suggested that an ELSI-like model should be developed and used to guide researchers working in nanotechnology. Many consider ELSI to be an ideal model because it is a "proactive" ethics framework. In most scientific research areas, ethics has had to play "catch up," because ethical guidelines were developed in response to cases where serious harm had already resulted. Prior to the ELSI Program, ethics was typically "reactive" in the sense that it "followed scientific developments" rather than informing scientific research.

Although many see the ELSI model as a vast improvement over traditional frameworks, where ethics was mainly an "afterthought," we noted some flaws in that ELSI model when applied to bioinformatics research. For example, we saw that recent technological developments, such as data mining and related computational techniques, seriously challenged ELSI's effectiveness in genetic/genomic research contexts. So, we concluded that this model should be updated or revised to respond to newer technologies.

The ELSI model employs a scheme that Moor and Weckert (2004) describe as an "ethics-first" framework. They believe that ethical frameworks of this kind have problems because they depend in large part on a "factual determination" of the specific harms and benefits in implementing the technology before an ethical assessment can be done. But, in the case of nanotechnology, the authors note that it is very difficult to know what the future will be in five or ten years, let alone twenty or more years. If we developed an ethics model along the lines of the ELSI framework, it might seem appropriate to put a moratorium on nanotechnology and nanocomputing research until we get all of the facts—especially those pertaining to Drexler's predictions about nanite assemblers. But Moor and Weckert point out that while a moratorium on future research would halt technology developments, it will not advance ethics in the area of nanotechnology.

Moor and Weckert also argue that turning back to what they call the "ethics-last model" is not desirable either. The authors note that once a technology is in place, much unnecessary harm may already have occurred. So, in Moor and Weckert's scheme, neither an ethics-first nor an ethics-last model is satisfactory for nanotechnology. Instead, they argue that ethics is something that needs to be *done continually* as "technology develops and as its potential consequences become better understood." The authors also point out that ethics is "dynamic" in that the factual component on which it relies has to be continually updated.

As we debate whether to continue to go forward with research and development in nanotechnology and nanocomputing, we can see how neither an ethics-first nor an ethics-last model is adequate. We agree with Moor and Weckert that it is necessary to establish a set of ethical guidelines that can be continually updated as new factual information about nanotechnology becomes available. To date, "molecular nanotechnology guidelines" have been proposed and implemented by the Foresight Institute, and the U.S. government has created the National Nanotechnology Initiative (NNI) to monitor and guide research in this field. These are an excellent start, but they will need to be updated continuously.

Because much of the funding for nanotechnology research thus far has come from government agencies, such as the National Science Foundation (NSF) and the Defense Advanced Research Projects Agency (DARPA), some worry that conflicts of interest involving the military and national defense initiatives can easily arise. Others worry that not all of the stakeholders are currently represented in the policy debate involving nanotechnology. For example, Andrew Chen (2002) believes that in addition to NSF and DARPA, other stakeholders include (independent and privately funded) researchers, explicit users of nanotechnology, and potentially everyone—insofar as all of us are or will eventually be affected by developments in nanotechnology. He proposes that a non-government advisory council be formed to monitor the research and help formulate a broader set of ethical guidelines and policies. We agree with Chen, but we should also note that ethical guidelines established by such a council will need to be continually updated in light of ongoing developments in nanotechnology.

▶ 12.5 FUTURE CHALLENGES AFFECTING AI: CYBORGS, BIONIC CHIP IMPLANTS, AND "MORAL MACHINES"

We have examined some ethical challenges posed by three converging technologies: AmI, bioinformatics, and nanocomputing. We saw that a critical (convergent) element in AmI is artificial intelligence (AI). In Chapter 11, we briefly examined AI in connection with questions about our sense of self and what it means to be human in an age of cybertechnology. In the remaining sections of Chapter 12, we examine some AI-related controversies affecting cyborgs and bionic chip implants, as well the question of whether we need to expand our sphere of moral consideration to include (at least certain kinds of) AI entities. Finally, we pose the question, Who is responsible for teaching AI entities, including (soft)bots and robots, right from wrong?

12.5.1 Cyborgs and Bionic Chip Implants

As we are implanted with more and more (AI-induced) bionic parts, are we becoming cyborgs? What kinds of policies should be in place to regulate bionic chip implants in humans? We briefly examine each question. First, we should note that implant technologies are by no means new. However, Weckert (2004) points out that while "conventional" implants in the form of devices designed to "correct" deficiencies have been around and used for some time, their purpose has been viewed as one of assisting patients in their goal of achieving "normal" states of vision, hearing, heartbeat, and so forth. These can be thought of as "therapeutic implants." Future chip plants, in the form of "enhancement implants" could be designed to make a normal person "super-human."[24] This possibility raises a controversy that some believe can be framed in terms of "enhancement vs. therapy" debate.

Moor (2005) points out that this distinction might suggest the basis for a policy that would limit unnecessary implants. He also notes that because the human body has "natural functions," some will argue that implanting chips in a body is acceptable as long as these implants "maintain and restore the body's natural functions." Moor suggests that a policy framed along the lines of a therapeutic-enhancement distinction will appeal to many because it would

> ... endorse the use of a chip that reduced dyslexia but would forbid the implanting of a deep blue chip for superior chess play. It would permit a chip implant to assist memory of Alzheimer patients but would not license implanting of a miniature digital camera that would record and play back what the implantee had just seen and heard.[25]

It would seem prudent to frame clear policies and laws now to address concerns that will inevitably arise with bionic chip implants. Describing some of the advantages and disadvantages of bionic implants of the future, especially with respect to questions about what it will mean to be human, Weckert (2006) asks:

> Do we want to be "superhuman" relative to our current abilities, with implants that enhance our senses, our memory and our reasoning ability? What would such implants do to our view of what it is to be human?[26]

With so many bionic parts becoming available, some worry that humans and machines could soon begin to merge into cyborgs. Ray Kurzweil (1999) has suggested that in the near future, the distinction between machines and humans may no longer be useful. And Moor (2005) believes the question we must continually reevaluate is "not whether we should become cyborgs, but rather what sort of cyborgs should we become." Andrew Clark (2003) argues that we already are cyborgs because of our dependency on technologies. He also suggests that in the future, we will likely find ourselves more and more closely tied to the technologies we have created and, eventually, we may reach a "post-human" or "trans-human" state. In response to concerns raised about cyborgs and the prospects of a "post-human" era, organizations such as the World Transhumanist Association have emerged. This organization addresses concerns involving the ethical use of technology to extend human capabilities.

12.5.2 Do We Need to Expand our Sphere of Moral Consideration?

Some AI entities, including (soft)bots and intelligent robots, are taking on human-like characteristics. As we noted in Chapter 11, AI entities of the not-too-distant future may even exhibit (human-like) consciousness. So we need to address the question of whether (at least some kinds of) these AI entities will merit moral consideration. And if they do, will we need to expand our current domain of moral consideration to include them? But these questions presuppose two additional, and perhaps more basic, questions:

    i. Which kinds of beings or entities deserve moral consideration?

    ii. Why do they warrant it?

Prior to the twentieth century, ethicists and lay persons in the Western world generally assumed that only human beings deserved moral consideration; all other entities—animals, trees, natural objects, etc.—were merely resources for humans to use (and abuse) as they saw fit. In other words, humans viewed these resources simply as something to be used and disposed of as they saw fit, because they believed they had no moral obligations toward these "resources."

By the mid-twentieth century, the assumption that moral consideration should be granted only to humans had been challenged on two separate fronts. One challenge comes from animal rights groups, who argue that animals, like humans, are sentient creatures and thus capable of feeling pleasure and pain. Based on this comparison, proponents for animal rights have argued that we should also grant ethical consideration to animals, in which case it would be morally wrong for humans to abuse animals or to treat them simply as resources.

On a second front, some environmentalists made an even bolder claim, arguing that we should extend ethical consideration to include new "objects," or entities. Hans Jonas (1984) argued that because modern technologies involving atomic and nuclear power have presented us with tools of destruction that could devastate our planet on a scale never before imaginable, we have to expand our sphere of moral obligation to include "new objects of moral consideration"—these include natural objects such as trees, land, and the environment itself, as well as abstract objects such as "future generations of humans" that will inherit the planet.

In the past fifty years or so, our thinking about who and what should be included in the sphere of moral obligation has evolved significantly. We have moved from a morality that grants consideration only to human beings to one that at least debates whether animals, land, and the entire ecosystem deserve moral consideration as well. Do we once again need to expand our sphere of moral consideration—this time to include non-natural or "artificial objects" such as AI entities?

Luciano Floridi and J. W. Sanders (2004) have suggested that we need to take seriously whether or not to grant moral consideration to at least certain kinds of informational objects or entities—what they call "artificial autonomous agents." Initially, one might find this assertion strange, perhaps even preposterous, but some sophisticated AI entities (sometimes also referred to as "AI agents") already exhibit a form of rationality that parallels, and in some cases exceeds, that of humans. (Because the concept of agency is complex and because the use of "artificial agent" in AI contexts is still considered controversial, we use the expressions "artificial entity" or "AI entity" instead.) The question that concerns us here is whether these artificial entities merit moral consideration because they exhibit rational characteristics. If our primary justification for granting moral consideration to humans is based on the premise that humans are rational entities, and if certain artificial entities also qualify as "rational entities," then we can make a compelling case for granting at least some moral consideration to them.

We should also note that robots of the near future will most likely exhibit sentient, as well as rational, characteristics; that is, robots, like humans and animals, would (arguably, at least) be capable of experiencing sensation and feeling. Perhaps, then, we will need to consider criteria in addition to mere rationality in determining whether to grant at least some degree of moral status to robots of the future.

▶ **SCENARIO 12–4:** Artificial Children

The movie *AI* is a story of an artificial boy who is physically indistinguishable from human boys and who appears to be capable of experiencing human-like emotion as well as displaying human-like intelligence. This "boy" needs the love of human parents and displays this need in a way that seems genuine and convincing. He is adopted by human parents, who later abandon him.[27] Does this "boy" deserve any moral consideration? Do the parents who adopted him have any clear moral obligations to their "child"? For example, do they have the right to discard "him" at their convenience, in the same way that they might discard a computer that no longer serves their needs and thus is no longer useful to them? ■

Of course, we could ask whether such a creature (or entity) should have been developed in the first place. But given the likelihood that artificial entities similar to the "boy" in the film *AI* will be developed, we need to seriously consider questions about which kinds of moral consideration, if any, they merit.

12.5.3 Designing "Moral Machines" of the Future

Assuming that we go ahead with the development of artificial entities, including intelligent robots, a related (and perhaps equally important) question also needs to be addressed: Who should be responsible for teaching these entities right from wrong? Can the appropriate instruction be accomplished through software code designed to implement agreed-upon ethical rules or guidelines?

In the 1940s, science fiction writer Isaac Asimov anticipated the need for ethical rules that would guide the robots of the future when he formulated his (now-classic) Three Laws of Robots:

1. A robot may not injure a human being, or through inaction, allow a human being to come to harm.

2. A robot must obey orders given it by human beings except where such orders would conflict with the First Law.

3. A robot must protect its own existence as long as such protection does not conflict with the First or Second Law.[28]

We can question whether the three laws articulated by Asimov are adequate to meet the kinds of challenges that robots and AI entities of the near future will likely present. The concerns initially posed by Asimov have since moved beyond the realm of science fiction, and many in the AI community believe that the design of "moral machines" is something that needs to be taken seriously now. Wendell Wallach and Colin Adam (2009) predict that within the next few years, there will be a "catastrophic incident" resulting from a sophisticated computer system making an important decision "independent of human oversight." For this reason, they believe that we need to build machines capable of making ethical decisions. But it is still not clear who is ultimately responsible for doing this.

Wallach and Adam, as well as many others in the AI community, believe that questions about who is responsible for ethical instruction of robots need to be addressed sooner rather than later. While questions of this kind have intrigued science fiction writers in the past, they may soon have more to do with practical concerns affecting everyday life than with mere speculation about the future.

The final sections of Chapter 12 clearly raise more questions than they answer. But these questions can help computer professionals to anticipate many of the challenges they face in designing and implementing intelligent machines. These questions also show why it is crucial that we articulate and approve clear policies to guide us in cyber-related research as we proceed in the twenty-first century.

► 12.6 CHAPTER SUMMARY

In this chapter we examined a cluster of social, ethical, and professional challenges affecting emerging and converging technologies. In particular, we examined controversies involving three broad areas of technological convergence: ambient intelligence (AmI), bioinformatics, and nanocomputing. We saw that AmI environments, made possible by pervasive computing and ubiquitous communication, raised concerns for freedom and autonomy as well as for privacy and surveillance. We then examined some ways that research in bioinformatics raised ethical concerns affecting privacy, informed consent, and intellectual property. We also speculated about ethical issues that may well arise because of developments in nanotechnology and nanocomputing, and we considered the question whether computer professionals should participate in research and development in this area, especially in light of some recent concerns raised by nanotechnology's critics. Finally, we considered whether we may need to expand our conventional moral framework to include ethical consideration for some AI entities.

► REVIEW QUESTIONS

1. What is "technological convergence" in the context of cybertechnology?
2. Why do some converging technologies raise special ethical and social issues?
3. Describe key aspects of pervasive (or ubiquitous) computing. How is it different from conventional or traditional computing?
4. What is ambient intelligence (AmI)?
5. What is ubiquitous communication, and what kinds of controversies does it raise?
6. What is an intelligent user interface (IUI), and how are IUIs different from traditional user interfaces?
7. What implications does AmI have for concerns involving individual freedom and autonomy, as well as for privacy and security?

8. What implications does AmI have for *technological dependency*?
9. What implications does AmI have for privacy, surveillance, and the "panopticon"?
10. What is bioinformatics, and how is it different from computational genomics?
11. Identify three kinds of ethical issues associated with bioinformatics.
12. How does the practice of storing personal genetic data in privately owned computer databases raise issues affecting information ownership and property-rights?
13. What is the ELSI (ethical, legal, and social implications) research program?
14. What is the Genetic Information Nondiscrimination Act (GINA)? Is it helpful in protecting the privacy of personal genetic data stored in computer databases?
15. What is nanotechnology?
16. What are nanocomputers?
17. What kinds of ethical and professional challenges do research and development in nanocomputing pose for computer professionals?
18. Why are clear and explicit ethical guidelines needed if research and development in nanocomputing and nanotechnology continue?
19. Why are bionic chip implants controversial?
20. What is meant by the "enhancement versus therapy debate" in the context of bionic chip implants?

▶ DISCUSSION QUESTIONS

1. As we proceed with cybertechnology research and development in the twenty-first century, continued technological convergence would seem to be inevitable. Few would reject most of the benefits and conveniences that have resulted from this phenomenon thus far—e.g., cell phones that take pictures, GPS (Global Positioning Systems) technology in automobiles that guide motorists, etc. Yet, we have also noted some controversial implications that convergent technologies can have for individual freedom, autonomy, and privacy. Can you think of any other social and ethical concerns that could also arise because of converging technologies? Identify three to five additional concerns that you believe might have some social and ethical implications.

2. Recall the scenario in Section 12.2 in which a young mother arrives at her "smart home." One might tend to be excited about the conveniences that "smart homes" (and other ambient-intelligence technologies) make possible. Imagine that next week you and your family will be moving into a home similar to the one described in this scenario. Make a list of three or more concerns that you might have, from an ethical, social, or personal point of view, as you prepare to move into this "intelligent environment." If you had the option to move either into this "smart home" or a traditional home, which would you choose? Explain.

3. In the case involving deCODE Genetics Inc., we examined some controversies surrounding the question, "Who should own the personal genetic information stored in deCODE's databases"? If organizations and corporations in the private sector are permitted to own that information, it seems that the privacy rights of individuals are threatened. If individuals retain ownership rights, on the other hand, some worry that corporations would have less of an incentive to invest in genetic/genomic research. In the deCODE case, would it have made sense to give the Icelandic government custodial rights over this information? If you were preparing to participate in a genomics study that employed computational techniques such as data mining tools, what kind of expectations would you have about ownership rights of your personal genetic data?

4. Assess the arguments that we examined for and against continued research in nanotechnology. Given the potential advantages and disadvantages involved in research and development in this area, which side in this debate do you find to be more plausible? Do the criteria provided by John Weckert for when research in a particular area should and should not be allowed in scientific research offer us clear guidelines with respect to research and development in nanotechnology and nanocomputing? What kind of an ethical framework is needed to guide research and development in this field?

▶ ESSAY/PRESENTATION QUESTIONS

1. According to Bert Gordijn, what are some of the optimistic visions involving nanotechnology? What are some of the pessimistic predictions involving nanotechnology that Gordijn describes? Identify and briefly describe the three nanoethics issues examined by James Moor and John Weckert. Why do some critics, such as Bill Joy, question whether we should continue nanotechnology research? What is the Precautionary Principle, as applied to scientific research? Can it be successfully applied to concerns involving research in nanotechnology? Why does John Weckert believe that we should "presume in favor of freedom" in scientific research?

2. Assess the arguments we examined for whether we need to expand our conventional moral framework to include at least some AI entities? Do you believe that these entities deserve moral consideration? If we develop artificial creatures, such as the artificial boy in the movie *AI*, which kinds of moral obligations do we have to them? For example, can we discard these entities in the same ways we currently discard computer hardware resources? And if we grant moral consideration to some AI entities but not to others, where should we draw the line? In other words, which kinds of criteria are relevant for moral consideration?

▶ ENDNOTES

1. Rheingold (1991), p. 61.
2. See, for example, Aarts and Marzano (2003); Brey (2005); and Weber et al. (2005).
3. A slightly longer version of this passage from Raisinghani et al. (2004) is cited in Brey (2005), p. 157.
4. See Weiser (1991) for his original description of this expression.
5. See Brey (2005) for a more thorough discussion of how AmI can both enhance and limit human control.
6. See Forster (1995). For a critical analysis of this work, see http://en.wikipedia.org/wiki/The_Machine_Stops.
7. For more detail, see J. Bentham. "Panopticon." In M. Bozovic, ed. *The Panopticon Writings* (London: Verso, 1995), pp. 29–95.
8. See Goodman (1998), p. 17.
9. For a more detailed analysis of these distinctions, see Tavani (2006).
10. Moor (2006), p. 110.
11. Goodman, p. 16.
12. This scenario is adapted from Tavani (2004). See also Stefansson (2001) and Taubes (2001).
13. My descriptions of these kinds of ethical issues in the next three sections draw from material in Tavani (2004, 2006).
14. For a detailed account, see Tavani (2006).
15. See http://www.genome.gov/24519851.
16. See, for example, http://en.wikipedia.org/wiki/Genetic_Information_Nondiscrimination_Act.
17. Regis (2009), p. 40.
18. Gordijn (2003), p. 4. The description of the six components of the "optimistic view" that is based on the account in Gordijn.
19. Ibid., pp. 5–6. The description of the six components of "pessimistic view" is based on the account in Gordijn.
20. Moor and Weckert (2004), p. 307.
21. Weckert and Moor (2004), p. 12.
22. Weckert (2006), p. 334.
23. Ibid., p. 335.
24. Weckert (2004), p. 693.
25. Moor (2005), p. 124.
26. Weckert (2006), p. 336.
27. This scenario is based on Steven Spielberg's 2001 film *AI*.
28. The Three Laws were introduced by Asimov in his short story "Runaround" in 1942.

▶ REFERENCES

Aarts, Emile, and Stefano Marzano, eds. 2003. *The New Everyday: Views on Ambient Intelligence.* Rotterdam, The Netherlands: 101 Publishers.

Baumer, David, Julia Brande Earp, and Fay Cobb Payton. 2006. "Privacy of Medical Records: IT Implications of HIPAA." In H. T. Tavani, ed. *Ethics, Computing, and Genomics*. Sudbury MA: Jones and Bartlett, pp. 137–52. Reprinted from *Computers and Society* 30 (2000): 40–47.

Berne, Rosalyn W. 2005. "Nanoethics." In C. Mitcham, ed. *Encyclopedia of Science, Technology, and Ethics*. Vol. 3. New York: Macmillan, pp. 1259–62.

Bohn, Jurgen, Vlad Coroama, Marc Langheinrich, Freidman Mattern, and Michael Rohs. 2005. "Social, Economic, and Ethical Implications of Ambient Intelligence and Ubiquitous Intelligence." In W. Weber, J. Rabaey, and E. Aarts, eds. *Ambient Intelligence*. New York: Springer.

Brey, Philip. 2005. "Freedom and Privacy in Ambient Intelligence." *Ethics and Information Technology* 7, no. 4: 157–66.

Bütschi, Danielle, Michèle Courant, and Lorenz M. Hilty. 2005. "Towards Sustainable Pervasive Computing." *IEEE Technology and Society Magazine* 21, no. 1: 7–8.

Čas, Johann. 2005. "Privacy in Pervasive Computing Environments—A Contradiction in Terms?" *IEEE Technology and Society Magazine* 21, no. 1: 24–33.

Chadwick, Ruth, and Antonio Marturano. 2006. "Computing, Genetics, and Policy: Theoretical and Practical Considerations." In H. T. Tavani, ed. *Ethics, Computing, and Genomics*. Sudbury MA: Jones and Bartlett, pp. 75–83.

Chen, Andrew. 2002. "The Ethics of Nanotechnology." Available at http://www.actionbioscience.org/newfrontiers/chen.html.

Clark, Andrew J. 2003. *Natural-Born Cyborgs: Minds, Technologies, and the Future of Human Intelligences*. New York: Oxford University Press.

Custers, Bart. 2006. "The Risks of Epidemiological Data Mining." In H. T. Tavani, ed. *Ethics, Computing, and Genomics*. Sudbury MA: Jones and Bartlett, pp. 153–65.

Drexler, K. Eric. 1986. *Engines of Creation: The Coming Era of Nanotechnology*. Garden City NY: Anchor/Doubleday.

Drexler, K. Eric. 1991. *Unbounding the Future: The Nanotechnology Revolution*. New York: Quill.

ELSI Research Program. National Human Genome Research Institute. Available at: http://www.genome.gov/10001618.

Floridi, Luciano, and J. W. Sanders. 2004. "On the Morality of Artificial Agents." *Minds and Machines* 14, no. 3: 349–79.

Foresight Nanotech Institute. 2004. *Foresight Guidelines on Molecular Nanotechnology. Version 4.0*. Available at http://www.foresight.org/guidelines/current/html.

Forster, E. M. 1995. "The Machine Stops." In D. G. Johnson and H. Nissenabum, eds. *Computing, Ethics, and Social Values*. Upper Saddle River NJ: Prentice Hall, pp. 694–713. Reprinted from *The Eternal Moment and Other Short Stories*. New York: Harcourt Brace, 1970.

Goodman, Kenneth W. 1998. "Bioethics and Health Informatics: An Introduction." In K. W. Goodman, ed. *Ethics, Computing, and Medicine: Informatics and the Transformation of Healthcare*. Cambridge UK: Cambridge University Press, pp. 1–31.

Gordijn, Bert. 2003. "Nanoethics: From Utopian Dreams and Apocalyptic Nightmares Towards a More Balanced View." In *Proceedings of the World Commission of the Ethics of Scientific Knowledge and Technology (COMEST): Third Session*. Available at http://portal.unesco.org/shs/fr/files/6603/10960368721Nanoethics.pdf/Nanoethics.pdf.

Greenfield, Adam. 2005. "Boxes and Arrows: All Watched Over by Machines of Loving Grace: Some Ethical Guidelines." Available at http://www.boxesandarrows.com/archives/all_watched_over-bymachines_of_loving_grace_some_ethical_guidelines_for_users_experience_in_ubiquitous-computing_settings_1.php.

Jonas, Hans. 1984. *The Imperative of Responsibility: In Search of an Ethics for the Technological Age*. Chicago: University of Chicago Press.

Joy, Bill. 2006. "Why the Future Doesn't Need Us." In M. E. Winston and R. D. Edelbach, eds. *Society, Ethics, and Technology*. 3rd ed. Florence KY: Wadsworth, pp. 216–32. Reprinted from *Wired* 8, no. 4 (2000).

Koehler, Andreas, and Claudia Som. 2005. "Effects of Pervasive Computing on Sustainable Development." *IEEE Technology and Society Magazine* 21, no. 1 (Spring): 15–23.

Kurzweil, Ray. 1999. *The Age of Spiritual Machines: When Computers Exceed Human Intelligence*. New York: Penguin.

Kurzweil, Ray. 2005. "Nanoscience, Nanotechnology, and Ethics: Promise and Peril." In C. Mitcham, ed. *Encyclopedia of Science, Technology, and Ethics*. Vol. 1. New York: Macmillan, pp. xli–xlvi.

Langheinrich, Marc. 2001. "Privacy by Design—Principles of Privacy-Aware Ubiquitous Systems." In *Proceedings of the Third International Conference on Ubiquitous Computing*. Springer-Verlag, pp. 273–91.

Marturano, Antonio. 2006. "Molecular Biologists as Hackers of Human Data: Rethinking Intellectual Property Rights for Bioinformatics Research." In H. T. Tavani, ed. *Ethics, Computing, and Genomics*. Sudbury MA: Jones and Bartlett, pp. 235–45. Reprinted from *Journal of Information, Communication, and Ethics in Society* 1 (2003)" 207–15.

Merkle, Ralph. 1997. "It's a Small, Small, Small, Small World." *Technology Review* 25 (February/March): 25–32.

Merkle, Ralph. 2001. "Nanotechnology: What Will it Mean?" *IEEE Spectrum* 38, no. 1 (January): 19–21.

Moor, James H. 2001. "The Future of Computer Ethics: You Ain't Seen Nothin' Yet!" *Ethics and Information Technology* 3, no. 2: 89–91.

Moor, James H. 2005. "Should We Computers Get Under Our Skin?" In R. Cavalier, ed. *The Impact of the Internet on Our Moral Lives*. Albany NY: State University of New York Press, pp. 121–38.

Moor, James H. 2006. "Using Genetic Information While Protecting the Privacy of the Soul." In H. T. Tavani, ed. *Ethics, Computing, and Genomics*. Sudbury MA: Jones and Bartlett, pp. 109–19. Reprinted from *Ethics and Information Technology* 1, no. 4 (1999): 257–63.

Moor, James H., and John Weckert. 2004. "Nanoethics: Assessing the Nanoscale from an Ethical Point of View." In D. Baird, A. Nordmann, and J. Schummer, eds. *Discovering the Nanoscale*. Amsterdam, The Netherlands: IOS Press, pp. 301–10.

O'Neill, Onora. 2002. *Autonomy and Trust in Bioethics*. Cambridge UK: Cambridge University Press.

Raisinghani, M., A. Benoit, J. Ding, M. Gomez, K. Gupta, V. Gusila, D. Power, and O. Schmedding. 2004. "Ambient Intelligence: Changing Forms of Human-Computer Interaction and Their Social Implications." *Journal of Digital Information* 5, no. 4 (Article No. 271): 8–24.

Regis, Ed. 2009. "Nanotechnology: The World's Smallest Radio." *Scientific American* 300, no. 3: 40–45.

Rheingold, Howard. 1991. *Virtual Reality*. New York: Touchstone Books.

Seeman, Nadrian C. 2004. "Nanotechnology and the Double Helix." *Scientific American* 290, no. 6: 64–75.

Smalley, Richard E. 2001. "Of Chemistry, Love, and Nanobots." *Scientific American* 285, no. 3: 76–77.

Stefansson, Kari. 2001. "Population Inc." Interview in *Technology Review* 104, no. 3: 50–55.

Taubes, Gary. 2001. "Your Genetic Destiny for Sale." *Technology Review* 104, no. 3: 40–46.

Tavani, Herman T. 2004. "Genomic Research and Data-Mining Technology: Implications for Personal Privacy and Informed Consent." *Ethics and Information Technology* 6, no. 1: 15–28.

Tavani, Herman T. 2006. "Ethics at the Intersection of Computing and Genomics." In H. T. Tavani, ed. *Ethics, Computing, and Genomics*. Sudbury MA: Jones and Bartlett, pp. 5–26.

Vedder, Anton. 2004. "KDD, Privacy, Individuality, and Fairness." In R. A. Spinello and H. T. Tavani, eds. *Readings in CyberEthics*. 2nd ed. Sudbury MA: Jones and Bartlett, pp. 462–70.

Wallach, Wendell, and Colin Adams. 2009. *Moral Machines: Teaching Robots Right from Wrong*. New York: Oxford University Press.

Weber, W., J. Rabaey, and E. Aarts, eds. 2005. *Ambient Intelligence*. New York: Springer.

Weckert, John. 2004. "Lilliputian Computer Ethics." In R. A. Spinello and H. T. Tavani, eds. *Readings in CyberEthics*. 2nd ed. Sudbury MA: Jones and Bartlett, pp. 690–97. Reprinted from *Metaphilosophy* 33, no. 3 (2002): 366–75.

Weckert, John. 2006. "The Control of Scientific Research: The Case of Nanotechnology." In H. T. Tavani, ed. *Ethics, Computing, and Genomics*. Sudbury MA: Jones and Bartlett, pp. 323–39. Reprinted from *Australian Journal of Professional and Applied Ethics* 3 (2001): 29–44.

Weckert, John, and James H. Moor. 2004. "Using the Precautionary Principle in Nanotechnology Policy Making." *Asia Pacific Nanotechnology Forum News Journal* 3, no. 4: 12–14.

Weisenbaum, Joseph. 1984. *Computer Power and Human Reason: From Judgment to Calculation*. New York: Penguin Books.

Weiser, Mark. 1991. "The Computer for the 21st Century." *Scientific American* 265, no. 3: 94–104.

Woodhouse, E. J. 2004. "Nanotechnology Controversies." *IEEE Technology and Society Magazine* 21, no. 4: 6–8.

► FURTHER READINGS

Allhoff, Fritz, Patrick Lin, James Moor, and John Weckert, eds. *Nanoethics: The Ethical and Social Implications of Nanotechnology*. Hoboken NJ: John Wiley and Sons, 2007.

Brey, Philip, Luciano Floridi, and Frances S. Grodzinsky, eds. *Ethics of New Information Technology*. Special Issue of *Ethics and Information Technology* 7, no. 3 (2005).

Cameron, Nigel M. de S., and M. Ellen Mitchell, eds. *Nanoscale: Issues and Perspectives for the Nano Century*. Hoboken NJ: John Wiley and Sons, 2007.

Clarke, Steve. "Future Technologies, Dystopic Futures and the Precautionary Principle." *Ethics and Information Technology* 7, no. 3 (2005): 121–26.

Himma, Kenneth E. Artificial Agency, Consciousness, and the Criteria for Moral Agency: What Properties Must an Artificial Agent Have to be a Moral Agent?" *Ethics and Information Technology* 11, no. 1 (2009): 19–29.

Johnson, Deborah G., and Thomas M. Powers. "Computers as Surrogate Agents." In J. van den Hoven and J. Weckert, eds. *Information Technology and Moral Philosophy*. Cambridge UK: Cambridge University Press, 2008, pp. 251–69.

Mills, Kirsty, and Charles Fleddermann. "Getting the Best from Nanotechnology: Approaching Social and Ethical Implications Openly and Proactively." *IEEE Technology and Society Magazine* 24, no. 4 (2005): 18–26.

Moor, James H. "Why We Need Better Ethics for Emerging Technologies." *Ethics and Information Technology* 7, no. 3 (2005): 111–19.

GLOSSARY

ACM Code of Ethics and Professional Conduct: A code of ethics endorsed by the Association for Computing Machinery.

accessibility privacy: A conception of privacy in terms of being let alone, or being free from intrusion into one's physical space; contrasted with decisional privacy and informational privacy.

ambient intelligence (AmI): A technology that senses changes in the environment and automatically adapts to these changes vis-à-vis the needs and preferences of users, while remaining in the background and thus being virtually invisible to users. See also *pervasive computing* and *ubiquitous communication*.

anonymity: In the context of cybertechnology, the ability to navigate the Internet and participate in online forums without having to reveal one's true identity.

applied ethics: A branch of ethical inquiry that examines practical (as opposed to theoretical) moral issues and problems. See also *ethical theory*.

artificial intelligence (AI): The field of study that examines relationships between machine intelligence and human intelligence. One branch of AI attempts to shed light on human intelligence by using cybertechnology to simulate it; another branch is concerned with constructing intelligent tools to assist humans in complex tasks. See also *expert systems*.

bioinformatics: A field concerned with the acquisition, storage, manipulation, analyses, and simulation of biological information on a computer, with the objective of making that information more understandable and useful.

biometrics: The biological identification of a person, which includes eyes, voice, hand prints, finger prints, retina patterns, and handwritten signatures.

blog (or Web log): A Web site that contains an online journal with reflections and comments; blogs may be further categorized as political blogs, personal blogs, corporate blogs, travel blogs, health blogs, literary blogs, and so forth. See also *blogosphere*.

blogosphere: A name given to the collective community of all *blogs*.

computer security: A branch of computer science concerned with both safeguarding computer systems (hardware and software resources) from attacks by malicious programs, such as viruses and worms, and protecting the integrity of the data resident in and transmitted between those systems from unauthorized access.

consequentialism: An ethical theory that appeals to consequences, outcomes, or ends as the essential criterion, or standard, used to justify particular actions and policies in a moral system. See also *utilitarianism.*

contract theory of ethics: A theory that ties a moral obligation to assist others to an express contract to do so. Contract theory is sometimes viewed as a minimalist theory of morality, because without an explicit contract, one would simply be required to do no harm to others; there is no obligation to actively assist others.

cookies: Text files that Web sites send to and retrieve from a Web visitor's computer system. Cookies technology enables Web site owners to collect information about a visitor's preferences while the visitor interacts with their Web sites.

Creative Commons (CC): A nonprofit organization whose aim is to expand the range of creative work available to others to legally build upon and share, via a set of licensing options intended to help artists and authors give others the freedom and creativity to build upon their creativity.

cultural relativism: A descriptive thesis stating that different cultures have different views about what is morally right or wrong. Many philosophers have argued that even if cultural relativism is true, it does not logically imply moral relativism, which is a normative position. See also *moral relativism.*

cyberbullying: A type of harassment (or bullying) that takes place online, via e-mail, text messaging, or online forums, such as social networking sites.

cybercrime: Criminal activity that is either made possible or significantly exacerbated by the use of computers and cybertechnology.

cyberethics: The field of study that examines moral, legal, and social issues involving cybertechnology.

cyberstalking: The use of cybertechnology to clandestinely track the movement and whereabouts of one or more individuals.

cybertechnology: A range of computing and information/communication technologies, from stand-alone computer systems to privately owned computer networks to the Internet.

cyberterrorism: The convergence of cyberspace and terrorism, covering a range of politically motivated hacking operations that can result in loss of life, severe economic loss, or both.

data mining: A computerized technique for unearthing implicit patterns in large databases to reveal statistical data and corresponding associations that can be used to construct consumer profiles.

dataveillance: A term coined by Roger Clarke to describe the combination of data monitoring (surveillance) techniques with data-recording techniques made possible by computer technology.

decisional privacy: A conception of privacy in terms of freedom from interference in one's choices and decisions; contrasted with accessibility privacy and informational privacy.

denial-of-service attacks: Repeated bogus requests to a Web site that are intended to disrupt services at that site. Denial-of-service attacks can be sent via third-party sites, from computer systems located in universities and organizations, to confuse the targeted sites about the source of the attacks.

deontological ethics: A theory of ethics that bases its moral system on duty or obligation rather than on consequences and outcomes that result from actions. Deontological ethical theories can be contrasted with consequentialist theories. See also *consequentialism.*

descriptive ethics: A branch of ethical inquiry that reports or describes the ethical principles and values held by various groups and individuals. Descriptive ethics is usually contrasted with normative ethics. See also *normative ethics.*

digital divide: The disparity between those who have (information haves) and those who do not have (information have-nots) computers and access to cybertechnology.

digital rights management (DRM): A technology that allows content owners to regulate the flow of information in digital media by blocking access to it via encryption mechanisms, and by enabling access to it through the use of passwords.

ethical theory: A branch of ethical inquiry dedicated to the study of philosophical frameworks for determining when actions and policies are morally right or morally wrong. Ethical theory, or theoretical ethics, is often contrasted with applied ethics. See also *applied ethics.*

ethics: The study of morality or a moral system. Normative ethics approaches the study of a moral system from the perspective of philosophy, religion, or law, whereas descriptive ethics typically examines morality from the perspective of social science. See also *morality, descriptive ethics,* and *normative ethics.*

expert system (ES): A computer program that is expert at performing one particular task traditionally performed by humans; developed from research in artificial intelligence. Because it is a computer program, an ES is different than a robot, which is a physical or mechanical system. See also *artificial intelligence* and *robotics.*

hacktivism: The convergence of political activism and computer hacking by which activists use cybertechnology to disrupt the operations of organizations.

identity theft: The act of taking another person's identity by using that person's name, social security number, credit card numbers, and so forth.

IEEE Code of Ethics: An ethical code sanctioned by the Institute of Electrical and Electronics Engineering.

inductive argument: An argument form in which the premises, when assumed true, are strong enough to suggest the likelihood of the argument's conclusion. Unlike deductive, or valid, arguments, the premises of an inductive argument cannot guarantee the conclusion.

informal logical fallacies: Fallacious arguments that commonly occur in everyday discourse. Because these fallacies are so common, they have familiar names such as *ad hominem*, *ad populum*, begging the question, and slippery slope.

information warfare (IW): Operations that target or exploit information media in order to win some objective over an adversary. IW, unlike conventional warfare, can be more disruptive than destructive; it can also use false information to deceive the enemy.

informational privacy: A conception of privacy in terms of control over the flow of one's personal information, including the collection and exchange of that information; contrasted with accessibility privacy and decisional privacy.

intellectual property: An intangible form of property that is protected by a system of laws such as patents, copyrights, trademarks, and trade secrets, through which authors and inventors are given ownership rights over their creative works (e.g., books, poems, songs) and inventions.

keystroke-monitoring software: A specialized form of audit-trail software that records every keystroke entered by a user.

location privacy: A relatively new category of privacy concerned with the use of embedded chips, RFID technology, and global positioning systems to track the location of individuals at any point in time.

logical argument: A form or structure of reasoning in which one or more statements (called premises) are used as evidence to support another statement, the conclusion.

macroethics: Concerned with the analysis of moral rules and policies at the societal level, as opposed to the level of individuals. See also *microethics*.

malware: A label that applies to a cluster of "malicious programs," including viruses, worms, Trojan horses, logic bombs, and so forth; malware can also include "spyware."

microethics: Concerned with the analysis of moral rules and directives at the level of individuals, as opposed to the societal level. See also *macroethics*.

moral absolutism: A view holding that there are absolute moral principles and that there is only one uniquely correct answer to every moral question.

moral objectivism: A compromise view between moral absolutism and moral relativism; moral objectivists believe that there are objective standards for evaluating moral claims, so that there can be agreement on the correct answers to many moral issues, but that there can also be more than one acceptable answer to some moral issues. See also *moral absolutism* and *moral relativism*.

moral relativism: The view that there are no universal moral norms or standards and that only the members of a particular group or culture are capable of evaluating the moral principles used within that group. See also *cultural relativism*.

morality: A system that comprises rules, principles, and values; at its core are rules of conduct for guiding action, and principles of evaluation for justifying those rules. See also *ethics*.

MMORPGs: Massively Multiplayer Online Role-Playing Games, which include popular games such *World of Warcraft* and *Second Life*.

nanotechnology: A field dedicated to the development of extremely small electronic circuits and mechanical devices built at the molecular level of matter.

normative ethics: A branch of ethical inquiry that is concerned with evaluating moral rules and principles by asking what ought to be the case, as opposed to descriptive ethics which simply reports what is the case (i.e., what individuals and cultures happen to believe) with respect to morally right and wrong behavior. See also *descriptive ethics*.

online communities: Computer-mediated social groups that interact in virtual space, as contrasted with traditional communities in which interaction occurs in physical space.

open source software: Software for operating systems and applications in which the source code is made freely available to use, modify, improve, and redistribute. Open source software, such as the Linux operating system, is contrasted with proprietary operating system software such as MS Windows.

P2P technology: Peer-to-peer technology, which enables two or more computers to share files through either a centralized directory such as Napster, or a decentralized system such as Morpheus, KaZaA, and Gnutella.

pervasive computing: A computing environment where information and communication technology are everywhere, for everyone, at all times. See also *ambient intelligence* and *ubiquitous communication*.

PETs: Privacy-Enhancing Technologies are tools that both protect a user's personal identity while the user interacts with the Web and protect the privacy of communications (such as e-mail) sent over the Internet.

phishing: A fraudulent use of e-mail to acquire a user's password, social security number, etc., to gain unauthorized access to information about the victim; often, the e-mail looks as if it was sent by an official site such as eBay or PayPal.

***prima facie* duty:** A type of moral duty that one has, all things being equal. David Ross provides a list of prima facie duties such as honesty, benevolence, justice, and so forth. Prima facie duties can be overridden by circumstances; these duties are contrasted with absolute duties.

RFID: Radio Frequency Identification is a technology that consists of a tag (microchip) containing an electronic circuit, which stores data, and an antenna that broadcasts data by radio waves in response to a signal from a reader.

risk analysis: A methodology used to make an informed decision about a product based on considerations such as cost. A costs-benefits model of risk assessment for software can include safety, reliability, schedule, budget, consumer demand, and so forth.

robotics: The field of research and development in robots and robotic parts/limbs. See also *expert systems*.

sexting: The use of cell phones (or similar handheld electronic devices) to send nude or semi-nude photos of oneself to others; in some cases these photos become widely distributed and can eventually end up on the Internet.

Social Networking Service (SNS): A Web-based service, such as Facebook or MySpace, which enables users to construct a profile and share information with other members (i.e., "friends") on the online forum.

softbots: Software robots and artificial agents (sometimes called bots) that perform highly specialized tasks on the Web. Metasearch engines (Web crawlers) and negotiation agents are examples of softbots.

spam: E-mail that is generally considered to be unsolicited, promotional, and sent in bulk to multiple users.

spyware: A type of software installed on users' computers without their knowledge that records information from the source computer and sends it to a destination computer.

ubiquitous communication: Aims at ensuring flexible and omnipresent communication possibilities between interlinked computer devices that can be stationed in various locations. See *ambient intelligence* and *pervasive computing*.

utilitarianism: A consequentialist ethical theory based on the principle that an act or policy is morally permissible if it produces the greatest good (usually measured in terms of happiness) for the greatest number of people affected by it. See also *consequentialism*.

valid argument: An argument form in which the premises, if assumed true, are sufficient to guarantee the truth of the conclusion.

virtual environment: An online (or computer-generated) environment, which is contrasted with an environment in physical space. Virtual environments, as opposed to virtual reality (VR) environments and applications, can be either two-dimensional (e.g., text-only) or three-dimensional. See also *virtual reality*.

virtual reality: A three-dimensional, interactive computer-generated environment, as contrasted with physical reality. See also *virtual environment*.

virtue ethics: A theory that stresses character development and the acquisition of "correct" moral habits as opposed to duty-based (deontological) and consequence-based (utilitarian) ethical theories, which stress obligation or duty and conformance with certain rules of action.

virus: A program that can insert executable copies of itself into other programs; also generically referred to as a malicious program or a rogue computer program. See also *worm*.

VSD: Value Sensitive Design, a theoretically grounded approach to the design of technology that accounts for human values in a principled and comprehensive manner throughout the design process.

worm: A program or program segment that searches computer systems for idle resources and then disables them by erasing various locations in memory; also generically referred to as a malicious program or a rogue computer program. See also *virus*.

INDEX